Windows Server Automation with PowerShell Cookbook

Fifth Edition

Powerful ways to automate, manage, and administrate
Windows Server 2022 using PowerShell 7.2

Thomas Lee

BIRMINGHAM—MUMBAI

Windows Server Automation with PowerShell Cookbook
Fifth Edition

Senior Publishing Product Manager: Aaron Tanna
Acquisition Editor – Peer Reviews: Gaurav Gavas
Project Editor: Meenakshi Vijay
Content Development Editor: Liam Draper
Copy Editor: Safis Editing
Technical Editor: Karan Sonawane
Proofreader: Safis Editing
Indexer: Subalakshmi Govindhan
Presentation Designer: Rajesh Shirsath
Developer Relations Marketing Executive: Meghal Patel

First published: March 2013
Second edition: September 2017
Third edition: February 2019
Fourth edition: July 2021
Fifth edition: January 2023
Production reference: 1270123

Published by Packt Publishing Ltd.
Livery Place
35 Livery Street
Birmingham
B3 2PB, UK.

ISBN 978-1-80461-423-5

www.packt.com

Contributors

About the author

Thomas Lee is a consultant, trainer, and writer from England and has been in the IT business since the late 1960s. After graduating from Carnegie Mellon University, Thomas joined ComShare, where he was a systems programmer building the Commander II time-sharing operating system, a forerunner of today's cloud computing paradigm. In the mid 1970s, he moved to ICL to work on the VME/K operating system. After a sabbatical in 1980 and 1981, he joined what is today known as Accenture, leaving in 1988 to run his own consulting and training business, which is still active today.

Thomas worked for Microsoft in Redmond to develop both multiple Microsoft official training courses and several chapters on DNS for the Windows Server 2003 Resource kit. Later, Thomas also worked for both QA (as Chief Technologist), and for Global Knowledge as Chief Architect. In both roles, he developed and delivered training for a variety of customers, including Microsoft.

Today, Thomas writes, trains, and consults. He is a site moderator and PowerShell group administrator at the popular SpiceWorks.com site. He is responsible for and a major contributor to the Microsoft PowerShell Community blog (https://devblogs.microsoft.com/powershell-community/).

Thomas holds numerous Microsoft certifications, including MCSE (one of the first in the world) and later versions, MCT (25 years), and has been awarded Microsoft's MVP award 17 times. Over the years, he has written and contributed to a variety of books on Windows and TCP/IP.

He lives today in a cottage in the English countryside with his family, a nice wine cellar, and a huge collection of live recordings by *The Grateful Dead* and *The Jerry Garcia Band*.

About the reviewer

Mike Roberts is a PowerShell ninja not only in his profession, but also teaches it on his blog: `https://gngr.ninja`. Through his blog, he hopes to inspire others by showing them what different technologies are capable of.

I am eternally grateful for the support of my family, and Destiny. Thank you!

Join our community on Discord

Join our community's Discord space for discussions with the author and other readers:

https://packt.link/SecNet

Table of Contents

Preface

PowerShell was first introduced to the world at the Professional Developer's conference in Los Angeles in 2003 by *Jeffrey Snover*. Monad, as it was originally known, represented a complete revolution in managing host servers. A white paper written around that time, *The Monad Manifesto* (refer to `http://www.jsnover.com/blog/2011/10/01/monad-manifesto/`), remains an amazing analysis of the problem at the time – that of managing large numbers of Windows Server systems. A key takeaway is that the GUI does not scale to the, whereas PowerShell can and does.

PowerShell has transformed the management of complex, network-based Windows infrastructure and, increasingly, non-Windows and cloud infrastructures. Knowledge of PowerShell and how to get the most from PowerShell is now obligatory for any IT professional. The popular adage continues to be true: Learn PowerShell or learn golf.

Windows PowerShell was developed on Windows for Windows administrators. PowerShell 7, the open-source successor, is also available for Mac and most of the more popular Linux distributions as well as Windows. This book, however, concentrates on PowerShell within a Windows environment.

This book takes you through the use of PowerShell 7.2 in various scenarios using many of the rich set of features included in Windows Server 2022. This preface introduces what is in the book, along with some tips on how to get the most out of it.

Who this book is for

This book is aimed at IT professionals, including system administrators, system engineers, architects, and consultants who need to understand PowerShell 7 to simplify and automate their daily tasks. The recipes in this book have been tested on the latest versions of Windows Server 2022.

What this book covers

Chapter 1, Installing and Configuring PowerShell 7, shows you how you can install and configure both PowerShell 7 and VS Code, which replaces the Windows PowerShell **Integrated Scripting Environment (ISE)** as well as installing a new font, Cascadia Code. This chapter also examines the PowerShell 7 environment, including examining the PSReadLine module.

Chapter 2, Managing PowerShell 7 in the Enterprise, looks at how you can use various PowerShell 7 features that might be more common within larger enterprises. These include the **Remote Server Administration Tools (RSAT)**, package management and the PowerShell Gallery, and creating a local module repository. The chapter also looks at PowerShell script signing, using short cuts, and working with archive (.zip) files.

Chapter 3, Exploring .NET, examines .NET, which provides the foundation for PowerShell 7. The chapter looks at .NET assemblies, classes, and methods. The chapter concludes with showing you how to create simple C#-based PowerShell extensions, as well as a full PowerShell cmdlet.

Chapter 4, Managing Active Directory, examines how to install, manage, and leverage Active Directory, including installing domains and child domains, managing AD objects, and leveraging Group Policy. This chapter also shows how you can use a CSV to create multiple AD user accounts.

Chapter 5, Managing Networking, shows you how to manage Windows networking with PowerShell. Networks are today central to almost every organization and this chapter looks at a variety of network-related tasks, including looking at new ways (with PowerShell) to do old things, such as setting up DNS, DHCP, and DHCP failover and load balancing.

Chapter 6, Implementing Enterprise Security, looks at security aspects within the context of an enterprise environment. The chapter looks at Just Enough Administration (JEA), which limits the actions an administrator can perform remotely). The chapter also looks at the event log, and PowerShell 7's script block logging, setting PowerShell 7 related Group policies and configuring a fine-grained AD password policy. The chapter concludes by looking at the Windows Defender AV product built into Windows Server.

Chapter 7, Managing Storage, looks at managing storage in Windows Server, including locally attached devices and Windows Storage Spaces. The chapter also looks at managing Storage Replica, a feature of Windows Server 2022.

Chapter 8, Managing Shared Data, examines different ways to share data and manage your shared data with Windows Server and PowerShell, including managing NTFS permissions, creating and securing SMB shares, and setting up and using iSCSI. The chapter concludes by looking at **File Server Resource Manager** (**FSRM**), a feature of Windows Server, and managing FSRM quotas, file screening, and reporting.

Chapter 9, Managing Printing, shows you how to manage printers, printer queues, and printer drivers as well as how to set up a printer pool. You will also examine how to print a test page.

Chapter 10, Exploring Windows Containers, shows you how to install the Containers feature in Windows Server 2022, and use sample containers you can download. You can use containers to create a website and create a custom container using a Docker file.

Chapter 11, Managing Hyper-V, demonstrates the use of Hyper-V. This chapter shows you how to build and deploy VMs with Hyper-V. This includes nested Hyper-V running a Hyper-V VM inside another Hyper-V VM, which is useful in many scenarios.

Chapter 12, Debugging and Troubleshooting Windows Server, looks at a number of aspects of both reactive and proactive troubleshooting. This includes using the PowerShell script debugger, getting events from the event log, and using the Best Practice Analyzer contained in Windows Server.

Chapter 13, Managing Window Server with Window Management Instrumentation (WMI), examines WMI and enables you to investigate WMI namespaces, classes, and class occurrences. You retrieve information from WMI classes, update WMI using WMI methods, and manage WMI events, including WMI permanent eventing.

Chapter 14, Managing Windows Update Services, examines how you can install, configure, and manage the **Windows Server Update Service** (**WSUS**). This chapter shows how to manage a Windows feature that has no PowerShell 7 commands and does not work natively in PowerShell 7.

To get the most out of this book

I designed and wrote this book based on some assumptions and with some constraints. Please read this section to understand how I intended the book to be used and what I have assumed about you. This should help you to get the most out of this book.

The first assumption I made in writing this book is that you know the very basics of Windows PowerShell. For that reason, this book is not a PowerShell tutorial. The recipes in this book make use of a wide range of PowerShell features, including WMI, Remoting, AD, and so on, but you need to know the basics of PowerShell. The book was developed using Windows 10/11 and Windows Server 2022.

The second, related, assumption is that you have a reasonable background in Windows infrastructure, including AD, networking, and storage. The recipes in each chapter provide an overview of the various technologies. I've tried to provide good links for more information on the topics in this book. The recipes are designed to show you the basics of how to manage aspects of Windows Server and how you might adapt them for your environment.

You start your exploration by installing and configuring PowerShell 7 and VS Code, and creating Hyper-V VMs to test out each chapter's recipes. I built and tested the recipes in this book step-by-step (i.e., not running the entire recipe as a single script file). If you run a recipe as a single step, some of the output may not be what you see here, due to how PowerShell formats objects.

Once you have any recipe working, try to re-factor the recipe's code into your own reusable functions. In some cases, we build simple functions as a guide to richer scripts you could build. Once you have working and useful functions, incorporate them into organizational or personal modules and reuse the code.

As any author knows, writing PowerShell scripts for publication in a book is a layout and production nightmare. To reduce the issues specifically with line width and line wrapping, I have made extensive use of methods that ensure the command line width fits in the book's chapters without wrapping. Many recipes use hash tables, property splatting, and other devices to ensure that every line of every recipe is 73 characters or less, and that there are no unintended line breaks. I hope there are not too many issues with layout!

Many of the cmdlets, commands, and object methods used in this book produce output that may not be all that helpful or useful, particularly in production. Some cmdlets generate output that would fill many pages of this book but with little added value. For this reason, many recipes pipe cmdlet output to `Out-Null`. Feel free to remove this where you want to see more details. I have also adjusted the output in many cases to avoid wasted white space. Thus, if you test a recipe, you may see the output that is laid out a bit differently, but it should contain the same information. Finally, remember that the specific output you see may be different based on your environment and the specific values you use in each step.

To write this book, I created a VM farm consisting of 14 Windows Server 2022 hosts. My main development host was a well-configured Windows 11 system (with 128 GB RAM, 2 x 16 core Xeon processors, and several fast SSDs). My host runs all the VMs in this book simultaneously. If your computing power is more modest, you can spin up just the VMs you need. I suggest you have a minimum of 16GB of RAM.

To assist in writing this book, I have also created a set of scripts that build the Hyper-V VMs, which I then used to develop and test the recipes in this book. I have published these scripts at: `https://github.com/doctordns/ReskitBuildScripts`. I have also published some details of the network of VMs created by using these scripts, complete with hostnames and IP addresses, at: `https://github.com/doctordns/ReskitBuildScripts/blob/master/ReskitNetwork.md`. The full set of VMs, at the end of writing this, took up around 500 GB of storage. Fortunately, storage is cheap! The GitHub repository has more details on the scripts and how to run them. If you have any issues with the scripts, please file an issue on GitHub and I can assist.

The build scripts are pretty easy to use, and I have added details on how to approach these scripts in the `Readme.md` file.

PowerShell 7 provides great feature coverage for managing Windows Server 2022 using Power-Shell. PowerShell offers considerable flexibility in what commands you use in your scripts. While PowerShell cmdlets are generally your first choice, in some cases, you need to dip down into .NET or into WMI to get to objects, properties, and methods that PowerShell cmdlets do not provide.

An important aspect of the recipes in this book is the use of third-party modules obtained from the PowerShell Gallery. A rich and vibrant PowerShell community has created a substantial amount of functionality for you to use. The PowerShell Gallery is a repository provided by Microsoft. With PowerShell, you can, download and use the resources available in the Gallery. The `NTFSSecurity` module, for example, makes it easier to manage the **Access Control List (ACL)** on NTFS files and folders.

I have tested all the code provided in this book. It worked when I tested it and did what it says (at least during the writing stage). I have taken some liberties regarding the layout and formatting of screenshots to cater to the book's production and printing process, but you should get the same results when you run these scripts.

The book production process is very complex, and errors can creep in during production. So if you find a step in any recipe that fails, file an issue in my GitHub repository for this book, and for generic issues, please post issues to the Spiceworks PowerShell forum at .

When writing the recipes, I use full cmdlet names with all parameter names spelled out in full. This approach makes the text a bit longer, but hopefully easier to read and understand. I have also used a variety of different ways you can achieve results.

In writing this book, I set out to create content around many features of Windows Server 2022. To publish the book, I have to avoid going too deep into every Windows Feature. I have had to decide which Windows Server features (and commands) to show and which not to cover since every chapter could easily have become its own book. To paraphrase Jeffrey Snover, *to ship is to choose*. I hope I chose well.

Some recipes in this book rely on you having run other recipes in previous chapters. These related recipes worked well when we wrote and tested them and hopefully work for you as well. If you have problems with any recipes, raise issues on my GitHub repository, and I can take a look and help.

Finally, there is a fine line between PowerShell and Windows Server features. To use PowerShell to manage any Windows feature, you need to understand the Windows feature as well as understand PowerShell. The chapters provide short overviews of the Windows Server features, and I have provided links to help you get more information. And as ever, Bing and Google are your best friends.

Download the example code files

The code bundle for the book is hosted on GitHub at `https://github.com/PacktPublishing/Windows-Server-Automation-with-PowerShell-Cookbook-5th-edition`. We also have other code bundles from our rich catalog of books and videos available at `https://github.com/PacktPublishing/`. Check them out!

The full and up-to-date repository for this book's scripts is at: `https://github.com/doctordns/PacktPS72/`.

Download the color images

We also provide a PDF file that has color images of the screenshots/diagrams used in this book. You can download it here: `https://packt.link/SlBcp`.

Conventions used

There are a number of text conventions used throughout this book.

`CodeInText`: Indicates code words in text, database table names, folder names, filenames, file extensions, pathnames, dummy URLs, user input, and Twitter handles. For example: " The `System.IO.FileInfo` class has a static method `new()` that enables you to create a new file."

Any command-line input or output is written as follows:

```
$Manifest = Get-Content -Path $Mod.Path
$Manifest | Select-Object -First 20
```

Bold: Indicates a new term, an important word, or words that you see on the screen. For instance, words in menus or dialog boxes appear in the text like this. For example: " Click on **Open File** to run the .NET SDK installer."

Warnings or important notes appear like this.

Tips and tricks appear like this.

Get in touch

Feedback from our readers is always welcome.

General feedback: Email feedback@packtpub.com and mention the book's title in the subject of your message. If you have questions about any aspect of this book, please email us at questions@packtpub.com.

Errata: Although we have taken every care to ensure the accuracy of our content, mistakes do happen. If you have found a mistake in this book, we would be grateful if you reported this to us. Please visit http://www.packtpub.com/submit-errata, click **Submit Errata**, and fill in the form. Alternatively post an issue in GitHub at https://github.com/doctordns/PacktPS72/issues.

Piracy: If you come across any illegal copies of our works in any form on the internet, we would be grateful if you would provide us with the location address or website name. Please contact us at copyright@packtpub.com with a link to the material.

If you are interested in becoming an author: If there is a topic that you have expertise in and you are interested in either writing or contributing to a book, please visit http://authors.packtpub.com.

Share your thoughts

Once you've read *Windows Server Automation with PowerShell Cookbook, Fifth Edition,* we'd love to hear your thoughts! Scan the QR code below to go straight to the Amazon review page for this book and share your feedback.

https://packt.link/r/1-804-61423-8

Your review is important to us and the tech community and will help us make sure we're delivering excellent quality content.

Download a free PDF copy of this book

Thanks for purchasing this book!

Do you like to read on the go but are unable to carry your print books everywhere? Is your eBook purchase not compatible with the device of your choice?

Don't worry, now with every Packt book you get a DRM-free PDF version of that book at no cost.

Read anywhere, any place, on any device. Search, copy, and paste code from your favorite technical books directly into your application.

The perks don't stop there, you can get exclusive access to discounts, newsletters, and great free content in your inbox daily

Follow these simple steps to get the benefits:

1. Scan the QR code or visit the link below

https://packt.link/free-ebook/9781804614235

2. Submit your proof of purchase
3. That's it! We'll send your free PDF and other benefits to your email directly

1

Installing and Configuring PowerShell 7

This chapter covers the following recipes:

- Installing PowerShell 7
- Installing PowerShell 7 Using Chocolatey
- Using the PowerShell 7 Console
- Building PowerShell 7 Profile Files
- Exploring Installation Artifacts
- Installing VS Code
- Installing the Cascadia Code Font
- Exploring PSReadLine

Introduction

Microsoft Windows PowerShell was first introduced to the public in 2003, and released formally, as Windows PowerShell v1, in 2006. Microsoft has released multiple versions of Windows PowerShell. Microsoft plans to support Windows PowerShell 5.1 for a long time, but no new features are likely.

In 2016, the PowerShell development team began working on an open-source version of PowerShell based on the open-source version of .NET Core (later renamed to just .NET). You can read the announcement by Jeffrey Snover here: `https://azure.microsoft.com/blog/powershell-is-open-sourced-and-is-available-on-linux/`. This new version is just PowerShell (or PowerShell 7).

The initial versions (PowerShell 6.X) represented, in effect, a proof of concept – you could run the core functions and features of PowerShell across the Windows, Mac, and Linux platforms. Those early versions also enabled the development team to implement all the necessary tooling to allow future development. But they were quite limited in supporting the rich needs of the IT professional community.

With the release of PowerShell 7.0 came improved parity with Windows PowerShell. A few modules did not work with PowerShell 7, and a few more operated via a compatibility mechanism. PowerShell 7.0 shipped in 2019 and was followed by version 7.1 and version 7.2 (released in late 2021). This book uses the term "PowerShell 7" to include PowerShell 7.0, 7.1, and 7.2. If there are version-specific issues, the chapters call those out specifically.

Microsoft does not include PowerShell 7 in Windows, thus you have to install it on each system. And as ever, you have options including direct from GitHub and via other installers such as Chocolatey.

Once you have installed PowerShell 7, you can use it just as you used the Windows PowerShell console to run commands or scripts. You can run it from a shortcut on the desktop, from the start panel, from a shortcut on the taskbar, or just run the executable. The name of the executable for PowerShell 7 is pwsh.exe (versus powershell.exe for Windows PowerShell).

Another important difference is that PowerShell 7 uses different profile file locations from Windows PowerShell. This feature allows you to customize your profiles to use the new PowerShell 7 features. And that, in turn, enables you to run both Windows PowerShell and PowerShell 7 side by side without interference.

Most IT pros who have used Windows PowerShell are familiar with the **Integrated Scripting Environment (ISE)**. The ISE was a great tool you used with Windows PowerShell. However, you cannot use the ISE with PowerShell 7. A very worthy successor to the ISE is **Visual Studio Code (VS Code)**, an open-source editing project that provides all the features of the ISE and a great deal more. Installation of VS Code is optional but relatively straightforward.

Microsoft also developed a new font, Cascadia Code, to coincide with the launch of VS Code. This font is a nice improvement over Courier or other mono-width fonts. All screenshots of working code in this book use this new font.

PSReadLine is a PowerShell module designed to provide color-coding of PowerShell scripts in the PowerShell 7 Console. The module, included with PowerShell 7 by default, makes editing at the command line easier and more on par with the features available in Linux shells. You can also use the later versions of PSReadLine with Windows PowerShell.

Systems used in the chapter

This chapter is all about getting you started with PowerShell 7 – installing and configuring your environment to make the most out of PowerShell 7. In this chapter, you use a single host, SRV1, as follows:

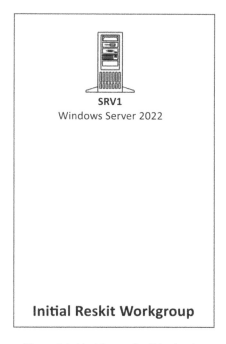

SRV1
Windows Server 2022

Initial Reskit Workgroup

Figure 1.1: Host in use for this chapter

In later chapters, you will use additional servers and promote SRV1 to be a domain-based server rather than being in a workgroup.

Installing PowerShell 7

As mentioned, PowerShell 7 is not installed in Windows by default, at least not at the time of writing. The PowerShell team made PowerShell 7.1 available from the Microsoft Store, which is useful to install PowerShell 7.1 or later on Windows 10/11 systems. Windows Server does not support the Microsoft Store.

You have other methods of installing PowerShell 7 on your systems. The first option is to use the Install-PowerShell.ps1 script, which you download from GitHub, as shown in this recipe. You can also use this recipe on Windows 10 hosts. This approach has the advantage of being the most up-to-date source of the latest versions of PowerShell.

Getting ready

This recipe uses SRV1, a Windows Server workgroup host. There are no features of applications loaded on this server (yet).

You can use either the Windows PowerShell console or the ISE for this recipe.

How to do it...

1. Setting an execution policy for Windows PowerShell

    ```
    Set-ExecutionPolicy -ExecutionPolicy Unrestricted -Force
    ```

2. Updating help text for Windows PowerShell

    ```
    Update-Help -Force | Out-Null
    ```

3. Ensuring the C:\Foo Folder exists

    ```
    $LFHT = @{
      ItemType    = 'Directory'
      ErrorAction = 'SilentlyContinue' # should it already exist
    }
    New-Item -Path C:\Foo @LFHT | Out-Null
    ```

4. Downloading PowerShell 7 installation script from GitHub

    ```
    Set-Location -Path C:\Foo
    $URI = 'https://aka.ms/install-powershell.ps1'
    Invoke-RestMethod -Uri $URI |
      Out-File -FilePath C:\Foo\Install-PowerShell.ps1
    ```

5. Viewing Installation Script Help

    ```
    Get-Help -Name C:\Foo\Install-PowerShell.ps1
    ```

6. Installing PowerShell 7.2

    ```
    $EXTHT = @{
      UseMSI                = $true
      Quiet                 = $true
      AddExplorerContextMenu = $true
      EnablePSRemoting      = $true
    }
    ```

```
C:\Foo\Install-PowerShell.ps1 @EXTHT | Out-Null
```

7. Installing the preview and daily builds (for the adventurous)

```
C:\Foo\Install-PowerShell.ps1 -Preview -Destination C:\PSPreview |
  Out-Null
C:\Foo\Install-PowerShell.ps1 -Daily   -Destination C:\PSDailyBuild
|
  Out-Null
```

8. Creating Windows PowerShell default profiles

```
# First the ISE
$URI = 'https://raw.githubusercontent.com/doctordns/PACKTPS72/
master' +
        '/scripts/goodies/Microsoft.PowerShell_Profile.ps1'
$ProfileFile    = $Profile.CurrentUserCurrentHost
New-Item -Path $ProfileFile -Force -WarningAction SilentlyContinue |
   Out-Null
(Invoke-WebRequest -Uri $URI -UseBasicParsing).Content |
  Out-File -FilePath  $ProfileFile
# Now profile for ConsoleHost
$ProfilePath    = Split-Path -Path $ProfileFile
$ChildPath      = 'Microsoft.PowerShell_profile.ps1'
$ConsoleProfile = Join-Path -Path $ProfilePath -ChildPath $ChildPath
(Invoke-WebRequest -Uri $URI -UseBasicParsing).Content |
  Out-File -FilePath  $ConsoleProfile
```

9. Checking versions of PowerShell 7 loaded

```
Get-ChildItem -Path C:\pwsh.exe -Recurse -ErrorAction
SilentlyContinue
```

How it works...

In *step 1*, you set the execution policy for Windows PowerShell to Unrestricted. This step, which produces no output, simplifies the installation and setup of PowerShell. In production, you may wish to set PowerShell's execution policy to be more restrictive.

Most of the scripts in this book should run successfully using a more restrictive setting. To simplify things, this recipe sets the execution policy to Unrestricted.

In *step 2*, you update the help text files for Windows PowerShell, which produces output like this:

```
PS C:\WINDOWS\system32> # 2. Update help text for Windows PowerShell
PS C:\WINDOWS\system32> Update-Help -Force |
                            Out-Null
Update-Help : Failed to update Help for the module(s) 'ConfigDefender, ConfigDefenderPerformance, Dism, Get-NetView,
              Kds, Microsoft.ServerCore.SConfig, NetQos, PcsvDevice, PKI, PSReadline, RemoteDesktop, StorageBusCache,
              VMDirectStorage, Whea, WindowsUpdate' with UI culture(s) {en-US} : Unable to retrieve the HelpInfo XML
              file for UI culture en-US.
              Make sure the HelpInfoUri property in the module manifest is valid or check your network connection
              and then try the command again.
At line:1 char:1
+ Update-Help -Force |
+ ~~~~~~~~~~~~~~~~~~~
    + CategoryInfo          : ResourceUnavailable: (:) [Update-Help], Exception
    + FullyQualifiedErrorId : UnableToRetrieveHelpInfoXml,Microsoft.PowerShell.Commands.UpdateHelpCommand
```

Figure 1.2: Updating help files

Note that after installing PowerShell 7, PowerShell prompts you to download help text (not shown in this figure) the first time you use Get-Help.

In *step 3*, you create a folder, C:\Foo. This book uses this folder as a place to put files used by the book's recipes. For example, this recipe stores the PowerShell installation file in this folder from which you execute the script to install PowerShell 7. Also, note that this step mixes spatting, using hash tables, and direct parameter specification. You can always mix and match.

With *step 4*, you download the PowerShell installation script from GitHub. Although you can look in C:\Foo to examine the script, this step produces no output.

The installation script is a PowerShell script. In *step 5*, you use Get-Help to get details on the script, as shown here:

```
PS C:\WINDOWS\system32> # 5. Viewing Installation Script Help
PS C:\WINDOWS\system32> Get-Help -Name C:\Foo\Install-PowerShell.ps1
Install-PowerShell.ps1 [-Destination <string>] [-Daily] [-DoNotOverwrite] [-AddToPath] [-Preview] [<CommonParameters>]
Install-PowerShell.ps1 [-UseMSI] [-Quiet] [-AddExplorerContextMenu] [-EnablePSRemoting] [-Preview] [<CommonParameters>]
```

Figure 1.3: Getting help information from the installation script

In *step 6*, you use the installation script to install PowerShell 7 on SRV1, with output like this:

```
PS C:\WINDOWS\system32> # 6. Installing PowerShell 7.2
PS C:\WINDOWS\system32> EXTHT = @{
                           UseMSI                  = $true
                           Quiet                   = $true
                           AddExplorerContextMenu  = $true
                           EnablePSRemoting        = $true
                        }
PS C:\WINDOWS\system32> C:\Foo\Install-PowerShell.ps1 @EXTHT | Out-Null

VERBOSE: About to download package from 'https://github.com/PowerShell/PowerShell/releases/download/v7.2.2/PowerShell-7.2.2-win-x64.msi'
```

Figure 1.4: Installing PowerShell 7

PowerShell 7 is a work in progress. On most weekdays, the PowerShell team builds updated versions of PowerShell. Monthly, the team also releases preview versions of the next major version. At time of writing, the current preview is 7.3 Preview 3 – but that should change by the time you read this and the team releases new previews. The daily and preview builds are usually very stable and allow you to try out new features that may be in the next major release. The daily build enables you to view progress on a specific bug or feature. You may find it useful to install both of these. Note that if you install preview/daily builds as shown in this recipe, you also need to ensure you keep them up to date as time goes by – Microsoft's update services do not update these side-by-side installations.

In *step 7*, you install the latest preview build along with the latest build of PowerShell, which looks like this:

```
PS C:\WINDOWS\system32> # 7. Installing the preview and daily builds (for the adventurous)
PS C:\WINDOWS\system32> C:\Foo\Install-PowerShell.ps1 -Preview -Destination C:\PSPreview |
                           Out-Null
Destination: C:\PSPreview
About to download package from 'https://github.com/PowerShell/PowerShell/releases/download/v7.3.0-preview.3/PowerShell-7.3.0-preview.3-win-x64.zip'
PowerShell has been installed at C:\PSPreview
PS C:\WINDOWS\system32> C:\Foo\Install-PowerShell.ps1 -Daily    -Destination C:\PSDailyBuild |
                           Out-Null
Destination: C:\PSDailyBuild
About to download package from 'https://pscoretestdata.blob.core.windows.net/v7-3-0-daily20220329-1/PowerShell-7.3.0-daily20220329.1-win-x64.zip'
PowerShell has been installed at C:\PSDailyBuild
```

Figure 1.5: Installing the preview and daily builds

PowerShell, like Windows PowerShell, uses profile files to enable you to configure PowerShell each time you run it (whether in the PowerShell console or as part of VS Code).

In *step 8*, you download sample PowerShell profile scripts and save them locally, which produces no output. This step assumes you are running the script from the ISE – the first part creates an ISE profile while the second establishes a PowerShell profile for the Console Host.

The executable name for PowerShell 7 is pwsh.exe. In *step 9*, you view the versions of this file as follows:

```
PS C:\Foo> # 9. Checking versions of PowerShell 7 loaded
Get-ChildItem -Path C:\pwsh.exe -Recurse -ErrorAction SilentlyContinue

    Directory: C:\Program Files\PowerShell\7

Mode                 LastWriteTime         Length Name
----                 -------------         ------ ----
-a----        08/03/2022     23:21         287632 pwsh.exe

    Directory: C:\PSDailyBuild

Mode                 LastWriteTime         Length Name
----                 -------------         ------ ----
-a----        29/03/2022     18:24         286104 pwsh.exe

    Directory: C:\PSPreview

Mode                 LastWriteTime         Length Name
----                 -------------         ------ ----
-a----        18/03/2022     17:04         281512 pwsh.exe
```

Figure 1.6: Checking PowerShell 7 versions loaded

As you can see, there are three versions of PowerShell 7 installed on SRV1: the latest full release, the latest preview, and the build of the day.

There's more...

In *step 1*, you update the execution policy for Windows PowerShell. While this simplifies the installation and configuration of hosts, it may be unduly permissive for your environment, and you can change it as needed. Don't forget, though, PowerShell's execution policy is not truly a security mechanism – it just slows down an inexperienced administrator. For a good explanation of PowerShell's Security Guiding Principles, see https://devblogs.microsoft.com/powershell/powershells-security-guiding-principles/.

In *step 2*, you updated the help files for Windows PowerShell. This step is optional, but later steps can prompt you to update your help files if you skip it. Installing the most up-to-date help files also adds many conceptual help topics to help you get more out of PowerShell.

In *step 4*, you use a shortened URL to download the `Install-PowerShell.ps1` script. When you use `Invoke-RestMethod`, PowerShell discovers the underlying target URL for the script. The short URL allows Microsoft and the PowerShell team to publish a well-known URL and then have the flexibility to move the target location should that be necessary. The target URL, at the time of writing, is `https://raw.githubusercontent.com/PowerShell/PowerShell/master/tools/install-powershell.ps1`.

In *step 6*, you use the installation script to install PowerShell 7 on SRV2. This step installs PowerShell 7.2.2, as you can see, using an MSI. The MSI, which you install silently without any user notification, updates the system execution path to add the PowerShell 7 installation folder. At the time of writing, the latest released version of PowerShell is 7.2.2. In *step 7*, you install the latest preview build (a foretaste of things to come in the next version of PowerShell) and the daily build (for the brave). The code here retrieves the latest supported version of PowerShell 7, plus the preview and daily builds. When you run this recipe, the versions you install are going to be later than what is shown here.

In *step 8*, you create two sample profile files: an ISE profile and a profile for the console host. Windows PowerShell uses the profile when you launch the PowerShell console. PowerShell 7 also uses the profile (when you run PowerShell 7 in the console or Microsoft Terminal).

In *step 9*, you can see that you have installed PowerShell 7 (into `C:\Program Files`) and the latest daily build and preview versions. The specific file versions you see may differ from the output shown here, reflecting the relentless progress of the PowerShell team.

Installing PowerShell 7 Using Chocolatey

Chocolatey is a third-party package management tool for Windows. Chocolatey has a large set of packages you can install, and the Chocolatey tool (`choco.exe`) provides a rich set of management features. You can install Chocolatey on both Windows Client machines (Windows 10/11 and earlier versions) and, as this recipe demonstrates, you can also install Chocolatey on Windows Server.

Chocolatey has a very large online registry of Windows packages that you can install, simplifying the deployment of applications in your environment. Read more about the company and its products at its website, `https://chocolatey.org/`.

Getting ready

You run this recipe on SRV1 after you have installed PowerShell 7. The method shown here installs PowerShell 7 using an MSI package. In the *Installing PowerShell 7* recipe, you installed PowerShell 7 using the MSI. With PowerShell already installed, this recipe installs Chocolatey but would fail gracefully attempting to reinstall PowerShell 7. If you want to test the installation of PowerShell 7 using Chocolatey, you should remove PowerShell 7.

Run this script using the PowerShell ISE.

How to do it...

1. Downloading the installation script for Chocolatey

```
$ChocoIns = 'C:\Foo\Install-Chocolatey.ps1'
$DI       = New-Object System.Net.WebClient
$DI.DownloadString('https://community.chocolatey.org/install.ps1') |
  Out-File -FilePath $ChocoIns
```

2. Viewing the installation help file

```
C:\Foo\Install-Chocolatey.ps1 -?
```

3. Installing Chocolatey

```
C:\Foo\Install-Chocolatey.ps1
```

4. Configuring Chocolatey

```
choco feature enable -n allowGlobalConfirmation
```

5. Finding PowerShell (PWSH) on Chocolatey

```
choco find pwsh
```

6. Installing PowerShell 7 using choco.exe

```
choco install powershell-core –force
```

How it works...

In *step 1*, you download the Chocolatey installation script. You need this script to install Chocolatey. This step produces no output.

In *step 2*, you use Get-Help to view the help information for the Chocolatey install script, with output like this:

```
PS C:\WINDOWS\system32> # 2. Viewing the installation help file
PS C:\WINDOWS\system32> C:\Foo\Install-Chocolatey.ps1 -?

NAME
    C:\Foo\Install-Chocolatey.ps1

SYNOPSIS
    Downloads and installs Chocolatey on the local machine.

SYNTAX
    C:\Foo\Install-Chocolatey.ps1 [-ChocolateyDownloadUrl <String>]
                                  [-ChocolateyVersion <String>]
                                  [-UseNativeUnzip]
                                  [-IgnoreProxy]
                                  [<CommonParameters>]

    C:\Foo\Install-Chocolatey.ps1 [-ChocolateyDownloadUrl <String>]
                                  [-ChocolateyVersion <String>]
                                  [-UseNativeUnzip]
                                  [-IgnoreProxy]
                                  [-ProxyUrl <String>]
                                  [-ProxyCredential <PSCredential>]
                                  [<CommonParameters>]


DESCRIPTION
    Retrieves the Chocolatey nupkg for the latest or a specified version, and
    downloads and installs the application to the local machine.


RELATED LINKS
    For organizational deployments of Chocolatey, please see
    https://docs.chocolatey.org/en-us/guides/organizations/organizational-deployment-guide

REMARKS
    To see the examples, type: "get-help C:\Foo\Install-Chocolatey.ps1 -examples".
    For more information, type: "get-help C:\Foo\Install-Chocolatey.ps1 -detailed".
    For technical information, type: "get-help C:\Foo\Install-Chocolatey.ps1 -full".
    For online help, type: "get-help C:\Foo\Install-Chocolatey.ps1 -online"
```

Figure 1.7: Viewing the Chocolatey installation script help details

In *step 3*, you use the installation script to download and install Chocolatey on SRV1. The output looks like this:

```
PS C:\WINDOWS\system32> # 3. Installing Chocolatey
PS C:\WINDOWS\system32> C:\Foo\Install-Chocolatey.ps1

Forcing web requests to allow TLS v1.2 (Required for requests to Chocolatey.org)
Getting latest version of the Chocolatey package for download.
Not using proxy.
Getting Chocolatey from https://community.chocolatey.org/api/v2/package/chocolatey/1.1.0.
Downloading https://community.chocolatey.org/api/v2/package/chocolatey/1.1.0 to
  C:\Users\ADMINI~1\AppData\Local\Temp\2\chocolatey\chocoInstall\chocolatey.zip
Not using proxy.
Extracting C:\Users\ADMINI~1\AppData\Local\Temp\2\chocolatey\chocoInstall\chocolatey.zip to
  C:\Users\ADMINI~1\AppData\Local\Temp\2\chocolatey\chocoInstall
Installing Chocolatey on the local machine
Creating ChocolateyInstall as an environment variable (targeting 'Machine')
  Setting ChocolateyInstall to 'C:\ProgramData\chocolatey'
WARNING: It's very likely you will need to close and reopen your shell
  before you can use choco.
Restricting write permissions to Administrators
We are setting up the Chocolatey package repository.
The packages themselves go to 'C:\ProgramData\chocolatey\lib'
  (i.e. C:\ProgramData\chocolatey\lib\yourPackageName).
A shim file for the command line goes to 'C:\ProgramData\chocolatey\bin'
  and points to an executable in 'C:\ProgramData\chocolatey\lib\yourPackageName'.

Creating Chocolatey folders if they do not already exist.

WARNING: You can safely ignore errors related to missing log files when
  upgrading from a version of Chocolatey less than 0.9.9.
  'Batch file could not be found' is also safe to ignore.
  'The system cannot find the file specified' - also safe.
chocolatey.nupkg file not installed in lib.
  Attempting to locate it from bootstrapper.
PATH environment variable does not have C:\ProgramData\chocolatey\bin in it. Adding...
Adding Chocolatey to the profile. This will provide tab completion, refreshenv, etc.
WARNING: Chocolatey profile installed. Reload your profile - type . $profile
Chocolatey (choco.exe) is now ready.
You can call choco from anywhere, command line or powershell by typing choco.
Run choco /? for a list of functions.
You may need to shut down and restart powershell and/or consoles
  first prior to using choco.
Ensuring Chocolatey commands are on the path
Ensuring chocolatey.nupkg is in the lib folder
```

Figure 1.8: Installing Chocolatey

In *step 4*, you use choco.exe to set certain feature options with the following output:

```
PS C:\WINDOWS\system32> # 4.Configuring Chocolatey
PS C:\WINDOWS\system32> choco feature enable -n allowGlobalConfirmation
Chocolatey v1.1.0
Enabled allowGlobalConfirmation
```

Figure 1.9: Setting Chocolatey global options

In *step 5*, you use choco.exe to find PowerShell packages that you can install using Chocolatey.

The output looks like this:

```
PS C:\WINDOWS\system32> # 5. Finding PowerShell (PWSH) on Chocolatey
PS C:\WINDOWS\system32> choco find pwsh
Chocolatey v1.1.0
pwsh 7.2.2 [Approved]
powershell.portable 7.1.3 [Approved] Downloads cached for licensed users
powershell-core 7.2.2 [Approved] Downloads cached for licensed users
powershell-preview 7.2.4.20210411 [Approved] Downloads cached for licensed users
4 packages found.
```

Figure 1.10: Finding PowerShell on Chocolatey

In *step 6*, you install PowerShell 7 using Chocolatey. There is a lot of output, which looks like this:

```
PS C:\WINDOWS\system32> # 6. Installing PowerShell-7 using choco.exe
PS C:\WINDOWS\system32> choco install powershell-core
Chocolatey v1.1.0
Installing the following packages:
powershell-core
By installing, you accept licenses for the packages.

Progress: Downloading powershell-core 7.2.2... 4%
Progress: Downloading powershell-core 7.2.2... 100%

powershell-core v7.2.2 [Approved]
powershell-core package files install completed. Performing other installation steps.
7.2.2
WARNING: If you started this package under PowerShell core, replacing an in-use version may be unpredictable, require mu
ltiple attempts or produce errors.
Downloading powershell-core 64 bit
  from 'https://github.com/PowerShell/PowerShell/releases/download/v7.2.2/PowerShell-7.2.2-win-x64.msi'

Progress: 0% - Saving 13.39 KB of 101.8 MB
Progress: 100% - Completed download of C:\Users\Administrator\AppData\Local\Temp\2\chocolatey\powershell-core\7.2.2\Powe
rShell-7.2.2-win-x64.msi (101.8 MB).
Download of PowerShell-7.2.2-win-x64.msi (101.8 MB) completed.
Hashes match.
Installing powershell-core...
powershell-core has been installed.
********************************************************************************
*  INSTRUCTIONS: Your system default WINDOWS PowerShell version has not been changed.
*    PowerShell CORE 7.2.2, was installed to: "C:\Program Files\PowerShell\7"
*    To start PowerShell Core 7.2.2, at a prompt or the start menu execute:
*       "pwsh.exe"
*    Or start it from the desktop or start menu shortcut installed by this package.
*    This is your new default version of PowerShell CORE (pwsh.exe).
********************************************************************************
********************************************************************************
*  As of OpenSSH 0.0.22.0 Universal Installer, a script is distributed that allows  *
*  setting the default shell for openssh. You could call it with code like this:    *
*    If (Test-Path "C:\Program Files\openssh-win64\Set-SSHDefaultShell.ps1")         *
*      {& "C:\Program Files\openssh-win64\Set-SSHDefaultShell.ps1" [PARAMETERS]}      *
*  Learn more with this:                                                             *
*    Get-Help "C:\Program Files\openssh-win64\Set-SSHDefaultShell.ps1"               *
*  Or here:                                                                          *
*    https://github.com/DarwinJS/ChocoPackages/blob/main/openssh/readme.md           *
********************************************************************************
 powershell-core may be able to be automatically uninstalled.
Environment Vars (like PATH) have changed. Close/reopen your shell to
 see the changes (or in powershell/cmd.exe just type `refreshenv`).
 The install of powershell-core was successful.
  Software installed as 'msi', install location is likely default.

Chocolatey installed 1/1 packages.
 See the log for details (C:\ProgramData\chocolatey\logs\chocolatey.log).

Enjoy using Chocolatey? Explore more amazing features to take your
experience to the next level at
 https://chocolatey.org/compare
```

Figure 1.11: Installing PowerShell 7

There's more...

In *step 1*, you open a new Windows PowerShell 7 console. Make sure you run the console as the local administrator.

In *step 6*, you install PowerShell 7 (7.2.2, as you can see in the output). The result shows the successful installation of PowerShell.

If you do not uninstall PowerShell 7, then when you run this step, you will see different output, indicating that you have already installed the product, and thus, the installation fails gracefully.

Using the PowerShell 7 Console

Once you have installed PowerShell 7, you can explore the PowerShell 7 console irrespective of your installation method. In the main, the PowerShell 7 console is similar to the Windows PowerShell console, but you should notice a few differences.

Getting ready

You run this recipe on SRV1 after you have installed PowerShell 7. You can install PowerShell 7 using the installation script (as in the *Installing PowerShell 7* recipe), Chocolatey (as in the *Installing PowerShell 7 using Chocolatey* recipe), or any other mechanism. You run this recipe in the PowerShell 7 console – pwsh.exe.

How to do it...

1. Viewing the PowerShell version

   ```
   $PSVersionTable
   ```

2. Viewing the $Host variable

   ```
   $Host
   ```

3. Looking at the PowerShell process (PWSH)

   ```
   Get-Process -Id $PID |
     Format-Custom -Property MainModule -Depth 1
   ```

4. Looking at resource usage statistics

   ```
   Get-Process -Id $PID |
     Format-List CPU,*Memory*
   ```

5. Updating the PowerShell 7 help files

```
$Before = Get-Help -Name about_*
Update-Help -Force | Out-Null
$After = Get-Help -Name about_*
$Delta = $After.Count - $Before.Count
"{0} Conceptual Help Files Added" -f $Delta
```

6. Determining available commands

```
Get-Command |
  Group-Object -Property CommandType
```

7. Examining the Path Variable

```
$env:path.split(';')
```

How it works...

In *step 1*, you view the PowerShell version information contained in `$PSVersionTable`, which produces output like this:

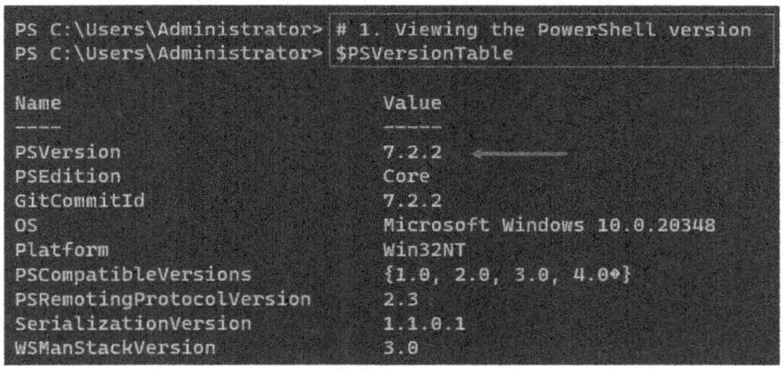

```
PS C:\Users\Administrator> # 1. Viewing the PowerShell version
PS C:\Users\Administrator> $PSVersionTable

Name                           Value
----                           -----
PSVersion                      7.2.2
PSEdition                      Core
GitCommitId                    7.2.2
OS                             Microsoft Windows 10.0.20348
Platform                       Win32NT
PSCompatibleVersions           {1.0, 2.0, 3.0, 4.0…}
PSRemotingProtocolVersion      2.3
SerializationVersion           1.1.0.1
WSManStackVersion              3.0
```

Figure 1.12: Viewing the $PSVersionTable variable

In *step 2*, you view the contents of the `$Host` variable, which contains details of the PowerShell host (i.e., the PowerShell 7 console), which looks like this:

```
PS C:\Users\Administrator> # 2. Viewing the $Host variable
PS C:\Users\Administrator> $Host

Name             : ConsoleHost  ←
Version          : 7.2.2  ←
InstanceId       : e9582c28-fc21-46fa-8e93-4c1738c9eed3
UI               : System.Management.Automation.Internal.Host.InternalHostUserInterface
CurrentCulture   : en-GB
CurrentUICulture : en-US
PrivateData      : Microsoft.PowerShell.ConsoleHost+ConsoleColorProxy
DebuggerEnabled  : True
IsRunspacePushed : False
Runspace         : System.Management.Automation.Runspaces.LocalRunspace
```

Figure 1.13: Viewing $Host

In *step 3*, you view the details of the PowerShell process (pwsh.exe) with output like this:

```
PS C:\Users\Administrator> # 3. Looking at the PowerShell process (PWSH)
PS C:\Users\Administrator> Get-Process -Id $PID |
                              Format-Custom -Property MainModule -Depth 1

class Process
{
  MainModule =
    class ProcessModule
      {
        ModuleName = pwsh.exe
        FileName = C:\Program Files\PowerShell\7\pwsh.exe  ←
        BaseAddress = 140702355292160
        ModuleMemorySize = 303104
        EntryPointAddress = 140702355373392
        FileVersionInfo = File:              C:\Program Files\PowerShell\7\pwsh.exe  ←
        InternalName:     pwsh.dll
        OriginalFilename: pwsh.dll
        FileVersion:      7.2.2.500
        FileDescription:  pwsh
        Product:          PowerShell
        ProductVersion:   7.2.2 SHA: 9027d1a433831dcabd8e108f65a893bec63b0c1b
        Debug:            False
        Patched:          False
        PreRelease:       False
        PrivateBuild:     False
        SpecialBuild:     False
        Language:         Language Neutral

        Site =
        Container =
        Size = 296
        Company = Microsoft Corporation
        FileVersion = 7.2.2.500
        ProductVersion = 7.2.2 SHA: 9027d1a433831dcabd8e108f65a893bec63b0c1b
        Description = pwsh
        Product = PowerShell
      }
}
```

Figure 1.14: Viewing the pwsh process

In *step 4*, you can observe the resources used by this process by using Get-Process and viewing the resource-related properties, with output like this:

```
PS C:\Users\Administrator> # 4. Looking at resource usage statistics
PS C:\Users\Administrator> Get-Process -Id $PID |
                           Format-List CPU,*Memory*

CPU                        : 2.71875
NonpagedSystemMemorySize64 : 66888
NonpagedSystemMemorySize   : 66888
PagedMemorySize64          : 48328704
PagedMemorySize            : 48328704
PagedSystemMemorySize64    : 428712
PagedSystemMemorySize      : 428712
PeakPagedMemorySize64      : 49778688
PeakPagedMemorySize        : 49778688
PeakVirtualMemorySize64    : 2204178198528
PeakVirtualMemorySize      : 859975680
PrivateMemorySize64        : 48328704
PrivateMemorySize          : 48328704
VirtualMemorySize64        : 2204171730944
VirtualMemorySize          : 853508096
```

Figure 1.15: Viewing the pwsh resource usage

It is always useful to get the most up-to-date help files, which you can do using Update-Help. In *step 5*, you update the PowerShell 7 help files and count the number of conceptual help files resulting from updating help. The output of this step looks like this:

```
PS C:\Users\Administrator> # 5. Updating the PowerShell 7 help files
PS C:\Users\Administrator> $Before = Get-Help -Name about_*
PS C:\Users\Administrator> Update-Help -Force | Out-Null
Update-Help: Failed to update Help for the module(s) 'ConfigDefenderPerformance, Dism, kds,
  NetQos, PcsvDevice, PRI, PSReadline, Whea, WindowsUpdate' with UI culture(s) {en-US} :
  One or more errors occurred. (Response status code does not indicate success:
  404 (The specified blob does not exist.).).
English-US help content is_available_and_can_be_installed using: Update-Help -UICulture en-US.
PS C:\Users\Administrator> $After = Get-Help -Name about_*
PS C:\Users\Administrator> $Delta = $After.Count - $Before.Count
PS C:\Users\Administrator> "{0} Conceptual Help Files Added" -f $Delta
136 Conceptual Help Files Added
```

Figure 1.16: Updating the PowerShell 7 help files

In *step 6*, you use Get-Command to determine the number of commands available to a newly installed version of PowerShell 7.2.2 (in this case!) on a freshly installed version of Windows Server 2022. The output looks like this:

```
PS C:\Users\Administrator> # 6. Determining available commands
PS C:\Users\Administrator> Get-Command |
                              Group-Object -Property CommandType


Count  Name      Group
-----  ----      -----
   58  Alias     {Add-AppPackage, Add-AppPackageVolume, Add-AppProvisionedPackage,...
 1136  Function  {A:, Add-BCDataCacheExtension, Add-DnsClientDohServerAddress...
  587  Cmdlet    {Add-AppxPackage, Add-AppxProvisionedPackage, Add-AppxVolume...}
```

Figure 1.17: Updating the PowerShell 7 help files

In the final step, *step 7*, you review the contents of the path environment variable, with output like this:

```
PS C:\WINDOWS\system32> # 7. Examining the Path Variable
PS C:\WINDOWS\system32> $env:path.split(';')
C:\WINDOWS\system32>
C:\WINDOWS
C:\WINDOWS\system32\Wbem
C:\WINDOWS\system32\WindowsPowerShell\v1.0
C:\WINDOWS\System32\OpenSSH\
C:\ProgramData\chocolatey\bin
C:\Program Files\PowerShell\7\
C:\Users\Administrator\AppData\Local\Microsoft\WindowsApps
```

Figure 1.18: Viewing the available commands in PowerShell 7

There's more...

In *step 1*, you examine the $PSVersion built-in variable. At the time of writing, the latest released version of PowerShell 7 is 7.2.2, as you can see in the output. However, when you run this step, you may discover you have installed a later version.

You run pwsh.exe to start PowerShell 7 via the console. PowerShell has a built-in variable, $PID, which holds the Windows process ID for the current PowerShell console. This variable can be useful if you have multiple consoles open at one time. You can use Get-Process, as shown in *step 2*, specifying the process ID, to get details of this PowerShell process.

Building PowerShell 7 Profile Files

Profile files are PowerShell scripts that PowerShell runs at startup. They are easy to create and support a range of deployment scenarios. They enable you to customize your PowerShell environment. See this article on Microsoft's PowerShell Community blog for more details on PowerShell profile files: https://devblogs.microsoft.com/powershell-community/how-to-make-use-of-powershell-profile-files/.

In this recipe, you examine profile files, download a sample PowerShell profile file, and install it on SRV1. This profile is just for the console. In a later recipe, you install VS Code and create a VS Code-specific profile.

Getting ready

You run this recipe on SRV1 after you have installed PowerShell 7. You should begin this recipe by opening up a PowerShell 7 console.

How to do it...

1. Discovering the profile filenames

```
$ProfileFiles = $PROFILE |  Get-Member -MemberType NoteProperty
$ProfileFiles | Format-Table -Property Name, Definition
```

2. Checking for the existence of each PowerShell profile file

```
Foreach ($ProfileFile in $ProfileFiles){
  "Testing $($ProfileFile.Name)"
  $ProfilePath = $ProfileFile.Definition.split('=')[1]
  If (Test-Path -Path $ProfilePath){
    "$($ProfileFile.Name) DOES EXIST"
    "At $ProfilePath"
  }
  Else {
    "$($ProfileFile.Name) DOES NOT EXIST"
  }
  ""
}
```

3. Discovering a Current User/Current Host profile

```
$CUCHProfile = $PROFILE.CurrentUserCurrentHost
"Current User/Current Host profile path: [$CUCHPROFILE]"
```

4. Creating a Current User/Current Host profile for the PowerShell 7 console

```
$URI = 'https://raw.githubusercontent.com/doctordns/PacktPS72/
master/' +
        'scripts/goodies/Microsoft.PowerShell_Profile.ps1'
New-Item $CUCHProfile -Force -WarningAction SilentlyContinue |
```

```
        Out-Null
    (Invoke-WebRequest -Uri $URI).Content |
      Out-File -FilePath $CUCHProfile
```

5. Exiting from the PowerShell 7 console

```
Exit
```

6. Restarting the PowerShell 7 console and viewing the profile output at startup

```
Get-ChildItem -Path $PROFILE
```

How it works...

In *step 1*, you use the $Profile built-in variable to obtain the filenames of the four profile files in PowerShell, with output like this:

```
PS C:\Users\Administrator> # 1. Discovering the profile file names
PS C:\Users\Administrator> $ProfileFiles = $PROFILE |  Get-Member -MemberType NoteProperty
PS C:\Users\Administrator> $ProfileFiles | Format-Table -Property Name, Definition

Name                    Definition
----                    ----------
AllUsersAllHosts        string AllUsersAllHosts=C:\Program Files\PowerShell\7\profile.ps1
AllUsersCurrentHost     string AllUsersCurrentHost=C:\Program Files\PowerShell\7\Microsoft.PowerShell_profile.ps1
CurrentUserAllHosts     string CurrentUserAllHosts=C:\Users\Administrator\Documents\PowerShell\profile.ps1
CurrentUserCurrentHost  string CurrentUserCurrentHost=C:\Users\Administrator\Documents\PowerShell\Microsoft.Power
```

Figure 1.19: Obtaining the PowerShell profile filenames

In *step 2*, you check to see which, if any, of the four profiles exist, with output like this:

```
PS C:\Users\Administrator> # 2. Checking for the existence of each PowerShell profile files
PS C:\Users\Administrator> Foreach ($ProfileFile in $ProfileFiles){
                               "Testing $($ProfileFile.Name)"
                               $ProfilePath = $ProfileFile.Definition.split('=')[1]
                                 If (Test-Path $ProfilePath){
                                   "$($ProfileFile.Name) DOES EXIST"
                                   "At $ProfilePath"
                                 }
                           Else {
                               "$($ProfileFile.Name) DOES NOT EXIST"
                           }
                           ""
                           }
Testing AllUsersAllHosts
AllUsersAllHosts DOES NOT EXIST

Testing AllUsersCurrentHost
AllUsersCurrentHost DOES NOT EXIST

Testing CurrentUserAllHosts
CurrentUserAllHosts DOES NOT EXIST

CurrentUserCurrentHost DOES NOT EXIST
```

Figure 1.20: Checking for the existence of the profile files

The profile file most IT pros use is the Current User/Current Host profile (aka $Profile). In *step 3*, you discover the filename for this profile file, with the following output:

```
PS C:\Users\Administrator> # 3. Discovering Current User/Current Host Profile
PS C:\Users\Administrator> $CUCHProfile = $PROFILE.CurrentUserCurrentHost
PS C:\Users\Administrator> "Current User/Current Host profile path: [$CUCHPROFILE]"
Current User/Current Host profile path: [C:\Users\Administrator\Documents\PowerShell\Microsoft.PowerShell_profile.ps1]
```

Figure 1.21: Viewing the name of the Current User/Current Host profile file

In *step 4*, you download a sample PowerShell console profile file from GitHub. This step creates no output. After making a new profile file, in *step 5*, you exit PowerShell 7. After restarting the console, in *step 6*, you view the details of this profile file. The output from this step looks like this:

```
PS C:\Foo> # 6. Restarting the PowerShell 7 console and viewing the profile output at startup
PS C:\Foo> Get-ChildItem -Path $PROFILE

    Directory: C:\Users\Administrator\Documents\PowerShell

Mode                 LastWriteTime         Length Name
----                 -------------         ------ ----
-a---          01/04/2022     12:01          1225 Microsoft.PowerShell_profile.ps1
```

Figure 1.22: Viewing the name of the Current User/Current Host profile file

There's more...

In *step 1*, you view the built-in profile filenames. As you can see, PowerShell has four profile files you can use. These files enable you to configure a given PowerShell host or all hosts for one or all users. As you can see in *step 2*, none of the four profile files exist by default.

In *step 4*, you create the Current User/Current Host profile file based on a code sample you download from GitHub. This profile file is a starting point and demonstrates many things you can do in a profile file.

In *step 6*, you view the profile file you created earlier. Also, notice that the prompt has changed – the current working directory when you start PowerShell is now C:\Foo.

Exploring Installation Artifacts

Installing PowerShell 7 creates some artifacts that may be useful to better understand how PowerShell 7 and Windows PowerShell differ. The installation folder for PowerShell, as well as the folders holding PowerShell modules, are different from Windows PowerShell.

Getting ready

You run this recipe on SRV1 after you have installed PowerShell 7 and have added a profile file.

How to do it...

1. Checking the version table for the PowerShell 7 console

    ```
    $PSVersionTable
    ```

2. Examining the PowerShell 7 installation folder

    ```
    Get-ChildItem -Path $env:ProgramFiles\PowerShell\7 -Recurse |
      Measure-Object -Property Length -Sum
    ```

3. Viewing the PowerShell 7 configuration JSON file

    ```
    Get-ChildItem -Path $env:ProgramFiles\PowerShell\7\powershell*.json
    |
      Get-Content
    ```

4. Checking the initial Execution Policy for PowerShell 7

    ```
    Get-ExecutionPolicy
    ```

5. Viewing module folders

    ```
    $I = 0
    $ModPath = $env:PSModulePath -split ';'
    $ModPath |
      Foreach-Object {
        "[{0:N0}]   {1}" -f $I++, $_
      }
    ```

6. Checking the modules

    ```
    $TotalCommands = 0
    Foreach ($Path in $ModPath){
      Try {
       $Modules = Get-ChildItem -Path $Path -Directory -ErrorAction Stop
         "Checking Module Path:  [$Path]"
      }
    ```

```
   catch [System.Management.Automation.ItemNotFoundException] {
     "Module path [$path] DOES NOT EXIST ON $(hostname)"
   }
   $TotalCommands = 0
   foreach ($Module in $Modules) {
     $Cmds = Get-Command -Module ($Module.name)
     $TotalCommands += $Cmds.Count
   }
 }
```

7. Viewing the totals of the commands and modules

```
$Mods = (Get-Module * -ListAvailable | Measure-Object).count
"{0} modules providing {1} commands" -f $Mods,$TotalCommands
```

How it works...

In *step 1*, you start the PowerShell 7 console on SRV1. The console should look like this:

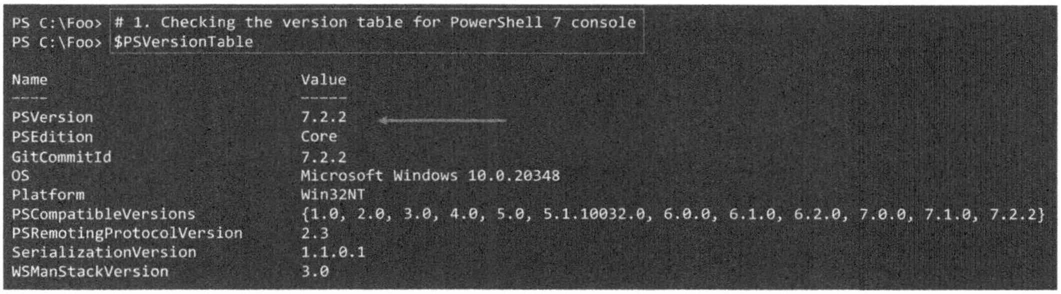

Figure 1.23: Checking PowerShell Version information

In *step 2*, you use Measure-Object to determine how many files exist in the PowerShell installation folder and how much space those files occupy on the disk. The output of this step looks like this:

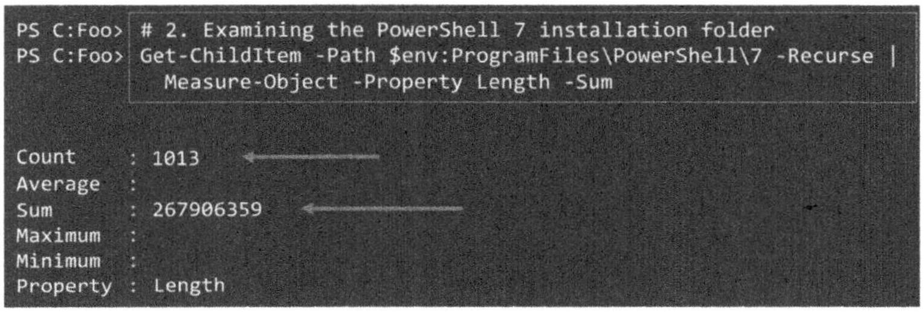

Figure 1.24: Examining the PowerShell 7 installation folder

PowerShell 7 uses the PWSH.JSON file (in the installation folder) to hold certain key settings. In *step 3*, you examine this file for PowerShell 7.2.2, with output like this:

```
PS C:\Foo> # 3. Viewing PowerShell 7 configuration JSON file
PS C:\Foo> Get-ChildItem -Path $env:ProgramFiles\PowerShell\7\powershell*.json |
              Get-Content
{
  "Microsoft.PowerShell:ExecutionPolicy": "RemoteSigned",
  "WindowsPowerShellCompatibilityModuleDenyList": [
    "PSScheduledJob",
    "BestPractices",
    "UpdateServices"
  ]
}
```

Figure 1.25: Viewing the PWSH.JSON configuration file

In *step 4*, you check the current execution policy for PowerShell 7, with output as follows:

```
PS C:\Foo> # 4. Checking initial Execution Policy for PowerShell 7
PS C:\Foo> Get-ExecutionPolicy
RemoteSigned   ◄
```

Figure 1.26: Checking the PowerShell 7 execution policy

PowerShell 7, by default, loads modules from a series of folders as described in the PowerShell variable $PSModulepath variable. In *step 5*, you display the default module folders for PowerShell 7, with output like this:

```
PS C:\Foo> # 5. Viewing module folders
PS C:\Foo> $I = 0
PS C:\Foo> $ModPath = $env:PSModulePath -split ';'
PS C:\Foo> $ModPath |
             Foreach-Object {
               [{0:N0}]   {1}  -f $I++, $_
             }
[0]   C:\Users\Administrator\Documents\PowerShell\Modules
[1]   C:\Program Files\PowerShell\Modules
[2]   c:\program files\powershell\7\Modules
[3]   C:\Program Files\WindowsPowerShell\Modules
[4]   C:\WINDOWS\system32\WindowsPowerShell\v1.0\Modules
```

Figure 1.27: Viewing the module folders for PowerShell 7

In *step 6*, you look at the modules in each module path and determine the total number of commands available via these modules. The output from this step looks like this:

```
PS C:\Foo> # 6. Checking the modules
PS C:\Foo> $TotalCommands = 0
PS C:\Foo> Foreach ($Path in $ModPath){
               Try { $Modules = Get-ChildItem -Path $Path -Directory -ErrorAction Stop
                   "Checking Module Path:  [$Path]"
               }
               Catch [System.Management.Automation.ItemNotFoundException] {
                 "Module path [$path] DOES NOT EXIST ON $(hostname)"
               }
               $TotalCommands = 0
               Foreach ($Module in $Modules) {
                 $Cmds = Get-Command -Module ($Module.name)
                 $TotalCommands += $Cmds.Count
               }
           }

Module path [C:\Users\Administrator\Documents\PowerShell\Modules] DOES NOT EXIST ON SRV1
Module path [C:\Program Files\PowerShell\Modules] DOES NOT EXIST ON SRV1
Checking Module Path:  [c:\program files\powershell\7\Modules]
Checking Module Path:  [C:\Program Files\WindowsPowerShell\Modules]
Checking Module Path:  [C:\WINDOWS\system32\WindowsPowerShell\v1.0\Modules]
```

Figure 1.28: Counting the commands available

In the final step in this recipe, *step 7*, you view the number of modules and commands provided in those modules, with output like this:

```
PS C:\Foo> # 7. Viewing totals of commands and modules
PS C:\Foo> $Mods = (Get-Module * -ListAvailable I Measure-Object).count
PS C:\Foo> "{0} modules providing {1} commands" -f $Mods,$TotalCommands
69 modules providing 1562 commands
```

Figure 1.29: Counting the commands available

There's more...

In *step 1*, you open a new Windows PowerShell console and view the PowerShell version details. In this case, this is version 7.2.2, although, by the time you read this, the PowerShell team may have created newer versions.

As you can see in *step 2*, the PowerShell pwsh.json file contains both the execution policy and a list of modules that PowerShell 7 should never attempt to load (as these three modules are known to not work with PowerShell 7, even using the Windows PowerShell compatibility mechanism). For reasons best known to themselves, the owners of these modules have declined the opportunity to port them over to work with PowerShell 7, although that may change.

In *step 4*, you view the current PowerShell 7 execution policy. Note that this policy is independent of the Windows PowerShell execution policy.

In *step 5*, you view the current module folders. This step uses .NET composite formatting and the PowerShell -f operator. PowerShell provides you with numerous ways to output this information that you may use, including simple variable expansion. Using the method shown in this step can give you more control over the formatting. You can see another example of this type of formatting in *step 7*.

Installing VS Code

The Windows PowerShell ISE was a great tool that Microsoft first introduced with Windows PowerShell v2 (and vastly improved with v3). This tool has reached feature completeness, and Microsoft has no plans for further development.

However, in its place is Visual Studio Code or VS Code. This open-source tool provides an extensive range of features for IT pros and others. For IT professionals, this should be your editor of choice. VS Code is highly customizable, as the range of extensions demonstrates. While there is a learning curve (as for any new product), VS Code contains all the features you found in the ISE and a lot more.

VS Code, and the available extensions, are works in progress and are constantly evolving and improving. Each new release brings additional features. A recent addition from Draw.IO, for example, is the ability to create diagrams directly in VS Code. Take a look at this post for more details on this diagram tool: `https://tfl09.blogspot.com/2020/05/over-weekend-i-saw-tweet-announcing-new.html`.

There is a wealth of extensions you might be able to use, depending on your workload. For more details on VS Code, see `https://code.visualstudio.com/`. And for more information on the many VS Code extensions, you might be able to use `https://code.visualstudio.com/docs/editor/extension-gallery#:~:text=You%20can%20browse%20and%20install,on%20the%20VS%20Code%20Marketplace`.

For many IT pros using PowerShell 7, an important extension is the PowerShell Integrated Console. This extension implements a separate PowerShell host, the Visual Studio Code Host. This extension implements the same four profile file files, which you can view. However, the AllUsers/This host and Current User/This Host profile files have the name `Microsoft.VSCode_profile.ps1`. These profile files mean you can use the PowerShell Console host (and its associated profile files) by default but use the VS Code Host when you edit PowerShell files. It is easy to get confused at first. Remember that you only see the VS Code host by default when you open a PowerShell file.

Getting ready

You run this recipe on SRV1 after you have installed PowerShell 7. You run the first part of this recipe in the PowerShell 7 console. Once you have completed installing VS Code, you do the remainder of this recipe using VS Code.

How to do it...

1. Downloading the VS Code installation script from the PS Gallery

```
$VscPath = 'C:\Foo'
$RV      = "2.8.5.208"
Install-PackageProvider -Name 'nuget' -RequiredVersion $RV -Force|
  Out-Null
Save-Script -Name Install-VSCode -Path $ VscPath
Set-Location -Path $ VscPath
```

2. Reviewing the installation help details

```
Get-Help -Name C:\Foo\Install-VSCode.ps1
```

3. Running the installation script and adding in some popular extensions

```
$Extensions =   'Streetsidesoftware.code-spell-checker',
                'yzhang.markdown-all-in-one',
                'hediet.vscode-drawio'
$InstallHT = @{
  BuildEdition        = 'Stable-System'
  AdditionalExtensions = $Extensions
  LaunchWhenDone      = $true
}
.\Install-VSCode.ps1 @InstallHT | Out-Null
```

4. Exiting from VS Code by clicking on File/Exit.

5. Restarting VS Code as an administrator.

6. Click on Start, type code, and hit return.

7. Opening a VS Code Terminal and running PowerShell 7 as administrator.

8. Use the Terminal menu to open a new terminal.

9.   Creating a profile file for VS Code

```
$SAMPLE =
  'https://raw.githubusercontent.com/doctordns/PACKT-PS7/master/' +
  'scripts/goodies/Microsoft.VSCode_profile.ps1'
(Invoke-WebRequest -Uri $Sample).Content |
  Out-File $Profile
```

10. Updating local user settings for VS Code

```
# 8. Updating local user settings for VS Code
$JSON = @'
{
  "workbench.colorTheme": "Visual Studio Light",
  "powershell.codeFormatting.useCorrectCasing": true,
  "files.autoSave": "onWindowChange",
  "files.defaultLanguage": "powershell",
  "editor.fontFamily": "'Cascadia Code',Consolas,'Courier New'",
  "workbench.editor.highlightModifiedTabs": true,
  "window.zoomLevel": 1
}
'@

$Path = $Env:APPDATA
$CP   = '\Code\User\Settings.json'
$Settings = Join-Path  $Path -ChildPath $CP
$JSON |
  Out-File -FilePath $Settings
```

11. Creating a shortcut to VS Code

```
$SourceFileLocation  = "$env:ProgramFiles\Microsoft VS Code\Code.
exe"
$ShortcutLocation    = "C:\foo\vscode.lnk"
# Create a  new wscript.shell object
$WScriptShell        = New-Object -ComObject WScript.Shell
$Shortcut            = $WScriptShell.
CreateShortcut($ShortcutLocation)
```

```
$Shortcut.TargetPath = $SourceFileLocation
# Save the Shortcut to the TargetPath
$Shortcut.Save()
```

12. Creating a shortcut to PowerShell 7

```
$SourceFileLocation  = "$env:ProgramFiles\PowerShell\7\pwsh.exe"
$ShortcutLocation    = 'C:\Foo\pwsh.lnk'
# Create a  new wscript.shell object
$WScriptShell        = New-Object -ComObject WScript.Shell
$Shortcut            = $WScriptShell.
CreateShortcut($ShortcutLocation)
$Shortcut.TargetPath = $SourceFileLocation
#Save the Shortcut to the TargetPath
$Shortcut.Save()
```

13. Building an updated Layout XML file

```
$XML = @'
<?xml version="1.0" encoding="utf-8"?>
<LayoutModificationTemplate
  xmlns="http://schemas.microsoft.com/Start/2014/LayoutModification"
  xmlns:defaultlayout=
    "http://schemas.microsoft.com/Start/2014/FullDefaultLayout"
  xmlns:start="http://schemas.microsoft.com/Start/2014/StartLayout"
  xmlns:taskbar="http://schemas.microsoft.com/Start/2014/
TaskbarLayout"
  Version="1">
<CustomTaskbarLayoutCollection>
<defaultlayout:TaskbarLayout>
<taskbar:TaskbarPinList>
 <taskbar:DesktopApp DesktopApplicationLinkPath="C:\Foo\vscode.lnk"
/>
 <taskbar:DesktopApp DesktopApplicationLinkPath="C:\Foo\pwsh.lnk" />
</taskbar:TaskbarPinList>
</defaultlayout:TaskbarLayout>
```

```
</CustomTaskbarLayoutCollection>
</LayoutModificationTemplate>
'@
$XML | Out-File -FilePath C:\Foo\Layout.Xml
```

14. Importing the start layout XML file. Note: You get an error if this is not run in an elevated session

```
Import-StartLayout -LayoutPath C:\Foo\Layout.Xml -MountPath C:\
```

15. Creating a profile file for the PWSH 7 consoles

```
$ProfileFolder = Join-Path ($Env:homeDrive+ $env:HOMEPATH)
'Documents\PowerShell'
$ProfileFile2   = 'Microsoft.PowerShell_Profile.ps1'
$ConsoleProfile = Join-Path -Path $ProfileFolder -ChildPath
$ProfileFile2
New-Item $ConsoleProfile -Force -WarningAction SilentlyContinue |
   Out-Null
$URI2 = 'https://raw.githubusercontent.com/doctordns/PACKT-PS7/
master/' +
        "scripts/goodies/$ProfileFile2"
(Invoke-WebRequest -Uri $URI2).Content |
  Out-File -FilePath  $ConsoleProfile
```

16. Logging off

```
logoff.exe
```

17. Logging into Windows to observe the updated taskbar

How it works...

In *step 1*, you get the VS Code installation script from the PS Gallery, which produces no output.
In *step 2*, you view the help information from the `Install-VSCode.ps1` script file, with output
like this:

```
PS C:\Foo> # 2. Reviewing the installation help details
PS C:\Foo> Get-Help -Name C:\Foo\Install-VSCode.ps1

NAME
    C:\Foo\Install-VSCode.ps1

SYNOPSIS
    Installs Visual Studio Code, the PowerShell extension, and optionally
    a list of additional extensions.

SYNTAX
    C:\Foo\Install-VSCode.ps1 [[-Architecture] <String>] [[-BuildEdition] <String>] [[-AdditionalExtensions]
    <String[]>] [-LaunchWhenDone] [-EnableContextMenus] [-WhatIf] [-Confirm] [<CommonParameters>]

DESCRIPTION
    This script can be used to easily install Visual Studio Code and the
    PowerShell extension on your machine.  You may also specify additional
    extensions to be installed using the -AdditionalExtensions parameter.
    The -LaunchWhenDone parameter will cause VS Code to be launched as
    soon as installation has completed.

    Please contribute improvements to this script on GitHub!

    https://github.com/PowerShell/vscode-powershell/blob/master/scripts/Install-VSCode.ps1


RELATED LINKS

REMARKS
    To see the examples, type: "Get-Help C:\Foo\Install-VSCode.ps1 -Examples"
    For more information, type: "Get-Help C:\Foo\Install-VSCode.ps1 -Detailed"
    For technical information, type: "Get-Help C:\Foo\Install-VSCode.ps1 -Full"
```

Figure 1.30: Viewing the Install-VSCode.ps1 help information

In *step 3*, you install VS Code, with output that looks like this:

```
PS C:\Foo> # 3. Running the installation script and adding in some popular extensions
PS C:\Foo> $Extensions =  'Streetsidesoftware.code-spell-checker',
                          'yzhang.markdown-all-in-one',
                          'hediet.vscode-drawio'
PS C:\Foo> $InstallHT = @{
              BuildEdition         = 'Stable-System'
              AdditionalExtensions = $Extensions
              LaunchWhenDone       = $true
           }
PS C:\Foo> .\Install-VSCode.ps1 @InstallHT
Installing extensions...
Installing extension 'ms-vscode.powershell'...
Extension 'ms-vscode.powershell' v2021.12.0 was successfully installed.

Installing extension Streetsidesoftware.code-spell-checker...
Installing extensions...
Installing extension 'streetsidesoftware.code-spell-checker'...
Extension 'streetsidesoftware.code-spell-checker' v2.1.11 was successfully installed.

Installing extension yzhang.markdown-all-in-one...
Installing extensions...
Installing extension 'yzhang.markdown-all-in-one'...
Extension 'yzhang.markdown-all-in-one' v3.4.0 was successfully installed.

Installing extension hediet.vscode-drawio...
Installing extensions...
Installing extension 'hediet.vscode-drawio'...
Extension 'hediet.vscode-drawio' v1.6.4 was successfully installed.

Installation complete, starting Visual Studio Code (64-bit)...
```

Figure 1.31: The PowerShell 7 console

After installing VS Code, the installation script starts VS Code (as an ordinary user) with output that looks like this:

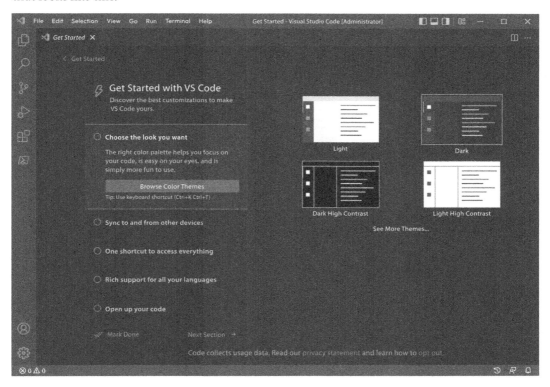

Figure 1.32: The initial VS Code window

In *step 4*, you exit out of this VS Code instance, and in *step 5*, you restart VS Code but run it as an administrator. With these two steps, you open VS Code as an administrator.

In *step 6*, you use the VS Code GUI to create a new terminal, with output like this:

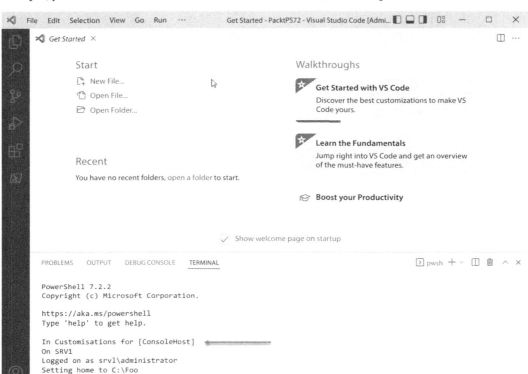

Figure 1.33: Running a new terminal

In the next steps, which generate no console output, you configure VS Code for your environment. In *step 7*, you create a new profile file specifically for the VS Code PowerShell extension. In *step 8*, you update the VS Code local user settings. In *step 9*, you create a shortcut to the VS Code executable (code.exe) and save it in C:\Foo. In *step 10*, you create a new shortcut for the PowerShell 7 console, which you also store in C:\Foo. In *step 11*, you build an XML file describing the Windows toolbar. In *step 12*, you import the new start bar layout (but note it does not take effect until you log in again). Then in *step 13*, you create profiles for the new PowerShell 7 console, also based on the downloaded profile file. Finally, in *step 14*, you log off SRV1.

In *step 15*, you log in again to Windows as the local administrator. When you log in, you can see the new Windows toolbar, with shortcuts for the PowerShell 7 console and VS Code, like this:

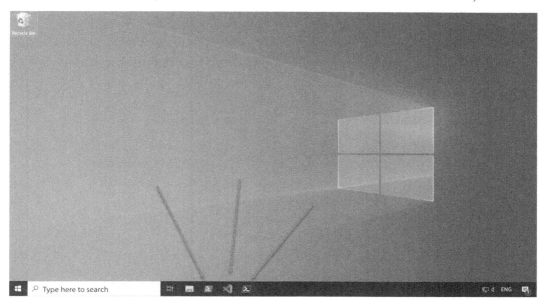

Figure 1.34: Viewing the updated Windows toolbar

There's more...

In *step 1*, you open a new Windows PowerShell 7 console. Make sure you run the console as the local administrator.

In *step 15*, you can see the updated Window toolbar with shortcuts to the Windows PowerShell console, VS Code, and the PowerShell 7 console.

Installing the Cascadia Code Font

Fonts, like color schemes in general, are a very personal thing. Some people love the comic sans font, for example, while others loathe it. Some love dark themes, and others don't. For programming, including PowerShell (with the console, VS Code, and possibly even Notepad), fixed-width fonts are easier to use. But the choice of which font is always a personal preference.

As part of the Visual Studio Code launch, Microsoft also created a new and free font that you can download and use at the PowerShell 7 console and inside VS Code. This recipe shows how you can download the font, install it, and set this font to be the default in VS Code.

This recipe shows how to install the Cascadia Code font, but you can choose many great fonts. See this article on (arguably!) the ten best fonts for use with VS Code: https://toastofcode.com/best-fonts-for-programming-with-vscode/.

And should you want to use a different font for VS Code, you can adapt this recipe to make use of whatever font you wish. Or use the VS Code settings menus to change the font as you may want.

How to do it...

1. Getting download locations

```
$CascadiaRelURL   =
        'https://github.com/microsoft/cascadia-code/releases'
$CascadiaRelease = Invoke-WebRequest -Uri $CascadiaRelURL
$Fileleaf         = ($CascadiaRelease.Links.href |
                      Where-Object { $_ -match $CascadiaFont } |
                      Select-Object -First 1)
$CascadiaPath    = 'https://github.com' + $FileLeaf
$CascadiaFile    = 'C:\Foo\CascadiaFontDL.zip'
```

2. Downloading the Cascadia Code font file archive

```
Invoke-WebRequest -Uri $CascadiaPath -OutFile $CascadiaFile
```

3. Expanding the font archive file

```
$FontFolder = 'C:\Foo\CascadiaCode'
Expand-Archive -Path $CascadiaFile -DestinationPath $FontFolder
```

4. Installing the Cascadia Code font

```
$FontFile = 'c:\Foo\CascadiaCode\ttf\CascadiaCode.ttf'
$FontShellApp = New-Object -Com Shell.Application
$FontShellNamespace = $FontShellApp.Namespace(0x14)
$FontShellNamespace.CopyHere($FontFile, 0x10)
```

How it works...

In *step 1*, you determine the location of the latest release of the font and set a variable to the location to download the font.

In *step 2*, you use Invoke-WebRequest to download the font archive. Then in *step 3*, you use Expand-Archive to expand the archive. Finally, in *step 4*, you install the Cascadia font.

The steps in this recipe produce no console output – but you can see the change in VS Code after you run these steps.

There's more...

In *step 1*, you determine the location of the latest release of the Cascadia Code font on GitHub. The font is heavily used and has been subject to minor updates and improvements over time. This step ensures you get the latest version. The remaining steps expand the downloaded archive and then install the font. Once you complete this recipe, you should observe the font inside VS Code.

In *step 2*, you download the latest version of the font – but as a ZIP archive, which, in *step 3*, you expand and then install (in *step 4*).

Exploring PSReadLine

Early versions of PowerShell were monochrome, although the terminal (`conhost.exe`) did provide some limited coloring. These versions of Windows PowerShell also lacked some of the cool features found in Linux shells.

With PowerShell 4, PowerShell included a new module, `PSReadLine`. The module provides a command-line editing experience that is on a par with the best of the Linux command shells (e.g., BASH). The PSReadLine module provides additional console editing features within both PowerShell 7 and Windows PowerShell.

When you type into a PowerShell console, `PSReadLine` intercepts your keystrokes to provide syntax coloring, simple syntax error notification, etc. `PSReadLine` enables you to customize your environment to suit your personal preferences. Some key features of the module include:

- Syntax coloring of the command-line entries
- Multiline editing
- History management
- Customizable key bindings
- Highly customizable

For an overview of PSReadLine, see `https://learn.microsoft.com/powershell/module/psreadline/about/about_psreadline`. And for more details, you can view the PSReadLine's GitHub README file: `https://github.com/PowerShell/PSReadLine/blob/master/README.md`.

There are several minor issues you may need to understand. One issue is the naming of this module. The original name of the module was PSReadline. At some point, the module's developers changed the module's name to PSReadLine (capitalizing the L character in the module name). Unfortunately, that change caused Update-Help to fail since there is case sensitivity in module names). You can fix this by manually updating the module's folder name from PSReadline to PSReadLine.

Another issue arises if you use VS Code. The PSReadLine module ships natively with PowerShell 7. If you use VS Code's PowerShell Integrated Terminal, you cannot load any newer version of PSReadline. At least until the development team updates the PowerShell extension to utilize the updated version of PSReadLine. This is by design. For *most* IT pros, this probably does not matter much. But you may find later versions of PSReadLine contains features you want – if so, you should be able to use the Preview (i.e., beta!) version of the PowerShell extension, which supports the latest version of PSReadLine.

A final issue relates to changes made at V2. With the module's V2 release, the dev team made some changes that were not backward compatible. But be aware that some older scripts may need adjusting. Many blog articles, for example, use the older V1 syntax for Set-PSReadLineOption, which fails with later versions of the module. You may still see the old syntax if you use your search engine to discover examples. Likewise, some of the examples in this recipe fail should you run them utilizing PSReadline V1. Over time, though, the documentation and blog posts should catch up.

You run this recipe on SRV1 after you have installed PowerShell 7. Run this recipe in VS Code after configuring VS Code and loading the Cascadia Code font.

How to do it...

1. Getting commands in the PSReadline module

   ```
   Get-Command -Module PSReadLine
   ```

2. Getting the first 10 PSReadLine key handlers

   ```
   Get-PSReadLineKeyHandler |
     Select-Object -First 10
       Sort-Object -Property Key |
         Format-Table -Property Key, Function, Description
   ```

3. Discovering a count of unbound key handlers

   ```
   $Unbound = (Get-PSReadLineKeyHandler -Unbound).count
   "$Unbound unbound key handlers"
   ```

4. Getting the PSReadline options

```
Get-PSReadLineOption
```

5. Determining the VS Code theme name

```
$Path       = $Env:APPDATA
$CP         = '\Code\User\Settings.json'
$JsonConfig = Join-Path  $Path -ChildPath $CP
$ConfigJSON = Get-Content $JsonConfig
$Theme = $ConfigJson |
          ConvertFrom-Json |
            Select-Object -ExpandProperty 'workbench.colorTheme'
```

6. Changing the VS Code colors

```
If ($Theme -eq 'Visual Studio Light') {
  Set-PSReadLineOption -Colors @{
    Member    = "'e[33m"
    Number    = "'e[34m"
    Parameter = "'e[35m"
    Command   = "'e[34m"
  }
}
```

How it works...

In *step 1*, you use Get-Command to discover commands in the PSReadLine module, with

```
PS C:\Foo> # 1.Getting commands in the PSReadLine module
PS C:\Foo> Get-Command -Module PSReadLine


CommandType     Name                         Version    Source
-----------     ----                         -------    ------
Function        PSConsoleHostReadLine        2.1.0      PSReadLine
Cmdlet          Get-PSReadLinekeyHandler     2.1.0      PSReadLine
Cmdlet          Get-PSReadLineOption         2.1.0      PSReadLine
Cmdlet          Remove-PSReadLinekeyHandler  2.1.0      PSReadLine
Cmdlet          Set-PSReadLinekeyHandler     2.1.0      PSReadLine
Cmdlet          Set-PSReadLineOption         2.1.0      PSReadLine
```

Figure 1.35: Discovering commands in the PSReadLine module

In *step 2*, you use Get-PSReadLineKeyHandler to discover some of the key handlers implemented by PSReadline, with output like this:

```
PS C:\Foo> # 2. Getting the first 10 PSReadLine key handlers
PS C:\Foo> Get-PSReadLineKeyHandler |
              Select-Object -First 10
                Sort-Object -Property Key |
                  Format-Table -Property Key, Function, Description

Basic editing functions
=========================

Key             Function            Description
---             --------            -----------
Enter           AcceptLine          Accept the input or move to the next line if input is missing a closing token.
Shift+Enter     AddLine             Move the cursor to the next line without attempting to execute the input
Backspace       BackwardDeleteChar  Delete the character before the cursor
Ctrl+h          BackwardDeleteChar  Delete the character before the cursor
Ctrl+Home       BackwardDeleteLine  Delete text from the cursor to the start of the line
Ctrl+Backspace  BackwardKillWord    Move the text from the start of the current or previous word to the cursor to the kill ring
Ctrl+w          BackwardKillWord    Move the text from the start of the current or previous word to the cursor to the kill ring
Ctrl+C          Copy                Copy selected region to the system clipboard.  If no region is selected, copy the whole line
Ctrl+c          CopyOrCancelLine    Either copy selected text to the clipboard, or if no text is selected, cancel editing the line with CancelLine.
Ctrl+x          Cut                 Delete selected region placing deleted text in the system clipboard
```

Figure 1.36: Viewing ten PSReadLine key handlers

In *step 3*, you calculate how many key handers are unbound and are available for you to use. The output from this step is:

```
PS C:\Foo> # 3. Discovering a count of unbound key handlers
PS C:\Foo> $Unbound = (Get-PSReadLinekeyHandler -Unbound).count
PS C:\Foo> "$Unbound unbound key handlers"
116 unbound key handlers
```

Figure 1.37: Counting unbound key handlers

PSReadLine has many options you can set. In *step 4*, you use the Get-PSReadLineOption command to view the option settings, with output like this:

```
PS C:\Foo> # 4. Getting the PSReadline options
PS C:\Foo> Get-PSReadLineOption

EditMode                              : Windows
AddToHistoryHandler                   : System.Func`2[System.String,System.Object]
HistoryNoDuplicates                   : True
HistorySavePath                       : C:\Users\Administrator\AppData\Roaming\Microsoft\Windows\
BellStyle                             : Audible
DingDuration                          : 50
DingTone                              : 1221
CommandsToValidateScriptBlockArguments : {ForEach-Object, %, Invoke-Command, icm, Measure-Command, New-Module, nmo,
                                          Register-EngineEvent,Register-ObjectEvent, Register-WMIEvent, Set-PSBreakpoint,
                                          sbp, Start-Job, sajb, Trace-Command, trcm,Use-Transaction, Where-Object, ?, where}
CommandValidationHandler              :
CompletionQueryItems                  : 100
MaximumKillRingCount                  : 10
ShowToolTips                          : True
ViModeIndicator                       : None
WordDelimiters                        : ;:,.[]{}()/\|^&*-=+'"---
AnsiEscapeTimeout                     : 100
PredictionSource                      : None
CommandColor                          : "`e[91m"
CommentColor                          : "`e[32m"
ContinuationPromptColor               : "`e[37m"
DefaultTokenColor                     : "`e[37m"
EmphasisColor                         : "`e[33m"
ErrorColor                            : "`e[91m"
KeywordColor                          : "`e[92m"
MemberColor                           : "`e[34m"
NumberColor                           : "`e[34m"
OperatorColor                         : "`e[35m"
ParameterColor                        : "`e[35m"
InlinePredictionColor                 : "`e[38;5;238m"
SelectionColor                        : "`e[30;47m"
StringColor                           : "`e[36m"
TypeColor                             : "`e[37m"
VariableColor                         : "`e[33m"
```

Figure 1.38: Counting unbound key handlers

In *step 5*, you determine the current VS Code theme, and in *step 6*, you change the PowerShell token colors, but only if the theme set is the Visual Studio Light theme. These two steps produce no console output.

There's more...

In *step 1*, you open a new Windows PowerShell console. Make sure you run the console as the local administrator.

In *step 3*, you view the first ten of the PSReadLine's key handlers. Using PowerShell, PSReadLine captures specific keyboard sequences (e.g., *Alt + L*) and uses an assigned key handler to carry out some action. Typing Alt + L clears the terminal window (in VS Code and the PowerShell console). PSReadline implements a range of key handers with plenty of room for you to customize the editing experience and provide significant customization of the shell. As you can see in *step 3*, you can use over 100 key combinations to implement your own customizations.

The screenshots throughout most of this book use this color theme. You could extend your profile files to update token colors each time you start a VS Code terminal.

Join our community on Discord

Join our community's Discord space for discussions with the author and other readers:

https://packt.link/SecNet

2

Managing PowerShell 7 in the Enterprise

This chapter covers the following recipes:

- Utilizing Windows PowerShell Compatibility
- Installing RSAT
- Exploring Package Management
- Exploring PowerShellGet and the PS Gallery
- Creating and Using a Local PowerShell Repository
- Establishing a Script Signing Environment
- Working With Shortcuts and the PSShortCut Module
- Working With Archive Files
- Searching for Files Using the Everything Search Tool

Introduction

For an IT professional in an enterprise environment (and even in smaller ones), PowerShell 7 provides a platform to manage your environment. Many of the commands you need to carry out typical operations come with PowerShell 7, augmented by the commands provided with Windows Server feature tools. In addition, you can obtain third-party modules to extend your capabilities.

Automation, today, means using commands that come from many sources. Some are built-in, but there are gaps. Those gaps can be filled by modules you can obtain from the community and via the PowerShell Gallery. In many cases, you can make use of .NET and WMI classes.

When all else fails, there is often a command-line tool.

As you blend these tools into your workflow, you need to be aware of how a given set of commands work as well as the objects returned. You also need to deal with the mismatch. The `Get-ADComputer` command, for example, returns the name of the computer in AD in the `Name` property. Most commands that interact with a given computer use the parameter `ComputerName`.

In building Windows Server 2022, Microsoft did not update most of the role/feature management tools to support PowerShell 7. These tools work natively in Windows PowerShell but many do not work directly in PowerShell 7. The reason for this is that Microsoft based Windows PowerShell on Microsoft's .NET Framework, whereas PowerShell 7 is based on the open source .NET. The .NET team did not port all the APIs from the .NET Framework into .NET. Thus many of the role/feature commands that you can run in Windows PowerShell do not run natively since .NET did not implement a certain .NET Framework.

To get around this, PowerShell 7 comes with a Windows PowerShell compatibility solution. When you attempt to use some of the older commands (i.e., those that live in the System32 Windows directory), PowerShell 7 creates a PowerShell remoting session on the current host based on a Windows PowerShell 5.1 endpoint. Then, using implicit remoting, PowerShell creates and imports a script module of proxy functions that invoke the underlying commands in the remoting session. This enables you to use commands, such as `Add-WindowsFeature`, more or less seamlessly. You will examine the Windows PowerShell compatibility feature in *Utilizing Windows PowerShell Compatibility*.

Most of Windows Server 2022's features and roles provide management tools you can use to manage the role or feature. You can also install and use these feature tools on any host allowing you to manage features across your network, as you can see in *Installing RSAT*.

You can also find and utilize third-party modules that can improve your PowerShell experience. PowerShell implements a set of built-in package management commands, as you can see in *Exploring Package Management*.

Some organizations create their own private package repositories. These enable their organizations to share corporate modules inside the corporate network. You will create a new package repository in the *Creating and Using a Local PowerShell Repository* recipe.

PowerShell 7, like Windows PowerShell, supports the use of digitally signed scripts. You can configure PowerShell to run only properly signed scripts as a way of improving the organization's security. It is straightforward to establish a code-signing environment, using self-signed certificates, as you investigate in the *Establishing a code-signing environment* recipe.

To simplify the use of commands in an interactive environment, you may find it convenient to create shortcuts you can place on the desktop or in a folder of shortcuts. In *Working With Shortcuts and the PSShortCut Module*, you will manage shortcuts.

A common problem you can face when automating your environment is the management of archive files. As you saw in *Installing Cascadia Code font,* you can often get components delivered as a ZIP file. In *Working With Archive Files*, you examine commands for managing these files.

Windows, Windows Server, and Windows applications have grown significantly both in scope and the files that support them. Sometimes, finding key files you need can be challenging, especially on larger file servers.

The system used in the chapter

This chapter is all about using PowerShell 7 in an enterprise environment and configuring your environment to make the most out of PowerShell 7. In this chapter, you use a single host, SRV1, as follows:

Figure 2.1: Host in use for this chapter

In later chapters, you will use additional servers and will promote SRV1 to be a domain-based server rather than being in a workgroup.

Utilizing Windows PowerShell Compatibility

The PowerShell 7 Windows Compatibility solution allows you to use older Windows PowerShell commands whose developers have not (yet) ported the commands to work natively in PowerShell 7. PowerShell 7 creates a special remoting session into a Windows PowerShell 5.1 endpoint, loads the modules into the remote session, then uses implicit remoting to expose proxy functions inside the PowerShell 7 session. This remoting session has a unique session name, WinPSCompatSession. Should you use multiple Windows PowerShell modules, PowerShell 7 loads them all into a single remoting session. Also, this session uses the "process" transport mechanism versus *Windows Remote Management (WinRM)*. WinRM is the core transport protocol used with PowerShell remoting. The process transport is the transport used to run background jobs; it has less overhead than using WinRM, so is more efficient.

An example of the compatibility mechanism is using Get-WindowsFeature, a cmdlet inside the ServerManager module. You use the command to get details of features that are installed, or not, inside Windows Server. You use other commands in the ServerManager module to install and remove features. Unfortunately, the Windows Server team has not yet updated this module to work within PowerShell 7. Via the compatibility solution, the commands in the ServerManager module enable you to add, remove, and view features. The Windows PowerShell compatibility mechanism allows you to use existing Windows PowerShell scripts in PowerShell 7, although with some very minor caveats.

When you invoke commands in PowerShell 7, PowerShell uses its command discovery mechanism to determine which module contains your desired command. In this case, that module is the ServerManager Windows PowerShell module. PowerShell 7 then creates the remoting session and, using implicit remoting, imports the commands in the module as proxy functions. You then invoke the proxy functions to accomplish your goal. For the most part, this is totally transparent. You use the module's commands, and they return the object(s) you request. A minor caveat is that the compatibility mechanism does not import Format-XML for the Windows PowerShell module. The result is that the default output of some objects is not the same. There is a workaround for this, which is to manually install Format-XML.

With implicit remoting, PowerShell creates a function inside a PowerShell 7 session with the same name and parameters as the actual command (in the remote session). Once you import the module into the compatibility session, you can view the function definition in the Function drive (`Get-Item Function:Get-WindowsFeature | Format-List -Property *`). The output shows the proxy function definition that PowerShell 7 creates when it imports the remote module.

When you invoke the command by name, e.g., `Get-WindowsFeature`, PowerShell runs the function. The function then invokes the remote cmdlet using the steppable pipeline. Implicit remoting is a complex feature that is virtually transparent in operation. You can read more about implicit remoting at `https://www.techtutsonline.com/implicit-remoting-windows-powershell/`.

And for more information on Windows PowerShell compatibility, see: `https://learn.microsoft.com/powershell/module/microsoft.powershell.core/about/about_windows_powershell_compatibility`.

Getting ready

You run this recipe on SRV1 after you have installed PowerShell 7.

How to do it...

1. Importing the `ServerManager` module

    ```
    Import-Module -Name ServerManager
    ```

2. Viewing module details

    ```
    Get-Module -Name ServerManager |
      Format-List
    ```

3. Displaying a Windows feature

    ```
    Get-WindowsFeature -Name 'TFTP-Client'
    ```

4. Running the same command in a remoting session

    ```
    $Session = Get-PSSession -Name WinPSCompatSession
    Invoke-Command -Session $Session -ScriptBlock {
      Get-WindowsFeature -Name 'TFTP-Client' |
        Format-Table
    }
    ```

5. Getting the path to Windows PowerShell modules

```
$Paths = $env:PSModulePath -split ';'
$S32Path = $Paths |
  Where-Object {$_.ToString() -match 'system32'}
"System32 path: [$S32Path]"
```

6. Displaying path to the format XML for the Server Manager module

```
$FXML = "$S32path/ServerManager"
$FF = Get-ChildItem -Path $FXML\*.format.ps1xml
"Format XML files:"
"    $($FF.Name)"
```

7. Updating format XML in PowerShell 7

```
Foreach ($fF in $FFFf) {
    Update-FormatData -PrependPath $fF.FullName}
```

8. Using the command with improved output

```
Get-WindowsFeature -Name TFTP-Client
```

How it works...

In *step 1*, you import the Server Manager module, with output like this:

```
PS C:\Foo> # 1. Importing the ServerManager Module
PS C:\Foo> Import-Module -Name ServerManager
WARNING: Module ServerManager is loaded in Windows PowerShell using
WinPSCompatSession remoting session; please note that all input and
output of commands from this module will be deserialized objects.
If you want to load this module into PowerShell please use
'Import-Module -SkipEditionCheck' syntax.
```

Figure 2.2: Importing the Server Manager module

In *step 2*, you use the Get-Module command to examine the Server Manager module's properties.
The output of this step looks like this:

```
PS C:\Foo> # 2. Viewing module details
PS C:\Foo> Get-Module -Name ServerManager |
               Format-List


Name               : ServerManager
Path               : C:\Users\Administrator\AppData\Local\Temp\2\remoteIpMoProxy_ServerManager_2.0.0.0_
                     localhost_c7b5e52a-1429-4fcf-841f-d8800a63ff9f\remoteIpMoProxy_ServerManager_2.0.0.0_
                     localhost_c7b5e52a-1429-4fcf-841f-d8800a63ff9f.psml
Description        : Implicit remoting for
ModuleType         : Script
Version            : 1.0
PreRelease         :
NestedModules      : {}
ExportedFunctions  : {Disable-ServerManagerStandardUserRemoting, Enable-ServerManagerStandardUserRemoting,
                     Get-WindowsFeature, Install-WindowsFeature, Uninstall-WindowsFeature}
ExportedCmdlets    :
ExportedVariables  :
ExportedAliases    : {Add-WindowsFeature, Remove-WindowsFeature}
```

Figure 2.3: Importing the Server Manager module

Now that you have loaded the Server Manager module, in *step 3*, you utilize one of the commands Get-WindowsFeature to view the details of a feature, with output like this:

```
PS C:\Foo> # 3. Displaying a Windows Feature
PS C:\Foo> Get-WindowsFeature -Name 'TFTP-Client'

Display Name         Name            Install State
------------         ----            -------------
                     TFTP-Client     Available
```

Figure 2.4: Displaying the TFTP-Client feature

In *step 4*, by comparison, you run the same command inside the Windows PowerShell remoting session with slightly different results – like this:

```
PS C:\Foo> # 4. Running the same command in a remoting session
PS C:\Foo> $Session = Get-PSSession -Name WinPSCompatSession
PS C:\Foo> Invoke-Command -Session $Session -ScriptBlock {
               Get-WindowsFeature -Name 'TFTP-Client' |
                   Format-Table
           }

Display Name         Name            Install State
------------         ----            -------------
[ ] TFTP Client      TFTP-Client     Available
```

Figure 2.5: Displaying the TFTP-Client feature inside the remoting session

With *step 5*, you determine and display the folder where Windows PowerShell modules can be found, with output like this:

```
PS C:\Foo> # 5. Getting the path to Windows PowerShell modules
PS C:\Foo> $Paths = $env:PSModulePath -split ';'
PS C:\Foo> $S32Path = $Paths |
             Where-Object {$_.ToString() -match 'system32'}
PS C:\Foo> "System32 path: [$S32Path]"
System32 path: [C:\WINDOWS\system32\WindowsPowerShell\v1.0\Modules]
```

Figure 2.6: Displaying the TFTP-Client feature inside the remoting session

In *step 6*, you find and display the Server Manager's display formatting XML file, with output like this:

```
PS C:\Foo> # 6. Displaying path to the format XML for Server Manager module
PS C:\Foo> $FXML = "$S32path/ServerManager"
PS C:\Foo> $FF = Get-ChildItem -Path $FXML\*.format.ps1xml
PS C:\Foo> "    $($FF.Name)"
PS C:\Foo> "Format XML files:"
Format XML files:
  Feature.format.ps1xml
```

Figure 2.7: Displaying the TFTP-Client feature inside the remoting session

In *step 7*, you import the display XML files – which produces no output. Finally, in *step 8*, you re-run the Get-WindowsFeature command. Since you have now imported the necessary display XML, you see output like this:

```
PS C:\Foo> # 8. Using the command with improved output
PS C:\Foo> Get-WindowsFeature -Name TFTP-Client

Display Name          Name          Install State
------------          ----          -------------
[ ] TFTP-Client       TFTP-Client      Available
```

Figure 2.8: Displaying the TFTP-Client feature inside PowerShell 7 session

There's more...

In *step 3*, you used the Get-WindowsFeature to view one feature. When you run this command, PowerShell runs the command in the compatibility session and returns the object(s) for display in PowerShell 7. However, as you may notice, the output is not the same as you would see normally in Windows PowerShell. This is because the Windows PowerShell compatibility does not, by default, add Format-XML to the current PowerShell session.

Once you have loaded the Server Manager's display XML, as you can see in *step 8*, running the Get-WindowsFeature command now produces the same nicely formatted output you can see in Windows PowerShell.

Installing RSAT

The **Remote Server Admin Tools (RSAT)** is a set of management tools you use to manage individual Windows Features. The RSAT are fundamental to administering the roles and features you can install on Windows Server. The Windows Server DNS Server feature, for example, comes with both an MMC and a module that you use to manage the DNS Server on a given host.

A nice thing about the commands in the ServerManager module – everything is a feature, meaning you do not know whether the tools manage a Windows feature or a Windows role.

Each feature in Windows Server can optionally have management tools, and most do. These tools include PowerShell cmdlets, functions, aliases, GUI **Microsoft Management Console (MMC)** files, and Win32 console applications. The DNS Server's RSAT tools include a PowerShell module, an MMC, as well as the command-line tool dnscmd.exe. While you probably do not need the console applications since you can use the cmdlets, that is not always the case. And you may have some older batch scripts that use those console applications.

You can also install the RSAT tools independently of a Windows Server feature on Windows Server. This recipe covers RSAT tool installation on Windows Server 2022.

As mentioned, PowerShell 7 is not installed in Windows by default, at least not at the time of writing. The PowerShell team made PowerShell 7.1 available from the Microsoft Store, which is useful to install PowerShell 7.1 or later on Windows 10/11 systems. Windows Server does not support the Microsoft store.

You have other methods of installing PowerShell 7 on your systems. The first option is to use Install-PowerShell.ps1, which you can download from GitHub, as shown in this recipe. You can also use this recipe on Windows 10 hosts. This approach has the advantage of being the most up-to-date source of the latest versions of PowerShell.

Getting ready

This recipe uses SRV1, a Windows Server workgroup host. There are no Windows features or server applications loaded on this server.

How to do it...

1. Displaying counts of available PowerShell commands

```
$CommandsBeforeRSAT = Get-Command
$CmdletsBeforeRSAT = $CommandsBeforeRSAT |
    Where-Object CommandType -eq 'Cmdlet'
$CommandCountBeforeRSAT = $CommandsBeforeRSAT.Count
$CmdletCountBeforeRSAT  = $CmdletsBeforeRSAT.Count
"On Host: [$(hostname)]"
"Commands available before RSAT installed [$CommandCountBeforeRSAT]"
"Cmdlets available before RSAT installed  [$CmdletCountBeforeRSAT]".
```

2. Getting command types returned by Get-Command

```
$CommandsBeforeRSAT |
  Group-Object -Property CommandType
```

3. Checking the object type details

```
$CommandsBeforeRSAT |
  Get-Member |
    Select-Object -ExpandProperty TypeName -Unique
```

4. Getting the collection of PowerShell modules and a count of modules before adding the RSAT tools

```
$ModulesBefore = Get-Module -ListAvailable
```

5. Displaying a count of modules available before adding the RSAT tools

```
$CountOfModulesBeforeRSAT = $ModulesBefore.Count
"$CountOfModulesBeforeRSAT modules available"
```

6. Getting a count of features actually available on SRV1

```
Import-Module -Name ServerManager -WarningAction SilentlyContinue
$Features = Get-WindowsFeature
$FeaturesInstalled = $Features |
                        Where-Object Installed
$RsatFeatures = $Features |
                    Where-Object Name -Match 'RSAT'
$RsatFeaturesInstalled = $Rsatfeatures |
                    Where-Object Installed
```

7. Displaying counts of features installed

```
"On Host [$(hostname)]"
"Total features available       [{0}]" -f $Features.Count
"Total features installed       [{0}]" -f $FeaturesInstalled.Count
"Total RSAT features available [{0}]" -f $RsatFeatures.Count
"Total RSAT features installed [{0}]" -f $RsatFeaturesInstalled.
Count
```

8. Adding all RSAT tools to SRV1

```
Get-WindowsFeature -Name *RSAT* |
  Install-WindowsFeature
```

9. Getting details of RSAT tools now installed on SRV1:

```
$FeaturesSRV1       = Get-WindowsFeature
$InstalledOnSRV1    = $FeaturesSRV1 | Where-Object Installed
$RsatInstalledOnSRV1 = $InstalledOnSRV1 | Where-Object Installed |
                       Where-Object Name -Match 'RSAT'
```

10. Displaying counts of commands after installing the RSAT tools

```
"After Installation of RSAT tools on SRV1"
$INS = 'Features installed on SRV1'
"$($InstalledOnSRV1.Count) $INS"
"$($RsatInstalledOnSRV1.Count) $INS"
```

11. Displaying RSAT tools on SRV1

```
$Modules = "$env:windir\system32\windowspowerShell\v1.0\modules"
$ServerManagerModules = "$Modules\ServerManager"
Update-FormatData -PrependPath "$ServerManagerModules\*.format.
ps1xml"
Get-WindowsFeature |
  Where-Object Name -Match 'RSAT'
```

12. Rebooting SRV1 and then logging on as the local administrator

```
Restart-Computer -Force
```

How it works...

In *step 1*, you use Get-Command to obtain all the existing commands available on SRV1. Then you create a count of the commands available as well as a count of the PowerShell cmdlets available to you, with output like this:

```
PS C:\Foo> # 1. Displaying counts of available PowerShell commands
PS C:\Foo> $CommandsBeforeRSAT = Get-Command
PS C:\Foo> $CmdletsBeforeRSAT = $CommandsBeforeRSAT   |
             Where-Object CommandType -eq 'Cmdlet'
PS C:\Foo> $CommandCountBeforeRSAT = $CommandsBeforeRSAT.Count
PS C:\Foo> $CmdletCountBeforeRSAT  = $CmdletsBeforeRSAT.Count
PS C:\Foo> "On Host: [$(hostname)]"
PS C:\Foo> "Total Commands available before RSAT installed [$CommandCountBeforeRSAT]"
PS C:\Foo> "Cmdlets available before RSAT installed        [$CmdletCountBeforeRSAT]"
On Host: [SRV1]
Commands available before RSAT installed [1809]
Cmdlets available before RSAT installed  [597]
```

Figure 2.9: Counting the available commands and cmdlets on SRV1

In *step 2*, you discover the different kinds of commands returned by Get-Command. The output looks like this:

```
PS C:\Foo> # 2. Getting command types returned by Get-Command
PS C:\Foo> $CommandsBeforeRSAT |
             Group-Object -Property CommandType

Count Name      Group
----- ----      -----
   58 Alias     {Add-AppPackage, Add-AppPackageVolume, Add-AppProvisionedPackage,…
 1154 Function  {A:, Add-BCDataCacheExtension, Add-DnsClientDohServerAddress, Add…
  597 Cmdlet    {Add-AppxPackage, Add-AppxProvisionedPackage, Add-AppxVolume, Add…
```

Figure 2.10: Viewing command types returned by Get-Command

In PowerShell, the Get-Command cmdlet returns occurrences of different object types to describe the available commands. As you saw in the previous step, there are three command types returned by default by Get-Command. There is a fourth command type, **Application**, which Get-Command does not return by default.

You can see the class names for those three command types in the output from *step 3*, which looks like this:

```
PS C:\Foo> # 3. Checking the object type details
PS C:\Foo> $CommandsBeforeRSAT |
             Get-Member |
               Select-Object -ExpandProperty TypeName -Unique
System.Management.Automation.AliasInfo
System.Management.Automation.FunctionInfo
System.Management.Automation.CmdletInf
```

Figure 2.11: Determining full object type names

In *step 4*, you get the modules available on SRV1, which returns no console output. In *step 5*, you display a count of the modules discovered, with output like this:

```
PS C:\Foo> # 5. Displaying a count of modules available
PS C:\Foo> #     before adding the RSAT tools
PS C:\Foo> $CountOfModulesBeforeRSAT = $ModulesBefore.Count
PS C:\Foo> "$CountOfModulesBeforeRSAT modules available"
75 modules available
```

Figure 2.12: Displaying the number of modules available

In *step 6*, you obtain a count of the features available on SRV1, which produces no output. In the following step, *step 7*, you display counts of the total features available and the number of RSAT tool sets available. The output from this step looks like this:

```
PS C:\Foo> # 7. Displaying counts of features installed
PS C:\Foo> "On Host [$(hostname)]"
PS C:\Foo> "Total features available      [{0}]"  -f $Features.count
PS C:\Foo> "Total features installed      [{0}]"  -f $FeaturesInstalled.count
PS C:\Foo> "Total RSAT features available [{0}]"  -f $RSATFeatures.count
PS C:\Foo> "Total RSAT features installed [{0}]"  -f $RSATFeaturesInstalled.count
On Host [SRV1]
Total features available      [266]
Total features installed      [12]
Total RSAT features available [50]
Total RSAT features installed [0]
```

Figure 2.13: Displaying the number of features and RSAT features available

In *step 8*, you install all the available features onto SRV1, with output like this:

```
PS C:\Foo> # 8. Adding ALL RSAT tools to SRV1
PS C:\Foo> Get-WindowsFeature -Name *RSAT* |
              Install-WindowsFeature

Success Restart Needed Exit Code      Feature Result
------- -------------- ---------      --------------
True    Yes            SuccessRestar… {BitLocker Drive Encryption, RAS Connection …
WARNING: You must restart this server to finish the installation process.
```

Figure 2.14: Adding all RSAT tools to SRV1

In *step 9*, you get details of all the features now available on SRV1, producing no output. In *step 10*, you obtain and display a count of the features, including RSAT features, on SRV1, with output like this:

```
PS C:\Foo> # 10. Displaying counts of commands after installing the RSAT tools
PS C:\Foo> "After Installation of RSAT tools on SRV1"
PS C:\Foo> $INS = 'Features installed on SRV1'
PS C:\Foo> "$($InstalledOnSRV1.Count) $INS"
PS C:\Foo> "$($RsatInstalledOnSRV1.Count) $INS"
After Installation of RSAT tools on SRV1
76 features installed on SRV1
50 RSAT features installed on SRV1
```

Figure 2.15: Counting features and RSAT features

In *step 11*, you use `Get-WindowsFeature` to display all the RSAT tools and their installation status, with output like this:

```
PS C:\Foo> # 11. Displaying RSAT tools on SRV1
PS C:\Foo> $MODS = "$env:windir\system32\windowspowerShell\v1.0\modules"
PS C:\Foo> $SMMOD = "$MODS\ServerManager"
PS C:\Foo> Update-FormatData -PrependPath "$SMMOD\*.format.ps1xml"
PS C:\Foo> Get-WindowsFeature |
               Where-Object Name -Match 'RSAT'
```

```
Display Name                                              Name                        Install State
------------                                              ----                        -------------
[X] Remote Server Administration Tools                    RSAT                        Installed
    [X] Feature Administration Tools                       RSAT-Feature-Tools          Installed
        [X] SMTP Server Tools                              RSAT-SMTP                   Installed
        [X] BitLocker Drive Encryption Administration …    RSAT-Feature-Tools-Bit…     Installed
            [X] BitLocker Drive Encryption Tools           RSAT-Feature-Tools-Bit…     Installed
            [X] BitLocker Recovery Password Viewer         RSAT-Feature-Tools-Bit…     Installed
        [X] BITS Server Extensions Tools                   RSAT-Bits-Server            Installed
        [X] DataCenterBridging LLDP Tools                  RSAT-DataCenterBridgin…     Installed
        [X] Failover Clustering Tools                      RSAT-Clustering             Installed
            [X] Failover Cluster Management Tools          RSAT-Clustering-Mgmt        Installed
            [X] Failover Cluster Module for Windows Po…    RSAT-Clustering-PowerS…     Installed
            [X] Failover Cluster Automation Server         RSAT-Clustering-Automa…     Installed
            [X] Failover Cluster Command Interface         RSAT-Clustering-CmdInt…     Installed
        [X] Network Load Balancing Tools                   RSAT-NLB                    Installed
        [X] Shielded VM Tools                              RSAT-Shielded-VM-Tools      Installed
        [X] SNMP Tools                                     RSAT-SNMP                   Installed
        [X] Storage Migration Service Tools                RSAT-SMS                    Installed
        [X] Storage Replica Module for Windows PowerSh…    RSAT-Storage-Replica        Installed
        [X] System Insights Module for Windows PowerSh…    RSAT-System-Insights        Installed
        [X] WINS Server Tools                              RSAT-WINS                   Installed
    [X] Role Administration Tools                          RSAT-Role-Tools             Installed
        [X] AD DS and AD LDS Tools                         RSAT-AD-Tools               Installed
            [X] Active Directory module for Windows Po…    RSAT-AD-PowerShell          Installed
            [X] AD DS Tools                                RSAT-ADDS                   Installed
                [X] Active Directory Administrative Ce…    RSAT-AD-AdminCenter         Installed
                [X] AD DS Snap-Ins and Command-Line To…    RSAT-ADDS-Tools             Installed
            [X] AD LDS Snap-Ins and Command-Line Tools     RSAT-ADLDS                  Installed
        [X] Hyper-V Management Tools                       RSAT-Hyper-V-Tools          Installed
        [X] Remote Desktop Services Tools                  RSAT-RDS-Tools              Installed
            [X] Remote Desktop Gateway Tools               RSAT-RDS-Gateway            Installed
            [X] Remote Desktop Licensing Diagnoser Too…    RSAT-RDS-Licensing-Dia…     Installed
        [X] Windows Server Update Services Tools           UpdateServices-RSAT         Installed
        [X] Active Directory Certificate Services Tools    RSAT-ADCS                   Installed
            [X] Certification Authority Management Too…    RSAT-ADCS-Mgmt              Installed
            [X] Online Responder Tools                     RSAT-Online-Responder       Installed
        [X] Active Directory Rights Management Service…    RSAT-ADRMS                  Installed
        [X] DHCP Server Tools                              RSAT-DHCP                   Installed
        [X] DNS Server Tools                               RSAT-DNS-Server             Installed
        [X] Fax Server Tools                               RSAT-Fax                    Installed
        [X] File Services Tools                            RSAT-File-Services          Installed
            [X] DFS Management Tools                        RSAT-DFS-Mgmt-Con           Installed
            [X] File Server Resource Manager Tools         RSAT-FSRM-Mgmt              Installed
            [X] Services for Network File System Manag…    RSAT-NFS-Admin              Installed
        [X] Network Controller Management Tools            RSAT-NetworkController      Installed
        [X] Network Policy and Access Services Tools       RSAT-NPAS                   Installed
        [X] Print and Document Services Tools              RSAT-Print-Services         Installed
        [X] Remote Access Management Tools                 RSAT-RemoteAccess           Installed
            [X] Remote Access GUI and Command-Line Too…    RSAT-RemoteAccess-Mgmt      Installed
            [X] Remote Access module for Windows Power…    RSAT-RemoteAccess-Powe…     Installed
        [X] Volume Activation Tools                        RSAT-VA-Tools               Installed
```

Figure 2.16: Displaying RSAT features on SRV1

In the final step in this recipe, *step 12*, you reboot the host creating no console output.

There's more...

The output from *step 1* shows there are 1,809 total commands and 597 cmdlets available on SRV1, before adding the RSAT tools. The actual number may vary, depending on what additional tools, features, or applications you might have added to SRV1 or the specific Windows Server version.

In *step 2* and *step 3*, you find the kinds of commands available and the object type name PowerShell uses to describe these different command types. When you have the class names, you can use your search engine to discover more details about each of these command types. There are two further types of command (**ExternalScript** and **Application**) but these are not returned by default.

In *step 8*, you install all RSAT tools and as you can see, Windows requires a reboot to complete the installation of the tools. Later, in *step 12*, you reboot SRV1 to complete the installation of these tools.

In *step 10*, you create the $INS variable, which you later use in the display of the results. This technique enables you to see the code without worrying about line breaks in the book!

In *step 11*, you display all the RSAT tools using Get-WindowsFeature. Strictly speaking, this step displays the Windows features that have "RSAT" somewhere in the feature name. As you can see, there is no standard for actual feature names. The output shows the individual tools as either Feature Administration tools or Role Administration tools, although that difference is not relevant in your using the Server Manager cmdlets.

Exploring Package Management

The PackageManagement PowerShell module provides tools that enable you to download and install software packages from a variety of sources. The module, in effect, implements a provider interface that software package management systems use to manage software packages.

You can use the cmdlets in the PackageManagement module to work with a variety of package management systems. This module, in effect, provides an API to package management providers such as PowerShellGet, discussed in the *Exploring PowerShellGet and PS Gallery* recipe.

The primary function of the PackageManagement module is to manage the set of software repositories in which package management tools can search, obtain, install, and remove packages. The module enables you to discover and utilize software packages from a variety of sources, including the PowerShell Gallery.

The modules in the various internet repositories, including the PowerShell Gallery, vary in quality. Some are excellent and are heavily used by the community, while others are less useful or of lower quality. Some are written by the PowerShell product team. Ensure you look carefully at any third-party module you put into production.

This recipe explores the `PackageManagement` module from SRV1.

Getting ready

You run this recipe on SRV1 after you have installed PowerShell 7.

How to do it...

1. Reviewing the cmdlets in the `PackageManagement` module

   ```
   Get-Command -Module PackageManagement
   ```

2. Reviewing installed providers with `Get-PackageProvider`

   ```
   Get-PackageProvider |
     Format-Table -Property Name,
                            Version,
                            SupportedFileExtensions,
                            FromTrustedSource
   ```

3. Examining available package providers

   ```
   $PROVIDERS = Find-PackageProvider
   $PROVIDERS |
       Select-Object -Property Name,Summary |
         Format-Table -AutoSize -Wrap
   ```

4. Discovering and counting available packages

   ```
   $PACKAGES = Find-Package
   "Discovered {0:N0} packages" -f $PACKAGES.Count
   ```

5. Showing the first 5 packages discovered

   ```
   $PACKAGES |
       Select-Object -First 5 |
         Format-Table -AutoSize -Wrap
   ```

6. Installing the ChocolateyGet provider

```
Install-PackageProvider -Name ChocolateyGet -Force |
  Out-Null
```

7. Verifying ChocolateyGet is in the list of installed providers

```
Import-PackageProvider -Name ChocolateyGet
Get-PackageProvider -ListAvailable |
  Select-Object -Property Name,Version
```

8. Discovering packages using the ChocolateyGet provider

```
$CPackages = Find-Package -ProviderName ChocolateyGet -Name *
"$($CPackages.Count) packages available via ChocolateyGet"
```

How it works...

In *step 1*, you use Get-Command to discover the cmdlets in the PackageManagement module, with output like this:

```
PS C:\Foo> # 1. Reviewing the cmdlets in the PackageManagement module
PS C:\Foo> Get-Command -Module PackageManagement

CommandType     Name                        Version    Source
-----------     ----                        -------    ------
Cmdlet          Find-Package                1.4.7      PackageManagement
Cmdlet          Find-PackageProvider        1.4.7      PackageManagement
Cmdlet          Get-Package                 1.4.7      PackageManagement
Cmdlet          Get-PackageProvider         1.4.7      PackageManagement
Cmdlet          Get-PackageSource           1.4.7      PackageManagement
Cmdlet          Import-PackageProvider      1.4.7      PackageManagement
Cmdlet          Install-Package             1.4.7      PackageManagement
Cmdlet          Install-PackageProvider     1.4.7      PackageManagement
Cmdlet          Register-PackageSource      1.4.7      PackageManagement
Cmdlet          Save-Package                1.4.7      PackageManagement
Cmdlet          Set-PackageSource           1.4.7      PackageManagement
Cmdlet          Uninstall-Package           1.4.7      PackageManagement
Cmdlet          Unregister-PackageSource    1.4.7      PackageManagement
```

Figure 2.17: The PowerShell 7 console

In *step 2*, you use the Get-PackageProvider cmdlet to view the package providers that you have
loaded and imported, with output like this:

```
PS C:\Foo> # 2. Reviewing installed providers with Get-PackageProvider
PS C:\Foo> Get-PackageProvider |
              Format-Table -Property Name,
                                     Version,
                                     SupportedFileExtensions,
                                     FromTrustedSource


Name          Version SupportedFileExtensions FromTrustedSource
----          ------- ----------------------- -----------------
NuGet         3.0.0.1 {nupkg}                              False
PowerShellGet 2.2.5.0 {}                                   False
```

Figure 2.18: Reviewing installed package providers

In *step 3*, you use the Find-PackageProviders cmdlet to find additional package providers. The
output looks like this:

```
PS C:\Foo> # 3. Examining available Package Providers
PS C:\Foo> $PROVIDERS = Find-PackageProvider
PS C:\Foo> $PROVIDERS |
              Select-Object -Property Name,Summary |
                Format-Table -AutoSize -Wrap

Name                     Summary
----                     -------
PowerShellGet            PowerShell module with commands for discovering, installing, updating and
                         publishing the PowerShell artifacts like Modules, DSC Resources, Role
                         Capabilities and Scripts.
ChocolateyGet            Package Management (OneGet) provider that facilitates installing
                         Chocolatey packages from any NuGet repository.
ContainerImage           This is a PackageManagement provider module which helps in discovering,
                         downloading and installing Windows Container OS images.
                         For more details and examples refer to our project site
                         at https://github.com/PowerShell/ContainerProvider.
NanoServerPackage        A PackageManagement provider to  Discover, Save and Install Nano Server
                         Packages on-demand
Chocolatier              Package Management (OneGet) provider that facilitates installing
                         Chocolatey packages from any NuGet repository.
WinGet                   Package Management (OneGet) provider that facilitates installing
                         WinGet packages from any NuGet repository.
DotNetGlobalToolProvider OneGet package provider for dotnet global tools.
```

Figure 2.19: Discovering additional package providers

You can use the Find-Package cmdlet to discover packages that you can download, install, and
use. In *step 4*, you discover packages available with output that resembles this:

```
PS C:\Foo> # 4. Discovering and counting available packages
PS C:\Foo> $PACKAGES = Find-Package
PS C:\Foo> "Discovered {0:N0} packages" -f $PACKAGES.Count

Discovered 7,880 packages
```

Figure 2.20: Counting available packages

In *step 5*, you view the details of five (the first five) packages you discovered in the prior step. The output looks like this:

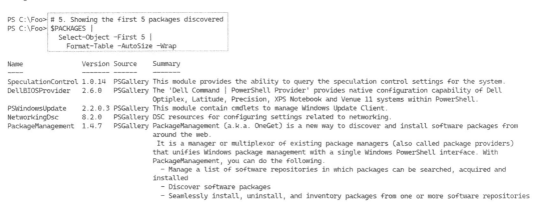

Figure 2.21: Viewing package summaries

In *step 6*, you install a new package provider – the ChocolateyGet provider. This step produces no output. In *step 7*, you view the currently imported package providers, with output like this:

```
PS C:\Foo> # 7. Verifying ChocolateyGet is in the list of installed providers
PS C:\Foo> Import-PackageProvider -Name ChocolateyGet
PS C:\Foo> Get-PackageProvider -ListAvailable |
             Select-Object -Property Name,Version

Name          Version
----          -------
ChocolateyGet 4.0.0.0
NuGet         3.0.0.1
PowerShellGet 2.2.5.0
PowerShellGet 1.0.0.1
```

Figure 2.22: Viewing package summaries

In the final step in this recipe, *step 8*, you discover all the currently available packages you can download using the ChocolatelyGet package provider – the output looks like this:

```
PS C:\Foo> # 8. Discovering Packages using the ChocolateyGet provider
PS C:\Foo> $CPackages = Find-Package -ProviderName ChocolateyGet -Name *
PS C:\Foo> "$($CPackages.Count) packages available via ChocolateyGet"
6842 packages available via ChocolateyGet
```

Figure 2.23: Counting packages available via the ChocolateyGet provider

There's more...

In *step 4,* you display a count of the packages available in the PS Gallery. By the time you read this, the number of packages is certain to rise. Package authors in the community are constantly adding new and improved packages to the PS Gallery. At the same time, since some users may have developed some automation on top of older providers, these too remain in the PS Gallery.

In *step 7*, you install the ChocolateyGet packaged provider. With this provider, you can discover and install packages from the Chocolatey repository in addition to the PowerShell Gallery. In *Chapter 1*, you used the Chocolatey command-line tool while in *step 8*, you find packages using the Find-Package cmdlet. The ChocolateyGet package provider is a wrapper around the command-line tool – and probably a lot easier to use for a simple case. The PowerShell Gallery and Chocolatey have many packages in common so you can probably find whatever packages you might need in either or both.

Exploring PowerShellGet and the PS Gallery

In a perfect world, PowerShell would come with a command that performed every single action any IT professional should ever need or want. But, as Jeffrey Snover (the inventor of PowerShell) says: *To Ship is To Choose*. And that means PowerShell itself, as well as Windows Server features, may not have every command you need. At a practical level, the various Windows feature teams, as well as the PowerShell team, do not have infinite resources to implement every good idea. And that is where the PowerShell community and the **PowerShell Gallery** (**PS Gallery**) come in.

The PS Gallery provides a huge range of PowerShell artifacts for you to leverage. To some degree, if you can conceive of a use for PowerShell, there are likely to be things in the Gallery to delight you. If you are a Grateful Dead fan, for example, there are some scripts to manage your live concert collection (https://www.powershellgallery.com/packages/gdscripts/1.0.4). If you need to generate nice-looking HTML reports, then you can use the PSWriteHTML module (https://www.powershellgallery.com/packages/PSWriteHTML/0.0.173).

PowerShellGet is a module that enables you to discover, install, update, and publish key PowerShell artifacts found in the PowerShell Gallery. The artifacts you can leverage include modules, scripts, and more. You can think of this module as an abstraction on top of the Package Management tools. You can read more about the module at: `https://learn.microsoft.com/powershell/module/powershellget`.

Getting ready

You run this recipe on SRV1 after you have installed PowerShell 7.

How to do it...

1. Reviewing the commands available in the PowerShellGet module

```
Get-Command -Module PowerShellGet
```

2. Discovering Find-* cmdlets in PowerShellGet module

```
Get-Command -Module PowerShellGet -Verb Find
```

3. Getting all commands, modules, DSC resources, and scripts

```
$Commands     = Find-Command
$Modules      = Find-Module
$DSCResources = Find-DscResource
$Scripts      = Find-Script
```

4. Reporting on results

```
"On Host [$(hostname)]"
"Commands found:       [{0:N0}]"  -f $Commands.Count
"Modules found:        [{0:N0}]"  -f $Modules.Count
"DSC Resources found:  [{0:N0}]"  -f $DSCResources.Count
"Scripts found:        [{0:N0}]"  -f $Scripts.Count
```

5. Discovering NTFS-related modules

```
$Modules |
  Where-Object Name -match NTFS
```

6. Installing the NTFSSecurity module

```
Install-Module -Name NTFSSecurity -Force
```

7. Reviewing module contents

    ```
    Get-Command -Module NTFSSecurity
    ```

8. Testing the Get-NTFSAccess cmdlet:

    ```
    Get-NTFSAccess -Path C:\Foo
    ```

9. Creating a download folder

    ```
    $DLFLDR = 'C:\Foo\DownloadedModules'
    $NIHT = @{
      ItemType = 'Directory'
      Path     = $DLFLDR
      ErrorAction = 'SilentlyContinue'
    }
    New-Item @NIHT | Out-Null
    ```

10. Downloading the PSLogging module

    ```
    Save-Module -Name PSLogging -Path $DLFLDR
    ```

11. Viewing the contents of the download folder

    ```
    Get-ChildItem -Path $DownloadFolder -Recurse -Depth 2 |
      Format-Table -Property FullName
    ```

12. Importing the PSLogging module

    ```
    $ModuleFolder = Join-Path -Path $DownloadFolder -ChildPath
    'PSLogging'
    Get-ChildItem -Path $ModuleFolder -Filter *.psm1 -Recurse |
        Select-Object -ExpandProperty FullName -First 1 |
            Import-Module -Verbose
    ```

13. Checking commands in the module

    ```
    Get-Command -Module PSLogging
    ```

How it works...

In *step 1*, you use the Get-Command cmdlet to investigate the commands in the PowerShellGet module, with output that should look like this:

```
PS C:\Foo> # 1. Reviewing the commands available in the PowerShellGet module
PS C:\Foo> Get-Command -Module PowerShellGet

CommandType   Name                             Version   Source
-----------   ----                             -------   ------
Function      Find-Command                     2.2.5     PowerShellGet
Function      Find-DscResource                 2.2.5     PowerShellGet
Function      Find-Module                      2.2.5     PowerShellGet
Function      Find-RoleCapability              2.2.5     PowerShellGet
Function      Find-Script                      2.2.5     PowerShellGet
Function      Get-CredsFromCredentialProvider  2.2.5     PowerShellGet
Function      Get-InstalledModule              2.2.5     PowerShellGet
Function      Get-InstalledScript              2.2.5     PowerShellGet
Function      Get-PSRepository                 2.2.5     PowerShellGet
Function      Install-Module                   2.2.5     PowerShellGet
Function      Install-Script                   2.2.5     PowerShellGet
Function      New-ScriptFileInfo               2.2.5     PowerShellGet
Function      Publish-Module                   2.2.5     PowerShellGet
Function      Publish-Script                   2.2.5     PowerShellGet
Function      Register-PSRepository            2.2.5     PowerShellGet
Function      Save-Module                      2.2.5     PowerShellGet
Function      Save-Script                      2.2.5     PowerShellGet
Function      Set-PSRepository                 2.2.5     PowerShellGet
Function      Test-ScriptFileInfo              2.2.5     PowerShellGet
Function      Uninstall-Module                 2.2.5     PowerShellGet
Function      Uninstall-Script                 2.2.5     PowerShellGet
Function      Unregister-PSRepository          2.2.5     PowerShellGet
Function      Update-Module                    2.2.5     PowerShellGet
Function      Update-ModuleManifest            2.2.5     PowerShellGet
Function      Update-Script                    2.2.5     PowerShellGet
Function      Update-ScriptFileInfo            2.2.5     PowerShellGet
```

Figure 2.24: The PowerShell 7 console

In *step 2*, you discover the cmdlets in the PowerShellGet module that have the Find verb, with output like this:

```
PS C:\Foo> # 2. Discovering Find-* cmdlets in PowerShellGet module
PS C:\Foo> Get-Command -Module PowerShellGet -Verb Find

CommandType   Name                 Version   Source
-----------   ----                 -------   ------
Function      Find-Command         2.2.5     PowerShellGet
Function      Find-DscResource     2.2.5     PowerShellGet
Function      Find-Module          2.2.5     PowerShellGet
Function      Find-RoleCapability  2.2.5     PowerShellGet
Function      Find-Script          2.2.5     PowerShellGet
```

Figure 2.25: Discovering the Find- cmdlets in the PowerShellGet module*

In *step 3*, which generates no output, you find all the commands, modules, DSC resources, and scripts in the PowerShell Gallery. In *step 4*, you report on the number of objects found in the PS Gallery, with output like this:

```
PS C:\Foo> # 4. Reporting on results
PS C:\Foo> "On Host [$(hostname)]"
PS C:\Foo> "Commands found:        [{0:N0}]"  -f $Commands.Count
PS C:\Foo> "Modules found:         [{0:N0}]"  -f $Modules.Count
PS C:\Foo> "DSC Resources found:   [{0:N0}]"  -f $DSCResources.Count
PS C:\Foo> "Scripts found:         [{0:N0}]"  -f $Sripts.Count

On Host [SRV1]
Commands found:        [146,638]
Modules found:         [7,886]
DSC Resources found:   [2,146]
Scripts found:         [1,545]
```

Figure 2.26: Discovering the Find-* cmdlets in the PowerShellGet module

In *step 5*, you examine the modules returned (in *step 3)* to see if any of them have "NTFS" in the module name. The output looks like this:

```
PS C:\Foo> # 5. Discovering NTFS-related modules
PS C:\Foo> $Modules |
             Where-Object Name -match NTFS

Version   Name                      Repository   Description
-------   ----                      ----------   -----------
4.2.6     NTFSSecurity              PSGallery    Windows PowerShell M…
1.4.1     cNtfsAccessControl        PSGallery    The cNtfsAccessContr…
1.0       NTFSPermissionMigration   PSGallery    This module is used …
```

Figure 2.27: Discovering NTFS-related modules in the PowerShell Gallery

Having discovered an NTFS-related module, in *step 6*, you install the module. This step creates no output. In *step 7*, you use Get-Command to discover the commands in the NTFSSecurity module, with output like this:

```
PS C:\Foo> # 7. Reviewing module contents
PS C:\Foo> Get-Command -Module NTFSSecurity

CommandType    Name                          Version   Source
-----------    ----                          -------   ------
Cmdlet         Add-NTFSAccess                4.2.6     NTFSSecurity
Cmdlet         Add-NTFSAudit                 4.2.6     NTFSSecurity
Cmdlet         Clear-NTFSAccess              4.2.6     NTFSSecurity
Cmdlet         Clear-NTFSAudit               4.2.6     NTFSSecurity
Cmdlet         Copy-Item2                    4.2.6     NTFSSecurity
Cmdlet         Disable-NTFSAccessInheritance 4.2.6     NTFSSecurity
Cmdlet         Disable-NTFSAuditInheritance  4.2.6     NTFSSecurity
Cmdlet         Disable-Privileges            4.2.6     NTFSSecurity
Cmdlet         Enable-NTFSAccessInheritance  4.2.6     NTFSSecurity
Cmdlet         Enable-NTFSAuditInheritance   4.2.6     NTFSSecurity
Cmdlet         Enable-Privileges             4.2.6     NTFSSecurity
Cmdlet         Get-ChildItem2                4.2.6     NTFSSecurity
Cmdlet         Get-DiskSpace                 4.2.6     NTFSSecurity
Cmdlet         Get-FileHash2                 4.2.6     NTFSSecurity
Cmdlet         Get-Item2                     4.2.6     NTFSSecurity
Cmdlet         Get-NTFSAccess                4.2.6     NTFSSecurity
Cmdlet         Get-NTFSAudit                 4.2.6     NTFSSecurity
Cmdlet         Get-NTFSEffectiveAccess       4.2.6     NTFSSecurity
Cmdlet         Get-NTFSHardLink              4.2.6     NTFSSecurity
Cmdlet         Get-NTFSInheritance           4.2.6     NTFSSecurity
Cmdlet         Get-NTFSOrphanedAccess        4.2.6     NTFSSecurity
Cmdlet         Get-NTFSOrphanedAudit         4.2.6     NTFSSecurity
Cmdlet         Get-NTFSOwner                 4.2.6     NTFSSecurity
Cmdlet         Get-NTFSSecurityDescriptor    4.2.6     NTFSSecurity
Cmdlet         Get-NTFSSimpleAccess          4.2.6     NTFSSecurity
Cmdlet         Get-Privileges                4.2.6     NTFSSecurity
Cmdlet         Move-Item2                    4.2.6     NTFSSecurity
Cmdlet         New-NTFSHardLink              4.2.6     NTFSSecurity
Cmdlet         New-NTFSSymbolicLink          4.2.6     NTFSSecurity
Cmdlet         Remove-Item2                  4.2.6     NTFSSecurity
Cmdlet         Remove-NTFSAccess             4.2.6     NTFSSecurity
Cmdlet         Remove-NTFSAudit              4.2.6     NTFSSecurity
Cmdlet         Set-NTFSInheritance           4.2.6     NTFSSecurity
Cmdlet         Set-NTFSOwner                 4.2.6     NTFSSecurity
Cmdlet         Set-NTFSSecurityDescriptor    4.2.6     NTFSSecurity
Cmdlet         Test-Path2                    4.2.6     NTFSSecurity
```

Figure 2.28: Discovering commands in the NTFSSecurity module

In *step 8*, you use a command from the NTFSSecurity module, Get-NTFSAccess, to view the access control list on the C:\Foo folder, which looks like this:

```
S C:\Foo> # 8. Testing the Get-NTFSAccess cmdlet
PS C:\Foo> Get-NTFSAccess -Path C:\Foo

    Path: C:\Foo (Inheritance enabled)

Account                 Access Rights        Applies to                     Type   IsInherited   InheritedFrom
-------                 -------------        ----------                     ----   -----------   -------------
NT AUTHORITY\SYSTEM     FullControl          ThisFolderSubfoldersAndF... Allow  True          C:
BUILTIN\Administrators  FullControl          ThisFolderSubfoldersAndF... Allow  True          C:
BUILTIN\Users           ReadAndExecute, ...  ThisFolderSubfoldersAndF... Allow  True          C:
BUILTIN\Users           CreateDirectories    ThisFolderAndSubfolders     Allow  True          C:
BUILTIN\Users           CreateFiles          ThisFolderAndSubfolders     Allow  True          C:
CREATOR OWNER           GenericAll           SubfoldersAndFilesOnly      Allow  True          C:
```

Figure 2.29: Using Get-NTFSAccess

As an alternative to installing fully a PS Gallery module, you might find it useful to download a module into a new folder. From there, you can investigate (and possibly improve it) before installing it in your environment. To do that, in *step 9*, you create a new download folder, creating no output. In *step 10*, you download the PSLogging module, which also produces no output.

In *step 11*, you discover the files contained in the PSLogging module with output like this:

```
PS C:\Foo> # 11. Viewing the contents of the download folder
PS C:\Foo> Get-ChildItem -Path $DownloadFolder -Recurse |
             Format-Table -Property FullName

FullName
--------
C:\Foo\DownloadedModules\PSLogging
C:\Foo\DownloadedModules\PSLogging\2.5.2
C:\Foo\DownloadedModules\PSLogging\2.5.2\PSLogging.psd1
C:\Foo\DownloadedModules\PSLogging\2.5.2\PSLogging.psm1
```

Figure 2.30: Discovering files contained in the PSLogging module

Finally, in *step 12*, you check the commands contained in this module with output like this:

```
PS C:\Foo> # 12. Checking commands in the module
PS C:\Foo> Get-Command -Module PSLogging

CommandType Name             Version Source
----------- ----             ------- ------
Function    Send-Log         0.0     PSLogging
Function    Start-Log        0.0     PSLogging
Function    Stop-Log         0.0     PSLogging
Function    Write-LogError   0.0     PSLogging
Function    Write-LogInfo    0.0     PSLogging
Function    Write-LogWarning 0.0     PSLogging
```

Figure 2.31: Discovering files contained in the PSLogging module

There's more...

In *step 2*, you discover the commands within the PowerShellGet module that enable you to find resources in the PS Gallery. There are 5 types of resources you can search for in the Gallery:

- Command – these are individual commands contained within the gallery. You can use Find-Command to help you discover the name of a module that might contain a command.

- Module – these are PowerShell modules. Some of which may not work in PowerShell 7 and some that may not work at all.

- DSC Resource – these are Windows PowerShell DSC resources. PowerShell 7 does not provide the rich DSC functions and features available with Windows PowerShell at this time.

- Script – these are complete PowerShell scripts. You can use them as-is or adapt them to your needs.

- Role Capability – this resource was meant for packages that enhance Windows roles but is little used in practice.

In *steps 3* and *step 4*, you discover the number of commands, modules, DSC Resources, and PowerShell scripts available in the gallery. Since there is constant activity, the numbers of PowerShell resources you discover are likely different from what you see in this book. Note that step 3 may take several minutes. If you plan to search for multiple modules, then downloading the details of *all* the modules makes subsequent searching quicker.

In *step 5*, you search the PS Gallery for modules whose name includes the string "NTFS". The modules returned may or may not be helpful for you. As you can see, the search returns the NTFSSecurity module that, in *steps 6* through *step 8*, you install and use.

Before you start using a PS Gallery module, it is a great idea to first download it and test it. In *step 9*, you create a new folder, and then in *step 10*, you download the module into this new folder. In *step 11*, you observe the contents of the module.

Since you have downloaded the module to a folder, not on the PSModulePath environment variable, PowerShell cannot find it automatically. Therefore, in *step 12*, you import the module manually. You then look at the commands available within the module.

The two modules you examined in this recipe are a tiny part of the PowerShell Gallery. As you discovered, there are thousands of modules, commands, and scripts. Some of those objects are not of the highest quality or may be of no use to you. But others are excellent additions to your module collection, as many recipes in this book demonstrate.

For most IT pros, the PowerShell Gallery is the go-to location for obtaining useful modules that avoid you having to reinvent the wheel. In some cases, you may develop a particularly useful module and then publish it to the PS Gallery to share with others. See https://learn.microsoft.com/powershell/scripting/gallery/concepts/publishing-guidelines for guidelines regarding publishing to the PS Gallery. And, while you are looking at that page, consider implementing the best practices suggested in any production script you develop.

Creating and Using a Local Package Repository

In the *Exploring PowerShellGet and PS Gallery* recipe, you saw how you could download PowerShell modules and more from the PS Gallery. You can install them, or save them for investigation. One nice feature is that after you install a module using Install-Module, you can later update the module using Update-Module.

As an alternative to using a public repository, you can create your own private repository. You can then use the commands in the PowerShellGet module to find, install, and manage your modules. A private repository allows you to create your modules and put them into a local repository for your IT professionals, developers, or other users to access.

There are several methods you can use to set up your internal package repository. One approach would be to use, a third-party tool such as ProGet from Inedo (see https://inedo.com/ for details on ProGet).

A simple way to create a repository is to set up an SMB file share. Then, you use the command Register-PSRepository to enable you to use the PowerShellGet commands to view this share as a PowerShell repository. You must register this repository for every host from which you access your repository. After you create the share and register the repository, you can publish your modules to the new repository using the Publish-Module command.

Once you set up a repository, you just need to ensure you use Register-PSRepository on any system that wishes to use this new repository, as you can see in this recipe.

Getting ready

Run this recipe on SRV1 after you have loaded PowerShell 7.

How to do it...

1. Creating a new repository folder

```
$PATH = 'C:\RKRepo'
New-Item -Path $PATH -ItemType Directory | Out-Null
```

2. Sharing the folder

```
$SMBHT = @{
  Name        = 'RKRepo'
  Path        = LPATH
  Description = 'Reskit Repository'
  FullAccess  = 'Everyone'
}
New-SmbShare @SMBHT
```

3. Registering the repository as trusted (on SRV1)

```
$Path = '\\SRV1\RKRepo'
$REPOHT = @{
  Name              = 'RKRepo'
  SourceLocation    = $Path
  PublishLocation   = $Path
  InstallationPolicy = 'Trusted'
}
Register-PSRepository @REPOHT
```

4. Viewing configured repositories

```
Get-PSRepository
```

5. Creating a Hello World module folder

```
$HWDIR = 'C:\HW'
New-Item -Path $HWDIR -ItemType Directory | Out-Null
```

6. Creating a very simple module

```
$HS = @"
Function Get-HelloWorld {'Hello World'}
Set-Alias -[Name GHW -=Value Get-HelloWorld
"@
$HS | Out-File $HWDIR\HW.psm1
```

7. Testing the module locally

```
Import-Module -Name $HWDIR\HW.PSM1 -Verbose
GHW
```

8. Creating a PowerShell module manifest for the new module

```
$NMHT = @{
  Path              = "$HWDIR\HW.psd1"
  RootModule        = 'HW.psm1'
  Description       = 'Hello World module'
  Author            = 'DoctorDNS@Gmail.com'
  FunctionsToExport = 'Get-HelloWorld'
  ModuleVersion     = '1.0.1'
}
New-ModuleManifest @NMHT
```

9. Publishing the module

```
Publish-Module -Path $HWDIR -Repository RKRepo -Force
```

10. Viewing the results of publishing

```
Find-Module -Repository RKRepo
```

11. Checking the repository's home folder

```
Get-ChildItem -Path $LPATH
```

How it works...

In *step 1*, you create a new folder on SRV1 to hold your new PowerShell repository, producing no output. In *step 2*, you use the `New-SmbShare` cmdlet to create a new share, with output like this:

```
PS C:\Foo> # 2. Sharing the folder
PS C:\Foo> $SMBHT = @{
              Name        = 'RKRepo'
              Path        = $PATH
              Description = 'Reskit Repository'
              FullAccess  = 'Everyone'
           }
PS C:\Foo> New-SmbShare @SMBHT

Name      ScopeName  Path         Description
----      ---------  ----         -----------
RKRepo    *          C:\RKRepo    Reskit Repository
```

Figure 2.32: The PowerShell 7 console

In *step 3*, you register this new SMB share as a new PowerShell repository, which creates no console output. In *step 4*, you view the configured PowerShell repositories, with output like this:

```
PS C:\Foo> # 4. Viewing configured repositories
PS C:\Foo> Get-PSRepository

Name        InstallationPolicy  SourceLocation
----        ------------------  --------------
RKRepo      Trusted             \\SRV1\RKRepo
PSGallery   Untrusted           https://www.powershellgallery.com/api/v2
```

Figure 2.33: Viewing configured repositories

To demonstrate using this new repository, in *step 5*, you first create a folder, and then in *step 6*, you create a simple module in this folder. These two steps produce no console output.

In *step 7*, you import and use the module, with output like this:

```
PS C:\Foo> # 7. Testing the module locally
PS C:\Foo> Import-Module -Name $HWDIR\HW.PSM1 -Verbose
VERBOSE: Importing function 'Get-HelloWorld'.
VERBOSE: Importing alias 'GHW'.
PS C:\Foo> GHW
Hello World
```

Figure 2.34: Testing HW module

In *step 8*, you create a module manifest, and in *step 9*, you publish the module to your repository. These two steps produce no output. In *step 10*, you use `Find-Module` to find the modules in your repository, with output like this:

```
PS C:\Foo> # 10. Viewing the results of publishing
PS C:\Foo> Find-Module -Repository RKRepo

Version   Name   Repository   Description
-------   ----   ----------   -----------
1.0.1     HW     RKRepo       Hello World module
```

Figure 2.35: Viewing the modules in the new repository

In *step 11*, you view the repository's home folder, with output like this:

```
PS C:\Foo> # 11. Checking the repository's home folder
PS C:\Foo> Get-ChildItem -Path $LPATH

    Directory: C:\RKRepo

Mode         LastWriteTime      Length  Name
----         -------------      ------  ----
-a---    25/04/2022    17:38       3462  HW.1.0.1.nupkg
```

Figure 2.36: Testing HW module

There's more...

In *step 1*, you create a folder on the C:\ drive to act as a repository that you then share. In production, you should probably put this share in a highly-available system with redundant disk drives.

In *step 3*, you set up an SMB share to act as a PowerShell repository on SRV1. You may need to adjust the value of the $Path variable in this step if you are testing this recipe on a host with a different name. Also, if you plan to use this repository on other systems, you need to explicitly register this repository on each host since registering a repository works on a system-by-system basis.

In *step 11*, you can see the NuGet package, which is your module. When you published the module, the cmdlet created and stored the NuGet package in the shared folder.

Establishing a Script Signing Environment

You can often find that it is essential to know if an application, or a PowerShell script, has been modified since it was released. You can use Windows Authenticode Digital Signatures for this purpose.

Authenticode is a Microsoft code-signing technology that identifies the publisher of Authenticode-signed software. Authenticode also verifies that the software has not been tampered with since it was signed and published.

You can also use Authenticode to digitally sign your script using a PowerShell command. You can then ensure PowerShell only runs digitally-signed scripts by setting an execution policy of `AllSigned` or `RemoteSigned`.

After you sign a PowerShell script, you can set PowerShell's execution policy to force PowerShell to test the script to ensure the digital signature is still valid and only run scripts that succeed. You can set PowerShell to do this either for all scripts (you set the execution policy to `AllSigned`) or only for scripts you downloaded from a remote site (by setting the execution policy to `RemoteSigned`). Setting the execution policy to `AllSigned` also means that your Profile files must be signed, or they do not run.

This sounds a beautiful thing, but it is worth remembering that even if you have the execution policy set to `AllSigned`, it's trivial to run any non-signed script. Simply bring your script into VS Code (or the Windows PowerShell ISE), select all the text in the script, then run that selected text. If an Execution policy of `RemoteSigned` is blocking a particular script you downloaded from the internet or from the PS Gallery, you can use the `Unblock-File` cmdlet to, in effect, turn a remote script into a local one. Script signing just makes it a bit harder, but not impossible, to run a script that has no signature or whose signature fails.

Signing a script is simple once you have a digital certificate issued by a **Certificate Authority (CA)**. You have three options for getting an appropriate code-signing certificate:

- Use a well-known public Certificate Authority such as Digicert (see `https://www.digicert.com/code-signing` for details of their code-signing certificates).
- Deploy an internal CA and obtain the certificate from your organization's CA.
- Use a self-signed certificate.

Public certificates are useful but generally not free. You can easily set up your own CA or use self-signed certificates. Self-signed certificates are great for testing out signing scripts and then using them, but possibly inappropriate for production use. All three of these methods can give you a certificate that you can use to sign PowerShell scripts.

This recipe shows how to sign and use digitally-signed scripts. The mechanisms in this recipe work on any of the three sources of signing key listed above. For simplicity, you use a self-signed certificate for this recipe.

Getting ready

You run this recipe on SRV1 after you have installed PowerShell 7.

How to do it...

1. Creating a script-signing self-signed certificate

```
$CHT = @{
  Subject           = 'Reskit Code Signing'
  Type              = 'CodeSigning'
  CertStoreLocation = 'Cert:\CurrentUser\My'
}
New-SelfSignedCertificate @CHT | Out-Null
```

2. Displaying the newly created certificate

```
$Cert = Get-ChildItem -Path Cert:\CurrentUser\my -CodeSigningCert
$Cert |
  Where-Object {$_.SubjectName.Name -match $CHT.Subject}
```

3. Creating and viewing a simple script

```
$Script = @"
  # Sample Script
  'Hello World from PowerShell 7!'
  "Running on [$(Hostname)]"
"@
$Script | Out-File -FilePath C:\Foo\Signed.ps1
Get-ChildItem -Path C:\Foo\Signed.ps1
```

4. Signing your new script

```
$SHT = @{
  Certificate = $cert
  FilePath    = 'C:\Foo\Signed.ps1'
}
Set-AuthenticodeSignature @SHT
```

5. Checking the script after signing

```
Get-ChildItem -Path C:\Foo\Signed.ps1
```

6. Viewing the signed script

```
Get-Content -Path C:\Foo\Signed.ps1
```

7. Testing the signature

```
Get-AuthenticodeSignature -FilePath C:\Foo\Signed.ps1 |
  Format-List
```

8. Running the signed script

```
C:\Foo\Signed.ps1
```

9. Setting the execution policy to all signed for this process

```
Set-ExecutionPolicy -ExecutionPolicy AllSigned -Scope Process
```

10. Running the signed script

```
C:\Foo\Signed.ps1
```

11. Copying certificate to the Current User Trusted Root store

```
$DestStoreName  = 'Root'
$DestStoreScope = 'CurrentUser'
$Type   = 'System.Security.Cryptography.X509Certificates.X509Store'
$MHT = @{
  TypeName = $Type
  ArgumentList  = ($DestStoreName, $DestStoreScope)
}
$DestStore = New-Object @MHT
$DestStore.Open(
  [System.Security.Cryptography.X509Certificates.
OpenFlags]::ReadWrite)
$DestStore.Add($Cert)
$DestStore.Close()
```

12. Checking the signature

```
Get-AuthenticodeSignature -FilePath C:\Foo\Signed.ps1 |
  Format-List
```

13. Running the signed script

```
C:\Foo\Signed.ps1
```

14. Copying certificate to the Trusted Publisher store

```
$DestStoreName  = 'TrustedPublisher'
$DestStoreScope = 'CurrentUser'
$Type   = 'System.Security.Cryptography.X509Certificates.X509Store'
$MHT = @{
  TypeName = $Type
  ArgumentList  = ($DestStoreName, $DestStoreScope)
}
$DestStore = New-Object  @MHT
$DestStore.Open(
  [System.Security.Cryptography.X509Certificates.
OpenFlags]::ReadWrite)
$DestStore.Add($Cert)
$DestStore.Close()
```

15. Running the signed script

```
C:\Foo\Signed.ps1
```

16. Resetting the Execution policy for this process

```
Set-ExecutionPolicy -ExecutionPolicy Unrestricted -Scope Process
```

How it works...

In *step 1*, you create a new self-signed certificate for code signing. This step creates no output. In *step 2*, you display the newly created certificate, with output like this:

```
PS C:\Foo> # 2. Displaying the newly created certificate
PS C:\Foo> $Cert = Get-ChildItem -Path Cert:\CurrentUser\my -CodeSigningCert
PS C:\Foo> $Cert |
            Where-Object {$_.SubjectName.Name -match $CHT.Subject}

  PSParentPath: Microsoft.PowerShell.Security\Certificate::CurrentUser\my

Thumbprint                               Subject                EnhancedKeyUsageList
----------                               -------                --------------------
55694D1AA117028A739E9F5CC7AEBBB1209D45E5  CN=Reskit Code Sign... Code Signing
```

Figure 2.37: Displaying the certificate

In *step 3*, you create a very simple script and view the script file's details, with the following output:

```
PS C:\Foo> # 3. Creating and viewing a simple script
PS C:\Foo> $Script = @"
             # Sample Script
             'Hello World from PowerShell 7!'
             "Running on [$(Hostname)]"
           "@
PS C:\Foo> $Script | Out-File -FilePath C:\Foo\Signed.ps1
PS C:\Foo> Get-ChildItem -Path C:\Foo\Signed.ps1


    Directory: C:\Foo

Mode                 LastWriteTime         Length Name
----                 -------------         ------ ----
-a---        26/04/2022     17:22              78 Signed.ps1
```

Figure 2.38: Displaying the certificate

With *step 4*, you sign the script using your newly created code-signing certificate. The output is as follows:

```
PS C:\Foo> # 4. Signing your new script
PS C:\Foo> $SHT = @{
             Certificate = $cert
             FilePath    = 'C:\Foo\Signed.ps1'
           }
PS C:\Foo> Set-AuthenticodeSignature @SHT
```

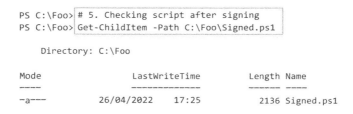

| Directory: C:\foo | | | |
SignerCertificate	Status	StatusMessage	Path
55694D1AA117028A739E9F5CC7AEBBB1209D45E5	UnknownError	A certificate chain processed, but terminated in a root certificate which is not trusted by the trust provider.	signed.ps1

Figure 2.39: Signing your script

In *step 5*, you view the file details for your newly signed script, with output like this:

```
PS C:\Foo> # 5. Checking script after signing
PS C:\Foo> Get-ChildItem -Path C:\Foo\Signed.ps1


    Directory: C:\Foo

Mode                 LastWriteTime         Length Name
----                 -------------         ------ ----
-a---        26/04/2022     17:25            2136 Signed.ps1
```

Figure 2.40: Signing your script

Next, in *step 6*, you view the contents of the script file, with output like this:

```
PS C:\Foo> # 6. Viewing the signed script
PS C:\Foo> Get-Content -Path C:\Foo\Signed.ps1

  # Sample Script
  'Hello World from PowerShell 7!'
  "Running on [SRV1]"

# SIG # Begin signature block
# MIIFeQYJKoZIhvcNAQcCoIIFajCCBWYCAQExCzAJBgUrDgMCGgUAMGkGCisGAQQB
# gjcCAQSgWzBZMDQGCisGAQQBgjcCAR4wJgIDAQAABBAfzDtgWUsITrck0sYpfvNR
# AgEAAgEAAgEAAgEAAgEAMCEwCQYFKw4DAhoFAAQUiXIZ7que8HGeN6y3v9batOmI
# VzygggMQMIIDDDCCAfSgAwIBAgIQESy8ARMRF6RNfapBk//p+zANBgkqhkiG9w0B
# AQsFADAeMRwwGgYDVQQDDBNSZXNraXQgQ29kZSBTaWduaW5nMB4XDTIyMDQyNjE2
# MTExM1oXDTIzMDQyNjE2MzExM1owHjEcMBoGA1UEAwwTUmVza2l0IENvZGUgU2ln
# bmluZzCCASIwDQYJKoZIhvcNAQEBBQADggEPADCCAQoCggEBAMQkI0Zo8ctEiPwd
# R5LdCw7QQ0WVK6gsqAvgXOpMVYe9V70Y+h3jyomxA3svRAKJVriyfsp+uEaCN5WS
# aT863u553qMBYkgvokJzmQIxWJVO1B1dBbSWutn9wihSjzaqUm3KWh/k8XS8ow9W
# KvWChT7Vn5fmsfX/6tXtmJxaG47DirWZUZ/9V4RJADQL24RT5SsE16WboCKanRAL
# can6OJK8OCbIQvM0uXne+7bv1n+3x+ZfBptJFB8Sf0CfGiUYe/q3P1rWZS+do1hd
# bPfRxca44SU4zxLSnllvIXeQgCTPe93NHPOFkgDblizhtbjFSF03SOdxj7UmOE1/
# RQcLy00CAwEAAaNGMEQwDgYDVR0PAQH/BAQDAgeAMBMGA1UdJQQMMAoGCCsGAQUF
# BwMDMB0GA1UdDgQWBBSbIu3CywcdPmTZRkdvE647Q6XrXjANBgkqhkiG9w0BAQsF
# AAOCAQEAphlEvSTYsxdBYWir+/3ShQ05454IfIIgAtNar9RTGmdobpeMdGTWIglS
# mXRUvnTGIWNPqEdd3m+Pm9hUwuW4Av/FOlMwIE0WsqvS5MoepKY6oinpaa4rUDZi
# XbLBTdutNTa4u7YExjVxYgOUXmdbGG0l/OjiWmqQ7BC40zmJr1LrJ+NfQkMDf9LR
# VjkrLX1MD/V6ZqZtJK57XjmX1VmiZeS0pNNpvvSIGE70/N37Bf9iBmg2HkLz/cmO
# Aqo6IrIHmK3UuG1VEjCPh7479KqwSEcqkGaVWTBuuA4xhfl5mjJXaK17MqCYD6bZ
# BpTrBLs1G3ULSeCqzVhSXPGGnSQ5AzGCAdMwggHPAgEBMDIwHjEcMBoGA1UEAwwT
# UmVza2l0IENvZGUgU2lnbmluZwIQESy8ARMRF6RNfapBk//p+zAJBgUrDgMCGgUA
# oHgwGAYKKwYBBAGCNwIBDDEKMAigAoAAoQKAADAZBgkqhkiG9w0BCQMxDAYKKwYB
# BAGCNwIBBDAcBgorBgEEAYI3AgELMQ4wDAYKKwYBBAGCNwIBFTAjBgkqhkiG9w0B
# CQQxFgQUtXvYPUYhpvHmSjkz4NMrIU+3M6QwDQYJKoZIhvcNAQEBBQAEggEAAo7K
# r2w2oNathBRiZ4mohR44DqMFgq5dfkbW9+wWg1Q5C2opNSWFPbKJWJJWRHv7r21P
# 0t0myr/TGo1MQ093afZPJvpeDP1pA/Gc+VNQJwk3YG6yl+HnhthaxuyNzHCZqDdX
# ydzTO5VazDdHIOUT63ZN8RDi7JZQ0lXHiPxSbpkoIvAkQJ5NPK6X/Rbi8YOu69/U
# Q71jptE0I9HYL8htjns0Mp41DHJp0pKPsL5JmNyilj6xj/vad0RrrPvrHhKbXWOP
# TAwvZro2J6BK0zSucHNnOX2AYpGdnvkVOYnCEa60nQg1EXBvkYH8M4PoY457UlCy
# qN+2J0RqrkyF1AF85Q==
# SIG # End signature block
```

Figure 2.41: Viewing the signed script

In *step 7*, you use the Get-AuthenticodeSignature to get the details of the file signature and view the results, as you can see here:

```
PS C:\Foo> # 7. Testing the signature
PS C:\Foo> Get-AuthenticodeSignature -FilePath C:\Foo\Signed.ps1 |
              Format-List

SignerCertificate      : [Subject]
                           CN=Reskit Code Signing

                         [Issuer]
                           CN=Reskit Code Signing

                         [Serial Number]
                           112CBC01131117A44D7DAA4193FFE9FB

                         [Not Before]
                           26/04/2022 17:11:13

                         [Not After]
                           26/04/2023 17:31:13

                         [Thumbprint]
                           55694D1AA117028A739E9F5CC7AEBBB1209D45E5

TimeStamperCertificate :
Status                 : UnknownError
StatusMessage          : A certificate chain processed, but terminated in
                         a root certificate which is not trusted by the
                         trust provider.
Path                   : C:\Foo\Signed.ps1
SignatureType          : Authenticode
IsOSBinary             : False
```

Figure 2.42: Viewing details of the script's digital signature

In *step 8*, you run the script with output like this:

```
PS C:\Foo> # 8. Running the signed script
PS C:\Foo> C:\Foo\Signed.ps1
Hello World from PowerShell 7!
Running on [SRV1]
```

Figure 2.43: Running the script

In *step 9*, you change the current process's Execution policy to AllSigned, which generates no console output. In *step 10* you run the script again with the output like this:

```
PS C:\Foo> # 10. Running the signed script
PS C:\Foo> C:\Foo\Signed.ps1
C:\Foo\Signed.ps1
Line |
   2 |  C:\Foo\Signed.ps1
     |  ~~~~~~~~~~~~~~~~~~
     | File C:\Foo\Signed.ps1 cannot be loaded. A certificate chain processed, but
       terminated in a root certificate which is not trusted by the trust provider.
```

Figure 2.44: Running the script

In *step 11*, you copy the self-signed certificate to the current user's trusted root CA certificate store. There is no output from the console, but when PowerShell attempts to add the certificate, Windows opens a security warning message box that looks like this:

Figure 2.45: Authorizing the addition of the certificate

In *step 12*, you recheck the script's digital signature, which looks like this:

Figure 2.46: Checking the script's digital signature

In *step 13*, you rerun the script file. Doing so generates a warning message, as you can see here:

```
PS C:\Foo> # 13. Running the signed script
PS C:\Foo> C:\Foo>:\Foo\Signed.ps1
Do you want to run software from this untrusted publisher?
File C:\Foo\Signed.ps1 is published by CN=Reskit Code Signing and is
not trusted on your system. Only run scripts from trusted publishers.
[V] Never run [D] Do not run [R] Run once [A] Always run [?] Help
(default is "Do not run"):
```

Figure 2.47: Rerunning the script

To resolve the warning message, in *step 14*, you copy the certificate to the current user's trusted publisher store. Then in *step 15*, you run the signed script successfully, as you can see in this output:

```
PS C:\Foo> # 15. Running the signed script
PS C:\Foo> C:\Foo\Signed.ps1
Hello World from PowerShell 7!
Running on [SRV1]
```

Figure 2.48: Rerunning the script

In the final step in this recipe, *step 16*, you reset the process level execution policy to Unrestricted.

There's more...

In *step 1*, you open a new Windows PowerShell console. Make sure you run the console as the local administrator.

In *step 4*, you sign the script using the newly created code-signing certificate. The output from this step shows that you signed the script with a certificate that was not issued by a trusted certificate authority. In *step 5*, you can see that the script file exists, but is now 2,136 bytes! To see why this relatively large file size, in *step 6*, you can see the script, with a large text block at the end holding the digital signature.

With *step 7*, you verify the signature on the script, which results in the same status message. The file is signed, but Windows does not (yet) trust the certificate authority that issued the code-signing certificate.

In *step 8*, you run the script. Despite the signature issue, the script runs fine, since you set the PowerShell execution policy to Unrestricted when you installed PowerShell. In *step 9*, you set the execution policy to Allsigned, and in *step 10*, you run the script. As you can see, PowerShell stops you from running the script due to the certificate chain issue.

In *step 11,* you copy the self-signed certificate into the current user's trusted root certificate store. You can only perform this copy action by using .NET objects as there are no cmdlets. When you invoke the `Add()` method, Windows displays a security warning. Note that Windows tends to display this dialog box *under* your PowerShell console or VS code. When you run this step, if the code seems to hang, check to see if the dialog box is hidden before agreeing to the addition to complete the step.

By copying the self-signed certificate to the trusted root store, Windows believes the code signing certificate is signed by a trusted CA. In *step 12,* you verify that the signature is trusted. Despite this, in *step 13,* you were sent a warning when you attempt to run the signed script. To avoid this warning, you copy the certificate to the current user's trusted publisher certificate store. With this done, in *step 15,* you rerun the script to observe that it now runs successfully.

In a production environment, you would more likely use either a public CA or an internal CA. If you use a public CA, then Windows *should* have that CA's certificate in the local host's trusted root store. You may need to add that certificate to the Trusted Publisher's store on each local host that you want to be able to run signed scripts. If you use an internal CA, you must ensure that each host is automatically enrolled for these certificates. For details on configuring certificate auto-enrollment, see: `https://learn.microsoft.com/windows-server/networking/core-network-guide/cncg/server-certs/configure-server-certificate-autoenrollment`.

Working With Shortcuts and the PSShortCut Module

A shortcut is a file that contains a pointer to another file or URL. You can place a shell link shortcut to some executable program, such as PowerShell, on your Windows desktop. When you click the shortcut in Windows Explorer, Windows runs the target program. You can also create a shortcut to a URL.

Shell link shortcuts have the extension `.LNK`, while URL shortcuts have the `.URL` extension. Internally, a file shortcut has a binary structure that is not directly editable. For more details on the internal format, see `https://learn.microsoft.com/openspecs/windows_protocols/ms-shllink/16cb4ca1-9339-4d0c-a68d-bf1d6cc0f943`.

The URL shortcut is a text document that you could edit with VS Code or Notepad. For more details on the URL shortcut file format, see `http://www.lyberty.com/encyc/articles/tech/dot_url_format_-_an_unofficial_guide.html`.

There are no built-in commands to manage shortcuts in PowerShell 7. As you saw earlier in this book, you can make use of older COM objects to create shortcuts. A more straightforward way is to use the PSShortCut module, which you can download from the PowerShell Gallery.

In this recipe, you discover shortcuts on your system and create shortcuts both to an executable file and a URL.

Getting ready

You run this recipe on SRV1 after you have installed PowerShell 7.

How to do it...

1. Finding the PSShortCut module

   ```
   Find-Module -Name '*Shortcut'
   ```

2. Installing the PSShortCut module

   ```
   Install-Module -Name PSShortcut -Force
   ```

3. Reviewing the PSShortCut module

   ```
   Get-Module -Name PSShortCut -ListAvailable |
     Format-List
   ```

4. Discovering commands in the PSShortCut module

   ```
   Get-Command -Module PSShortCut
   ```

5. Discovering all shortcuts on SRV1

   ```
   $SHORTCUTS = Get-Shortcut
   "Shortcuts found on $(hostname): [{0}]" -f $SHORTCUTS.Count
   ```

6. Discovering PWSH shortcuts

   ```
   $SHORTCUTS | Where-Object Name -match '^PWSH'
   ```

7. Discovering URL shortcut

   ```
   $URLSC = Get-Shortcut -FilePath *.url
   $URLSC
   ```

8. Viewing the content of shortcut

```
$URLSC | Get-Content
```

9. Creating a URL shortcut

```
$NEWURLSC  = 'C:\Foo\Google.url'
$TARGETURL = 'https://google.com'
New-Item -Path $NEWURLSC | Out-Null
Set-Shortcut -FilePath $NEWURLSC -TargetPath $TARGETURL
```

10. Using the URL shortcut

```
& $NEWURLSC
```

11. Creating a file shortcut

```
$CMD  = Get-Command -Name notepad.exe
$NP   = $CMD.Source
$NPSC = 'C:\Foo\NotePad.lnk'
New-Item -Path $NPSC | Out-Null
Set-Shortcut -FilePath $NPSC -TargetPath $NP
```

12. Using the shortcut

```
& $NPSC
```

How it works...

In *step 1*, you use the Find-Module cmdlet to discover any modules with the string "Shortcut" in the module name. The output looks like this:

```
PS C:\Foo> # 1. Finding the PSShortCut module
PS C:\Foo> Find-Module -Name '*Shortcut'

Version   Name                          Repository   Description
-------   ----                          ----------   -----------
2.2.0     DSCR_Shortcut                 PSGallery    PowerShell DSC Resource to create shortcut file.
0.2.1     PSAdvancedShortcut            PSGallery    Advanced shortcut appliance to create and modify shortcut file properties that are not easily…
2.2.0     Remove-iCloudPhotosShortcut   PSGallery    A PowerShell module for removing iCloud Photos shortcuts from This PC and Quick access on Win…
1.0.6     PSShortcut                    PSGallery    This module eases working with Windows shortcuts (LNK and URL) files.
0.1.0     oneShortcut                   PSGallery    PowerShell module to query, create, and remove OneDrive shortcuts to SharePoint document libr…
```

Figure 2.49: Rerunning the script

In *step 2*, you install the PSShortCut module, producing no output. After you have the module
installed, in *step 3*, you examine the module details, with output like this:

```
PS C:\Foo> # 3. Reviewing PSShortcut module
PS C:\Foo> Get-Module -Name PSShortCut -ListAvailable |
             Format-List

Name               : PSShortcut
Path               : C:\Users\Administrator\Documents\PowerShell\Modules\PSShortcut\1.0.6\PSShortcut.psd1
Description        : This module eases working with Windows shortcuts (LNK and URL) files.
ModuleType         : Script
Version            : 1.0.6
PreRelease         :
NestedModules      : {}
ExportedFunctions  : {Get-Shortcut, Set-Shortcut}
ExportedCmdlets    :
ExportedVariables  :
ExportedAliases    :
```

Figure 2.50: Viewing module details

In *step 4*, you use Get-Command to confirm the names of the commands in the module, with output
like this:

```
PS C:\Foo> # 4. Discovering commands in PSShortcut module
PS C:\Foo> Get-Command -Module PSShortcut

CommandType   Name            Version    Source
-----------   ----            -------    ------
Function      Get-Shortcut    1.0.6      PSShortcut
Function      Set-Shortcut    1.0.6      PSShortcut
```

Figure 2.51: Using Get-Command to find the commands in the PSShortCut module

As shown in *step 5*, you can search the entire host to discover all the shortcuts on the server, with
results like this:

```
PS C:\Foo> # 5. Discovering all shortcuts on SRV1
PS C:\Foo> $SHORTCUTS = Get-Shortcut
PS C:\Foo> "Shortcuts found on $(hostname): [{0}]" -f $SHORTCUTS.Count
Shortcuts found on SRV1: [261]
```

Figure 2.52: Finding shortcuts on SRV1

In *step 6*, you discover the shortcut to PowerShell 7 (which you created in *Chapter 1*). The output is like this:

```
PS C:\Foo> # 6. Discovering PWSH shortcuts
PS C:\Foo> $SHORTCUTS | Where-Object Name -match '^PWSH'

    Directory: C:\Users\Administrator\AppData\Roaming\Microsoft\Internet Explorer\Quick Launch\User Pinned\TaskBar

Mode           LastWriteTime      Length Name
----           -------------      ------ ----
-a---      09/04/2022    16:11       1030 pwsh.lnk
```

Figure 2.53: Discovering shortcuts to PowerShell 7

In *step 7*, you use the Get-Shortcut command to find all the URL shortcuts, with output like this:

```
PS C:\Foo> # 7. Discovering URL shortcut
PS C:\Foo> $URLSC = Get-Shortcut -FilePath *.url
PS C:\Foo> $URLSC

    Directory: C:\Users\Administrator\Favorites

Mode            LastWriteTime       Length Name
----            -------------       ------ ----
-a---       31/03/2022    17:30        208 Bing.url
```

Figure 2.54: Discovering URL shortcuts

In *step 8*, you view the contents of the shortcut, with output like this:

```
PS C:\Foo> # 8. Viewing content of shortcut
PS C:\Foo> $URLSC | Get-Content
[{000214A0-0000-0000-C000-000000000046}]
Prop3=19,2
[InternetShortcut]
IDList=
URL=http://go.microsoft.com/fwlink/p/?LinkId=255142
IconIndex=0
IconFile=%ProgramFiles%\Internet Explorer\Images\bing.ico
```

Figure 2.55: Viewing the contents of a URL shortcut

In *step 9*, you create a new URL shortcut, which generates no console output. In *step 10*, you use the URL shortcut. This step produces no console output, but you do see the Edge browser popping up, like this:

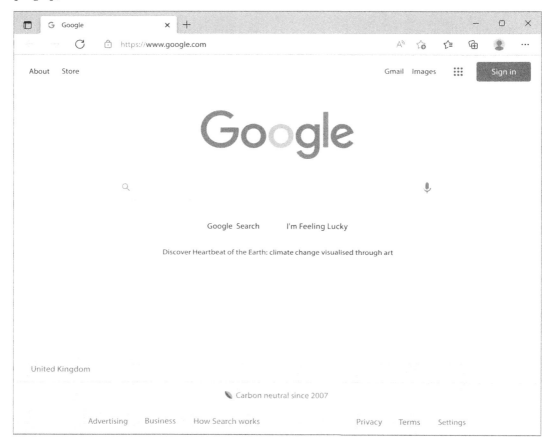

Figure 2.57: Using a shortcut to Google

In *step 11*, you create a new file-based URL (pointing to notepad.exe, which generates no output. Then in *step 12*, you use the shortcut. This step produces no output, but you should see Notepad pop up, like this:

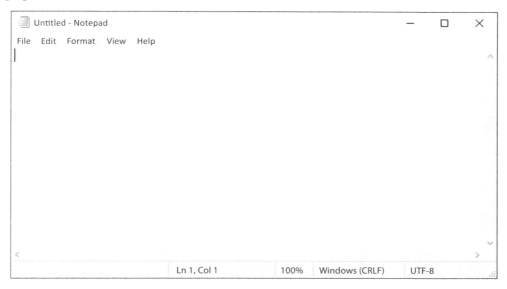

Figure 2.57: Using the shortcut to Notepad

There's more...

In *step 7*, you find URL shortcuts and as you can see, there is just one, to Bing. The Windows installer created this when it installed Windows Server on this host.

In *step 8*, you examine the contents of a URL shortcut. Unlike link shortcut files, which have a binary format and are not fully readable, URL shortcuts are text files. For an unofficial guide to the format of these files, see http://www.lyberty.com/encyc/articles/tech/dot_url_format_-_an_unofficial_guide.html.

Working With Archive Files

Since the beginning of the PC era, users have employed a variety of file compression mechanisms. An early method used the ZIP file format, initially implemented by PKWare's PKZip program quickly became a near-standard for data transfer. A later Windows version, WinZip, became popular. With Windows 98, Microsoft provided built-in support for ZIP archive files. Today, Windows supports ZIP files up to 2GB in total size. You can find more information about the ZIP file format at https://en.wikipedia.org/wiki/Zip_(file_format).

Numerous developers, over the years, have provided alternative compression schemes and associated utilities, including WinRAR and 7-Zip. WinZip and WinRAR are both excellent programs but are commercial programs. 7-Zip is a freeware tool that is also popular. All three offer their own compression mechanisms (with associated file extension) and support the others as well.

For details on WinZip, see `https://www.winzip.com/win/en`, for information on WinRAR, see `https://www.win-rar.com`, and for more on 7-Zip, see `https://www.7-zip.org`. Each of the compression utilities offered by these groups also supports compression mechanisms from other environments such as TAR.

In this recipe, you will look at PowerShell 7's built-in commands to manage archive files. The commands work only with ZIP files. You can find a PowerShell module for 7Zip at `https://github.com/thoemmi/7Zip4Powershell`, although the module is old and has not been updated in many years.

Getting ready

You run this recipe on SRV1 after you have installed PowerShell 7.

How to do it...

1. Getting the archive module

   ```
   Get-Module -Name Microsoft.Powershell.Archive -ListAvailable
   ```

2. Discovering commands in the archive module

   ```
   Get-Command -Module Microsoft.PowerShell.Archive
   ```

3. Making a new folder

   ```
   $NIHT = @{
     Name      = 'Archive'
     Path      = 'C:\Foo'
     ItemType  = 'Directory'
     ErrorAction = 'SilentlyContinue'
   }
   New-Item @NIHT | Out-Null
   ```

4. Creating files in the archive folder

```
$Contents = "Have a Nice day with PowerShell and Windows Server" *
1000
1..100 |
  ForEach-Object {
    $FName = "C:\Foo\Archive\Archive_$_.txt"
    New-Item -Path $FName -ItemType File  | Out-Null
    $Contents | Out-File -FilePath $FName
}
```

5. Measuring files to archive

```
$Files = Get-ChildItem -Path 'C:\Foo\Archive'
$Count = $Files.Count
$LenKB = (($Files | Measure-Object -Property length -Sum).Sum)/1mb
"[{0}] files, occupying {1:n2}mb" -f $Count, $LenKB
```

6. Compressing a set of files into an archive

```
$AFILE1 = 'C:\Foo\Archive1.zip'
Compress-Archive -Path $Files -DestinationPath "$AFile1"
```

7. Compressing a folder containing files

```
$AFILE2 = 'C:\Foo\Archive2.zip'
Compress-Archive -Path "C:\Foo\Archive" -DestinationPath $AFile2
```

8. Viewing the archive files

```
Get-ChildItem -Path $AFILE1, $AFILE2
```

9. Viewing archive content with Windows Explorer

```
explorer.exe $AFILE1
```

10. Viewing the second archive with Windows Explorer

```
explorer.exe $AFILE2
```

11. Making a new output folder

```
$Opath = 'C:\Foo\Decompressed'
$NIHT2 = @{
  Path        = $Opath
```

```
     ItemType    = 'Directory'
     ErrorAction = 'SilentlyContinue'
}
New-Item @NIHT2 | Out-Null
```

12. Decompress the `Archive1.zip` archive

```
Expand-Archive -Path $AFILE1 -DestinationPath $Opath
```

13. Measuring the size of the decompressed files

```
$Files = Get-ChildItem -Path $Opath
$Count = $Files.Count
$LenKB = (($Files |
         Measure-Object -Property length -Sum).Sum)/1mb
"[{0}] decompressed files, occupying {1:n2}mb" -f $Count, $LenKB
```

How it works...

In *step 1*, you get details of the `Microsoft.Powershell.Archive` module, with output like this:

```
PS C:\Foo> # 1. Getting archive module
PS C:\Foo> Get-Module -Name Microsoft.Powershell.Archive –ListAvailable

    Directory: C:\program files\powershell\7\Modules

ModuleType Version PreRelease Name                           PSEdition ExportedCommands
---------- ------- ---------- ----                           --------- ----------------
Manifest   1.2.5              Microsoft.PowerShell.Archive   Desk      {Compress-Archive, Expand-Archive}
```

Figure 2.58: Using the shortcut to Notepad

In *step 2*, you use `Get-Command` to discover additional details about the commands contained in the Archive module, with output like this:

```
PS C:\Foo> # 2. Discovering commands in archive module
PS C:\Foo> Get-Command –Module Microsoft.PowerShell.Archive

CommandType  Name              Version  Source
-----------  ----              -------  ------
Function     Compress-Archive  1.2.5    Microsoft.PowerShell.Archive
Function     Expand-Archive    1.2.5    Microsoft.PowerShell.Archive
```

Figure 2.59: Viewing the commands in the Microsoft.PowerShell.Archive module

To prepare to use the archiving commands, in *step 3*, you create a hash table to hold the parameters to `New-Item` to create a new folder. In *step 4*, you populate the folder with a set of files. These two steps produce no output.

In *step 5,* you get a count of the files in the folder and the space they occupy, with output like this:

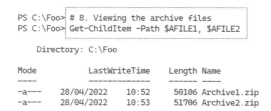

```
PS C:\Foo> # 5. Measuring files to archive
PS C:\Foo> $Files = Get-ChildItem -Path 'C:\Foo\Archive'
PS C:\Foo> $Count = $Files.Count
PS C:\Foo> $LenKB = (($Files | Measure-Object -Property length -Sum).Sum)/1mb
PS C:\Foo> "[{0}] files, occupying {1:n2}mb" -f $Count, $LenKB
[100] files, occupying 4.77mb
```

Figure 2.60: Measuring the files to be compressed

In *step 6,* you compress a set of files into an archive file, and in *step 7,* you compress a folder (containing files) into another archive file. These two steps produce no output. In *step 8,* you view the two archive files, with output like this:

```
PS C:\Foo> # 8. Viewing the archive files
PS C:\Foo> Get-ChildItem -Path $AFILE1, $AFILE2


    Directory: C:\Foo


Mode                 LastWriteTime         Length Name
----                 -------------         ------ ----
-a---        28/04/2022     10:52          50106 Archive1.zip
-a---        28/04/2022     10:53          51706 Archive2.zip
```

Figure 2.61: Viewing the archive files

In *step 9,* you view the first archive file in Windows File Explorer, with output like this:

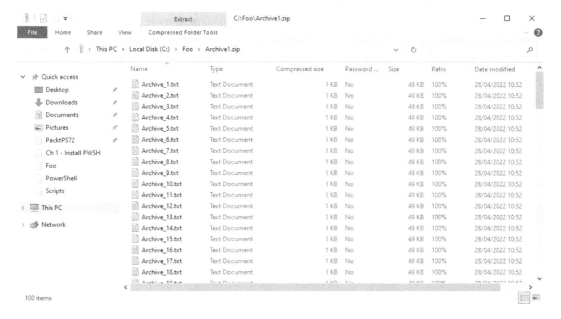

Figure 2.62: Viewing Archive1.zip

In *step 10*, you view the second archive file, which looks like this:

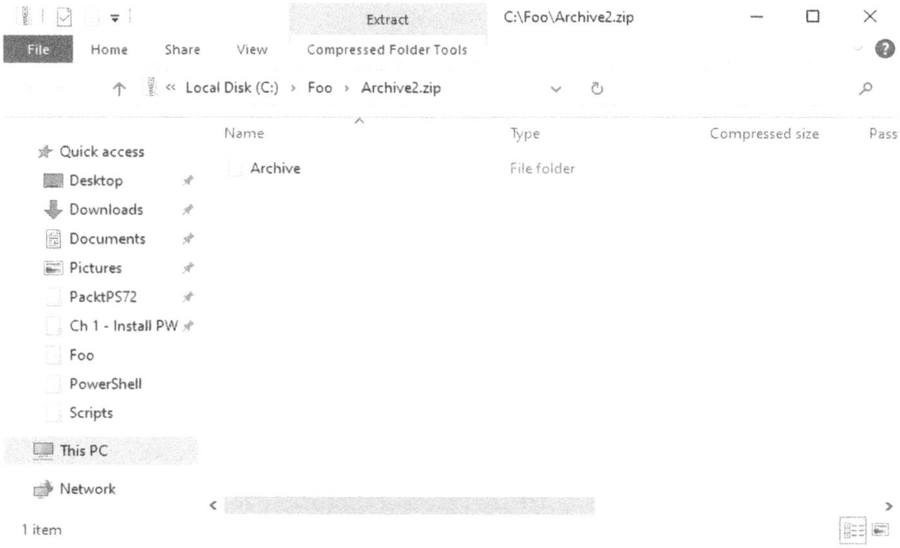

Figure 2.63: Viewing Archive1.zip

To demonstrate expanding an archive, in *step 11*, you create a new folder (C:\Foo\Decompressed), which generates no console output, In *step 12*, you use Expand-Archive to decompress the files within the archive to the specified destination folder, which also generates no output.

In the final step, *step 13*, you count the decompressed files with output like this:

```
PS C:\Foo> # 13. Measuring the size of the decompressed files
PS C:\Foo> $Files = Get-ChildItem -Path $Opath
PS C:\Foo> $Count = $Files.Count
PS C:\Foo> $LenKB = (($Files |
                    Measure-Object -Property length -Sum).Sum)/1mb
PS C:\Foo> "[{0}] decompressed files, occupying {1:n2}mb" -f $Count, $LenKB
[100] decompressed files, occupying 4.77mb
```

Figure 2.64: Viewing Archive1.zip

There's more...

In *step 1* and *step 2*, you can see the Archive module has two commands internally. As you can see, the module details returned by Get-Module show the module to have two commands. In the next step, Get-Command confirms the module has the two commands but that these are PowerShell functions and not PowerShell cmdlets. If you navigate to the folder containing this module, you can see both the module manifest (Microsoft.PowerShell.Archive.psd1) and the module file that defines the exported functions (Microsoft.PowerShell.Archive.psm1).

In *step 9*, you created the archive file `Archive1.zip`, which contains 100 files. In *step 12*, you used `Expand-Archive` to expand the files from the archive into the specified folder. As you can see in *step 13*, the files previously compressed into an archive are now decompressed and in the destination path.

Searching for Files Using the Everything Search Tool

Void Tools is a software company that produced the Everything search tool. Most IT pros run it from the GUI but there is a community module to help you use this tool using PowerShell. The Everything tool and the PowerShell community have developed a nice little product that you can easily leverage in PowerShell. The Everything applications return fully qualified filenames for those files on your system whose names meet a specified pattern. You can use either a wild card (e.g., `*.PS1`) or a regular expression (e.g., `'\.PS1$'`) as a pattern. There is also an add-on module that provides an easy-to-use PowerShell COMMAND.

The key benefit is that it is very fast. On a large Windows host with say one million total files, it might take 10-12 seconds to return a list of all the files on that system. To find all the `.PS1` files on the system drive would take under 100 milliseconds. By comparison, using `Get-ChildItem` would take several minutes.

If you are managing a large file server, tools like Everything could be very useful. And for a bit of light relief, you can bring up the GUI, specify ALL files, and sort files by date modified. After a second or two, you can watch as Windows and Windows applications create and update files on your system. Do you know what all those files are?

This recipe first downloads and installs the Everything tool and the `PSEverything` module from the PowerShell Gallery. Then you use the tool to find files on the system.

For more details on the Everything tool, see `https://www.voidtools.com/`. For the latest downloads, you can view the download page at `https://www.voidtools.com/downloads/`. And for more information about installing Everything, see a great support article at `https://www.voidtools.com/forum/viewtopic.php?f=5&t=5673&p=15546`. The tool provides a large range of installation options that you can use, depending on your needs.

Getting ready

You run this recipe on SRV1 after you have installed PowerShell 7.

How to do it...

1. Getting download locations

```
$ELoc  = 'https://www.voidtools.com/downloads'
$Release = Invoke-WebRequest -Uri $ELoc # Get all
$FLoc  = 'https://www.voidtools.com'
$EPath = $FLOC + ($Release.Links.href |
            Where-Object { $_ -match 'x64' } |
              Select-Object -First 1)
$EFile = 'C:\Foo\EverythingSetup.exe'
```

2. Downloading the Everything installer

```
Invoke-WebRequest -Uri $EPath -OutFile $EFile -verbose
```

3. Install Everything

```
$Iopt = "-install-desktop-shortcut -install-service"
$Iloc = 'C:\Program Files\Everything'
.\EverythingSetup.exe /S -install-options  $Iipt /D=$Iopt
```

4. Open the GUI for the first time

```
& "C:\Program Files\Everything\Everything.exe"
```

5. Finding the PSEverything module

```
Find-Module -Name PSEverything
```

6. Installing the PSEverything module

```
Install-Module -Name PSEverything -Force
```

7. Discovering commands in the module

```
Get-Command -Module PSEverything
```

8. Getting a count of files in folders below C:\Foo

```
Search-Everything |
  Get-Item |
    Group-Object DirectoryName |
      Where-Object name -ne '' |
        Format-Table -property Name, Count
```

9. Finding PowerShell scripts using wild cards

```
Search-Everything *.ps1 |
   Measure-Object
```

10. Finding all PowerShell scripts using regular expression

```
Search-Everything -RegularExpression '\.ps1$' -Global |
   Measure-Object
```

How it works...

In *step 1*, you set the locations for the download of the Everything tool. Then in *step 2*, you download the installation package. With *step 3*, you perform a silent install of the tool onto SRV1. With *step 4*, you open the Everything GUI. This produces no console output but you do see the following popup:

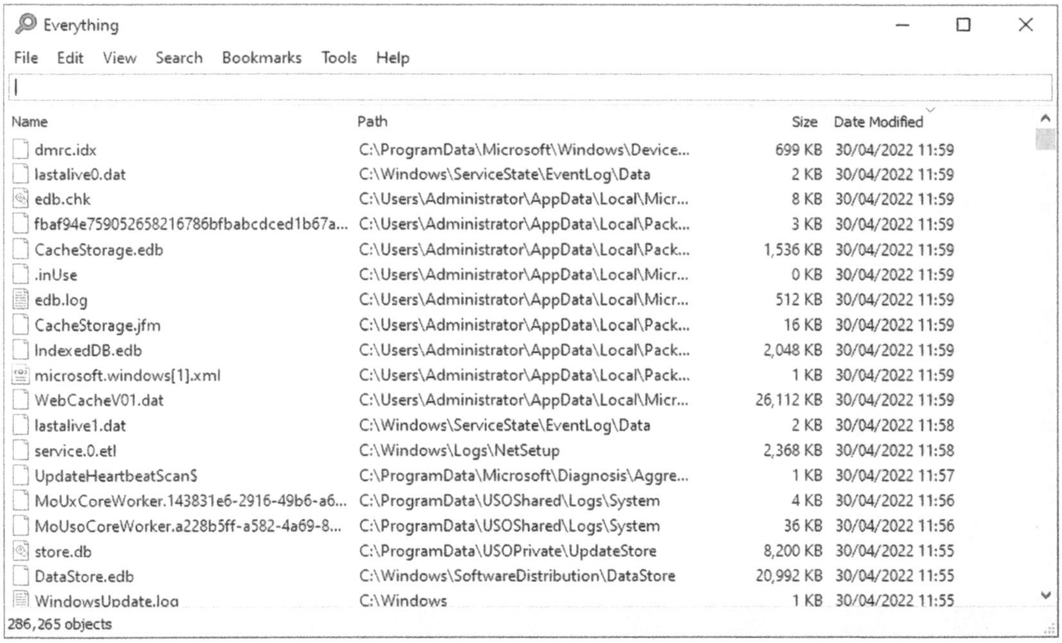

Figure 2.65: Everything GUI

With *step 5*, you find the PSEverything module with output like this:

```
PS C:\Foo> # 5. Find the PSEverything module
PS C:\Foo> Find-Module -Name PSEverything

Version    Name           Repository    Description
-------    ----           ----------    -----------
3.3.0      PSEverything   PSGallery     Powershell access to Everything - Blazingly fast file system se...
```

Figure 2.66: Finding the PSEverything module

In *step 6*, you install the module, which generates no console output. In *step 7* you view the commands in the module with output like this:

```
PS C:\Foo> # 7. Find commands in the module
PS C:\Foo> Get-Command -Module PSEverything

CommandType     Name                              Version    Source
-----------     ----                              -------    ------
Cmdlet          Search-Everything                 3.3.0      PSEverything
Cmdlet          Select-EverythingString           3.3.0      PSEverything
```

Figure 2.67: Getting the commands in the PSEverything module

```
PS C:\Foo> # 8. Getting a count of files in folders below C:\Foo
PS C:\Foo> Search-Everything |
             Get-Item |
               Group-Object DirectoryName |
                 Where-Object name -ne '' |
                   Format-Table -Property Name, Count

Name                                         Count
----                                         -----
C:\Foo                                          17
C:\Foo\Archive                                 100
C:\Foo\CascadiaCode\otf\static                  48
C:\Foo\CascadiaCode\ttf                          8
C:\Foo\CascadiaCode\ttf\static                  48
C:\Foo\CascadiaCode\woff2                         8
C:\Foo\CascadiaCode\woff2\static                48
C:\Foo\Decompressed                            100
C:\Foo\DownloadedModules\PSLogging\2.5.2         3
```

Figure 2.68: Counting the files in each folder below C:\Foo on SRV1

In *step 8*, you search for all the *.PS1 files at and below C:\Foo, then return a count, with output like this:

```
PS C:\Foo> # 9. Finding PowerShell scripts using wild cards
PS C:\Foo> Search-Everything *.ps1 |
             Measure-Object

Count              : 4
Average            :
Sum                :
Maximum            :
Minimum            :
StandardDeviation  :
Property           :
```

*Figure 2.69: Counting the *.PS1 files in and below C:\Foo*

In the final step in this recipe, *step 10*, you count the total number of files on SRV1 whose filename matches the regular expression "\.ps1$" – which is the equivalent of the wild card used in the prior step. The output from this step looks like this:

```
PS C:\Foo> # 10. Finding all PowerShell scripts using regular expression
PS C:\Foo> Search-Everything -RegularExpression '\.ps1$' -Global |
             Measure-Object

Count              : 1629
Average            :
Sum                :
Maximum            :
Minimum            :
StandardDeviation  :
Property           :
```

*Figure 2.70: Counting the *.PS1 files on SRV1*

There's more...

In *step 1*, you set variables that correspond to the location from which you can download the Everything installation package. This location was correct at the time of writing – but may have changed.

The screenshot for *step 4* shows the Everything GUI with the files sorted with the most recently changed files at the top of the window. Note the number of files that Windows changes every minute! Do you know what these files are or why Windows is changing them? Answers on a postcard, please.

In *step 8*, you view the folders below C:\Foo and the files contained in each folder. You created these folders and files by performing the recipes in this book. If you skipped any of the prior recipes, loaded different modules, etc., you may see different output.

The Search-Everything cmdlet returns the filenames that match a specified pattern. The cmdlet does not search inside any of the files. As you see in *step 7*, there is another command in the module, Select-EverythingString, which does search inside the files found.

Join our community on Discord

Join our community's Discord space for discussions with the author and other readers:

https://packt.link/SecNet

3

Exploring .NET

This chapter covers the following recipes:

- Exploring .NET Assemblies
- Exploring .NET Classes
- Leveraging .NET Methods
- Creating a C# Extension
- Creating a cmdlet

Introduction

Microsoft first launched .NET Framework in June 2000, with the code name Next Generation Windows Services. Amidst a barrage of marketing zeal, Microsoft seemed to add the .NET moniker to every product in its portfolio: Windows .NET Server (later renamed Windows Server 2003), Visual Studio.NET, and even MapPoint .NET.

.NET Framework provided application developers with a host of underlying features and technologies on which to base their applications. These worked well then (20+ years ago), but newer features later emerged based on advances in the underlying technologies. For example, **Simple Object Access Protocol (SOAP)** and XML-based web services have given way to **Representational State Transfer (REST)** and **JavaScript Object Notation (JSON)**.

Microsoft made considerable improvements to .NET Framework with each release and added new features based on customer feedback. .NET Framework started as closed-source, but Microsoft transitioned .NET to open source, aka .NET Core. PowerShell 7.2 is based on .NET 6.0.

An issue that emerged over time was that .NET became fragmented across different OSs and the web. To resolve this problem, Microsoft created .NET 5.0 and dropped "core" moniker. They released this version both on the web and across hardware platforms such as ARM. The intention from now on is to move to a single .NET across all platforms and form factors, thus simplifying application development. See `https://www.zdnet.com/article/microsoft-takes-a-major-step-toward-net-unification-with-net-5-0-release/` for some more detail on this.

It is important to note that both .NET 6.0 and PowerShell 7.2 have **long-term support (LTS)**. Microsoft intends to support these two products for three years, as described in this article: `https://devblogs.microsoft.com/dotnet/announcing-net-6/`. Many larger organizations prefer products with a longer support horizon.

For the application developer, .NET provides a rich **Application Program Interface (API)**, a programming model, plus associated tools and runtime. .NET is an environment in which developers can develop rich applications and websites across multiple platforms.

PowerShell sits on top of and makes heavy use of .NET. Some cmdlets are just a thin wrapper around .NET objects. For the IT professional, .NET provides the underpinnings of PowerShell but is otherwise mostly transparent. You use cmdlets to carry out actions. While these cmdlets use .NET to carry out their work, you are generally unaware of how PowerShell works under the hood. For example, you can use `Get-Process` without worrying about how that cmdlet obtains the details of the processes.

In some cases, there is no cmdlet available to you to carry out some action, but you can use .NET classes and methods to achieve it. For example, if you are creating an Active Directory cross-forest trust. So in some cases, knowing how to use .NET classes and their associated methods can be useful.

In some cases, you may wish to extend what is available by creating a .NET class (e.g., using C#) or developing a full PowerShell cmdlet. It is quite easy to download the tools and build a cmdlet. You might have a calculation of a bit of C# code that performs a particular task. Rather than taking the time to convert it to PowerShell and possibly taking a performance hit, you can wrap the code easily and create a class. Then you can add this to the PowerShell environment and use the class directly from PowerShell. And, if you are developing line-of-business applications, you could also create a full C# cmdlet.

Here is a high-level illustration of the components of .NET.

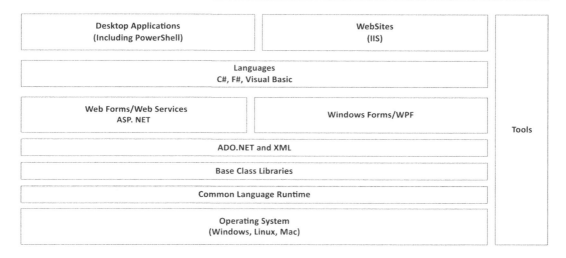

.Net Architecture

Figure 3.1: .NET components

The key components of .NET in this diagram are:

- **Operating system** – The .NET story begins with the operating system. The operating system provides the fundamental operations of your computer. .NET leverages the OS components. The .NET team supports .NET 6.0, the basis for PowerShell 7.2, on Windows, Linux, and the Apple Mac. .NET also runs on the ARM platform, enabling you to get PowerShell on ARM. See `https://github.com/dotnet/core/blob/main/release-notes/6.0/supported-os.md` for a full list of the operating systems supported.

- **Common Language Runtime (CLR)** – The CLR is the core of .NET, the managed code environment in which all .NET applications run (including PowerShell). The CLR delivers a managed execution environment and type safety and code access security. The CLR manages memory, threads, objects, resource allocation/de-allocation, and garbage collection. For an overview of the CLR, see `https://learn.microsoft.com/dotnet/standard/clr`. The CLR also contains the **Just-In-Time (JIT)** compiler and the class loader (responsible for loading classes into an application at runtime). For the PowerShell user, the CLR "just works."

- **Base Class Libraries (BCLs)** – .NET comes with numerous base class libraries, the fundamental built-in features you can use to build .NET applications. Each BCL is a DLL that contains .NET classes and types. The installer adds the .NET Framework components into PowerShell's installation folder when you install PowerShell. PowerShell developers use these libraries to implement PowerShell cmdlets. You can also call classes in the BCL directly from within PowerShell. It is the BCLs that enable you to reach into .NET.

- **WMI, COM, Win32** – Traditional application development technologies you can access via PowerShell. Within PowerShell, you can run programs that use these technologies and access them from the console or via a script. Your scripts can be a mixture of cmdlets, .NET, WMI, COM, and Win32 if necessary.

- **Languages** – This is the language that a cmdlet and application developer uses to develop PowerShell cmdlets. You can use various languages based on your preferences and skill set. Most cmdlet developers use C#, although using any .NET supported language would work, such as VB.NET. The original PowerShell development team designed the PowerShell language based on C#. You can describe PowerShell as on the glide scope down to C#. Understanding C# can be useful since there is a lot of documentation with examples in C#.

- **PowerShell** – PowerShell sits on top of these other components. From PowerShell, you can use cmdlets developed using a supported language. And you can use both BCL and WMI/COM/Win32.

Before diving into using .NET, there are some terms you should understand:

- **Class** – A class is a definition of some kind of object: the System.String defines a string while the System.Diagnostics.Process class defines a Windows process. Developers typically use C#, but you have options.

- **Assembly** – An assembly is a collection of types and resources used by an application and contains rich metadata about what the assembly includes. Most assemblies you use are .DLL files that a developer compiled for you previously – you add them using the Add-Type command. A neat feature is that you can also use Add-Type and supply just the source code – the cmdlet does the compilation for you at runtime!

- **Class instances** – You can have multiple instances of a given class, such as the processes on a system. A class instance can have properties, methods, events, and more. A property is some attribute of a class instance. For example, the StartTime property on a process object holds the process's start time. A method is some action that .NET can take on a given instance. A process instance, for example, has a Kill() method that immediately terminates the process (and does NOT ask you if you are sure!).

- **Static properties and methods** – Many classes have static properties and methods. Static properties relate to the class as opposed to a class instance. The System.Int32 class has a static property, MaxValue, that holds a value of the largest value that you can carry in a 32-bit integer instance. The System.IO.FileInfo class has a static method new() that enables you to create a new file.

In the chapter, you examine .NET assemblies, classes, and methods.

The system used in the chapter

This chapter is about using PowerShell 7 to explore .NET. In this chapter, you use a single host, SRV1, as follows:

Figure 3.2: Host in use for this chapter

In later chapters, you will use additional servers and will promote SRV1 to be a domain-based server rather than being in a workgroup.

Exploring .NET Assemblies

With .NET, an assembly holds compiled code that .NET can run. An assembly can be either a **Dynamic Link Library (DLL)** or an executable. As you can see in this recipe, cmdlets and .NET classes are generally contained in DLLs. Each assembly also includes a manifest that describes what is in the assembly and compiled code.

Most PowerShell modules and most PowerShell commands use assemblies of compiled code. When PowerShell loads any module, the module manifest (the .PSD1 file) lists the assemblies that make up the module. For example, the `Microsoft.PowerShell.Management` module provides many core PowerShell commands such as `Get-ChildItem` and `Get-Process`. This module's manifest lists a nested module (i.e., `Microsoft.PowerShell.Commands.Management.dll`) as the assembly containing the actual commands. PowerShell automatically loads this DLL file for you whenever it loads the module.

A great feature of PowerShell is the ability for you to invoke a .NET class method directly or to obtain a static .NET class value (or even execute a static method). The syntax for calling a .NET method or a .NET field, demonstrated in numerous recipes in this book, is to enclose the class name in square brackets and then follow it with two ":" characters (that is: "::") followed by the name of the method or static field (such as `[System.Int32]::MaxValue`).

In this recipe, you examine the assemblies loaded into PowerShell 7 and compare them with the behavior in Windows PowerShell. You also look at a module and the assembly that implements the commands in the module. The recipe illustrates some of the differences between PowerShell 7 and Windows PowerShell and how they co-exist with .NET.

Getting ready

You run this recipe on SRV1 after you have installed PowerShell 7.

How to do it...

1. Counting loaded assemblies

    ```
    $Assemblies = [System.AppDomain]::CurrentDomain.GetAssemblies()
    "Assemblies loaded: {0:n0}" -f $Assemblies.Count
    ```

2. Viewing first 10

    ```
    $Assemblies | Select-Object -First 10
    ```

3. Checking assemblies in Windows PowerShell

    ```
    $B = {
      [System.AppDomain]::CurrentDomain.GetAssemblies()
    }
    $PS51 = New-PSSession -UseWindowsPowerShell
    ```

```
$Assin51 = Invoke-Command -Session $PS51 -ScriptBlock $SB
"Assemblies loaded in Windows PowerShell: {0:n0}" -f $Assin51.Count
```

4. Viewing `Microsoft.PowerShell` assemblies

```
$Assin51 |
  Where-Object FullName -Match "Microsoft\.Powershell" |
    Sort-Object -Property Location
```

5. Exploring the `Microsoft.PowerShell.Management` module

```
$AllTheModulesOnThisSystem =
  Get-Module -Name Microsoft.PowerShell.Management -ListAvailable
$AllTheModuleOnThisYstgewjm  | Format-List
```

6. Viewing module manifest

```
$Manifest = Get-Content -Path $Mod.Path
$Manifest | Select-Object -First 20
```

7. Discovering the module's assembly

```
Import-Module -Name Microsoft.PowerShell.Management
$Match = $Manifest | Select-String Modules
$Line = $Match.Line
$DLL = ($Line -Split '"')[1]
Get-Item -Path $PSHOME\$DLL
```

8. Viewing associated loaded assembly

```
$Assemblies2 = [System.AppDomain]::CurrentDomain.GetAssemblies()
$Assemblies2 | Where-Object Location -match $DLL
```

9. Getting details of a PowerShell command inside a module DLL

```
$Commands = $Assemblies |
              Where-Object Location -match Commands.Management\.dll
$Commands.GetTypes() |
  Where-Object Name -match "Addcontentcommand$"
```

How it works...

In *step 1*, you use the `GetAssemblies()` static method to return all the assemblies currently loaded by PowerShell. Then you output a count of the assemblies presently loaded, which looks like this:

```
PS C:\Foo> # 1. Counting loaded assemblies
PS C:\Foo> $Assemblies = [System.AppDomain]::CurrentDomain.GetAssemblies()
PS C:\Foo> "Assemblies loaded: {0:n0}" -f $Assemblies.Count
Assemblies loaded: 86
```

Figure 3.3: Counting loaded assemblies

In *step 2*, you look at the first ten loaded assemblies, with output like this:

```
PS C:\Foo> # 2. Viewing first 10
PS C:\Foo> $Assemblies | Select-Object -First 10

GAC    Version     Location
---    -------     --------
False  v4.0.30319  C:\Program Files\PowerShell\7\System.Private.CoreLib.dll
False  v4.0.30319  C:\Program Files\PowerShell\7\pwsh.dll
False  v4.0.30319  C:\Program Files\PowerShell\7\System.Runtime.dll
False  v4.0.30319  C:\Program Files\PowerShell\7\Microsoft.PowerShell.ConsoleHost.dll
False  v4.0.30319  C:\Program Files\PowerShell\7\System.Management.Automation.dll
False  v4.0.30319  C:\Program Files\PowerShell\7\System.Threading.Thread.dll
False  v4.0.30319  C:\Program Files\PowerShell\7\System.Runtime.InteropServices.dll
False  v4.0.30319  C:\Program Files\PowerShell\7\System.Threading.dll
False  v4.0.30319  C:\Program Files\PowerShell\7\System.Diagnostics.Process.dll
False  v4.0.30319  C:\Program Files\PowerShell\7\System.Text.RegularExpressions.dll
```

Figure 3.4: Viewing the first ten loaded assemblies

In *step 3*, you examine the assemblies loaded into Windows PowerShell 5.1, which looks like this:

```
PS C:\Foo> # 3. Checking assemblies in Windows PowerShell
PS C:\Foo> $ScriptBlock = {
              [System.AppDomain]::CurrentDomain.GetAssemblies()
           }
PS C:\Foo> $PS51 = New-PSSession -UseWindowsPowerShell
PS C:\Foo> $Assin51 = Invoke-Command -Session $PS51 -ScriptBlock $ScriptBlock
PS C:\Foo> "Assemblies loaded in Windows PowerShell: {0:n0}" -f $Assin51.Count

Assemblies loaded in Windows PowerShell: 16
```

Figure 3.5: Counting assemblies loaded in Windows PowerShell

In *step 4*, you examine the `Microsoft.PowerShell.*` assemblies in PowerShell 5.1, which looks like this:

```
PS C:\Foo> # 4. Viewing Microsoft.PowerShell assemblies
PS C:\Foo> $Assin51 |
              Where-Object FullName -Match "Microsoft\.Powershell" |
                Sort-Object -Property Location

GAC    Version     Location                                                          PSComputerName
---    -------     --------                                                          --------------
True   v4.0.30319  C:\WINDOWS\Microsoft.Net\assembly\GAC_MSIL\Microsoft.PowerS… localhost
True   v4.0.30319  C:\WINDOWS\Microsoft.Net\assembly\GAC_MSIL\Microsoft.PowerS… localhost
```

Figure 3.6: Examining the Microsoft.PowerShell.* assemblies in Windows PowerShell

The `Microsoft.PowerShell.Management` PowerShell module contains numerous core PowerShell commands. In *step 6*, you examine the details of this module, as returned by `Get-Module`, with output like this:

Figure 3.7: Examining the Microsoft.PowerShell.Management module

In *step 6*, you view the module manifest for the `Microsoft.PowerShell.Management` PowerShell module. The figure below shows the first twenty lines of the manifest, which look like this:

```
PS C:\Foo> # 6. Viewing module manifest
PS C:\Foo> $Manifest = Get-Content -Path $Mod.Path
PS C:\Foo> $Manifest | Select-Object -First 20
@{
GUID="EEFCB906-B326-4E99-9F54-8B4BB6EF3C6D"
Author="PowerShell"
CompanyName="Microsoft Corporation"
Copyright="Copyright (c) Microsoft Corporation."
ModuleVersion="7.0.0.0"
CompatiblePSEditions = @("Core")
PowerShellVersion="3.0"
NestedModules="Microsoft.PowerShell.Commands.Management.dll"
HelpInfoURI = 'https://aka.ms/powershell72-help'
FunctionsToExport = @()
AliasesToExport = @("gcb", "gin", "gtz", "scb", "stz")
CmdletsToExport=@("Add-Content",
    "Clear-Content",
    "Get-Clipboard",
    "Set-Clipboard",
    "Clear-ItemProperty",
    "Join-Path",
    "Convert-Path",
    "Copy-ItemProperty",
```

Figure 3.8: Examining the module manifest for the Microsoft.PowerShell.Management module

In *step 7*, you import the `Microsoft.PowerShell.Management` module, extract the name of the DLL implementing the module, and discover its supporting DLL, with output like this:

```
PS C:\Foo> # 7. Discovering the module's assembly
PS C:\Foo> Import-Module -Name Microsoft.PowerShell.Management
PS C:\Foo> $Match = $Manifest | Select-String Modules
PS C:\Foo> $Line = $Match.Line
PS C:\Foo> $DLL = ($Line -Split '"')[1]
PS C:\Foo> Get-Item -Path $PSHOME\$DLL

    Directory: C:\Program Files\PowerShell\7

Mode         LastWriteTime     Length Name
----         -------------     ------ ----
-a---    08/03/2022    23:22   1134480 Microsoft.PowerShell.Commands.Management.dll
```

Figure 3.9: Examining a module's supporting DLL

In *step 8*, you find the assembly that contains the cmdlets in the `Microsoft.PowerShell.Management` module, which looks like this:

```
PS C:\Foo> # 8. Viewing associated loaded assembly
PS C:\Foo> $Assemblies2 = [System.AppDomain]::CurrentDomain.GetAssemblies()
PS C:\Foo> $Assemblies2 | Where-Object Location -match $DLL

GAC    Version   Location
---    -------   --------
False  v4.0.30319  C:\Program Files\PowerShell\7\Microsoft.PowerShell.Commands.Management.dll
```

Figure 3.10: Examining a module's supporting DLL

In *step 9*, you discover the name of the class that implements the Add-Content command, which looks like this:

```
PS C:\Foo> # 9. Getting details of a PowerShell command inside a module DLL
PS C:\Foo> $Commands = $Assemblies |
             Where-Object Location -match Commands.Management\.dll
PS C:\Foo> $Commands.GetTypes() |
             Where-Object Name -match "Addcontentcommand$"

IsPublic IsSerial Name              BaseType
-------- -------- ----              --------
True     False    AddContentCommand  Microsoft.PowerShell.Commands.WriteContentCommandBase
```

Figure 3.11: Examining a module's supporting DLL

There's more...

In this recipe, you have seen the .NET assemblies used by PowerShell. These consist of both .NET Framework assemblies (i.e., the BCLs) and the assemblies that implement PowerShell commands. For example, you find the Add-Content cmdlet in the PowerShell module Microsoft.PowerShell. Management.

In *step 1*, you use the GetAssemblies() static method to return all the assemblies currently loaded by PowerShell 7.2. As you can see, the syntax is different from calling PowerShell cmdlets.

In *steps 3* and *step 4*, you obtain and view the assemblies loaded by Windows PowerShell 5.1. As you can see, Windows PowerShell and PowerShell 7.2 load different assemblies.

In *step 6*, you view the first 20 lines of the module manifest for the Microsoft.PowerShell. Management module. The output cuts off the complete list of cmdlets exported by the module and the long digital signature for the module manifest. In the output, you can see that the Microsoft. PowerShell.Management.dll contains the Add-Content command.

In *step 7*, you discover the DLL, which implements, among others, the Add-Content cmdlet, and in *step 8*, you can see that the assembly is loaded. In *step 9*, you can discover that the Add-Content PowerShell cmdlet is implemented by the AddContentCommand class within the Assembly's DLL. For the curious, navigate to https://github.com/PowerShell/PowerShell/blob/master/src/ Microsoft.PowerShell.Commands.Management/commands/management/AddContentCommand.cs, where you can read the source code for this cmdlet.

Exploring .NET Classes

With .NET, a class defines an object in terms of properties, methods, etc. Objects and object occurrences are fundamental to PowerShell, where cmdlets produce and consume objects. The Get-Process command returns objects of the System.Diagnostics.Process class. When you use Get-ChildItem to return files and folders, the output is a set of objects based on the System. IO.FileInfo and System.IO.DirectoryInfo classes.

In most cases, your console activities and scripts use the objects created automatically by PowerShell commands. But you can also use the New-Object command to create occurrences of any class as necessary. This book shows numerous examples of creating an object using New-Object.

Within .NET, you have two kinds of object definitions: .NET classes and .NET types. A type defines a simple object that lives, at runtime, on your CPU's stack. Classes, being more complex, live in the global heap. The global heap is a large area of memory that .NET uses to hold object occurrences during a PowerShell session. In almost all cases, the difference between type and class is probably not overly relevant to IT professionals using PowerShell.

After a script or even a part of a script has run, .NET can tidy up the global heap in a process known as garbage collection. The garbage collection process is also not important for IT professionals (in most cases). The scripts you see in this book, for example, are not generally impacted by the garbage collection process, nor are most production scripts. For more information on the garbage collection process in .NET, see https://learn.microsoft.com/dotnet/standard/ garbage-collection/.

There are cases where the GC process can impact performance. For example, the System.Array class creates objects of fixed length within the global heap. If you add an item to an array, .NET creates a new copy of the array (including the addition) and marks the old one for removal. If you add a few items to the array, the performance hit is negligible. But if you are adding millions of occurrences, the performance can suffer significantly. You can use the ArrayList class to avoid this, which supports adding/removing items from an array without the performance penalty.

For more information on GC and performance, see `https://learn.microsoft.com/dotnet/standard/garbage-collection/performance`.

In .NET, occurrences of every class or type can include members, including properties, methods, and events. A property is an attribute of an occurrence of a class. An occurrence of the `System.IO.FileInfo` object, for example, has a `FullName` property. A method is effectively a function you can call that can do something to an object occurrence. You look at .NET methods in "Leveraging .NET Methods recipe." With .NET, an event can happen to an object occurrence, such as when Windows generates an event when a Windows process terminates. This book does not cover .NET events; however, a later chapter in this book discusses using WMI events.

You can quickly determine an object's class (or type) by piping the output of any cmdlet, or an object, to the `Get-Member` cmdlet. The `Get-Member` cmdlet uses a feature of .NET, reflection, to look inside and give you a definitive statement of what that object contains. This feature is invaluable – instead of guessing where in some piece of string output your script can find the full name of a file, you can discover the `FullName` property, a string, or the `Length` property, which is unambiguously an integer. Reflection and the `Get-Member` cmdlet help you to discover the properties and other members of a given object.

As mentioned earlier, .NET classes can have static properties and static methods. Static properties/methods are aspects of the class of a whole as opposed to a specific class instance. A static property is a fixed constant value, such as the maximum and minimum values for a 32-bit signed integer or the value of Pi. A static method is independent of any specific instance. For example, the `Parse()` method of the `INT32` class can parse a string to ensure it is a value 32-bit signed integer. In most cases, you use static methods to create object instances or do something related to the class, such as parsing a string to determine if it is a valid 32-bit integer.

This recipe looks at some everyday objects created automatically by PowerShell. The recipe also examines the static fields of the [Int] .NET class.

Getting ready

You run this recipe on SRV1 after you have installed PowerShell 7.

How to do it...

1. Creating a `FileInfo` object

   ```
   $File = Get-ChildItem -Path $PSHOME\pwsh.exe
   $File
   ```

2. Discovering the underlying class

   ```
   $Type = $File.GetType().FullName
   ".NET Class name: $Type"
   ```

3. Getting member types of `FileInfo` object

   ```
   $File |
     Get-Member |
       Group-Object -Property MemberType |
         Sort-Object -Property Count -Descending
   ```

4. Discovering properties of a Windows service

   ```
   Get-Service |
     Get-Member -MemberType Property
   ```

5. Discovering the underlying type of an integer

   ```
   $I = 42
   $IntType  = $I.GetType()
   $TypeName = $IntType.FullName
   $BaseType = $IntType.BaseType.Name
   ".NET Class name      : $TypeName"
   ".NET Class base type : $BaseType"
   ```

6. Looking at Process objects

   ```
   $Pwsh = Get-Process -Name pwsh |
     Select-Object -First 1
   $Pwsh |
     Get-Member |
       Group-Object -Property MemberType |
         Sort-Object -Property Count -Descending
   ```

7. Looking at static properties within a class

```
$Max = [Int32]::MaxValue
$Min = [Int32]::MinValue
"Minimum value [$Min]"
"Maximum value [$Max]"
```

How it works...

In *step 1*, you use the Get-ChildItem cmdlet to return a Fileinfo object. When you examine the object created by the cmdlet, it looks like this:

```
PS C:\Foo> # 1. Creating a Fileinfo object
PS C:\Foo> $FILE = Get-ChildItem -Path $PSHOME\pwsh.exe
PS C:\Foo> $FILE

    Directory: C:\Program Files\PowerShell\7

Mode              LastWriteTime         Length Name
----              -------------         ------ ----
-a---         08/03/2022     23:21      287632 pwsh.exe
```

Figure 3.12: Creating a FileInfo object

In *step 2*, you use the Get-Type() method to return the full class name of the $File object, which looks like this:

```
PS C:\Foo> # 2. Discovering the underlying class
PS C:\Foo> $Type = $FILE.GetType().FullName
PS C:\Foo> ".NET Class name: $Type"
.NET Class name: System.IO.FileInfo
```

Figure 3.13: Viewing the underlying class name

In *step 3*, you get the different types of members in an instance of a FileInfo class. You can see the other member types in the output like this:

```
PS C:\Foo> # 3. Getting member types of Fileinfo object
PS C:\Foo> $File |
             Get-Member |
               Group-Object -Property MemberType |
                 Sort-Object -Property Count -Descending

Count Name           Group
----- ----           -----
   23 Method          {System.IO.StreamWriter AppendText(), System.IO.FileInfo CopyTo(string destFileName), System.IO.FileInfo Copy…
   16 Property        {System.IO.FileAttributes Attributes {get;set;}, datetime CreationTime {get;set;}, datetime CreationTimeUtc {…
    6 NoteProperty    {string PSChildName=pwsh.exe, PSDriveInfo PSDrive=C, bool PSIsContainer=False, string PSParentPath=Microsoft.…
    3 CodeProperty    {System.String LinkType{get=GetLinkType;}, System.String Mode{get=Mode;}, System.String ModeWithoutHardLink{g…
    2 ScriptProperty  {System.Object BaseName {get=if ($this.Extension.Length -gt 0){$this.Name.Remove($this.Name.Length - $this.Ex…
    1 AliasProperty   {Target = LinkTarget}
```

Figure 3.14: Viewing the member types of a FileInfo object

In *step 4*, you examine the properties of an object representing a Windows service, looking like this:

```
PS C:\Foo> # 4. Discovering properties of a Windows service
PS C:\Foo> Get-Service |
              Get-Member -MemberType Property


   TypeName: System.Service.ServiceController#StartupType

Name                    MemberType Definition
----                    ---------- ----------
BinaryPathName          Property   System.String {get;set;}
CanPauseAndContinue     Property   bool CanPauseAndContinue {get;}
CanShutdown             Property   bool CanShutdown {get;}
CanStop                 Property   bool CanStop {get;}
Container               Property   System.ComponentModel.IContainer Container {get;}
DelayedAutoStart        Property   System.Boolean {get;set;}
DependentServices       Property   System.ServiceProcess.ServiceController[] DependentServices {get;}
Description             Property   System.String {get;set;}
DisplayName             Property   string DisplayName {get;set;}
MachineName             Property   string MachineName {get;set;}
ServiceHandle           Property   System.Runtime.InteropServices.SafeHandle ServiceHandle {get;}
ServiceName             Property   string ServiceName {get;set;}
ServicesDependedOn      Property   System.ServiceProcess.ServiceController[] ServicesDependedOn {get;}
ServiceType             Property   System.ServiceProcess.ServiceType ServiceType {get;}
Site                    Property   System.ComponentModel.ISite Site {get;set;}
StartType               Property   System.ServiceProcess.ServiceStartMode StartType {get;}
StartupType             Property   Microsoft.PowerShell.Commands.ServiceStartupType {get;set;}
Status                  Property   System.ServiceProcess.ServiceControllerStatus Status {get;}
UserName                Property   System.String {get;set;}
```

Figure 3.15: Viewing the properties of a Windows service object

In *step 5*, you examine the underlying type of a 32-bit integer, with output like this:

```
PS C:\Foo> # 5. Discovering the underlying type of an integer
PS C:\Foo> $I = 42
PS C:\Foo> $IntType  = $I.GetType()
PS C:\Foo> $TypeName = $IntType.FullName
PS C:\Foo> $BaseType = $IntType.BaseType.Name
PS C:\Foo> ".NET Class name       : $TypeName"
PS C:\Foo> ".NET Class base type : $BaseType"

.NET Class name       : System.Int32
.NET Class base type : ValueType
```

Figure 3.16: Viewing the class name for a 32-bit integer

In *step 6*, you look at the different member types within an object representing a Windows process, with the following output:

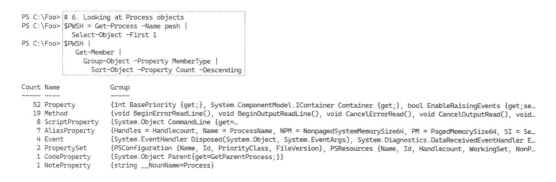

```
PS C:\Foo> # 6. Looking at Process objects
PS C:\Foo> $PWSH = Get-Process -Name pwsh |
             Select-Object -First 1
PS C:\Foo> $PWSH |
             Get-Member |
               Group-Object -Property MemberType |
                 Sort-Object -Property Count -Descending

Count Name            Group
----- ----            -----
   52 Property        {int BasePriority {get;}, System.ComponentModel.IContainer Container {get;}, bool EnableRaisingEvents {get;se…
   19 Method          {void BeginErrorReadLine(), void BeginOutputReadLine(), void CancelErrorRead(), void CancelOutputRead(), void…
    8 ScriptProperty  {System.Object CommandLine {get=…
    7 AliasProperty   {Handles = Handlecount, Name = ProcessName, NPM = NonpagedSystemMemorySize64, PM = PagedMemorySize64, SI = Se…
    4 Event           {System.EventHandler Disposed(System.Object, System.EventArgs), System.Diagnostics.DataReceivedEventHandler E…
    2 PropertySet     {PSConfiguration {Name, Id, PriorityClass, FileVersion}, PSResources {Name, Id, Handlecount, WorkingSet, NonP…
    1 CodeProperty    {System.Object Parent{get=GetParentProcess;}}
    1 NoteProperty    {string __NounName=Process}
```

Figure 3.17: Viewing the member types of a process object

In the final step in this recipe, *step 7*, you examine two static properties of an Int32 object, with output like this:

```
PS C:\Foo> # 7. Looking at static properties within a class
PS C:\Foo> $Max = [Int32]::MaxValue
PS C:\Foo> $Min = [Int32]::MinValue
PS C:\Foo> "Minimum value [$Min]"
PS C:\Foo> "Maximum value [$Max]"
Minimum value [-2147483648]
Maximum value [2147483647]
```

Figure 3.18: Viewing the static properties of a 32-bit integer

There's more...

In *step 1*, you create a FileInfo object representing pwsh.exe. This object's full type name is System.IO.FileInfo. In .NET, classes live in namespaces and, in general, namespaces equate to DLLs. In this case, the object is in the System.IO namespace, and the class is contained in the System.IO.FileSystem.DLL.

As you use your favorite search engine to learn more about .NET classes that might be useful, note that many sites describe the class without the namespace, simply as the FileInfo class, while others spell out the class as System.IO.FileInfo. If you are using .NET class names in your scripts, a best practice is to spell out the full class name. You can discover namespace and DLL details by examining the class's documentation – in this case, https://learn.microsoft.com/dotnet/api/system.io.fileinfo.

In *step 6*, you examine the different member types you can find on a class or class instance for a process object. Some of the members you can see come directly from the underlying .NET object. Others, such as ScriptProperty, AliasProperty, and CodeProperty, are added by PowerShell's **Extensible Type System** (**ETS**). With the ETS, the developers extend the .NET object with, in effect, additional properties which IT pros may find more useful. You can read about the ETS here: https://powershellstation.com/2009/09/15/powershell-ets-extended-type-system.

Exploring .NET Methods

With .NET, a method is some action that a .NET object occurrence (an instance method) or the class (a static method) can perform. These methods form the basis for many PowerShell cmdlets. For example, you can stop a Windows process by using the Stop-Process cmdlet. The cmdlet then uses the Kill() method of the associated Process object. As a general best practice, you should use cmdlets wherever possible. You should only use .NET classes and methods directly where there is no alternative.

.NET methods can be beneficial for performing some operations that have no PowerShell cmdlet support. And it can be useful too from the command line, for example, when you wish to kill a process. IT professionals are all too familiar with processes that are not responding and need to be killed, something you can do at the GUI using Task Manager. Or, with PowerShell, you can use the Stop-Process cmdlet. At the command line, where brevity is useful, you can use Get-Process to find the process you want to stop and pipe the output to each process's Kill() method. PowerShell then calls the object's Kill() method. To help IT professionals, the PowerShell team created the Kill alias to the Stop-Process cmdlet.

Another great example is encrypting files. Windows's NTFS filesystem includes support for the **Encrypting File System** (**EFS**) feature. EFS lets you encrypt or decrypt files on your computer with encryption based on X.509 certificates. For details on the EFS and how it works, see https://learn.microsoft.com/windows/win32/fileio/file-encryption.

At present, there are no cmdlets to encrypt or decrypt files. The System.IO.FileInfo class, however, has two methods you can use: Encrypt() and Decrypt(). These instance methods encrypt and decrypt a file based on EFS certificates (which Windows can automatically generate). You can use these .NET methods to encrypt or decrypt a file without using the GUI.

As you saw in the *Examining .NET Classes* recipe, you can pipe any object to the Get-Member cmdlet to discover the methods for the object. Discovering the specific property names and property value types is simple and easy – no guessing or prayer-based text parsing, so beloved by Linux admins.

Getting ready

You run this recipe on SRV1 after you have installed PowerShell 7.

How to do it...

1. Starting Notepad

    ```
    notepad.exe
    ```

2. Obtaining methods on the Notepad process

    ```
    $Notepad = Get-Process -Name Notepad
    $Notepad | Get-Member -MemberType Method
    ```

3. Using the Kill() method

    ```
    $Notepad |
      ForEach-Object {$_.Kill()}
    ```

4. Confirming Notepad process is destroyed

    ```
    Get-Process -Name Notepad
    ```

5. Creating a new folder and some files

    ```
    $Path = 'C:\Foo\Secure'
    New-Item -Path $Path -ItemType directory -ErrorAction
    SilentlyContinue |
      Out-Null
    1..3 | ForEach-Object {
      "Secure File" | Out-File "$Path\SecureFile$_.txt"
    }
    ```

6. Viewing files in $Path folder

    ```
    $Files = Get-ChildItem -Path $Path
    $Files | Format-Table -Property Name, Attributes
    ```

7. Encrypting the files

    ```
    $Files | ForEach-Object Encrypt
    ```

8. Viewing file attributes

```
Get-ChildItem -Path $Path |
  Format-Table -Property Name, Attributes
```

9. Decrypting the files

```
$Files| ForEach-Object {
  $_.Decrypt()
}
```

10. Viewing the file attributes

```
Get-ChildItem -Path $Path |
  Format-Table -Property Name, Attributes
```

How it works...

In *step 1*, you start the Windows Notepad application. There is no console output, but you do see Notepad pop up like this:

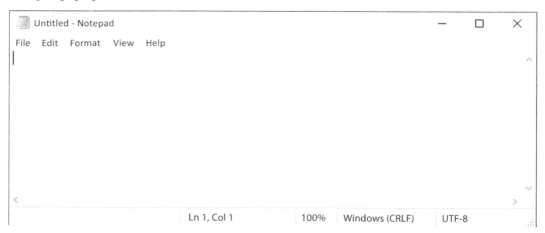

Figure 3.19: Starting Notepad

In *step 2*, you obtain the methods from the object representing the Notepad process, with output like this:

```
PS C:\Foo> # 2. Obtaining methods on the Notepad process
PS C:\Foo> $Notepad = Get-Process -Name Notepad
PS C:\Foo> $Notepad | Get-Member -MemberType Method


   TypeName: System.Diagnostics.Process

Name                        MemberType Definition
----                        ---------- ----------
BeginErrorReadLine          Method     void BeginErrorReadLine()
BeginOutputReadLine         Method     void BeginOutputReadLine()
CancelErrorRead             Method     void CancelErrorRead()
CancelOutputRead            Method     void CancelOutputRead()
Close                       Method     void Close()
CloseMainWindow             Method     bool CloseMainWindow()
Dispose                     Method     void Dispose(), void IDisposable.Dispose()
Equals                      Method     bool Equals(System.Object obj)
GetHashCode                 Method     int GetHashCode()
GetLifetimeService          Method     System.Object GetLifetimeService()
GetType                     Method     type GetType()
InitializeLifetimeService   Method     System.Object InitializeLifetimeService()
Kill                        Method     void Kill(), void Kill(bool entireProcessTree)
Refresh                     Method     void Refresh()
Start                       Method     bool Start()
ToString                    Method     string ToString()
WaitForExit                 Method     void WaitForExit(), bool WaitForExit(int milliseconds)
WaitForExitAsync            Method     System.Threading.Tasks.Task WaitForExitAsync(System.Threading.CancellationToken cancellationToken)
WaitForInputIdle            Method     bool WaitForInputIdle(), bool WaitForInputIdle(int milliseconds)
```

Figure 3.20: Viewing Notepad's methods

With *step 3*, you use the process's Kill() method to kill the Notepad process, which generates no console output, but you see the Notepad window disappear. In *step 4*, you confirm that the Notepad process no longer exists, with output like this:

```
PS C:\Foo> # 4. Confirming Notepad process is destroyed
PS C:\Foo> Get-Process -Name Notepad
Get-Process: Cannot find a process with the name "Notepad". Verify the process name and call the cmdlet again.
```

Figure 3.21: Ensuring the Notepad process no longer exists

To illustrate encrypting and decrypting files using .NET methods, in *step 5*, you create a new folder and some files, which creates no output. In *step 6*, you view the attributes of the three files created, with output like this:

```
PS C:\Foo> # 6. Viewing files in $Path folder
PS C:\Foo> $Files = Get-ChildItem -Path $Path
PS C:\Foo> $Files | Format-Table -Property Name, Attributes


Name             Attributes
----             ----------
SecureFile1.txt    Archive
SecureFile2.txt    Archive
SecureFile3.txt    Archive
```

Figure 3.22: Viewing newly created files and their attributes

In *step 7*, you use the Encrypt() method to encrypt the files, generating no output. In *step 8*, you view the files and their attributes again, with this output:

```
PS C:\Foo> # 8. Viewing file attributes
PS C:\Foo> Get-ChildItem -Path $Path |
              Format-Table -Property Name, Attributes


Name                    Attributes
----                    ----------
SecureFile1.txt  Archive  Encrypted
SecureFile2.txt  Archive  Encrypted
SecureFile3.txt  Archive  Encrypted
```

Figure 3.23: Viewing encrypted files and file attributes

In *step 9*, you decrypt the previously encrypted files, generating no output. In the final step, *step 10*, you examine the file attributes to ensure that the files are now decrypted, with the following results:

```
PS C:\Foo> # 10. Viewing the -File attributes
PS C:\Foo> Get-Childltem -Path $Path |
              Format-Table -Property Name, Attributes


Name             Attributes
----             ----------
SecureFile1.txt    Archive
SecureFile2.txt    Archive
SecureFile3.txt    Archive
```

Figure 3.24: Viewing decrypted files and file attributes

There's more...

In *step 2*, you view the methods you can invoke on a process object. As shown in the figure, one of those methods is the Kill() method. In *step 3*, you use that method to stop the Notepad process. The Kill() method is an instance method, meaning you invoke it to kill (stop) a specific process. You can read more about this .NET method at https://learn.microsoft.com/dotnet/api/system.diagnostics.process.kill.

The output in *step 4* illustrates an error occurring within VS Code. If you use the PowerShell 7 console, you may see a slightly different output, although with the same actual error message.

In *steps 7* and *step 9*, you use the FileInfo objects (created by Get-ChildItem) and call the Encrypt() and Decrypt() methods. These steps demonstrate using a .NET method to achieve some objectives without specific cmdlets.

Best practice suggests always using cmdlets where you can. You should also note that the syntax in the two steps is different. In *step 7*, you use a more modern syntax which calls the `Encrypt` method for each file. In *step 9*, you use an older syntax that does the same, albeit with more characters. Both syntax methods work.

In *step 7*, while you get no console output, Windows may generate a popup (aka Toast) to tell you that you should back up your encryption key. Backing up the key is a good idea. If you lose the key, you lose all access to the file(s) – so be very careful.

Creating a C# Extension

For most day-to-day operations, the commands provided by PowerShell, from Windows features, or third-party modules, provide all the functionality you need to manage your systems. In some cases, as you saw in the *Leveraging .NET Methods* recipe, commands do not exist to achieve your goal. In those cases, you can use the methods provided by .NET.

There are also cases where you need to perform more complex operations without a PowerShell cmdlet or direct .NET support. You may, for example, have a component of an ASP.NET web application written in C#, but you now wish to repurpose it for administrative scripting purposes.

PowerShell makes it easy to add a class, based on .NET language source code, into a PowerShell session. You supply the C# code, and PowerShell creates a .NET class that you can use the same way you use .NET methods (and using virtually the same syntax). You use the `Add-Type` cmdlet and specify the C# code for your class/type(s). PowerShell compiles the code and loads the resultant class into your PowerShell session.

An essential aspect of .NET methods is that a method can have multiple definitions or calling sequences. Known and method overloads, these different definitions allow you to invoke a method using different sets of parameters. This is not dissimilar to PowerShell's use of parameter sets. For example, the `System.String` class, which PowerShell uses to hold strings, contains the `Trim()` method. You use that method to remove extra characters, usually space characters, from the start or end of a string (or both). The `Trim()` method has three different definitions, which you view in this recipe. Each overloaded definition trims characters from a string slightly differently. To view more details on this method, and the three overloaded definitions, see `https://learn.microsoft.com/dotnet/api/system.string.trim`.

In this recipe, you create and use two simple classes with static methods.

Getting ready

You run this recipe on SRV1 after you have installed PowerShell 7.

How to do it...

1. Examining overloaded method definition

    ```
    ("a string").Trim
    ```

2. Creating a C# class definition in here string

    ```
    $NewClass = @"
    namespace Reskit {
       public class Hello {
         public static void World() {
             System.Console.WriteLine("Hello World!");
         }
        }
       }
    "@
    ```

3. Adding the type into the current PowerShell session

    ```
    Add-Type -TypeDefinition $NewClass
    ```

4. Examining method definition

    ```
    [Reskit.Hello]::World
    ```

5. Using the class's method

    ```
    [Reskit.Hello]::World()
    ```

6. Extending the code with parameters

    ```
    $NewClass2 = @"
    using System;
    using System.IO;
    namespace Reskit {
      public class Hello2  {
        public static void World() {
          Console.WriteLine("Hello World!");
        }
    ```

```
        public static void World(string name) {
          Console.WriteLine("Hello " + name + "!");
        }
      }
    }
    "@
```

7. Adding the type into the current PowerShell session

   ```
   Add-Type -TypeDefinition $NewClass2
   ```

8. Viewing method definitions

   ```
   [Reskit.Hello2]::World
   ```

9. Calling with no parameters specified

   ```
   [Reskit.Hello2]::World()
   ```

10. Calling new method with a parameter

    ```
    [Reskit.Hello2]::World('Jerry')
    ```

How it works...

In *step 1*, you examine the definitions of the Trim() method for a string, with output like this:

```
PS C:\Foo> # 1. Examining overloaded method definition
PS C:\Foo> ("a string").Trim

OverloadDefinitions
-------------------
string Trim()
string Trim(char trimChar)
string Trim(Params char[] trimChars)
```

Figure 3.25: Viewing the Trim() methods on System.String

In *step 2*, you create a C# class definition for the Hello class that contains one method (World()). In *step 3*, you add this class to the current PowerShell session. These two steps create no output at the console.

In *step 4*, you examine the new class's method signature with output like this:

```
PS C:\Foo> # 4. Examining method definition
PS C:\Foo> [Reskit.Hello]::World

OverloadDefinitions
-------------------
static void World()
```

Figure 3.26: Viewing the World() method definition on the newly created class

In *step 5*, you use the method, with output like this:

```
PS C:\Foo> # 5. Using the class's method
PS C:\Foo> [Reskit.Hello]::World()
Hello World!
```

Figure 3.27: Using the World() method

In *step 6*, you define a more complex class definition for the Hello class, this time with two method definitions for the World method. In *step 7*, you add this new class definition to your current PowerShell session. These two steps generate no console output.

In *step 8*, you examine the two method signatures with output like this:

```
PS C:\Foo> # 8. Viewing method definitions
PS C:\Foo> [Reskit.Hello2]::World

OverloadDefinitions
-------------------
static void World()
static void World(string name)
```

Figure 3.28: Viewing the new method definitions for Hello2

In *step 9*, you invoke the World() method on the Hello2 class – with output like this:

```
PS C:\Foo> # 9. Calling with no parameters specified
PS C:\Foo> [Reskit.Hello2]::World()
Hello World!
```

Figure 3.29: Viewing the new method definitions for Hello2

In *step 10*, you call the new method but specify a string as a parameter. The output of this step is as follows:

```
PS C:\Foo> # 10. Calling new method with a parameter
PS C:\Foo> [Reskit.Hello2]::World('Jerry')
Hello Jerry!
```

Figure 3.30: Calling the new method with a parameter

There's more...

There are several ways you discover method overloads. In *step 1*, you examine the different definitions of a method, the `Trim()` method of the `System.String` class. This step creates a pseudo-object containing a string and then looks at the method definitions for that class.

PowerShell creates an unnamed object (in the .NET managed heap) in this step. As soon as the command is complete, .NET marks the memory as reclaimable. At some point later, .NET runs the GC process to reclaim the memory used by this temporary object and re-organizes the managed heap.

As you can see, there are three overloaded definitions – three different ways you can invoke the `Trim()` method. You use the first overloaded definition to remove both leading and trailing space characters from a string, probably the most common usage of `Trim()`. With the second definition, you specify a specific character and .NET removes any leading or trailing occurrences of that character. With the third definition, you specify an array of characters to trim from the start or end of the string. The last two definitions are less useful in most cases, although it depends on your needs. The extra flexibility is useful.

In *step 3*, you used the `Add-Type` cmdlet to add the class definition into your current workspace. The cmdlet compiles the C# code, creates, and then loads a DLL, enabling you to use the classes. If you intend to use this add-in regularly, you could add *step 2* and *step 3* to your PowerShell profile file. Alternatively, if you use this method within a script, you could add the steps to the start of the script.

As you can see from the C# code in *step 6*, you can add multiple definitions to a method. Overloaded methods can provide great value for both classes within .NET or in your code. The .NET method documentation, which you can find at `https://learn.microsoft.com`, is mainly oriented toward developers rather than IT professionals. If you have issues with a .NET method, feel free to fire off a query on one of the many PowerShell support forums, such as the PowerShell group at Spiceworks: `https://community.spiceworks.com/programming/powershell`.

Creating a cmdlet

As noted previously in this chapter, for most operations, the commands and cmdlets available to you natively provide all the functionality you need. In the *Creating a C# Extension* recipe, you saw how you could create a class definition and add it to PowerShell. In some cases, you may wish to expand on the class definition and create a custom cmdlet.

Creating a compiled cmdlet requires you to either use a tool such as Visual Studio or use the free tools provided by Microsoft as part of the .NET Core **Software Development Kit (SDK)**. The free tools in the SDK are more than adequate to help you to create a cmdlet using C#. Microsoft's Visual Studio, whether the free community edition or the commercial releases, is a rich and complex tool whose inner workings are well outside the scope of this book.

As in the *Creating a C# Extension* recipe, an important question you should be asking is when/ why should you create a cmdlet? Aside from the perennial "because you can" excuse, there are reasons why an extension or a cmdlet might be a good idea. You can create a cmdlet to improve performance. In some cases, a compiled cmdlet is faster than doing operations using a PowerShell script. For some applications, using a cmdlet is to perform a specific action may be difficult or not possible directly. PowerShell does not have support for asynchronous operations and **Language Independent Query (LINQ)**, which are more straightforward in C#. A developer could write the cmdlet in C#, allowing you to use it easily with PowerShell.

To create a cmdlet, you need to install the .NET SDK. The SDK is a free download you get via the internet. The SDK contains all the tools you need to create a cmdlet. Sadly, there is no easy way to download and install the SDK programmatically – you need to use the Windows GUI – you have to use your browser and navigate to a web page, then download and run the SDK installer.

Getting ready

You run this recipe on SRV1 after you have installed PowerShell 7.

How to do it...

1. Installing the .NET SDK

2. Creating the cmdlet folder

    ```
    New-Item -Path C:\Foo\Cmdlet -ItemType Directory -Force
    Set-Location C:\Foo\Cmdlet
    ```

3. Creating a new class library project

    ```
    dotnet new classlib --name SendGreeting
    ```

4. Viewing contents of new folder

    ```
    Set-Location -Path .\SendGreeting
    Get-ChildItem
    ```

5. Creating and displaying global.json

```
dotnet new globaljson
Get-Content -Path .\global.json
```

6. Adding PowerShell package

```
$SourceName = 'Nuget.org https://api.nuget.org/v3/index.json'
dotnet nuget add source --name $SourceName
dotnet add package PowerShellStandard.Library
```

7. Create the cmdlet source file

```
$Cmdlet = @"
using System.Management.Automation;  // Windows PowerShell assembly.
namespace Reskit
{
  // Declare the class as a cmdlet
  // Specify verb and noun = Send-Greeting
  [Cmdlet(VerbsCommunications.Send, "Greeting")]
  public class SendGreetingCommand : PSCmdlet
  {
    // Declare the parameters for the cmdlet.
    [Parameter(Mandatory=true)]
    public string Name
    {
      get { return name; }
      set { name = value; }
    }
    private string name;
    // Override the ProcessRecord method to process the
    // supplied name and write a geeting to the user by
    // calling the WriteObject method.
    protected override void ProcessRecord()
    {
      WriteObject("Hello " + name + " - have a nice day!");
    }
  }
}
```

```
"@
$Cmdlet | Out-File .\SendGreetingCommand.cs
```

8. Removing the unused class file

```
Remove-Item -Path .\Class1.cs
```

9. Building the cmdlet

```
dotnet build
```

10. Importing the DLL holding the cmdlet

```
$DLLPath = '.\bin\Debug\net6.0\SendGreeting.dll'
Import-Module -Name $DLLPath
```

11. Examining the module's details

```
Get-Module SendGreeting
```

12. Using the cmdlet

```
Send-Greeting -Name 'Jerry Garcia'
```

How it works...

In *step 1*, you install the .NET SDK. You begin by using the browser to navigate to the .NET download site, which looks like this:

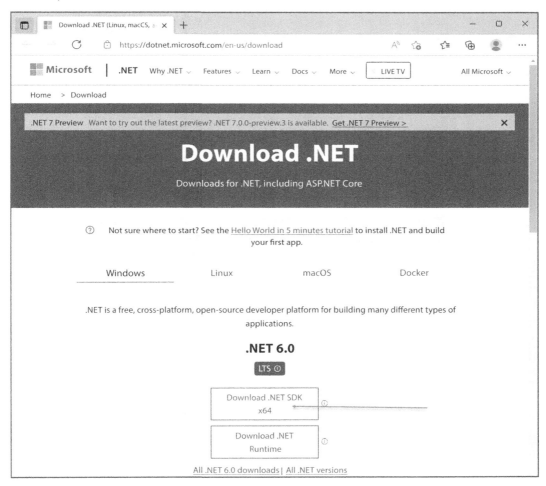

Figure 3.31: Downloading the .NET SDK

If you click on the button, your browser should download the installation program. When the browser finishes the download, you should see something like this:

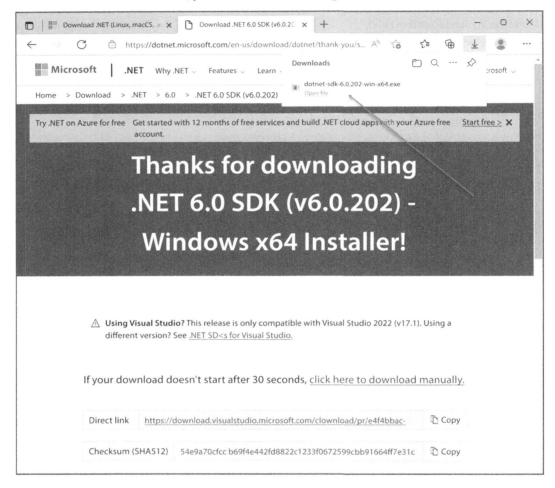

Figure 3.32: Downloading the .NET SDK

Click on **Open File** to run the .NET SDK installer. You should now see an option to install the SDK like this:

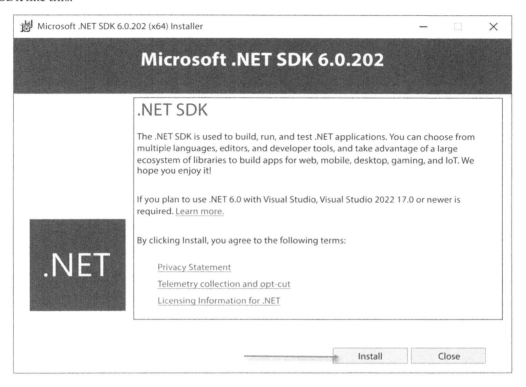

Figure 3.33: Installing the .NET SDK

When you click on the **Install** button, the installation program installs the SDK and, when complete, shows you the following dialog box:

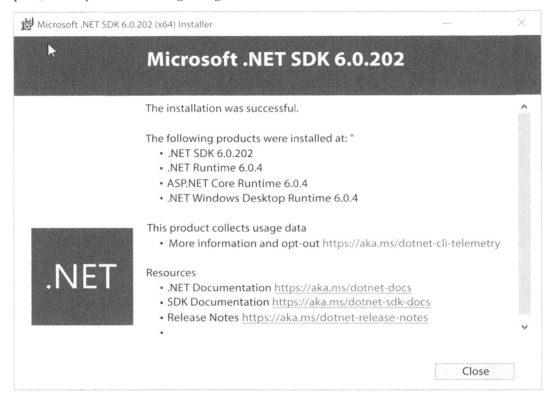

Figure 3.34: Completing the installation of the .NET SDK

Once you have the SDK installed, you need to restart PowerShell to carry out the remainder of this recipe.

In *step 2*, you create a new folder (C:\Foo\Cmdlet), which you use for developing your cmdlet. This step generates the following output:

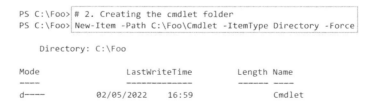

Figure 3.35: Creating the cmdlet folder

In *step 3*, you create a new class library project for your cmdlet, which generates the following output:

```
PS C:\Foo> # 3. Creating a new class library project
PS C:\Foo> Set-Location C:\Foo\Cmdlet
PS C:\Foo\Cmdlet> dotnet new classlib --name SendGreeting

Welcome to .NET 6.0!
---------------------
SDK Version: 6.0.202

Telemetry
---------
The .NET tools collect usage data in order to help us improve your experience. It is collected
by Microsoft and shared with the community. You can opt-out of telemetry by setting the
DOTNET_CLI_TELEMETRY_OPTOUT environment variable to '1' or 'true' using your favorite shell.

Read more about .NET CLI Tools telemetry: https://aka.ms/dotnet-cli-telemetry


------------------
Installed an ASP.NET Core HTTPS development certificate.
To trust the certificate run 'dotnet dev-certs https --trust' (Windows and macOS only).
Learn about HTTPS: https://aka.ms/dotnet-https
------------------
Write your first app: https://aka.ms/dotnet-hello-world
Find out what's new: https://aka.ms/dotnet-whats-new
Explore documentation: https://aka.ms/dotnet-docs
Report issues and find source on GitHub: https://github.com/dotnet/core
Use 'dotnet --help' to see available commands or visit: https://aka.ms/dotnet-cli
------------------------------------------------------------------------------------
The template "Class Library" was created successfully.

Processing post-creation actions...
Running 'dotnet restore' on C:\Foo\Cmdlet\SendGreeting\SendGreeting.csproj...
  Determining projects to restore...
  Restored C:\Foo\Cmdlet\SendGreeting\SendGreeting.csproj (in 95 ms).
Restore succeeded.
```

Figure 3.36: Creating a new .NET project for your cmdlet

In *step 4*, you view the contents of the folder contents, which look like this:

```
PS C:\Foo\Cmdlet> # 4. Viewing contents of new folder
PS C:\Foo\Cmdlet> Set-Location -Path .\SendGreeting
PS C:\Foo\Cmdlet\SendGreeting> Get-ChildItem

    Directory: C:\Foo\Cmdlet\SendGreeting

Mode                 LastWriteTime         Length Name
----                 -------------         ------ ----
d----         02/05/2022     16:20                obj
-a---         02/05/2022     16:20             57 Class1.cs
-a---         02/05/2022     16:20            215 SendGreeting.csproj
```

Figure 3.37: Viewing the contents of the cmdlet project's folder

To tell the .NET build engine which version of .NET to compile your cmdlet against, you create a `global.json` file within your project, as shown in *step 5*. The step displays the following output:

```
PS C:\Foo\Cmdlet\SendGreeting> # 5. Creating and displaying global.json
PS C:\Foo\Cmdlet\SendGreeting> dotnet new globaljson
The template "global.json file" was created successfully.
PS C:\Foo\Cmdlet\SendGreeting> Get-Content -Path .\global.json
{
  "sdk": {
    "version": "6.0.202"
  }
}
```

Figure 3.38: Creating and viewing the global.json file

In *step 6*, you add the PowerShell package to the cmdlet's project with the following output:

```
PS C:\Foo\Cmdlet\SendGreeting> # 6. Adding PowerShell package
PS C:\Foo\Cmdlet\SendGreeting> $Sourcename = 'Nuget.org https://api.nuget.org/v3/index.json'
PS C:\Foo\Cmdlet\SendGreeting> dotnet nuget add source --name $SourceName
Package source with Name: nuget.org added successfully.
PS C:\Foo\Cmdlet\SendGreeting> dotnet add package PowerShellStandard.Library
  Determining projects to restore...
  Writing C:\Users\Administrator\AppData\Local\Temp\2\tmpCD91.tmp
info : Adding PackageReference for package 'PowerShellStandard.Library' into
       project 'C:\Foo\Cmdlet\SendGreeting\SendGreeting.csproj'.
info :   GET https://api.nuget.org/v3/registration5-gz-semver2/powershellstandard.library/index.json
info :   OK https://api.nuget.org/v3/registration5-gz-semver2/powershellstandard.library/index.json 133ms
info : Restoring packages for C:\Foo\Cmdlet\SendGreeting\SendGreeting.csproj...
info :   GET https://api.nuget.org/v3-flatcontainer/powershellstandard.library/index.json
info :   OK https://api.nuget.org/v3-flatcontainer/powershellstandard.library/index.json 133ms
info :   GET https://api.nuget.org/v3-flatcontainer/powershellstandard.library/5.1.1/
          powershellstandard.library.5.1.1.nupkg
info :   OK https://api.nuget.org/v3-flatcontainer/powershellstandard.library/5.1.1/
          powershellstandard.library.5.1.1.nupkg 54ms
info : Installed PowerShellStandard.Library 5.1.1 from https://api.nuget.org/v3/index.json with content hash
       e31xJjG+Kjbv6YF3Yq6D4Dl3or8v7LrNF41k3CXrWozW6hR1zcOe5KYuZJaGSiAgLnwP8wcW+I3+IWEzMPZKXQ==.
info : Package 'PowerShellStandard.Library' is compatible with all the specified frameworks in
       project 'C:\Foo\Cmdlet\SendGreeting\SendGreeting.csproj'.
info : PackageReference for package 'PowerShellStandard.Library' version '5.1.1' added to
       file 'C:\Foo\Cmdlet\SendGreeting\SendGreeting.csproj'.
info : Writing assets file to disk. Path: C:\Foo\Cmdlet\SendGreeting\obj\project.assets.json
log  : Restored C:\Foo\Cmdlet\SendGreeting\SendGreeting.csproj (in 820 ms).
```

Figure 3.39: Adding the PowerShell package to the cmdlet's project

In *step 7*, you create a source file containing your cmdlet's C# code. In *step 8*, you remove an unneeded class file previously created by the dotnet program. These two steps produce no output.

In *step 9*, you use the dotnet.exe program to build your cmdlet, with output like this:

```
PS C:\Foo\Cmdlet\SendGreeting> # 9. Building the cmdlet
PS C:\Foo\Cmdlet\SendGreeting> dotnet build
Microsoft (R) Build Engine version 17.1.1+a02f73656 for .NET
Copyright (C) Microsoft Corporation. All rights reserved.

  Determining projects to restore...
  All projects are up-to-date for restore.
  SendGreeting -> C:\Foo\Cmdlet\SendGreeting\bin\Debug\net6.0\SendGreeting.dll

Build succeeded.
    0 Warning(s)
    0 Error(s)

Time Elapsed 00:00:03.79
```

Figure 3.40: Building your cmdlet

In *step 10*, you import the DLL, built by the previous step, that holds your cmdlet. This step creates no output. PowerShell treats this DLL as a binary Powershell module, and in *step 11*, you use the Get-Module cmdlet to see the module's details, with output like this:

```
PS C:\Foo\Cmdlet\SendGreeting> # 11. Examining the module's details
PS C:\Foo\Cmdlet\SendGreeting> Get-Module SendGreeting

ModuleType Version    PreRelease Name         ExportedCommands
---------- -------    ---------- ----         ----------------
Binary     1.0.0.0               SendGreeting  Send-Greeting
```

Figure 3.41: Caption please

In *step 12*, you use your cmdlet with a value specified for the cmdlet's -Name parameter, with output like this:

```
PS C:\Foo\Cmdlet\SendGreeting> # 12. Using the cmdlet
PS C:\Foo\Cmdlet\SendGreeting> Send-Greeting -Name 'Jerry Garcia'
Hello Jerry Garcia - have a nice day!
```

Figure 3.42: Using the Send-Greeting cmdlet

There's more...

In *step 1*, you download the .NET 6.0 SDK. You need this tool kit to create a cmdlet. There is no obvious way to automate the installation, so you need to run the installer and click through its GUI to install the .NET SDK.

In *step 3*, you create a new class library project. This step also makes the SendGreeting.csproj file, as you can see. This file is a Visual Studio .NET C# project file that contains details about the files included in your cmdlet project, assemblies referenced from your code, and more. For more information on the project file, see https://learn.microsoft.com/aspnet/web-forms/overview/deployment/web-deployment-in-the-enterprise/understanding-the-project-file.

In *step 5*, you create the global.json file. If you do not create this file, the dotnet command will compile your cmdlet with the latest version of .NET loaded on your system. Using this file tells the project build process to use a specific version of .NET Core (such as version 6.0). For an overview of this file, https://learn.microsoft.com/en-us/dotnet/core/tools/global-json.

In *step 9*, you compile your source code file and create a DLL containing your cmdlet. This step compiles all the source code files in the folder to create the DLL. Therefore, you could have multiple cmdlets in separate source code files and build the entire set in one operation.

In *step 11*, you can see that the module, SendGreeting, is a binary module. A binary module is one just loaded directly from a DLL. Using DLLs as binary modules is fine for testing, but in production you should use manifest modules not pure binary module.

You can get more details on manifest files from https://learn.microsoft.com/powershell/scripting/developer/module/how-to-write-a-powershell-module-manifest. You should also move the module, module manifest, and any other module contents such as help files to a supported module location. You might also consider publishing the completed module to either the PowerShell gallery or your internal repository.

Join our community on Discord

Join our community's Discord space for discussions with the author and other readers:

https://packt.link/SecNet

4

Managing Active Directory

This chapter covers the following recipes:

- Installing a Forest Root Domain
- Testing an AD Installation
- Installing a Replica Domain Controller
- Installing a Child Domain
- Creating and Managing AD Users and Groups
- Managing AD Computers
- Adding/Removing Users Using a CSV Files
- Creating Group Policy Objects
- Reporting on AD Computers
- Reporting on AD Users
- Managing AD Replication

Introduction

A core component of almost all organizations' IT infrastructure is **Active Directory** (**AD**). AD provides access control, user and system customization, and a wealth of directory and other services. Microsoft first introduced AD with Windows 2000 and has improved and expanded the product with each successive release of Windows Server.

At the core is **Active Directory Domain Services** (**AD DS**). Over the years, Microsoft has made "AD" more of a brand than a single feature. There are four additional Windows Server features under the AD brand:

- **AD Certificate Services (AD-CS)** – this allows you to issue X.509 certificates for your organization. For an overview of AD-CS, see `https://learn.microsoft.com/previous-versions/windows/it-pro/windows-server-2012-r2-and-2012/hh831740(v=ws.11)`.

- **AD Federation Services (AD-FS)** – this feature enables you to federate identity with other organizations to facilitate interworking. You can find an overview of AD-FS at `https://learn.microsoft.com/previous-versions/windows/it-pro/windows-server-2012-r2-and-2012/hh831502(v=ws.11)`.

- **AD Lightweight Directory Services (AD-LDS)** – this provides rich directory services for use by applications. You can find an overview of AD-LDS at `https://learn.microsoft.com/previous-versions/windows/it-pro/windows-server-2012-r2-and-2012/hh831593(v=ws.11)`.

- **AD Rights Management Services (AD-RMS)** – RMS enables you to control the rights to document access to limit information leakage. For an overview of RMS, see `https://learn.microsoft.com/previous-versions/windows/it-pro/windows-server-2012-r2-and-2012/hh831364(v=ws.11)`.

Note that the overview documents above are older documents based on Windows Server 2012. The documentation teams have not updated them fully to reflect the latest Windows Server version at the time of writing. The overview and the essential operation of these features remain mostly unchanged, and the documents remain a good reference for each AD feature.

Active Directory's domain service is complex, and there are a lot of moving parts. With AD, you have a logical structure consisting of Forests, Domains, Domain Trees, and Organizational Units. You also have the physical structure, including Domain Controllers and Global Catalog Servers. There is also a replication mechanism to replicate objects across your domain. For a deeper look at the architecture of AD, see `https://activereach.net/support/knowledge-base/connectivity-networking/understanding-active-directory-its-architecture/`.

A forest is a top-level container that houses one or more domains. A forest is a security boundary. If you need to operate between forests, you can set up cross-forest trusts to enable interworking between multiple forests. AD uses DNS names as the basis for forest and domain names, and both AD domain controllers and AD clients use DNS to find the IP address of domain controllers. For this reason, DNS is a critical part of your AD infrastructure.

A domain is a collection of objects, including users, computers, policies, etc. You create a forest by installing the forest's first domain controller. In AD domains, trees are collections of domains that you group in a hierarchical structure. Most organizations use a single domain (and thus a single domain tree) within a single forest.

For very large organizations, another common approach is to have a single (empty) forest root domain and multiple child domains (typically based on geography). AD supports having multiple non-contiguous domain trees with a forest, but the best practice is to avoid them.

A **domain controller** (**DC**) is a Windows Server running AD and holding the objects for a given domain. ALL domains must have at least one DC, although best practice is always to have at least two. You install the AD DS service onto your server, then promote the server to be a DC. You can also have DCs within a forest running older versions of Windows Server.

The **global catalog** (**GC**) is a partial replica of objects from every domain in an object to enable searching. Microsoft Exchange, for example, uses the GC heavily. You can have the GC service on some or all DCs in your forest. Generally, you install the GC facility while promoting a Windows server to be a DC, but fewer GCs might be preferable to reduce replication traffic for very large domains.

Using AD Domain Services (or AD) and PowerShell, you can deploy your domain controllers throughout your organization. Use the *Installing Active Directory and forest root domain* recipe to install a forest root domain controller and establish an AD Forest. That recipe converts DC1 as a workgroup server into a DC – the first DC in the Reskit.Org forest.

You can install Windows features and manage services using PowerShell in a domain environment using PowerShell remoting, which requires authentication. From one machine, you use PowerShell remoting to perform operations on other systems, and for that, you need the correct credentials for the remote machine. Sometimes, you may encounter the well-understood Kerberos double hop problem for which the Credential Security Subsystem Provider can be a solution. For a better explanation of this issue, see https://learn.microsoft.com/powershell/scripting/learn/remoting/ps-remoting-second-hop.

In this book, you use a domain, Reskit.Org, for most of the recipes. In this chapter, you establish the forest root domain and a child domain. You also create users, groups, and Organizational units, which you rely on in later chapters.

Once you have the first DC in your Reskit.Org forest, you should add a replica DC to ensure reliable domain operations. In *Installing a Replica Domain Controller*, you add a second DC to your domain. In *Installing a Child Domain*, you extend the forest and add a child domain to your forest.

The AD service uses a database of objects, including users, computers, and Groups. In the *Creating and Managing AD Users and Groups* recipe, you create, move, and remove user and group objects, and create and use Organizational Units (OUs).

In *Managing Active Directory computers*, you manage the computers in your Active Directory, including joining workgroup systems to the domain. In the *Adding/Removing Users Using a CSV Files* recipe, you add users to your AD using a comma-separated value file containing users' details.

Group Policy is another important feature of Active Directory. With Group Policy, you can define policies for users and computers that Windows applies automatically to the user and/or computer. In the *Creating Group Policy Objects* recipe, you create a simple GPO and apply that policy.

Active Directory can use multiple DCs for both load balancing and fault tolerance. These DCs must be synchronized across the forest whenever you change any AD object. AD replication performs that function. In *Managing AD Replication*, you examine tools to help you manage and troubleshoot replication. For a fuller look at AD replication, see `https://social.technet.microsoft.com/wiki/contents/articles/4592.how-active-directory-replication-works.aspx`.

In the recipes *Reporting on AD Computers* and *Reporting on AD Users*, you examine AD to find details on computers that have not started up or logged onto the domain. You also look at user accounts for users who are members of special security groups (such as enterprise administrators). These two recipes help keep your AD free of stale objects and reduce potential security risks.

The systems used in the chapter

The recipes in this chapter create the `Reskit.Org` forest with a parent and a child domain and a total of three DCs as follows:

Figure 4.1: Host in use for this chapter

In later chapters, you will use additional servers and will promote SRV1 to be a domain-based server rather than being in a workgroup.

Installing a Forest Root Domain

Installing Active Directory and DNS has always been reasonably straightforward. You can always use the Server Manager GUI, but using PowerShell is easier to automate. You create an AD forest by creating your first domain controller.

To create a DC, you start with a system running Windows Server. You then add the AD DS services Windows feature to the server and the management tools. Then you use the management tools to promote DC1 to be your first DC (aka DC1.Reskit.Org) within the Reskit.Org domain.

Getting ready

You run this recipe on DC1 after installing PowerShell 7 and VS Code.

How to do it...

1. Installing the AD Domain Services feature and management tools

```
Install-WindowsFeature -Name AD-Domain-Services
-IncludeManagementTools
```

2. Importing the ADDSDeployment module

```
Import-Module -Name ADDSDeployment
```

3. Examining the commands in the ADDSDeployment module

```
Get-Command -Module ADDSDeployment
```

4. Create a secure password for the Administrator

```
$PasswordHT = @{
  String      = 'Pa$$w0rd'
  AsPlainText = $true
  Force       = $true
}
$PSS = ConvertTo-SecureString @PasswordHT
```

5. Test the DC Forest installation starting on DC1

```
$ForestHT= @{
  DomainName              = 'Reskit.Org'
  InstallDNS              = $true
  NoRebootOnCompletion    = $true
  SafeModeAdministratorPassword = $PSS
  ForestMode              = 'WinThreshold'
  DomainMOde              = 'WinThreshold'
}
Test-ADDSForestInstallation @ForestHT -WarningAction
SilentlyContinue
```

6. Create theforest root DC on DC1

```
$NewActiveDirectoryParameterHashTable = @{
    DomainName                      = 'Reskit.Org'
    SafeModeAdministratorPassword   = $PSS
    InstallDNS                      = $true
    DomainMode                      = 'WinThreshold'
    ForestMode                      = 'WinThreshold'
    Force                           = $true
    NoRebootOnCompletion            = $true
    WarningAction                   = 'SilentlyContinue'
}
Install-ADDSForest @NewActiveDirectoryParameterHashTble
```

7. Check the key AD and related services

```
Get-Service -Name DNS, Netlogon
```

8. Check DNS zones

```
Get-DnsServerZone
```

9. Restart DC1 to complete promotion

```
Restart-Computer -Force
```

How it works...

In *step 1*, you install the AD Domain Services feature. This feature enables you to deploy a server as a domain controller. The output of this command looks like this:

```
PS C:\Foo> # 1. Installing the AD Domain Services feature and management tools
PS C:\Foo> Install-WindowsFeature -Name AD-Domain-Services -IncludeManagementTools

Success Restart Needed Exit Code Feature Result
------- -------------- --------- --------------
True    No             Success   {Active Directory Domain Services, Group Pot...
```

Figure 4.2: Installing the ADDS feature and management tools

In *step 2*, you manually import the ADDSDeployment module. Since PowerShell does not support this module natively, this step loads the module using the Windows PowerShell compatibility feature, which is why you see a warning message in the output of this command, which looks like this:

```
PS C:\Foo> # 2. Importing the ADDeployment module
PS C:\Foo> Import-Module -Name ADDSDeployment
WARNING: Module ADDSDeployment is loaded in Windows PowerShell using WinPSCompatSession remoting
session; please note that all input and output of commands from this module will be deserialized
objects. If you want to load this module into PowerShell please use 'Import-Module -SkipEditionCheck'
syntax.
```

Figure 4.3: Importing the ADDSDeployment module

In *step 3*, you use the Get-Command cmdlet to discover the commands contained in the ADDSDeployment module, which looks like this:

```
PS C:\Foo> # 3. Examining the commands in the ADDSDeployment module
PS C:\Foo> Get-Command -Module ADDSDeployment

CommandType    Name                                              Version   Source
-----------    ----                                              -------   ------
Function       Add-ADDSReadOnlyDomainControllerAccount           1.0       ADDSDeployment
Function       Install-ADDSDomain                                1.0       ADDSDeployment
Function       Install-ADDSDomainController                      1.0       ADDSDeployment
Function       Install-ADDSForest                                1.0       ADDSDeployment
Function       Test-ADDSDomainControllerInstallation             1.0       ADDSDeployment
Function       Test-ADDSDomainControllerUninstallation           1.0       ADDSDeployment
Function       Test-ADDSDomainInstallation                       1.0       ADDSDeployment
Function       Test-ADDSForestInstallation                       1.0       ADDSDeployment
Function       Test-ADDSReadOnlyDomainControllerAccountCreation  1.0       ADDSDeployment
Function       Uninstall-ADDSDomainController                    1.0       ADDSDeployment
```

Figure 4.4: Discovering the commands within the ADDSDeployment module

With *step 4*, you create a secure string password to use as the Administrator password in the domain you are creating. This step produces no output.

Before you promote a server to be a DC, it can be useful to test to ensure that a promotion would be successful as far as possible. In *step 5*, you use the Test-ADDSForestInstallation command to check whether you can promote DC1 to be a DC in the Reskit.Org domain. The output of this command looks like this:

```
PS C:\Foo> # 5. Testing DC Forest installation starting on DC1
PS C:\Foo> $ForestHT = @{
               DomainName              = 'Reskit.Org'
               InstallDNS              = $true
               NoRebootOnCompletion = $true
               SafeModeAdministratorPassword = $PSS
               ForestMode              = 'WinThreshold'
               DomainMOde              = 'WinThreshold'
           }
PS C:\Foo> Test-ADDSForestInstallation @ForestHT -WarningAction SilentlyContinue

RunspaceId     : 463237a4-f04b-41a6-b871-bd2da91e68fe
Message        : Operation completed successfully
Context        : Test.VerifyDcPromoCore.DCPromo.General.3
RebootRequired : False
Status         : Success
```

Figure 4.5: Testing DC forest installation

In *step 6*, you promote DC1 as the first domain controller in a new domain, Reskit.Org. The output looks like this:

```
PS C:\Foo> # 6. Creating Forest Root DC on DC1
PS C:\Foo> $NewActiveDirectoryParameterHashTable = @{
               DomainName                    = 'Reskit.Org'
               SafeModeAdministratorPassword = $PSS
               InstallDNS                    = $true
               DomainMode                    = 'WinThreshold'
               ForestMode                    = 'WinThreshold'
               Force                         = $true
               NoRebootOnCompletion          = $true
               WarningAction                 = 'SilentlyContinue'
           }
PS C:\Foo> Install-ADDSForest @NewActiveDirectoryParameterHashTable
RunspaceId     : 463237a4-f04b-41a6-b871-bd2da91e68fe
Message        : You must restart this computer to complete the operation.

Context        : DCPromo.General.4
RebootRequired : True
Status         : Success
```

Figure 4.6: Testing DC forest installation - part two

With the promotion complete, you can check the critical services required for Active Directory. Checking the Netlogon and DNS services, which you do in *step 7*, should look like this:

```
PS C:\Foo> # 7. Checking key AD and related services
PS C:\Foo> Get-Service -Name DNS, Netlogon

Status    Name        DisplayName
------    ----        -----------
Running   DNS         DNS Server
Stopped   Netlogon    Netlogon
```

Figure 4.7: Checking the DNS and Netlogon services

In *step 8*, you use the Get-DnsServerZone cmdlet to see the zones currently available on DC1 and their status. Before rebooting after the DC promotion, the output from this step looks like this:

```
PS C:\Foo> # 8. Checking DNS zones
PS C:\Foo> Get-DnsServerZone

ZoneName              ZoneType   IsAutoCreated   IsDsIntegrated   IsReverseLookupZone   IsSigned
--------              --------   -------------   --------------   -------------------   --------
_msdcs.Reskit.Org     Primary    False           False            False                 False
0.in-addr.arpa        Primary    True            False            True                  False
127.in-addr.arpa      Primary    True            False            True                  False
255.in-addr.arpa      Primary    True            False            True                  False
Reskit.Org            Primary    False           False  ←——————   False                 False
```

Figure 4.8: Checking the DNS zones available

In *step 9*, you run the Restart-Computer command, which generates no actual output. To complete the promotion process, you need to reboot DC1. After the reboot, you should be able to log in to the Reskit.Org domain as the Domain Administrator (using the password specified in this recipe).

There's more...

In *step 1*, you install the AD DS feature and the management tools, including the ADDSDeployment module. In *step 2*, you load the module, which, as you can see, PowerShell loads using the Windows PowerShell compatibility feature. Although the modules' commands work, the output does not appear as nicely formatted as you might observe running these commands within Windows PowerShell. The Import-Module command does not import the module's display XML, but you can do that manually should you need to. As shown, you can always import the XML manually. The key thing to look at is the success or failure of the key deployment steps, so this is probably not a major problem (and there is a workaround!).

Throughout the recipes in this book, you use the string Pa$$w0rd as a password for each host and for most core AD users you create. The book uses these steps and this password for simplicity – since Reskit.Org is not a real production domain, the risks are minimal. The steps that contain a plain text version of a weak password, as you see in *step 4*, are not best practice for production.

In *step 5*, you test whether Windows can promote DC1 to be a DC. As you can see from the message, the command completed the test successfully. This success means that you can proceed to install AD on this host. And in *step 8*, you run Install-ADDSForest to promote DC1. By default, this step would cause the host to reboot after completing the promotion process, but in this case, you do not reboot. This approach allows you to examine the results of the step before rebooting.

In *step 7*, you can see that the DNS service is available and running. The Netlogon service, which is the service that implements AD, runs on each DC.

In *step 8*, you see the zones available on DC1's DNS service. You installed this service when you promoted DC1. As you can see, before the reboot, the DNS service is running, but the Reskit.Org zone is not AD integrated because there is no AD service running. After the reboot, this property should change.

Testing an AD installation

In *Installing an Active Directory forest root domain*, you installed AD on DC1. In that recipe, you installed AD initially without rebooting, then did some basic testing, followed by a reboot. After the required reboot, it is useful to check to ensure that your domain and domain controller are fully up, running, and working correctly. In this recipe, you examine core aspects of the AD infrastructure on your first DC.

Getting ready

You run this recipe on DC1, the first domain controller in the Reskit.Org domain, after you have promoted it to be a DC. You promoted DC1 as a domain controller in the Reskit.Org domain in *Installing an Active Directory forest root domain*. Log on as Reskit\Administrator using the password set in the previous recipe, Pa$$w0rd.

How to do it...

1. Examine the Root Directory Service Entry (DSE)

   ```
   Get-ADRootDSE -Server DC1.Reskit.Org
   ```

2. Viewing AD forest details

   ```
   Get-ADForest
   ```

3. Viewing AD Domain details

   ```
   Get-ADDomain -Current LocalComputer
   ```

4. Checking Netlogon, ADWS, and DNS services

   ```
   Get-Service NetLogon, ADWS, DNS
   ```

5. Getting initial AD users

   ```
   Get-ADUser -Filter * |
     Sort-Object -Property Name |
       Format-Table -Property Name, DistinguishedName
   ```

6. Getting initial AD groups

    ```
    Get-ADGroup -Filter *  |
      Sort-Object -Property GroupScope, Name |
        Format-Table -Property Name, GroupScope
    ```

7. Examining Enterprise Admins group membership

    ```
    Get-ADGroupMember -Identity 'Enterprise Admins'
    ```

8. Checking DNS zones on DC1

    ```
    Get-DnsServerZone -ComputerName DC1
    ```

9. Testing domain name DNS resolution

    ```
    Resolve-DnsName -Name Reskit.Org
    ```

How it works...

In *step 1*, after you complete the installation of AD and reboot DC1 (and log in), you examine the AD DSE, which looks like this:

```
PS C:\Foo> # 1. Examining Root Directory Service Entry (DSE)
PS C:\Foo> Get-ADRootDSE -Server DC1.Reskit.Org

configurationNamingContext    : CN=Configuration,DC=Reskit,DC=Org
currentTime                   : 03/05/2022 19:00:28
defaultNamingContext          : DC=Reskit,DC=Org
dnsHostName                   : DC1.Reskit.Org
domainControllerFunctionality : Windows2016
domainFunctionality           : Windows2016Domain
dsServiceName                 : CN=NTDS Settings,CN=DC1,CN=Servers,CN=Default-First-Site-Name,
                                  CN=Sites,CN=Configuration,DC=Reskit,DC=Org
forestFunctionality           : Windows2016Forest
highestCommittedUSN           : 12829
isGlobalCatalogReady          : {TRUE}
isSynchronized                : {TRUE}
ldapServiceName               : Reskit.Org:dc1$@RESKIT.ORG
namingContexts                : {DC=Reskit,DC=Org, CN=Configuration,DC=Reskit,DC=Org,
                                  CN=Schema,CN=Configuration,DC=Reskit,DC=Org,
                                  DC=DomainDnsZones,DC=Reskit,DC=Org, DC=ForestDnsZones,DC=Reskit,DC=Org}
rootDomainNamingContext       : DC=Reskit,DC=Org
schemaNamingContext           : CN=Schema,CN=Configuration,DC=Reskit,DC=Org
serverName                    : CN=DC1,CN=Servers,CN=Default-First-Site-Name,CN=Sites,
                                  CN=Configuration,DC=Reskit,DC=Org
subschemaSubentry             : CN=Aggregate,CN=Schema,CN=Configuration,DC=Reskit,DC=Org
supportedCapabilities         : {1.2.840.113556.1.4.800 (LDAP_CAP_ACTIVE_DIRECTORY_OID),
                                  1.2.840.113556.1.4.1670 (LDAP_CAP_ACTIVE_DIRECTORY_V51_OID),
                                  1.2.840.113556.1.4.1791 (LDAP_CAP_ACTIVE_DIRECTORY_LDAP_INTEG_OID),
                                  1.2.840.113556.1.4.1935 (LDAP_CAP_ACTIVE_DIRECTORY_V61_OID),
                                  1.2.840.113556.1.4.2080, 1.2.840.113556.1.4.2237}
supportedControl              : {1.2.840.113556.1.4.319 (LDAP_PAGED_RESULT_OID_STRING),
                                  1.2.840.113556.1.4.801 (LDAP_SERVER_SD_FLAGS_OID),
```

Figure 4.9: Examining the Root DSE

In *step 2*, you use `Get-ADForest` to return core information about the `Reskit.Org` forest, with output like this:

```
PS C:\Foo> # 2. Viewing AD forest details
PS C:\Foo> Get-ADForest

ApplicationPartitions : {DC=ForestDnsZones,DC=Reskit,DC=Org, DC=DomainDnsZones,DC=Reskit,DC=Org}
CrossForestReferences : {}
DomainNamingMaster    : DC1.Reskit.Org  ◄─────────
Domains               : {Reskit.Org}
ForestMode            : Windows2016Forest
GlobalCatalogs        : {DC1.Reskit.Org} ◄─────────
Name                  : Reskit.Org
PartitionsContainer   : CN=Partitions,CN=Configuration,DC=Reskit,DC=Org
RootDomain            : Reskit.Org
SchemaMaster          : DC1.Reskit.Org  ◄─────────
Sites                 : {Default-First-Site-Name}
SPNSuffixes           : {}
UPNSuffixes           : {}
```

Figure 4.10: Viewing AD Forest details

In *step 3*, you use the `Get-ADDomain` command to get details about the `Reskit.Org` domain, with output like this:

```
PS C:\Foo> # 3. Viewing AD Domain details
PS C:\Foo> Get-ADDomain -Current LocalComputer

AllowedDNSSuffixes                 : {}
ChildDomains                       : {}
ComputersContainer                 : CN=Computers,DC=Reskit,DC=Org
DeletedObjectsContainer            : CN=Deleted Objects,DC=Reskit,DC=Org
DistinguishedName                  : DC=Reskit,DC=Org
DNSRoot                            : Reskit.Org  ◄─────────
DomainControllersContainer         : OU=Domain Controllers,DC=Reskit,DC=Org
DomainMode                         : Windows2016Domain
DomainSID                          : S-1-5-21-3837990179-1095414155-523858238
ForeignSecurityPrincipalsContainer : CN=ForeignSecurityPrincipals,DC=Reskit,DC=Org
Forest                             : Reskit.Org
InfrastructureMaster               : DC1.Reskit.Org  ◄─────────
LastLogonReplicationInterval       :
LinkedGroupPolicyObjects           : {CN={31B2F340-016D-11D2-945F-00C04FB984F9},
                                     CN=Policies,CN=System,DC=Reskit,DC=Org}
LostAndFoundContainer              : CN=LostAndFound,DC=Reskit,DC=Org
ManagedBy                          :
Name                               : Reskit
NetBIOSName                        : RESKIT
ObjectClass                        : domainDNS
ObjectGUID                         : 641ac984-a9e6-410f-9f41-d8be35cc217b
ParentDomain                       :
PDCEmulator                        : DC1.Reskit.Org  ◄─────────
PublicKeyRequiredPasswordRolling   : True
QuotasContainer                    : CN=NTDS Quotas,DC=Reskit,DC=Org
ReadOnlyReplicaDirectoryServers    : {}
ReplicaDirectoryServers            : {DC1.Reskit.Org} ◄─────────
RIDMaster                          : DC1.Reskit.Org  ◄─────────
SubordinateReferences              : {DC=ForestDnsZones,DC=Reskit,DC=Org,
                                      DC=DomainDnsZones,DC=Reskit,DC=Org,
                                      CN=Configuration,DC=Reskit,DC=Org}
SystemsContainer                   : CN=System,DC=Reskit,DC=Org
UsersContainer                     : CN=Users,DC=Reskit,DC=Org
```

Figure 4.11: Viewing AD Domain details

In *step 4*, you check on three key services for AD: Active Directory Web Services, DNS, and Netlogon. You see output like this:

```
PS C:\Foo> # 4. Checking Netlogon, ADWS, and DNS services
PS C:\Foo> Get-Service NetLogon, ADWS, DNS

Status    Name       DisplayName
------    ----       -----------
Running   ADWS       Active Directory Web Services
Running   DNS        DNS Server
Running   Netlogon   Netlogon
```

Figure 4.12: Viewing the status of key services

In *step 5*, you view the AD users created by the AD installation process, with output like this:

```
PS C:\Foo> # 5. Getting initial AD users
PS C:\Foo> Get-ADUser -Filter * |
             Sort-Object -Property Name |
               Format-Table -Property Name, DistinguishedName

Name           DistinguishedName
----           -----------------
Administrator  CN=Administrator,CN=Users,DC=Reskit,DC=Org
Guest          CN=Guest,CN=Users,DC=Reskit,DC=Org
krbtgt         CN=krbtgt,CN=Users,DC=Reskit,DC=Org
```

Figure 4.13: Viewing initial AD users

When you created the forest, the AD installer also created a large number of AD groups, which you view in *step 6*. The output of this step looks like this:

```
PS C:\Foo> # 6. Getting initial AD groups
PS C:\Foo> Get-ADGroup -Filter * |
              Sort-Object -Property GroupScope,Name |
              Format-Table -Property Name, GroupScope

Name                                              GroupScope
----                                              ----------
Access Control Assistance Operators               DomainLocal
Account Operators                                 DomainLocal
Administrators                                     DomainLocal
Allowed RODC Password Replication Group           DomainLocal
Backup Operators                                  DomainLocal
Cert Publishers                                   DomainLocal
Certificate Service DCOM Access                   DomainLocal
Cryptographic Operators                           DomainLocal
Denied RODC Password Replication Group            DomainLocal
Distributed COM Users                             DomainLocal
DnsAdmins                                         DomainLocal
Event Log Readers                                 DomainLocal
Guests                                            DomainLocal
Hyper-V Administrators                            DomainLocal
IIS_IUSRS                                         DomainLocal
Incoming Forest Trust Builders                    DomainLocal
Network Configuration Operators                   DomainLocal
Performance Log Users                             DomainLocal
Performance Monitor Users                         DomainLocal
Pre-Windows 2000 Compatible Access                DomainLocal
Print Operators                                   DomainLocal
RAS and IAS Servers                               DomainLocal
RDS Endpoint Servers                              DomainLocal
RDS Management Servers                            DomainLocal
RDS Remote Access Servers                         DomainLocal
Remote Desktop Users                              DomainLocal
Remote Management Users                           DomainLocal
Replicator                                        DomainLocal
Server Operators                                  DomainLocal
Storage Replica Administrators                    DomainLocal
Terminal Server License Servers                   DomainLocal
Users                                             DomainLocal
Windows Authorization Access Group                DomainLocal
Cloneable Domain Controllers                           Global
DnsUpdateProxy                                         Global
Domain Admins                                          Global
Domain Computers                                       Global
Domain Controllers                                     Global
Domain Guests                                          Global
Domain Users                                           Global
Group Policy Creator Owners                            Global
Key Admins                                             Global
Protected Users                                        Global
Read-only Domain Controllers                           Global
Enterprise Admins                                   Universal
Enterprise Key Admins                               Universal
Enterprise Read-only Domain Controllers             Universal
Schema Admins                                       Universal
```

Figure 4.14: Viewing initial AD groups

The Enterprise Admins group is a very high-security group within AD. Membership of this group gives significant rights to systems and services within a domain. In *step 7*, you examine the initial membership of this group, with output like this:

```
PS C:\Foo> # 7. Examining Enterprise Admins group membership
PS C:\Foo> Get-ADGroupMember -Identity 'Enterprise Admins'

distinguishedName : CN=Administrator,CN=Users,DC=Reskit,DC=Org
name              : Administrator
objectClass       : user
objectGUID        : 1d9f4694-5a75-42eb-82f2-7fdf3d4b98d0
SamAccountName    : Administrator
SID               : S-1-5-21-3837990179-1095414155-523858238-500
```

Figure 4.15: Viewing Enterprise Admin group membership

In *step 8*, after you reboot your workgroup server to become a domain controller, you recheck the DNS zones available from DC1, with output like this:

```
PS C:\Foo> # 8. Checking DNS zones on DC1
PS C:\Foo> Get-DnsServerZone -ComputerName DC1

ZoneName          ZoneType  IsAutoCreated  IsDsIntegrated  IsReverseLookupZone  IsSigned
--------          --------  -------------  --------------  -------------------  --------
_msdcs.Reskit.Org Primary   False          True            False                False
0.in-addr.arpa    Primary   True           False           True                 False
127.in-addr.arpa  Primary   True           False           True                 False
255.in-addr.arpa  Primary   True           False           True                 False
Reskit.Org        Primary   False          True  ◄───────  False                False
```

Figure 4.16: Checking DNS zones

The final check, in *step 9*, is to test DNS to ensure that you can resolve the AD domain name. The output resembles this:

```
PS C:\Foo> # 9. Testing domain name DNS resolution
PS C:\Foo> Resolve-DnsName -Name Reskit.Org

Name        Type  TTL  Section   IPAddress
----        ----  ---  -------   ---------
Reskit.Org  AAAA  600  Answer    2a02:8010:6386:0:f55d:e38c:ceb0:8efb
Reskit.Org  A     600  Answer    10.10.10.10
```

Figure 4.17: Checking DNS resolution

There's more...

In *step 1*, you viewed the Root DSE for the Reskit.Org domain. Active Directory implements a **Lightweight Directory Access Protocol (LDAP)** directory service for domain activities. The DSE is a component of LDAP directories and contains information about your directory structure. Windows allows access to the Root DSE without requiring authentication.

The DSE includes much information about your AD forest, which might help an attacker. Thus, the best practice is never to expose an AD DC to the internet if you can possibly help it. For a more detailed look at the Root DSE, see `https://learn.microsoft.com/windows/win32/adschema/rootdse`.

The ADWS service, which you investigate in *step 4*, implements an important web service. The AD PowerShell commands use this web service to get information and make changes to your AD. If this service is not running, AD commands do not work. You should always check to ensure the service has started before using the AD cmdlets.

In *step 6*, you saw the groups created by the promotion process. These groups have permissions associated and thus are useful. Before adding users to these groups, consider reviewing the groups and determining (and possibly changing) the permissions and rights assigned to them.

In *step 8*, you examine the DNS zones available from DC1. As you can see, the Reskit.Org domain is now AD integrated. After creating the AD forest, Windows integrates this zone into AD as part of the reboot.

In *step 9*, you check the resolution of the domain name. In this case, you see both IPv6 and IPv4 addresses.

Installing a Replica Domain Controller

In *Installing an Active Directory forest root domain*, you installed AD on DC1. If you have just one DC, then that DC is a single point of failure. If the DC goes down with a single domain controller, you cannot manage or log in to the domain. It is always a best practice to install at least two DCs. If you are using VMs for your DCs, you should also ensure that each DC VM is on a separate virtualization host – otherwise, the VM host is a single point of failure.

To add a second DC to your domain, you run `Install-ADDSDomainController` on another host, that is DC2. This cmdlet is similar to `Install-ADDSForest` in terms of parameters. It is useful to conduct tests to ensure the second DC's promotion can succeed as with creating your first DC.

In this recipe, you promote a host, DC2, to be the second DC in the Reskit.Org domain. Like creating your first DC, after you promote DC2 to be a DC, you need to reboot the server before processing. And after the reboot, it is useful to ensure the promotion process was successful.

Getting ready

You run this recipe on DC2, a domain-joined server on which you have installed PowerShell 7 and VS Code. You should log in to DC2 as Reskit\Administrator, a member of the Enterprise Admins group.

Note that if you are using the Reskit.Org build scripts from GitHub, make sure you build the DC2 M after you have created DC1 and promoted it to be a domain controller.

How to do it...

1. Importing the ServerManager module

   ```
   Import-Module -Name ServerManager -WarningAction SilentlyContinue
   ```

2. Checking DC1 can be resolved

   ```
   Resolve-DnsName -Name DC1.Reskit.Org -Type A
   ```

3. Testing the network connection to DC1

   ```
   Test-NetConnection -ComputerName DC1.Reskit.Org -Port 445
   Test-NetConnection -ComputerName DC1.Reskit.Org -Port 389
   ```

4. Adding the AD DS features on DC2

   ```
   Install-WindowsFeature -Name AD-Domain-Services
   -IncludeManagementTools
   ```

5. Promoting DC2 to be a DC

   ```
   Import-Module -Name ADDSDeployment -WarningAction SilentlyContinue
   $User       = "Administrator@Reskit.Org"
   $Password   = 'Pa$$w0rd'
   $PWSString  = ConvertTo-SecureString -String $Password -AsPlainText
   -Force
   $CredRK = [PSCredential]::New($User,$PWSString)
   $INSTALLHT = @{
     DomainName                     = 'Reskit.Org'
     SafeModeAdministratorPassword  = $PSS
     SiteName                       = 'Default-First-Site-Name'
   ```

```
        NoRebootOnCompletion           = $true
        InstallDNS                     = $false
        Credential                     = $CredRK
        Force                          = $true
    }
    Install-ADDSDomainController @INSTALLHT | Out-Null
```

6. Checking the computer objects in AD

```
Get-ADComputer -Filter *  |
    Format-Table DNSHostName, DistinguishedName
```

7. Rebooting DC2 manually

```
Restart-Computer -Force
```

8. Checking DCs in Reskit.Org

```
$SearchBase = 'OU=Domain Controllers,DC=Reskit,DC=Org'
Get-ADComputer -Filter * -SearchBase $SearchBase  -Properties *  |
    Format-Tale -Property DNSHostName, Enabled
```

9. Viewing Reskit.Org domain DCs

```
Get-ADDomain |
    Format-Table -Property Forest, Name,
                           ReplicaDirectoryServers
```

How it works...

In *step 1*, you import the ServerManager module, which creates no output. With *step 2*, you ensure that you can resolve your DC's address, which is, at this point, the only DC in the Reskit.Org domain. The output looks like this:

```
PS C:\Foo> # 2. Checking DC1 can be resolved
PS C:\Foo> Resolve-DnsName -Name DC1.Reskit.Org -Type A

Name              Type  TTL   Section  IPAddress
----              ----  ---   -------  ---------
DC1.Reskit.Org    A     3600  Answer   10.10.10.10
```

Figure 4.18: Resolving DC1's DNS entry

After confirming that you can resolve the IP address of DC1, in *step 3*, you check if you can connect to two key ports on DC1 (445 and 389). The output looks like this:

```
PS C:\Foo> # 3. Testing the network connection to DC1
PS C:\Foo> Test-NetConnection -ComputerName DC1.Reskit.Org -Port 445

ComputerName    : DC1.Reskit.Org
RemoteAddress   : 10.10.10.10
RemotePort      : 445
InterfaceAlias  : Ethernet
SourceAddress   : 10.10.10.11
TcpTestSucceeded : True  ←────────


PS C:\Foo> Test-NetConnection -ComputerName DC1.Reskit.Org -Port 389

ComputerName    : DC1.Reskit.Org
RemoteAddress   : 10.10.10.10
RemotePort      : 389
InterfaceAlias  : Ethernet
SourceAddress   : 10.10.10.11
TcpTestSucceeded : True  ←────────
```

Figure 4.19: Checking key ports are available on DC1

As you saw, when promoting DC1 to be your first DC, you need to add the ADDSDeployment Windows feature to DC2 before you can promote the DC. You add this feature in *step 4*, with output that looks like this:

```
PS C:\Foo> # 4. Adding the AD DS features on DC2
PS C:\Foo> Install-WindowsFeature -Name AD-Domain-Services -IncludeManagementTools

Success Restart Needed Exit Code  Feature Result
------- -------------- ---------  --------------
True    No             Success    {Active Directory Domain Services, Group Pol…
```

Figure 4.20: Adding AD Domain Sevices to DC2

In *step 5*, you promote DC2 to be a DC and ensure that the DC does not reboot after this step completes. There is no output from this step.

Before rebooting DC2 to complete the DC promotion process, in *step 6*, you check to see the computer objects now in the AD, including your new replica DC. This step ensures that DC2 is now in the correct place in AD. The output of this step is like this:

```
PS C:\Foo> # 6. Checking the computer objects in AD
PS C:\Foo> Get-ADComputer -Filter * |
             Format-Table DNSHostName, DistinguishedName

DNSHostName     DistinguishedName
-----------     -----------------
DC1.Reskit.Org  CN=DC1,OU=Domain Controllers,DC=Reskit,DC=Org
DC2.Reskit.Org  CN=DC2,OU=Domain Controllers,DC=Reskit,DC=Org
```

Figure 4.21: Adding AD Domain Sevices to DC2 - part two

In *step 7*, you reboot DC2, which produces no console output, to complete the promotion of this host to be a replica DC.

After DC2 completes the reboot process, you log in as the domain administrator (Reskit\ Administrator). After you log in, in *step 8*, you use Get-ADComputer to check the hosts in the Domain Controllers OU. You can see that the OU contains both DC1 and DC2. You see output like this:

```
PS C:\Foo> # 8. Checking DCs in Reskit.Org
PS C:\Foo> $SearchBase = '0U=Domain Controllers,DC=Reskit,DC=Org'
PS C:\Foo> Get-ADComputer -Filter * -SearchBase $SearchBase - Properties * |
             Format-Table -Property DNSHostName, Enabled

DNSHostName       Enabled
-----------       -------
DC1.Reskit.Org    True
DC2.Reskit.Org    True
```

Figure 4.22: Viewing AD Computers in the Domain Controllers OU

In the final step in this recipe, *step 9*, you use the Get-ADDomain command to view the details of the forest, the domain, and the replica DCs, with output like this:

```
PS C:\Foo> # 9. Viewing Reskit.Org domain DCs
PS C:\Foo> Get-ADDomain |
             Format-Table -Property Forest, Name,
                                     ReplicaDirectoryServers

Forest      Name   ReplicaDirectoryServers
------      ----   -----------------------
Reskit.Org  Reskit {DC1.Reskit.Org, DC2.Reskit.Org}
```

Figure 4.23: Viewing forest, domain, and replica DC information

There's more...

In *step 1*, you import the ServerManager module manually. This step loads the module using the Windows PowerShell compatibility solution described earlier. As you have seen in earlier recipes, this module is not supported natively with PowerShell 7.

In *step 3*, you check to ensure DC2 can connect to DC1 over ports 445 and 389. Windows uses TCP port 445 for SMB file sharing. The Group Policy Agent on each domain-joined host uses this port to retrieve Group Policy details from the SYSVOL share on DC1. LDAP uses port 389 to perform actions against a DC, such as adding a new user or checking group membership. Both ports need to be open and contactable if the promotion of DC2 is to be successful.

In *step 6*, you retrieve all computer accounts currently in your AD. The AD DC promotion process ensures that this host's computer account is now in the Domain Controllers OU by default. The location of a DC in an OU is essential as it enables your new DC to apply the group policy settings on this OU. If DC2 is a workgroup computer and not joined to the domain, the promotion process creates this account in the appropriate Domain Controllers OU. If DC2 were a domain member, then the promotion process would move the computer account into the Domain Controllers OU.

Mistakes are easy to make, but also (usually) easy to correct. In this recipe, before promoting DC2 to be a DC, you check to ensure that the prerequisites are in place before the promotion. Then you confirm that you have configured your forest, domain, and domain controllers correctly. Likewise, the checks in the last two steps are not strictly necessary. If nothing else, they're just more evidence of the successful creation of a replica DC.

These steps are probably redundant since most AD promotions "just work." Nevertheless, the additional checks ensure you discover and resolve any issues that might affect the promotion or cause the AD to not work correctly after a not fully successful promotion (for whatever reason).

Installing a Child Domain

In *Installing a Replica Domain Controller*, you added a DC to an existing domain. With all the pre-requisites like DNS in place, the promotion process is simple and quick.

An AD forest can contain more than one domain, with one domain having zero, one, or more child domains. This architecture provides for delegated administration and reduction in replication traffic across a global network. Like creating a replica DC, creating a new child domain is simple, as you can see in this recipe.

Best practice calls for a contiguous namespace of domains, where the additional domain is a child of another existing domain. In this recipe, you create a child domain, UK.Reskit.Org. You begin with the domain joined server UKDC1 and with this recipe, convert it to be the first DC in a new child domain, UK.Reskit.Org. In doing so, the hostname changes from UKDC1.Reskit.Org to UKDC1.UK.Reskit.Org.

The steps in this recipe are very similar to those in *Installing a replica directory domain controller*.

Getting ready

You run this recipe on SRV1 after you have installed PowerShell 7.

How to do it...

1. Importing the ServerManager module

   ```
   Import-Module -Name ServerManager -WarningAction SilentlyContinue
   ```

2. Checking DC1 can be resolved

   ```
   Resolve-DnsName -Name DC1.Reskit.Org -Type A
   ```

3. Checking network connection to DC1

   ```
   Test-NetConnection -ComputerName DC1.Reskit.Org -Port 445
   Test-NetConnection -ComputerName DC1.Reskit.Org -Port 389
   ```

4. Adding the AD DS features on UKDC1

   ```
   $Features = 'AD-Domain-Services'
   Install-WindowsFeature -Name $Features -IncludeManagementTools
   ```

5. Creating a credential and installation hash table

   ```
   Import-Module -Name ADDSDeployment -WarningAction SilentlyContinue
   $URK     = "Administrator@Reskit.Org"
   $PW      = 'Pa$$w0rd'
   $PSS     = ConvertTo-SecureString -String $PW -AsPlainText -Force
   $CredRK = [PSCredential]::New($URK,$PSS)
   $INSTALLHT      = @{
     NewDomainName                      = 'UK'
     ParentDomainName                   = 'Reskit.Org'
     DomainType                         = 'ChildDomain'
     SafeModeAdministratorPassword = $PSS
     ReplicationSourceDC                = 'DC1.Reskit.Org'
     Credential                         = $CredRK
     SiteName                           = 'Default-First-Site-Name'
     InstallDNS                         = $false
     Force                              = $true
   }
   ```

6. Installing child domain

```
Install-ADDSDomain @INSTALLHT
```

7. Looking at the AD forest

```
Get-ADForest -Server UKDC1.UK.Reskit.Org
```

8. Looking at the UK domain

```
Get-ADDomain -Server UKDC1.UK.Reskit.Org
```

9. Checking on user accounts in UK domain

```
Get-ADUser -Filter *   |
    Format-Table -Property SamAccountName, DistinguishedName
```

10. Checking on user accounts in parent domain

```
Get-ADUser -Filter * -Server DC1.Reskit.Org |
    Format-Table -Property SamAccountName, DistinguishedName
```

How it works...

In *step 1*, you load the ServerManager module. As discussed in earlier recipes, this module is not natively supported by PowerShell 7. This step, which produces no output, loads the module using the Windows PowerShell compatibility solution.

When you create a new domain and new domain controller (using UKDC1, for example), the server needs to contact the holder of the Domain Naming FSMO role, the DC responsible for the forest's changes. In *step 2*, you check to ensure you can resolve this host, DC1, which looks like this:

```
PS C:\Foo> # 2. Checking DC1 can be resolved
PS C:\Foo> Resolve-DnsName -Name DC1.Reskit.Org -Type A

Name              Type  TTL   Section  IPAddress
----              ----  ---   -------  ---------
DC1.Reskit.Org    A     3600  Answer   10.10.10.10
```

Figure 4.24: Viewing forest, domain, and replica DC information - part two

In *step 3*, you check that you can connect to ports 445 and 389 on DC1. These two ports are fundamental to AD operations. The output looks like this:

```
PS C:\Foo> # 3. Checking network connection to DC1
PS C:\Foo> Test-NetConnection -ComputerName DC1.Reskit.Org -Port 445

ComputerName     : DC1.Reskit.Org
RemoteAddress    : 10.10.10.10
RemotePort       : 445
InterfaceAlias   : Ethernet
SourceAddress    : 10.10.10.12
TcpTestSucceeded : True


PS C:\Foo> Test-NetConnection -ComputerName DC1.Reskit.Org -Port 389

ComputerName     : DC1.Reskit.Org
RemoteAddress    : 10.10.10.10
RemotePort       : 389
InterfaceAlias   : Ethernet
SourceAddress    : 10.10.10.12
TcpTestSucceeded : True
```

Figure 4.25: Testing network connection to DC1

In *step 4*, you add the AD DS feature to UKDC1, with output like this:

```
PS C:\Foo> # 4. Adding the AD DS -features on UKDC1
PS C:\Foo> $Features = 'AD-Domain-Services'
PS C:\Foo> Install-WindowsFeature -Name $Features -IncludeManagementTools

Success Restart Needed Exit Code Feature Result
------- -------------- --------- --------------
True    No             Success   {Active Directory Domain Services, Group Pol...
```

Figure 4.26: Adding the AD DS feature to UKDC1

In *step 5*, you create a hash table of the parameters to create your child domain. This step creates no output. In *step 6*, you make UKDC1 the first DC in the UK.Reskit.Org domain, creating no console output. After this step, the host reboots, and you can log in as UK\Administrator for the remainder of this recipe.

After rebooting, in *step 7*, you use Get-ADForest to view the details of the forest, including the GC servers in the forest. The output of this step looks like this:

```
PS C:\Foo> # 7. Looking at the AD forest
PS C:\Foo> Get-ADForest -Server UKDC1.UK.Reskit.Org
ApplicationPartitions  : {DC=ForestDnsZones,DC=Reskit,DC=Org, DC=DomainDnsZones,DC=Reskit,DC=Org}
CrossForestReferences  : {}
DomainNamingMaster     : DC1.Reskit.Org
Domains                : {Reskit.Org, UK.Reskit.Org}
ForestMode             : Windows2016Forest
GlobalCatalogs         : {DC1.Reskit.Org, DC2.Reskit.Org, UKDC1.UK.Reskit.Org}
Name                   : Reskit.Org
PartitionsContainer    : CN=Partitions,CN=Configuration,DC=Reskit,DC=Org
RootDomain             : Reskit.Org
SchemaMaster           : DC1.Reskit.Org
Sites                  : {Default-First-Site-Name}
SPNSuffixes            : {}
UPNSuffixes            : {}
```

Figure 4.27: Viewing AD forest details

In *step 8*, you examine the details of the UK domain using Get-ADDomain, with output like this:

```
PS C:\Foo> # 8. Looking at the UK domain
PS C:\Foo> Get-ADDomain -Server UKDC1.UK.Reskit.Org

AllowedDNSSuffixes                  : {}
ChildDomains                        : {}
ComputersContainer                  : CN=Computers,DC=UK,DC=Reskit,DC=Org
DeletedObjectsContainer             : CN=Deleted Objects,DC=UK,DC=Reskit,DC=Org
DistinguishedName                   : DC=UK,DC=Reskit,DC=Org
DNSRoot                             : UK.Reskit.Org
DomainControllersContainer          : OU=Domain Controllers,DC=UK,DC=Reskit,DC=Org
DomainMode                          : Windows2016Domain
DomainSID                           : S-1-5-21-2334424375-2449464812-1680912663
ForeignSecurityPrincipalsContainer  : CN=ForeignSecurityPrincipals,DC=UK,DC=Reskit,DC=Org
Forest                              : Reskit.Org
InfrastructureMaster                : UKDC1.UK.Reskit.Org
LastLogonReplicationInterval        :
LinkedGroupPolicyObjects            : {CN={31B2F340-016D-11D2-945F-00C04FB984F9},CN=Policies,CN=System,DC=UK,DC=Reskit,DC=Org}
LostAndFoundContainer               : CN=LostAndFound,DC=UK,DC=Reskit,DC=Org
ManagedBy                           :
Name                                : UK
NetBIOSName                         : UK
ObjectClass                         : domainDNS
ObjectGUID                          : 247c3c57-6869-4347-9594-04fe466542ae
ParentDomain                        : Reskit.Org
PDCEmulator                         : UKDC1.UK.Reskit.Org
PublicKeyRequiredPasswordRolling    : True
QuotasContainer                     : CN=NTDS Quotas,DC=UK,DC=Reskit,DC=Org
ReadOnlyReplicaDirectoryServers     : {}
ReplicaDirectoryServers             : {UKDC1.UK.Reskit.Org}
RIDMaster                           : UKDC1.UK.Reskit.Org
SubordinateReferences               : {}
SystemsContainer                    : CN=System,DC=UK,DC=Reskit,DC=Org
UsersContainer                      : CN=Users,DC=UK,DC=Reskit,DC=Org
```

Figure 4.28: Viewing details of the UK domain

In *step 9*, you check the user account objects contained in the new UK domain, with output like this:

```
PS C:\Foo> # 9. Checking on user accounts in UK domain
PS C:\Foo> Get-ADUser -Filter * |
             Format-Table -Property SamAccountName, DistinguishedName

SamAccountName DistinguishedName
-------------- -----------------
Administrator  CN=Administrator,CN=Users,DC=UK,DC=Reskit,DC=Org
Guest          CN=Guest,CN=Users,DC=UK,DC=Reskit,DC=Org
krbtgt         CN=krbtgt,CN=Users,DC=UK,DC=Reskit,DC=Org
RESKIT$        CN=RESKIT$,CN=Users,DC=UK,DC=Reskit,DC=Org
```

Figure 4.29: Viewing user accounts in the UK domain

In *step 10*, you check on the user accounts in the parent domain, Reskit.Org, with output like this:

```
PS C:\Foo> # 10. Checking on user accounts in parent domain
PS C:\Foo> # Get-ADUser -Filter * -Server DC1.Reskit.Org |
             Format-Table -Property SamAccountName, DistinguishedName

SamAccountName DistinguishedName
-------------- -----------------
Administrator  CN=Administrator,CN=Users,DC=Reskit,DC=Org
Guest          CN=Guest,CN=Users,DC=Reskit,DC=Org
krbtgt         CN=krbtgt,CN=Users,DC=Reskit,DC=Org
UK$            CN=UK$,CN=Users,DC=Reskit,DC=Org
```

Figure 4.30: Viewing user accounts in the Reskit.Org domain

There's more...

In *step 2*, you check that you can resolve the IP address for DC1, the Domain Naming FSMO role holder. You could call Get-ADForest and obtain the hostname from the DomainNamingMaster property.

In *step 5*, you promote UKDC1 to be the first DC in a new child domain, UK.Reskit.Org. Unlike in the two previous DC promotions (that is, promoting DC1 and DC2), in this step, you allow Windows to reboot after Windows completes the DC promotion. This step can take quite a while – potentially 10 minutes or more, so be patient.

In *step 7*, you use Get-ADForest to examine details of the forest as stored on UKDC1. As you can see in the figure, these details now show your new domain (UK.Reskit.Org) in the Domains property. Also, by default, you can see that UKDC1.UK.Reskit.Org is also a Global Catalog server.

Creating and Managing AD Users and Groups

After you have created your forest/domain and your domain controllers, you can begin to manage the core objects in AD, namely, users, groups, computers, and OUs. User and computer accounts identify a specific user or computer. Windows uses these objects to enable the computer and the user to log on securely using passwords held in AD.

AD Groups enable you to collect users and computers into a single (group) account that simplifies setting access controls on resources such as files or file shares. As you saw in *Testing an AD installation*, the AD promotion process creates many potentially useful groups when you create a new forest.

Organizational Units enable you to partition users, computers, and groups into separate container OUs. OUs provide you with essential roles in your AD. The first is role delegation. You can delegate the management of any OU (and child OUs) to be carried out by different groups.

For example, you could create a top-level OU called UK in the Reskit.Org domain. You could then delegate permissions to the objects in this OU to a group, such as UKAdmins, enabling any group member to manage AD objects in and below the UK OU. You can delegate permissions to another group, such as the North America Admins group.

The second role played by OUs is to act as a target for Group Policy Objects. You could create a group policy object for the IT team and apply it to the IT OU. You could create a separate OU and GPOs that apply to only the computer and user objects in that OU. Thus, each user and computer in a given OU are configured based on the GPO.

In this recipe, you examine AD users and group objects. In a later recipe, *Managing AD Computers*, you explore managing AD computers. And in *Creating Group Policy Objects*, you assign a Group Policy to an OU you create in this recipe.

Getting ready

You run this recipe on DC1, a domain controller in the Reskit.Org domain. You have previously installed PowerShell 7 and VS Code on this DC.

How to do it...

1. Createing a hash table for general user attributes

```
$PW  = 'Pa$$w0rd'
$PSS = ConvertTo-SecureString -String $PW -AsPlainText -Force
$NewUserHT = @{}
$NewUserHT.AccountPassword      = $PSS
$NewUserHT.Enabled              = $true
$NewUserHT.PasswordNeverExpires = $true
$NewUserHT.ChangePasswordAtLogon = $false
```

2. Creating two new users

```
# First user
$NewUserHT.SamAccountName    = 'ThomasL'
$NewUserHT.UserPrincipalName = 'thomasL@reskit.org'
$NewUserHT.Name              = 'ThomasL'
$NewUserHT.DisplayName       = 'Thomas Lee (IT)'
New-ADUser @NewUserHT
# Second user
$NewUserHT.SamAccountName    = 'RLT'
```

```
$NewUserHT.UserPrincipalName = 'rlt@reskit.org'
$NewUserHT.Name              = 'Rebecca Tanner'
$NewUserHT.DisplayName       = 'Rebecca Tanner (IT)'
New-ADUser @NewUserHT
```

3. Creating an OU for IT

```
$OUHT = @{
    Name        = 'IT'
    DisplayName = 'Reskit IT Team'
    Path        = 'DC=Reskit,DC=Org'
}
New-ADOrganizationalUnit @OUHT
```

4. Moving users into the OU

```
$MHT1 = @{
    Identity   = 'CN=ThomasL,CN=Users,DC=Reskit,DC=ORG'
    TargetPath = 'OU=IT,DC=Reskit,DC=Org'
}
Move-ADObject @MHT1
$MHT2 = @{
    Identity = 'CN=Rebecca Tanner,CN=Users,DC=Reskit,DC=ORG'
    TargetPath = 'OU=IT,DC=Reskit,DC=Org'
}
Move-ADObject @MHT2
```

5. Creating a third user directly in the IT OU

```
$NewUserHT.SamAccountName    = 'JerryG'
$NewUserHT.UserPrincipalName = 'jerryg@reskit.org'
$NewUserHT.Description       = 'Virtualization Team'
$NewUserHT.Name              = 'Jerry Garcia'
$NewUserHT.DisplayName       = 'Jerry Garcia (IT)'
$NewUserHT.Path              = 'OU=IT,DC=Reskit,DC=Org'
New-ADUser @NewUserHT
```

6. Adding two users who get removed later

```
# First user to be removed
$NewUserHT.SamAccountName    = 'TBR1'
```

```
$NewUserHT.UserPrincipalName = 'tbr@reskit.org'
$NewUserHT.Name              = 'TBR1'
$NewUserHT.DisplayName       = 'User to be removed'
$NewUserHT.Path              = 'OU=IT,DC=Reskit,DC=Org'
New-ADUser @NewUserHT
# Second user to be removed
$NewUserHT.SamAccountName     = 'TBR2'
$NewUserHT.UserPrincipalName  = 'tbr2@reskit.org'
$NewUserHT.Name               = 'TBR2'
New-ADUser @NewUserHT
```

7. Viewing existing AD users

```
Get-ADUser -Filter *  -Property *|
   Format-Table -Property Name, Displayname, SamAccountName
```

8. Removing via a Get | Remove pattern

```
Get-ADUser -Identity 'CN=TBR1,OU=IT,DC=Reskit,DC=Org' |
   Remove-ADUser -Confirm:$false
```

9. Removing a user directly

```
$RUHT = @{
  Identity = 'CN=TBR2,OU=IT,DC=Reskit,DC=Org'
  Confirm  = $false}
Remove-ADUser @RUHT
```

10. Updating a user object

```
$TLHT =@{
  Identity     = 'ThomasL'
  OfficePhone  = '4416835420'
  Office       = 'Cookham HQ'
  EmailAddress = 'ThomasL@Reskit.Org'
  GivenName    = 'Thomas'
  Surname      = 'Lee'
  HomePage     = 'Https://tfl09.blogspot.com'
}
Set-ADUser @TLHT
```

11. Viewing updated user

```
Get-ADUser -Identity ThomasL -Properties * |
  Format-Table -Property DisplayName,Name,Office,
                          OfficePhone,EmailAddress
```

12. Creating a new domain local group

```
$NGHT = @{
  Name        = 'IT Team'
  Path        = 'OU=IT,DC=Reskit,DC=org'
  Description = 'All members of the IT Team'
  GroupScope  = 'DomainLocal'
}
New-ADGroup @NGHT
```

13. Adding all the users in the IT OU into the IT Team group

```
$SB = 'OU=IT,DC=Reskit,DC=Org'
$ItUsers = Get-ADUser -Filter * -SearchBase $SB
Add-ADGroupMember -Identity 'IT Team'  -Members $ItUsers
```

14. Display members of the IT Team group

```
Get-ADGroupMember -Identity 'IT Team' |
  Format-Table SamAccountName, DistinguishedName
```

How it works...

You use the New-ADUser cmdlet to create a new AD user. Due to the amount of information you wish to hold for any user you create, the number of parameters you might need to pass to New-ADUser can make for very long code lines. To get around that, you create a hash table of parameters and parameter values and then use it to create the user. In *step 1*, you create such a hash table, which produces no output.

In *step 2*, you add to the hash table you created in the previous step and create two new AD users. This step creates no output.

With *step 3*, you create a new OU, IT, which produces no output. Next, in *step 4*, which also creates no output, you move the two previously created users into the IT OU. You use this OU to collect user and computer objects for the IT department of Reskit.Org.

Rather than creating a user (which, by default, places the new user object in the *Users* container in your AD) and later moving it to an OU, you can create a new user object directly in an OU. In *step 5*, you create a third new user directly in the IT OU, which creates no output.

In *step 6*, which generates no output, you create two additional users, which you use later in the recipe.

In *step 7*, you retrieve all the AD users and display their Name, DisplayName, and SamAccountName properties, with output like this:

```
PS C:\Foo> # 7. Viewing existing AD users
PS C:\Foo> Get-ADUser -Filter *  -Property *|
             Format-Table -Property Name, Displayname, SamAccountName

Name                 Displayname              SamAccountName
----                 -----------              --------------
Administrator                                 Administrator
Guest                                         Guest
krbtgt                                        krbtgt
UK$                                           UK$
ThomasL              Thomas Lee (IT)          ThomasL
Rebecca Tanner       Rebecca Tanner (IT)      RLT
Jerry Garcia         Jerry Garcia (IT)        JerryG
TBR1                 User to be removed       TBR1
TBR2                 User to be removed       TBR2
```

Figure 4.31: Viewing user accounts in the Reskit.Org domain

There are two broad patterns for removing a user. The first pattern (known as Get | Remove) has you find the AD user(s) you wish to remove and pipe them to the Remove-ADuser cmdlet. In *step 8*, you use this pattern to find, then remove the TBR1 user. This step produces no output.

With *step 9*, you remove a user by specifying the full distinguished name of the TBR2 user. This step also produces no output.

In *step 10*, you use Set-ADUser to update the properties of a user, such as an email address, office, and home page. This step also produces no console output. After updating the user, in *step 11*, you view details about the user, as you can see here:

```
PS C:\Foo> # 11. Viewing updated user
PS C:\Foo> Get-ADUser -Identity ThomasL -Properties * |
             Format-Table -Property DisplayName,Name,Office,
                                     OfficePhone,EmailAddress

DisplayName       Name     Office    OfficePhone EmailAddress
-----------       ----     ------    ----------- ------------
Thomas Lee (IT)   ThomasL  Cookham HQ 4416835420  ThomasL@Reskit.Org
```

Figure 4.32: Viewing user accounts in the Reskit.Org domain - part two

In *step 12*, you create a new Domain Local Group called IT Team within the IT OU. In *step 13*, you add all the users within the IT OU to this new group. These two steps produce no output.

In *step 14,* you use Get-ADGroupMember to display details of the members of the group, with output like this:

```
PS C:\Foo> # 14. Display members of the IT Team group
PS C:\Foo> Get-ADGroupMember -Identity 'IT Team' |
             Format-Table SamAccountName, DistinguishedName

SamAccountName DistinguishedName
-------------- -----------------
JerryG         CN=Jerry Garcia,OU=IT,DC=Reskit,DC=Org
RLT            CN=Rebecca Tanner,OU=IT,DC=Reskit,DC=Org
ThomasL        CN=ThomasL,OU=IT,DC=Reskit,DC=Org
```

Figure 4.33: Viewing group members

There's more...

In *step 7*, you see the users in the Reskit.Org domain. Note the user UK$. This user relates to the child domain (UK.Reskit.Org). It is not, as such, an actual user. The $ character at the end of the username indicates it's a hidden user but fundamental to supporting the child domain. Don't be tempted to tidy up and remove this user account – that would break the child domain structure.

As you see in this recipe, the cmdlets you use to add or modify a user, group, or OU create no output, which cuts down on the output you have to wade through. Some cmdlets and cmdlet sets would output details of the objects created, updated, or possibly deleted. Consider the lack of output for AD cmdlets as a feature!

Managing AD Computers

Before you can log in to a host as a domain user, such as Reskit\JerryG, that host computer must be a domain member. In AD, computer objects represent domain-joined computers that can use the domain to authenticate user login. When a domain-joined computer starts up, it contacts a domain controller to authenticate itself. The computer logs into the domain and creates a secure channel to the DC. Once Windows establishes this secure channel, Windows can log a user on. Under the covers, Windows uses the secure channel to negotiate the user logon.

In terms of managing AD, computer objects are similar to user objects, albeit with different properties. The cmdlets to manage AD computer objects are similar to those used to manage AD user accounts.

You created and configured SRV1, a workgroup computer, in the recipes in earlier chapters. In this recipe, you work with AD computers and add SRV1 to the Reskit.Org domain. For the remainder of the chapters in this book, SRV1 is a member server, so you need to add this host to the Reskit. Org domain.

Getting ready

You run this recipe on DC1, a domain controller in the Reskit.Org domain. This recipe also uses SRV1, which, as noted above, starts as a non-domain joined Windows Server 2022 host. The recipe also uses UKDC1, the child domain's DC. You have previously installed PowerShell 7 and VS Code on each host and log in as Reskit\Administrator.

How to do it...

1. Getting computers in the Reskit Domain

```
Get-ADComputer -Filter * |
    Format-Table -Property Name, DistinguishedName
```

2. Getting computers in the UK Domain

```
Get-ADComputer -Filter * -Server UKDC1.UK.Reskit.Org |
    Format-Table -Property Name, DistinguishedName
```

3. Creating a new computer in the Reskit.Org domain

```
$NCHT = @{
    Name            = 'Wolf'
    DNSHostName     = 'Wolf.Reskit.Org'
    Description     = 'One for Jerry'
    Path            = 'OU=IT,DC=Reskit,DC=Org'
}
New-ADComputer @NCHT
```

4. Creating credential object for SRV1

```
$ASRV1     = 'SRV1\Administrator'
$PSRV1     = 'Pa$$w0rd'
$PSSRV1    = ConvertTo-SecureString -String $PSRV1 -AsPlainText
-Force
$CredSRV1 = [pscredential]::New($ASRV1, $PSSRV1)
```

5. Creating a script block to join SRV1 to the Reskit domain

```
$SB = {
  $ARK    = 'Reskit\Administrator'
  $PRK    = 'Pa$$w0rd'
  $PSRK   = ConvertTo-SecureString -String $PRK -AsPlainText -Force
  $CredRK = [pscredential]::New($ARK, $PSRK)
  $DJHT = @{
    DomainName = 'Reskit.Org'
    OUPath     = 'OU=IT,DC=Reskit,DC=Org'
    Credential = $CredRK
    Restart    = $false
  }
    Add-Computer @DJHT
}
```

6. Testing to ensure SRV1 is online

```
Test-NetConnection -ComputerName SRV1
Test-NetConnection -ComputerName SRV1 -port 5985
```

7. Joining the computer to the domain

```
Set-Item -Path WSMan:\localhost\Client\TrustedHosts -Value '*'
-Force
Invoke-Command -ComputerName SRV1 -Credential $CredSRV1 -ScriptBlock
$SB
```

8. Restarting SRV1

```
Restart-Computer -ComputerName SRV1 -Credential $CredSRV1 -Force
```

9. Viewing the resulting computer accounts for Reskit.Org

```
Get-ADComputer -Filter * -Properties DNSHostName |
  Format-Table
```

How it works...

In *step 1*, you use Get-ADComputer to check the computers that you have added to the Reskit domain, with output like this:

```
PS C:\Foo> # 1. Getting computers in the Reskit Domain
PS C:\Foo> Get-ADComputer -Filter * |
             Format-Table -Property Name, DistinguishedName

Name   DistinguishedName
----   -----------------
DC1    CN=DC1,OU=Domain Controllers,DC=Reskit,DC=Org
DC2    CN=DC2,OU=Domain Controllers,DC=Reskit,DC=Org
UKDC1  CN=UKDC1,CN=Computers,DC=Reskit,DC=Org
```

Figure 4.34: Viewing computers in the Reskit domain

In *step 2*, you use Get-ADComputer to get the computer accounts in the UK.Reskit.Org domain, with output like this:

```
PS C:\Foo> # 2. Getting computers in the UR Domain
PS C:\Foo> Get-ADComputer -Filter * -Server URDC1 UK.Reskit.Org |
             Format-Table -Property Name, DistinguishedName

Name   DistinguishedName
----   -----------------
UKDC1  CN=UKDC1,OU=Domain Controllers,DC=UK,DC=Reskit,DC=Org
```

Figure 4.35: Viewing computers in the UK child domain

To demonstrate creating a compute account in AD, in *step 3*, you create a new computer object, Wolf, for the Reskit domain. This step creates no console output.

In *step 4*, you create a credential object you use in the next step. *Step 5* creates a script block you run on SRV1 to make the host a domain member. These two steps produce no console output.

In *step 6*, you use Test-NetConnection to check that SRV1 is online, and you can make a connection to the WinRM port, which produces output like this:

```
PS C:\Foo> # 6. Testing to ensure SRV1 is on line
PS C:\Foo> Test-NetConnection -ComputerName SRV1

ComputerName            : SRV1
RemoteAddress           : 10.10.1.13
InterfaceAlias          : Ethernet 2
SourceAddress           : 10.10.1.2
PingSucceeded           : True
PingReplyDetails (RTT)  : 0 ms

PS C:\Foo> Test-NetConnection -ComputerName SRV1 -port 5985

ComputerName     : SRV1
RemoteAddress    : 10.10.10.50
RemotePort       : 5985
InterfaceAlias   : Ethernet
SourceAddress    : 10.10.10.10
TcpTestSucceeded : True
```

Figure 4.36: Testing the connection to SRV2

In *step 7*, you invoke the script block ($SB) on SRV1 to join that host to the Reskit domain. This step produces no output. In *step 8*, you restart SRV1 with no console output. If you are running SRV1 as a VM and connecting to the server using tools such as VMconnect, you should see the VM reboot. After the reboot – log in as Reskit\Administrator.

In *step 9*, you use Get-ADComputer to check on the computers in the Reskit domain, which has output like this:

```
PS C:\Foo> # 9. Viewing the resulting computer accounts for Reskit.Org
PS C:\Foo> Get-ADComputer -Filter * -Properties DNSHostName |
             Format-Table

Name   DNSHostName        Enabled
----   -----------        -------
DC1    DC1.Reskit.Org        True
DC2    DC2.Reskit.Org        True
UKDC1  UKDC1.Reskit.Org     False
Wolf   Wolf.Reskit.Org       True
SRV1   SRV1.Reskit.Org       True
```

Figure 4.37: Viewing Reskit AD computer objects

There's more...

There are two broad ways of adding a Windows computer to an AD domain. The first is to log on to the computer to be added and join the domain using Add-Computer. You must have logged in with credentials that have the permissions needed to add a computer to a domain (i.e., the domain administrator).

You also need the credentials that enable you to log on to the system itself. Alternatively, you can create a computer object in AD in advance. This approach is known as pre-staging. You need administrator credentials to add the computer object to the domain, but once you have pre-staged the account, any user can join the computer to the domain.

 In *step 1* and *step 2*, you use Get-ADComputer to get the computer accounts in the Reskit and the UK (child) domain. Note that in parent domains (Reskit), you have a computer account related to the child domain (UK), and in the child domain, you can see a computer account for the parent domain. These accounts are fundamental to the operation of a multi-domain forest – do NOT touch them unless you want to experiment with domain recovery!

In *step 3*, you pre-stage the Wolf computer. A user able to log on to Wolf could then use Add-Computer (or the GUI) to add the host to the domain. In *step 4*, you add a computer to a domain using domain administrator credentials.

Adding/Removing Users Using a CSV Files

Adding users (or computers) is straightforward, as you saw in the two previous recipes. These methods are great for adding one or two users/computers, but if you have a larger number of users or computers to add, this can become long-winded.

Spiceworks (https://www.spiceworks.com/) is an excellent site for IT professionals to learn more and get their problems solved. Spiceworks has a busy PowerShell support forum, which you can access at https://community.spiceworks.com/programming/powershell. A frequently asked (and answered) question at Spiceworks is: How do I add multiple users using an input file? This recipe does just that.

You start by creating a CSV file containing details of the users you want to add. In production, you would add additional fields to the rows in the CSV and amend the recipe script to add these property values to each user you create.

This recipe uses a CSV file of users to add to AD, with a limited set of properties and values. In production, you would most likely extend the information contained in the CSV based on your business needs and the information you want to store in AD. You can extend this method to add computers to AD and to create/populate AD groups.

Getting ready

You run this recipe on DC1, a domain controller in the Reskit domain on which you have installed PowerShell 7 and VS Code. Log in to DC1 as Reskit\Administrator. You should also have DC1 and DC2 up and running.

This recipe creates and uses a CSV file. As an alternative to using *step 1* in the recipe, you can also download the CSV from this book's GitHub repository at https://github.com/doctordns/PacktPS72/blob/main/Scripts/Goodies/Users.Csv. If you download it from GitHub, make sure you store it in C:\Foo\Users.csv.

How to do it...

1. Creating a CSV file

```
$CSVData = @'
FirstName,Initials,LastName,UserPrincipalName,Alias,Description,
Password
P, D, Rowley, PDR, Peter, Data Team, Christmas42
C, F, Smith, CFS, Claire, Receptionist, Christmas42
Billy, Bob, JoeBob, BBJB, BillyBob, One of the Bobs, Christmas42
Malcolm, D, Duewrong, Malcolm, Malcolm, Mr. Danger, Christmas42
'@
$CSVData | Out-File -FilePath C:\Foo\Users.Csv
```

2. Importing and displaying the CSV

```
$Users = Import-CSV -Path C:\Foo\Users.Csv |
  Sort-Object -Property Alias
$Users | Format-Table
```

3. Adding the users using the CSV

```
$Users |
  ForEach-Object -Parallel {
    $User = $_
    # Create a hash table of properties to set on created user
    $Prop = @{}
    # Fill in values
    $Prop.GivenName       = $User.FirstName
    $Prop.Initials        = $User.Initials
```

```
        $Prop.Surname            = $User.LastName
        $Prop.UserPrincipalName = $User.UserPrincipalName + "@Reskit.
    Org"
        $Prop.Displayname        = $User.FirstName.Trim() + " " +
                                     $User.LastName.Trim()
        $Prop.Description        = $User.Description
        $Prop.Name               = $User.Alias
        $PW = ConvertTo-SecureString -AsPlainText $User.Password -Force
        $Prop.AccountPassword    = $PW
        $Prop.ChangePasswordAtLogon = $true
        $Prop.Path               = 'OU=IT,DC=Reskit,DC=ORG'
        $Prop.Enabled            = $true
        #  Now Create the User
        New-ADUser @Prop
        # Finally, Display User Created
        "Created $($Prop.Name)"
    }
```

4. Showing all users in AD (Reskit.Org)

```
Get-ADUser -Filter * -Property Description |
    Format-Table -Property Name, UserPrincipalName, Description
```

How it works...

In *step 1*, which produces no output, you create a simple CSV file, which you save to C:\Foo\
Users.CSV.

In *step 2*, you import this newly created CSV file and display the information it contains, which
looks like this:

```
PS C:\Foo> # 2. Importing and displaying the CSV
PS C:\Foo> $Users = Import-CSV -Path C:\Foo\Users.Csv |
             Sort-Object -Property Alias
PS C:\Foo> $Users | Format-Table

FirstName Initials LastName UserPrincipalName Alias    Description      Password
--------- -------- -------- ----------------- -----    -----------      --------
Billy     Bob      JoeBob   BBJB              BillyBob One of the Bobs Christmas42
C         F        Smith    CFS               Claire   Receptionist    Christmas42
Malcolm   D        Duewrong Malcolm           Malcolm  Mr. Danger      Christmas42
P         D        Rowley   PDR               Peter    Data Team       Christmas42
```

Figure 4.38: Viewing CSV contents

In *step 3*, you add each user contained in the CSV into AD. You add the users using `New-ADUser`, which itself produces no output. This step also displays additional output to show the users you added, which looks like this:

```
PS C:\Foo> # 3. Adding the users using the CSV
PS C:\Foo> $Users |
             ForEach-Object -Parallel {
               $User = $_
               # Create a hash table of properties to set on created user
               $Prop = @{}
               # Fill in values
               $Prop.GivenName          = $User.FirstName
               $Prop.Initials           = $User.Initials
               $Prop.Surname            = $User.LastName
               $Prop.UserPrincipalName = $User.UserPrincipalName + "@Reskit.Org"
               $Prop.Displayname        = $User.FirstName.Trim() + " " +
                                          $User.LastName.Trim()
               $Prop.Description        = $User.Description
               $Prop.Name               = $User.Alias
               $PW = ConvertTo-SecureString -AsPlainText $User.Password -Force
               $Prop.AccountPassword    = $PW
               $Prop.ChangePasswordAtLogon = $true
               $Prop.Path                  = 'OU=IT,DC=Reskit,DC=ORG'
               $Prop.Enabled            = $true
               # Now Create the User
               New-ADUser @Prop
               # Finally, Display User Created
               "Created $($Prop.Name)"
             }
```

```
Created BillyBob
Created Malcolm
Created Claire
Created Peter
```

Figure 4.39: Adding new users to the Reskit domain

In *step 4*, you view the AD users in the `Reskit` domain, with output like this:

```
PS C:\Foo> # 4. Showing all users in AD (Reskit.Org)
PS C:\Foo> Get-ADUser -Filter * -Property Description |
             Format-Table -Property Name, UserPrincipalName, Description
```

```
Name            UserPrincipalName   Description
----            -----------------   -----------
Administrator                       Built-in account for administering the computer/domain
Guest                               Built-in account for guest access to the computer/domain
krbtgt                              Key Distribution Center Service Account
UK$
ThomasL         thomasL@reskit.org
Rebecca Tanner  rlt@reskit.org
Jerry Garcia    jerryg@reskit.org   Virtualization Team
BillyBob        BBJB@Reskit.Org     One of the Bobs
Malcolm         Malcolm@Reskit.Org  Mr. Danger
Claire          CFS@Reskit.Org      Receptionist
Peter           PDR@Reskit.Org      Data Team
```

Figure 4.40: Adding new users to the Reskit domain

There's more...

In *step 3*, you add users based on the CSV. You add these users explicitly to the IT OU, using the parameter -Path (as specified in the $Prop hash table). In production, when adding users that could reside in different OUs, you should extend the CSV to include the distinguished name of the OU into which you wish to add each user.

Also in *step 3*, you use the Foreach-Object-Parallel command. Since it takes AD a bit of time to add each user, you can add users in parallel, thus speeding up the total time to add all the users.

Creating Group Policy Objects

In Windows AD, GPO allows you to define computer and user configuration settings that AD applies to each system/user. GPOs ensure a system remains configured per policy. Each time a domain-joined computer starts up or a domain user logs in, the local Group Policy agent on your computer obtains the group policy settings from AD and ensures they are applied. Additionally, the group policy client re-applies policies at regular intervals.

In this recipe, you start by creating a group policy object within Active Directory. You then configure the GPO, enabling computers in the IT organizational unit to use PowerShell scripts on those systems or set a specific screen saver.

You can configure thousands of settings for a user or computer through group policy. Microsoft has created a spreadsheet that lists the policy settings, which you can download from https://www.microsoft.com/en-us/download/101451. At the time of writing, the spreadsheet covers the Group Policy template files delivered with the Windows 10 May 2020 update (aka Windows 10 2004).

Once you create and configure your GPO object, you link the policy object to the OU you want to configure. You can apply a GPO to the domain, to a specific AD site, or to an OU (or child OU). You can also assign any GPO to multiple OUs, simplifying your OU design.

The configuration of a GPO typically results in Windows generating information that a host's group policy agent (the code that applies the GPO objects) can access. This information tells the agent how to work. Settings made through administrative templates use registry settings inside Registry.POL files. The group policy agent obtains the policy details from the SYSVOL share on a domain controller and applies them whenever a user logs on or off or when a computer starts up or shuts down.

The group policy module also produces nice-looking reports describing the group policy objects on your system. There are default HTML reports that give you a quick look at the GPOs on your system.

You can also get that same information as XML and create your own more customized reports.

Getting ready

You run this recipe on DC1, a domain controller in the Reskit.Org domain. You created this DC in *Installing an Active Directory forest root domain* and after creating and populating the IT OU.

How to do it...

1. Creating a new Group Policy object

```
$Pol = New-GPO -Name ITPolicy -Comment "IT GPO" -Domain Reskit.Org
```

2. Ensuring just computer settings are enabled

```
$Pol.GpoStatus = 'UserSettingsDisabled'
```

3. Configuring the policy with two registry-based settings

```
$EPHT1= @{
  Name     = 'ITPolicy'
  Key      = 'HKLM\Software\Policies\Microsoft\Windows\PowerShell'
  ValueName = 'ExecutionPolicy'
  Value    = 'Unrestricted'
  Type     = 'String'
}
Set-GPRegistryValue @EPHT1 | Out-Null
$EPHT2= @{
  Name     = 'ITPolicy'
  Key      = 'HKLM\Software\Policies\Microsoft\Windows\PowerShell'
  ValueName = 'EnableScripts'
  Type     = 'DWord'
  Value    = 1
}
Set-GPRegistryValue @EPHT2 | Out-Null
```

4. Creating a screen saver GPO

```
$Pol2 = New-GPO -Name 'Screen Saver Time Out'
$Pol2.GpoStatus   = 'ComputerSettingsDisabled'
$Pol2.Description = '15 minute timeout'
```

5. Setting a Group Policy enforced registry value

```
$EPHT3= @{
  Name     = 'Screen Saver Time Out'
  Key      = 'HKCU\Software\Policies\Microsoft\Windows\'+
              'Control Panel\Desktop'
  ValueName = 'ScreenSaveTimeOut'
  Value    = 900
  Type     = 'DWord'
}
Set-GPRegistryValue @EPHT3 | Out-Null
```

6. Linking both GPOs to the IT OU

```
$GPLHT1 = @{
  Name     = 'ITPolicy'
  Target   = 'OU=IT,DC=Reskit,DC=org'
}
New-GPLink @GPLHT1 | Out-Null
$GPLHT2 = @{
  Name     = 'Screen Saver Time Out'
  Target   = 'OU=IT,DC=Reskit,DC=org'
}
New-GPLink @GPLHT2 | Out-Null
```

7. Displaying the GPOs in the domain

```
Get-GPO -All -Domain Reskit.Org |
  Sort-Object -Property DisplayName |
    Format-Table -Property Displayname, Description, GpoStatus
```

8. Creating and viewing a GPO Report

```
$RPath = 'C:\Foo\GPOReport1.HTML'
Get-GPOReport -All -ReportType Html -Path $RPath
Invoke-Item -Path $RPath
```

9. Getting report in XML format

```
$RPath2 = 'C:\Foo\GPOReport2.XML'
Get-GPOReport -All -ReportType XML -Path $RPath2
$XML = [xml] (Get-Content -Path $RPath2)
```

10. Create a simple GPO report

```
$RPath2 = 'C:\Foo\GPOReport2.XML'
$FMTS = "{0,-33}  {1,-30} {2,-10} {3}"
$FMTS -f 'Name','Linked To', 'Enabled', 'No Override'
$FMTS -f '----','---------', '-------', '-----------'
$XML.report.GPO |
  Sort-Object -Property Name |
    ForEach-Object {
      $Gname = $_.Name
      $SOM = $_.linksto.SomPath
      $ENA = $_.linksto.enabled
      $NOO = $_.linksto.nooverride
      $FMTS -f $Gname, $SOM, $ENA, $NOO
    }
```

How it works...

Like many AD-related cmdlets, the cmdlets you use to manage Group Policy objects do not produce much output.

In *step 1*, you create a new GPO in the Reskit.Org domain. This step creates an empty GPO in the domain that is not yet linked to any OU and thus does not apply to any computer or user.

In *step 2*, you disable user settings, which allows the GPO client to ignore any user settings. Doing so can make the client's GPO processing a bit faster.

In *step 3*, you set this GPO to have two specific registry-based values. When a computer starts up, the GPO processing on that client computer ensures that these two registry values are set on the client. During Group Policy refresh (which happens approximately every 2 hours), the group policy agent enforces the value contained in the policy.

In *step 4* and *step 5*, you create a new GPO and set a screen saver timeout of 900 seconds.

In *step 6*, you link the two GPOs to the IT Organizational unit. GPO processing ignores the GPO until you link the GPOs to an OU (or to the domain or a domain site).

In this recipe, *step 1* through *step 6* produces no output.

In *step 7*, you use Get-GPO to get and display the details of the GPOs in the domain, which looks like this:

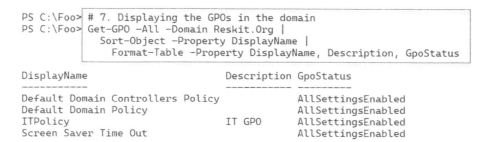

```
PS C:\Foo> # 7. Displaying the GPOs in the domain
PS C:\Foo> Get-GPO -All -Domain Reskit.Org |
              Sort-Object -Property DisplayName |
                Format-Table -Property DisplayName, Description, GpoStatus
```

```
DisplayName                        Description GpoStatus
-----------                        ----------- ---------
Default Domain Controllers Policy              AllSettingsEnabled
Default Domain Policy                          AllSettingsEnabled
ITPolicy                           IT GPO      AllSettingsEnabled
Screen Saver Time Out                          AllSettingsEnabled
```

Figure 4.41: Adding new users to the Reskit domain - part two

In *step 8*, you use the Get-GPOReport cmdlet to generate an HTML report on policy objects in the domain. This step displays the results, creating a nicely formatted report, which looks like this:

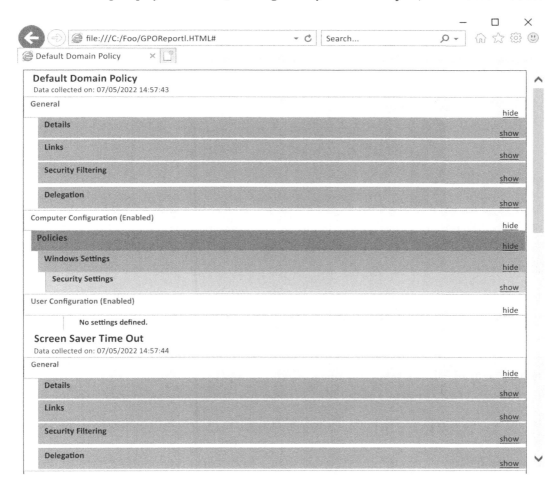

Figure 4.42: Viewing a GPO report

In *step 9*, you use the `Get-GPOReport` cmdlet to get information about the GPOs on your system and return this information as XML. This step produces no console output.

Then, in *step 10*, you use PowerShell to produce a nicely formatted report customized for your needs, which looks like this:

```
PS C:\Foo> # 10. Creating simple GPO report
PS C:\Foo> $RPath2 = 'C:\Foo\GPOReport2.XML'
PS C:\Foo> $FMTS = "{0,-33}  {1,-30} {2,-10} {3}"
PS C:\Foo> $FMTS -f 'Name','Linked To', 'Enabled', 'No Override'
PS C:\Foo> $FMTS -f '----','---------', '-------', '-----------'
PS C:\Foo> $XML.report.GPO |
             Sort-Object -Property Name |
               ForEach-Object {
                 $Gname = $_.Name
                 $SOM = $_.linksto.SomPath
                 $ENA = $_.linksto.enabled
                 $NOO = $_.linksto.nooverride
                 $FMTS -f $Gname, $SOM, $ENA, $NOO
             }
```

```
Name                              Linked To                          Enabled    No Override
----                              ---------                          -------    -----------
Default Domain Controllers Policy Reskit.Org/Domain Controllers      true       false
Default Domain Policy             Reskit.Org                         true       false
ITPolicy                          Reskit.Org/IT                      true       false
Screen Saver Time Out             Reskit.Org/IT                      true       false
```

Figure 4.43: Creating a customized GPO report

There's more...

In *step 8*, you see the output from the `Get-GPOReport` cmdlet from Internet Explorer. At the time of writing, the Edge browser does not render the output as nicely as you might want. What may look like a bug in the graphic is just how Edge (again at the time of writing) renders this HTML document.

In *step 9*, you use the `Get-GPOReport` command to obtain a report of all GPOs in the domain returned as XML. The XML returned contains details of the GPO links as a property which includes many sub-properties. To create nice-looking output, you create a format string you use to display each row of your report, including report header lines. You first use this format string to make the two report header lines for the report. In practice, you might need to adjust the composite formatting strings (`$FMTS`) to ensure the widths of each column are appropriate for your environment.

In *step 10*, you report on the GPOs in the `Reskit` domain using .NET composite string formatting using the `-f` operator. Using .NET composite formatting enables you to create nice-looking customized output when the objects returned by a cmdlet are not in a form to be used directly with `Format-Table`.

The Format-Table and Format-List cmdlets are of the most use when each object has simple properties. When an object has properties that are objects which also have properties, the format commands do not surface these (sub) properties. In this case, you must obtain the details manually of the GPO links for each GPO and generate your report lines based on those results. While the report layout works well for this specific set of GPOs, should you have GPOs with longer names, or linked to deeper organizational units, you may need to adjust the format string you set in *step 10*.

Reporting on AD Users

Monitoring Active Directory is a necessary, albeit time-consuming, task. With larger numbers of users and computers to manage, you need all the help you can get, and PowerShell makes it easy to keep track of things.

If a user has not logged on for a reasonable period, the account could be a security risk. Likewise, a user with membership in a privileged account (for example, Enterprise Admins) could be used by an attacker. IT professionals know how easy it is to put someone in a high privilege group rather than set up more fine-grained permissions using something like Just Enough Administration (see *Implementing JEA* in *Chapter 8*).

Regular reporting can help focus on accounts that could be usefully deactivated, removed from a security group, or possibly removed altogether.

In this recipe, you obtain all the accounts in AD and examine potential security risks.

Getting ready

After running the recipes in this chapter, you run this recipe on DC1, a DC in the Reskit.Org domain. You should also have installed PowerShell 7 and VS Code on this host.

How to do it...

1. Defining a function Get-ReskitUser to return objects related to users in the Reskit.Org domain

```
Function Get-ReskitUser {
# Get PDC Emulator DC
$PrimaryDC = Get-ADDomainController -Discover -Service PrimaryDC
# Get Users
$ADUsers = Get-ADUser -Filter * -Properties * -Server $PrimaryDC
# Iterate through them and create $Userinfo hash table:
Foreach ($ADUser in $ADUsers) {
```

```
      # Create a userinfo HT
      $UserInfo = [Ordered] @{}
      $UserInfo.SamAccountname = $ADUser.SamAccountName
      $UserInfo.DisplayName    = $ADUser.DisplayName
      $UserInfo.Office         = $ADUser.Office
      $UserInfo.Enabled        = $ADUser.Enabled
      $UserInfo.LastLogonDate  = $ADUser.LastLogonDate
      $UserInfo.ProfilePath    = $ADUser.ProfilePath
      $UserInfo.ScriptPath     = $ADUser.ScriptPath
      $UserInfo.BadPWDCount     = $ADUser.badPwdCount
      New-Object -TypeName PSObject -Property $UserInfo
      }
    } # end of function
```

2. Getting the users

```
    $RKUsers = Get-ReskitUser
```

3. Building the report header

```
    $RKReport = ''   # first line of the report
    $RkReport += "*** Reskit.Org AD Report'n"
    $RKReport += "*** Generated [$(Get-Date)]'n"
    $RKReport += "********************************'n'n"
```

4. Reporting on disabled users

```
    $RkReport += "*** Disabled Users'n"
    $RKReport += $RKUsers |
        Where-Object {$_.Enabled -NE $true} |
            Format-Table -Property SamAccountName, Displayname |
                Out-String
```

5. Reporting on users who have not recently logged on

```
    $OneWeekAgo = (Get-Date).AddDays(-7)
    $RKReport += "'n*** Users Not logged in since $OneWeekAgo'n"
    $RkReport += $RKUsers |
        Where-Object {$_.Enabled -and $_.LastLogonDate -le $OneWeekAgo}
    |
            Sort-Object -Property LastlogonDate |
```

```
            Format-Table -Property SamAccountName,lastlogondate |
                Out-String
```

6. Discovering users with a high number of invalid password attempts

```
$RKReport += "'n*** High Number of Bad Password Attempts'n"
$RKReport += $RKUsers | Where-Object BadPwdCount -ge 5 |
    Format-Table -Property SamAccountName, BadPwdCount |
        Out-String
```

7. Adding another report header line for this part of the report and creating an empty array of privileged users

```
$RKReport += "'n*** Privileged  User Report'n"
$PUsers = @()
```

8. Querying the Enterprise Admins/Domain Admins/Scheme Admins groups for members and adding them to the $Pusers array

```
# Get Enterprise Admins group members
$Members = Get-ADGroupMember -Identity 'Enterprise Admins'
-Recursive |
    Sort-Object -Property Name
$PUsers += foreach ($Member in $Members) {
    Get-ADUser -Identity $Member.SID -Properties * |
        Select-Object -Property Name,
                @{Name='Group';expression={'Enterprise Admins'}},
                whenCreated,LastLogonDate
}
# Get Domain Admins group members
$Members =
  Get-ADGroupMember -Identity 'Domain Admins' -Recursive |
    Sort-Object -Property Name
$PUsers += Foreach ($Member in $Members)
    {Get-ADUser -Identity $member.SID -Properties * |
        Select-Object -Property Name,
                @{Name='Group';expression={'Domain Admins'}},
                WhenCreated, Lastlogondate,SamAccountName
}
# Get Schema Admins members
```

```
$Members =
  Get-ADGroupMember -Identity 'Schema Admins' -Recursive |
    Sort-Object Name
$PUsers += Foreach ($Member in $Members) {
    Get-ADUser -Identity $member.SID -Properties * |
        Select-Object -Property Name,
            @{Name='Group';expression={'Schema Admins'}},
            WhenCreated, LastLogonDate,SamAccountName
}
```

9. Adding the special users to the report

```
$RKReport += $PUsers | Out-String
```

10. Displaying the final report

```
$RKReport
```

How it works...

All the steps except the last one produce no output in this recipe. The first steps create a report, which you view in the final step.

In *step 1*, you create a function, Get-ReskitUser, which creates a set of user objects related to each user in your AD. In *step 2*, you use the function to populate an array, $RKUsers, containing users and necessary details for your report.

In *step 3*, you build the header for the report, and then in *step 4*, you build a report section on disabled users, adding details of disabled user accounts. In *step 5*, you add details of users that have not logged on within the last seven days. In *step 6*, you add details of users who have had more than five unsuccessful login attempts.

The final section of the report lists members of crucial AD groups. With *step 7,* you create a header for this section. Then, with *step 8* and *step 9*, you add details of members of these groups.

Once these steps are complete, in step *10*, you can view the output of the report, which looks like this:

```
PS C:\Foo> # 10. Displaying the final report
PS C:\Foo> $RKReport
*** Reskit.Org AD Report
*** Generated [05/07/2022 21:51:09]
*******************************

*** Disabled Users

SamAccountName DisplayName
-------------- -----------
Guest
krbtgt

*** Users Not logged in since 04/30/2022 21:51:09

SamAccountName LastLogonDate
-------------- -------------
UK$
RLT
JerryG
BillyBob
Claire
Peter

*** High Number of Bad Password Attempts

SamAccountName BadPWDCount
-------------- -----------
ThomasL                  7
Malcolm                  9

*** Privileged  User Report

Name          Group            whenCreated         LastLogonDate
----          -----            -----------         -------------
Administrator Enterprise Admins 03/05/2022 13:51:52 03/05/2022 13:58:10
Malcolm       Enterprise Admins 06/05/2022 16:00:42 06/05/2022 16:22:42
ThomasL       Enterprise Admins 06/05/2022 17:23:46 07/05/2022 18:01:48
Administrator Domain Admins     03/05/2022 13:51:52 03/05/2022 13:58:10
ThomasL       Domain Admins     06/05/2022 17:23:46 07/05/2022 18:01:48
Administrator Schema Admins     03/05/2022 13:51:52 03/05/2022 13:58:10
```

Figure 4.44: Viewing the final Users report

There's more...

In *step 1*, you create a function to retrieve users. This function allows you to reformat the properties as needed, improving the output in your report.

In *step 3* through *step 9*, you build the report contents by adding to a variable holding the report. These steps show you how to create highly customized reports for your domain.

In *step 10*, you see the final report. Note that the users Malcolm and ThomasL have a high number of failed login attempts but logged in at some point successfully. If you log in using a domain account and an incorrect password, AD rejects the login and increases the bad attempt count. However, AD zeros the bad logon count once you log in successfully. You might also ask why both those users are members of the Enterprise Admins group!

In this recipe, you use simple arrays or strings to create parts of and the entire report. These objects are of the type System.Array. This type of array in PowerShell has some performance issues if you add a large number of items to an array. A more performant approach would be to use the System.Collections.ArrayList object but that would mean the steps changing to use the .ADD method and be more complex code. For this particular case, the performance implications are not significant. Should the reports start to increase in size (e.g. thousands of lines), you might wish to make the change. For more details on the array list, see https://pipe.how/new-arraylist/.

Reporting on AD Computers

Monitoring AD user accounts is an important task, and as you saw in *Reporting on AD Users*, you can automate monitoring with PowerShell. Monitoring computer accounts can also be useful. And with larger numbers of computers to manage, you need all the help you can get.

A computer that has not logged on for an extended period could represent a security risk or could be a lost/stolen computer. It could also be a system you have not rebooted after applying patches and updates.

This recipe creates a report of computers that have not logged on or that you have not rebooted for a while.

One challenge in developing scripts like this is creating meaningful test data. If you wish to generate a test report showing a system that has not logged on for over 6 months, you might have to wait for 6 months to get the necessary data. This recipe offers a way around that, if only for testing purposes.

Getting ready

You run this recipe on SRV1 after you have installed PowerShell 7. You should also have DC1, a domain controller in the domain, up and running.

How to do it...

1. Creating example computer accounts in the AD

```
$NCHT1 = @{
    Name        = 'NLIComputer1_1week'
    Description = 'Computer last logged in 1 week ago'
}
New-ADComputer @NCHT1
$NCHT2 = @{
  Name        = 'NLIComputer2_1month'
  Description = 'Computer last logged in 1 week ago'
}
New-ADComputer @NCHT2
$NCHT3 = @{
  Name        = 'NLIComputer3_6month'
  Description = 'Computer last logged in 1 week ago'
}
New-ADComputer @NCHT3
```

2. Creating some constants for later comparison

```
$OneWeekAgo   = (Get-Date).AddDays(-7)
$OneMonthAgo  = (Get-Date).AddMonths(-1)
$SixMonthsAgo = (Get-Date).AddMonths(-6)
```

3. Defining a function to create sample data

```
Function Get-RKComputers {
$ADComputers = Get-ADComputer -Filter * -Properties LastLogonDate
$Computers = @()
foreach ($ADComputer in $ADComputers) {
  $Name = $ADComputer.Name
  # Real computers and last logon date
  if ($adComputer.name -NotMatch "^NLI") {
    $LLD = $ADComputer.LastLogonDate
  }
  Elseif ($ADComputer.Name -eq "NLIComputer1_1week")  {
    $LLD = $OneWeekAgo.AddMinutes(-30)
  }
```

```
  Elseif ($ADComputer.Name -eq "NLIComputer2_1month")  {
    $LLD = $OneMonthAgo.AddMinutes(-30)
  }
  Elseif ($ADComputer.Name -eq "NLIComputer3_6month")  {
    $LLD = $SixMonthsAgo.AddMinutes(-30)
  }
  $Computers += [pscustomobject] @{
    Name = $Name
    LastLogonDate = $LLD
  }
}
$Computers
}
```

4. Building the report header

```
$RKReport = ''              # Start of report
$RKReport += "*** Reskit.Org AD Daily AD Computer Report'n"
$RKReport += "*** Generated [$(Get-Date)]'n"
$RKReport += "***********************************'n'n"
```

5. Getting Computers in RK AD using Get-RKComputers

```
$Computers = Get-RKComputers
```

6. Getting computers that have never logged on

```
$RKReport += "Computers that have never logged on'n"
$RkReport += "Name                   LastLogonDate'n"
$RkReport += "----                   -------------'n"
$RKReport += Foreach($Computer in $Computers) {
  If ($null -eq $Computer.LastLogonDate) {
   "{0,-22}  {1}  'n" -f $Computer.Name, "Never"
  }
}
```

7. Reporting on computers who have not logged on in over 6 months

```
$RKReport += "'nComputers that have not logged in over 6 months'n"
$RkReport += "Name                   LastLogonDate'n"
$RkReport += "----                   -------------'n"
```

```
$RKReport +=
foreach($Computer in $Computers) {
  If (($Computer.LastLogonDate -lt $SixMonthsAgo) -and
      ($null -ne $Computer.LastLogonDate)) {
("'n{0,-23}  {1}  'n" -f $Computer.Name, $Computer.LastLogonDate)
  }
}
```

8. Reporting on computer accounts that have not logged for 1-6 months

```
$RKReport += "'n'nComputers that have not logged in 1-6 months'n"
$RkReport += "Name                       LastLogonDate'n"
$RkReport += "----                       -------------"
$RKReport +=
foreach($Computer in $Computers) {
  If (($Computer.LastLogonDate -ge $SixMonthsAgo) -and
      ($Computer.LastLogonDate -lt $OneMonthAgo) -and
        ($null -ne $Computer.LastLogonDate)) {
   "'n{0,-22}  {1}  " -f $Computer.Name, $Computer.LastLogonDate
  }
}
```

9. Reporting on computer accounts that have not logged in the past 1 week to one month ago

```
$RKReport += "'n'nComputers that have between one week "
$RKReport += "and one month ago'n"
$RkReport += "Name                       LastLogonDate'n"
$RkReport += "----                       -------------"
$RKReport +=
foreach($Computer in $Computers) {
  If (($Computer.LastLogonDate -ge $OneMonthAgo) -and
      ($Computer.LastLogonDate -lt $OneWeekAgo) -and
        ($null -ne $Computer.LastLogonDate)) {
   "'n{0,-22}  {1}  " -f $Computer.Name, $Computer.LastLogonDate
  }
}
```

10. Displaying the report

```
$RKReport
```

How it works...

In this recipe, all but the final step produce no output. Some of the steps exist to enable you to test the report that this recipe generates. Some of these steps might not be necessary for real life, as you already have enough real-life data to create a complete report.

In *step 1*, you create three AD computer accounts. You use these accounts to simulate computers that have not logged on for a while, thus enabling you to view a complete report. If you re-run this recipe or this step, adding these accounts produces errors since the accounts already exist. You could modify this step to check to see if the accounts exist before creating them.

In *step 2*, you create three time constants, representing the time 7 days ago, 1 month ago, and 6 months ago. This step lets you test if a given user account has not longed on in that period.

In *step 3*, you create a new function, Get-RKComputers. This function returns a list of all the computer accounts in AD along with their last logon time.

In *step 4*, you begin the report by creating a report header.

In *step 5*, you call the Get-RKComputers function and populate the $Computers array (all the computers available).

In *step 6* through *step 9*, you add details to the report of computers who have never logged on, have not logged on for over 6 months, have not logged on in 1-6 months, and computers that have not logged on in 1 week-1 month.

In the final step, *step 10*, you display the report created by the earlier steps. The output of this step looks like this:

```
PS C:\Foo> # 10. Displaying the report
PS C:\Foo> $RKReport
*** Reskit.Org AD Daily AD Computer Report
*** Generated [05/08/2022 21:31:52]
***********************************

Computers that have never logged on
Name                    LastLogonDate
----                    -------------
Wolf                    Never

Computers that have not logged in over 6 months
Name                    LastLogonDate
----                    -------------

NLIComputer3_6month      08/11/2021 21:00:04


Computers that have not logged in 1-6 months
Name                    LastLogonDate
----                    -------------
NLIComputer2_1month     08/04/2022 21:00:04

Computers that have between one week and one month ago
Name                    LastLogonDate
----                    -------------
NLIComputer1_1week      01/05/2022 21:00:04
```

Figure 4.45: Viewing the final computer report

There's more...

In *step 3*, you create a function to get the computer accounts in AD. This function returns an array of computer names and the last login date and includes values for the three test computer accounts' previous logon dates. In production, you might amend this function to return computer accounts from just certain OUs. You could also extend this function to test whether each computer is online by testing a network connection or checking to see if there is a DNS A record for the computer to detect stale computer accounts.

In *step 5* through *step 9*, you create a report by adding text lines to the $RKReport variable. You need to add CRLF characters before or after each line of text when you add each line to the report. Ensuring each report line begins in the right place can be challenging in creating reports using the technique shown by this recipe.

Managing AD Replication

Active Directory uses a special database to support its operations. The database is a distributed, multi-master database with convergence – every DC in every domain stores this database in the file C:\Windows\NTDS\ntds.dit.

Every DC in any domain holds a complete copy of this database. If you add a new user or change a user's office, that change occurs on just one DC (initially). AD replication makes the change in all database copies. In this way, the database remains consistent over time and across all DCs.

AD replication is based on partitions – a slice of the overall database. AD can replicate each partition separately. There are several partitions in AD:

- **Schema partition** – This holds the AD schema that defines each object that AD stores in the database. The schema also defines the properties of all these objects.

- **Configuration partition** – This holds the details of the structure of the domain.

- **Domain partition** – This partition, also known as the domain naming context, contains the objects relating to a domain (users, groups, OUs, etc.). The objects in this partition are defined based on the schema.

- **Application partition** – Some applications, such as DNS, store objects in your AD and rely on AD replication to replicate the values.

There are two types of replication: intra-site replication and inter-site replication. Intra-site replication happens between DCs in a given AD site, while inter-site replication occurs between different AD sites.

You can create different topologies for replication, including:

- **Ring** – Each DC in a site has at least two inbound replication partners. When any change is made to any DC, that DC notifies its replication partners that it has a change. Those DCs can then replicate that change (if they have not seen it before). AD by default ensures there are not more than three hops within the replication topology. If you have a large number of DCs (more than 7), AD automatically creates additional replication links to keep the hop count below 3.

- **Full mesh** – With this topology, all DCs replicate to all other DCs. Full mesh replication keeps the database in sync with a minimum replication delay, but can be more expensive in terms of bandwidth (and DC utilization). It is not scalable.

- **Hub and spoke** – You might use this approach in enormous organizations where a "spoke" DC replicates with a central hub DC. The hub DC then replicates the change to all other spoke DCs in your organization. Hub and spoke can reduce replication for widely dispersed implementations.

- **Hybrid** – Here, you can combine any of these based on business needs.

By default, AD replication uses a ring topology. If your business needs dictate, you can adopt different topologies requiring additional configuration.

In most smaller organizations (such as `Reskit.Org`), replication is set up and operates automagically. But for large and distributed organizations, replication can be quite complicated as you attempt to balance being totally up to date against the cost of geographical bandwidth. If you have DCs on several continents, you want to collect those changes and make them simultaneously, say every 4 hours. But that means the remote DC would have out-of-date information for a period. As a general rule of thumb, you should design replication to happen faster than a person can fly between your AD sites served by a DC. If you change your password, say in London, then as long as the changes occur within 16 hours when you fly to Brisbane, Australia, the Australian DCs contain the replicated password. Thus, you can log in with the new password immediately upon landing in Brisbane.

For more information on AD replication concepts, see `https://learn.microsoft.com/windows-server/identity/ad-ds/get-started/replication/active-directory-replication-concepts`.

For any sizeable organization, the design and planning of AD is vital – see `https://docs.microsoft.com/windows-server/identity/ad-ds/plan/ad-ds-design-and-planning` for more information on the planning and design work necessary.

Traditionally, you use many Win32 console applications to manage and troubleshoot replication, including `repadmin.exe`, which broadly replaces an earlier command, `replmon.exe`. See the following for details on the `repadmin.exe` command (and replication): `https://techcommunity.microsoft.com/t5/ask-the-directory-services-team/getting-over-replmon/ba-p/396687`.

With the advent of PowerShell and the PowerShell Active Directory module, you can now perform many of the functions of `repadmin.exe` using PowerShell cmdlets.

In this recipe, you examine replication details and see it in action.

Getting ready

You run this recipe on DC1, a domain controller in the Reskit.Org domain. You should also have DC2 and UKDC1 available and online at the start of testing this recipe. You must have installed PowerShell 7 and VS Code on all these hosts.

How to do it...

1. Checking replication partners for DC1

```
Get-ADReplicationPartnerMetadata -Target DC1.Reskit.Org     |
    Format-List -Property Server, PartnerType, Partner,
                         Partition, LastRep*
```

2. Checking AD replication partner metadata in the domain

```
Get-ADReplicationPartnerMetadata -Target Reskit.Org -Scope Domain |
    Format-Table -Property Server, P*Type, Last*
```

3. Investigating group membership metadata

```
$REPLHT = @{
  Object              = (Get-ADGroup -Identity 'IT Team')
  Attribute           = 'Member'
  ShowAllLinkedValues = $true
  Server              = (Get-ADDomainController)
}
Get-ADReplicationAttributeMetadata @REPLHT |
    Format-Table -Property A*NAME, A*VALUE, *TIME
```

4. Adding two users to the group and removing one

```
Add-ADGroupMember -Identity 'IT Team' -members Malcolm
Add-ADGroupMember -Identity 'IT Team' -members Claire
Remove-ADGroupMember -Identity 'IT Team' -members Claire
-Confirm:$False
```

5. Checking updated metadata

```
# From DC1
Get-ADReplicationAttributeMetadata @REPLHT |
  Format-Table -Property A*NAME,A*VALUE, *TIME
# From DC2
Get-ADReplicationAttributeMetadata -Server DC2 @REPLHT |
  Format-Table -Property A*NAME,A*VALUE, *TIME
```

6. Make a change to a user

```
$User = 'Malcolm'
Get-ADUser -Identity $User |
  Set-ADUser -Office 'Marin Office'
```

7. Checking updated metadata

```
$O = Get-ADUser -Identity $User
# From DC1
Get-ADReplicationAttributeMetadata -Object $O -Server DC1 |
  Where-Object AttributeName -match 'Office'
# From DC2
Get-ADReplicationAttributeMetadata -Object $O -Server DC2 |
  Where-Object AttributeName -match 'Office'
```

8. Examine Replication partners for both DC1, UKDC1

```
Get-ADReplicationConnection |
  Format-List -Property Name,ReplicateFromDirectoryServer
Get-ADReplicationConnection -Server UKDC1 |
  Format-List -Property Name,ReplicateFromDirectoryServer
```

9. Use repadmin to check the replication summary

```
repadmin /replsummary
```

How it works...

In *step 1*, you check to discover replication partners for DC1. With only two DCs in the Reskit domain (DC1 and DC2), the output of this step looks like this:

```
PS C:\Foo> # 1. Checking replication partners for DC1
PS C:\Foo> Get-ADReplicationPartnerMetadata -Target DC1.Reskit.Org   |
              Format-List -Property Server, PartnerType, Partner,
                             Partition, LastRep*

Server                : DC1.Reskit.Org
PartnerType           : Inbound
Partner               : CN=NTDS
                        Settings,CN=DC2,CN=Servers,CN=Default-First-Site-Name,CN=Sites,CN=Configuration,DC=Reskit,DC=Org
Partition             : DC=Reskit,DC=Org
LastReplicationAttempt : 08/05/2022 23:47:46
LastReplicationResult  : 0
LastReplicationSuccess : 08/05/2022 23:47:46
```

Figure 4.46: Viewing DC1 replication partners (for the Reskit.Org domain)

In *step 2*, you get the AD replication partner metadata in the Reskit domain, with output like this:

```
PS C:\Foo> # 2. Checking AD replication partner metadata in the domain
PS C:\Foo> Get-ADReplicationPartnerMetadata -Target Reskit.Org -Scope Domain |
              Format-Table -Property Server, P*Type, Last*

Server          PartnerType LastChangeUsn LastReplicationAttempt LastReplicationResult LastReplicationSuccess
------          ----------- ------------- ---------------------- --------------------- ----------------------
DC1.Reskit.Org  Inbound     29228 08/05/2022 23:47:46                               0 08/05/2022 23:47:46
DC2.Reskit.Org  Inbound     20987 08/05/2022 23:48:24                            1722 08/05/2022 20:25:4
```

Figure 4.47: Viewing DC1 replication metadata

In *step 3*, you view the AD replication metadata for the group membership for a group (IT Team), with output like this:

```
PS C:\Foo> # 3. Investigating group membership metadata
PS C:\Foo> $REPLHT = @{
              Object              = (Get-ADGroup -Identity 'IT Team')
              Attribute           = 'Member'
              ShowAllLinkedValues = $true
              Server              = (Get-ADDomainController)
           }
PS C:\Foo> Get-ADReplicationAttributeMetadata @REPLHT |
              Format-Table -Property A*NAME, A*VALUE, *TIME

AttributeName AttributeValue                              FirstOriginatingCreateTime LastOriginatingChangeTime LastOriginatingDeleteTime
------------- --------------                              -------------------------- ------------------------- -------------------------
member        CN=Jerry Garcia,OU=IT,DC=Reskit,DC=Org      06/05/2022 17:28:42        06/05/2022 17:28:42       01/01/1601 00:00:00
member        CN=Rebecca Tanner,OU=IT,DC=Reskit,DC=Org    06/05/2022 17:28:42        06/05/2022 17:28:42       01/01/1601 00:00:00
member        CN=ThomasL,OU=IT,DC=Reskit,DC=Org           06/05/2022 17:28:42        06/05/2022 17:28:42       01/01/1601 00:00:00
```

Figure 4.48: Viewing group membership metadata

In *step 4*, you add two users to a group, then remove one, creating no console output. In *step 5*, you look again at the group metadata, which reflects the change to group status, as you can see here:

```
PS C:\Foo> # 5 Checking updated metadata
PS C:\Foo> Get-ADReplicationAttributeMetadata @REPLHT |
             Format-Table -Property A*NAME,A*VALUE, *TIME


AttributeName  AttributeValue                              FirstOriginatingCreateTime  LastOriginatingChangeTime  LastOriginatingDeleteTime
-------------  --------------                              --------------------------  -------------------------  -------------------------
member         CN=Claire,OU=IT,DC=Reskit,DC=Org            08/05/2022 23:52:38         09/05/2022 00:25:01        09/05/2022 00:25:01
member         CN=Malcolm,OU=IT,DC=Reskit,DC=Org           08/05/2022 23:52:38         09/05/2022 00:25:01        01/01/1601 00:00:00
member         CN=Jerry Garcia,OU=IT,DC=Reskit,DC=Org      06/05/2022 17:28:42         06/05/2022 17:28:42        01/01/1601 00:00:00
member         CN=Rebecca Tanner,OU=IT,DC=Reskit,DC=Org    06/05/2022 17:28:42         06/05/2022 17:28:42        01/01/1601 00:00:00
member         CN=ThomasL,OU=IT,DC=Reskit,DC=Org           06/05/2022 17:28:42         06/05/2022 17:28:42        01/01/1601 00:00:00
```

Figure 4.49: Viewing group membership metadata after group changes

In *step 6*, you update the details of a given user, generating no output. In *step 7*, you check the replication metadata for this user to see what was changed. You view the replication data from both DC1 and DC2 with output that looks like this:

```
PS C:\Foo> # 7. Checking updated metadata
PS C:\Foo> $O = Get-ADUser -Identity $User
PS C:\Foo> # From DC1
PS C:\Foo> Get-ADReplicationAttributeMetadata -Object $O -Server DC1 |
             Where-Object AttributeName -match 'Office'

AttributeName                                   : physicalDeliveryOfficeName
AttributeValue                                  : Marin Office
FirstOriginatingCreateTime                      :
IsLinkValue                                     : False
LastOriginatingChangeDirectoryServerIdentity    : CN=NTDS Settings,CN=DC1,CN=Servers,CN=Default-First-Site-Name,CN=Sites,CN=Configur
                                                  ation,DC=Reskit,DC=Org
LastOriginatingChangeDirectoryServerInvocationId : d5f95fc9-5fad-4290-a08f-4dff5b62bfbf
LastOriginatingChangeTime                       : 09/05/2022 11:39:48
LastOriginatingChangeUsn                        : 23224
LastOriginatingDeleteTime                       :
LocalChangeUsn                                  : 23224
Object                                          : CN=Malcolm,OU=IT,DC=Reskit,DC=Org
Server                                          : DC1.Reskit.Org
Version                                         : 3


PS C:\Foo> # From DC2
PS C:\Foo> Get-ADReplicationAttributeMetadata -Object $O -Server DC2 |
             Where-Object AttributeName -match 'Office'

AttributeName                                   : physicalDeliveryOfficeName
AttributeValue                                  : Marin Office
FirstOriginatingCreateTime                      :
IsLinkValue                                     : False
LastOriginatingChangeDirectoryServerIdentity    : CN=NTDS Settings,CN=DC1,CN=Servers,CN=Default-First-Site-Name,CN=Sites,CN=Configur
                                                  ation,DC=Reskit,DC=Org
LastOriginatingChangeDirectoryServerInvocationId : d5f95fc9-5fad-4290-a08f-4dff5b62bfbf
LastOriginatingChangeTime                       : 09/05/2022 11:39:48
LastOriginatingChangeUsn                        : 23224
LastOriginatingDeleteTime                       :
LocalChangeUsn                                  : 34015
Object                                          : CN=Malcolm,OU=IT,DC=Reskit,DC=Org
Server                                          : DC2.Reskit.Org
```

Figure 4.50: Viewing user change details

In *step 8*, you view the details of replication partners for both DC1 and the child DC, UKDC1, with output like this:

```
PS C:\Foo> # 8. Examine Replication partners for both DC1, UKDC1
PS C:\Foo> Get-ADReplicationConnection |
           Format-List -Property Name,ReplicateFromDirectoryServer

Name                      : bae320e1-f2af-4530-aac5-647ced3129a4
ReplicateFromDirectoryServer : CN=NTDS
                            Settings,CN=DC2,CN=Servers,CN=Default-First-Site-Name,CN=Sites,CN=Configuration,DC=Reskit,DC=Org

Name                      : c70c8749-56db-4990-93f6-db482e6be3b9
ReplicateFromDirectoryServer : CN=NTDS
                            Settings,CN=UKDC1,CN=Servers,CN=Default-First-Site-Name,CN=Sites,CN=Configuration,DC=Reskit,DC=Org


PS C:\Foo> Get-ADReplicationConnection -Server UKDC1 |
>>    Format-List -Property Name,ReplicateFromDirectoryServer

Name                      : 9c16d02c-8297-4b8a-89e9-fc63b7bccde1
ReplicateFromDirectoryServer : CN=NTDS
                            Settings,CN=DC1,CN=Servers,CN=Default-First-Site-Name,CN=Sites,CN=Configuration,DC=Reskit,DC=Org

Name                      : 05c0c646-9b40-4bcf-bb59-f3a2418333f4
ReplicateFromDirectoryServer : CN=NTDS
                            Settings,CN=DC2,CN=Servers,CN=Default-First-Site-Name,CN=Sites,CN=Configuration,DC=Reskit,DC=Org
```

Figure 4.51: Viewing replication partners for DC1 and UKDC1

In the final step in this recipe, *step 9*, you use the repadmin console application to view an overview of replication in the forest, with output like this:

```
PS C:\Foo> # 9. Use repadmin to check replication summary
PS C:\Foo> repadmin /replsummary
Replication Summary Start Time: 2022-05-09 13:28:14

Beginning data collection for replication summary, this may take awhile:
   ......

Source DSA          largest delta    fails/total %%    error
  DC1                   34m:16s       0 /   7      0
  DC2                   43m:02s       0 /   7      0
  UKDC1                 43m:02s       0 /   6      0

Destination DSA     largest delta    fails/total %%    error
  DC1                   43m:02s       0 /   7      0
  DC2                   34m:16s       0 /   7      0
  UKDC1                 31m:24s       0 /   6      0
```

Figure 4.52: Viewing replication status for the Reskit forest

There's more...

In *step 1*, you view the replication partner(s) for the Reskit domain. With just two DCs in the Reskit domain, you would expect DC1 and DC2 to be replication partners for each other. And in *step 2*, you can see that replication for the domain is up to date.

In *step 3*, you view the metadata related to the group membership of the IT Team group. So far, you can see that AD records three changes to the membership of this group (which happened when you added these three users to the group in an earlier recipe). In *step 4*, you add two users to the group and remove one. In *step 5*, you again view the metadata to see you (or someone!) added Malcolm and Claire to the group and immediately removed Claire.

Also note that, in *step 4*, you use wild cards to pull out properties. This approach saves space in published works, but you may wish to spell out the full property names in production code.

As another example of replication, in *step 6*, you change a user's Office property, then in *step 7*, you examine the replication metadata. You can see that someone made a change to this user, changing their office name.

In *step 9*, you use the repadmin tool and verify that there are currently no replication issues in the forest.

Join our community on Discord

Join our community's Discord space for discussions with the author and other readers:

```
https://packt.link/SecNet
```

5

Managing Networking

This chapter covers the following recipes:

- Configuring IP Addressing
- Testing Network Connectivity
- Installing DHCP
- Using DHCP
- Configuring DHCP Scopes and Options
- Implementing DHCP Fail Over/Load Balancing
- Configuring a DHCP Reservation
- Implementing DNS in the Enterprise
- Configuring DNS Forwarding
- Managing DNS Zones and Resource Records

Introduction

Every organization's heart is its network—the infrastructure that enables your client and server systems to interoperate. Windows has included networking features since the early days of Windows for Workgroups 3.1 (and earlier with Microsoft LAN Manager).

One thing worth noting is that even in the cloud age, "the network" isn't going anywhere. The cloud is really just resources in someone else's network, and you still need the network to communicate. The role of enabling a client to connect to a server does not really change when you have servers (and clients) now in the cloud.

Every server or workstation in your environment must have a correct IP configuration. While IPv6 is gaining in popularity, most organizations rely on IPv4. In the *Configuring IP Addressing* recipe, we look at setting a network interface's IPv4 configuration, including DNS settings.

Many organizations assign a static IPv4 address to most server systems. The servers used throughout this book, for example, use static IP addresses. For client hosts and some servers, an alternative to assigning a static IP address is to use **Dynamic Host Configuration Protocol (DHCP)**. DHCP is a network protocol that enables a workstation to lease an IP address (and release it when the lease expires). You set up a DHCP server to issue IP address configuration to clients using the *Installing DHCP* recipe.

Once you have installed your DHCP server, you can use the *Configuring DHCP Scopes and Options* recipe to set up the details that your DHCP server is to hand out to clients. In the *Configuring DHCP failover and load balancing* recipe, we deploy a second DHCP server and configure it to act as a failover/load balancing DHCP service.

You can create a DHCP reservation as an alternative to manually configuring a host's IP details. The reservation means the DHCP server delivers a specific IP address to a particular host. In "*Creating a DHCP Reservation*," you configure SRV2 to get its IP configuration from the DHCP server.

Another key service in all organizations is DNS, the Domain Name System. In *Deploying DNS in the Enterprise*, you install and configure DNS within the Reskit network. In *Configuring DNS forwarding*, you see how to set up DNS forwarders, which can be useful in larger enterprises.

In this chapter's final recipe, *Managing DNS Zones and Resource Records*, you configure the DNS server on DC1 with zones and additional resource records.

The systems used in the chapter

This chapter is about networking in an enterprise. The recipes in this chapter make use of numerous hosts as follows:

Reskit.Org Forest

Figure 5.1: Hosts in use for this chapter

Configuring IP Addressing

By default, Windows uses DHCP to configure all NICs that the Windows installation process discovers when installing Windows. Once you complete the installation of Windows, you can use the control panel applet (ncpa.cpl), the network shell console application (netsh.exe), or PowerShell to set IP configuration manually. In this recipe, you set the IP address details for SRV2 and ensure the host registers DNS names in the Reskit.Org DNS domain (on the DNS service running on DC1).

Setting up any host requires setting an IP address, a subnet mask, and a default gateway, which you do in the first part of this recipe. Then you configure SRV2 (a workgroup host) to register with the DNS server on DC1.Reskit.Org as SRV2.Reskit.Org (despite it *not* being a member of the domain yet!).

This approach raises some challenges. When you default create DC1.Reskit.Org as a DC, the domain promotion process sets the domain's DNS zone to allow only secure updates that domain members can make. That means a workgroup host cannot register. You can overcome this by setting the zone to allow all updates. But this could be dangerous as it enables ANY host to, potentially, register their address. A second challenge is that since SRV2 is not a domain member, remoting to DC1 fails by default. A solution to that issue is to set the WinRM service to trust all hosts. Configuring WinRM to disregard server authentication has security implications you should consider before using this approach in production.

Getting ready

You run this recipe on SRV2 after you have installed PowerShell 7. The recipe starts with SRV2 being a workgroup host, not a domain member. In this recipe, after configuring an IP address, the recipe also adds SRV2 to the Reskit domain.

How to do it...

1. Discovering the adapter, adapter interface, and adapter interface index

```
$IPType    = 'IPv4'
$Adapter   = Get-NetAdapter -Name Ethernet |
                Where-Object Status -eq 'Up'
$Interface = $Adapter |
                Select-Object -First 1
                    Get-NetIPInterface -AddressFamily $IPType
$Index     = $Interface.IfIndex
Get-NetIPAddress -InterfaceIndex $Index -AddressFamily $IPType |
   Format-Table -Property Interface*, IPAddress, PrefixLength
```

2. Setting a new IP address for the NIC

```
$IPConfigHT = @{
   InterfaceIndex = $Index
   PrefixLength   = 24
   IPAddress      = '10.10.10.51'
   DefaultGateway = '10.10.10.254'
   AddressFamily  = $IPType
}
New-NetIPAddress @IPConfigHT
```

3. Verifying the new IP address

```
Get-NetIPAddress -InterfaceIndex $Index -AddressFamily $IPType |
  Format-Table IPAddress, InterfaceIndex, PrefixLength
```

4. Setting the DNS server IP address

```
$CAHT = @{
  InterfaceIndex  = $Index
  ServerAddresses = '10.10.10.10'
}
Set-DnsClientServerAddress @CAHT
```

5. Verifying the new IP configuration

```
Get-NetIPAddress -InterfaceIndex $Index -AddressFamily $IPType |
  Format-Table
```

6. Testing that SRV2 can see the domain controller

```
Test-NetConnection -ComputerName DC1.Reskit.Org |
  Format-Table
```

7. Creating a credential for DC1

```
$U    = 'Reskit\Administrator'
$PPT  = 'Pa$$w0rd'
$PSS  = ConvertTo-SecureString -String $ppt -AsPlainText -Force
$Cred = [pscredential]::new($U,$PSS)
```

8. Setting WinRM on SRV2 to trust DC1

```
$TPPATH = 'WSMan:\localhost\Client\TrustedHosts'
Set-Item -Path $TPPATH -Value 'DC1' -Force
Restart-Service -Name WinRM -Force
```

9. Enabling non-secure updates to Reskit.Org DNS domain

```
$DNSSSB = {
  $SBHT = @{
    Name          = 'Reskit.Org'
    DynamicUpdate = 'NonsecureAndSecure'
  }
```

```
      Set-DnsServerPrimaryZone @SBHT
  }
  Invoke-Command -ComputerName DC1 -ScriptBlock $DNSSSB -Credential
  $Cred
```

10. Ensuring the host registers within the Reskit.Org DNS zone

```
$DNSCHT = @{
  InterfaceIndex                 = $Index
  ConnectionSpecificSuffix       = 'Reskit.Org'
  RegisterThisConnectionsAddress = $true
  UseSuffixWhenRegistering       = $true
}
Set-DnsClient  @DNSCHT
```

11. Registering the host IP address at DC1

```
Register-DnsClient
```

12. Pre-staging SRV2 in AD

```
$SB = {New-ADComputer -Name SRV2}
Invoke-Command -ComputerName DC1 -ScriptBlock $SB
```

13. Testing that the DNS server on DC1.Reskit.Org correctly resolves SRV2

```
Resolve-DnsName -Name SRV2.Reskit.Org -Type 'A' -Server DC1.Reskit.
Org
```

14. Checking the computer account in the AD

```
Invoke-Command -ComputerName DC1 -ScriptBlock {
                      Get-ADComputer -Identity SRV2}
```

15. Adding SRV2 to the domain and restarting

```
Add-Computer -DomainName Reskit.Org -Credential $Cred
Restart-Computer
```

How it works...

In *step 1*, you use the Get-NetAdapter, Get-NetIPInterface, and Get-NETIPaddress cmdlets to retrieve the IP configuration of the NIC in SRV2. By default, Hyper-V VMs have a single NIC, and, again, by default, Windows sets this NIC to get its configuration from DHCP.

The output of this step looks like this:

```
PS C:\Foo> # 1. Discovering the adapter, adapter interface and adapter interface index
PS C:\Foo> $IPType   = 'IPv4'
PS C:\Foo> $Adapter  = Get-NetAdapter |  Where-Object Status -eq 'Up'
PS C:\Foo> $Interface = $Adapter | Get-NetIPInterface -AddressFamily $IPType
PS C:\Foo> $Index    = $Interface.IfIndex
PS C:\Foo> Get-NetIPAddress -InterfaceIndex $Index -AddressFamily $IPType |
           Format-Table -Property Interface*, IPAddress, PrefixLength
```

```
InterfaceAlias InterfaceIndex IPAddress       PrefixLength
-------------- -------------- ---------       ------------
Ethernet                    5 169.254.118.167           16
```

Figure 5.2: Discovering IP address information

In *step 2*, you use the `New-NetIPAddress` cmdlet to set the host's NIC to have a static IP address (`10.10.10.51`). The output looks like this:

```
PS C:\Foo> # 2. Setting a new IP address for the NIC
PS C:\Foo> $IPHT = @{
               InterfaceIndex = $Index
               PrefixLength   = 24
               IPAddress      = '10.10.10.51'
               DefaultGateway = '10.10.10.254'
               AddressFamily  = $IPType
           }
PS C:\Foo> New-NetIPAddress @IPHT
```

```
IPAddress         : 10.10.10.51
InterfaceIndex    : 5
InterfaceAlias    : Ethernet
AddressFamily     : IPv4
Type              : Unicast
PrefixLength      : 24
PrefixOrigin      : Manual
SuffixOrigin      : Manual
AddressState      : Tentative
ValidLifetime     : Infinite ([TimeSpan]::MaxValue)
PreferredLifetime : Infinite ([TimeSpan]::MaxValue)
SkipAsSource      : False
PolicyStore       : ActiveStore

IPAddress         : 10.10.10.51
InterfaceIndex    : 5
InterfaceAlias    : Ethernet
AddressFamily     : IPv4
Type              : Unicast
PrefixLength      : 24
PrefixOrigin      : Manual
SuffixOrigin      : Manual
AddressState      : Invalid
ValidLifetime     : Infinite ([TimeSpan]::MaxValue)
PreferredLifetime : Infinite ([TimeSpan]::MaxValue)
SkipAsSource      : False
PolicyStore       : PersistentStore
```

Figure 5.3: Discovering IP address information

In *step 3*, you verify the IP address by using Get-NetIPAddress, with output like this:

```
PS C:\Foo> # 3. Verifying the new IP address
PS C:\Foo> Get-NetIPAddress -InterfaceIndex $Index -AddressFamily $IPType |
             Format-Table IPAddress, InterfaceIndex, PrefixLength


IPAddress    InterfaceIndex PrefixLength
---------    -------------- ------------
10.10.10.51               5           24
```

Figure 5.4: Confirming the NIC IP address

Next, in *step 4,* you set the NIC to use the DNS server at 10.10.10.10 – DC1.Reskit.Net. The step produces no console output. In *step 5*, you verify the IP configuration with output like this:

```
PS C:\Foo> # 5. Verifying the new IP configuration
PS C:\Foo> Get-NetIPAddress -InterfaceIndex $Index -AddressFamily $IPType |
             Format-Table

ifIndex IPAddress   PrefixLength PrefixOrigin SuffixOrigin AddressState PolicyStore
------- ---------   ------------ ------------ ------------ ------------ -----------
5       10.10.10.51           24 Manual       Manual       Preferred    ActiveStore
```

Figure 5.5: Confirming IP address configuration

Now that you have a working IP address for the NIC, you can use Test-NetConnection to check the connection to DC1. The output of this step looks like this:

```
PS C:\Foo> # 6. Testing that SRV2 can see the domain controller
PS C:\Foo> Test-NetConnection -ComputerName DC1.Reskit.Org |
             Format-Table

ComputerName    RemotePort RemoteAddress PingSucceeded PingReplyDetails (RTT) TcpTestSucceeded
------------    ---------- ------------- ------------- ---------------------- ----------------
DC1.Reskit.Org 0           10.10.10.10   True          0 ms                    False
```

Figure 5.6: Confirming IP address configuration

In *step 7*, you create a credential object for the Reskit\Administrator user. In *step 8*, you set the WinRM service on SRV2 to trust DC1, and then you restart the service. In *step 9*, you configure the DNS server on DC1 to accept both secure and non-secure updates for the Reskit.Org domain. In *step 10*, you configure the DNS client on SRV2 to register its IP address using the suffix Reskit.Org. With *step 11*, you force the registration on DC1's DNS server. In *step 12*, you create an account for SRV2 in the Reskit domain. These six steps produce no console output.

In *step 13*, you test the DNS server to check it resolves SRV2.Reskit.Org, with the following output:

```
PS C:\Foo> # 13. Testing the DNS server on DC1.Reskit.Org correctly resolves SRV2
PS C:\Foo> Resolve-DnsName -Name SRV2.Reskit.Org -Type 'A' -Server DC1.Reskit.Org

Name              Type   TTL   Section   IPAddress
----              ----   ---   -------   ---------
SRV2.Reskit.Org   A      1200  Answer    10.10.10.51
```

Figure 5.7: Confirming resolution of SRV2.Reskit.Org

With *step 14*, you invoke the Get-ADComputer command on DC1 to verify the AD account details for SRV2. The output of this step looks like this:

```
PS C:\Foo> # 14. Checking the computer account in the AD
PS C:\Foo> Invoke-Command -ComputerName DC1 -ScriptBlock {
                Get-ADComputer -Identity SRV2}

PSComputerName    : DC1
RunspaceId        : 4f45b87c-b5df-4d35-b87d-f2f1cfbf72b4
DistinguishedName : CN=SRV2,CN=Computers,DC=Reskit,DC=Org
DNSHostName       :
Enabled           : True
Name              : SRV2
ObjectClass       : computer
ObjectGUID        : 7b0128ff-7a95-4cf8-a8e2-cd7257928661
SamAccountName    : SRV2$
SID               : S-1-5-21-3837990179-1095414155-523858238-3101
UserPrincipalName :
```

Figure 5.8: Confirming AD account for SRV2

In the final step in this recipe, you add SRV2 to the Reskit.Org domain and then restart the computer. Since the restart-computer command follows directly after you add the computer to the domain, you may not see any message as SRV2 restarts. If you are very quick, you might see the output here:

```
PS C:\Foo> # 15. Adding SRV2 to the domain and restarting
PS C:\Foo> Add-Computer -DomainName Reskit.Org -Credential $Cred
WARNING: The changes will take effect after you restart the computer SRV2
```

Figure 5.9: Joining SRV2 to the domain and rebooting

There's more...

In *step 1*, you discover the IP address of the host NIC. As you can see in the figure, the address is in the 169.254.0.0/16 subnet. This IP address is an Automatic Private IP Addressing or APIPA address. That is normal in a network with no DHCP server and a newly installed host. To understand more about APIPA, you can view this document: https://docs.microsoft.com/windows-server/troubleshoot/how-to-use-automatic-tcpip-addressing-without-a-dh.

In *steps 2* through *4*, you reconfigure the NIC in SRV2 to have a specific IP address and DNS server address. *Step 6* ensures that SRV2 can connect to the DC (DC1).

In *step 7*, you create a credential object that you later use when invoking commands on the domain controller. In *step 8*, you set the WinRM service to trust DC1. By default, WinRM connections use domain membership or SSL for server authentication – the Trusted Hosts setting tells Windows not to carry out server authentication. Configuring this setting is necessary for the following steps in the recipe. But once you have completed these steps (and joined SRV2 to the domain), you should revert this setting.

Testing Network Connectivity

In today's connected world, network connectivity is vital. When you add a new server to your infrastructure, it is useful to ensure that the server can connect to and use the network.

In this recipe, you perform necessary network connectivity tests on the newly installed SRV2 host. You should ensure that full connectivity exists before adding a server to the domain.

Getting ready

This recipe uses SRV2, a domain-joined host. You gave this host a static IP address in "*Configuring IP Addressing*."

How to do it...

1. Verifying SRV2 itself is up, and that loopback is working

    ```
    Test-Connection -ComputerName SRV2 -Count 1 -IPv4
    ```

2. Testing connection to local host's WinRM port

    ```
    Test-NetConnection -ComputerName SRV2 -CommonTCPPort WinRM
    ```

3. Testing basic connectivity to DC1

    ```
    Test-Connection -ComputerName DC1.Reskit.Org -Count 1
    ```

4. Checking connectivity to SMB port on DC1

    ```
    Test-NetConnection -ComputerName DC1.Reskit.Org -CommonTCPPort SMB
    ```

5. Checking connectivity to the LDAP port on DC1

```
Test-NetConnection -ComputerName DC1.Reskit.Org -Port 389
```

6. Examining the path to a remote server on the internet

```
$NetConnectionHT = @{
    ComputerName     = 'WWW.Packt.Com'
    TraceRoute       = $true
    InformationLevel = 'Detailed'
}
Test-NetConnection @NetConnectionHT     # Check our wonderful
publisher
```

How it works...

In *step 1*, you verify that SRV2's loopback adapter works and that the basic TCP/IP stack is up and working. The output looks like this:

```
PS C:\Foo> # 1. Verifying SRV2 itself is up, and that loopback is working
PS C:\Foo> Test-Connection -ComputerName SRV2 -Count 1 -IPv4

   Destination: SRV2

Ping Source     Address         Latency BufferSize Status
                                (ms)      (B)
---- ------     -------         ------- ---------- ------
   1 SRV2       10.10.10.51           0         32 Success
```

Figure 5.10: Verifying SRV2 itself is up and that loopback is working

In *step 2*, you check to ensure that the WinRM port is open and working, with output like this:

```
PS C:\Foo> # 2. Testing connection to local host's WinRM port
PS C:\Foo> Test-NetConnection -ComputerName SRV2 -CommonTCPPort WinRM

ComputerName    : SRV2
RemoteAddress   : fe80::b5le:f281:f518:76a7%5
RemotePort      : 5985
InterfaceAlias  : Ethernet
SourceAddress   : fe80::b5le:f281:f518:76a7%5
TcpTestSucceeded : True
```

Figure 5.11: Checking the WinRM port

In the `Reskit.Org` network, DC1 is a domain controller and a DNS server. In *step 3*, you test the connectivity to this critical enterprise server, with output like this:

```
PS C:\Foo> # 3. Testing basic connectivity to DC1
PS C:\Foo> Test-Connection -ComputerName DC1.Reskit.Org -Count 1

   Destination: DC1.Reskit.Org

Ping Source    Address        Latency BufferSize Status
                                 (ms)      (B)
---- ------    -------        ------- ---------- ------
   1 SRV2      10.10.10.10          0         32 Success
```

Figure 5.12: Testing basic connectivity to DC1

All domain-joined hosts need to access the SYSVOL share on a DC in any domain environment to download the group policy `.POL` files. In *step 4*, you test that SRV2 can access the SMB port, port 445, on the DC, with output like this:

```
PS C:\Foo> # 4. Checking connectivity to SMB port on DC1
PS C:\Foo> Test-NetConnection -ComputerName DC1.Reskit.Org -CommonTCPPort SMB

ComputerName     : DC1.Reskit.Org
RemoteAddress    : 10.10.10.10
RemotePort       : 445
InterfaceAlias   : Ethernet
SourceAddress    : 10.10.10.51
TcpTestSucceeded : True
```

Figure 5.13: Checking connectivity to SMB port on DC1

In *step 5*, you test that SRV2 can access DC1 on the LDAP port, port 389, with the following output:

```
PS C:\Foo> # 5. Checking connectivity to the LDAP port on DC1
PS C:\Foo> Test-NetConnection -ComputerName DC1.Reskit.Org -Port 389

ComputerName     : DC1.Reskit.Org
RemoteAddress    : 10.10.10.10
RemotePort       : 389
InterfaceAlias   : Ethernet
SourceAddress    : 10.10.10.51
TcpTestSucceeded : True
```

Figure 5.14: Checking connectivity to the LDAP port on DC1

In *step 6,* you check connectivity with the internet and test the network path to the publisher's website at `www.packt.com`.

The output is:

```
PS C:\Foo> # 6. Examining the path to a remote server on the Internet
PS C:\Foo> $NCHT = @{
              ComputerName     = 'WWW.Packt.Com'
              TraceRoute       = $true
              InformationLevel = 'Detailed'
           }
PS C:\Foo> Test-NetConnection @NCHT    # Check our wonderful publisher

ComputerName            : WWW.Packt.Com
RemoteAddress           : 141.193.213.20
NameResolutionResults   : 141.193.213.20
                          141.193.213.21
InterfaceAlias          : Ethernet 2
SourceAddress           : 10.10.1.17
NetRoute (NextHop)      : 10.10.1.100
PingSucceeded           : True
PingReplyDetails (RTT)  : 9 ms
TraceRoute              : 10.10.1.100
                          51.148.72.22
                          51.148.73.160
                          51.148.73.153
                          5.57.81.75
                          141.101.71.2
                          141.193.213.20
```

Figure 5.15: Examining the path to a remote server on the internet

There's more...

This recipe's steps confirm the host can accept connections over WinRM and can contact the DC for core activities. You could add several additional tests, such as testing that you can access the DNS server and resolve DNS queries.

This recipe uses two cmdlets to test the connection with another host: Test-NetConnection and Test-Connection. These two cmdlets have different parameters and perform similar but not identical functions. For example, Test-NetConnection tests the ability to connect to a specific TCP port on the remote host. And the Test-Connection cmdlet allows you to specify testing of the connection over IPv4 vs. IPv6. The Test-NetConnection command, as you can see in *step 2*, uses IPv6 and IPv4, although, in practice, IPv6 seems to be a bit faster. Mileage may vary, of course.

In *step 6*, you test the internet connectivity to our publisher's website (www.packt.com). Since we are just testing the connectivity to this site, you only need to specify the actual computer name and do not need the HTTP or HTTPS prefix.

Installing DHCP

Each server needs a unique IP address and other configuration options to configure on a server-by-server basis. You configured SRV2 with a static IP address in a previous recipe and tested its connectivity to the rest of the Reskit network. You can configure client computers running Windows 10 or other OSs manually, although this can be a huge and challenging task in large organizations.

DHCP enables a DHCP client to automate its IP configuration and other networking details from a DHCP server. DHCP automates IP configuration, avoids all the manual configuration work, and avoids the inevitable issues arising from manual IP configuration.

Windows and most other client operating systems, including Linux and Apple Macs, have a built-in DHCP client. Windows Server also includes a DHCP Server service you can install to provide DHCP services to the clients. You can install DHCP using Server Manager and configure the service using the DHCP GUI application. Alternatively, you can automate the installation of DHCP, as you can see in this recipe. In the next recipe, *Configuring DHCP Scopes and Options*, you configure the DHCP service to issue IP addresses in a specific range. You also configure DHCP to provide DHCP clients with other IP address configuration options, such as the subnet mask, default gateway, and the DNS server IP address or addresses.

Getting ready

This recipe uses DC1, a domain controller in the Reskit.Org domain. You should have installed AD on this host and configured it as per earlier recipes.

How to do it...

1. Installing the DHCP feature on DC1 and adding the management tools

   ```
   Import-Module -Name ServerManager -WarningAction SilentlyContinue
   Install-WindowsFeature -Name DHCP -IncludeManagementTools
   ```

2. Adding DC1 to trusted DHCP servers and adding the DHCP security group

   ```
   Import-Module -Name DHCPServer -WarningAction SilentlyContinue
   Add-DhcpServerInDC
   Add-DHCPServerSecurityGroup
   ```

3. Letting DHCP know it's all configured

   ```
   $DHCPHT = @{
   ```

```
        Path  = 'HKLM:\SOFTWARE\Microsoft\ServerManager\Roles\12'
        Name  = 'ConfigurationState'
        Value = 2
    }
    Set-ItemProperty @DHCPHT
```

4. Restarting the DHCP server

    ```
    Restart-Service -Name DHCPServer -Force
    ```

5. Testing service availability

    ```
    Get-Service -Name DHCPServer |
        Format-List -Property *
    ```

How it works...

In *step 1*, you import the ServerManager module. PowerShell 7 recognizes this is an older Windows PowerShell module and imports the module via the Windows PowerShell compatibility mechanism introduced in the *Utilizing Windows PowerShell compatibility* recipe in *Chapter 2*. This step also uses Install-WindowsFeature to add the DHCP Server service to DC1. The output from this step looks like this:

```
PS C:\Foo> # 1. Installing the DHCP feature on DC1 and add the management tools
PS C:\Foo> Import-Module -Name ServerManager -WarningAction SilentlyContinue
PS C:\Foo> Install-WindowsFeature -Name DHCP -IncludeManagementTools

Success Restart Needed Exit Code    Feature Result
------- -------------- ---------    --------------
True    No             Success      {DHCP Server, DHCP Server Tools}
```

Figure 5.16: Installing the DHCP Server service on DC1

In *step 2*, you add DC1 to the set of authorized DHCP servers in the domain and add the DHCP security groups to the DHCP server, which produces no output to the console. The groups that this command adds are the DHCP Users and DHCP Administrators security groups. For more details on these groups, see https://secureidentity.se/delegate-dhcp-admins-in-the-domain/.

In *step 3*, you set a registry entry to tell Windows that all post-deployment DHCP configuration activities are complete. The GUI installation process takes you through this automatically. When installing DHCP via PowerShell, you need to set the registry entry to complete the configuration, which produces no output.

Once you have completed the configuration activities, restart the DHCP service, as shown in *step 4*. Once restarted, the DHCP service can issue IP configuration to DHCP clients. For this to happen, you must also have specified the configuration information in the *Configuring DHCP Scopes and Options* recipe. Depending on the speed of your CPU and storage system and how you have configured the VM, you may see the following output from this step:

```
PS C:\Foo> # 4. Restarting DHCP server
PS C:\Foo> Restart-Service -Name DHCPServer -Force
WARNING: Waiting for service 'DHCP Server (DHCPServer)' to start...
WARNING: Waiting for service 'DHCP Server (DHCPServer)' to start...
PS C:\Foo>
```

Figure 5.17: Restarting the DHCP Server service on DC1

In *step 5*, you complete this recipe by ensuring that the DHCP service has started. The output of this step looks like this:

```
PS C:\Foo> # 5. Testing service availability
PS C:\Foo> Get-Service -Name DHCPServer |
           Format-List -Property *

UserName              : NT AUTHORITY\NetworkService
Description           : Performs TCP/IP configuration for DHCP clients, including dynamic assignments of
                        IP addresses, specification of the WINS and DNS servers, and connection-specific
                        DNS names. If this service is stopped, the DHCP server will not perform
                        TCP/IP configuration for clients. If this service is disabled, any services
                        that explicitly depend on it will fail to start.
DelayedAutoStart      : False
BinaryPathName        : C:\WINDOWS\system32\svchost.exe -k DHCPServer -p
StartupType           : Automatic
Name                  : DHCPServer
RequiredServices      : {RpcSs, Tcpip, SamSs, EventLog, EventSystem}
CanPauseAndContinue   : True
CanShutdown           : True
CanStop               : True
DisplayName           : DHCP Server
DependentServices     : {}
MachineName           : .
ServiceName           : DHCPServer
ServicesDependedOn    : {RpcSs, Tcpip, SamSs, EventLog, EventSystem}
StartType             : Automatic
ServiceHandle         : Microsoft.Win32.SafeHandles.SafeServiceHandle
Status                : Running
ServiceType           : Win32OwnProcess, Win32ShareProcess
Site                  :
Container             :
```

Figure 5.18: Testing DHCP service availability

There's more...

When the Windows DHCP service starts, it checks to ensure the server is on the DHCP server list authorized in the domain. This server list ensures that the DHCP service does not start on any non-authorized DHCP server. Adding DC1 to the list of authorized servers can help guard against rogue DHCP servers.

In *step 5*, you check the DHCP service. Get-Service output includes a description of the service and the path name to the actual service executable. As you can see, the DHCP service does not run in its own process. Instead, it runs inside svchost.exe, which is why you cannot explicitly view the service's process when using Get-Process.

Configuring DHCP Scopes and Options

Installing DHCP is straightforward, as you saw in the *"Installing DHCP"* recipe – you add the Windows feature and then carry out two small configuration steps. The extra steps enable you to use the relevant security groups and avoid the Server Manager GUI message that there are configuration steps not yet performed. You probably do not need to take these extra steps in most cases.

Before your DHCP server can provide IP address configuration information to clients, you must create a DHCP scope and options. A DHCP scope is a range of DHCP addresses your DHCP server can give out for a given IP subnet. DHCP options are specific configuration options your DHCP server provides, such as the DNS server's IP address and the IPv4 default gateway.

Depending on your organization's needs, you can set DHCP options at a scope level or server level. For example, you would most likely specify a default gateway in the scope options, with DNS server address(es) set at the server level. But as ever, mileage varies!

You create a new scope for the 10.10.10.0/24 subnet in this recipe and specify options at both the scope and server level.

Getting ready

You run this recipe on SRV1 after you have installed PowerShell 7.

How to do it...

1. Importing the DHCP Server module

```
Import-Module DHCPServer -WarningAction SilentlyContinue
```

2. Creating an IPv4 scope

```
$SCOPEHT = @{
  Name         = 'ReskitOrg'
  StartRange   = '10.10.10.150'
  EndRange     = '10.10.10.199'
  SubnetMask   = '255.255.255.0'
  ComputerName = 'DC1.Reskit.Org'
}
Add-DhcpServerV4Scope @SCOPEHT
```

3. Getting IPv4 scopes from the server

```
Get-DhcpServerv4Scope -ComputerName DC1.Reskit.Org
```

4. Setting server-wide option values

```
$OPTION1HT = @{
  ComputerName = 'DC1.Reskit.Org' # DHCP Server to Configure
  DnsDomain    = 'Reskit.Org'     # Client DNS Domain
  DnsServer    = '10.10.10.10'    # Client DNS Server
}
Set-DhcpServerV4OptionValue @OPTION1HT
```

5. Setting a scope-specific option

```
$OPTION2HT = @{
  ComputerName = 'DC1.Reskit.Org' # DHCP Server to Configure
  Router       = '10.10.10.254'
  ScopeID      = '10.10.10.0'
}
Set-DhcpServerV4OptionValue @OPTION2HT
```

6. Viewing server options

```
Get-DhcpServerv4OptionValue | Format-Table -AutoSize
```

7. Viewing scope-specific options

```
Get-DhcpServerv4OptionValue -ScopeId '10.10.10.0' |
  Format-Table -AutoSize
```

8. Viewing DHCPv4 option definitions

```
Get-DhcpServerv4OptionDefinition | Format-Table -AutoSize
```

How it works...

In *step 1*, you import the DHCPServer module. This step, which produces no output, loads the module using the Windows PowerShell compatibility solution. When you installed DHCP (in *Installing DHCP*), you added the management tools, including this module. However, the DHCP team has not yet made this module compatible with PowerShell 7. You read about the Windows PowerShell compatibility solution in *Chapter 2*. This step produces no console output.

In *step 2*, you create a new DHCP scope for IPv4 addresses. The scope enables the DHCP server to issue IP addresses in the range of 10.10.10.150 – 10.10.10.199. This step produces no output.

In *step 3*, you use Get-DHCPServerIPV4Scope to retrieve details of all the DHCP scopes you have defined on DC1. The output of this step looks like this:

```
PS C:\Foo> # 3. Getting IPV4 scopes from the server
PS C:\Foo> Get-DhcpServerv4Scope -ComputerName DC1.Reskit.Org

ScopeId      SubnetMask     Name       State   StartRange     EndRange        LeaseDuration
-------      ----------     ----       -----   ----------     --------        -------------
10.10.10.0   255.255.255.0  ReskitOrg  Active  10.10.10.150   10.10.10.199
```

Figure 5.19: Viewing IPv4 scopes on DC1's DHCP Server

In *step 4*, you set two server-wide DHCP options, creating no output. These are options and values offered to all clients of any DHCP scope defined on this server. In *step 5*, you specify a scope option. These two steps also produce no output.

In *step 6*, you view the DHCP server-wide options with output that looks like this:

```
PS C:\Foo> # 6. Viewing server options
PS C:\Foo> Get-DhcpServerv4OptionValue | Format-Table -AutoSize

OptionId Name             Type        Value          VendorClass UserClass PolicyName
-------- ----             ----        -----          ----------- --------- ----------
15       DNS Domain Name  String      {Reskit.Org}
6        DNS Servers      IPv4Address {10.10.10.10}
```

Figure 5.20: Viewing DHCP server-wide options

With *step 7*, you view the DHCP options you have set on the 10.10.10.10 scope, which looks like this:

```
PS C:\Foo> # 7. Viewing scope specific options
PS C:\Foo> Get-DhcpServerv4OptionValue -ScopeId '10.10.10.0' |
              Format-Table -AutoSize

OptionId Name   Type        Value          VendorClass UserClass PolicyName
-------- ----   ----        -----          ----------- --------- ----------
51       Lease  DWord       {691200}
3        Router IPv4Address {10.10.10.254}
```

Figure 5.21: Viewing DHCP server-wide options

In Windows Server 2022, Microsoft includes 66 pre-defined DHCP option definitions. You can use these options to provide option values to DHCP clients. Most of these options are of little use and are, in many cases, purely historical and not used widely. That said, these options help you to provide support for niche and uncommon scenarios.

To view the set of options Windows defines by default, in *step 8*, you use the geGet-Dhcp-Serverv4OptionDefinition command.

The output from this command looks like this:

```
PS C:\Foo> # 8. Viewing DHCPv4 option definitions
PS C:\Foo> Get-DhcpServerv4OptionDefinition | Format-Table -AutoSize

Name                                             OptionId  Type         VendorClass MultiValued
----                                             --------  ----         ----------- -----------
Classless Static Routes                          121       BinaryData               False
Subnet Mask                                      1         IPv4Address              False
Time Offset                                      2         DWord                    False
Router                                           3         IPv4Address              True
Time Server                                      4         IPv4Address              True
Name Servers                                     5         IPv4Address              True
DNS Servers                                      6         IPv4Address              True
Log Servers                                      7         IPv4Address              True
Cookie Servers                                   8         IPv4Address              True
LPR Servers                                      9         IPv4Address              True
Impress Servers                                  10        IPv4Address              True
Resource Location Servers                        11        IPv4Address              True
Host Name                                        12        String                   False
Boot File Size                                   13        Word                     False
Merit Dump File                                  14        String                   False
DNS Domain Name                                  15        String                   False
Swap Server                                      16        IPv4Address              False
Root Path                                        17        String                   False
Extensions Path                                  18        String                   False
IP Layer Forwarding                              19        Byte                     False
Nonlocal Source Routing                          20        Byte                     False
Policy Filter Masks                              21        IPv4Address              True
Max DG Reassembly Size                           22        Word                     False
Default IP Time-to-live                          23        Byte                     False
Path MTU Aging Timeout                           24        DWord                    False
Path MTU Plateau Table                           25        Word                     True
MTU Option                                       26        Word                     False
All subnets are local                            27        Byte                     False
Broadcast Address                                28        IPv4Address              False
Perform Mask Discovery                           29        Byte                     False
Mask Supplier Option                             30        Byte                     False
Perform Router Discovery                         31        Byte                     False
Router Solicitation Address                      32        IPv4Address              False
Static Route Option                              33        IPv4Address              True
Trailer Encapsulation                            34        Byte                     False
ARP Cache Timeout                                35        DWord                    False
Ethernet Encapsulation                           36        Byte                     False
TCP Default Time-to-live                         37        Byte                     False
Keepalive Interval                               38        DWord                    False
Keepalive Garbage                                39        Byte                     False
NIS Domain Name                                  40        String                   False
NIS Servers                                      41        IPv4Address              True
NTP Servers                                      42        IPv4Address              True
Vendor Specific Info                             43        BinaryData               False
WINS/NBNS Servers                                44        IPv4Address              True
Rebinding (T2) Time Value                        59        DWord                    False
NIS+ Domain Name                                 64        String                   False
NIS+ Servers                                     65        IPv4Address              True
Boot Server Host Name                            66        String                   False
Bootfile Name                                    67        String                   False
Mobile IP Home Agents                            68        IPv4Address              True
Simple Mail Transport Protocol (SMTP) Servers    69        IPv4Address              True
Post Office Protocol (POP3) Servers              70        IPv4Address              True
Network News Transport Protocol (NNTP) Servers   71        IPv4Address              True
World Wide Web (WWW) Servers                      72        IPv4Address              True
Finger Servers                                   73        IPv4Address              True
Internet Relay Chat (IRC) Servers                74        IPv4Address              True
StreetTalk Servers                               75        IPv4Address              True
StreetTalk Directory Assistance (STDA) Servers   76        IPv4Address              True
```

Figure 5.22: Viewing DHCPv4 option definitions

There's more...

In *step 2*, you create a new scope and give it a scope name. However, as you can see in *step 5* and elsewhere, the DHCP cmdlets do not provide a -DHCPScopeName parameter. Instead, you specify a ScopeID. In general, this is the subnet for the IP addresses in the scope, 10.10.10.0/24. But even then, as you can see in *step 7*, the cmdlet accepts any IP address in the 10.10.10.0/24 subnet as the subnet ID, including 10.10.10.10 as shown.

In *step 6*, you view the pre-defined DHCP options available to your DHCP server. The IETF defined these options in RFC 2132 (https://www.rfc-editor.org/rfc/rfc2132.html). It is worth pointing out that just because a DHCP option exists, there is no way to make software use the DHCP options. For example, you could configure a scope (or the server) to issue option 72, WWW servers. But at present, no browser makes use of this option. Additionally, Windows does not appear to use or request that option.

Using DHCP

After installing the DHCP service and configuring scope(s) and option values, your DHCP service can issue IP configuration data to any client on the network. Any IP client you attach to the physical subnet can ask for and receive IP confirmation details. Since the DHCP protocol acts at the IP level, the protocol performs no authentication when any DHCP client uses the protocol to request IP configuration details.

In *Configuring IP Addressing*, you set a static IP address for SRV2. In this recipe, you reconfigure this server to obtain a DHCP-based IP address (and options you specify in *Configuring DHCP Scopes and Options*).

Getting ready

You run this recipe on SRV2 after installing PowerShell 7 and after you have installed and configured DHCP (and have defined a new DHCP scope and associated options).

How to do it...

1. Adding DHCP RSAT tools

```
Import-Module -Name ServerManager -WarningAction SilentlyContinue
Install-WindowsFeature -Name RSAT-DHCP
```

2. Importing the DHCP module

    ```
    Import-Module -Name DHCPServer -WarningAction SilentlyContinue
    ```

3. Viewing the scopes on DC1

    ```
    Get-DhcpServerv4Scope -ComputerName DC1
    ```

4. Getting V4 scope statistics from DC1

    ```
    Get-DhcpServerv4ScopeStatistics -ComputerName DC1
    ```

5. Discovering a free IP address

    ```
    Get-DhcpServerv4FreeIPAddress -ComputerName dc1 -ScopeId 10.10.10.42
    ```

6. Getting SRV2 NIC configuration

    ```
    $NIC = Get-NetIPConfiguration -InterfaceAlias 'Ethernet'
    ```

7. Getting the IP interface

    ```
    $NIC |
      Get-NetIPInterface |
        Where-Object AddressFamily -eq 'IPv4'
    ```

8. Enabling DHCP on the NIC

    ```
    $NIC |
      Get-NetIPInterface |
        Where-Object AddressFamily -eq 'IPv4' |
          Set-NetIPInterface -Dhcp Enabled
    ```

9. Checking the IP address assigned

    ```
    Get-NetIPAddress -InterfaceAlias "Ethernet" |
      Where-Object AddressFamily -eq 'IPv4'
    ```

10. Viewing updated V4 scope statistics from DC1

    ```
    Get-DhcpServerv4ScopeStatistics -ComputerName DC1
    ```

11. Discovering the next free IP address

    ```
    Get-DhcpServerv4FreeIPAddress -ComputerName dc1 -ScopeId 10.10.10.42
    ```

12. Checking IPv4 DNS name resolution

```
Resolve-DnsName -Name SRV2.Reskit.Org -Type A
```

How it works...

In *step 1*, you install the RSAT-DHCP feature to add the DHCP server's PowerShell module on SRV2, with output like this:

```
PS C:\Foo> # 1. Adding DHCP RSAT tools
PS C:\Foo> Import-Module -Name ServerManager -WarningAction SilentlyContinue
PS C:\Foo> Install-WindowsFeature -Name RSAT-DHCP
Success Restart Needed Exit Code Feature Result
------- -------------- --------- --------------
True    No             Success   {Remote Server Administration Tools, DHCP Se...
```

Figure 5.23: Installing DHCP tools on SRV2

Like many Windows Server 2022 native PowerShell modules, the DHCP server module is incompatible with .NET, and you cannot import it directly into PowerShell 7. You can use this module via the compatibility mechanism noted in *Chapter 2*. In *step 2*, you explicitly load this module using Import-Module, which creates no output.

In *step 3*, you look at the scopes available on DC1 (the DHCP server you installed in *Installing DHCP*). The output looks like this:

```
PS C:\Foo> # 3. Viewing the scopes on DC1
PS C:\Foo> Get-DhcpServerv4Scope -ComputerName DC1

ScopeId     SubnetMask     Name      State   StartRange     EndRange       LeaseDuration
-------     ----------     ----      -----   ----------     --------       -------------
10.10.10.0  255.255.255.0  ReskitOrg Active  10.10.10.150   10.10.10.199
```

Figure 5.24: Installing DHCP tools on SRV2

In *step 4*, you examine the scope statistics for the DHCP scope you created in *Configuring DHCP Scopes and Options*, which produces output like this:

```
PS C:\Foo> # 4. Getting V4 scope statistics from DC1
PS C:\Foo> Get-DhcpServerv4ScopeStatistics -ComputerName DC1

ScopeId     Free  InUse  PercentageInUse  Reserved  Pending  SuperscopeName
-------     ----  -----  ---------------  --------  -------  --------------
10.10.10.0  50    0      0                0         0
```

Figure 5.25: Viewing scope statistics

In *step 5*, you use the `Get-DhcpServerv4FreeIPAddress` cmdlet to find the first available free IP address in the scope. The output resembles this:

```
PS C:\Foo> # 5. Discovering a free IP address
PS C:\Foo> Get-DhcpServerv4FreeIPAddress -ComputerName dc1 -ScopeId 10.10.10.42
10.10.10.150
```

Figure 5.26: Getting the next free IPv4 address in the DHCP scope

In *step 6*, you get the NIC details and store them in the $NIC variable, producing no output. Note that you specify the `InterfaceIndex` of 6, which should be your VM's NIC.

In *step 7*, you use that variable to get details of the NIC, with output like this:

```
PS C:\Foo> # 7. Getting IP interface
PS C:\Foo> $NIC |
            Get-NetlPlnterface   |
              Where-Object AddressFamily -eq 'IPv4'

ifIndex InterfaceAlias  AddressFamily NlMtu(Bytes) InterfaceMetric Dhcp     ConnectionState PolicyStore
------- --------------  ------------- ------------ --------------- ----     --------------- -----------
5       Ethernet        IPv4                  1500              15 Disabled Connected       ActiveStore
```

Figure 5.27: Getting IP interface details

In *step 8*, you change the NIC to get configuration details via DHCP. This step creates no output.

In *step 9*, you view the NIC's updated IPv4 address, assigned by DHCP. The output looks like this:

```
PS C:\Foo> # 9. Checking IP address assigned
PS C:\Foo> Get-NetIPAddress -InterfaceAlias "Ethernet"   |
            Where-Object AddressFamily -eq 'IPv4'

IPAddress          : 10.10.10.150
InterFaceIndex     : 5
InterFaceAlias     : Ethernet
AddressFamily      : IPv4
Type               : Unicast
PrefixLength       : 24
PrefixOrigin       : Dhcp
SuffixOrigin       : Dhcp
AddressState       : Preferred
ValidLifetime      : 7.23:59:23
PreferredLifetime  : 7.23:59:23
SkipAsSource       : False
PolicyStore        : ActiveStore
```

Figure 5.28: Checking the IP address assigned

In *step 10*, you re-examine the scope statistics with output like this:

```
PS C:\Foo> # 10. Getting updated V4 scope statistics from DC1
PS C:\Foo> Get-DhcpServerv4ScopeStatistics -ComputerName DC1

ScopeId      Free InUse PercentageInUse Reserved Pending SuperscopeName
-------      ---- ----- --------------- -------- ------- --------------
10.10.10.0   49   1     2               0        0
```

Figure 5.29: Getting updated V4 scope statistics from DC1

With *step 11*, you re-check to discover the next free IP address in the DHCP scope, with output like this:

```
PS C:\Foo> # 11. Discovering the next free IP address
PS C:\Foo> Get-DhcpServerv4FreeIPAddress -ComputerName dc1 -ScopeId 10.10.10.42
10.10.10.151
```

Figure 5.30: Discovering the next free IP address

In the final step, *step 12*, you check to ensure that SRV2 has registered its new IP address in the DNS server on DC1. The output looks like this:

```
PS C:\Foo> # 12. Checking IPv4 DNS name resolution
PS C:\Foo> Resolve-DnsName -Name SRV2.Reskit.Org -Type A

Name             Type TTL  Section  IPAddress
----             ---- ---  -------  ---------
SRV2.Reskit.Org  A    1200 Question 10.10.10.150
```

Figure 5.31: Checking IPv4 DNS name resolution

There's more...

In this recipe, you use the DHCP server cmdlets to get information from the DHCP server on DC1. These cmdlets retrieve information about the IP address scopes hosted on your DHCP server, including the next free IP address. You can also get statistics on the DHCP scope on the server, including free and used addresses.

In *step 7*, you get the IP interface details to allow you, in *step 8*, to convert the NIC from a static IP address to a dynamic address configuration based on DHCP.

In *step 9*, you view the DHCP-supplied IP address information for SRV2. If you perform *step 8* and immediately run *step 9*, you may find that the NIC shows an APIPA IP address in the 169.254.0.0/24 subnet. This address is transient as Windows configures the DHCP-supplied address. When you change to DHCP (as in *step 8*), Windows first removes any static address and gives the NIC an APIPA address.

Windows then contacts the DHCP server and negotiates an address, which can take a few seconds. So be patient.

Configuring a DHCP Reservation

DHCP enables you to create an IP address reservation which means you can create an IP config-uration for a specific host. If you need to change a host's IP address later, you can just change the DHCP reservation (and refresh the DHCP lease on the host). You might have, for example, a printer that gets its IP configuration via DHCP.

For more information on DHCP reservations, see: `https://learn.microsoft.com/en-us/powershell/module/dhcpserver/add-dhcpserverv4reservation?view=windowsserver2022-ps`

Getting ready

You run this recipe on SRV2. This host is a domain-joined server on which you have loaded both PowerShell 7 and VS Code. In *Configuring IP Addressing*, you configured the NIC in this host to have a static IP address. Later, in *Using DHCP*, you gave SRV2 a DHCP address.

How to do it...

1. Importing the DHCP Server module explicitly

   ```
   Import-Module -Name DHCPServer
   ```

2. Getting NIC's MAC address for NIC in SRV2

   ```
   $SB = {Get-NetAdapter -Name 'Ethernet'}
   $Nic = Invoke-command -ComputerName SRV2 -ScriptBlock $SB
   $MAC = $Nic.MacAddress
   ```

3. Creating a DHCP reservation for SRV2

   ```
   $NewResHT = @{
     ScopeId     = '10.10.10.0'
     IPAddress   = '10.10.10.199'
     ClientId    = $Mac
     ComputerName = 'DC1'
   }
   Add-DhcpServerv4Reservation @NewResHT
   ```

4. Renewing the IP address in SRV2

```
Invoke-Command -ComputerName SRV2 -ScriptBlock {
    ipconfig /renew
}
```

5. Testing the net connection to SRV2

```
Clear-DnsClientCache
Resolve-DnsName -Name SRV2.Reskit.Org -Type A
Test-Connection -TargetName SRV2.Reskit.Org
```

How it works...

In *step 1*, you import the DHCP Server PowerShell module explicitly. There is some console output like this:

```
PS C:\Foo> # 1. Importing the DHCP Server module explicitly
PS C:\Foo> Import-Module -Name DHCPServer
WARNING: Module DHCPServer is loaded in Windows PowerShell using WinPSCompatSession
remoting session; please note that all input and output of commands from this
module will be deserialized objects. If you want to load this module into
PowerShell please use 'Import-Module -SkipEditionCheck' syntax.
```

Figure 5.32: Importing the DHCP Server module

In *step 2*, you get the MAC address for the NIC. In *step 3*, you use this MAC address to create a DHCP reservation. These two steps produce no console output.

In *step 4*, which you run from DC1, you remotely invoke ipconfig.exe to release and then renew the DHCP-supplied address for SRV2. You are using PowerShell remoting to invoke this command on SRV2 – but once SRV2 changes its IP address, the remoting channel breaks. So you see no actual output other than PowerShell attempting to recreate the remoting channel.

In *step 5*, you check to see whether you can resolve SRV2 to its new address and connect to it with output like this:

```
PS C:\Foo> # 5.Testing net connection to SRV2
PS C:\Foo> Clear-DnsClientCache
PS C:\Foo> Resolve-DnsName -Name SRV2.Reskit.Org -Type A

Name                Type TTL  Section IPAddress
----                ---- ---  ------- ---------
SRV2.Reskit.Org A    1200 Answer  10.10.10.199

PS C:\Foo> Test-Connection -TargetName SRV2.Reskit.Org

   Destination: SRV2.Reskit.Org

Ping Source Address      Latency(ms) BufferSize(B) Status
---- ------ -------      ----------- ------------- ------
   1 DC1    10.10.10.199           0            32 Success
   2 DC1    10.10.10.199           0            32 Success
   3 DC1    10.10.10.199           1            32 Success
   4 DC1    10.10.10.199           0            32 Success
```

Figure 5.33: Testing network connection to SRV2

There's more...

In *step 1*, you explicitly import the DHCP Server module. Importing the module also generates a warning message about PowerShell loading the module using the compatibility mechanism. You read about the Windows PowerShell compatibility mechanism in *Chapter 2*. Also, in the output from this step, you see the suggestion to use the parameter -SkipEditionCheck. This advice is usually unhelpful as it does not tend to work in practice. The DHCP Server module works fine using the compatibility mechanism.

A DHCP reservation reserves a specific IP address for a host with a particular MAC address. So in *step 2*, you get the MAC address for the host's NIC, and then in *step 3*, you reserve a specific address for this MAC address.

In *step 4*, you run `ipconfig.exe` on SRV2 and renew the IP address from DHCP. The DHCP server then sends SRV2 the IP address you configured in the reservation. The network stack on SRV2 then changes the IP address accordingly, which immediately breaks the remoting channel. The result is that this step works fine – SRV2 gets the reserved IP address – but you see some error messages. Although the `ipconfig` command worked fine (SRV2 has an updated IP address), you see an error on DC1. If you wanted a more controllable method, you could use the `Restart-Computer` command and specify both the `-Wait` and `-For` parameters to restart SRV2 and, from the script, wait until there is PowerShell connectivity.

Implementing DHCP Fail Over/Load Balancing

As shown in previous recipes, installing and configuring a single on-premises DHCP server is straightforward. However, a single DHCP server represents a single point of failure, which is never a good thing. The solution is always to have a second DHCP server with as much independence as possible from the first server. That would include running the second DHCP service on a separate host (physical or virtual) on different subnets and using independent power and networking components.

In earlier versions of Windows, one approach to fault tolerance was to stand up two DHCP servers and define the necessary scopes on each DHCP host. You split the full set of IP addresses and allowed each server to have part of that set. The traditional "wisdom" was to do an 80/20 split (have 80% of the scope supplied by your primary DHCP server and 20% on the backup server).

Independent DHCP servers are an error-prone approach and were never ideal since these separate servers did not coordinate scope details. That 80/20 "rule" was a recommendation for one specific customer scenario (a large firm in the Pacific Northwest) and possibly was not meant to become a best practice.

In Windows Server 2012, Microsoft added a DHCP failover and load balancing mechanism that simplified deploying DHCP in an organization. You can now set up two DHCP servers, define a DHCP scope, and allow both servers to work in tandem.

In this recipe, you install DHCP on a second server, DC2, and then configure and use the failover and load balancing capabilities of Windows Server.

This recipe uses the two DCs you have installed, DC1 and DC2. You should also have installed DHCP on DNS ("*Installing DHCP*") and configured a DNS zone (*Configuring DHCP Scopes and Options*).

Getting ready

You run this recipe on DC2 after you have installed PowerShell 7. You should have created a DHCP server on DC1, created a scope, and created a reservation in that scope for the SRV2.

How to do it...

1. Installing the DHCP server feature on DC2

```
Import-Module -Name ServerManager -WarningAction SilentlyContinue
$FEATUREHT = @{
  Name                 = 'DHCP'
  IncludeManagementTools = $True
}
Install-WindowsFeature @FEATUREHT
```

2. Letting DHCP know it is fully configured

```
$IPHT = @{
  Path  = 'HKLM:\SOFTWARE\Microsoft\ServerManager\Roles\12'
  Name  = 'ConfigurationState'
  Value = 2
}
Set-ItemProperty @IPHT
```

3. Authorizing the DHCP server in AD

```
Import-Module -Name DHCPServer -WarningAction 'SilentlyContinue'
Add-DhcpServerInDC -DnsName DC2.Reskit.Org
```

4. Viewing authorized DHCP servers in the Reskit domain

```
Get-DhcpServerInDC
```

5. Configuring failover and load balancing

```
$FAILOVERHT = @{
  ComputerName      = 'DC1.Reskit.Org'
  PartnerServer     = 'DC2.Reskit.Org'
  Name              = 'DC1-DC2'
  ScopeID           = '10.10.10.0'
  LoadBalancePercent = 60
  SharedSecret      = 'j3RryIsTheB3est!'
```

```
    Force              = $true
    Verbose            = $True
  }
  Invoke-Command -ComputerName DC1.Reskit.Org -ScriptBlock {
    Add-DhcpServerv4Failover @Using:FAILOVERHT
  }
```

6. Getting active scopes (from both servers!)

```
$DHCPServers = 'DC1.Reskit.Org', 'DC2.Reskit.Org'
$DHCPServers |
  ForEach-Object {
    "Server: $_" | Format-Table
    Get-DhcpServerv4Scope -ComputerName $_ | Format-Table
  }
```

7. Viewing DHCP server statistics from both DHCP Servers

```
$DHCPServers |
  ForEach-Object {
    "Server: $_" | Format-Table
    Get-DhcpServerv4ScopeStatistics -ComputerName $_  | Format-Table
  }
```

8. Viewing DHCP reservations from both DHCP Servers

```
$DHCPServers |
  ForEach-Object {
    "Server: $_" | Format-Table
    Get-DhcpServerv4Reservation -scope 10.10.10.42 -ComputerName $_
|
      Format-Table
  }
```

How it works...

Before configuring a DHCP failover relationship, you first install and configure DHCP on DC2. In *step 1*, you install the DHCP Server feature on DC2 with the following output:

```
PS C:\Foo> # 1. Installing the DHCP server feature on DC2
PS C:\Foo> Import-Module -Name ServerManager -WarningAction SilentlyContinue
PS C:\Foo> $FEATUREHT = @{
               Name                 = 'DHCP'
               IncludeManagementTools = $True
           }
PS C:\Foo> Install-WindowsFeature @FEATUREHT

Success Restart Needed Exit Code     Feature Result
------- -------------- ---------     --------------
True    No             Success       {DHCP Server, DHCP Server Tools}
```

Figure 5.34: Adding the DHCP Server feature to DC2

In *step 2*, you let DHCP know it is now fully configured. In *step 3*, you authorize DC2 to be a DHCP server in AD. These two steps create no output.

In *step 4*, you view the authorized DHCP servers in the domain with the following output:

```
PS C:\Foo> # 4. Viewing authorized DHCP servers in the Reskit domain
PS C:\Foo> Get-DhcpServerinDC

IPAddress     DnsName
---------     -------
10.10.10.10   dc1.reskit.org
10.10.10.11   dc2.reskit.org
```

Figure 5.35: Adding the DHCP Server feature to DC2

In *step 5*, you create a failover/load balancing relationship between DC1 and DC2. The verbose output is as follows:

```
PS C:\Foo> # 5. Configuring fail-over and load balancing
PS C:\Foo> $FAILOVERHT = @{
            ComputerName       = 'DC1.Reskit.Org'
            PartnerServer      = 'DC2.Reskit.Org'
            Name               = 'DC1-DC2'
            ScopeID            = '10.10.10.0'
            LoadBalancePercent = 60
            SharedSecret       = 'j3RryIsTheB3est!'
            Force              = $true
            Verbose            = $True
          }
PS C:\Foo> Invoke-Command -ComputerName DC1.Reskit.Org -ScriptBlock {
               Add-DhcpServerv4Failover @Using:FAILOVERHT
           }
```

```
VERBOSE: A new failover relationship will be created between servers DC1.Reskit.Org and DC2.Reskit.Org. The
configuration of the specified scopes on server DC1.Reskit.Org will be replicated to the partner server.
VERBOSE: Add scopes on partner server DC2.Reskit.Org ................................In progress.
VERBOSE: Update properties for scope 10.10.10.0 (1 of 1) on partner server DC2.Reskit.Org ............In progress.
VERBOSE: Update properties for scope 10.10.10.0 (1 of 1) on partner server DC2.Reskit.Org ............Successful.
VERBOSE: Update delay offer for scope 10.10.10.0 (1 of 1) on partner server DC2.Reskit.Org ...........In progress.
VERBOSE: Update delay offer for scope 10.10.10.0 (1 of 1) on partner server DC2.Reskit.Org ...........Successful.
VERBOSE: Update NAP properties for scope 10.10.10.0 (1 of 1) on partner server DC2.Reskit.Org .........In progress.
VERBOSE: Update NAP properties for scope 10.10.10.0 (1 of 1) on partner server DC2.Reskit.Org ........Successful.
VERBOSE: Update superscope for scope 10.10.10.0 (1 of 1) on partner server DC2.Reskit.Org ............In progress.
VERBOSE: Update superscope for scope 10.10.10.0 (1 of 1) on partner server DC2.Reskit.Org ............Successful.
VERBOSE: Update IP ranges for scope 10.10.10.0 (1 of 1) on partner server DC2.Reskit.Org .............In progress.
VERBOSE: Update IP ranges for scope 10.10.10.0 (1 of 1) on partner server DC2.Reskit.Org .............Successful.
VERBOSE: Update exclusions for scope 10.10.10.0 (1 of 1) on partner server DC2.Reskit.Org ............In progress.
VERBOSE: Update exclusions for scope 10.10.10.0 (1 of 1) on partner server DC2.Reskit.Org ............Successful.
VERBOSE: Update reservations for scope 10.10.10.0 (1 of 1) on partner server DC2.Reskit.Org ..........In progress.
VERBOSE: Update reservations for scope 10.10.10.0 (1 of 1) on partner server DC2.Reskit.Org ..........Successful.
VERBOSE: Update policies for scope 10.10.10.0 (1 of 1) on partner server DC2.Reskit.Org ..............In progress.
VERBOSE: Update policies for scope 10.10.10.0 (1 of 1) on partner server DC2.Reskit.Org ..............Successful.
VERBOSE: Update options for scope 10.10.10.0 (1 of 1) on partner server DC2.Reskit.Org ...............In progress.
VERBOSE: Update options for scope 10.10.10.0 (1 of 1) on partner server DC2.Reskit.Org ...............Successful.
VERBOSE: Add scopes on partner server DC2.Reskit.Org ................................Successful.
VERBOSE: Disable scopes on partner server DC2.Reskit.Org ...........................In progress.
VERBOSE: Disable scopes on partner server DC2.Reskit.Org ...........................Successful.
VERBOSE: Creation of failover configuration on partner server DC2.Reskit.Org .........In progress.
VERBOSE: Creation of failover configuration on partner server DC2.Reskit.Org ........Successful.
VERBOSE: Creation of failover configuration on host server DC1.Reskit.Org ...........In progress.
VERBOSE: Creation of failover configuration on host server DC1.Reskit.Org ...........Successful.
VERBOSE: Activate scopes on partner server DC2.Reskit.Org ..........................In progress.
VERBOSE: Activate scopes on partner server DC2.Reskit.Org ..........................Successful.
```

Figure 5.36: Creating a DHCP failover relationship

In *step 6*, you retrieve and view the active scopes on both DHCP servers with the following output:

```
PS C:\Foo> # 6. Getting active scopes (from both servers!)
PS C:\Foo> $DHCPServers = 'DC1.Reskit.Org', 'DC2.Reskit.Org'
PS C:\Foo> $DHCPServers |
             ForEach-Object {
               "Server: $_" | Format-Table
               Get-DhcpServerv4Scope -ComputerName $_ | Format-Table
             }

Server: DC1.Reskit.Org

ScopeId      SubnetMask      Name      State  StartRange     EndRange      LeaseDuration
-------      ----------      ----      -----  ----------     --------      -------------
10.10.10.0   255.255.255.0   ReskitOrg Active 10.10.10.150   10.10.10.199

Server: DC2.Reskit.Org

ScopeId      SubnetMask      Name      State  StartRange     EndRange      LeaseDuration
-------      ----------      ----      -----  ----------     --------      -------------
10.10.10.0   255.255.255.0   ReskitOrg Active 10.10.10.150   10.10.10.199
```

Figure 5.37: Viewing active scopes on both DHCP servers

In *step 7*, you use the Get-DhcpServerV4ScopeStatistics command to retrieve details about the scopes on both servers, with output like this:

```
PS C:\Foo> # 7. Viewing DHCP server statistics from both DHCP Servers
PS C:\Foo> $DHCPServers |
             ForEach-Object {
               "Server: $_" | Format-Table
               Get-DhcpServerv4ScopeStatistics -ComputerName $_  | Format-Table
             }

Server: DC1.Reskit.Org

ScopeId      Free InUse PercentageInUse Reserved Pending SuperscopeName
-------      ---- ----- --------------- -------- ------- --------------
10.10.10.0   49   1     2               1        0

Server: DC2.Reskit.Org

ScopeId      Free InUse PercentageInUse Reserved Pending SuperscopeName
-------      ---- ----- --------------- -------- ------- --------------
10.10.10.0   49   1     2               1        0
```

Figure 5.38: Viewing scope statistics on both DHCP servers

In *step 8*, you view the DHCP reservations on each server with the following output:

```
PS C:\Foo> # 8. Viewing DHCP reservations from both DHCP Servers
PS C:\Foo> $DHCPServers |
             ForEach-Object {
               "Server: $_" | Format-Table
               Get-DhcpServerv4Reservation -scope 10.10.10.42 -ComputerName $_  |
                 Format-Table
             }

Server: DC1.Reskit.Org

IPAddress     ScopeId     ClientId         Name             Type Description
---------     -------     --------         ----             ---- -----------
10.10.10.199 10.10.10.42 00-15-5d-01-01-4c SRV2.Reskit.Org Both

Server: DC2.Reskit.Org

IPAddress     ScopeId     ClientId         Name             Type Description
---------     -------     --------         ----             ---- -----------
10.10.10.199 10.10.10.42 00-15-5d-01-01-4c SRV2.Reskit.Org Both
```

Figure 5.39: Viewing DHCP reservations from both DHCP servers

There's more...

Unlike in *Installing DHCP*, in this recipe, you do not add the DHCP-related local security groups on DC2. If you plan to delegate administrative privileges, you may wish to add those groups as you did in the earlier recipe.

In *step 5*, you establish a load balancing and failover relationship between the two DHCP servers. By using the -Verbose switch for the Add-DhcpServerV4Failover cmdlet, you can see what the command does, step by step. As you can see in the output, this command copies full details of all the scopes on DC1 to DC2. You should note you create DHCP failover relationships on a scope-by-scope basis.

Depending on your needs, you can configure different relationships between DHCP servers using the -ServerRole parameter. For more details on this parameter and others that you can use to fine-tune the relationship between the two partners, see https://learn.microsoft.com/powershell/module/dhcpserver/add-dhcpserverv4failover.

The DHCP failover feature provides several additional settings to control precisely when to fail over and for how long (and when to failback). These settings allow you to manage, for example, what might happen during a planned reboot of your DHCP server.

Implementing DNS in the Enterprise

When you installed Active Directory in *Chapter 4*, you created a single DNS server on DC1. When you added a replica DC, DC2, and the child domain with UKDC1, you did not set up any additional DNS server in your forest. You always want to configure your clients and servers to use at least two DNS servers. In an enterprise organization, this is a best practice. For servers with a static DNS setting, you should also update the DHCP DNS server option settings to ensure that your DHCP servers provide two DNS server entries to DHCP clients.

In most organizations, there are several DNS service configuration options you may wish to set. These include whether to allow DNS server recursion on the server, the maximum size of the DNS cache, and whether to use **Extended DNS (EDNS)**.

EDNS (also referred to as EDNS0 or, more recently, EDNS(0)) is an extension mechanism that enables more recent DNS servers to interact with older servers that may not be capable of specific actions. For more details on EDNS(0), see `https://en.wikipedia.org/wiki/ Extension_mechanisms_for_DNS#:~:text=Extension%20mechanisms%20for%20DNS%20 (EDNS,increasing%20functionality%20of%20the%20protocol`.

This recipe is a starting point. There are other DNS server options you may wish to consider updating, such as DNS Security. Additionally, you may need to reconfigure other servers and update the static IP address settings (to point to both DNS servers). And finally, in the `Reskit.Org` forest, you should also be updating the child domain `UK.Reskit.Org`.

In this recipe, you update the domain-wide DNS settings in the Reskit.Org domain. These settings configure DC2's DNS service in the same way as DC1, update DNS server configuration settings, and configure both DC1 and DC2 to use both DNS servers. You also update the DHCP zone to supply both DNS server addresses.

In *Configuring IP Addressing*, you configured SRV2, a workgroup host, to update DNS. You configured the Reskit.Org zone on DC1 to allow non-domain members to update their DNS registrations using dynamic DNS. This configuration is not a best-practice configuration. In the final steps in this recipe, you update the DNS zones for Reskit.Org to allow only secure updates.

Getting ready

You run this recipe on DC2, with DC1 and SRV2 also operational. You run this recipe after setting up DNS on both DC1 and DC2 and implementing DHCP.

How to do it...

1. Installing the DNS feature on DC2

    ```
    Import-Module -Name ServerManager -WarningAction SilentlyContinue
    Install-WindowsFeature -Name DNS -IncludeManagementTools
    ```

2. Creating a script block to set DNS Server Options

    ```
    $SB1 = {
      # Enable recursion on this server
      Set-DnsServerRecursion -Enable $true
      # Configure DNS Server cache maximum size
      Set-DnsServerCache  -MaxKBSize 20480  # 28 MB
      # Enable EDNS
      $EDNSHT = @{
        EnableProbes    = $true
        EnableReception = $true
      }
      Set-DnsServerEDns @EDNSHT
      # Enable Global Name Zone
      Set-DnsServerGlobalNameZone -Enable $true
    }
    ```

3. Reconfiguring DNS on DC2 and DC1

    ```
    Invoke-Command -ScriptBlock $SB1
    Invoke-Command -ScriptBlock $SB1 -ComputerName DC1
    ```

4. Creating a script block to configure DC2 to have two DNS servers

    ```
    $SB2 = {
      $NIC =
        Get-NetIPInterface -InterfaceAlias "Ethernet" -AddressFamily
    IPv4
      $DNSSERVERS = ('127.0.0.1','10.10.10.10')
      $DNSHT = @{
        InterfaceIndex  = $NIC.InterfaceIndex
        ServerAddresses = $DNSSERVERS
      }
    ```

```
    Set-DnsClientServerAddress @DNSHT
    Start-Service -Name DNS
}
```

5. Configuring DC2 to have two DNS servers

```
Invoke-Command -ScriptBlock $SB2
```

6. Creating a script block to configure DC1 to have two DNS servers

```
$SB3 = {
  $NIC =
    Get-NetIPInterface -InterfaceAlias "Ethernet" -AddressFamily
IPv4
  $DNSSERVERS = ('127.0.0.1','10.10.10.11')
  $DNSHT = @{
    InterfaceIndex  = $NIC.InterfaceIndex
    ServerAddresses = $DNSSERVERS
  }
  Set-DnsClientServerAddress @DNSHT
  Start-Service -Name DNS
}
```

7. Configuring DC1 to have two DNS servers

```
Invoke-Command -ScriptBlock $SB3 -ComputerName DC1
```

8. Updating DHCP scope to add 2 DNS entries

```
$DNSOPTIONHT = @{
  DnsServer    = '10.10.10.11',
                 '10.10.10.10'    # Client DNS Servers
  DnsDomain    = 'Reskit.Org'
  Force        = $true
}
Set-DhcpServerV4OptionValue @DNSOPTIONHT -ComputerName DC1
Set-DhcpServerV4OptionValue @DNSOPTIONHT -ComputerName DC2
```

9. Getting DNS service details

```
$DNSRV = Get-DNSServer -ComputerName DC2.Reskit.Org
```

10. Viewing recursion settings

```
$DNSRV |
  Select-Object -ExpandProperty ServerRecursion
```

11. Viewing server cache settings

```
$DNSRV |
  Select-Object -ExpandProperty ServerCache
```

12. Viewing EDNS settings

```
$DNSRV |
  Select-Object -ExpandProperty ServerEdns
```

13. Setting the `Reskit.Org` zone to be secure only

```
$DNSSSB = {
  $SBHT = @{
    Name          = 'Reskit.Org'
    DynamicUpdate = 'Secure'
  }
  Set-DnsServerPrimaryZone @SBHT
}
Invoke-Command -ComputerName DC1 -ScriptBlock $DNSSSB
Invoke-Command -ComputerName DC2 -ScriptBlock $DNSSSB
```

14. Resolving SRV2 on DC2

```
Resolve-DnsName -Name SRV2 -Type A -Server DC2
```

How it works...

In *step 1*, you install the DNS feature on DC2, with output like this:

```
PS C:\Foo> # 1. Installing the DNS feature on DC2
PS C:\Foo> Import-Module -Name ServerManager -WarningAction SilentlyContinue
PS C:\Foo> Install-WindowsFeature -Name DNS -IncludeManagementTools

Success Restart Needed Exit Code  Feature Result
------- -------------- ---------  --------------
True    No             Success    {DNS Server, DNS Server Tools}
```

Figure 5.40: Installing DNS feature on DC2

In *step 2*, you create a script block that contains commands to configure DNS server options. In *step 3*, you run this script block on both DC1 and DC2, creating no output.

In *step 4*, you create another script block that sets the IP configuration for the host NIC to have two DNS servers. In *step 5*, you run this script block to reconfigure DC2, which creates no output.

In *steps 6* and *step 7*, you reconfigure the static IP setting on DC1 to have two DNS servers. This step also creates no output.

In *step 8*, you update the defined scope (10.10.10.0) on both DHCP servers to supply two DNS server IP addresses to clients of your DHCP server. This step produces no output.

Now that you have reconfigured DNS, in *step 9*, you get and view the DNS server details from DC2. This step produces no output. In *step 10*, you view the DNS server recursion settings with output like this:

```
PS C:\Foo> # 10. Viewing recursion settings
PS C:\Foo> $DNSRV |
             Select-Object -ExpandProperty ServerRecursion

Enable                  True
AdditionalTimeout(s)    4
RetryInterval(s)        3
Timeout(s)              8
SecureResponse          True
```

Figure 5.41: Viewing DNS Server recursion settings

In *step 11*, you examine the DNS server cache settings, with output like this:

```
PS C:\Foo> # 11. Viewing server cache settings
PS C:\Foo> $DNSRV |
             Select-Object -ExpandProperty ServerCache

MaxTTL                             : 1.00:00:00
MaxNegativeTTL                     : 00:15:00
MaxRBSize                          : 20480
EnablePollutionProtection          : True
LockingPercent                     : 100
StoreEmptyAuthenticationResponse   : True
IgnorePolicies                     : False
```

Figure 5.42: Viewing DNS Server cache settings

In *step 12*, you view the EDNS settings on DC2, with output like this:

```
PS C:\Foo> # 12. Viewing ENDS Settings
PS C:\Foo> $DNSRV |
              Select-Object -ExpandProperty ServerEdns

CacheTimeout EnableProbes EnableReception
------------ ------------ ---------------
00:15:00     True         True
```

Figure 5.43: Viewing DNS Server EDNS settings

In *step 13*, you change the DNS zone for Reskit.Org on both DC1 and DC2 to only accept secure dynamic updates, creating no output.

As a final DNS check, you use `Resolve-DnsName` to return any A records for `SRV2.Reskit.Org`, which produces output like this:

```
PS C:\Foo> # 14. Resolving SRV2.Reskit.Org on DC2
PS C:\Foo> Resolve-DnsName -Name SRV2.Reskit.Org -Type A -Server DC2

Name             Type TTL  Section IPAddress
----             ---- ---  ------- ---------
SRV2.Reskit.Org  A    1200 Answer  10.10.10.199
```

Figure 5.44: Resolving SRV2.Reskit.Org's A record

There's more...

In this recipe, you begin by installing and configuring DNS on DC2. Then you set DNS server options on both DNS servers (DC1 and DC2). You configure your domain controllers to point to themselves first and then to the other DNS servers second. Configuring DNS in this manner is a best practice.

In the earlier DHCP-related recipes, you configured your DHCP servers to provide a single DNS server IP address to DHCP clients as part of an IP lease. In *step 8*, you update the DHCP scope provided by DC1 and DC2 to provide two DNS server IP addresses when offering an IP configuration to a DHCP client.

At the end of this recipe, you obtain and view the DNS server recursion, server cache, and EDNS settings on DC2. You could extend these steps by examining the settings on DC1 and comparing them to ensure consistent configuration on both DNS servers.

In *Configuring IP Addressing*, you used a workgroup computer, SRV2, and enabled it to register with DNS by setting the DNS zone domain to accept insecure updates. Using non-secure DNS updates is not a best practice as it could allow a rogue computer to "steal" a real DNS name.

In a later recipe, you added SRV2 to the Reskit.Org domain. Therefore, you can now configure the DNS AD-integrated zones to accept only secure updates (i.e., only from domain-joined computers). In *step 13*, you ensure that the Reskit.Org DNS domain only allows secure updates.

Finally, in *step 14*, you resolve SRV2.Reskit.Org from DC2. You originally created, via dynamic DNS update, the DNS A record for SRV2 on the DNS server on DC1. Now that you have created a new DNS service on DC2, and since the Reskit.Org zone is AD-integrated, DNS can resolve all records from the DNS zone from either DNS server. You can see in the figure that SRV2 has the DHCP-provided IP address (10.10.10.199).

In this recipe, you set up DNS for use in the Reskit.Org domain and for DHCP clients in that domain. But, you did not make any DNS-related changes to the UK.Reskit.Org sub-domain. This means that the DC in that domain, UKDC1.UK.Reskit.Org, still uses just DC1 for its DNS. In production, you would want at least a second DC for this sub-domain and update DNS server address settings for servers in the UK domain (and ensure any DHCP leases include two DNS server IP addresses). This additional work is similar to what you did in this recipe.

Another production aspect regards the replication of AD-integrated DNS zones. In this chapter, you created a DNS zone for Reskit.Org. The recipes you used in this chapter set that zone to be AD integrated and replicated to every DC in the Reskit.Org forest. If you change the zone content (for example, adding a new static host A record), the updates are stored within AD. AD then replicates the changes to DC1 and DC2, as well as to UKDC1. By default, Windows replicates all AD-integrated zone data to every DC in the forest, but you can change that. Depending on your usage scenario, you may wish to adjust the zone replication scope for AD-integrated zones. For more details on AD-integrated DNS zones, see https://learn.microsoft.com/windows-server/identity/ad-ds/plan/active-directory-integrated-dns-zones.

Managing DNS Zones and Resource Records

The DNS service enables you to resolve names to other information. The most common use of DNS is to resolve a hostname to its IP (IPv4 or IPv6) addresses. But different name resolutions, such as determining email servers or anti-spam, also rely on DNS.

DNS servers hold zones. A DNS zone is a container for a set of Resource Records (RRs) related to a specific DNS domain. If you use an email client to send mail, for example, to DoctorDNS@Gmail.com, the email client uses DNS to discover an email server to which to send the mail. When you enter www.packt.com, your browser uses DNS to resolve that website name into an IP address and contacts the server at that IP address.

Before using DNS to hold a RR, you must create a DNS forward lookup zone. A zone is integral to a global (or internal) DNS namespace. You can configure different zones to hold other parts of your namespace. You could, for example, have one zone containing RRs for the Reskit.Org on DC1 and DC2 while delegating to a new sub-zone, uk.reskit.org, on UKDC1. In *Chapter 4*, you added a child domain to the Reskit.Org forest, UK.Reskit.Net.

A reverse lookup zone does the reverse – you use it to obtain a hostname from its IP address. You may find reverse lookup zones useful, but you do not need them for most domain usage. The old NSlookup nslookup.exe command is one tool that uses the reverse lookup zone, for example. For more details on DNS in Windows, see https://learn.microsoft.com/windows-server/networking/dns/dns-top.

Traditionally, DNS stores and obtains zone details from files on the DNS server. When the DNS service starts up, it reads these zone files and updates the files as needed when it receives updates. If you have multiple DNS servers, you must configure your service to perform replication to ensure all DNS servers are in sync.

With Windows 2000, Microsoft added AD-integrated zones. DNS stores the DNS data for these zone types within AD. These zones replicate their zone data via AD replication, which simplifies the setup. This also means that when you created the AD service on DC1, DNS created a zone in the DNS server on DC1 and replicated the zone data to all DCs in a forest. For more information on AD-integrated zones, see https://learn.microsoft.com/windows-server/identity/ad-ds/plan/active-directory-integrated-dns-zones.

In this recipe, you create a forward and reverse look up zone on DC1. Then you add RRs in those zones. Once added, you test DNS resolution.

Getting ready

You run this recipe on DC1 after installing and configuring DNS.

How to do it...

1. Creating a new primary forward DNS zone for Cookham.Net

```
$ZHT1 = @{
  Name               = 'Cookham.Net'
  ResponsiblePerson  = 'dnsadmin.cookham.net.'
  ReplicationScope   = 'Domain'
  ComputerName       = 'DC1.Reskit.Org'
}
```

```
Add-DnsServerPrimaryZone @ZHT1 -Verbose
```

2. Creating a reverse lookup zone

```
$ZHT2 = @{
  NetworkID         = '10.10.10.0/24'
  ResponsiblePerson = 'dnsadmin.reskit.org.'
  ReplicationScope  = 'Forest'
  ComputerName      = 'DC1.Reskit.Org'
}
Add-DnsServerPrimaryZone @ZHT2
```

3. Registering DNS for DC1 and DC2

```
Register-DnsClient
Invoke-Command -ComputerName DC2 -ScriptBlock {Register-DnsClient}
```

4. Checking the DNS zones on DC1

```
Get-DNSServerZone -ComputerName DC1 | ft -AutoSize
```

5. Adding Resource Records to the Cookham.Net zone

```
# Adding an A record
$RRHT1 = @{
  ZoneName       = 'Cookham.Net'
  A              = $true
  Name           = 'Home'
  AllowUpdateAny = $true
  IPv4Address    = '10.42.42.42'
}
Add-DnsServerResourceRecord @RRHT1
# Adding a Cname record
$RRHT2 = @{
  ZoneName      = 'Cookham.Net'
  Name          = 'MAIL'
  HostNameAlias = 'Home.Cookham.Net'
}
Add-DnsServerResourceRecordCName @RRHT2
# Adding an MX record
$MXHT = @{
```

```
          Preference    = 10
          Name          = '.'
          TimeToLive    = '4:00:00'
          MailExchange  = 'Mail.Cookham.Net'
          ZoneName      = 'Cookham.Net'
      }
      Add-DnsServerResourceRecordMX @MXHT
```

6. Restarting the DNS service to ensure replication

```
      Restart-Service -Name DNS
      $SB = {Restart-Service -Name DNS}
      Invoke-Command -ComputerName DC2 -ScriptBlock $SB
```

7. Checking results of RRs in the Cookham.Net zone

```
      Get-DnsServerResourceRecord -ZoneName 'Cookham.Net' | ft -auto
```

8. Testing DNS resolution on DC2 andDC1

```
      # Testing The CNAME from DC1
      Resolve-DnsName -Server DC1.Reskit.Org -Name 'Mail.Cookham.Net'
      # Testing the MX on DC2
      Resolve-DnsName -Server DC2.Reskit.Org -Name 'Cookham.Net'
```

9. Testing the reverse lookup zone

```
      Resolve-DnsName -Name '10.10.10.10'
```

How it works...

In *step 1*, which you run on DC1, you create a new primary forward lookup DNS zone for the DNS domain Cookham.Net. Using the -Verbose switch creates output from this step, like this:

```
PS C:\Foo> # 1. Creating a new primary forward DNS zone for Cookham.Net
PS C:\Foo> $ZHT1 = @{
              Name              = 'Cookham.Net'
              ResponsiblePerson = 'dnsadmin.cookham.net.'
              ReplicationScope  = 'Domain'
              ComputerName      = 'DC1.Reskit.Org'
           }
PS C:\Foo> Add-DnsServerPrimaryZone @ZHT1 -Verbose
VERBOSE: Adding DNS primary (AD integrated/file-backed forward/reverse lookup) zone Cookham.Net on DC1.Reskit.Org server.
VERBOSE: AllowUpdate successfully set on server DC1.Reskit.Org.
```

Figure 5.45: Creating a new DNS zone

In *step 2*, you create a primary reverse lookup zone for 10.10.10.0/24. In *step 3*, you run the Register-DNSClient on both DC1 and DC2. This ensures that both DCs have updated their DNS details. These two steps produce no console output.

In *step 4*, you check on the DNS zones held by the DNS service on DC1. The output looks like this:

```
PS C:\Foo> # 4. Checking the DNS zones on DC1
PS C:\Foo> Get-DNSServerZone -ComputerName DC1

ZoneName                ZoneType IsAutoCreated IsDsIntegrated IsReverseLookupZone IsSigned
--------                -------- ------------- -------------- ------------------- --------
_msdcs.Reskit.Org       Primary  False         True           False               False
0.in-addr.arpa          Primary  True          False          True                False
10.10.10.in-addr.arpa   Primary  False         True           True                False
127.in-addr.arpa        Primary  True          False          True                False
255.in-addr.arpa        Primary  True          False          True                False
Cookham.Net             Primary  False         True           False               False
Reskit.Org              Primary  False         True           False               False
TrustAnchors            Primary  False         True           False               Fals
```

Figure 5.46: Checking DNS zones on DC1

In *step 5*, you add three RRs to Cookham.net: an A record, a CNAME record, and an MX record. In *step 6*, you restart the DNS service on both DC1 and DC2 to ensure replication has ensured both DNS servers are up to date. These two steps generate no console output.

In *step 7*, you get all the DNS resource records for Cookham.Net, which look like this:

```
PS C:\Foo> # 4. Checking the DNS zones on DC1
PS C:\Foo> Get-DNSServerZone -ComputerName DC1

ZoneName                ZoneType IsAutoCreated IsDsIntegrated IsReverseLookupZone IsSigned
--------                -------- ------------- -------------- ------------------- --------
_msdcs.Reskit.Org       Primary  False         True           False               False
0.in-addr.arpa          Primary  True          False          True                False
10.10.10.in-addr.arpa   Primary  False         True           True                False
127.in-addr.arpa        Primary  True          False          True                False
255.in-addr.arpa        Primary  True          False          True                False
Cookham.Net             Primary  False         True           False               False
Reskit.Org              Primary  False         True           False               False
TrustAnchors            Primary  False         True           False               False
```

Figure 5.47: Checking DNS RRs for Cookham.Net

In *step 8*, you test DNS name resolution from DC1 and DC2. You first resolve the Mail.Cookham.Net CNAME RR from DC1, then check the MX record from DC2.

The output from these two commands is as follows:

```
PS C:\Foo> # 8. Testing DNS resolution on DC2, DC1
PS C:\Foo> # Testing The CNAME from DC1
PS C:\Foo> Resolve-DnsName -Server DC1.Reskit.Org -Name 'Mail.Cookham.Net'

Name              Type  TTL  Section  NameHost
----              ----  ---  -------  --------
Mail.Cookham.Net  CNAME 3600 Answer   Home.Cookham.Net

Name       : Home.Cookham.Net
QueryType  : A

PS C:\Foo> # Testing the MX on DC2
PS C:\Foo> Resolve-DnsName -Server DC2.Reskit.Org -Name 'Cookham.Net'

Name         Type TTL  Section   PrimaryServer   NameAdministrator    SerialNumber
----         ---- ---  -------   -------------   -----------------    ------------
Cookham.Net  SOA  3600 Authority dc2.reskit.org  dnsadmin.Cookham.Net 4
```

Figure 5.48: Checking DNS name resolution from DC1 and DC2

In *step 9*, you test the reverse lookup zone and resolve `10.10.10.10` into a domain name like this:

```
PS C:\Foo> # 9. Testing the reverse lookup zone
PS C:\Foo> Resolve DnsName -Name '10.10.10.10'

Name                     Type TTL  Section  NameHost
----                     ---- ---  -------  --------
10.10.10.10.in-addr.arpa. PTR  1200 Question DC1.Reskit.Org
```

Figure 5.49: Testing the reverse lookup zone on DC2

There's more...

In *step 5*, you create some new RRs for the `Cookham.Net` zone, which you test in later steps. To ensure that AD and DNS replicate the new RRs from, in this case, DC1 to DC2, in *step 6*, you restart the DNS service on both DCs. This ensures that Windows replicates the zone information stored in AD if AD has not already replicated that information.

Configuring DNS Forwarding

When a DNS server gets a query for a **resource record** (**RR**) not held by the server, it can use recursion to discover a DNS server that can resolve the RR. If, for example, you use `Resolve-DNSName` to resolve `www.packt.com`, the configured DNS server may not hold a zone that would help. Your DNS service then looks to the DNS root servers to discover a DNS server that can via the recursion process. Eventually, the process finds a DNS server that can resolve the RR. Your DNS server then caches these details locally in the DNS server cache.

If you are resolving publicly available names, this process works great. But you might have internally supplied DNS names that DNS can't resolve via the mechanism. An example might be when two companies merge. There may be internal hostnames (e.g., intranet.kapoho.com and intranet.reskit.org) that your organization's internal DNS servers can resolve but are not available from publicly-facing DNS servers. In that scenario, you can set up conditional forwarding. Conditional forwarding enables one DNS server to forward a query to a DNS server or set of servers and not use recursion. You can learn a bit more about conditional forwarding here: https://medium.com/tech-jobs-academy/dns-forwarding-and-conditional-forwarding-f3118bc93984.

An alternative to using conditional forwarding is to use stub zones. You can learn more about the differences between conditional forwarding and stub zones here: https://blogs.msmvps.com/acefekay/2018/03/20/what-should-i-use-a-stub-conditional-forwader-forwarder-or-secondary-zone/.

Getting ready

In this recipe, you use DC1, a domain controller and DNS server for Reskit.Org. You have previously promoted DC1 to be a DC and installed/configured DNS using recipes earlier in this chapter and book.

How to do it...

1. Obtaining the IP addresses of DNS servers for Packt.com

```
$NameServers = Resolve-DnsName -Name Packt.Com -Type NS |
  Where-Object Name -eq 'Packt.com'
$NameServers
```

2. Obtaining the IPv4 addresses for these hosts

```
$NameServerIPs = foreach ($Server in $NS) {
  (Resolve-DnsName -Name $Server.NameHost -Type A).IPAddress
}
$NameServerIPs
```

3. Adding a conditional forwarder on DC1

```
$CFHT = @{
  Name          = 'Packt.Com'
  MasterServers = $NSIPS
}
Add-DnsServerConditionalForwarderZone @CFHT
```

4. Checking zone on DC1

    ```
    Get-DnsServerZone -Name Packt.Com
    ```

5. Testing conditional forwarding

    ```
    Resolve-DNSName -Name WWW.Packt.Com -Server DC1 |
     Format-Table
    ```

How it works...

In *step 1*, you resolve the name servers serving the Packt.com domain on the internet, and then you display the results like this:

```
PS C:\Foo> # 1. Obtaining the IP addresses of DNS servers for Packt.Com
PS C:\Foo> $NameServers = Resolve-DnsName -Name Packt.Com -Type NS |
              Where-Object Name -eq 'Packt.Com'
PS C:\Foo> $NameServers

Name           Type  TTL   Section  NameHost
----           ----  ---   -------  --------
Packt.Com      NS    1461  Answer   eva.ns.cloudflare.Com
Packt.Com      NS    1461  Answer   max.ns.cloudflare.Com
```

Figure 5.50: Obtaining IP addresses of DNS servers for Packt.Com

In *step 2*, you use the DNS servers you just retrieved and resolved their IPv4 addresses from the hostnames (which you got in *step 1*). This step produces the following output:

```
PS C:\Foo> # 2. Obtaining the IPV4 addresses for these hosts
PS C:\Foo> $NameServerIPs = foreach ($Server in $NS) {
              (Resolve-DnsName -Name $Server.NameHost -Type A),IPAddress
           }
PS C:\Foo> $NameServerIPs
108.162.192.114
172.64.32.114
173.245.58.114
108.162.193.132
172.64.33.132
173.245.59.132
```

Figure 5.51: Obtaining IPv4 addresses of DNS servers for Packt.Com

In *step 3*, which generates no output, you create a DNS forwarding zone for Packt.com, which you populate with the IP addresses returned in *step 2*.

In *step 4*, you view the conditional forwarder domain defined on DC1, with output like this:

```
PS C:\Foo> # 4. Checking zone on DC1
PS C:\Foo> Get-DnsServerZone -Name Packt.Com

ZoneName    ZoneType    IsAutoCreated   IsDsIntegrated   IsReverseLookupZone   IsSigned
--------    --------    -------------   --------------   -------------------   --------
Packt.Com   Forwarder   False           False            False
```

Figure 5.52: Checking zone on DC1

With the final step, *step 5*, you resolve www.packt.com like this:

```
PS C:\Foo> # 5. Testing conditional forwarding
PS C:\Foo> Resolve-DNSName -Name WWW.Packt.Com -Server DC1 |
               Format-Table

Name            Type   TTL Section NameHost
----            ----   --- ------- --------
WWW.Packt.Com   CNAME  300 Answer  packtcommerce.wpengine.Com

Name        : packtcommerce.wpengine.Com
QueryType   : A
TTL         : 120
Section     : Answer
IP4Address  : 34.105.173.16
```

Figure 5.53: Testing conditional forwarding

There's more...

In *step 1*, you discover the name server names for the DNS servers that serve Packt.com. In this case, these servers are part of Cloudflare's distributed DNS service. For more information on how this service works, see https://www.cloudflare.com/dns/.

In *step 2*, you resolve those DNS server names into IP addresses. In *step 3*, you create a conditional forwarding domain that forwards queries for packt.com (such as www.packt.com) to one of the six IP addresses you saw in *step 2*.

In *step 4*, you view the conditional forwarding zone on DC1. Since the zone is not DS integrated, DNS does not replicate it to DC2. In production, you should repeat *step 3* on DC2.

In *step 5*, you resolve www.packt.com via conditional forwarding.

Join our community on Discord

Join our community's Discord space for discussions with the author and other readers:

`https://packt.link/SecNet`

6

Implementing Enterprise Security

This chapter covers the following recipes:

- Implementing **Just Enough Administration (JEA)**
- Examining Applications and Services Logs
- Discovering Logon Events in the Event Log
- Deploying PowerShell Group Policies
- Using PowerShell Script Block Logging
- Configuring AD Password Policies
- Managing Windows Defender Antivirus

Introduction

Security within every organization is vital. The threats faced by most organizations are nearly constant. With today's threat model, with attacks from any number of attackers, you need to ensure every aspect of your organization is secure, from physical security to the security of your network and computer infrastructure.

Since the earliest times, security-savvy folks have preached the gospel of security in-depth. Having as many layers as realistic as possible and is a good thing. As the theory goes – the bad guys have to defeat all your layers to defeat you, while you only need to hold one to stay safe.

PowerShell is a powerful tool for IT professionals wanting to be secure and stay secure. There is so much you can do with PowerShell to help your organization deploy excellent security over your network and computer infrastructure. This chapter looks at several ways to use PowerShell to improve your Windows infrastructure's security.

JEA is a Windows feature that enables you to implement fine-grained administration, giving users just enough power to do their job and no more. A core objective of JEA is to reduce the number of users who are members of very high-privilege groups, including the local administrators, domain admins, and enterprise admins groups. The idea is you specify precisely what a user can do, and JEA makes it so.

In Windows, almost every component logs information to Windows event logs. These include the classic logs (first implemented with Windows NT 3.1) and the application and services logs that Microsoft added to Windows Vista. The logs provide a massive amount of information to help you manage your systems. One particular type of event that can be of interest is logon events – who logged on and when. You can use this information to track unusual or suspicious logins.

Using Group Policy, you can manage certain aspects of PowerShell 7 (and Windows PowerShell). With attackers increasingly using fileless PowerShell attacks, script block logging is one way of detecting suspicious behavior. You can use these event log entries for active detection by deploying a **security information and event management** (**SIEM**) tool, such as Solar Windows Security Event Manager or RSA NetWitness. Or you can store the events for manual review. As an alternative to a Group Policy setting, you can configure script block logging using registry settings, which helps for workgroup hosts (e.g., in the DMZ).

A critical security consideration for any sized organization is your password policy. You have considerable flexibility over your Windows password policies. Windows 11 and Windows Server 2022 have a default password policy that you can change. You can update your default domain password policy if you want longer or shorter passwords and complex or non-complex passwords. For those cases where you wish to have a different password policy for specific users, you can use AD's fine-grained password feature that enables you to set a password policy for a user or group.

Windows Server 2022 and Windows 11 have a built-in antivirus and antimalware product, **Microsoft Defender Antivirus** (**MDA**). This feature was formerly just Microsoft Defender. MDA is part of a more extensive suite of products under the umbrella name of Microsoft Defender for Endpoint. Windows 10/11 and Windows Server come with a Defender module to help you manage Defender on a server. See `https://www.microsoft.com/microsoft-365/security/endpoint-defender` for more information.

The systems used in the chapter

This chapter uses two systems: DC1 and SRV1, and should have the second domain controller, DC2, online like this:

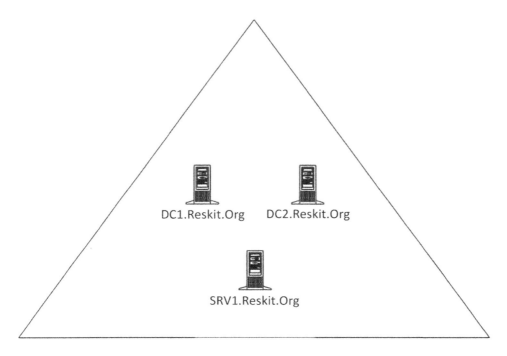

Reskit.Org domain

Figure 6.1: Hosts in use for this chapter

Implementing Just Enough Administration (JEA)

Just Enough Administration, also known as **JEA**, is a security framework that allows you to implement fine-grained administrative delegation. With JEA, you enable a user to have just enough administrative power to do their job, and no more. JEA is a more secure alternative to just adding users to the domain administrator or enterprise administrator groups.

With JEA, you could, for example, enable a junior administrator the right to access your domain controllers to administer the DNS service on the domain controller. JEA allows you to constrain what the user can do on the protected server. For example, you could allow the user to stop and start the DNS service (using Stop-Service and Start-Service) but no other services.

JEA makes use of three objects:

- **JEA role capabilities file (.psrc)**: This file defines a role in terms of its capabilities. You would configure the JEA role RKDnsAdmins to define a limited set of cmdlets that the role has access to on the domain controller, namely those related to administering DNS on a domain controller.

- **JEA session configuration file (.pssc)**: This file defines who can access a PowerShell remoting session and what they can do within the session. The session configuration file defines the JEA session's actions in the role capabilities file. Individuals can use JEA-protected remoting to do only what the role capabilities file dictates. You could allow anyone in the RKDnsAdmins domain security group to access the server using a JEA endpoint.

- **A PowerShell remoting endpoint**: Once you have the role capabilities and session configuration files created, you register the JEA endpoint to the server you are protecting with JEA.

Once the JEA endpoint is registered, a user who is a member of the domain security group, RKDnsAdmins, can use Invoke-Command or Enter-PsSession, specifying the remote server and the JEA-protected endpoint to access the protected server. Once inside the remoting session, the user can run the commands defined by the role capabilities.

The following diagram shows the components of JEA:

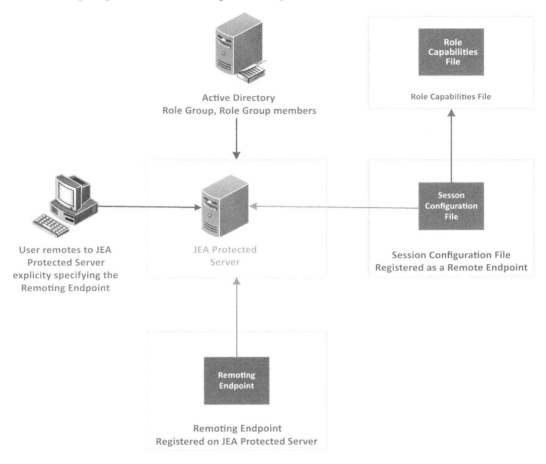

Figure 6.2: JEA components

Getting ready

This recipe uses DC1, a domain controller in the Reskit.Org domain on which you set up JEA for inbound connections. In earlier chapters, you installed DC1 as a domain controller and configured users, groups, and OUs. You run this recipe on DC1.

You would typically use a client computer to access the DC to manage DNS in production. For this recipe, adding an extra client host is replaced by using DC1 to test JEA without requiring an additional host. Of course, in production, you should test JEA on a client host.

How to do it...

1. Creating a transcripts folder

```
New-Item -Path C:\JEATranscripts -ItemType Directory |
    Out-Null
```

2. Creating a role capabilities folder

```
$Capabilities= "C:\JEACapabilities"
New-Item -Path $Capabilities -ItemType Directory |
    Out-Null
```

3. Creating a JEA session configuration folder

```
$SCF = 'C:\JEASessionConfiguration'
New-Item -Path $SCF -ItemType Directory |
    Out-Null
```

4. Creating DNSAdminsJEA as a global security group

```
$DNSGHT = @{
    Name           = 'DNSAdminsJEA'
    Description    = 'DNS Admins for JEA'
    GroupCategory = 'Security'
    GroupScope     = 'Global'
}
New-ADGroup @DNSGHT
Get-ADGroup -Identity 'DNSAdminsJEA' |
    Move-ADObject -TargetPath 'OU=IT, DC=Reskit, DC=Org'
```

5. Adding JerryG to the DNS Admins group

```
$ADGHT = @{
    Identity  = 'DNSAdminsJEA'
    Members   = 'JerryG'
}
Add-ADGroupMember @ADGHT
```

6. Creating a JEA role capabilities file

```
$RCF = Join-Path -Path $Capabilities -ChildPath "DnsAdmins.psrc"
$RCHT = @{
```

```
          Path            = $RCF
          Author          = 'Reskit Administration'
          CompanyName     = 'Reskit.Org'
          Description     = 'DnsAdminsJEA role capabilities'
          AliasDefinition = @{Name='gh';Value='Get-Help'}
          ModulesToImport = 'Microsoft.PowerShell.Core','DnsServer'
          VisibleCmdlets  = (@{ Name       = 'Restart-Computer';
                               Parameters  = @{Name = 'ComputerName'}
                               ValidateSet = 'DC1, DC2'},
                             'DNSSERVER\*',
                           @{ Name          = 'Stop-Service';
                               Parameters   = @{Name = 'DNS'}},
                           @{ Name          = 'Start-Service';
                               Parameters   = @{Name = 'DNS'}}
                           )
          VisibleExternalCommands = ('C:\Windows\System32\whoami.exe',
                                     'C:\Windows\System32\ipconfig.exe')
          VisibleFunctions = 'Get-HW'
          FunctionDefinitions = @{
            Name = 'Get-HW'
            Scriptblock = {'Hello JEA World'}}
        }
        New-PSRoleCapabilityFile @RCHT
```

7. Creating a JEA session configuration file

```
        $P    = Join-Path -Path $SCF -ChildPath 'DnsAdmins.pssc'
        $RDHT = @{
          'DnsAdminsJEA' =
              @{'RoleCapabilityFiles' =
                'C:\JEACapabilities\DnsAdmins.psrc'}
        }
        $PSCHT= @{
          Author            = 'DoctorDNS@Gmail.Com'
          Description       = 'Session Definition for DnsAdminsJEA'
          SessionType       = 'RestrictedRemoteServer'   # ie JEA!
          Path              = $P      # Role Capabilties file
          RunAsVirtualAccount = $true
```

```
      TranscriptDirectory = 'C:\JeaTranscripts'
      RoleDefinitions     = $RDHT      # tk role mapping
    }
    New-PSSessionConfigurationFile @PSCHT
```

8. Testing the session configuration file

```
    Test-PSSessionConfigurationFile -Path $P
```

9. Enabling remoting on DC1

```
    Enable-PSRemoting -Force |
      Out-Null
```

10. Registering the JEA session configuration remoting endpoint

```
    $SCHT = @{
      Path  = $P
      Name  = 'DnsAdminsJEA'
      Force = $true
    }
    Register-PSSessionConfiguration @SCHT
```

11. Viewing remoting endpoints

```
    Get-PSSessionConfiguration   |
      Format-Table -Property Name, PSVersion, Run*Account
```

12. Verifying what the user can do

```
    $SCHT = @{
      ConfigurationName = 'DnsAdminsJEA'
      Username          = 'Reskit\JerryG'
    }
    Get-PSSessionCapability  @SCHT |
      Sort-Object -Property Module
```

13. Creating the credentials for user JerryG

```
    $U    = 'JerryG@Reskit.Org'
    $P    = ConvertTo-SecureString 'Pa$$w0rd' -AsPlainText -Force
    $Cred = [PSCredential]::New($U,$P)
```

14. Defining three script blocks and an invocation splatting hash table

```
$SB1   = {Get-Command}
$SB2   = {Get-HW}
$SB3   = {Get-Command -Name   '*-DNSSERVER*'}
$ICMHT = @{
  ComputerName      = 'DC1.Reskit.Org'
  Credential        = $Cred
  ConfigurationName = 'DnsAdminsJEA'
}
```

15. Geting commands available within the JEA session

```
Invoke-Command -ScriptBlock $SB1 @ICMHT |
  Sort-Object -Property Module |
    Select-Object -First 15
```

16. Invoking a JEA-defined function in a JEA session as JerryG

```
Invoke-Command -ScriptBlock $SB2 @ICMHT
```

17. Getting DNSServer commands available to JerryG

```
$C = Invoke-Command -ScriptBlock $SB3 @ICMHT
"$($C.Count) DNS commands available"
```

18. Examining the contents of the transcripts folder

```
Get-ChildItem -Path $PSCHT.TranscriptDirectory
```

19. Examining a transcripts

```
Get-ChildItem -Path $PSCHT.TranscriptDirectory |
  Select-Object -First 1  |
    Get-Content
```

How it works...

In *step 1*, you create a new folder to hold JEA transcripts. In *step 2*, you create a folder to store JEA role capabilities files. And in *step 3*, you create a folder to hold JEA session configuration files. Next, in *step 4*, you create a new global security group, DNSAdminsJEA. Then in *step 5*, you add the user JerryG to the newly created DNSAdminsJEA security group. This step creates no console output.

In *step 6*, you create a new JEA role capabilities file. In *step 7*, you create the JEA session configuration file. These two steps, which finish the basic JEA setup, produce no console output.

In *step 8*, you use the Test-PSSessionConfigurationFile cmdlet to ensure the session configuration file is valid. This step creates some rather simple output, like this:

```
PS C:\Foo> # 8. Testing the session configuration file
PS C:\Foo> Test-PSSessionConfigurationFile -Path $P
True
```

Figure 6.3: Testing the session configuration file

In *step 9*, you use Enable-PSRemoting to ensure you have DC1 set up for PowerShell remoting. This command produces a warning message like this:

```
PS C:\Foo> # 9. Enabling remoting on DC1
PS C:\Foo> Enable-PSRemoting -Force |
              Out Null
WARNING: PowerShell remoting has been enabled only for PowerShell 6+
configurations and does not affect Windows PowerShell remoting
configurations. Run this cmdlet in Windows PowerShell to affect all
PowerShell remoting configurations.
```

Figure 6.4: Ensuring remoting is active on DC1

In *step 10*, you register the JEA session configuration remoting endpoint with output like this:

```
PS C:\Foo> # 10. Registering the JEA session configuration remoting endpoint
PS C:\Foo> $SCHT = @{
              Path = $P
              Name = 'DnsAdminsJEA'
              Force = $true
           }
PS C:\Foo> Register-PSSessionConfiguration @SCHT

   WSManConfig: Microsoft.WSMan.Management\WSMan::localhost\Plugin

Type       keys                 Name
----       ----                 ----
Container  {Name=DnsAdminsJEA}  DnsAdminsJEA
```

Figure 6.5: Registering the JEA remoting endpoint

In *step 11*, you use the Get-PSSessionConfiguration command to display the PowerShell remoting
endpoints available, with output like this:

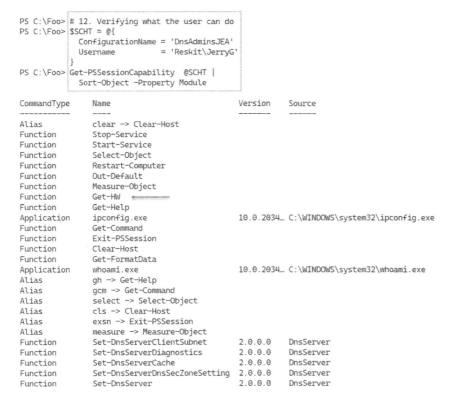

```
PS C:\Foo> # 11. Viewing remoting endpoints
PS C:\Foo> Get-PSSessionConfiguration  |
              Format-Table -Property Name, PSVersion, Run*Account

Name                   PSVersion RunAsVirtualAccount
----                   --------- -------------------
DnsAdminsJEA           7.2       True
PowerShe11.7           7.2       false
PowerShe11.7.2.5.7.2             false
```

Figure 6.6: Viewing PowerShell remoting endpoints

With *step 12*, you use the Get-PSSessionCapability command to determine what commands,
if any, the JerryG user can use within the JEA session, with output like this (truncated for publication):

```
PS C:\Foo> # 12. Verifying what the user can do
PS C:\Foo> $SCHT = @{
              ConfigurationName = 'DnsAdminsJEA'
              Username          = 'Reskit\JerryG'
           }
PS C:\Foo> Get-PSSessionCapability @SCHT |
              Sort-Object -Property Module

CommandType    Name                          Version     Source
-----------    ----                          -------     ------
Alias          clear -> Clear-Host
Function       Stop-Service
Function       Start-Service
Function       Select-Object
Function       Restart-Computer
Function       Out-Default
Function       Measure-Object
Function       Get-HW
Function       Get-Help
Application    ipconfig.exe                  10.0.2034_  C:\WINDOWS\system32\ipconfig.exe
Function       Get-Command
Function       Exit-PSSession
Function       Clear-Host
Function       Get-FormatData
Application    whoami.exe                    10.0.2034_  C:\WINDOWS\system32\whoami.exe
Alias          gh -> Get-Help
Alias          gcm -> Get-Command
Alias          select -> Select-Object
Alias          cls -> Clear-Host
Alias          exsn -> Exit-PSSession
Alias          measure -> Measure-Object
Function       Set-DnsServerClientSubnet     2.0.0.0     DnsServer
Function       Set-DnsServerDiagnostics      2.0.0.0     DnsServer
Function       Set-DnsServerCache            2.0.0.0     DnsServer
Function       Set-DnsServerDnsSecZoneSetting 2.0.0.0    DnsServer
Function       Set-DnsServer                 2.0.0.0     DnsServer
```

Figure 6.7: Viewing available commands for JerryG

In *step 13*, you create a PowerShell credential object for JerryG. In *step 14*, you create three script blocks and an invocation hash table for use in later steps, producing no output. There are numerous ways to create your credential. The approach shown here, especially as it contains the actual user name and password, is far from best practice. A better approach to obtaining credentials would be to use the Secrets module – see https://devblogs.microsoft.com/powershell-community/how-to-use-the-secret-modules/ for more details.

In *step 15*, you invoke the $SB1 script block inside a JEA session (to DC1, as JerryG), with output (truncated) like this:

```
PS C:\Foo> # 15. Getting commands available within the JEA session
PS C:\Foo> Invoke-Command -ScriptBlock $SB1 @ICMHT |
             Sort-Object -Property Module |
               Select-Object -First 15

CommandType   Name                              Version   Source      PSComputerName
-----------   ----                              -------   ------      --------------
Function      Get-HW                                                  DC1.Reskit.Org
Function      Get-Help                                                DC1.Reskit.Org
Function      Get-FormatData                                          DC1.Reskit.Org
Function      Stop-Service                                            DC1.Reskit.Org
Function      Measure-Object                                          DC1.Reskit.Org
Function      Start-Service                                           DC1.Reskit.Org
Function      Out-Default                                             DC1.Reskit.Org
Function      Get-Command                                             DC1.Reskit.Org
Function      Exit-PSSession                                          DC1.Reskit.Org
Function      Restart-Computer                                        DC1.Reskit.Org
Function      Clear-Host                                              DC1.Reskit.Org
Function      Select-Object                                           DC1.Reskit.Org
Function      Add-DnsServerClientSubnet         2.0.0.0   DnsServer   DC1.Reskit.Org
Function      Reset-DnsServerZoneKeyMasterRole  2.0.0.0   DnsServer   DC1.Reskit.Org
Function      Restore-DnsServerPrimaryZone      2.0.0.0   DnsServer   DC1.Reskit.Org
```

Figure 6.8: Getting commands available within the JEA session

In *step 16*, you invoke the $SB2 script block in the JEA session. This script block calls the Get-HW function defined in the JEA role capabilities file. The output of this step looks like this:

```
PS C:\Foo> # 16. Invoking a JEA-defined function in a JEA session as JerryG
PS C:\Foo> Invoke-Command -ScriptBlock SSB2 @ICMHT
Hello JEA World
```

Figure 6.9: Invoking a JEA-defined function in a JEA session as JerryG

In *step 17*, you invoke the $SB3 script block, which counts the number of commands available in the DNS server module, which the user JerryG has permission to use.

The output is like this:

```
PS C:\Foo> # 17. Getting DNSServer commands available to JerryG
PS C:\Foo> $C = Invoke-Command -ScriptBlock $SB3 @ICMHT
PS C:\Foo> "$($C.Count) DNS commands available"
131 DNS commands available
```

Figure 6.10: Counting the number of DNS commands available to JerryG

When you set up JEA, you indicated that JEA should create a transcript for each JEA session. In *step 18*, you examine the transcripts in the transcript folder, with output like this:

```
PS C:\Foo> # 18. Examining the contents of the transcripts folder
PS C:\Foo> Get-ChildItem -Path $PSCHT.TranscriptDirectory

    Directory: C:\JEATranscripts

Mode        LastWriteTime    Length Name
----        -------------    ------ ----
-a---  28/06/2022    17:08   12819 PowerShell_transcript.DC1.lLTY91d2.20220628170803.txt
-a---  28/06/2022    17:02   12845 PowerShell_transcript.DC1.n+EhEOfS.20220628170207.txt
-a---  28/06/2022    17:06   13108 PowerShell_transcript.DC1.Uaexd6D5.20220628170559.txt
-a---  28/06/2022    17:07     779 PowerShell_transcript.DC1.xs+t5kPA.20220628170730.txt
```

Figure 6.11: Examining the transcript folder contents

In the final step, *step 19*, in this recipe, you examine the first transcript in the transcripts folder, with output (truncated for publishing) that should look like this:

```
PS C:\Foo> # 19. Examining a transcript
PS C:\Foo> Get-ChildItem -Path $PSCHT.TranscriptDirectory |
             Select-Object -First 1  |
               Get-Content
WSManStackVersion: 3.0
**********************
PS>CommandInvocation(Get-Command): "Get-Command"
>> ParameterBinding(Get-Command): name="Name"; value="*-DNSSERVER*"
>> ParameterBinding(Get-Command): name="ListImported"; value="False"
>> ParameterBinding(Get-Command): name="ShowCommandInfo"; value="False"

CommandType    Name                                        Version    Source
-----------    ----                                        -------    ------
Function       Add-DnsServerClientSubnet                   2.0.0.0    DnsServer
Function       Add-DnsServerConditionalForwarderZone       2.0.0.0    DnsServer
Function       Add-DnsServerDirectoryPartition             2.0.0.0    DnsServer
Function       Add-DnsServerForwarder                      2.0.0.0    DnsServer
Function       Add-DnsServerPrimaryZone                    2.0.0.0    DnsServer
Function       Add-DnsServerQueryResolutionPolicy          2.0.0.0    DnsServer
```

Figure 6.12: Examining the transcripts

There's more...

In *step 1*, you run a command but pipe the output to Out-Null. This is one of several ways to run the cmdlet and avoid seeing the output from that command. Another way you could write this line is like this:

```
$Null = New-Item -Path C:\JEATranscripts -ItemType Directory
```

For more details on this, see https://powerwisescripting.blog/2020/04/15/powershell-null-vs-out-null.

In *step 6*, you create a JEA role capabilities file. In this file, you specify what actions a user can perform within a JEA session. This file defines the commands a user can run, modules they can load, specific JEA session-specific functions they can access, and more. You can, for example, specify that the JEA user can run a cmdlet that takes parameters, but you only allow specific parameter values. For instance, you could enable the user to start a service using Start-Service, but only the DNS service and not any other service. If you are deploying JEA in an enterprise, you might have many servers and services managed with JEA sessions and a disparate user base. In such cases, you may wish to create a platform for your deployment to simplify creating the role definitions and your JEA deployment in general.

In *step 9*, you use the Enable-PSRemoting command. This command ensures you enable WinRM remoting and creates two standard PowerShell 7 remoting endpoints, in addition to the one you create in *step 10*.

In *step 15*, you run $SB1 inside a JEA session on DC1. This script invokes Get-Command to list all the commands available to any member of the DNSAdminsJEA group. The output is truncated in the figure to take up less space for publishing. The complete output lists all the commands available.

In *step 16*, you use the Get-HW function defined in the JEA role capabilities file. This function only exists within the JEA session.

In *step 18*, you examine the transcripts in the JEA transcripts folder. Depending on what you have done so far, you may see a different number of transcripts. Each transcript represents one use of a JEA session. The transcript contains full details of the user's commands inside the session and documents that the user initiated the session and when. The transcript provides valuable information for subsequent analysis where needed.

In the final step, *step 19*, you examine one of the JEA session transcripts. In *Figure 6.12*, you see the transcript generated by *step 15*. You must also manage the transcripts folder, including archiving or removing older transcripts. And if you are implementing JEA widely, you may wish to develop some summary reporting based on each transcript's contents, including which users used any JEA session and when.

Examining Applications and Services Logs

Since the first version of Windows NT in 1993, anytime anything happens on a Windows, the component responsible writes details to an event log. In the earlier versions of Windows Server, there were four different Windows logs:

- Application – holds events related to software you have installed on the server
- Security – holds events related to the security of your server
- Setup – holds events related to **Knowledge Base (KB)** installation and events that occurred during installation activities
- System – holds events that relate to this system, such as system start and system shutdown

In addition to these logs, other applications and features can add additional logs. You can see the classic and additional logs using the Windows Powershell Get-Eventlog cmdlet.

With Windows Vista, Microsoft significantly improved the event logging features, including adding the applications and Services logs. This provides you with more than four hundred individual logs (although not all are enabled by default). These extra logs allow Windows components to write to application-specific logs rather than the system or application classic event logs. Individual application-specific logs make finding application-specific issues easier to find. You can use Get-Event to examine the classic event logs, and, with PowerShell 7, you use Get-WinEvent to work with all of the event logs, including these newer ones.

In this recipe, you examine both the classic event logs and the applications and Services Logs and get log event details from both sets of event logs.

Getting ready

You run this recipe on SRV1, a domain-joined server. You used SRV1 in earlier chapters, on which you installed PowerShell 7. You should ensure you log in as the domain administrator (Reskit\ Administrator).

How to do it...

1. Registering PowerShell event log provider

   ```
   & $PSHOME\RegisterManifest.ps1
   ```

2. Discovering classic event logs on SRV1

   ```
   Get-EventLog -LogName *
   ```

3. Discovering and measuring all event logs on this host

   ```
   $Logs = Get-WinEvent -ListLog *
   "There are $($Logs.Count) total event logs on SRV1"
   ```

4. Discovering and measuring all event logs on DC1

   ```
   $SB1     = {Get-WinEvent -ListLog *}
   $LogsDC1 = Invoke-Command -ComputerName DC1 -ScriptBlock $SB1
   "There are $($LogsDC1.Count) total event logs on DC1"
   ```

5. Discovering SRV1 log member details

   ```
   $Logs | Get-Member
   ```

6. Measuring enabled logs on SRV1

   ```
   $Logs |
     Where-Object IsEnabled |
       Measure-Object |
         Select-Object -Property Count
   ```

7. Measuring enabled logs on DC1

   ```
   $LogsDC1 |
     Where-Object IsEnabled |
       Measure-Object |
         Select-Object -Property Count
   ```

8. Measuring enabled logs that have records on SRV1

   ```
   $Logs |
     Where-Object IsEnabled |
       Where-Object RecordCount -gt 0 |
         Measure-Object |
   ```

```
          Select-Object -Property Count
```

9. Discovering PowerShell-related logs

```
$Logs |
   Where-Object LogName -match 'Powershell'
```

10. Examining PowerShellCore event log

```
Get-WinEvent -LogName 'PowerShellCore/Operational' |
   Select-Object -First 10
```

How it works...

By default, Windows disabled the PowerShell event logs. In *step 1*, you run a script that enables these logs, which generates no console output.

With *step 2*, you use Get-EventLog to discover the classic event logs on SRV1, with output like this:

```
PS C:\Foo> # 2. Discovering classic event logs on SRV1
PS C:\Foo> Get-EventLog -LogName *

Max(K) Retain OverflowAction        Entries Log
------ ------ --------------        ------- ---
20,480      0 OverwriteAsNeeded       1,241 Application
20,480      0 OverwriteAsNeeded           0 HardwareEvents
   512      7 OverwriteOlder              0 Internet Explorer
20,480      0 OverwriteAsNeeded           0 Key Management Service
20,480      0 OverwriteAsNeeded      10,334 Security
20,480      0 OverwriteAsNeeded       7,692 System
15,360      0 OverwriteAsNeeded         475 Windows PowerShell
```

Figure 6.13: Discovering classic event logs on SRV1

In *step 3*, you use the Get-WinEvent to return all the event logs on this host and provide a count of available event logs, with output like this:

```
PS C:\Foo> # 3. Discovering and measuring all event logs on this host
PS C:\Foo> $Logs = Get-WinEvent -ListLog *
PS C:\Foo> "There are $($Logs.Count) total event logs on SRV1"
There are 423 total event logs on SRV1
```

Figure 6.14: Discovering all event logs on SRV1

In *step 4*, you use `Get-WinEvent` remotely to provide details of the event logs available on the domain controller, DC1, with output like this:

```
PS C:\Foo> # 4. Discovering and measuring all event logs on DC1
PS C:\Foo> $SB1    = {Get-WinEvent -ListLog *}
PS C:\Foo> $LogsDC1 = Invoke-Command -ComputerName DC1 -ScriptBlock SSB1
PS C:\Foo> "There are $($LogsDC1.Count) total event logs on DC1"
There are 415 total event logs on DC1
```

Figure 6.15: Discovering all event logs on DC1

In *step 5*, you use `Get-Member` to determine the properties available for the event logs, with output like this:

```
PS C:\Foo> # 5. Discovering SRV1 log member details
PS C:\Foo> $Logs | Get-Member


   TypeName: System.Diagnostics.Eventing.Reader.EventLogConfiguration

Name                            MemberType   Definition
----                            ----------   ----------
Dispose                         Method       void Dispose(), void IDisposable.Dispose()
Equals                          Method       bool Equals(System.Object obj)
GetHashCode                     Method       int GetHashCode()
GetType                         Method       type GetType()
SaveChanges                     Method       void SaveChanges()
ToString                        Method       string ToString()
FileSize                        NoteProperty long FileSize=1118208
IsLogFull                       NoteProperty bool IsLogFull=False
LastAccessTime                  NoteProperty datetime LastAccessTime=30/06/2022 12:45:34
LastWriteTime                   NoteProperty datetime LastWriteTime=30/06/2022 12:45:34
OldestRecordNumber              NoteProperty long OldestRecordNumber=1
RecordCount                     NoteProperty long RecordCount=475
IsClassicLog                    Property     bool IsClassicLog {get;}
IsEnabled                       Property     bool IsEnabled {get;set;}
LogFilePath                     Property     string LogFilePath {get;set;}
LogIsolation                    Property     System.Diagnostics.Eventing.Reader.EventLogIsolation LogIsolation {get;}
LogMode                         Property     System.Diagnostics.Eventing.Reader.EventLogMode LogMode {get;set;}
LogName                         Property     string LogName {get;}
LogType                         Property     System.Diagnostics.Eventing.Reader.EventLogType LogType {get;}
MaximumSizeInBytes              Property     long MaximumSizeInBytes {get;set;}
OwningProviderName              Property     string OwningProviderName {get;}
ProviderBufferSize              Property     System.Nullable[int] ProviderBufferSize {get;}
ProviderControlGuid             Property     System.Nullable[guid] ProviderControlGuid {get;}
ProviderKeywords                Property     System.Nullable[long] ProviderKeywords {get;set;}
ProviderLatency                 Property     System.Nullable[int] ProviderLatency {get;}
ProviderLevel                   Property     System.Nullable[int] ProviderLevel {get;set;}
ProviderMaximumNumberOfBuffers  Property     System.Nullable[int] ProviderMaximumNumberOfBuffers {get;}
ProviderMinimumNumberOfBuffers  Property     System.Nullable[int] ProviderMinimumNumberOfBuffers {get;}
ProviderNames                   Property     System.Collections.Generic.IEnumerable[string] ProviderNames {get;}
SecurityDescriptor              Property     string SecurityDescriptor {get;set;}
```

Figure 6.16: Discovering event log object properties

As noted above, Windows does now enable all event logs by default. In *step 6*, you count the enabled event logs (on SRV1) with output like this:

```
PS C:\Foo> # 6. Measuring enabled logs on SRV1
PS C:\Foo> $Logs |
               Where-Object IsEnabled |
                 Measure-Object |
                   Select-Object -Property Count

Count
-----
  343
```

Figure 6.17: Counting enabled event logs on SRV1

With *step 7*, you count the enabled event logs for DC1 with this output:

```
PS C:\Foo> # 7. Measuring enabled logs on DC1
PS C:\Foo> $LogsDC1 |
               Where-Object IsEnabled |
                 Measure-Object |
                   Select-Object -Property Count

Count
-----
  340
```

Figure 6.18: Counting enabled event logs on DC1

In *step 9*, you discover the PowerShell (and Windows PowerShell) related event logs with this output:

```
PS C:\Foo> # 9. Discovering PowerShell-related logs
PS C:\Foo> $Logs |
             Where-Object LogName -match 'Powershell'

LogMode     MaximumSizeInBytes RecordCount LogName
-------     ------------------ ----------- -------
Circular              15728640         475 Windows PowerShell
Circular              15728640        2630 PowerShellCore/Operational
Circular              15728640         401 Microsoft-Windows-PowerShell/Operational
Retain              1048985600           0 Microsoft-Windows-PowerShell/Admin
Circular               1052672           0 Microsoft-Windows-PowerShell-DesiredStateConfiguration-FileDownloadManager/Operational
```

Figure 6.19: Discovering PowerShell-related event logs available on SRV1

In *step 10*, you examine the ten most recent event log entries in the `PowerShell/Operational` event log, with the following output:

```
PS C:\Foo> # 10. Examining PowerShellCore event log
PS C:\Foo> Get-WinEvent -LogName 'PowerShellCore/Operational' |
              Select-Object -First 10

   ProviderName: PowerShellCore

TimeCreated                      Id LevelDisplayName Message
-----------                      -- ---------------- -------
30/06/2022 12:50:31           12039 Information      Modifying activity Id and correlating
30/06/2022 12:50:31            8196 Information      Modifying activity Id and correlating
30/06/2022 12:50:30           12039 Information      Modifying activity Id and correlating
30/06/2022 12:50:30            8196 Information      Modifying activity Id and correlating
30/06/2022 12:50:30           12039 Information      Modifying activity Id and correlating
30/06/2022 12:50:30            8196 Information      Modifying activity Id and correlating
30/06/2022 12:50:30           12039 Information      Modifying activity Id and correlating
30/06/2022 12:50:30            8196 Information      Modifying activity Id and correlating
30/06/2022 12:50:30           12039 Information      Modifying activity Id and correlating
30/06/2022 12:50:30            8196 Information      Modifying activity Id and correlating
```

Figure 6.20: Viewing more recent event entries in the PowerShell/Operational log on SRV1

There's more…

In *step 3* and *step 4*, you get a count of the number of event logs on SRV1 and DC1. As you can see, the number of logs differs on different hosts. Different Windows features and applications can add additional event logs for your use. In *step 6* and *step 7*, you also see the number of enabled logs on both systems. And with *step 8*, you see how many enabled logs (on SRV1) actually contain event log entries.

In *step 10*, you view the most recent event log entries in the PowerShell entries.

Discovering Logon Events in the Event Log

Each time you attempt to log on to Windows, whether you are successful or not, Windows logs the attempt in the security log. These log events can help determine who logged into a computer and when.

Windows defines several different logon types. A logon type of 2 indicates a local console login (logging on to a physical host), while a logon type of 10 indicates a logon over RDP. Other logon types include service logon (type 5), batch or scheduled task (type 4), and console unlock (type 7).

You can read about this in more detail in this article: `https://learn.microsoft.com/windows-server/security/windows-authentication/windows-logon-scenarios`. Note that this document is somewhat outdated, and Microsoft has not updated it for later versions of Windows.

With that said, the information continues to be correct.

In this recipe, you use PowerShell to examine the Security event log and look at the logon events.

Getting ready

You run this recipe on DC1, a domain controller in the Reskit.Org forest.

How to do it...

1. Getting security log events

   ```
   $SecLog = Get-WinEvent -ListLog Security
   "Security Event log entries:    [{0,10:N0}]" -f $Seclog.RecordCount
   ```

2. Getting all Windows Security log event details

   ```
   $SecEvents = Get-WinEvent -LogName Security
   "Found $($SecEvents.count) security events on DC1"
   ```

3. Examining Security event log event members

   ```
   $SecEvents |
     Get-Member
   ```

4. Summarizing security events by event ID

   ```
   $SecEvents |
     Sort-Object -Property Id |
       Group-Object -Property ID |
         Sort-Object -Property Name |
           Format-Table -Property Name, Count
   ```

5. Getting all successful logon events on DC1

   ```
   $Logons = $SecEvents | Where-Object ID -eq 4624    # logon event
   "Found $($Logons.Count) logon events on DC1"
   ```

6. Getting all failed logon events on DC1

   ```
   $FLogons = $SecEvents | Where-Object ID -eq 4625    # failed logon
   event
   "Found $($FLogons.Count) failed logon events on DC1"
   ```

7. Creating a summary array of successful logon events

```
$LogonEvents = @()
Foreach ($Logon in $Logons) {
  $XMLMSG = [xml] $Logon.ToXml()
  $Text = '#text'
  $HostName   = $XMLMSG.Event.EventData.data.$Text[1]
  $HostDomain = $XMLMSG.Event.EventData.data.$Text[2]
  $Account    = $XMLMSG.Event.EventData.data.$Text[5]
  $AcctDomain = $XMLMSG.Event.EventData.data.$Text[6]
  $LogonType  = $XMLMSG.Event.EventData.data.$Text[8]
  $LogonEvent = New-Object -Type PSCustomObject -Property @{
      Account   = "$AcctDomain\$Account"
      Host      = "$HostDomain\$Hostname"
      LogonType = $LogonType
      Time      = $Logon.TimeCreated
  }
  $LogonEvents += $logonEvent
}
```

8. Summarizing successful logon events on DC1

```
$LogonEvents |
  Group-Object -Property LogonType |
    Sort-Object -Property Name |
      Select-Object -Property Name,Count
```

9. Creating a summary array of failed logon events on DC1

```
$FLogonEvents = @()
Foreach ($FLogon in $FLogons) {
  $XMLMSG = [xml] $FLogon.ToXml()
  $Text = '#text'
  $HostName   = $XMLMSG.Event.EventData.data.$Text[1]
  $HostDomain = $XMLMSG.Event.EventData.data.$Text[2]
  $Account    = $XMLMSG.Event.EventData.data.$Text[5]
  $AcctDomain = $XMLMSG.Event.EventData.data.$Text[6]
  $LogonType  = $XMLMSG.Event.EventData.data.$Text[8]
  $LogonEvent = New-Object -Type PSCustomObject -Property @{
```

```
            Account    = "$AcctDomain\$Account"
            Host       = "$HostDomain\$Hostname"
            LogonType  = $LogonType
            Time       = $FLogon.TimeCreated
        }
        $FLogonEvents += $LogonEvent
    }
```

10. Summarizing failed logon events on DC1

```
    $FLogonEvents |
      Group-Object -Property Account |
        Sort-Object -Property Name |
          Format-Table Name, Count
```

How it works...

In *step 1*, you use the Get-WinEvent cmdlet to retrieve details about the security log on DC1. Then you display the number of events in the Security event log. The output looks like this:

```
PS C:\Foo> # 1. Getting Security log events
PS C:\Foo> $SecLog = Get-WinEvent -ListLog Security
PS C:\Foo> "Security Event log entries:    [{10,10:N0}]" -f $Seclog.RecordCount
Security Event log entries:    [    80,792]
```

Figure 6.21: Getting security log events

In *step 2*, you use Get-WinEvent to retrieve all events from the security log and display a count of the events returned, with output like this:

```
PS C:\Foo> # 2. Getting all Windows Security log event details
PS C:\Foo> $SecEvents = Get-WinEvent -LogName Security
PS C:\Foo> "Found $C$SecEvents.count) security events on DC1"
Found 80792 security events on DC1
```

Figure 6.22: Getting all Windows security log event details

The Get-WinEvent cmdlet returns objects that contain individual event log entries. Each object is of the type System.Diagnostics.Eventing.Reader.EventLogRecord.

In *step 3*, you view the members of this .NET object class with output like this:

```
PS C:\Foo> # 3: Examining Security event log event members
PS C:\Foo> $SecEvents |
              Get-Member

   TypeName: System.Diagnostics.Eventing.Reader.EventLogRecord

Name                     MemberType   Definition
----                     ----------   ----------
Dispose                  Method       void Dispose(), void IDisposable.Dispose()
Equals                   Method       bool Equals(System.Object obj)
FormatDescription        Method       string FormatDescription(), string FormatDescription(System.Collections.
                                          Generic.IEnumerable[System.Object] values)
GetHashCode              Method       int GetHashCode()
GetPropertyValues        Method       System.Collections.Generic.IList[System.Object] GetPropertyValues(System.
                                          Diagnostics.Eventing.Reader.EventLogPropertySelector propertySelector)
GetType                  Method       type GetType()
ToString                 Method       string ToString()
ToXml                    Method       string ToXml()
Message                  NoteProperty string Message=An account was logged off.…
ActivityId               Property     System.Nullable[guid] ActivityId {get;}
Bookmark                 Property     System.Diagnostics.Eventing.Reader.EventBookmark Bookmark {get;}
ContainerLog             Property     string ContainerLog {get;}
Id                       Property     int Id {get;}
Keywords                 Property     System.Nullable[long] Keywords {get;}
KeywordsDisplayNames     Property     System.Collections.Generic.IEnumerable[string] KeywordsDisplayNames {get;}
Level                    Property     System.Nullable[byte] Level {get;}
LevelDisplayName         Property     string LevelDisplayName {get;}
LogName                  Property     string LogName {get;}
MachineName              Property     string MachineName {get;}
MatchedQueryIds          Property     System.Collections.Generic.IEnumerable[int] MatchedQueryIds {get;}
Opcode                   Property     System.Nullable[short] Opcode {get;}
OpcodeDisplayName        Property     string OpcodeDisplayName {get;}
ProcessId                Property     System.Nullable[int] ProcessId {get;}
Properties               Property     System.Collections.Generic.IList[System.Diagnostics.Eventing.Reader.
                                          EventProperty] Properties {get;}
ProviderId               Property     System.Nullable[guid] ProviderId {get;}
ProviderName             Property     string ProviderName {get;}
Qualifiers               Property     System.Nullable[int] Qualifiers {get;}
RecordId                 Property     System.Nullable[long] RecordId {get;}
RelatedActivityId        Property     System.Nullable[guid] RelatedActivityId {get;}
Task                     Property     System.Nullable[int] Task {get;}
TaskDisplayName          Property     string TaskDisplayName {get;}
ThreadId                 Property     System.Nullable[int] ThreadId {get;}
TimeCreated              Property     System.Nullable[datetime] TimeCreated {get;}
UserId                   Property     System.Security.Principal.SecurityIdentifier UserId {get;}
Version                  Property     System.Nullable[byte] Version {get;}
```

Figure 6.23: Examining Security event log entry members

Once you have retrieved the events in the security log, you can examine the different security event types held in the ID field of each log record. In *step 4*, you view and count the different event IDs in the security log. The output from this step, truncated for publication, looks like this:

```
PS C:\Foo> # 4. Summarizing security events by event ID
PS C:\Foo> $SecEvents |
              Sort-Object -Property Id |
                Group-Object -Property ID |
                  Sort-Object -Property Name |
                    Format-Table -Property Name, Count

Name Count
---- -----
1100     7
1101     2
4608    11
4616    23
4624 23829
4625     5
4634 22346
4647     6
4648   171
4662   242
4672 21887
4688   122
4696    11
4713     1
```

Figure 6.24: Summarizing security events by event ID

There are two logon-related events you might track, particularly on important servers. Log entries with an event ID of 4624 represent successful logon events, while 4625 represents failed logons. In *step 5*, you get ALL the successful logon events, with output like this:

```
PS C:\Foo> # 5. Getting all successful logon events on DC1
PS C:\Foo> $Logons = $SecEvents | Where-Object ID -eq 4624    # logon event
PS C:\Foo> "Found $($Logons.Count) logon events on DC1"
Found 23829 logon events on DC1
```

Figure 6.25: Getting all successful logon events on DC1

In *step 6*, you count the number of logon failures on DC1, which looks like this:

```
PS C:\Foo> # 6. Getting all failed logon events on DC1
PS C:\Foo> $FLogons = $SecEvents | Where-Object ID -eq 4625    # failed logon event
PS C:\Foo> "Found $($FLogons.Count) failed logon events on DC1"
Found 5 failed logon events on DC1
```

Figure 6.26: Getting all failed logon events on DC1

In *step 7*, you create an array summarizing the successful logons. This step produces no output. In *step 8*, you summarize the successful logon events showing how many logon events occurred by each type.

The output of this step looks like this:

```
PS C:\Foo> # 8. Summarizing successful logon events on DC1
PS C:\Foo> $LogonEvents |
             Group-Object -Property LogonType |
               Sort-Object -Property Name |
                 Select-Object -Property Name,Count


Name Count
---- -----
0       11
10       6
2       99
3    22383
5     1328
7        2
```

Figure 6.27: Summarizing successful logon events on DC1 by logon type

In *step 9*, you summarize the failed logon events on DC1. You display the details of unsuccessful logons with *step 10*, which looks like this:

```
PS C:\Foo> # 10. Summarizing failed logon events on DC1
PS C:\Foo> $FLogonEvents |
             Group-Object -Property Account |
               Sort-Object -Property Name |
                 Format-Table Name, Count


Name                    Count
----                    -----
Reskit\Malcolm            2
Reskit\BobbyW             3
```

Figure 6.28: Summarizing failed logon events on DC1 by user name

There's more...

In *step 1*, you retrieve a summary of the events in the security log and display the number of events in the log. In *step 2*, you retrieve and count the number of entries. As shown in the figures above, the counts do not match. The event counts may differ since Windows constantly logs additional events to the security log. The additional events are events generated by background tasks or services. This minor discrepancy is not unexpected and is harmless.

In *step 3*, you view the members of log event objects. You can discover more about the members of the class at `https://learn.microsoft.com/dotnet/api/system.diagnostics.eventing.reader.eventlogrecord`.

In *step 6*, you obtain unsuccessful logon events. To get unsuccessful logons, you must ensure you have attempted to log on to DC1 but with invalid credentials. As you see in the output of *step 10* in *Figure 6.28*, two users were involved with the recent unsuccessful logon attempts on DC1. Depending on which user you have attempted to log in to this server (and failed), the results you see in this step may differ from the above figure.

In *step 7*, you parse the XML log data to create a summary array. To create this array, you need to know which XML data item corresponds to the hostname, account name, etc. Note that this step uses normal PowerShell arrays. You could have used the [System.Arraylist] type, which would be a bit more performant. For some background into the array versus arraylist types, see https://learn.microsoft.com/en-us/powershell/scripting/learn/deep-dives/everything-about-arrays?view=powershell-7.2.

Deploying PowerShell Group Policies

AD supports group policies. Group policies are groups of policies you can deploy to control a user or computer environment. The policies define what a given user can and cannot do on a given Windows computer. For example, you can create a **Group Policy Object (GPO)** that defines what screen saver to use, allow the user to see the Control Panel, or specify a default PowerShell execution policy. There are over 2,500 individual settings that you can deploy.

After you create a GPO and specify the policies to deploy, you can apply the GPO to an **Organizational Unit (OU)** in your domain (or to the domain as a whole to a specific AD site). An OU is a container object within the AD that can contain other OUs and leaf objects such as AD users, computers, or group objects. You use OUs to support the deployment of GPOs and the delegation of AD administration.

GPOs provide considerable flexibility in restricting what users can do on a workstation or a server. You can apply a GPO to a specific OU, the domain, or an AD site. Additionally, you can specify whether policies within a given GPO are to apply to users, computers, or both.

With Windows PowerShell 5.1, Microsoft included a set of five Group Policy settings. The PowerShell team has extended the policies you can use with PowerShell 7. Installing PowerShell 7, even on a DC, does not also install the necessary GPO administrative template files. So you need to install them yourself if you choose to use them.

You can find the policy template files and a script to install them in the PowerShell home folder ($PSHOME). After installing PowerShell 7 on your domain controller, you run the installation script in the $PSHOME folder and install the policy definitions. If you use one, you either do this on all DCs or the central policy store.

For some details on PowerShell 7's group policies, see https://learn.microsoft.com/ powershell/module/microsoft.powershell.core/about/about_group_policy_settings.

In this recipe, you discover the files necessary to add PowerShell 7 GPO support, run the installer, then create a GPO to deploy a set of PowerShell-related policies.

Getting ready

You run this recipe on DC1 after installing PowerShell 7 and Visual Studio. DC1 is a domain controller in the Reskit.Org domain you used in earlier chapters.

How to do it...

1. Discovering the GPO-related files

```
Get-ChildItem -Path $PSHOME -Filter *Core*Policy*
```

2. Installing the PowerShell 7 group policy files

```
$LOC = $PSHOME + '\InstallPSCorePolicyDefinitions.ps1'
& $LOC -VERBOSE
```

3. Creating and displaying a new GPO for the IT group

```
$PshGPO = New-GPO -Name 'PowerShell GPO for IT'
```

4. Enabling module logging

```
$GPOKEY1 =
    'HKCU\Software\Policies\Microsoft\PowerShellCore\ModuleLogging'
$GPOHT1 = @{
  DisplayName    = $PshGPO.DisplayName
  Key            = $GPOKEY1
  Type           = [Microsoft.Win32.RegistryValueKind]::DWord
  ValueName      = 'EnableModuleLogging'
  Value          = 1
}
Set-GPRegistryValue @GPOHT1 | Out-Null
```

5. Configuring module names to log

```
$GPOHT2 = @{
  DisplayName    = $PshGPO.DisplayName
```

```
    Key             = "$GPOKEY1\ModuleNames"
    Type            = [Microsoft.Win32.RegistryValueKind]::String
    ValueName       = 'ITModule1', 'ITModule2'
    Value           = 'ITModule1', 'ITModule2'
  }
  Set-GPRegistryValue @GPOHT2 | Out-Null
```

6. Enabling script block logging

```
  $GPOKey3 =
    'HKCU\Software\Policies\Microsoft\PowerShellCore\
  ScriptBlockLogging'
  $GPOHT3  = @{
      DisplayName     = $PshGPO.DisplayName
      Key             = $GPOKEY3
      Type            = [Microsoft.Win32.RegistryValueKind]::DWord
      ValueName       = 'EnableScriptBlockLogging'
      Value           = 1
    }
  Set-GPRegistryValue @GPOHT3 | Out-Null
```

7. Enabling Unrestricted Execution Policy

```
  $GPOKey4 =
    'HKCU\Software\Policies\Microsoft\PowerShellCore'
  # create the key value to enable
  $GPOHT4 =  @{
      DisplayName     = $PshGPO.DisplayName
      Key             = $GPOKEY4
      Type            = [Microsoft.Win32.RegistryValueKind]::DWord
      ValueName       = 'EnableScripts'
      Value           = 1
    }
    Set-GPRegistryValue @GPOHT4 | Out-Null
  # Set the default
  $GPOHT4 = @{
    DisplayName     = $PshGPO.DisplayName
    Key             = "$GPOKEY4"
    Type            = [Microsoft.Win32.RegistryValueKind]::String
```

```
   ValueName      = 'ExecutionPolicy'
   Value          = 'Unrestricted'
}
Set-GPRegistryValue @GPOHT4
```

8. Assigning GPO to IT OU

```
$Target = "OU=IT, DC=Reskit, DC=Org"
New-GPLink -DisplayName $PshGPO.Displayname -Target $Target |
   Out-Null
```

9. Creating and viewing an RSOP report (after logging in as JerryG!)

```
$RSOPHT = @{
   ReportType = 'HTML'
   Path       = 'C:\Foo\GPOReport.Html'
   User       = 'Reskit\Jerryg'
}
Get-GPResultantSetOfPolicy @RSOPHT
& $RSOPHT.Path
```

How it works...

In *step 1*, you discover the PowerShell 7 GPO-related files, with output like this:

```
PS C:\Foo> # 1. Discovering the GPO-related files
PS C:\Foo> Get-ChildItem -Path $PSHOME -Filter *Core*Policy*


    Directory: C:\Program Files\PowerShell\7

Mode          LastWriteTime Length Name
----          ------------- ------ ----
-a--- 15/06/2022    17:24   17386 InstallPSCorePolicyDefinitions.ps1
-a--- 15/06/2022    17:08    9675 PowerShellCoreExecutionPolicy.adml
-a--- 15/06/2022    17:08    6198 PowerShellCoreExecutionPolicy.admx
```

Figure 6.29: Discovering the GPO-related files

In *step 2*, you create a string to hold the location of the GPO installation file. Then you run this file to install the GPO files, which look like this:

```
PS C:\Foo> # 2. Installing the PowerShell 7 group policy files
PS C:\Foo> $LOC = $PSHOME + '\InstallPSCorePolicyDefinitions.ps1'
PS C:\Foo> & $LOC -VERBOSE
VERBOSE: Copying C:\Program Files\PowerShell\7\PowerShellCoreExecutionPolicy.admx
  to C:\WINDOWS\PolicyDefinitions
VERBOSE: PowerShellCoreExecutionPolicy.admx was installed successfully
VERBOSE: Copying C:\Program Files\PowerShell\7\PowerShellCoreExecutionPolicy.adml
  to C:\WINDOWS\PolicyDefinitions\en-US
VERBOSE: PowerShellCoreExecutionPolicy.adml was installed successfully
```

Figure 6.30: Installing the PowerShell 7 group policy files

In *step 3*, you create a new GPO object and view it, which produces this output:

```
PS C:\Foo> # 3. Creating and displaying a new GPO for the IT group
PS C:\Foo> $GPOName = 'PowerShell GPO for IT'
PS C:\Foo> $PshGPO = New-GPO -Name $GPOName
PS C:\Foo> Get-GPO -Name $GPOName

DisplayName      : PowerShell GPO for IT
DomainName       : Reskit.Org
Owner            : RESKIT\Domain Admins
Id               : 694960eb-41a8-43de-95e1-1a12ffe4006e
GpoStatus        : AllSettingsEnabled
Description      :
CreationTime     : 01/07/2022 13:59:47
ModificationTime : 01/07/2022 14:03:30
UserVersion      :
ComputerVersion  :
WmiFilter        :
```

Figure 6.31: Creating and displaying a new GPO object for the IT group

In *step 4*, you configure the GPO to enable module logging, and in *step 5*, you configure the module names to log. In *step 6*, you enable script block logging, and in *step 7*, you configure the GPO to allow an Unrestricted PowerShell execution policy. These four steps produce no output.

In *step 8*, you assign this GPO to the IT OU, creating no output. In the final step, *step 9*, you create and view a resultant set of policy reports, which looks like this:

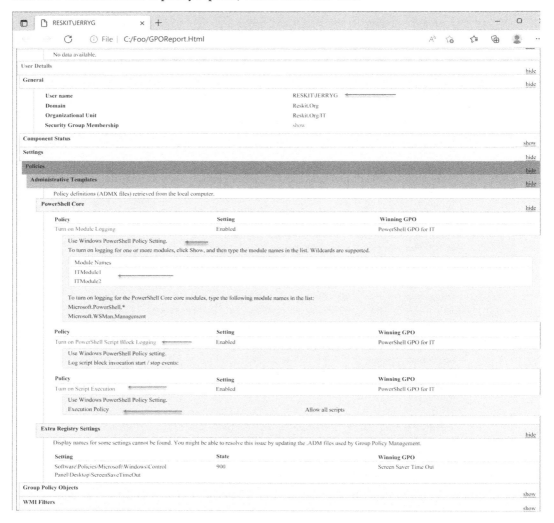

Figure 6.32: Viewing an RSOP report

There's more...

This recipe creates a new GPO, configures the GPO object with specific policy values, and then assigns it to the IT OU in the Reskit.Org domain. When any user in the IT group logs on, PowerShell performs the specified logging and uses an Unrestricted execution policy. You can see in the RSOP report, produced in *step 9*, which policy settings PowerShell applies.

In *step 9*, you create an RSOP report. To ensure you get sensible output, you must ensure that the user JerryG has logged into the DC (as noted in the step heading). That way, you can generate a meaningful RSOP report.

Using PowerShell Script Block Logging

In the *Deploying PowerShell group policies* recipe, you saw how you could deploy policies related to PowerShell 7. One of these policies, Script Block Logging, causes PowerShell 7 to generate log events whenever you execute a script block that PowerShell deems noteworthy. PowerShell does not log ALL script blocks, only those that can change the system's state.

There are two ways you can use to implement script block logging. The first and possibly best approach is to use GPOs to enforce logging on some or all hosts. You can also configure the local registry to enable script block logging. Modifying the local registry mimics a GPO by setting the appropriate registry settings on a host. You can use the Group Policy editor – it does provide a nice interface to the policies but you can't automate the GUI. The GUI may be more convenient if you need to make a single policy change to a single GPO. But if you are making changes to or creating more policies, using a PowerShell script may be more productive.

Getting ready

You run this recipe on SRV1, a domain-joined Windows host in the Reskit.Org domain. You must log in as a Reskit\Administrator, a member of the domain administrators group.

How to do it...

1. Clearing PowerShell Core operational log

```
wevtutil.exe cl 'PowerShellCore/Operational'
```

2. Enabling script block logging for the current user

```
$SBLPath = 'HKCU:\Software\Policies\Microsoft\PowerShellCore' +
            '\ScriptBlockLogging'
if (-not (Test-Path $SBLPath))  {
        $null = New-Item $SBLPath -Force
    }
Set-ItemProperty $SBLPath -Name EnableScriptBlockLogging -Value '1'
```

3. Examining the PowerShell Core event log for 4104 events

```
Get-Winevent -LogName 'PowerShellCore/Operational' |
  Where-Object Id -eq 4104
```

4. Examining logged event details

```
Get-Winevent -LogName 'PowerShellCore/Operational' |
  Where-Object Id -eq 4104  |
    Select-Object -First 1 |
      Format-List -Property ID, Logname, Message
```

5. Creating another script block that PowerShell does not log

```
$SBtolog = {Get-CimInstance -Class Win32_ComputerSystem | Out-Null}
$Before = Get-WinEvent -LogName 'PowerShellCore/Operational'
Invoke-Command -ScriptBlock $SBtolog
$After = Get-WinEvent -LogName 'PowerShellCore/Operational'
```

6. Comparing the events before and after you invoke the command

```
"Before:  $($Before.Count) events"
"After :  $($After.Count) events"
```

7. Removing registry policy entry

```
Remove-Item -Path $SBLPath
```

How it works...

In *step 1*, you use the wevtutil.exe console application to clear the PowerShell Core operational log. In *step 2*, you update the registry to enable script block logging for the currently logged-on user (Reskit\Administrator). These steps produce no output.

In *step 3*, you examine the PowerShell Core log for 4104 events, with output like this:

```
PS C:\Foo> # 3. Examining the PowerShell Core event log for 4104 events
PS C:\Foo> Get-Winevent -LogName 'PowerShellCore/Operational' |
             Where-Object Id -eq 4104

    ProviderName: PowerShellCore

TimeCreated          Id  LevelDisplayName  Message
-----------          --  ----------------  -------
10/07/2022 15:39:03  4104  Warning          Creating Scriptblock text (1 of 1):…
10/07/2022 15:39:03  4104  Warning          Creating Scriptblock text (1 of 1):…
10/07/2022 15:37:21  4104  Warning          Creating Scriptblock text (1 of 1):…
10/07/2022 15:37:21  4104  Warning          Creating Scriptblock text (1 of 1):…
```

Figure 6.33: Examining the PowerShell Core event log for 4104 events

In *step 4*, you view the details of one of the event log entries you saw in the previous step, with output that looks like this:

```
PS C:\Foo> # 4. Examining logged event details
PS C:\Foo> Get-Winevent -LogName 'PowerShellCore/Operational' |
             Where-Object Id -eq 4104 |
               Select-Object -First 1 |
                 Format-List -Property ID, Logname, Message

Id      : 4104
LogName : PowerShellCore/Operational
Message : Creating Scriptblock text (1 of 1):
          Set-ItemProperty $SBLPath -Name EnableScriptBlockLogging -Value '1'

          ScriptBlock ID: 0ea65eb3-e6b5-4b36-9ceb-d8076b9e80a4
```

Figure 6.34: Examining logged event details

In *step 5*, you create and execute another script block. This step gets a count of the event log entries before and after you execute the script block. In this case, this script block is one that PowerShell does not consider important enough to log. This step produces no output, but in *step 6*, you view the before and after counts like this:

```
PS C:\Foo> # 6. Comparing the events before and after you invoke the command
PS C:\Foo> "Before:  $($Before.Count) events"
Before:  4 events
PS C:\Foo> "After :  $($After.Count) events"
After :  4 events
```

Figure 6.35: Comparing events in the PowerShell event log

In the final step, *step 7*, you remove the policy entry from the registry, producing no output.

There's more...

In *step 1*, you use the wevtutil.exe console application to clear an event log. With Windows PowerShell, you can use the Clear-EventLog cmdlet that you can use to clear an event log. This cmdlet does not exist in PowerShell 7, which is why you use a Win32 console application to clear the event log. As an alternative, you could use PowerShell remoting, create a remoting session to the current machine using a Windows PowerShell endpoint, and run the Clear-EventLog command in that session.

In *step 6*, you can see that the script block you executed did not result in PowerShell logging the script block. By not logging every script block, you reduce the amount of logging PowerShell needs to perform (and the work you need to do to review the logs).

Configuring AD Password Policies

Passwords are essential for security as they help ensure that a person is who they say they are and thus are allowed to perform an action such as logging on to a host or editing a file. Password policies allow you to define your password attributes, including the minimum length and whether complex passwords are required. You can also set the number of times a user can enter an invalid password before that user is locked out (and a lockout duration). For more details on improving authentication security, see https://www.microsoftpressstore.com/articles/article.aspx?p=2224364&seqNum=2.

In AD, you can apply a default domain password policy. This policy applies to all users in the domain. In most cases, this is adequate for the organization. But in some cases, you may wish to apply a more stringent password policy to certain users or groups of users. You can use AD's fine-grained password policy to manage these more restrictive passwords. A "fine-grained" policy is one you can apply to just a single user or an OU, as opposed to every user in the domain.

Getting ready

You run this recipe on DC1, a domain controller in the Reskit.Org domain. You must log in as a domain administrator.

How to do it...

1. Discovering the current domain password policy

    ```
    Get-ADDefaultDomainPasswordPolicy
    ```

2. Discovering if there is a fine-grained password policy for JerryG

    ```
    Get-ADFineGrainedPasswordPolicy -Identity 'JerryG'
    ```

3. Updating the default password policy

    ```
    $DPWPHT = [Ordered] @{
        LockoutDuration           = '00:45:00'
        LockoutObservationWindow  = '00:30:00'
        ComplexityEnabled         = $true
        ReversibleEncryptionEnabled = $false
        MinPasswordLength         = 6
    }
    Get-ADDefaultDomainPasswordPolicy -Current LoggedOnUser |
      Set-ADDefaultDomainPasswordPolicy @DPWPHT
    ```

4. Checking updated default password policy

```
Get-ADDefaultDomainPasswordPolicy
```

5. Creating a fine-grained password policy

```
$PD = 'DNS Admins Group Fine-grained Password Policy'
$FGPHT = @{
  Name                    = 'DNSPWP'
  Precedence              = 500
  ComplexityEnabled       = $true
  Description             = $PD
  DisplayName             = 'DNS Admins Password Policy'
  LockoutDuration         = '0.12:00:00'
  LockoutObservationWindow = '0.00:42:00'
  LockoutThreshold        = 3
}
New-ADFineGrainedPasswordPolicy @FGPHT
```

6. Assigning the policy to DNSAdmins

```
$DNSADmins = Get-ADGroup -Identity DNSAdmins
$ADDHT = @{
  Identity = 'DNSPWP'
  Subjects = $DNSADmins
}
Add-ADFineGrainedPasswordPolicySubject  @ADDHT
```

7. Assigning the policy to JerryG

```
$Jerry = Get-ADUser -Identity JerryG
Add-ADFineGrainedPasswordPolicySubject -Identity DNSPWP -Subjects
$Jerry
```

8. Checking on policy applications for the group

```
Get-ADGroup 'DNSAdmins' -Properties * |
  Select-Object -Property msDS-PSOApplied
```

9. Checking on policy applications for the user

```
Get-ADUser JerryG -Properties * |
  Select-Object -Property msDS-PSOApplied
```

10. Getting DNS Admins policy

```
Get-ADFineGrainedPasswordPolicy -Identity DNSPWP
```

11. Checking on JerryG's resultant password policy

```
Get-ADUserResultantPasswordPolicy -Identity JerryG
```

How it works...

In *step 1*, you retrieve and display the default AD password policy, which looks like this:

```
PS C:\Foo> # 1. Discovering the current domain password policy
PS C:\Foo> Get-ADDefaultDomainPasswordPolicy

ComplexityEnabled             : True
DistinguishedName             : DC=Reskit,DC=Org
LockoutDuration               : 00:30:00
LockoutObservationWindow      : 00:30:00
LockoutThreshold              : 0
MaxPasswordAge                : 42.00:00:00
MinPasswordAge                : 1.00:00:00
MinPasswordLength             : 7
objectClass                   : {domainDNS}
objectGuid                    : ceb54656-2e25-4bec-b0f1-1c562e03230e
PasswordHistoryCount          : 24
ReversibleEncryptionEnabled   : False
```

Figure 6.36: Discovering the current domain password policy

In *step 2,* you check to see if there are any fine-grained password policies for the user JerryG, which looks like this:

```
PS C:\Foo> # 2. Discovering if there is a fine-grained password policy for JerryG
PS C:\Foo> Get-ADFineGrainedPasswordPolicy -Identity 'JerryG'
Get-ADFineGrainedPasswordPolicy: Cannot find an object with identity: 'JerryG' under: 'DC=Reskit,DC=Org'.
```

Figure 6.37: Checking for fine-grained password policies

In *step 3*, you update the default password policy for the domain, changing a few settings. This produces no output. In *step 4*, you review the updated default password policy, which looks like this:

```
PS C:\Foo> # 4. Checking updated default password policy
PS C:\Foo> Get-ADDefaultDomainPasswordPolicy

ComplexityEnabled            : True
DistinguishedName            : DC=Reskit,DC=Org
LockoutDuration              : 00:45:00
LockoutObservationWindow     : 00:30:00
LockoutThreshold             : 0
MaxPasswordAge               : 42.00:00:00
MinPasswordAge               : 1.00:00:00
MinPasswordLength            : 6
objectClass                  : {domainDNS}
objectGuid                   : ceb54656-2e25-4bec-b0f1-1c562e03230e
PasswordHistoryCount         : 24
ReversibleEncryptionEnabled  : False
```

Figure 6.38: Checking the updated default password policy

In *step 5*, you create a new fine-grained password policy with some overrides to the default domain policy you looked at above. In *step 6*, you assign the policy to the DNS Admins group, and in *step 7*, you apply this policy explicitly to the user JerryG. These three steps create no output.

In *step 8*, you check on the policy application for the DNSAdmins group, which looks like this:

```
PS C:\Foo> # 8. Checking on policy application for the group
PS C:\Foo> Get-ADGroup 'DNSAdmins' -Properties * |
             Select-Object -Property msDS-PSOApplied

msDS-PSOApplied
---------------
{CN=DNSPWP,CN=Password Settings Container,CN=System,DC=Reskit,DC=Org}
```

Figure 6.39: Checking the policy application for the DNS Admins group

In *step 9*, you check on the password policy applied to the user JerryG, which looks like this:

```
PS C:\Foo> # 9. Checking on policy application for the user
PS C:\Foo> Get-ADUser JerryG -Properties * |
             Select-Object -Property msDS-PSOApplied

msDS-PSOApplied
---------------
{CN=DNSPWP,CN=Password Settings Container,CN=System,DC=ReskitIDC=Org}
```

Figure 6.40: Checking on policy application for the user

In *step 10*, you examine the DNS Admins password policy, with output like this:

```
PS C:\Foo> # 10. Getting DNS Admins policy
PS C:\Foo> Get-ADFineGrainedPasswordPolicy -Identity DNSPWP

AppliesTo                   : {CN=Jerry Garcia,OU=IT,DC=Reskit,DC=Org, CN=DnsAdmins,CN=Users,DC=Reskit,DC=Org}
ComplexityEnabled           : True
DistinguishedName           : CN=DNSPWP,CN=Password Settings Container,CN=System,DC=Reskit,DC=Org
LockoutDuration             : 12:00:00
LockoutObservationWindow    : 00:42:00
LockoutThreshold            : 3
MaxPasswordAge              : 42.00:00:00
MinPasswordAge              : 1.00:00:00
MinPasswordLength           : 7
Name                        : DNSPWP
ObjectClass                 : msDS-PasswordSettings
ObjectGUID                  : f75e3310-6526-4957-b697-550c749b9717
PasswordHistoryCount        : 24
Precedence                  : 500
ReversibleEncryptionEnabled : True
```

Figure 6.41: Getting the DNS Admins password policy

In the final step in this recipe, *step 11*, you examine the resulting password policy for the user JerryG, which looks like this:

```
PS C:\Foo> # 11. Checking on JerryG's resultant password policy
PS C:\Foo> Get-ADUserResultantPasswordPolicy -Identity JerryG

AppliesTo                   : {CN=Jerry Garcia,OU=IT,DC=Reskit,DC=Org, CN=DnsAdmins,CN=Users,DC=Reskit,DC=Org}
ComplexityEnabled           : True
DistinguishedName           : CN=DNSPWP,CN=Password Settings Container,CN=System,DC=Reskit,DC=Org
LockoutDuration             : 12:00:00
LockoutObservationWindow    : 00:42:00
LockoutThreshold            : 3
MaxPasswordAge              : 42.00:00:00
MinPasswordAge              : 1.00:00:00
MinPasswordLength           : 7
Name                        : DNSPWP
ObjectClass                 : msDS-PasswordSettings
ObjectGUID                  : f75e3310-6526-4957-b697-550c749b9717
PasswordHistoryCount        : 24
Precedence                  : 500
ReversibleEncryptionEnabled : True
```

Figure 6.42: Checking JerryG's resultant password policy

There's more...

In *step 1*, you view the existing default domain password policy. The settings you see in this step were created by the installation process when you installed Windows Server on DC1.

In *step 2*, you attempt to find a fine-grained password policy that would apply to the user JerryG. As you can see from the output, there is no existing policy in AD.

In *step 5*, you create a new fine-grained password policy assigned to the DNS Admins group (in *step 6*) and JerryG (in *step 7*). This assignment ensures the policy applies to JerryG, whether or not this user is a DNS Admins group member.

In *step 11*, you see the password policy settings for the user JerryG. These settings derive from the default domain policy plus the settings you specified in the DNSPWP policy. In theory, you could have a user with effective password policy settings coming for multiple policy objects (e.g., a GPO for the domain, one for an OU, etc.), although you should avoid such complexity. A better approach would be to create specific AD security groups that contain the users you need to have a different policy and apply the policy to the group.

Managing Windows Defender Antivirus

Microsoft Defender Antivirus is the next-generation protection component of Microsoft Defender for Endpoint. Defender Antivirus provides antivirus and antimalware facilities. The product also does some packet analysis to detect network-level attacks.

The Windows installation process installs Defender on Windows 10, Windows 11, and Windows Server 2022 by default. You can subsequently remove Defender should you wish. For more details on Defender in Windows Server, see `https://learn.microsoft.com/en-us/ microsoft-365/security/defender-endpoint/microsoft-defender-antivirus-on-windows- server?view=o365-worldwide`.

Testing any antivirus or antimalware application can be difficult. On the one hand, you want to ensure that the product, Defender, in this case, is working. But at the same time, you don't want to infect a server. One solution is to create a test file. The **European Institute for Computer Anti-Virus Research (EICAR)** has created a simple set of test files you can use to ensure your antivirus product works. EICAR has created several versions of this file, including a text file and an executable. These files are harmless, but as you see, they trigger Defender.

Getting ready

You run this recipe on DC1, a domain controller in the Reskit.Org domain.

How to do it...

1. Ensuring Defender and tools are associated and installed

```
$DHT = @{
  Name                  = 'Windows-Defender'
  IncludeManagementTools = $true
```

```
  }
  $Defender = Install-WindowsFeature @DHT
  If ($Defender.RestartNeeded -eq 'Yes') {
    Restart-Computer
  }
```

2. Discovering the cmdlets in the Defender module

```
  Import-Module -Name Defender
  Get-Command -Module Defender
```

3. Checking the Defender service status

```
  Get-Service  -Name WinDefend
```

4. Checking the operational status of Defender on this host

```
  Get-MpComputerStatus
```

5. Getting and counting threat catalog

```
  $ThreatCatalog = Get-MpThreatCatalog
  "There are $($ThreatCatalog.count) threats in the catalog"
```

6. Viewing five threats in the catalog

```
  $ThreatCatalog |
    Select-Object -First 5 |
      Format-Table -Property SeverityID, ThreatID, ThreatName
```

7. Enabling key Defender settings

```
  # Enable real-time monitoring
  Set-MpPreference -DisableRealtimeMonitoring 0
  # Enable sample submission
  Set-MpPreference -SubmitSamplesConsent Always
  # Enable checking signatures before scanning
  Set-MpPreference -CheckForSignaturesBeforeRunningScan 1
  # Enable email scanning
  Set-MpPreference -DisableEmailScanning 0
```

8. Creating a false positive threat

```
  $TF = 'C:\Foo\FalsePositive1.Txt'
```

```
$FP = 'X5O!P%@AP[4\PZX54(P^)7CC)7}$EICAR-' +
      'STANDARD-ANTIVIRUS-TEST-FILE!$H+H*'
$FP | Out-File -FilePath $TF
Get-Content -Path $TF
```

9. Running a quick scan on C:\Foo

```
$ScanType = 'QuickScan'
Start-MpScan -ScanType $ScanType -ScanPath C:\Foo
```

10. Viewing detected threats

```
Get-MpThreat
```

How it works...

In *step 1*, you use the Install-WindowsFeature command to ensure that you have installed both Defender and the management tools. The management tools include a PowerShell module you can use to manage Defender. This step may require a reboot. If so, this step reboots DC1 without producing any output.

In *step 2*, you look at the Defender module to discover the cmdlets contained in the module. The output looks like this:

```
PS C:\Foo> # 2. Discovering the cmdlets in the Defender module
PS C:\Foo> Import-Module -Name Defender
WARNING: Module Defender is loaded in Windows PowerShell using WinPSCompatSession
 remoting session; please note that all input and output of commands from
 this module will be deserialized objects. If you want to load this module
 into PowerShell please use 'Import-Module -SkipEditionCheck' syntax.
PS C:\Foo> Get-Command -Module Defender

CommandType     Name                    Version     Source
-----------     ----                    -------     ------
Function        Add-MpPreference        1.0         Defender
Function        Get-MpComputerStatus    1.0         Defender
Function        Get-MpPreference        1.0         Defender
Function        Get-MpThreat            1.0         Defender
Function        Get-MpThreatCatalog     1.0         Defender
Function        Get-MpThreatDetection   1.0         Defender
Function        Remove-MpPreference     1.0         Defender
Function        Remove-MpThreat         1.0         Defender
Function        Set-MpPreference        1.0         Defender
Function        Start-MpScan            1.0         Defender
Function        Start-MpWDOScan         1.0         Defender
Function        Update-MpSignature      1.0         Defender
```

Figure 6.43: Discovering the cmdlets in the Defender module

In *step 3*, you check the status of the WinDefend service. You should see the following output:

```
PS C:\Foo> # 3. Checking the Defender service status
PS C:\Foo> Get-Service  -Name WinDefend

Status    Name       DisplayName
------    ----       -----------
Running   WinDefend  Microsoft Defender Antivirus Service
```

Figure 6.44: Checking the Defender service status

You use the Get-MpComputerstatus cmdlet to get the status of Defender on the local computer in *step 4*. The output looks like this:

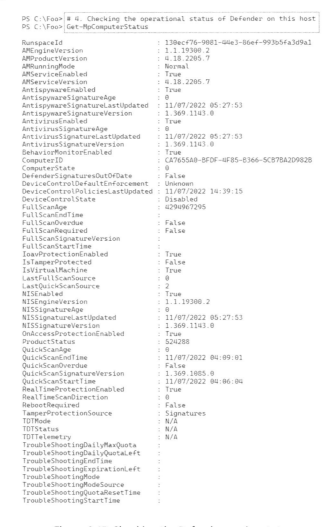

```
PS C:\Foo> # 4. Checking the operational status of Defender on this host
PS C:\Foo> Get-MpComputerStatus

RunspaceId                         : 130ecf76-9081-44e3-86ef-993b5fa3d9a1
AMEngineVersion                    : 1.1.19300.2
AMProductVersion                   : 4.18.2205.7
AMRunningMode                      : Normal
AMServiceEnabled                   : True
AMServiceVersion                   : 4.18.2205.7
AntispywareEnabled                 : True
AntispywareSignatureAge            : 0
AntispywareSignatureLastUpdated    : 11/07/2022 05:27:53
AntispywareSignatureVersion        : 1.369.1143.0
AntivirusEnabled                   : True
AntivirusSignatureAge              : 0
AntivirusSignatureLastUpdated      : 11/07/2022 05:27:53
AntivirusSignatureVersion          : 1.369.1143.0
BehaviorMonitorEnabled             : True
ComputerID                         : CA7655A0-BFDF-4F85-B366-5CB7BA2D982B
ComputerState                      : 0
DefenderSignaturesOutOfDate        : False
DeviceControlDefaultEnforcement    : Unknown
DeviceControlPoliciesLastUpdated   : 11/07/2022 14:39:15
DeviceControlState                 : Disabled
FullScanAge                        : 4294967295
FullScanEndTime                    :
FullScanOverdue                    : False
FullScanRequired                   : False
FullScanSignatureVersion           :
FullScanStartTime                  :
IoavProtectionEnabled              : True
IsTamperProtected                  : False
IsVirtualMachine                   : True
LastFullScanSource                 : 0
LastQuickScanSource                : 2
NISEnabled                         : True
NISEngineVersion                   : 1.1.19300.2
NISSignatureAge                    : 0
NISSignatureLastUpdated            : 11/07/2022 05:27:53
NISSignatureVersion                : 1.369.1143.0
OnAccessProtectionEnabled          : True
ProductStatus                      : 524288
QuickScanAge                       : 0
QuickScanEndTime                   : 11/07/2022 04:09:01
QuickScanOverdue                   : False
QuickScanSignatureVersion          : 1.369.1085.0
QuickScanStartTime                 : 11/07/2022 04:06:04
RealTimeProtectionEnabled          : True
RealTimeScanDirection              : 0
RebootRequired                     : False
TamperProtectionSource             : Signatures
TDTMode                            : N/A
TDTStatus                          : N/A
TDTTelemetry                       : N/A
TroubleShootingDailyMaxQuota       :
TroubleShootingDailyQuotaLeft      :
TroubleShootingEndTime             :
TroubleShootingExpirationLeft      :
TroubleShootingMode                :
TroubleShootingModeSource          :
TroubleShootingQuotaResetTime      :
TroubleShootingStartTime           :
```

Figure 6.45: Checking the Defender service status

Defender uses details of individual threats that it stores in a threat catalog. Windows Update regularly updates this catalog as needed. In *step 5*, you produce a count of the number of threats in the catalog, which looks like this:

```
PS C:\Foo> # 5. Getting and counting threat catalog
PS C:\Foo> $ThreatCatalog = Get-MpThreatCatalog
PS C:\Foo> "There are $($ThreatCatalog.count) threats in the catalog"
There are 234010 threats in the catalog
```

Figure 6.46: Getting and counting the threat catalog

In *step 6*, you examine the first five threats in the Defender threat catalog, which looks like this:

```
PS C:\Foo> # 6. Viewing five threats in the catalog
PS C:\Foo> $ThreatCatalog |
             Select-Object -First 5 |
               Format-Table -Property SeverityID, ThreatID, ThreatName

SeverityID ThreatID ThreatName
---------- -------- ----------
         5     1605 Dialer:Win32/Aconti
         5     1622 MonitoringTool:Win32/ActiveKeylogger
         5     1624 Dialer:Win32/ActiveStripPlayer
         5     1625 MonitoringTool:Win32/ActivityXCustomControl
         5     1626 MonitoringTool:Win32/ActivityMonitor
```

Figure 6.47: Viewing the first five threats in the catalog

In *step 7*, you configure four important Defender settings. You can use the Set-MpPreference cmdlet to configure a range of preference settings for Windows Defender scans and updates. You can modify exclusion file name extensions, paths, or processes and specify the default action for high, moderate, and low threat levels. You can view more details at: https://learn.microsoft. com/powershell/module/defender/set-mppreference.

In *step 8*, you attempt to create a file that Defender regards as a threat. This file comes from the EICAR and, as you can see, is a benign text file. When you run this step, you see an error message, and you may notice a Defender popup warning you that it has discovered a threat. The output from this step looks like this:

```
PS C:\Foo> # 8. Creating a false positive threat
PS C:\Foo> $TF = 'C:\Foo\FalsePositive1.Txt'
PS C:\Foo> $FP = 'X5O!P%@AP[4\PZX54(P^)7CC)7}$EICAR-' +
                 'STANDARD-ANTIVIRUS-TEST-FILE!$H+H*'
PS C:\Foo> $FP | Out-File -FilePath $TF
PS C:\Foo> Get-Content -Path $TF
Get-Content: Operation did not complete successfully because the file contains
 a virus or potentially unwanted software. : 'C:\Foo\FalsePositive1.Txt'
```

Figure 6.48: Creating and viewing a false positive file

In *step 9*, you use Start-MpScan to run a quick scan on the C:\Foo folder where you attempted to create the test threat file. This step also produces no output.

In *step 10*, you view all the threats detected by Defender, which looks like this:

```
PS C:\Foo> # 10. Viewing detected threats
PS C:\Foo> Get-MpThreat

RunspaceId         : 130ecf76-9081-44e3-86ef-993b5fa3d9a1
CategoryID         : 42
DidThreatExecute   : False
IsActive           : False
Resources          :
RollupStatus       : 1
SchemaVersion      : 1.0.0.0
SeverityID         : 5
ThreatID           : 2147519003
ThreatName         : Virus:DOS/EICAR_Test_File
TypeID             : 0
```

Figure 6.49: Viewing all detected threats

There's more...

In *step 2*, you manually import the Defender module. This module is not directly compatible with PowerShell 7. PowerShell uses Windows PowerShell compatibility to expose the commands to PowerShell 7.

In *step 5*, you get a count of the number of threats Defender is aware of today (that is, at the time of writing). When you run this step, you should see a higher number, reflecting newly discovered threats. It is worth noting that this step can take a long time to run.

With *step 8*, you attempt to create a file that Defender recognizes as a threat. This file is the EICAR test file, which is harmless, but you can use it to test the basic functioning of Defender. In *step 10*, you view the threats Defender detected, and you can see it is the file identified as an EICAR_Test_File.

Join our community on Discord

Join our community's Discord space for discussions with the author and other readers:

`https://packt.link/SecNet`

7

Managing Storage

This chapter covers the following recipes:

- Managing Disks
- Managing File Systems
- Exploring PowerShell Providers and the FileSystem Provider
- Managing Storage Replica
- Deploying Storage Spaces

Introduction

Windows Server 2022 provides a range of features that allow access to various storage and storage devices. Windows supports spinning disks, USB memory sticks, and SSD devices (including NVMe SSD devices). These storage options provide you with great flexibility.

Before using a storage device to hold files, you need to create partitions or volumes on the device and then format these drives/volumes. Before formatting, you need to initialize a disk and define which partitioning method to use. You have two choices:

- **Master Boot Record (MBR)**
- **GUID Partition Table (GPT)**

These days, most PCs use the GPT disk type for hard drives and SSDs. GPT is more robust and allows for volumes bigger than 2 TB. The older MBR disk type is used typically by older PCs and removable drives such as memory cards or external disk drives.

For a good discussion of the differences between these two mechanisms, see `https://www.howtogeek.com/193669/whats-the-difference-between-gptand-mbr-when-partitioning-a-drive/`.

Once you create a volume on a storage device, you can format the volume. Windows supports five file systems you can use: ReFS, NTFS, exFAT, UDF, and FAT32. For details on the latter four, see `https://learn.microsoft.com/windows/win32/fileio/filesystem-functionality-comparison`. The ReFS filesystem is more recent and is based on NFTS but lacks some features your file server might need (for example, ReFS does not support encrypted files, which you may wish to support). A benefit of the ReFS file system is the automatic integrity checking. For a comparison between the ReFS and NTFS file systems, see `https://www.iperiusbackup.net/en/refs-vs-ntfs-differences-and-performance-comparison-when-to-use/`. You'll examine partitioning and formatting volumes in the *Managing Disks* recipe.

NTFS (and ReFS) volumes allow you to create **access control lists** (**ACLs**) that control access to files and folders stored in Windows volumes. Each ACL has one or more **Access Control Entries** (**ACEs**). Each ACE in an ACL defines a specific permission for some account (for example, setting **Read only** for members of the DNS Admins group). In general, you want ACLs to have as few ACEs as possible. Longer ACLs can be challenging to keep up to date, represent a potential security issue, and impact performance.

Managing ACLs with PowerShell is somewhat tricky. PowerShell lacks rich support for managing ACLs and ACL inheritance, although .NET does provide the necessary classes you need to manage ACLs. To simplify the management of ACLs on NTFS volumes, as you'll see in the *Managing NTFS Permissions* recipe in *Chapter 8*, you can download and use a third-party module, *NTFSSecurity*.

Storage Replica is a feature of Windows Server that replicates any volume to a remote system. Storage Replica is only available with the Windows Server Datacenter edition. In *Managing Storage Replica*, you'll create a replication partnership between two hosts and enable Windows Server to keep the replica up to date.

Storage Spaces is a technology provided by Microsoft in the Windows Client (Windows 10 and Windows 11) and recent versions of Windows Server that can help you protect against a disk drive's failure. Storage Spaces provides software RAID, which you'll investigate in *Deploying Storage Spaces*.

The systems used in the chapter

In this chapter, you'll use two servers: SRV1 and SRV2. Both are running Windows Server 2022 Datacenter edition. The servers are member servers in the Reskit.Org domain served by the two Domain controllers, DC1 and DC2, as shown here:

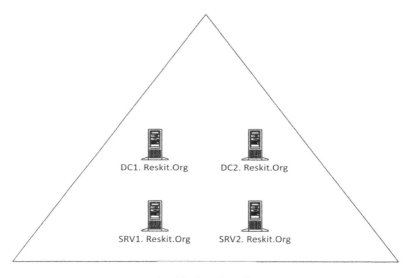

Reskit.Org domain

Figure 7.1: Hosts in use for this chapter

Managing Disks

Windows Server 2022 requires a computer with at least one storage drive (in most cases, this is your C:\ drive). You can connect a storage device using different bus types, such as IDE, SATA, SAS, and USB. Before you can utilize a storage device in Windows, you need to initialize it and create a partitioning scheme.

You can use two partitioning schemes: the older format of MBR and the more recent GPT. The MBR scheme, first introduced with the PC DOS 2 in 1983, had some restrictions. For example, the largest partition supported with MBR is 2 TB. And to create more than four primary partitions, you would need an extended partition and then create additional partitions inside the extended partition. For larger disk devices, this can be inefficient.

The GPT scheme enabled much larger drives (OS-imposed partition limits) and up to 128 partitions per drive. You typically use GPT partitioning with Windows Server. If you built the VMs for the servers you use to test the recipes, each VM has a single GPT partitioned (virtual) disk.

In this chapter, you'll use eight new virtual disk devices in the server, SRV1, and examine the disks and the partitions/volumes on SRV1.

Getting ready

This recipe uses SRV1, a domain-joined host in the Reskit.Org domain, on which you have installed PowerShell 7 and VS Code. You also use SRV2 and should have DC1 online as well.

Before this chapter, you configured SRV1 with a single boot/system drive (the C: drive). The recipes in this chapter use eight additional disks. You must add these disks to the SRV1 host before running this recipe.

Assuming you are using Hyper-V to create your VMs, you can run the following script on your Hyper-V host to add the new disks to the SRV1 and SRV2 VMs:

```
# 0. Add new disks to the SRV1, SRV2 VMs
# Run this step on the VM host
# Assumes a single C: on SCSI Bus 0
# This step creates a new SCSI controller to hold the new disks

#
# 0.1 Turning off the VMs
Get-VM -Name SRV1, SRV2 | Stop-VM -Force

# 0.2 Getting Path for hard disks for SRV1, SRV2
$Path1    = Get-VMHardDiskDrive -VMName SRV1
$Path2    = Get-VMHardDiskDrive -VMName SRV2
$VMPath1 = Split-Path -Parent $Path1.Path
$VMPath2 = Split-Path -Parent $Path2.Path

# 0.3 Creating 8 virtual disks on VM host
0..7 | ForEach-Object {
  New-VHD -Path $VMPath1\SRV1-D$_.vhdx -SizeBytes 64gb -Dynamic |
    Out-Null
  New-VHD -Path $VMPath2\SRV2-D$_.vhdx -SizeBytes 64gb -Dynamic |
```

```powershell
    Out-Null
}

# 0.4 Adding disks to SRV1, SRV2
# Create the next SCSI controller on SRV1/SRV2
Add-VMScsiController -VMName SRV1
[int] $SRV1Controller =
  Get-VMScsiController -VMName SRV1 |
    Select-Object -Last 1 |
      Select-Object -ExpandProperty ControllerNumber
Add-VMScsiController -VMName SRV2
[int] $SRV2Controller =
  Get-VMScsiController -VMName SRV1 |
    Select-Object -Last 1 |
        Select-Object -ExpandProperty ControllerNumber

# Now add the disks to each VM
0..7 | ForEach-Object {
  $DHT1 = @{
    VMName           = 'SRV1'
    Path             = "$VMPath1\SRV1-D$_.vhdx"
    ControllerType   = 'SCSI'
    ControllerNumber = $SRV1Controller
  }
  $DHT2 = @{
    VMName           = 'SRV2'
    Path             =  "$VMPath2\SRV2-D$_.vhdx"
    ControllerType   = 'SCSI'
    ControllerNumber =  $SRV2Controller
  }
  Add-VMHardDiskDrive @DHT1
  Add-VMHardDiskDrive @DHT2
}

# 0.5 Checking VM disks for SRV1, SRV2
Get-VMHardDiskDrive -VMName SRV1 | Format-Table
Get-VMHardDiskDrive -VMName SRV2 | Format-Table
```

```
# 0.6 Restarting VMs
Start-VM -VMName SRV1
Start-VM -VMName SRV2
```

If you download the scripts for this book from GitHub, the script for the recipe contains this preparation step.

Once you have created the eight new disks for the two VMs, you can begin the recipe on SRV1.

How to do it...

1. Displaying the disks on SRV1

    ```
    Get-Disk
    ```

2. Get first usable disk

    ```
    $Disk = Get-Disk |
                Where-Object PartitionStyle -eq Raw |
                  Select-Object -First 1
    $Disk | Format-List
    ```

3. Initializing the first available disk

    ```
    $Disk |
        Initialize-Disk -PartitionStyle GPT
    ```

4. Re-displaying all disks in SRV1

    ```
    Get-Disk
    ```

5. Viewing volumes on SRV1

    ```
    Get-Volume | Sort-Object -Property DriveLetter
    ```

6. Viewing partitions on SRV1

    ```
    Get-Partition
    ```

7. Examining details of a volume

    ```
    Get-Volume | Select-Object -First 1 | Format-List
    ```

8. Examining details of a partition

    ```
    Get-Partition | Select-Object -First 1 | Format-List
    ```

9. Formatting and initializing the second disk as MBR

```
$Disk2 = Get-Disk |
            Where-Object PartitionStyle -eq Raw |
                Select-Object -First 1
$Disk2 |
    Initialize-Disk -PartitionStyle MBR
```

10. Examining disks in SRV1

```
Get-Disk
```

How it works...

In *step 1*, you use the Get-Disk command to view the disks available in SRV1, with output like this:

```
PS C:\Foo> # 1. Displaying the disks on SRV1
PS C:\Foo> Get-Disk

Number Friendly Name     Serial Number HealthStatus OperationalStatus Total Size Partition Style
------ -------------     ------------- ------------ ----------------- ---------- ---------------
0      Msft Virtual Disk               Healthy      Online             128 GB GPT
1      Msft Virtual Disk               Healthy      Offline             64 GB RAW
2      Msft Virtual Disk               Healthy      Offline             64 GB RAW
3      Msft Virtual Disk               Healthy      Offline             64 GB RAW
4      Msft Virtual Disk               Healthy      Offline             64 GB RAW
5      Msft Virtual Disk               Healthy      Offline             64 GB RAW
6      Msft Virtual Disk               Healthy      Offline             64 GB RAW
7      Msft Virtual Disk               Healthy      Offline             64 GB RAW
8      Msft Virtual Disk               Healthy      Offline             64 GB RAW
```

Figure 7.2: Displaying disk details

In *step 2*, you get the first usable disks and examine the details of the disk, with output like this:

```
PS C:\Foo> # 2. Get first usable disk
PS C:\Foo> $Disk = Get-Disk |
            Where-Object PartitionStyle -eq Raw |
            Select-Object -First 1
PS C:\Foo> $Disk | Format-List

UniqueId          : 60022480E8258902AEAD5E128062318A
Number            : 1
Path              : \\?\scsi#disk&ven_msft&prod_virtual_disk#
                    5&2132ca1&0&000000#{53f56307-b6bf-11d0-94f2-00a0c91efb8b}
Manufacturer      : Msft
Model             : Virtual Disk
SerialNumber      :
Size              : 64 GB
AllocatedSize     : 0
LogicalSectorSize : 512
PhysicalSectorSize : 4096
NumberOfPartitions : 0
PartitionStyle    : RAW
IsReadOnly        : True
IsSystem          : False
IsBoot            : False
```

Figure 7.3: Displaying disk details of the first usable disk

In *step 3*, you initialize this disk using the GPT partition scheme. This step produces no output.

In *step 4*, you view the disks again on SRV1, with output like this:

```
PS C:\Foo> # 4. Re-displaying all disks in SRV1
PS C:\Foo> Get-Disk

Number Friendly Name      Serial Number HealthStatus OperationalStatus Total Size Partition Style
------ -------------      ------------- ------------ ----------------- ---------- ---------------
0      Msft Virtual Disk                Healthy      Online               128 GB GPT
1      Msft Virtual Disk                Healthy      Online                64 GB GPT
2      Msft Virtual Disk                Healthy      Offline               64 GB RAW
3      Msft Virtual Disk                Healthy      Offline               64 GB RAW
4      Msft Virtual Disk                Healthy      Offline               64 GB RAW
5      Msft Virtual Disk                Healthy      Offline               64 GB RAW
6      Msft Virtual Disk                Healthy      Offline               64 GB RAW
7      Msft Virtual Disk                Healthy      Offline               64 GB RAW
8      Msft Virtual Disk                Healthy      Offline               64 GB RAW
```

Figure 7.4: Viewing existing disk volumes on SRV1

In *step 5,* you use the Get-Volume command to view the partitions on SRV1, with the following output:

```
PS C:\Foo> # 5. Viewing volumes on SRV1
PS C:\Foo> Get-Volume | Sort-Object -Property DriveLetter

DriveLetter FriendlyName FileSystemType DriveType HealthStatus OperationalStatus SizeRemaining      Size
----------- ------------ -------------- --------- ------------ ----------------- -------------      ----
                         FAT32          Fixed     Healthy      OK                   67.25 MB      96 MB
C                        NTFS           Fixed     Healthy      OK                  111.25 GB   127.9 GB
```

Figure 7.5: Viewing existing volumes on SRV1

In *step 6*, you use the Get-Partition command to view all the partitions on SRV1, which creates the following output:

```
PS C:\Foo> # 6. Viewing partitions on SRV1
PS C:\Foo> Get-Partition

   DiskPath: \\?\scsi#disk&ven_msft&prod_virtual_disk#5&1ebf9ebb&0&000000#
             {53f56307-b6bf-11d0-94f2-00a0c91efb8b}

PartitionNumber DriveLetter Offset        Size Type
--------------- ----------- ------        ---- ----
1               C           1048576    127.9 GB Basic
2                           137333047296  100 MB System

   DiskPath: \\?\scsi#disk&ven_msft&prod_virtual_disk#5&2132ca1&0&000000#
             {53f56307-b6bf-11d0-94f2-00a0c91efb8b}

PartitionNumber DriveLetter Offset     Size Type
--------------- ----------- ------     ---- ----
1                           17408   15.98 MB Reserved
```

Figure 7.6: Viewing all partitions on SRV1

In *step 7*, you examine the properties of a disk, with output like this:

```
PS C:\Foo> # 7. Examining details of a volume
PS C:\Foo> Get-Volume | Select-Object -First 1 | Format-List

ObjectId                 : {1}\\SRV1\root/Microsoft/Windows/Storage/Providers_v2\
                           WSP_Volume.ObjectId="{004bc44d-ede2-11ec-a79c-806e6f6e6963}:
                           VO:\\?\Volume{ebeaff83-af69-11ec-be24-5cf37091be18}\"
PassThroughClass         :
PassThroughIds           :
PassThroughNamespace     :
PassThroughServer        :
UniqueId                 : \\?\Volume{ebeaff83-af69-11ec-be24-5cf37091be18}\
AllocationUnitSize       : 4096
DedupMode                : NotAvailable
DriveLetter              : C
DriveType                : Fixed
FileSystem               : NTFS
FileSystemLabel          :
FileSystemType           : NTFS
HealthStatus             : Healthy
OperationalStatus        : OK
Path                     : \\?\Volume{ebeaff83-af69-11ec-be24-5cf37091be18}\
Size                     : 137331994624
SizeRemaining            : 119453777920
PSComputerName           :
```

Figure 7.7: Viewing Volume properties

In *step 8*, you view the properties of a partition, with output like this:

```
PS C:\Foo> # 8. Examining details of a partition
PS C:\Foo> Get-Partition | Select-Object -First 1 | Format-List

UniqueId              : {00000000-0000-0000-0000-100000000000}6002248005588E716BE40737CCDCDD7C
AccessPaths           : {C:\, \\?\Volume{ebeaff83-af69-11ec-be24-5cf37091be18}\}
DiskNumber            : 0
DiskPath              : \\?\scsi#disk&ven_msft&prod_virtual_disk#5&1ebf9ebb&0&000000#
                        {53f56307-b6bf-11d0-94f2-00a0c91efb8b}
DriveLetter           : C
Guid                  : {ebeaff83-af69-11ec-be24-5cf37091be18}
IsActive              : False
IsBoot                : True
IsHidden              : False
IsOffline             : False
IsReadOnly            : False
IsShadowCopy          : False
IsDAX                 : False
IsSystem              : False
NoDefaultDriveLetter  : False
Offset                : 1048576
OperationalStatus     : Online
PartitionNumber       : 1
Size                  : 127.9 GB
Type                  : Basic
```

Figure 7.8: Viewing partition details

In *step 9*, you get the next unpartitioned disk and initialize it using the MBR formatting scheme. This step creates no output.

In *step 10*, you again view the disks available on SRV1, including the two disks you just partitioned. The output looks like this:

```
PS C:\Foo> # 10. Examining disks in SRV1
PS C:\Foo> Get-Disk

Number Friendly Name      Serial Number HealthStatus OperationalStatus Total Size Partition Style
------ -------------      ------------- ------------ ----------------- ---------- ---------------
0      Msft Virtual Disk                Healthy      Online              128 GB   GPT
1      Msft Virtual Disk                Healthy      Online               64 GB   GPT
2      Msft Virtual Disk                Healthy      Online               64 GB   MBR
3      Msft Virtual Disk                Healthy      Offline              64 GB   RAW
4      Msft Virtual Disk                Healthy      Offline              64 GB   RAW
5      Msft Virtual Disk                Healthy      Offline              64 GB   RAW
6      Msft Virtual Disk                Healthy      Offline              64 GB   RAW
7      Msft Virtual Disk                Healthy      Offline              64 GB   RAW
8      Msft Virtual Disk                Healthy      Offline              64 GB   RAW
```

Figure 7.9: Viewing disks on SRV1

There's more...

In *step 1*, you view all the disks in SRV1. The first disk, disk 0, is your C:\ drive. You created this as part of the process of installing Windows Server 2022. In *step 2,* you get the first of the eight disk devices you added to SRV1 at the start of this recipe. However, before you can use this disk in Windows, you need to initialize the disk, which you do in *step 3*. When you initialize a disk, you specify the partitioning scheme, which in this case is GPT. Initializing the disk does not create any partitions or volumes. You can see, in *step 4*, that the disk has a partition scheme.

In *steps 5* and *6*, you verify that there is only one volume or partition on SRV1 (i.e., the C: drive on disk 0).

The terms "partition" and "volume" in Windows are, in effect, the same thing. But due to history, you can use two different commands to create and manage volumes and partitions., In *step 7*, you review the properties of a volume, while in *step 8*, you examine the properties of a Windows disk partition.

In most cases, you initialize storage devices in your system using GPT, a more robust and flexible scheme. But you may wish to use the older MBR partition scheme, for example, for removable storage devices you intend to use on hosts that do not support GPT.

Managing File Systems

To use a storage device, whether a spinning disk, CD/DVD device, or a solid-state device, you must format that device/drive with a file system. You must also have initialized the disk with a partitioning scheme, as you saw in the *Managing Disks* recipe.

In most cases, you use NTFS as the file system of choice. It is robust and reliable and provides efficient access control. NTFS also provides file encryption and compression. An alternative is the ReFS file system. This file system might be a good choice for some specialized workloads. For example, you might use the ReFS file system on a Hyper-V host to hold VM virtual hard drives. Additionally, for interoperability with devices like video and still cameras, you might need to use the FAT, FAT32, or exFAT file system.

For more details on the difference between NTFS, FAT, FAT32, and ExFAT file systems, see `https://` `medium.com/hetman-software/the-difference-between-ntfs-fat-fat32-and-exfat-file-` `systems-ec5172c60ccd`. And for more information about the ReFS file system, see `https://learn.` `microsoft.com/windows-server/storage/refs/refs-overview`.

Getting ready

This recipe uses `SRV1`, a domain-joined host in the `Reskit.Org` domain, on which you have installed PowerShell 7 and VS Code. You also have `DC1` online. In the *Managing Disks* recipe, you added eight virtual disks to the `SRV1`. Then, also in the *Managing Disks* recipe, you initialized the first two. In this recipe, you'll create specific volumes on these two disks.

How to do it...

1. Getting second disk

```
$Disk = Get-Disk | Select-Object -Skip 1 -First 1
$Disk | Format-List
```

2. Creating a new volume in this disk

```
$NewVolumeHT1   = @{
  DiskNumber    = $Disk.Disknumber
  DriveLetter   = 'S'
  FriendlyName  = 'Files'
}
New-Volume @NewVolumeHT1
```

3. Getting next available disk to use on SRV1

```
$Disk2 = Get-Disk |
           Where-Object PartitionStyle -eq 'MBR' |
             Select-Object -First 1
$Disk2 | Format-List
```

4. Creating 4 new partitions on the third (MBR) disk

```
$UseMaxHT= @{UseMaximumSize = $true}
New-Partition -DiskNumber $Disk2.DiskNumber -DriveLetter W -Size 1gb
New-Partition -DiskNumber $Disk2.DiskNumber -DriveLetter X -Size
15gb
New-Partition -DiskNumber $Disk2.DiskNumber -DriveLetter Y -Size
15gb
New-Partition -DiskNumber $Disk2.DiskNumber -DriveLetter Z @UseMaxHT
```

5. Formatting each partition

```
$FormatHT1 = @{
  DriveLetter        = 'W'
  FileSystem         = 'FAT'
  NewFileSystemLabel = 'w-fat'
}
Format-Volume @FormatHT1
$FormatHT2 = @{
  DriveLetter        = 'X'
  FileSystem         = 'exFAT'
  NewFileSystemLabel = 'x-exFAT'
}
Format-Volume @FormatHT2
$FormatHT3 = @{
  DriveLetter        = 'Y'
  FileSystem         = 'FAT32'
  NewFileSystemLabel = 'Y-FAT32'
}
Format-Volume  @FormatHT3
$FormatHT4 = @{
  DriveLetter        = 'Z'
  FileSystem         = 'ReFS'
  NewFileSystemLabel = 'Z-ReFS'
}
Format-Volume @FormatHT4
```

6.   Getting all volumes on SRV1

```
Get-Volume | Sort-Object -Property DriveLetter
```

How it works...

In *step 1*, you obtain the second disk on SRV1 and display the disk details. You initialized this disk previously using the GPT partitioning scheme. The output looks like this:

```
PS C:\Foo> # 1. Getting the second disk
PS C:\Foo> $Disk = Get-Disk | Select-Object -Skip 1 -First 1
PS C:\Foo> $Disk | Format-List

UniqueId            : 60022480E8258902AEAD5E128062318A
Number              : 1
Path                : \\?\scsi#disk&ven_msft&prod_virtual_disk#5&2132ca1&0&000000#
                      {53f56307-b6bf-11d0-94f2-00a0c91efb8b}
Manufacturer        : Msft
Model               : Virtual Disk
SerialNumber        :
Size                : 64 GB
AllocatedSize       : 17825792
LogicalSectorSize   : 512
PhysicalSectorSize  : 4096
NumberOfPartitions  : 1
PartitionStyle      : GPT
IsReadOnly          : False
IsSystem            : False
IsBoot              : False
```

Figure 7.10: Getting the next RAW disk on SRV1

In *step 2*, you use the Create-Volume to create an S: volume/partition on the second disk in SRV1, with output like this:

```
PS C:\Foo> # 2. Creating a new volume in this disk
PS C:\Foo> $NewVolumeHT1  = @{
      DiskNumber    = $Disk.Disknumber
      DriveLetter   = 'S'
      FriendlyName  = 'Files'
      }
PS C:\Foo> New-Volume @NewVolumeHT1
```

DriveLetter	FriendlyName	FileSystemType	DriveType	HealthStatus	OperationalStatus	SizeRemaining	Size
S	Files	NTFS	Fixed	Healthy	OK	63.84 GB	63.98 GB

Figure 7.11: Creating the S: volume

In *step 3*, you get the third disk on SRV1, the disk you initialized in the prior recipe, with an MBR partitioning scheme. The output of this step is as follows:

```
PS C:\Foo> # 3. Getting next available disk to use on SRV1
PS C:\Foo> $Disk2 = Get-Disk |
              Where-Object PartitionStyle -eq 'MBR' |
              Select-Object -First 1
PS C:\Foo> $Disk2 | Format-List

UniqueId            : 60022480F74243AB1AD9CFB6E1B06E28
Number              : 2  ◄———
Path                : \\?\scsi#disk&ven_msft&prod_virtual_disk#5&2132ca1&0&000001#
                      {53f56307-b6bf-11d0-94f2-00a0c91efb8b}
Manufacturer        : Msft
Model               : Virtual Disk
SerialNumber        :
Size                : 64 GB
AllocatedSize       : 2097152
LogicalSectorSize   : 512
PhysicalSectorSize  : 4096
NumberOfPartitions  : 0
PartitionStyle      : MBR  ◄———
IsReadOnly          : False
IsSystem            : False
IsBoot              : False
```

Figure 7.12: Getting the next disk

In *step 4*, you use the `New-Partition` cmdlet to create four new partitions on disk 2, with output like this:

```
PS C:\Foo> # 4. Creating 4 new partitions on third (MBR) disk
PS C:\Foo> $UseMaxHT= @{UseMaximumSize = $true}
PS C:\Foo> New-Partition -DiskNumber $Disk2.DiskNumber -DriveLetter W -Size 1gb

   DiskPath: \\?\scsi#disk&ven_msft&prod_virtual_disk#5&2132ca1&0&000001#
             {53f56307-b6bf-11d0-94f2-00a0c91efb8b}

PartitionNumber  DriveLetter Offset  Size Type
---------------  ----------- ------  ---- ----
1                W           1048576  1 GB Logical

PS C:\Foo> New-Partition -DiskNumber $Disk2.DiskNumber -DriveLetter X -Size 15gb

   DiskPath: \\?\scsi#disk&ven_msft&prod_virtual_disk#5&2132ca1&0&000001#
             {53f56307-b6bf-11d0-94f2-00a0c91efb8b}

PartitionNumber  DriveLetter Offset      Size Type
---------------  ----------- ------      ---- ----
2                X           1074790400 15 GB Logical

PS C:\Foo> New-Partition -DiskNumber $Disk2.DiskNumber -DriveLetter Y -Size 15gb

   DiskPath: \\?\scsi#disk&ven_msft&prod_virtual_disk#5&2132ca1&0&000001#
             {53f56307-b6bf-11d0-94f2-00a0c91efb8b}

PartitionNumber  DriveLetter Offset       Size Type
---------------  ----------- ------       ---- ----
3                Y           17180917760 15 GB Logical

PS C:\Foo> New-Partition -DiskNumber $Disk2.DiskNumber -DriveLetter Z @UseMaxHT

   DiskPath: \\?\scsi#disk&ven_msft&prod_virtual_disk#5&2132ca1&0&000001#
             {53f56307-b6bf-11d0-94f2-00a0c91efb8b}

PartitionNumber  DriveLetter Offset       Size Type
---------------  ----------- ------       ---- ----
4                Z           33288093696 33 GB Logical
```

Figure 7.13: Creating partitions on disk 2

Now that you have initialized this disk and created partitions, you need to format those partitions using a specific file system. In *step 5*, you format the partitions you created in the previous step, with output like this:

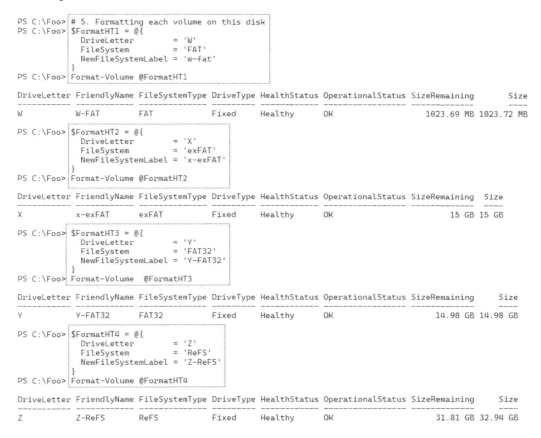

Figure 7.14: Formatting partitions on disk 2

In *step 7*, you use the Get-Volume command to view the partitions you have created on SRV1 (thus far!). The output from this step is as follows:

```
PS C:\Foo> # 7. Getting all volumes on SRV1
PS C:\Foo> Get-Volume | Sort-Object DriveLetter

DriveLetter FriendlyName FileSystemType DriveType HealthStatus OperationalStatus SizeRemaining      Size
----------- ------------ -------------- --------- ------------ ----------------- -------------      ----
                         FAT32          Fixed     Healthy      OK                     67.25 MB      96 MB
C                        NTFS           Fixed     Healthy      OK                    111.23 GB   127.9 GB
S           Files        NTFS           Fixed     Healthy      OK                     63.84 GB   63.98 GB
W           W-FAT        FAT            Fixed     Healthy      OK               1023.69 MB 1023.72 MB
X           x-exFAT      exFAT          Fixed     Healthy      OK                        15 GB      15 GB
Y           Y-FAT32      FAT32          Fixed     Healthy      OK                     14.98 GB   14.98 GB
Z           Z-ReFS       ReFS           Fixed     Healthy      OK                     31.81 GB   32.94 GB
```

Figure 7.15: Viewing volumes on disk 2

There's more...

In *step 1*, you get the next available disk on the server. This disk is the second on SRV1, as seen in the previous recipe (*Figure 7.9*).

In *step 4*, you create four partitions on the disk. In this step, you create the $UseMaxHT hash table variable to simplify and shorten the final command. This step illustrates how you can mix parameters/values and hash tables when using a cmdlet. This approach can simplify some scripts.

In this recipe, with disk 2, you used the MBR-partitioned disk and created four small partitions, each with a different file system. In practice, you would not usually create multiple MBR-based partitions on a single storage device.

Exploring PowerShell Providers and the FileSystem Provider

One innovation in PowerShell that IT professionals soon learn to love is PowerShell providers. A provider is a component that provides access to specialized data stores for easy management. The provider makes the data appear in a drive with a path similar to how you access files in file stores.

PowerShell 7.2 comes with the following providers:

- **Registry**: provides access to registry keys and registry values (https://learn.microsoft.com/powershell/module/microsoft.powershell.core/about/about_registry_provider).

- **Alias**: provides access to PowerShell's command aliases (https://learn.microsoft.com/powershell/module/microsoft.powershell.core/about/about_alias_provider).

- **Environment**: provides access to Windows environment variables (https://learn.microsoft.com/powershell/module/microsoft.powershell.core/about/about_environment_provider).

- **FileSystem**: provides access to files in a partition (https://learn.microsoft.com/powershell/module/microsoft.powershell.core/about/about_filesystem_provider).

- **Function**: provides access to PowerShell's function definitions (https://learn.microsoft.com/powershell/module/microsoft.powershell.core/about/about_function_provider).

- **Variable:** provides access to PowerShell's variables (https://learn.microsoft.com/powershell/module/microsoft.powershell.core/about/about_variable_provider).

- **Certificate**: provides access to the current user and local host's X.509 digital certificate stores (`https://learn.microsoft.com/powershell/module/microsoft.powershell.security/about/about_certificate_provider`).

- **WSMan**: provides a configuration surface for you to configure the WinRM service (`https://learn.microsoft.com/powershell/module/microsoft.wsman.management/about/about_wsman_provider`).

The key advantage of PowerShell providers is that you do not need a set of cmdlets for each underlying data store. Instead, you use `Get-Item` or `Get-ChildItem` with any provider to return provider-specific data, as you can see in this recipe.

Other applications can add providers to a given host. For example, the IIS administration module creates an IIS: drive, and the Active Directory module creates an AD: drive.

And if you have organization-unique data stores, you could create a customized provider. The SHiPS module, available from the PowerShell gallery, enables you to build a provider using PowerShell. As an example of the SHiPS platform's capabilities, you can use a sample provider from the CimPSDrive module. This module contains a provider for the CIM repository. For more information on the SHiPS platform, see `https://github.com/PowerShell/SHiPS/tree/development/docs`. For more details on the CimPSDrive provider, see `https://github.com/PowerShell/CimPSDrive`.

Getting ready

This recipe uses SRV1, a domain-joined host in the `Reskit.Org` domain. You used this server in previous recipes in this chapter. This recipe also uses the disks you added before the *Managing Disks* recipe.

How to do it...

1. Getting providers

   ```
   Get-PSProvider
   ```

2. Getting drives from the registry provider

   ```
   Get-PSDrive | Where-Object Provider -match 'Registry'
   ```

3. Looking at a registry key

   ```
   $Path = 'HKLM:\SOFTWARE\Microsoft\Windows NT\CurrentVersion'
   Get-Item -Path $Path
   ```

4. Getting the registered owner

    ```
    (Get-ItemProperty -Path $Path -Name RegisteredOwner).RegisteredOwner
    ```

5. Counting aliases in the `Alias:` drive

    ```
    Get-Item Alias:* | Measure-Object
    ```

6. Finding aliases for `Remove-Item`

    ```
    Get-ChildItem Alias:* |
       Where-Object ResolvedCommand -match 'Remove-Item$'
    ```

7. Counting environment variables on SRV1

    ```
    Get-Item ENV:* | Measure-Object
    ```

8. Displaying the Windows installation folder

    ```
    "Windows installation folder is [$env:windir]"
    ```

9. Checking on `FileSystem` provider drives on SRV1

    ```
    Get-PSProvider -PSProvider FileSystem |
       Select-Object -ExpandProperty Drives |
          Sort-Object -Property Name
    ```

10. Getting home folder for the `FileSystem` provider

    ```
    $HomeFolder = Get-PSProvider -PSProvider FileSystem |
       Select-Object -ExpandProperty Home
    $HomeFolder
    ```

11. Checking `Function` drive

    ```
    Get-Module | Remove-Module -WarningAction SilentlyContinue
    $Functions = Get-ChildItem -Path Function:
    "Functions available [$($Functions.Count)]"
    ```

12. Creating a new function

    ```
    Function Get-HelloWorld {'Hello World'}
    ```

13. Checking the Function drive again

```
$Functions2 = Get-ChildItem -Path Function:
"Functions now available [$($Functions2.Count)]"
```

14. Viewing function definition

```
Get-Item Function:\Get-HelloWorld | Format-List *
```

15. Counting the variables available

```
$Variables = Get-ChildItem -Path Variable:
"Variables defined [$($Variables.count)]"
```

16. Getting trusted root certificates for the local machine

```
Get-ChildItem -Path Cert:\LocalMachine\Root |
    Format-Table FriendlyName, Thumbprint
```

17. Examining ports in use by WinRM

```
Get-ChildItem -Path WSMan:\localhost\Client\DefaultPorts
Get-ChildItem -Path WSMan:\localhost\Service\DefaultPorts
```

18. Setting Trusted Hosts

```
Set-Item WSMan:\localhost\Client\TrustedHosts -Value '*' -Force
```

19. Installing SHiPS and CimPSDrive modules

```
Install-Module -Name SHiPS, CimPSDrive -Force
```

20. Importing the CimPSDrive module and creating a drive

```
Import-Module -Name CimPSDrive
New-PSDrive -Name CIM -PSProvider SHiPS -Root CIMPSDrive#CMRoot
```

21. Examining BIOS using the CimPSDrive module

```
Get-ChildItem CIM:\Localhost\CIMV2\Win32_Bios
```

How it works...

In *step 1*, you use Get-PSProvider to view all the PowerShell providers that are currently on SRV1. The output looks like this:

```
PS C:\Foo> # 1. Getting PowerShell providers
PS C:\Foo> Get-PSProvider

Name          Capabilities                            Drives
----          ------------                            ------
Registry      ShouldProcess                           {HKLM, HKCU}
Alias         ShouldProcess                           {Alias}
Environment   ShouldProcess                           {Env}
FileSystem    Filter, ShouldProcess, Credentials {C, Temp, S, W, X, Y, Z}
Function      ShouldProcess                           {Function}
Variable      ShouldProcess                           {Variable}
Certificate   ShouldProcess                           {Cert}
WSMan         Credentials                             {WSMan}
```

Figure 7.16: Viewing the PowerShell providers on SRV1

A provider can provide one or more drives. In *step 2*, you use the Get-PSDrive cmdlet to discover the drives currently provided by the registry provider, with output like this:

```
PS C:\Foo> # 2. Getting drives from the registry provider
PS C:\Foo> Get-PSDrive | Where-Object Provider -match 'Registry'

Name Used (GB) Free (GB) Provider Root              CurrentLocation
---- --------- --------- -------- ----              ---------------
HKCU                               Registry HKEY_CURRENT_USER
HKLM                               Registry HKEY_LOCAL_MACHINE
```

Figure 7.17: Viewing the drives in the registry provider

In *step 4*, you use the registry provider to retrieve the registry holding the registered owner. The Windows installation process writes a value to the registry containing the name of the system's owner. The output of this step looks like this:

```
PS C:\Foo> # 4. Getting registered owner
PS C:\Foo> (Get-ItemProperty -Path $Path -Name RegisteredOwner).RegisteredOwner
Book Readers
```

Figure 7.18: Obtaining the registered owner via the registry

In *step 5*, you use the PowerShell alias provider to count the number of aliases, with output like this:

```
PS C:\Foo> # 5. Counting aliases in the Alias: drive
PS C:\Foo> Get-Item Alias:* | Measure-Object

Count              : 164
Average            :
Sum                :
Maximum            :
Minimum            :
StandardDeviation  :
Property           :
```

Figure 7.19: Counting the number of aliases on SRV1

In *step 6*, you use the Get-ChildItem command against the alias provider to discover the aliases to the Remove-Item command, with output like this:

```
PS C:\Foo> # 6. Finding aliases for Remove-Item
PS C:\Foo> Get-Childitem Alias:* |
             Where-Object ResolvedCommand -match 'Remove-Item$'

CommandType    Name                                        Version    Source
-----------    ----                                        -------    ------
Alias          ri -> Remove-Item
Alias          rm -> Remove-Item
Alias          rmdir -> Remove-Item
Alias          del -> Remove-Item
Alias          erase -> Remove-Item
Alias          rd -> Remove-Item
```

Figure 7.20: Discovering aliases to the Remove-Item command

In *step 7*, you use the environment variable provider to count the number of environment variables, with output like this:

```
PS C:\Foo> # 7. Counting environment variables on SRV1
PS C:\Foo> Get-Item ENV:* | Measure-Object

Count              : 45
Average            :
Sum                :
Maximum            :
Minimum            :
StandardDeviation  :
Property           :
```

Figure 7.21: Counting the environment variables on SRV1

In *step 8*, you use the environment variable provider to retrieve the name of the Windows installation folder, with output like this:

```
PS C:\Foo> # 8. Displaying Windows installation folder
PS C:\Foo> "Windows installation folder is [$env:windir]"
Windows installation folder is [C:\WINDOWS]
```

Figure 7.22: Counting the environment variables

A provider enables you to create drives, which you can think of as placeholders within the underlying data store. In *step 9*, you use the Get-PSProvider command to retrieve the drives surfaced by the FileSystem provider, with output like this:

```
PS C:\Foo> # 9. Checking on FileSystem provider drives on SRV1
PS C:\Foo> Get-PSProvider -PSProvider FileSystem |
              Select-Object -ExpandProperty Drives |
              Sort-Object -Property Name

Name Used (GB) Free (GB) Provider   Root                                              CurrentLocation
---- --------- --------- --------   ----                                              ---------------
C        16.68    111.22 FileSystem C:\                                                           Foo
S         0.14     63.84 FileSystem S:\
Temp     16.68    111.22 FileSystem C:\Users\administrator.RESKIT\AppData\Local\Temp\
W         0.00      1.00 FileSystem W:\
X         0.00     15.00 FileSystem X:\
Y         0.00     14.98 FileSystem Y:\
Z         1.16     31.78 FileSystem Z:\
```

Figure 7.23: Getting drives in the FileSystem provider

Each provider enables you to define a "home drive." You can use the Set-Location command and specify a path of ~ to move to the home drive. In *Chapter 1*, you created a new PowerShell profile and set the home drive for the FileSystem provider (in *Installing and Configuring PowerShell*). In *step 10*, you get the home drive for the FileSystem provider. The output of this step looks like this:

```
PS C:\Foo> # 10. Getting home folder for FileSystem provider
PS C:\Foo> $HomeFolder = Get-PSProvider -PSProvider FileSystem |
              Select-Object -ExpandProperty Home
PS C:\Foo> $HomeFolder
C:\Foo  ◀──────
```

Figure 7.24: Getting the FileSystem provider home folder

In *step 11*, you remove all modules, removing any aliases defined by the loaded modules. Then you get and count the functions in the Function: drive, with output like this:

```
PS C:\Foo> # 11. Checking Function drive
PS C:\Foo> Get-Module | Remove-Module -WarningAction SilentlyContinue
PS C:\Foo> $Functions = Get-ChildItem -Path Function:
PS C:\Foo> "Functions available [$($Functions.Count)]"
Functions available [36]
```

Figure 7.25: Getting and counting functions available

To test the alias provider, in *step 12*, you create a simple function. This step generates no output.

In *step 13*, you check the Function: drive again to view the number of functions available after adding a function. The output of this step looks like this:

```
PS C:\Foo> # 13. Checking Function drive again
PS C:\Foo> $Functions2 = Get-ChildItem -Path Function:
PS C:\Foo> "Functions now available [$($Functions2.Count)]"
Functions now available [37]
```

Figure 7.26: Getting and counting functions available again

Objects returned from the Function provider contain several properties, not the least of which is the function definition. In *step 14*, you view the function definition for the Get-HelloWorld function held in the Function: drive. The output looks like this:

```
PS C:\Foo> # 14. Counting defined variables
PS C:\Foo> $Variables = Get-ChildItem -Path Variable:
PS C:\Foo> "Variables defined [$C$Variables.count)]"
Variables defined [70]
```

Figure 7.27: Getting the function definition from the Function: drive

The Variable: provider enables you to manipulate PowerShell variables. In *step 15*, you count the variables available in the current PowerShell session, with output like this:

```
PS C:\Foo> # 15. Counting defined variables
PS C:\Foo> $Variables = Get-ChildItem -Path Variable:
PS C:\Foo> "Variables defined [$($Variables.count)]"
Variables defined [70]
```

Figure 7.28: Counting variables on SRV1

The certificate provider enables you to manipulate X.509 digital certificates stored in the current user or system certificate stores. In *step 16*, you get the certificates from the current user's trusted root certificate store, with output like this:

```
PS C:\Foo> # 16. Getting trusted root certificates for the local machine
PS C:\Foo> Get-ChildItem -Path Cert:\LocalMachine\Root |
             Format-Table FriendlyName, Thumbprint

FriendlyName                                          Thumbprint
------------                                          ----------
Microsoft Root Certificate Authority                  CDD4EEAE6000AC7F40C3802C171E30148030C072
Thawte Timestamping CA                                BE36A4562FB2EE05DBB3D32323ADF445084ED656
Microsoft Root Authority                              A43489159A520F0D93D032CCAF37E7FE20A8B419
                                                      92B46C76E13054E104F230517E6E504D43AB10B5
Microsoft Root Certificate Authority 2011             8F43288AD272F3103B6FB1428485EA3014C0BCFE
Microsoft Authenticode(tm) Root                       7F88CD7223F3C813818C994614A89C99FA3B5247
Microsoft Root Certificate Authority 2010             3B1EFD3A66EA28B16697394703A72CA340A05BD5
Microsoft ECC TS Root Certificate Authority 2018      31F9FC8BA3805986B721EA7295C65B3A44534274
Microsoft Timestamp Root                              245C97DF7514E7CF2DF8BE72AE957B9E04741E85
VeriSign Time Stamping CA                             18F7C1FCC3090203FD5BAA2F861A754976C8DD25
Microsoft ECC Product Root Certificate Authority 2018 06F1AA330B927B753A40E68CDF22E34BCBEF3352
Microsoft Time Stamp Root Certificate Authority 2014  0119E81BE9A14CD8E22F40AC118C687ECBA3F4D8
DigiCert Global Root G2                               DF3C24F9BFD666761B268073FE06D1CC8D4F82A4
DST Root CA X3                                        DAC9024F54D8F6DF94935FB1732638CA6AD77C13
GlobalSign Root CA - R3                               D69B561148F01C77C54578C10926DF5B856976AD
DigiCert Baltimore Root                               D4DE20D05E66FC53FE1A50882C78DB2852CAE474
Sectigo (AAA)                                         D1EB23A46D17D68FD92564C2F1F1601764D8E349
ISRG Root X1                                          CABD2A79A1076A31F21D253635CB039D4329A5E8
GlobalSign Root CA - R1                               B1BC968BD4F49D622AA89A81F2150152A41D829C
Starfield Class 2 Certification Authority             AD7E1C28B064EF8F6003402014C3D0E3370EB58A
DigiCert                                              A8985D3A65E5E5C4B2D7D66D40C6DD2FB19C5436
Entrust.net                                           8CF427FD790C3AD166068DE81E57EFBB932272D4
VeriSign Class 3 Public Primary CA                    742C3192E607E424EB4549542BE1BBC53E6174E2
DigiCert                                              5FB7EE0633E259DBAD0C4C9AE6D38F1A61C7DC25
VeriSign                                              4EB6D578499B1CCF5F581EAD56BE3D9B6744A5E5
VeriSign Universal Root Certification Authority       3679CA35668772304D30A5FB873B0FA77BB70D54
Go Daddy Class 2 Certification Authority              2796BAE63F1801E277261BA0D77770028F20EEE4
QuoVadis Root CA 2 G3                                 093C61F38B8BDC7D55DF7538020500E125F5C836
DigiCert                                              0563B8630D62D75ABBC8AB1E4BDFB5A899B24D43
```

Figure 7.29: Getting certificates from the current user's trusted publisher certificate store

In PowerShell 7, the WinRM service provides the underpinnings for PowerShell remoting. Remoting uses WinRM to send PowerShell commands to a remote host and receive a response. With WinRM, you configure the WinRM client and WinRM server by updating items in the WSMan: drive. You can view the ports used by the WSMan client and WSMan server services on the SRV1 host, as shown in *step 1*. The output looks like this:

```
PS C:\Foo> # 17. Examining ports in use by WinRM
PS C:\Foo> Get-ChildItem -Path WSMan:\localhost\Client\DefaultPorts

   WSManConfig: Microsoft.WSMan.Management\WSMan::localhost\Client\DefaultPorts

Type            Name    SourceOfValue   Value
----            ----    -------------   -----
System.String   HTTP                    5985
System.String   HTTPS                   5986
```

Figure 7.30: Getting WSMan service ports

To show how you can configure WinRM, in *step 18*, you set WinRM to trust explicitly any remote host by setting the TrustedHosts item in the WSMan: drive. There is no output from this step.

Creating a provider in native C# is often a daunting step. But you can simplify the creation of customized providers by using the SHiPS module. One module created using SHiPS is CimPSDrive. This module contains a CIM database provider enabling you to navigate the WMI database using PowerShell item commands. In *step 20*, you install the SHiPS and CimPSDrive modules, creating no output. Then in *step 21*, you import the CimPSDrive module and create a drive, which looks like this:

```
PS C:\Foo> # 21. Importing the CimPSDrive module and creating a drive
PS C:\Foo> Import-Module -Name CimPSDrive
PS C:\Foo> New-PSDrive -Name CIM -PSProvider SHiPS -Root CIMPSDrive#CMRoot

Name Used (GB) Free (GB) Provider Root              CurrentLocation
---- --------- --------- -------- ----              ---------------
CIM                                SHiPS    CIMPSDrive#CMRoot
```

Figure 7.31: Importing the CimPSDrive module and creating a drive

In *step 22*, you use the newly created CIM PSDrive and examine the values of the Win32_Bios class, with output like this:

```
PS C:\Foo> # 22. Examining BIOS using the CimPSDrive module
PS C:\Foo> Get-ChildItem CIM:\Localhost\CIMV2\Win32_Bios

SMBIOSBIOSVersion : Hyper-V UEFI Release v4.1
Manufacturer      : Microsoft Corporation
Name              : Hyper-V UEFI Release v4.1
SerialNumber      : 1292-4012-4928-5640-9420-3487-94
Version           : VRTUAL - 1
PSComputerName    : localhost
```

Figure 7.32: Viewing a WMI class

There's more...

In *step 4,* you use the registry provider to return the registered owner of this system. The Windows installation process sets this value when you install the OS. If you use the Resource Kit build scripts on GitHub, the unattended XML files provide a user name and organization. Of course, you can change this in the XML or subsequently (by editing the registry).

In *step 11,* you check PowerShell's Function: drive. This drive holds an entry for every function within a PowerShell session. Since PowerShell has no *Remove-Function* command, to remove a function from your PowerShell session, you remove its entry (Remove-Item -Path Function:<functon to remove).

Step 16 lets you view the trusted root CA certificates in the local machine's certificate store. Depending on your organization's needs, you can add or remove certificates from this store – but be very careful. Microsoft maintains these root certificates as part of the Microsoft Root Certificate Program, which supports the distribution of root certificates, enabling customers to trust Windows products. You can read more about this program at https://learn.microsoft.com/ security/trusted-root/program-requirements.

In *step 18,* you set the WinRM TrustedHosts item to "*," which means that whenever PowerShell negotiates a remoting connection with a remote host, it trusts the remote host machine is who it says it is and is not an imposter. Setting TrustedHosts like this can have security implications – you should be careful about when and where you modify this setting.

The SHiPS framework, which you install in *step 19,* is a module that helps you to develop a provider. This framework can be useful in enabling you to create new providers to unlock data in your organization. The framework is available, as you see in this recipe, from the PowerShell Gallery or from GitHub at https://github.com/PowerShell/SHiPS. For a deeper explanation of the SHiPS framework, see https://4sysops.com/archives/create-a-custom-powershell-provider/.

Managing Storage Replica

Storage Replica (SR) is a feature of Windows Server 2022 that replicates storage volumes to other systems. SR is only available with the Windows Server 2022 Datacenter edition.

You typically use SR to maintain a complete replica of one or more disk volumes, typically for disaster recovery. SR works on a volume basis. Once you configure SR and create a replication partnership, SR replicates all the files in a volume, for example, the F: drive, to a disk on another host, for instance, SRV2. After setting up the SR partnership, as you update the F: drive, Windows automatically updates the target drive on SRV2.

However, you cannot see the files on SRV2. An SR partnership also requires a drive on the source and destination hosts for internal logging.

Getting ready

You'll use both SRV1 and SRV2 in this recipe. After adding and configuring additional virtual disks to this host, you'll run this recipe on SRV1, a domain-joined host in the Reskit.Org domain. You must have installed PowerShell 7 and VS Code on this host. This recipe uses the S: drive you created earlier on SRV1 in managing disks, plus a new G: drive, which you created on disk number 3. You also create the corresponding disks on SRV2.

How to do it...

1. Getting disk number of the disk holding the S partition

```
$Part = Get-Partition -DriveLetter S
"S drive on disk [$($Part.DiskNumber)]"
```

2. Creating S: drive on SRV2

```
$ScriptBlock = {
  Initialize-Disk -Number $using:Part.DiskNumber -PartitionStyle GPT
  $NVHT = @{
   DiskNumber   = $using:Part.DiskNumber
    FriendlyName = 'Files'
    FileSystem   = 'NTFS'
    DriveLetter  = 'S'
  }
  New-Volume @NVHT
}
Invoke-Command -ComputerName SRV2 -ScriptBlock $ScriptBlock
```

3. Creating content on S: on SRV1

```
1..100 | ForEach-Object {
  $NewFldr = "S:\CoolFolder$_"
  New-Item -Path $NewFldr -ItemType Directory | Out-Null
  1..100 | ForEach-Object {
    $NewFile = "$NewFldr\CoolFile$_"
    "Cool File" | Out-File -PSPath $NewFile
  }
}
```

4. Counting files/folders on S

```
Get-ChildItem -Path S:\ -Recurse | Measure-Object
```

5. Examining the S: drive remotely on SRV2

```
$ScriptBlock2 = {
  Get-ChildItem -Path S:\ -Recurse |
    Measure-Object
}
Invoke-Command -ComputerName SRV2 -ScriptBlock $ScriptBlock2
```

6. Adding the storage replica feature to SRV1

```
Add-WindowsFeature -Name Storage-Replica -IncludeManagementTools |
  Out-Null
```

7. Adding the storage replica feature to SRV2

```
$SB= {
  Add-WindowsFeature -Name Storage-Replica | Out-Null
}
Invoke-Command -ComputerName SRV2 -ScriptBlock $SB
```

8. Restarting SRV2 and wait for the restart

```
$RSHT = @{
  ComputerName = 'SRV2'
  Force        = $true
}
Restart-Computer @RSHT -Wait -For WinRM
```

9. Restarting SRV1 to finish the installation process

```
Restart-Computer
```

10. Creating a G: volume on disk 3 on SRV1

```
$ScriptBlock3 = {
  Initialize-Disk -Number 3 -PartitionStyle GPT | Out-Null
  $VolumeHT = @{
    DiskNumber   =  3
    FriendlyName = 'SRLOGS'
```

```
      DriveLetter  = 'G'
    }
    New-Volume @VolumeHT
  }
  Invoke-Command -ComputerName SRV1 -ScriptBlock $ScriptBlock3
```

11. Creating a G: volume on SRV2

```
  Invoke-Command -ComputerName SRV2 -ScriptBlock $ScriptBlock3
```

12. Viewing volumes on SRV1

```
  Get-Volume | Sort-Object -Property Driveletter
```

13. Viewing volumes on SRV2

```
  Invoke-Command -Computer SRV2 -ScriptBlock {
      Get-Volume | Sort-Object -Property Driveletter
  }
```

14. Creating an SR replica partnership

```
  $NewSRHT =  @{
    SourceComputerName       = 'SRV1'
    SourceRGName             = 'SRV1RG1'
    SourceVolumeName         = 'S:'
    SourceLogVolumeName      = 'G:'
    DestinationComputerName  = 'SRV2'
    DestinationRGName        = 'SRV2RG1'
    DestinationVolumeName    = 'S:'
    DestinationLogVolumeName = 'G:'
    LogSizeInBytes           = 2gb
  }
  New-SRPartnership @NewSRHT
```

15. Examining the volumes on SRV2

```
  $ScriptBlock3 = {
    Get-Volume |
      Sort-Object -Property DriveLetter |
        Format-Table}
  Invoke-Command -ComputerName SRV2 -ScriptBlock $ScriptBlock3
```

16. Reversing the replication

```
$ReverseHT = @{
  NewSourceComputerName    = 'SRV2'
  SourceRGName             = 'SRV2RG1'
  DestinationComputerName  = 'SRV1'
  DestinationRGName        = 'SRV1RG1'
  Confirm                  = $false
}
Set-SRPartnership @ReverseHT
```

17. Viewing the SR partnership

```
Get-SRPartnership
```

18. Examining the files remotely on SRV2

```
$ScriptBlock4 = {
  Get-ChildItem -Path S:\ -Recurse |
    Measure-Object
}
Invoke-Command -ComputerName SRV2 -ScriptBlock $ScriptBlock4
```

How it works...

In *step 1*, you get the disk number of the disk holding the S: partition, with output like this:

```
PS C:\Foo> # 1. Getting disk number of the disk holding the S partition
PS C:\Foo> $Part = Get-Partition -DriveLetter S
PS C:\Foo> "S drive on disk [$C$Part.DiskNumber)]"
S drive on disk [1]
```

Figure 7.33: Viewing a WMI class

In *step 2*, you create a new S: volume on SRV2. This step produces output like this:

```
PS C:\Foo> # 2. Creating S: drive on SRV2
PS C:\Foo> $ScriptBlock = {
             Initialize-Disk -Number $using:Part.DiskNumber -PartitionStyle GPT
             $NewVolHT = @{
             DiskNumber   =   $using:Part.DiskNumber
              FriendlyName = 'Files'
              FileSystem   = 'NTFS'
              DriveLetter  = 'S'
             }
             New-Volume @NweVolHT
           }
PS C:\Foo> Invoke-Command -ComputerName SRV2 -ScriptBlock $ScriptBlock


DriveLetter FriendlyName FileSystemType DriveType HealthStatus OperationalStatus SizeRemaining      Size PSComputerName
----------- ------------ -------------- --------- ------------ ----------------- -------------      ---- --------------
S           Files        NTFS           Fixed     Healthy      OK                     63.89 GB 63.98 GB SRV2
```

Figure 7.34: Creating S: on SRV2

In *step 3*, you create folders and files on SRV1, which creates no output. In *step 4*, you count the number of files and folders on the S: drive, with output like this:

```
PS C:\Foo> # 4. Counting files/folders on S:
PS C:\Foo> Get-ChildItem -Path S:\ -Recurse | Measure-Object

Count             : 10100
Average           :
Sum               :
Maximum           :
Minimum           :
StandardDeviation :
Property          :
```

Figure 7.35: Viewing the files on S: on SRV1

In *step 5*, you examine the files and folders on the S: drive on SRV2, with output like this:

```
PS C:\Foo> # 5. Examining the same drives remotely on SRV2
PS C:\Foo> $ScriptBlock2 = {
             Get-ChildItem -Path S:\ -Recurse |
               Measure-Object
           }
PS C:\Foo> Invoke-Command -ComputerName SRV2 -ScriptBlock $ScriptBlock2

Count          : 0
Average        :
Sum            :
Maximum        :
Minimum        :
Property       :
PSComputerName : SRV2
```

Figure 7.36: Viewing the files on SRV2

Now that you have the S: drive created on both SRV1 and SRV2 and have created content, in *step 6*, you add the Storage Replica feature to SRV1, creating the following output:

```
PS C:\Foo> # 6. Adding the storage replica feature to SRV1
PS C:\Foo> Add-WindowsFeature -Name Storage-Replica | Out-Null
WARNING: You must restart this server to finish the installation process
```

Figure 7.37: Adding Storage Replica to SRV1

In *step 7*, you add the Storage Replica feature to SRV2, generating similar output, like this:

```
PS C:\Foo> # 7. Adding the Storage Replica Feature to SRV2
PS C:\Foo> $SB= {
               Add-WindowsFeature -Name Storage-Replica | Out-Null
           }
PS C:\Foo> Invoke-Command -ComputerName SRV2 -ScriptBlock $SB

WARNING: You must restart this server to finish the installation process.
```

Figure 7.38: Adding Storage Replica to SRV2

In *step 8*, you restart SRV2. Then, in *step 9*, you restart SRV1. Neither step produces console output.

In *step 10*, you create a new G: volume on SRV1 (to hold Storage Replica log files), with output like this:

```
PS C:\Foo> # 10. Creating a G: volume in disk 3 on SRV1
PS C:\Foo> $ScriptBlock3 = {
               Initialize-Disk -Number 3 | Out-Null
               $VolumeHT = @{
                 DiskNumber   = 3
                 FriendlyName = 'SRLOGS'
                 DriveLetter  = 'G'
               }
               New-Volume @VolumeHT
           }
PS C:\Foo> Invoke-Command -ComputerName SRV1 -ScriptBlock $ScriptBlock3

DriveLetter FriendlyName FileSystemType DriveType HealthStatus OperationalStatus SizeRemaining     Size PSComputerName
----------- ------------ -------------- --------- ------------ ----------------- -------------     ---- --------------
G           SRLOGS       NTFS           Fixed     Healthy      OK                63.84 GB 63.98 GB SRV1
```

Figure 7.39: Creating a G: volume on SRV1

In *step 11*, you create a G: volume on SRV2, with output like this:

```
PS C:\Foo> # 11. Creating G: volume on SRV2
PS C:\Foo> Invoke-Command -ComputerName SRV2 -ScriptBlock $ScriptBlock3

DriveLetter FriendlyName FileSystemType DriveType HealthStatus OperationalStatus SizeRemaining     Size PSComputerName
----------- ------------ -------------- --------- ------------ ----------------- -------------     ---- --------------
G           SRLOGS       NTFS           Fixed     Healthy      OK                63.89 GB 63.98 GB SRV2
```

Figure 7.40: Creating a G: volume on SRV2

In *step 12*, you examine the volumes on SRV1, with output like this:

```
PS C:\Foo> # 12. Viewing volumes on SRV1
PS C:\Foo> Get-Volume | Sort-Object -Property Driveletter

DriveLetter FriendlyName FileSystemType DriveType HealthStatus OperationalStatus SizeRemaining        Size
----------- ------------ -------------- --------- ------------ ----------------- -------------        ----
                         FAT32          Fixed     Healthy      OK                   67.25 MB       96 MB
C                        NTFS           Fixed     Healthy      OK                  111.61 GB     127.9 GB
G           SRLOGS       NTFS           Fixed     Healthy      OK                   63.84 GB     63.98 GB
S           Files        NTFS           Fixed     Healthy      OK                   63.83 GB     63.98 GB
W           W-FAT        FAT            Fixed     Healthy      OK                1023.66 MB   1023.72 MB
X           x-exFAT      exFAT          Fixed     Healthy      OK                      15 GB        15 GB
Y           Y-FAT32      FAT32          Fixed     Healthy      OK                   14.98 GB     14.98 GB
Z           Z-ReFS       ReFS           Fixed     Healthy      OK                   31.78 GB     32.94 GB
```

Figure 7.41: Viewing volumes on SRV1

In *step 13,* you examine the volumes on SRV2, with output like this:

```
PS C:\Foo> # 13. Viewing volumes on SRV2
PS C:\Foo> Invoke-Command -Computer SRV2 -Scriptblock {
             Get-Volume | Sort-Object -Property Driveletter
           }

DriveLetter FriendlyName FileSystemType DriveType HealthStatus OperationalStatus SizeRemaining      Size PSComputerName
----------- ------------ -------------- --------- ------------ ----------------- -------------      ---- --------------
                         FAT32          Fixed     Healthy      OK                   67.26 MB     96 MB SRV2
C                        NTFS           Fixed     Healthy      OK                  115.03 GB 127.9 GB SRV2
G           SRLOGS       NTFS           Fixed     Healthy      OK                   63.89 GB 63.98 GB SRV2
S           Files        NTFS           Fixed     Healthy      OK                   63.89 GB 63.98 GB SRV2
```

Figure 7.42: Viewing volumes on SRV2

In *step 14*, you use the New-SRPartnership command to create a new Storage Replica partnership, creating the following output:

```
PS C:\Foo> # 14. Creating an SR replica group
PS C:\Foo> $NewSRHT =  @{
             SourceComputerName        = 'SRV1'
             SourceRGName              = 'SRV1RG2'
             SourceVolumeName          = 'S:'
             SourceLogVolumeName       = 'G:'
             DestinationComputerName   = 'SRV2'
             DestinationRGName         = 'SRV2RG2'
             DestinationVolumeName     = 'S:'
             DestinationLogVolumeName  = 'G:'
             LogSizeInBytes            = 2gb
           }
PS C:\Foo> New-SRPartnership @SRHT

RunspaceId              : 0da18bca-0a49-4f1a-9bbf-cdd44129984c
DestinationComputerName : SRV2
DestinationRGName       : SRV2RG2
Id                      : 5c52459b-38a9-44ae-8ebd-867d6e19ece0
SourceComputerName      : SRV1
SourceRGName            : SRV1RG2
```

Figure 7.43: Creating a Storage Replica partnership

In *step 15*, you examine the volumes again on SRV2, with output like this:

```
PS C:\Foo> # 15. Examining the volumes on SRV2
PS C:\Foo> $ScriptBlock3 = {
             Get-Volume |
               Sort-Object -Property DriveLetter |
                 Format-Table
           }
PS C:\Foo> Invoke-Command -ComputerName SRV2 -ScriptBlock $ScriptBlock3

DriveLetter FriendlyName FileSystemType DriveType HealthStatus OperationalStatus SizeRemaining      Size
----------- ------------ -------------- --------- ------------ ----------------- -------------      ----
                         FAT32          Fixed     Healthy      OK                    67.26 MB      96 MB
C                        NTFS           Fixed     Healthy      OK                   115.03 GB   127.9 GB
G           SRLOGS       NTFS           Fixed     Healthy      OK                    61.89 GB  63.98 GB
S                        Unknown        Fixed     Healthy      Unknown                    0 B       0 B
```

Figure 7.44: Examining the volumes on SRV2

Thus far, in this recipe, you have created an SR partnership, replicating the S: volume from SRV1 to SRV2. In the next step, *step 16*, you reverse the replication – replicating the S: volume from SRV2 to SRV1, which creates no output.

In *step 17*, you view the now-reversed SR partnership, with the following output:

```
PS C:\Foo> # 17. Viewing the SR Partnership
PS C:\Foo> Get-SRPartnership

RunspaceId              : 0da18bca-0a49-4f1a-9bbf-cdd44129984c
DestinationComputerName : SRV1
DestinationRGName       : SRV1RG2
Id                      : 5c52459b-38a9-44ae-8ebd-867d6e19ece0
SourceComputerName      : SRV2
SourceRGName            : SRV2RG2
```

Figure 7.45: Examining the reversed SR partnership

There's more...

In the first five steps in this recipe, you create and review content on SRV1, which you intend to have Storage Replica replicate to SRV2. In practice, the data you are replicating would be the files in a file server or represent other files you want to synchronize.

In *step 8*, you reboot SRV2 remotely. If this is the first time you have rebooted SRV2 remotely using PowerShell, you may find that the command never returns, even when SRV2 is demonstrably up and running. Just kill off the current PowerShell console (or close VS code) and open a new console to continue the recipe.

After creating the SR partnership, you can reverse the replication. Before you reverse the replication, you should ensure that the initial replication has been completed – depending on the size of the SR replications, it could take quite a while. You can use the command (Get-SRGroup).Replicas. ReplicationStatus to check the status of the initial replication.

Deploying Storage Spaces

Storage Spaces is a technology in Windows 10/11 and Windows Server that implements software RAID. You can add multiple physical drives to your server or workstation, and create fault-tolerant volumes for your host. You can read more about Storage Spaces at https://learn.microsoft.com/windows-server/storage/storage-spaces/overview.

You can use Storage Spaces on a single host or server to protect against unexpected disk drive failures. You should note that Storage Spaces is separate from **Storage Spaces Direct (S2D)**. S2D enables you to create a virtual SAN with multiple hosts providing SMB3 access to a scale-out file server.

Getting ready

You run this recipe on SRV1, a domain-joined host in the Reskit.Org domain. You also need DC1, a domain controller for the Reskit.Org domain. This recipe uses the five virtual disks you added to SRV1 earlier in the chapter, at the start of the *Managing Disks* recipe.

How to do it...

1. Viewing the disks available for pooling

```
$Disks = Get-PhysicalDisk -CanPool $true
$Disks | Sort-Object -Property Deviceid
```

2. Creating a storage pool

```
$NewPoolHT = @{
  FriendlyName                  = 'RKSP'
  StorageSubsystemFriendlyName  = "Windows Storage*"
  PhysicalDisks                 = $Disks
}
New-StoragePool @NewPoolHT
```

3. Creating a mirrored hard disk named Mirror1

```
$VDisk1HT = @{
  StoragePoolFriendlyName   = 'RKSP'
  FriendlyName              = 'Mirror1'
  ResiliencySettingName     = 'Mirror'
  Size                      = 8GB
  ProvisioningType          = 'Thin'
```

```
    }
    New-VirtualDisk @VDisk1HT
```

4. Creating a three-way mirrored disk named `Mirror2`

```
    $VDisk2HT = @{
        StoragePoolFriendlyName    = 'RKSP'
        FriendlyName               = 'Mirror2'
        ResiliencySettingName      = 'Mirror'
        NumberOfDataCopies         = 3
        Size                       = 8GB
        ProvisioningType           = 'Thin'
    }
    New-VirtualDisk @VDisk2HT
```

5. Creating a volume in `Mirror1`

```
    Get-VirtualDisk  -FriendlyName 'Mirror1' |
      Get-Disk |
        Initialize-Disk -PassThru |
          New-Partition -AssignDriveLetter -UseMaximumSize |
            Format-Volume
```

6. Creating a volume in `Mirror2`

```
    Get-VirtualDisk  -FriendlyName 'Mirror2' |
      Get-Disk |
        Initialize-Disk -PassThru |
          New-Partition -AssignDriveLetter -UseMaximumSize |
            Format-Volume
```

7. Viewing volumes on SRV1

```
    Get-Volume | Sort-Object -Property DriveLetter
```

How it works...

In *step 1*, you examine the disks available for polling within SRV1. The output should look something like this:

```
PS C:\Foo> # 1. Viewing disks available for pooling
PS C:\Foo> $Disks = Get-PhysicalDisk -CanPool $true
PS C:\Foo> $Disks | Sort-Object -Property Deviceid

Number FriendlyName      SerialNumber MediaType   CanPool OperationalStatus HealthStatus Usage       Size
------ ------------      ------------ ---------   ------- ----------------- ------------ -----       ----
4      Msft Virtual Disk              Unspecified True    OK                Healthy      Auto-Select 64 GB
5      Msft Virtual Disk              Unspecified True    OK                Healthy      Auto-Select 64 GB
6      Msft Virtual Disk              Unspecified True    OK                Healthy      Auto-Select 64 GB
7      Msft Virtual Disk              Unspecified True    OK                Healthy      Auto-Select 64 GB
8      Msft Virtual Disk              Unspecified True    OK                Healthy      Auto-Select 64 GB
```

Figure 7.46: Viewing disks available for pooling on SRV1

In *step 2*, you use the `New-StoragePool` cmdlet to create a new storage pool using the five disks you discovered in the previous step. The output looks like this:

```
PS C:\Foo> # 2. Creating a storage pool
PS C:\Foo> $NewPoolHT = @{
    FriendlyName                = 'RKSP'
    StorageSubsystemFriendlyName = "Windows Storage*"
    PhysicalDisks               = $Disks
}
PS C:\Foo> New-StoragePool @NewPoolHT

FriendlyName OperationalStatus HealthStatus IsPrimordial IsReadOnly     Size AllocatedSize
------------ ----------------- ------------ ------------ ----------     ---- -------------
RKSP         OK                Healthy      False        False      317.42 GB       1.25 GB
```

Figure 7.47: Creating a new storage pool

In *step 3*, you create a new storage space called `Mirror1`. This storage space is effectively a virtual disk within a storage pool. The output of this step looks like this:

```
PS C:\Foo> # 3. Creating a mirrored hard disk named Mirror1
PS C:\Foo> $VDisk1HT = @{
    StoragePoolFriendlyName  = 'RKSP'
    FriendlyName             = 'Mirror1'
    ResiliencySettingName    = 'Mirror'
    Size                     = 8GB
    ProvisioningType         = 'Thin'
}
PS C:\Foo> New-VirtualDisk @VDdisk1HT

FriendlyName ResiliencySettingName FaultDomainRedundancy OperationalStatus HealthStatus Size FootprintOnPool StorageEfficiency
------------ --------------------- --------------------- ----------------- ------------ ---- --------------- -----------------
Mirror1      Mirror                1                     OK                Healthy      8 GB         1.5 GB            33.33%
```

Figure 7.48: Creating a new mirrored disk inside Storage Spaces

In *step 4*, you create a three-way mirrored disk called `Mirror2`. The output of this step looks like this:

```
PS C:\Foo> # 4. Creating a three way mirrored disk named Mirror2
PS C:\Foo> $VDisk2HT = @{
               StoragePoolFriendlyName    = 'RKSP'
               FriendlyName               = 'Mirror2'
               ResiliencySettingName      = 'Mirror'
               NumberOfDataCopies         = 3
               Size                       = 8GB
               ProvisioningType           = 'Thin'
           }
PS C:\Foo> New-VirtualDisk @VDisk2HT
```

FriendlyName	ResiliencySettingName	FaultDomainRedundancy	OperationalStatus	HealthStatus	Size	FootprintOnPool	StorageEfficiency
Mirror2	Mirror	2	OK	Healthy	8 GB	1.5 GB	16.67%

Figure 7.49: Creating a three-way mirrored storage space

In *step 5*, you create a new volume in the `Mirror1` storage space, which looks like this:

```
PS C:\Foo> # 5. Creating a volume in Mirror1
PS C:\Foo> Get-VirtualDisk  -FriendlyName 'Mirror1' |
             Get-Disk |
               Initialize-Disk -PassThru |
                 New-Partition -AssignDriveLetter -UseMaximumSize |
                   Format-Volume
```

DriveLetter	FriendlyName	FileSystemType	DriveType	HealthStatus	OperationalStatus	SizeRemaining	Size
D		NTFS	Fixed	Healthy	OK	7.95 GB	7.98 GB

Figure 7.50: Creating a new disk volume inside the Mirror1 storage space

In *step 6*, you create another new volume. You create the volume in the three-way mirror storage space, `Mirror2`, with output like this:

```
PS C:\Foo> # 6. Creating a volume in Mirror2
PS C:\Foo> Get-VirtualDisk  -FriendlyName 'Mirror2' |
             Get-Disk |
               Initialize-Disk -PassThru |
                 New-Partition -AssignDriveLetter -UseMaximumSize |
                   Format-Volume
```

DriveLetter	FriendlyName	FileSystemType	DriveType	HealthStatus	OperationalStatus	SizeRemaining	Size
E		NTFS	Fixed	Healthy	OK	7.95 GB	7.98 GB

Figure 7.51: Creating a new disk volume inside the Mirror2 storage space

In the final step in this recipe, *step 7*, you use the Get-Volume command to view all the volumes available in SRV1, with output like this:

```
PS C:\Foo> # 7.  Viewing volumes on SRV1
PS C:\Foo> Get-Volume | Sort-Object -Property DriveLetter

DriveLetter FriendlyName FileSystemType DriveType HealthStatus OperationalStatus SizeRemaining        Size
----------- ------------ -------------- --------- ------------ ----------------- -------------        ----
                         FAT32          Fixed     Healthy      OK                   67.24 MB         96 MB
C                        NTFS           Fixed     Healthy      OK                  108.07 GB      127.9 GB
D                        NTFS           Fixed     Healthy      OK                    7.95 GB       7.98 GB
E                        NTFS           Fixed     Healthy      OK                    7.95 GB       7.98 GB
G           SRLOGS       NTFS           Fixed     Healthy      OK                   61.84 GB      63.98 GB
S                        Unknown        Fixed     Healthy      Unknown                   0 B           0 B
W           W-FAT        FAT            Fixed     Healthy      OK                 1023.66 MB    1023.72 MB
X           x-exFAT      exFAT          Fixed     Healthy      OK                      15 GB         15 GB
Y           Y-FAT32      FAT32          Fixed     Healthy      OK                   14.98 GB      14.98 GB
Z           Z-ReFS       ReFS           Fixed     Healthy      OK                   31.78 GB      32.94 GB
```

Figure 7.52: Viewing disk volumes available on SRV1

There's more...

In *step 1*, you get the disks available for pooling with Storage Spaces. The output assumes you have performed the recipes earlier in this chapter (e.g., creating volumes, etc.).

In *steps 5* and *step 6*, you create two new disk volumes in SRV1. The first is the D: drive, which you created in the mirror set Mirror1, and the second is the E: drive, a disk volume you create in the three-way mirror storage space. The drive you create in Mirror1 is resilient to losing a single disk, whereas the E: drive created in the Mirror2 storage space can sustain two disk failures and still provide full access to your information.

Join our community on Discord

Join our community's Discord space for discussions with the author and other readers:

https://packt.link/SecNet

8

Managing Shared Data

This chapter covers the following recipes:

- Managing NTFS File and Folder Permissions
- Securing Your SMB File Server
- Creating and Securing SMB Shares
- Accessing SMB Shares
- Creating an iSCSI Target
- Using an iSCSI Target
- Implementing FSRM Filestore Quotas
- Implementing FSRM Filestore reporting
- Implementing FSRM Filestore Screening

Introduction

Sharing data with other users on your network has been a feature of computer operating systems from the very earliest days of computing. This chapter looks at Windows Server 2022 features that enable you to share files and folders and use your shared data.

Microsoft's LAN Manager was the company's first network offering. It enabled client computers to create, manage, and share files securely. LAN Manager's protocol to provide this client/server functionality was an early version of the **Server Message Block (SMB)** protocol.

SMB is a file-level storage protocol running over TCP/IP. With the SMB protocol, you can share files and folders securely and reliably. To increase reliability for SMB servers, you can install a cluster and cluster the file server role.

A simple cluster solution is an active-passive solution – you have one cluster member sitting by if the other member fails. This solution works great as long as the underlying data is accessible. **Scale-Out File Server (SOFS)** is an active-active clustering-based solution. Both nodes of the cluster can serve cluster clients.

This chapter shows you how to implement and leverage the features of sharing data between systems in Windows Server 2022.

In the first recipe, *Managing NTFS File and Folder Permissions*, you use the NTFSSecurity third-party module to set **Access Control List (ACL)** and ACL inheritance for files held in NTFS from FS1. In the following recipe, *Securing Your SMB File Server*, you deploy a hardened SMB file server. You run that recipe on FS1.

iSCSI is a popular **Storage Area Networking (SAN)** technology. Many SAN vendors provide iSCSI as a way to access data stored in a SAN. There are two aspects to iSCSI: the server (the iSCSI target) and the client (the iSCSI initiator). With the *Creating an iSCSI Target* recipe, you create an iSCSI target on the SS1 server, while in the *Using an iSCSI Target* recipe, you make use of that shared iSCSI disk from FS1.

File System Resource Manager (FSRM) is a Windows Server feature that helps you manage file servers. You can use FSRM to set user quotas for folders, create file screens, and produce rich reports.

Several servers are involved in the recipes in this chapter—each recipe describes the specific server(s) you use for that recipe. As with other chapters in this book, all the servers are members of the Reskit.Org domain on which you have loaded PowerShell 7 and VS Code. You can install them by using the Reskit.Org setup scripts on GitHub.

The systems used in the chapter

There are two new servers, SS1 and FS, plus the existing SRV1. All servers run Windows Server 2022 Datacenter edition. The servers are member servers in the Reskit.Org domain served by the two domain controllers, DC1 and DC2, as shown here:

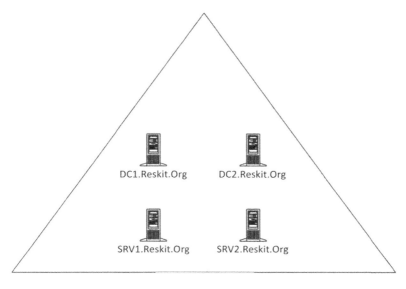

Reskit.Org domain

Figure 8.1: Hosts in use for this chapter

Managing NTFS File and Folder Permissions

Every file and folder in an NTFS file system has an **ACL**. The ACL contains a set of **Access Control Entries (ACEs)**. Each ACE defines permission to a file or folder for an account. For example, you could give the Sales AD global group full control of a file.

NTFS also allows a file or folder to inherit permission from its parent folder. If you create a new folder and then create a file within that new folder, the new file inherits the parent folder's permissions. You can manage the ACL to add or remove permissions, and you can modify inheritance.

There's limited PowerShell support for managing NTFS permissions. PowerShell does have the Get-ACL and Set-ACL cmdlets, but creating the individual ACEs and managing inheritance requires using .NET Framework (by default). A more straightforward approach is to use a third-party module, NTFSSecurity, which makes managing ACEs and ACLs, including dealing with inheritance, a lot easier. In this recipe, you download and use this module. This recipe uses the NTFSSecurity module, which simplifies the management of NTFS ACLs. As an alternative, .NET has some basic classes you can use to create ACEs in memory. You can then use the cmdlets to add the ACE to an ACL. For a deeper look at using .NET classes with the Set-ACL command, look at https://adamtheautomator.com/ntfs-permissions/.

You can also find additional examples in the Set-ACL documentation at: https://learn. microsoft.com/powershell/module/microsoft.powershell.security/set-acl

Getting ready

This recipe uses FS1, a domain-joined host in the Reskit.Org domain, on which you have installed PowerShell 7 and VS Code. You also need DC1 online. You also need to add a disk to this host. Assuming you are using Hyper-V to run the FS1 host, you can add the disk with the following code (run on the Hyper-V Host):

1. Stop the VM

   ```
   Get-VM -Name FS1 | Stop-VM -Force
   ```

2. Get the path for hard disks for SRV1 and SRV2

   ```
   $Path1   = Get-VMHardDiskDrive -VMName FS1
   $VMPath1 = Split-Path -Parent $Path1.Path
   ```

3. Create a new VHDX

   ```
   New-VHD -Path $VMPath1\FS1-F.vhdx -SizeBytes 64gb -Dynamic
   ```

4. Add a new SCSI controller to FS1

   ```
   Add-VMScsiController -VMName FS1
   [int] $FS1Controller =
     Get-VMScsiController -VMName FS1 |
       Select-Object -Last 1 |
         Select-Object -ExpandProperty ControllerNumber
   ```

5. Add the VHDX to the VM

   ```
   $DiskHT = @{
     VMName           = 'FS1'
     Path             = "$VMPath1\FS1-F.vhdx"
     ControllerType   = 'SCSI'
     ControllerNumber = $FS1Controller
   }
   Add-VMHardDiskDrive @DiskHT
   ```

6. Restart the VM

   ```
   Start-VM -Name FS1
   ```

You may need to wait a few seconds before logging in to FS1 to run this recipe.

How to do it...

1. Getting and initializing the new disk and creating an F: volume

```
$Disk = Get-Disk |
            Where-Object PartitionStyle -eq Raw |
              Select-Object -First 1
$Disk |
   Initialize-Disk -PartitionStyle GPT
$NewVolumeHT1   = @{
   DiskNumber   = $Disk.DiskNumber
   DriveLetter  = 'F'
   FriendlyName = 'FS Files'
}
New-Volume @NewVolumeHT1 | Out-Null
```

2. Downloading the NTFSSecurity module from PSGallery

```
Install-Module NTFSSecurity -Force
```

3. Getting commands in the module

```
Get-Command -Module NTFSSecurity
```

4. Creating a new folder and a file in the folder

```
New-Item -Path F:\Secure1 -ItemType Directory |
     Out-Null
"Secure" | Out-File -FilePath F:\Secure1\Secure.Txt
Get-ChildItem -Path F:\Secure1
```

5. Viewing ACL of the folder

```
Get-NTFSAccess -Path F:\Secure1 |
   Format-Table -AutoSize
```

6. Viewing ACL of the file

```
Get-NTFSAccess F:\Secure1\Secure.Txt |
   Format-Table -AutoSize
```

7. Creating the Sales group in AD if it does not exist

```
$ScriptBlock= {
  try {
    Get-ADGroup -Identity 'Sales' -ErrorAction Stop
  }
  catch {
    New-ADGroup -Name Sales -GroupScope Global |
      Out-Null
  }
}
Invoke-Command -ComputerName DC1 -ScriptBlock $ScriptBlock
```

8. Displaying Sales AD group

```
Invoke-Command -ComputerName DC1 -ScriptBlock {
                                  Get-ADGroup -Identity Sales}
```

9. Adding explicit full control for DomainAdmins

```
$AddAdminHT= @{
  Path        = 'F:\Secure1'
  Account     = 'Reskit\Domain Admins'
  AccessRights = 'FullControl'
}
Add-NTFSAccess @AddAdminHT
```

10. Removing Builtin\Users access from the Secure.Txt file

```
$RemoveUsersHT = @{
  Path        = 'F:\Secure1\Secure.Txt'
  Account     = 'Builtin\Users'
  AccessRights = 'FullControl'
}
Remove-NTFSAccess @RemoveUsersHT
```

11. Removing inherited rights for the folder

```
$RemoveInheritRHT = @{
  Path                     = 'F:\Secure1'
  RemoveInheritedAccessRules = $True
}
Disable-NTFSAccessInheritance @RemoveInheritRHT
```

12. Adding Sales group access to the folder

```
$AddHT = @{
  Path         = 'F:\Secure1\'
  Account      = 'Reskit\Sales'
  AccessRights = 'FullControl'
}
Add-NTFSAccess @AddHT
```

13. Getting ACL of the Secure1 folder

```
Get-NTFSAccess -Path F:\Secure1 |
  Format-Table -AutoSize
```

14. Getting resulting ACL on the Secure.Txt file

```
Get-NTFSAccess -Path F:\Secure1\Secure.Txt |
  Format-Table -AutoSize
```

How it works...

In *step 1*, you create a new volume on the disk added in the *Getting ready* section. This step is similar to those performed in the *Managing disks* recipe in *Chapter 7*. The step produces no output.

In *step 2*, you use the Install-Module command to download the NTFSSecurity module from the PowerShell Gallery. This step produces no output.

In *step 3*, you use the Get-Command cmdlet to discover the cmdlets inside the NTFSSecurity module, with output like this:

```
PS C:\Foo> # 3. Getting commands in the module
PS C:\Foo> Get-Command -Module NTFSSecurity

CommandType  Name                             Version  Source
-----------  ----                             -------  ------
Cmdlet       Add-NTFSAccess                   4.2.6    NTFSSecurity
Cmdlet       Add-NTFSAudit                    4.2.6    NTFSSecurity
Cmdlet       Clear-NTFSAccess                 4.2.6    NTFSSecurity
Cmdlet       Clear-NTFSAudit                  4.2.6    NTFSSecurity
Cmdlet       Copy-Item2                       4.2.6    NTFSSecurity
Cmdlet       Disable-NTFSAccessInheritance    4.2.6    NTFSSecurity
Cmdlet       Disable-NTFSAuditInheritance     4.2.6    NTFSSecurity
Cmdlet       Disable-Privileges               4.2.6    NTFSSecurity
Cmdlet       Enable-NTFSAccessInheritance     4.2.6    NTFSSecurity
Cmdlet       Enable-NTFSAuditInheritance      4.2.6    NTFSSecurity
Cmdlet       Enable-Privileges                4.2.6    NTFSSecurity
Cmdlet       Get-ChildItem2                   4.2.6    NTFSSecurity
Cmdlet       Get-DiskSpace                    4.2.6    NTFSSecurity
Cmdlet       Get-FileHash2                    4.2.6    NTFSSecurity
Cmdlet       Get-Item2                        4.2.6    NTFSSecurity
Cmdlet       Get-NTFSAccess                   4.2.6    NTFSSecurity
Cmdlet       Get-NTFSAudit                    4.2.6    NTFSSecurity
Cmdlet       Get-NTFSEffectiveAccess          4.2.6    NTFSSecurity
Cmdlet       Get-NTFSHardLink                 4.2.6    NTFSSecurity
Cmdlet       Get-NTFSInheritance              4.2.6    NTFSSecurity
Cmdlet       Get-NTFSOrphanedAccess           4.2.6    NTFSSecurity
Cmdlet       Get-NTFSOrphanedAudit            4.2.6    NTFSSecurity
Cmdlet       Get-NTFSOwner                    4.2.6    NTFSSecurity
Cmdlet       Get-NTFSSecurityDescriptor       4.2.6    NTFSSecurity
Cmdlet       Get-NTFSSimpleAccess             4.2.6    NTFSSecurity
Cmdlet       Get-Privileges                   4.2.6    NTFSSecurity
Cmdlet       Move-Item2                       4.2.6    NTFSSecurity
Cmdlet       New-NTFSHardLink                 4.2.6    NTFSSecurity
Cmdlet       New-NTFSSymbolicLink             4.2.6    NTFSSecurity
Cmdlet       Remove-Item2                     4.2.6    NTFSSecurity
Cmdlet       Remove-NTFSAccess                4.2.6    NTFSSecurity
Cmdlet       Remove-NTFSAudit                 4.2.6    NTFSSecurity
Cmdlet       Set-NTFSInheritance              4.2.6    NTFSSecurity
Cmdlet       Set-NTFSOwner                    4.2.6    NTFSSecurity
Cmdlet       Set-NTFSSecurityDescriptor       4.2.6    NTFSSecurity
Cmdlet       Test-Path2                       4.2.6    NTFSSecurity
```

Figure 8.2: Reviewing the commands in the NTFSSecurity module

In *step 4*, you create a new folder and a new file on the newly created F: volume. The output from this step looks like this:

```
PS C:\Foo> # 4. Creating a new folder and a file in the folder
PS C:\Foo> New-Item -Path F:\Secure1 -ItemType Directory |
              Out-Null
PS C:\Foo> "Secure" | Out-File -FilePath F:\Secure1\Secure.Txt
PS C:\Foo> Get-ChildItem -Path F:\Secure1


    Directory: F:\Secure1

Mode          LastWriteTime   Length Name
----          -------------   ------ ----
-a---    10/08/2022    13:55        8 Secure.Txt
```

Figure 8.3: Creating a new folder and file in F:

In *step 5*, you use the Get-NTFSAccess command to view the ACL of the F:\Secure1 folder, with output like this:

```
PS C:\Foo> # 5. Viewing ACL of the folder
PS C:\Foo> Get-NTFSAccess -Path F:\Secure1 |
              Format-Table -AutoSize

    Path: F:\Secure1 (Inheritance enabled)
```

Account	Access Rights	Applies to	Type	IsInherited	InheritedFrom
BUILTIN\Administrators	FullControl	ThisFolderOnly	Allow	False	
BUILTIN\Administrators	FullControl	ThisFolderSubfoldersAndFiles	Allow	True	F:
NT AUTHORITY\SYSTEM	FullControl	ThisFolderSubfoldersAndFiles	Allow	True	F:
CREATOR OWNER	GenericAll	SubfoldersAndFilesOnly	Allow	True	F:
BUILTIN\Users	ReadAndExecute, Synchronize	ThisFolderSubfoldersAndFiles	Allow	True	F:
BUILTIN\Users	CreateDirectories	ThisFolderAndSubfolders	Allow	True	F:
BUILTIN\Users	CreateFiles	ThisFolderAndSubfolders	Allow	True	F:

Figure 8.4: Viewing the ACL of the F:\Secure folder

In *step 6*, you view the ACL for the Secure.Txt file, producing output like this:

```
PS C:\Foo> # 6. Viewing ACL of the file
PS C:\Foo> Get-NTFSAccess F:\Secure1\Secure.Txt |
              Format-Table -AutoSize

    Path: F:\Secure1\Secure.Txt (Inheritance enabled)
```

Account	Access Rights	Applies to	Type	IsInherited	InheritedFrom
BUILTIN\Administrators	FullControl	ThisFolderOnly	Allow	True	F:
NT AUTHORITY\SYSTEM	FullControl	ThisFolderOnly	Allow	True	F:
BUILTIN\Users	ReadAndExecute, Synchronize	ThisFolderOnly	Allow	True	F:

Figure 8.5: Viewing the ACL of the Secure.Txt file

In *step 7*, you create and run a script block on DC1. The code in the script block checks to see if your AD has a Sales group and, if not, creates the AD group.

In the next step, *step 8*, you view the `Sales` group by running a second script block on the domain controller, with output like this:

```
PS C:\Foo> # 8. Displaying Sales AD Group
PS C:\Foo> Invoke-Command -ComputerName DC1 -ScriptBlock {
                                    Get-ADGroup -Identity Sales}

PSComputerName    : DC1
RunspaceId        : 50ee7037-cd9f-4270-b663-96cca880c708
DistinguishedName : CN=Sales,CN=Users,DC=Reskit,DC=Org
GroupCategory     : Security
GroupScope        : Global
Name              : Sales
ObjectClass       : group
ObjectGUID        : 7f426f57-c616-4555-8e75-d1c8a6d60a33
SamAccountName    : Sales
SID               : S-1-5-21-140053678-4069492383-922506915-3602
```

Figure 8.6: Viewing the Sales group

In *step 9*, you use the `Add-NTFSAccess` cmdlet to give the domain admins full control over the folder. In *step 10*, you remove the `Builtin\Users` group from the `Secure.Txt` file. Then, in *step 11*, you remove all inherited rights to the folder. Finally, in *step 12*, you give the `Sales` group full control over the folder (and, via inheritance, to files in the folder). These four steps produce no console output.

In *step 13*, you view the updated ACL for the Secure1 folder, with output like this:

```
PS C:\Foo> # 13. Getting ACL of the Securel folder
PS C:\Foo> Get-NTFSAccess -Path F:\Securel |
              Format-Table -AutoSize

    Path: F:\Securel (Inheritance disabled)

Account                    Access Rights Applies to                            Type  IsInherited InheritedFrom
-------                    ------------- ----------                            ----  ----------- -------------
BUILTIN\Administrators FullControl   ThisFolderOnly                        Allow False
RESKIT\Domain Admins   FullControl   ThisFolderSubfoldersAndFiles Allow False
RESKIT\Sales           FullControl   ThisFolderSubfoldersAndFiles Allow False
```

Figure 8.7: Viewing the ACL for the Secure1 folder

In the final step, *step 14*, you view the resulting ACL on the Secure.Txt file with output like this:

```
PS C:\Foo> # 14. Getting resulting ACL on the Secure1.Txt file
PS C:\Foo> Get-NTFSAccess -Path F:\Secure1\Secure.Txt |
             Format-Table -AutoSize

    Path: F:\Secure1\Secure.Txt (Inheritance enabled)


Account                   Access Rights Applies to      Type  IsInherited InheritedFrom
-------                   ------------- ----------      ----  ----------- -------------
RESKIT\Domain Admins FullControl   ThisFolderOnly Allow True          F:\Secure1
RESKIT\Sales              FullControl   ThisFolderOnly Allow True          F:\Secure1
```

Figure 8.8: Viewing the ACL for the Secure.Txt file

There's more...

As you can see in *step 3*, in *Figure 8.2*, there are several cmdlets in the NTFSSecurity module. You can use these cmdlets to set up the ACL on a file or folder and the **System ACL (SAC)** that enables you to audit file or folder access. There are also some improved cmdlets, such as Get ChildItem2 and Get-Item2, which you may find helpful.

In *steps 9* through *step 14*, update the ACL for the Secure1 folder and the text file, Secure.Txt, you created earlier. These steps demonstrate how you use the cmdlets in the NTFSSecurity module to update folder and file ACLs and may not be the best approach for your organization.

Securing Your SMB File Server

To create a file server, you first need to install the necessary features to the server and then harden it. You use the Add-WindowsFeature cmdlet to add the Windows features required for a file server. You can then use the Set-SmbServerConfiguration cmdlet to update the configuration to suit your organization's needs.

Security is a good thing, but, as always, be careful! By locking down your SMB file server too hard, you can lock some users out of the server. Since your file server can contain sensitive information, you must take reasonable steps to avoid some of the expected attack mechanisms and adopt the best security practices.

Windows file servers (and file server clients) use the SMB protocol. This protocol has gone through several significant improvements over the years. The original version, SMB 1.0, has many weaknesses and, in general, should be removed and not used. When you install Windows Server 2022, the installer turns SMB 1.0 off. But it never hurts to double-check and disable SMB 1.0 explicitly.

Before you lock down any of the server configurations, be sure to test your changes. You should remember that if you disable SMB 1.0, you may find that older computers (for example, those running Windows XP) lose access to shared data. By the time you read this book, this should not be an issue for most, but not all, organizations. If you do enable SMB 1.0, do so carefully.

Getting ready

This recipe uses FS1, a domain-joined host in the Reskit.Org domain, on which you have installed PowerShell 7 and VS Code.

How to do it...

1. Adding File Server features to FS1

    ```
    $FeaturesHT = 'FileAndStorage-Services',
                  'File-Services',
                  'FS-FileServer',
                  'RSAT-File-Services'
    Add-WindowsFeature -Name $FeaturesHT
    ```

2. Viewing the SMB server settings

    ```
    Get-SmbServerConfiguration
    ```

3. Turning off SMB1

    ```
    $ConfigHT1 = @{
      EnableSMB1Protocol = $false
      Confirm            = $false
    }
    Set-SmbServerConfiguration @ConfigHT1
    ```

4. Turning on SMB signing and encryption

    ```
    $ConfigHT2 = @{
        RequireSecuritySignature = $true
        EnableSecuritySignature  = $true
        EncryptData              = $true
    ```

```
            Confirm                 = $false
        }
        Set-SmbServerConfiguration @ConfigHT2
```

5. Turning off default server and workstations shares

```
        $ConfigHT3 = @{
            AutoShareServer        = $false
            AutoShareWorkstation   = $false
            Confirm                = $false
        }
        Set-SmbServerConfiguration @ConfigHT3
```

6. Turning off server announcements

```
        $ConfigHT4 = @{
            ServerHidden   = $true
            AnnounceServer = $false
            Confirm        = $false
        }
        Set-SmbServerConfiguration @ConfigHT4
```

7. Restarting SMB Server service with the new configuration

```
        Restart-Service LanManServer -Force
```

How it works...

In *step 1*, you add the file server features to FS1, with output like this:

```
PS C:\Foo> # 1. Adding File Server features to FS1
PS C:\Foo> $Features = 'FileAndStorage-Services',
                       'File-Services',
                       'FS-FileServer',
                       'RSAT-File-Services'
PS C:\Foo> Add-WindowsFeature -Name $Features

Success Restart Needed Exit Code Feature Result
------- -------------- --------- --------------
True    No             Success   {File and iSCSI Services, File Server, Remot…
```

Figure 8.9: Adding features to FS1

In *step 2,* you use the Get-SmbServerConfiguration cmdlet to return the SMB server settings for SRV2, which looks like this:

```
PS C:\Foo> # 2. Viewing the SMB server settings
PS C:\Foo> Get-SmbServerConfiguration

AnnounceComment                            :
AnnounceServer                             : False
AsynchronousCredits                        : 512
AuditSmb1Access                            : False
AutoDisconnectTimeout                      : 15
AutoShareServer                            : True
AutoShareWorkstation                       : True
CachedOpenLimit                            : 10
DisableSmbEncryptionOnSecureConnection     : True
DurableHandleV2TimeoutInSeconds            : 180
EnableAuthenticateUserSharing              : False
EnableDownlevelTimewarp                    : False
EnableForcedLogoff                         : True
EnableLeasing                              : True
EnableMultiChannel                         : True
EnableOplocks                              : True
EnableSecuritySignature                    : False
EnableSMB1Protocol                         : False
EnableSMB2Protocol                         : True
EnableStrictNameChecking                   : True
EncryptData                                : False
IrpStackSize                               : 15
KeepAliveTime                              : 2
MaxChannelPerSession                       : 32
MaxMpxCount                                : 50
MaxSessionPerConnection                    : 16384
MaxThreadsPerQueue                         : 20
MaxWorkItems                               : 1
NullSessionPipes                           :
NullSessionShares                          :
OplockBreakWait                            : 35
PendingClientTimeoutInSeconds              : 120
RejectUnencryptedAccess                    : True
RequireSecuritySignature                   : False
ServerHidden                               : True
Smb2CreditsMax                             : 8192
```

Figure 8.10 Viewing SMB server configuration

In *step 3,* you turn off SMB 1.0 explicitly. In *step 4,* you turn on digital signing and encrypting of all SMB-related data packets. With *step 5,* you turn off the default server and workstation shares, and with *step 6,* you turn off SMB server announcements to improve security. These four steps produce no output.

In *step 7,* which also produces no output, you restart the LanManServer service, which is the Windows service that provides SMB file sharing. The changes you made in the earlier step only take effect after you restart this service.

There's more...

In *steps 3* through *6*, you update the configuration of the SMB service to be more secure. The SMB 1.0 protocol has long been considered unsafe. By default, the Windows OS setup process never turns on version 1, but it's a good idea to ensure you turn it off. Digitally signing and encrypting all SMB packets protects against someone using a network sniffer to view data packets. SMB server announcements could provide more information to a potential network hacker about the services on your network.

In *step 7*, after making changes to the SMB service configuration, you restart the LanManWorkstation service. You must restart this service to implement any changes to the file server configuration.

Creating and Securing SMB Shares

With your file server service set up, the next step in deploying a file server is to create SMB shares and then secure them. For decades, administrators have used the net.exe command to set up shared folders and more. This command continues to work in Windows Server 2022 (and Windows 10/11), but you may find the SMB cmdlets easier to use, particularly if you're automating large-scale SMB server deployments.

This recipe looks at creating and securing shares on a Windows Server 2022 platform using the PowerShell SMBServer module. You also use cmdlets from the NTFSSecurity module (a third-party module you previously downloaded from the PSGallery).

You run this recipe on the file server (FS1) that you set up and hardened in the *Securing Your SMB File Server* recipe. You create and share a folder (F:\ITShare) on the file server in this recipe. Then, you create a file in the C:\ITShare folder and set the ACL for the files to be the same for the share. You use the Set-SMBPathAcl cmdlet to do this. You then review the ACL for both the folder and the file.

This recipe uses a security group, Sales, which you created in the Reskit.Org domain in a previous step. In this recipe, you also use the Get-NTFSAccess cmdlet from NTFSSecurity, a third-party module you can download from the PowerShell Gallery. See the *Managing NTFS File and Folder Permissions* recipe for more details about this module and download instructions.

Getting ready

This recipe uses FS1, a domain-joined host in the Reskit.Org domain, on which you have installed PowerShell 7 and VS Code. You should also have DC1 online.

How to do it...

1. Discovering existing shares and access rights

```
Get-SmbShare -Name * |
  Get-SmbShareAccess |
    Format-Table -GroupBy Name
```

2. Creating and sharing a new folder

```
New-Item -Path F: -Name ITShare -ItemType Directory |
  Out-Null
New-SmbShare -Name ITShare -Path F:\ITShare
```

3. Updating the share to have a description

```
$NoCnfHT = @{Confirm=$False}
Set-SmbShare -Name ITShare -Description 'File Share for IT' @NoCnfHT
```

4. Setting folder enumeration mode

```
$FldrEnumHT = @{
  Name                  = 'ITShare'
  FolderEnumerationMode = 'AccessBased'
  Force                 = $True
}
Set-SMBShare @FldrEnumHT
```

5. Setting encryption on for the ITShare share

```
Set-SmbShare -Name ITShare -EncryptData $true -Force
```

6. Removing all access to ITShare share for the Everyone group

```
$AdminHT1 = @{
  Name        = 'ITShare'
  AccountName = 'Everyone'
  Confirm     = $false
}
Revoke-SmbShareAccess @AdminHT1
```

7. Adding Reskit\Administrators to have read permission

```
$AdminHT2 = @{
```

```
    Name        = 'ITShare'
    AccessRight = 'Read'
    AccountName = 'Reskit\ADMINISTRATOR'
    ConFirm     = $false
  }
  Grant-SmbShareAccess @AdminHT2
```

8. Adding system full access

```
$AdminHT3 = @{
    Name        = 'ITShare'
    AccessRight = 'Full'
    AccountName = 'NT Authority\SYSTEM'
    Confirm     = $False
}
Grant-SmbShareAccess  @AdminHT3 | Out-Null
```

9. Setting Creator/Owner to Full Access

```
$AdminHT4 = @{
    Name        = 'ITShare'
    AccessRight = 'Full'
    AccountName = 'CREATOR OWNER'
    Confirm     = $False
}
Grant-SmbShareAccess @AdminHT4  | Out-Null
```

10. Granting Sales group read access, SalesAdmins has Full access

```
$AdminHT5 = @{
    Name        = 'ITShare'
    AccessRight = 'Read'
    AccountName = 'Sales'
    Confirm     = $false
}
Grant-SmbShareAccess @AdminHT5 | Out-Null
```

11. Reviewing share access

```
Get-SmbShareAccess -Name ITShare |
  Sort-Object AccessRight
```

12. Set file ACL to be same as share ACL

    ```
    Set-SmbPathAcl -ShareName 'ITShare'
    ```

13. Creating a file in `F:\ITShare`

    ```
    'File Contents' | Out-File -FilePath F:\ITShare\File.Txt
    ```

14. Setting file ACL to be same as share ACL

    ```
    Set-SmbPathAcl -ShareName 'ITShare'
    ```

15. Viewing file ACL

    ```
    Get-NTFSAccess -Path F:\ITShare\File.Txt |
      Format-Table -AutoSize
    ```

How it works...

In *step 1*, you use `Get-SmbShare` to discover the current SMB shares on FS1 and which accounts have access to those shares. The output looks like this:

```
PS C:\Foo> # 1. Discovering existing shares and access rights
PS C:\Foo> Get-SmbShare -Name * |
             Get-SmbShareAccess |
               Format-Table -GroupBy Name

   Name: IPC$

Name ScopeName AccountName               AccessControlType AccessRight
---- --------- -----------               ----------------- -----------
IPC$ *         BUILTIN\Administrators    Allow             Full
IPC$ *         BUILTIN\Backup Operators  Allow             Full
IPC$ *         NT AUTHORITY\INTERACTIVE  Allow             Full
```

Figure 8.11: Viewing SMB shares on FS1

In *step 2*, you create a new folder (`F:\ITShare`) and use the `New-SMB` share to share that folder (using default permissions). The output from this step looks like this:

```
PS C:\Foo> # 2. Creating and sharing a new folder
PS C:\Foo> New-Item -Path F: -Name ITShare -ItemType Directory |
             Out-Null
PS C:\Foo> New-SmbShare -Name ITShare -Path F:\ITShare

Name     ScopeName Path       Description
----     --------- ----       -----------
ITShare  *         F:\ITShare
```

Figure 8.12: Creating a new share on FS1

Having created the share, you next configure access to the share. In *step 3*, you modify the share to have a description. With *step 4*, you set access-based enumeration on the share. Then, in *step 5*, you ensure Windows encrypts all data transferred via the share. These two steps create no console output.

Next, with *step 6*, you remove access to the ITShare for the Everyone group. The output from this step looks like this:

```
PS C:\Foo> # 6. Removing all access to ITShare share for the Everyone group
PS C:\Foo> $AdminHT1 = @{
             Name        = 'ITShare'
             AccountName = 'Everyone'
             Confirm     = $false
           }
PS C:\Foo> Revoke-SmbShareAccess @AdmlinHT1

Name     ScopeName AccountName AccessControlType AccessRight
----     --------- ----------- ---------------- -----------
ITShare  *         Everyone    Deny             Full
```

Figure 8.13: Removing access to the Everyone group

In *step 7*, you grant the Reskit\Administrator account read permission on the ITShare share, creating the following output:

```
PS C:\Foo> # 7. Adding Reskit\Administrators to have read permission
PS C:\Foo> $AHT2 = @{
             Name        = 'ITShare'
             AccessRight = 'Read'
             AccountName = 'Reskit\ADMINISTRATOR'
             ConFirm     = $false
           }
PS C:\Foo> Grant-SmbShareAccess @AHT2

Name     ScopeName AccountName           AccessControlType AccessRight
----     --------- -----------           ---------------- -----------
ITShare  *         RESKIT\Administrator  Allow            Read
```

Figure 8.14: Removing access to the Everyone group

With *step 8*, you give the OS full access to the share. Finally, in *step 9*, you grant the creator or owner of any file/folder full access to the file. These seven configuration steps produce no output.

In *step 11*, you review the access to the share, which produces output like this:

```
PS C:\Foo> # 11. Reviewing share access
PS C:\Foo> Get-SmbShareAccess -Name ITShare |
             Sort-Object AccessRight

Name        ScopeName  AccountName              AccessControlType AccessRight
----        ---------  -----------              ----------------- -----------
ITShare *              NT AUTHORITY\SYSTEM      Allow             Full
ITShare *              CREATOR OWNER            Allow             Full
ITShare *              RESKIT\Administrator     Allow             Read
ITShare *              RESKIT\Sales             Allow             Read
```

Figure 8.15: Viewing share access

Now that you have configured access to the share, in *step 12*, you use the Set-SMBPathAcl command to make the NTFS permissions match the SMB share permissions. In *step 13*, you create a new file in the folder shared as ITShare and then ensure, in *step 14*, that the file itself has the same ACL as the share. These three steps produce no output.

In *step 15*, you view the file, F:\ITShare\File.Txt, which produces output like this:

```
PS C:\Foo> # 15. Viewing file ACL
PS C:\Foo> Get-NTFSAccess –Path F:\ITShare\File.Txt |
             Format-Table –AutoSize

    Path: F:\ITShare\File.Txt (Inheritance enabled)


Account                  Access Rights                       Applies to     Type  IsInherited InheritedFrom
-------                  -------------                       ----------     ----  ----------- -------------
BUILTIN\Administrators   FullControl                         ThisFolderOnly Allow True        F:\ITShare
NT AUTHORITY\SYSTEM      FullControl                         ThisFolderOnly Allow True        F:\ITShare
RESKIT\Administrator     ReadAndExecute, Synchronize ThisFolderOnly Allow True        F:\ITShare
RESKIT\Sales             ReadAndExecute, Synchronize ThisFolderOnly Allow True        F:\ITShare
BUILTIN\Users            ReadAndExecute, Synchronize ThisFolderOnly Allow True        F:
```

Figure 8.16: Viewing the File ACL

There's more...

In *step 1*, you examine the shares available on FS1. In the *Securing Your SMB File Server* recipe, you configured the SMB service to remove the default shares on FS1. The only share you see in *step 1* is the IPC$ share, which Windows uses for the named pipes communication mechanism. For more details about this share, see https://learn.microsoft.com/troubleshoot/windows-server/networking/inter-process-communication-share-null-session.

In *step 4*, you set access-based enumeration for the ITShare share. This setting means that any user viewing files or folders within the share only sees objects to which they have access.

This setting improves security and minimizes administrative questions, such as "What is this file/folder, and why can't I have access to this file/folder?".

In *step 5*, you set encryption for the ITShare share. This step ensures that Windows performs data encryption on any data transferred across this share. You can set this by default at the server level or, in this case, at the share level.

In the final step, *step 15*, you view the resultant ACL for the file F:\ITShare\File.Txt. The ACL results from the changes you made in the prior steps. You need to adjust the specific permissions added and removed to meet the needs of your organization. Note that this recipe shows you how to change the ACLs, modify ACL inheritance, and view the results.

Accessing SMB Shares

In the *Creating and Securing SMB Shares* recipe, you created a share on FS1. Data you access using SMB file sharing acts and feels like accessing local files via Windows Explorer or the PowerShell console, as you see in this recipe.

In this recipe, you access the ITShare share on FS1 from SRV1.

Getting ready

This recipe uses SRV1, a domain-joined host in the Reskit.Org domain, on which you have installed PowerShell 7 and VS Code. You also use FS1 and should have DC1 online. You previously created SMB shares on FS1, which you use in this recipe.

How to do it...

1. Examining the SMB client's configuration on SRV1

   ```
   Get-SmbClientConfiguration
   ```

2. Setting Signing of SMB packets

   ```
   $ConfirmHT = @{Confirm=$false}
   Set-SmbClientConfiguration -RequireSecuritySignature $True @
   ConfirmHT
   ```

3. Examining SMB client's network interface

   ```
   Get-SmbClientNetworkInterface |
       Format-Table
   ```

4. Examining the shares provided by FS1

   ```
   net view \\FS1
   ```

5. Creating a drive mapping, mapping R: to the share on server FS1

   ```
   New-SmbMapping -LocalPath R: -RemotePath \\FS1\ITShare
   ```

6. Viewing the shared folder mapping

   ```
   Get-SmbMapping
   ```

7. Viewing the shared folder contents

   ```
   Get-ChildItem -Path R:
   ```

8. Viewing existing connections

   ```
   Get-SmbConnection
   ```

How it works...

In *step 1*, you examine details of the SMB client configuration on SRV1, with output like this:

```
PS C:\Foo> # 1. Examining the SMB client's configuration on SRV1
PS C:\Foo> Get-SmbClientConfiguration

SkipCertificateCheck                     : False
ConnectionCountPerRssNetworkInterface    : 4
DirectoryCacheEntriesMax                 : 16
DirectoryCacheEntrySizeMax               : 65536
DirectoryCacheLifetime                   : 10
DormantFileLimit                         : 1023
EnableBandwidthThrottling                : True
EnableByteRangeLockingOnReadOnlyFiles    : True
EnableInsecureGuestLogons                : True
EnableLargeMtu                           : True
EnableLoadBalanceScaleOut                : True
EnableMultiChannel                       : True
EnableSecuritySignature                  : True
ExtendedSessionTimeout                   : 1000
FileInfoCacheEntriesMax                  : 64
FileInfoCacheLifetime                    : 10
FileNotFoundCacheEntriesMax              : 128
FileNotFoundCacheLifetime                : 5
ForceSMBEncryptionOverQuic               : False
KeepConn                                 : 600
MaxCmds                                  : 50
MaximumConnectionCountPerServer          : 32
OplocksDisabled                          : False
RequireSecuritySignature                 : False
SessionTimeout                           : 60
UseOpportunisticLocking                  : True
WindowSizeThreshold                      : 1
```

Figure 8.17: Examing SMB client information

In *step 2*, you ensure that SRV1 requires signed SMB packets, irrespective of the settings on the SMB server (FS1). There is no output from this step.

In *step 3*, you examine details of the client NIC on SRV1, with output that looks like this:

```
PS C:\Foo> # 3. Examining SMB client's network interface
PS C:\Foo> Get-SmbClientNetworkInterface |
            Format-Table

Interface Index RSS Capable RDMA Capable Speed  IpAddresses                                Friendly Name
--------------- ----------- ------------ -----  -----------                                -------------
7               True        False        10 Gbps {fe80::8d9c:754b:9c00:54, 10.10.10.101}  Ethernet
```

Figure 8.18: Viewing NIC on SRV1

In *step 4*, you use the net.exe command to view the shares provided by the FS1 host. The output from this step looks like this:

```
PS C:\Foo> # 4. Examining the shares provided by FS1
PS C:\Foo> net view \\FS1
Shared resources at \\FS1

Share name   Type  Used as  Comment
-------------------------------------------------------------------------------
ITShare      Disk  R:       File Share for IT
The command completed successfully.
```

Figure 8.19: Viewing shares offered by FS1

In *step 5*, you create a new drive mapping on SRV1, mapping the R: drive to \\FS1\ITShare, which creates output that looks like this:

```
PS C:\Foo> # 5. Creating a drive mapping, mapping R: to the share on server FS1
PS C:\Foo> New-SmbMapping -LocalPath R: -RemotePath \\FS1\ITShare

Status Local Path Remote Path
------ ---------- -----------
OK     R:         \\FS1\ITShare
```

Figure 8.20: Creating a drive mapping

In *step 6*, you view the SMB drive mappings on SRV1, which look like this:

```
PS C:\Foo> # 6. Viewing the shared folder mapping
PS C:\Foo> Get-SmbMapping

Status Local Path Remote Path
------ ---------- -----------
OK     R:         \\FS1\ITShare
```

Figure 8.21: Viewing the shared folder mapping

In *step 7*, you view the contents of the share to reveal the file you created in *Creating and Securing SMB Shares*, with output like this:

```
PS C:\Foo> # 7. Viewing the shared folder contents
PS C:\Foo> Get-ChildItem -Path R:

    Directory: R:\

Mode              LastWriteTime     Length Name
----              -------------     ------ ----
-a---     13/08/2022     11:23         15 File.Txt
```

Figure 8.22: Viewing the contents of the shared folder

In *step 8*, you view all existing SMB connections from SRV1. This step produces the following output:

```
PS C:\Foo> # 8. Viewing existing connections
PS C:\Foo> Get-SmbConnection

ServerName ShareName UserName              Credential            Dialect NumOpens
---------- --------- --------              ----------            ------- --------
FS1        ITShare   RESKIT\Administrator  RESKIT\Administrator  3.1.1   1
```

Figure 8.23: Viewing existing SMB connections from SRV1

There's more...

In *step 4*, you use the net.exe command. The SMBShare module does not provide a PowerShell cmdlet that retrieves the shares offered by a remote host. As an alternative to using net.exe to discover remote shares, you could create a script block to retrieve the shares from a local host. Then use Invoke-Command to send that script block to a server to obtain the shares. Some just find using net.exe easier.

Creating an iSCSI Target

iSCSI is an industry-standard protocol that implements block storage over a TCP/IP network. With iSCSI, the server, or target, provides a volume shared via iSCSI to an iSCSI client, also known as the iSCSI initiator.

In the original SCSI protocol, you use the term **Logical Unit Number (LUN)** to refer to a single physical disk attached to the SCSI bus. With iSCSI, you give each remotely shared volume an iSCSI LUN. Once connected to the iSCSI target, the iSCSI client sees the LUN as another disk device attached to the local system. From the iSCSI client, you can manage the disk just like locally attached storage.

Windows Server 2022 includes iSCSI target (server) and iSCSI initiator (client) features. Windows installs the initiator software by default, and you can add the target feature to Windows Server systems.

To use iSCSI, you need an iSCSI target on a server and an iSCSI initiator on another server (or client) system to access the iSCSI target. You can use both Microsoft and third-party initiators and targets, although if you mix and match, you need to test very carefully that the combination works in your environment.

With iSCSI, a target is a single disk that the client accesses using the iSCSI client. An iSCSI target server hosts one or more targets, where each iSCSI target is equivalent to a LUN on a fiber channel SAN.

You could use iSCSI in a cluster of Hyper-V servers. The servers in the cluster can use the iSCSI initiator to access an iSCSI target. Used via the cluster shared volume, the shared iSCSI target is shared between nodes in a failover cluster that enables the VMs in that cluster to be highly available.

Getting ready

This recipe uses SS1, a domain-joined host in the Reskit.Org domain, on which you have installed PowerShell 7 and VS Code.

How to do it...

1. Installing the iSCSI target feature on SS1

```
Import-Module -Name ServerManager -WarningAction SilentlyContinue
Install-WindowsFeature FS-iSCSITarget-Server
```

2. Restarting the computer

```
Restart-Computer
```

3. Exploring iSCSI target server settings

```
Get-IscsiTargetServerSetting
```

4. Creating a folder on SS1 to hold the iSCSI virtual disk

```
$NewFolderHT = @{
  Path        = 'C:\iSCSI'
  ItemType    = 'Directory'
  ErrorAction = 'SilentlyContinue'
}
New-Item @NewFolderHT | Out-Null
```

5. Creating an iSCSI virtual disk (aka a LUN)

```
$VDiskPath = 'C:\iSCSI\ITData.Vhdx'
$VDHT = @{
   Path        = $VDiskPath
   Description = 'LUN For IT Group'
   SizeBytes   = 500MB
 }
New-IscsiVirtualDisk @VDHT
```

6. Setting the iSCSI target, specifying who can initiate an iSCSI connection

```
$TargetName = 'ITTarget'
$NewTargetHT = @{
  TargetName   = $TargetName
  InitiatorIds = 'IQN:*'
}
New-IscsiServerTarget @NewTargetHT
```

7. Creating iSCSI disk target mapping LUN name to a local path

```
$TargetHT = @{
  TargetName = $TargetName
  Path       = $VDiskPath
}
Add-IscsiVirtualDiskTargetMapping @TargetHT
```

How it works...

In *step 1*, you install the iSCSI target feature on the SS1 server, with output like this:

```
PS C:\Foo> # 1. Installing the iSCSI target feature on SS1
PS C:\Foo> Import-Module -Name ServerManager -WarningAction SilentlyContinue
PS C:\Foo> Install-WindowsFeature FS-iSCSITarget-Server

Success Restart Needed Exit Code      Feature Result
------- -------------- ---------      --------------
True    Yes            SuccessRestar... {File and iSCSI Services, File Server, iSCSI...
WARNING: You must restart this server to finish the installation process.
```

Figure 8.24: Installing the iSCSI target feature on SS1

In *step 2*, you restart SS1 to complete the installation of the iSCSI target feature. This step creates no output.

In *step 3*, you examine the iSCSI target server settings, with output that looks like this:

```
PS C:\Foo> # 3. Exploring iSCSI target server settings
PS C:\Foo> Get-IscsiTargetServerSetting

RunspaceId                : dcd86396-786d-435e-a056-6f3b7b1d94b8
ComputerName              : SS1.Reskit.Org
IsClustered               : False
Version                   : 10.0
DisableRemoteManagement   : False
Portals                   : {+10.10.1.17:3260, -[fe80::5817:e84:6e63:f824%6]:32601
```

Figure 8.25: Exploring the iSCSI target server settings

In *step 4*, you create a folder on SS1 to hold the iSCSI virtual disk, which creates no output. In *step 5*, you create an iSCSI virtual disk (essentially a LUN) with output that looks like this:

```
PS C:\Foo> # 5. Creating an iSCSI virtual disk (aka a LUN)
PS C:\Foo> $VDiskPath = 'C:\iSCSI\ITData.Vhdx'
PS C:\Foo> $VDHT = @{
    Path        = $VDiskPath
    Description = 'LUN For IT Group'
    SizeBytes   = 500MB
}
PS C:\Foo> New-IscsiVirtualDisk @VDHT

RunspaceId          : dcd86396-786d-435e-a056-6f3b7b1d94b8
ClusterGroupName    :
ComputerName        : SS1.Reskit.Org
Description         : LUN For IT Group
DiskType            : Dynamic
HostVolumeId        : {BF124141-EFEA-11EC-BE5E-E454E88CB586}
LocalMountDeviceId  :
OriginalPath        :
ParentPath          :
Path                : C:\iSCSI\ITData.Vhdx
SerialNumber        : C8C701D3-E94C-40FF-B195-72B091357B4C
Size                : 524288000
SnapshotIds         :
Status              : NotConnected
VirtualDiskIndex    : 1694099853
```

Figure 8.26: Creating an iSCSI virtual disk on SS1

In *step 6*, you specify which computers can use the virtual iSCSI target, with output like this:

```
PS C:\Foo> # 6. Setting the iSCSI target, specifying who can initiate an iSCSI connection
PS C:\Foo> $TargetName = 'ITTarget'
PS C:\Foo> $NewTargetHT = @{
             TargetName   = $TargetName
             InitiatorIds = 'IQN:*'
           }
PS C:\Foo> New-IscsiServerTarget @NewTargetHT
```

```
RunspaceId                     : dcd86396-786d-435e-a056-6f3b7b1d94b8
ChapUserName                   :
ClusterGroupName               :
ComputerName                   : SS1.Reskit.Org
Description                    :
EnableChap                     : False
EnableReverseChap              : False
EnforceIdleTimeoutDetection    : True
FirstBurstLength               : 65536
IdleDuration                   : 00:00:00
InitiatorIds                   : {Iqn:*}
LastLogin                      :
LunMappings                    : {}
MaxBurstLength                 : 262144
MaxReceiveDataSegmentLength    : 65536
ReceiveBufferCount             : 10
ReverseChapUserName            :
Sessions                       : {}
Status                         : NotConnected
TargetIqn                      : iqn.1991-05.com.microsoft:ss1-ittarget-target
TargetName                     : ITTarget
```

Figure 8.27: Specifying which hosts can access the iSCSI virtual disk

In the final step, *step 6*, you specify the disk target mapping, which generates no output. This step creates a mapping between an iSCSI target name (ITTarget) and the local path where you stored the virtual iSCSI hard disk.

There's more…

By default, Windows does not install the iSCSI target feature, but as you can see in *step 1*, you use Install-WindowsFeature to add the feature to this storage server.

When you create an iSCSI target, you create the target name and the target virtual hard drive separately, and then, in *step 6*, you map the iSCSI target name to the file location. In production, you would use a separate set of (fault-tolerant) disks to hold the iSCSI information, possibly using storage spaces to create fault-tolerant virtual disks.

Using an iSCSI Target

Windows and Windows Server provide a built-in iSCSI client component you use to access almost any iSCSI target, as previously mentioned.

In the *Creating an iSCSI Target* recipe, you created an iSCSI target. The target is a disk you can access remotely via an iSCSI client. To make use of the remotely shared disk via iSCSI, you attach it to the iSCSI server and start using the disk as if it were locally attached.

Getting ready

This recipe uses FS1, a domain-joined host in the Reskit.Org domain, on which you have installed PowerShell 7 and VS Code. This recipe also uses SS1 (the host holding the iSCSI target), and you should have DC1 online. You previously created an iSCSI target (on SS1), and now you use the built-in iSCSI initiator to access the iSCSI disk. You run this recipe on FS1.

How to do it...

1. Adjusting the iSCSI service to autostart, then start the service

```
Set-Service MSiSCSI -StartupType 'Automatic'
Start-Service MSiSCSI
```

2. Setting up the portal to SS1

```
$PortalHT = @{
  TargetPortalAddress     = 'SS1.Reskit.Org'
  TargetPortalPortNumber  = 3260
}
New-IscsiTargetPortal @PortalHT
```

3. Finding and viewing the ITTarget on the portal

```
$Target  = Get-IscsiTarget |
               Where-Object NodeAddress -Match 'ITTarget'
$Target
```

4. Connecting to the target on SS1

```
$ConnectHT = @{
  TargetPortalAddress = 'SS1.Reskit.Org'
  NodeAddress         = $Target.NodeAddress
}
Connect-IscsiTarget  @ConnectHT
```

5. Viewing the iSCSI disk from FS1 on SRV1

```
$RemoteDisk =  Get-Disk |
```

```
     Where-Object BusType -eq 'iscsi'
$RemoteDisk |
   Format-Table -AutoSize
```

6. Turning disk online and making disk R/W

```
$RemoteDisk |
   Set-Disk -IsOffline  $False
$RemoteDisk |
   Set-Disk -Isreadonly $False
```

7. Formatting the volume on SS1

```
$NewVolumeHT = @{
   FriendlyName = 'ITData'
   FileSystem   = 'NTFS'
   DriveLetter  = 'I'
}
$RemoteDisk |
   New-Volume @NewVolumeHT
```

8. Using the drive as a local drive

```
Set-Location -Path I:
New-Item -Path I:\  -Name ITData -ItemType Directory |
   Out-Null
'Testing 1-2-3' |
   Out-File -FilePath I:\ITData\Test.Txt
Get-ChildItem I:\ITData
```

How it works...

In *step 1*, you set the iSCSI service to start automatically when SRV1 starts, and then you explicitly start the iSCSI service. This step creates no console output.

In *step 2*, you set up the iSCSI portal to SS1, which looks like this:

```
PS C:\Foo> # 2. Setting up the portal to SS1
PS C:\Foo> $PortalHT = @{
              TargetPortalAddress    = 'SS1.Reskit.Org'
              TargetPortalPortNumber = 3260
           }
PS C:\Foo> New-IscsiTargetPortal @PortalHT

RunspaceId              : 903f3c98-40a9-4094-9360-2a710fd27b3a
InitiatorInstanceName   :
InitiatorPortalAddress  :
IsDataDigest            : False
IsHeaderDigest          : False
TargetPortalAddress     : SS1.Reskit.Org
TargetPortalPortNumber  : 3260
```

Figure 8.28: Setting up the iSCSI portal to SS1

In *step 3*, you find and view the ITTarget LUN from SS1. The output looks like this:

```
PS C:\Foo> # 3. Finding and viewing the ITTarget on the portal
PS C:\Foo> $Target  = Get-IscsiTarget |
                        Where-Object NodeAddress -Match 'ITTarget'
PS C:\Foo> $Target

RunspaceId  : 903f3c98-40a9-4094-9360-2a710fd27b3a
IsConnected : False
NodeAddress : iqn.1991-05.com.microsoft:ss1-ittarget-target
```

Figure 8.29: Viewing the ITTarget portal to SS1

In *step 4*, you connect from SRV1 to the iSCSI target on SS1, which looks like this:

```
PS C:\Foo> # 4. Connecting to the target on SS1
PS C:\Foo> $ConnectHT = @{
              TargetPortalAddress = 'SS1.Reskit.Org'
              NodeAddress         = $Target.NodeAddress
           }
PS C:\Foo> Connect-IscsiTarget  @ConnectHT

RunspaceId             : 903f3c98-40a9-4094-9360-2a710fd27b3a
AuthenticationType     : NONE
InitiatorInstanceName  : ROOT\ISCSIPRT\0000_0
InitiatorNodeAddress   : iqn.1991-05.com.microsoft:fs1.reskit.org
InitiatorPortalAddress : 0.0.0.0
InitiatorSideIdentifier : 400001370000
IsConnected            : True
IsDataDigest           : False
IsDiscovered           : False
IsHeaderDigest         : False
IsPersistent           : False
NumberOfConnections    : 1
SessionIdentifier      : ffffe7045daff010-4000013700000002
TargetNodeAddress      : iqn.1991-05.com.microsoft:ss1-ittarget-target
TargetSideIdentifier   : 0100
```

Figure 8.30: Connecting to the iSCSI target on SS1

In *step 5*, you use `Get-Disk` to view the iSCSI disk from SRV1, which looks like this:

```
PS C:\Foo> # 5. Viewing the iSCSI disk from FS1 on SS1
PS C:\Foo> $RemoteDisk =  Get-Disk |
             Where-Object BusType -eq 'iscsi'
PS C:\Foo> $RemoteDisk |
             Format-Table -AutoSize

Number Friendly Name    Serial Number                          HealthStatus OperationalStatus Total Size Partition Style
------ -------------    -------------                          ------------ ----------------- ---------- ---------------
2      MSFT Virtual HD C8C701D3-E94C-40FF-B195-72B091357B4C Healthy      Offline              500 MB RAW
```

Figure 8.31: Viewing the iSCSI target disk

In *step 6*, you ensure the iSCSI disk is online and set to `Read/Write` – a step that generates no output. In *step 7*, you create a new volume on the iSCSI disks, which looks like this:

```
PS C:\Foo> # 7. Formatting the volume on SS1
PS C:\Foo> $NewVolumeHT = @{
             FriendlyName = 'ITData'
             FileSystem   = 'NTFS'
             DriveLetter  = 'I'
           }
PS C:\Foo> $RemoteDisk |
             New-Volume @NewVolumeHT

DriveLetter FriendlyName FileSystemType DriveType HealthStatus OperationalStatus SizeRemaining      Size
----------- ------------ -------------- --------- ------------ ----------------- -------------      ----
I           ITData       NTFS           Fixed     Healthy      OK                467.73 MB 483.93 MB
```

Figure 8.32: Viewing the iSCSI target disk

In the final step in this recipe, *step 8*, you create a folder in the iSCSI disk. Then you create a file and view the file, which looks like this:

```
PS C:\Foo> # 8. Using the drive as a local drive
PS C:\Foo> Set-Location -Path I:
PS I:\> New-Item -Path I:\  -Name ITData -ItemType Directory |
           Out-Null
PS I:\> 'Testing 1-2-3' |
           Out-File -FilePath I:\ITData\Test.Txt
PS I:\> Get-ChildItem I:\ITData

    Directory: I:\ITData

Mode            LastWriteTime   Length Name
----            -------------   ------ ----
-a---     19/08/2022     20:26      15 Test.Txt
```

Figure 8.33: Using the iSCSI target disk

There's more...

Using an iSCSI disk is straightforward – connect to the iSCSI target and manage the disk volume locally. Once connected, you can format it with a file system and then use it to store data.

In production, you may not be using a Windows Server host to serve as an iSCSI target. For example, many SAN vendors add iSCSI target features to their SAN offerings. With a SAN offering, you can use the Windows iSCSI initiator to access the SAN via iSCSI. However, some SAN vendors may provide an updated iSCSI initiator for you to use. If you choose to mix and match vendors for the target and initiators, you must test the proposed environment carefully.

Implementing FSRM Filestore Quotas

File Server Resource Manager (FSRM) is a feature of Windows Server that assists you in managing file servers. FSRM has three key sub-features:

- **Quota management**: With FSRM, you can set soft or hard quotas on volumes and folders. Soft quotas allow users to exceed an allowance, while hard quotas stop users from exceeding an allowance. You can configure a quota with thresholds and threshold actions. If a user exceeds 65% of the quota allowance, FSRM can send an email, while at 90%, you log an event in the event log or run a program. You have different actions for different quota levels. This recipe shows how to use quotas.

- **File screening**: You can set up a file screen and stop users from saving screened files. For example, you could screen for MP3 or FLAC files – should a user attempt to save a file (say, `jg75-02-28D1T1.flac`), the file screen rejects the request and doesn't allow the user to save the file.

- **Reporting**: FSRM enables you to create a wealth of storage reports that can be highly useful for management purposes.

In this recipe, you install FSRM on FS1, perform some general configuration, and then work with soft and hard quotas.

Getting ready

This recipe uses FS1, a domain-joined host in the Reskit.Org domain, on which you have installed PowerShell 7 and VS Code. You should have DC1 online to provide authentication for FS1.

FSRM has features that send email messages to an SMTP server. To test these features, as shown in this recipe, you need an email server so FSRM can send emails. In this recipe, you use SMTP.Reskit.Org. There are several ways to implement this SMTP server. You can, for example, use **Internet Information Server (IIS)** within Windows Server to forward emails to an external SMTP email server. Note that Microsoft has removed the IIS SMTP relay feature in Server 2022, so you may need to use an older version of Windows Server.

You could also set up a Linux mail forwarder (see https://www.plesk.com/blog/various/ setting-up-and-configuring-a-linux-mail-server/ for more details on how to do this).

This recipe configures FSRM to send mail to a host (SMTP.Reskit.Org), which then forwards the mail.

How to do it...

1. Installing FSRM feature on FS1

```
Import-Module -Name ServerManager -WarningAction 'SilentlyContinue'
$InstallIHT = @{
  Name                  = 'FS-Resource-Manager'
  IncludeManagementTools = $True
  WarningAction          = 'SilentlyContinue'
}
Install-WindowsFeature @InstallIHT
```

2. Viewing default FSRM settings

```
Get-FsrmSetting
```

3. Setting SMTP settings in FSRM

```
$SMTPHT = @{
  SmtpServer        = 'SMTP.Reskit.Org'
  FromEmailAddress  = 'FSAdmin@Reskit.Org'
  AdminEmailAddress = 'FSAdmin@Reskit.Org'
}
Set-FsrmSetting @SMTPHT
```

4. Sending a test email to check the setup

```
$TestHT = @{
  ToEmailAddress = 'FSAdmin@Reskit.Org'
  Confirm        = $false
}
Send-FsrmTestEmail  @TestHT
```

5. Creating a new FSRM quota template for a 10 MB hard limit

```
$QuotaHT1 = @{
  Name       = '10 MB Reskit Quota'
```

```
      Description = 'Filestore Quota (10mb)'
      Size        = 10MB
    }
    New-FsrmQuotaTemplate @QuotaHT1
```

6. Viewing available FSRM quota templates

```
    Get-FsrmQuotaTemplate |
      Format-Table -Property Name, Description, Size, SoftLimit
```

7. Creating a new folder on which to apply a quota

```
    If (-Not (Test-Path C:\Quota)) {
      New-Item -Path C:\Quota -ItemType Directory    |
        Out-Null
    }
```

8. Building an FSRM action

```
    $MailBody = @'
    User [Source Io Owner] has exceeded the [Quota Threshold]% quota
    threshold for the quota on [Quota Path] on server [Server].
    The quota limit is [Quota Limit MB] MB, and [Quota Used MB] MB
    currently is in use ([Quota Used Percent]% of limit).
    '@
    $NewActionHT = @{
      Type       = 'Email'
      MailTo     = 'Doctordns@gmail.Com'
      Subject    = 'FSRM Over limit [Source Io Owner]'
      Body       = $MailBody
    }
    $Action1 = New-FsrmAction @NewActionHT
```

9. Creating an FSRM threshold

```
    $Thresh = New-FsrmQuotaThreshold -Percentage 85 -Action $Action1
```

10. Building a quota for the C:\Quota folder

```
    $NewQuotaHT1 = @{
      Path       = 'C:\Quota'
      Template   = '10 MB Reskit Quota'
```

```
    Threshold = $Thresh
}
New-FsrmQuota @NewQuotaHT1
```

11. Testing the 85% soft quota limit on C:\Quota

```
Get-ChildItem -Path C:\Quota -Recurse |
  Remove-Item -Force      # for testing purposes!
$Text1 = '+'.PadRight(8MB)
# Make a first file - under the soft quota
$Text1 | Out-File -FilePath C:\Quota\Demo1.Txt
# Now create a second file to take the user over the soft quota
$Text2 = '+'.PadRight(.66MB)
$Text2 | Out-File -FilePath C:\Quota\Demo2.Txt
```

12. Testing the hard limit quota

```
$Text1 | Out-File -FilePath C:\Quota\Demo3.Txt
```

13. Viewing the contents of the C:\Quota folder

```
Get-ChildItem -Path C:\Quota
```

How it works...

In *step 1*, you use the Install-WindowsFeature cmdlet to add the FS-ResourceManager feature to FS1, which looks like this:

```
PS C:\Foo> # 1. Installing FS Resource Manager feature on FS1
PS C:\Foo> Import-Module -Name ServerManager -WarningAction 'SilentlyContinue'
PS C:\Foo> $InstallIHT = @{
              Name                 = 'FS-Resource-Manager'
              IncludeManagementTools = $True
              WarningAction        = 'SilentlyContinue'
           }
PS C:\Foo> Install-WindowsFeature @InstallIHT
```

```
Success Restart Needed Exit Code    Feature Result
------- -------------- ---------    --------------
True    No             Success      {File Server Resource Manager, Remote Server...
```

Figure 8.34: Installing the FSRM feature to FS1

In *step 2*, you view the default FSRM settings with output like this:

```
PS C:\Foo> # 2. Viewing default FSRM settings
PS C:\Foo> Get-FsrmSetting

AdminEmailAddress                        :
CommandNotificationLimit                 : 60
EmailNotificationLimit                   : 60
EventNotificationLimit                   : 60
FromEmailAddress                         :
ReportClassificationFormat               : DHtml
ReportClassificationLog                  : {ClassificationsInLogFile, ErrorsInLogFile}
ReportClassificationMailTo               :
ReportFileGroupIncluded                  :
ReportFileOwnerFilePattern               :
ReportFileOwnerUser                      :
ReportFileScreenAuditDaysSince           : 0
ReportFileScreenAuditEnable              : False
ReportFileScreenAuditUser                :
ReportLargeFileMinimum                   : 5242880
ReportLargeFilePattern                   :
ReportLeastAccessedFilePattern           :
ReportLeastAccessedMinimum               : 90
ReportLimitMaxDuplicateGroup             : 100
ReportLimitMaxFile                       : 1000
ReportLimitMaxFileGroup                  : 10
ReportLimitMaxFileScreenEvent            : 1000
ReportLimitMaxFilesPerDuplicateGroup     : 10
ReportLimitMaxFilesPerFileGroup          : 100
ReportLimitMaxFilesPerOwner              : 100
ReportLimitMaxFilesPerPropertyValue      : 100
ReportLimitMaxOwner                      : 10
ReportLimitMaxPropertyValue              : 10
ReportLimitMaxQuota                      : 1000
ReportLocationIncident                   : C:\StorageReports\Incident
ReportLocationOnDemand                   : C:\StorageReports\Interactive
ReportLocationScheduled                  : C:\StorageReports\Scheduled
ReportMostAccessedFilePattern            :
ReportMostAccessedMaximum                : 7
ReportNotificationLimit                  : 60
ReportPropertyFilePattern                :
ReportPropertyName                       :
ReportQuotaMinimumUsage                  : 0
Server                                   : Reserved
SmtpServer                               :
PSComputerName                           :
```

Figure 8.35: Viewing FSRM default settings

In *step 3*, you set FSRM's SMTP details, including the SMTP server name and the From and Admin addresses. This step produces no output. In *step 3*, you use the Send-FsrmTestEmail cmdlet to test SMTP email handling.

This step has no console output but does generate an email, which should look something like this:

Figure 8.36: Test email received from FSRM

Now that you have installed and configured FSRM, in *step 5*, you create a new FSRM quota template for a 10 MB hard quota limit. The output from this step looks like this:

```
PS C:\Foo> # 5. Creating a new FSRM quota template for a 10MB hard limit
PS C:\Foo> $QuotaHT1 = @{
             Name        = '10 MB Reskit Quota'
             Description = 'Filestore Quota (10mb)'
             Size        = 10MB
           }
PS C:\Foo> New-FsrmQuotaTemplate @QuotaHT1

Description           : Filestore Quota (10mb)
Name                  : 10 MB Reskit Quota
Size                  : 10485760
SoftLimit             : False
Threshold             :
UpdateDerived         : False
UpdateDerivedMatching : False
PSComputerName        :
```

Figure 8.37: Creating an FSRM quota template

In *step 6*, you view the available FSRM quota templates with output like this:

```
PS C:\Foo> # 6. Viewing available FSRM quota templates
PS C:\Foo> Get-FsrmQuotaTemplate |
             Format-Table -Property Name, Description, Size,` SoftLimit

Name                              Description                   Size SoftLimit
----                              -----------                   ---- ---------
100 MB Limit                                               104857600     False
200 MB Limit Reports to User                              209715200     False
Monitor 200 GB Volume Usage                             214748364800      True
Monitor 500 MB Share                                      524288000      True
200 MB Limit with 50 MB Extension                         209715200     False
250 MB Extended Limit                                     262144000     False
2 GB Limit                                               2147483648     False
5 GB Limit                                               5368709120     False
10 GB Limit                                             10737418240     False
Monitor 3 TB Volume Usage                             3298534883328      True
Monitor 5 TB Volume Usage                             5497558138880      True
Monitor 10 TB Volume Usage                           10995116277760      True
10 MB Reskit Quota                Filestore Quota (10mb)     10485760     False
```

Figure 8.38: Viewing available FSRM quota templates

In *step 7*, you create a new folder, C:\Quota\, which you can use to test file store quotas. In *step 8*, you build an FSRM action that sends an email whenever a user exceeds the quota. In *step 9*, you create an FSRM threshold (how much of the soft quota limit a user can use before triggering a quota violation). These three steps produce no console output.

In *step 10*, you build a quota for the C:\Quota folder, with output that looks like this:

```
PS C:\Foo> # 10. Building a quota for the C:\Quota folder
PS C:\Foo> $NewQuotaHT1 = @{
             Path      = 'C:\Quota'
             Template  = '10 MB Reskit Quota'
             Threshold = $Thresh
           }
PS C:\Foo> New-FsrmQuota @NewQuotaHT1

Description     :
Disabled        : False
MatchesTemplate : False
Path            : C:\Quota
PeakUsage       : 1024
Size            : 10485760
SoftLimit       : False
Template        : 10 MB Reskit Quota
Threshold       : {MSFT_FSRMQuotaThreshold}
Usage           : 1024
PSComputerName  :
```

Figure 8.39: Building a quota for the C:\Quota folder

In *step 11*, you test the 85% soft quota limit. First, you create a new file (C:\Quota\Demo1.Txt)
under the size of the soft quota limit. Thus, FSRM allows you to save the file.

Then, you create a second file (C:\Quota\Demo2.Txt) that uses up more than the soft quota limit
– but since the quota is a soft one, you can save the file. There is no console output from this step,
but FSRM detects you have exceeded the soft limit quota for this folder and generates an email
message that looks like this:

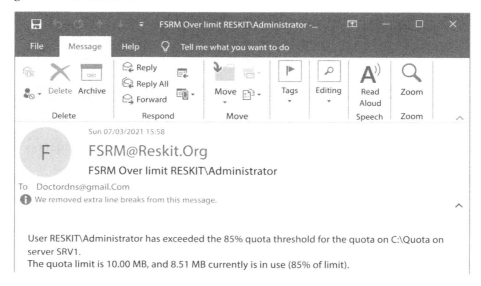

Figure 8.40: Exceeding soft quota limit email

In *step 12*, you attempt to create an additional file, C:\Quota\Demo3.txt, by outputting the $Text1
array to a file, which results in you exceeding the hard quota limit. You see the following output:

```
PS C:\Foo> # 12. Testing the hard limit quota
PS C:\Foo> $Test1 | Out-File -FilePath C:\Quota\Demo3.Txt
out-lineoutput: There is not enough space on the disk. : 'C:\Quota\Demo3.Txt'
```

Figure 8.41: Testing the hard quota limit

In *step 13*, you examine the files in the C:\Quota folder, which looks like this:

```
PS C:\Foo> # 13. Viewing the contents of the C:\Quota folder
PS C:\Foo> Get-ChildItem -Path C:\Quota


    Directory: C:\Quota

Mode            LastWriteTime       Length Name
----            -------------       ------ ----
-a---     26/08/2022     17:16      8388610 Demo1.Txt
-a---     26/08/2022     17:16       692062 Demo2.Txt
-a---     26/08/2022     17:17      1441792 Demo3.Txt
```

Figure 8.42: Viewing the C:\Quota folder

There's more...

In this recipe, you installed and configured FSRM, then defined and tested both a soft and a hard FSRM quota. With the soft quota, you configured FSRM to send an email to inform the recipient that they exceeded a quota. You might want to send an email to either an administrator or a user who has exceeded the quota thresholds.

For the hard quota, FSRM writes application event-log entries and stops the user from saving excess data. The quotas set in this recipe are very small and probably not of much use in production. But changing the step to have a quota of 10 GB is straightforward and might be more appropriate.

In *step 1*, you install a new Windows feature to FS1. From time to time, you may see the installation process just stall and not complete. In some cases, FSRM can require extra reboots to install the feature and tools. In such cases, re-running the command in a new PowerShell console or rebooting the server enables you to add features.

In *step 5*, you create a new FSRM quota template. You can see this new template in the output generated by *step 6*. Note that this quota template is for a hard, not a soft, limit.

In *step 10*, you create a new FSRM quota. If for some reason you get an error from this step, you may need to reboot the host then re-try the quota creation.

In *step 13*, you examine the C:\Quota folder. Notice that with the third file (which you attempted to create in *step 12*), Windows has saved some but not all of the file's intended contents. Suppose you are planning on imposing hard quotas. In that case, you must ensure users understand the implications of exceeding any hard quota limits and the potential for corrupting data (e.g., saving just half of a spreadsheet of a document).

Implementing FSRM Filestore Reporting

A useful and often overlooked feature of the FSRM component is reporting. You can generate FSRM reports immediately (also known as interactive) or at a scheduled time. The latter causes FSRM to create reports on a weekly or monthly basis. FSRM defines several basic report types that you can use.

FSRM produces reports with a fixed layout that you cannot change. FSRM can return the same data contained in the HTML report but as an XML document. You can then use the XML document to create the report the way you need it.

Getting ready

This recipe uses FS1, a domain-joined host in the Reskit.Org domain, on which you have installed PowerShell 7 and VS Code. In the previous recipe, *Implementing FSRM quotas*, you have installed FSRM on FS1.

How to do it...

1. Creating a new FSRM storage report for large files on C:\ on FS1

```
$NewReportHT = @{
  Name            = 'Large Files on FS1'
  NameSpace       = 'C:\'
  ReportType      = 'LargeFiles'
  LargeFileMinimum = 10MB
  Interactive     = $true
}
New-FsrmStorageReport @NewReportHT
```

2. Getting existing FSRM reports

```
Get-FsrmStorageReport * |
  Format-Table -Property Name, NameSpace,
                           ReportType, ReportFormat
```

3. Viewing interactive reports available on FS1

```
$Path = 'C:\StorageReports\Interactive'
Get-ChildItem -Path $Path
```

4. Viewing the report

```
$Rep = Get-ChildItem -Path $Path\*.html
Invoke-Item -Path $Rep
```

5. Extracting key information from the FSRM XML output

```
$XMLFile   = Get-ChildItem -Path $Path\*.xml
$XML       = [XML] (Get-Content -Path $XmlFile)
$Files     = $XML.StorageReport.ReportData.Item
$Files | Where-Object Path -NotMatch '^Windows|^Program|^Users'|
  Format-Table -Property name, path,
    @{ Name ='Sizemb'
       Expression = {(([int]$_.size)/1mb).tostring('N2')}},
       DaysSinceLastAccessed -AutoSize
```

6. Creating a monthly task in task scheduler

```
$Date = Get-Date '04:20'
$NewTaskHT = @{
  Time    = $Date
  Monthly = 1
}
$Task = New-FsrmScheduledTask @NewTaskHT
$NewReportHT = @{
  Name            = 'Monthly Files by files group report'
  Namespace       = 'C:\'
  Schedule        = $Task
  ReportType      = 'FilesbyFileGroup'
  FileGroupINclude = 'Text Files'
  LargeFileMinimum = 25MB
}
New-FsrmStorageReport @NewReportHT | Out-Null
```

7. Getting details of the task

```
Get-ScheduledTask |
  Where-Object TaskName -Match 'Monthly' |
    Format-Table -AutoSize
```

8. Running the task now

```
Get-ScheduledTask -TaskName '*Monthly*' |
   Start-ScheduledTask
Get-ScheduledTask -TaskName '*Monthly*'
```

9. Viewing the report in the `StorageReports` folder

```
$Path   = 'C:\StorageReports\Scheduled'
$Report = Get-ChildItem -Path $Path\*.html
$Report
```

10. Viewing the report

```
Invoke-item -Path $Report
```

How it works...

In *step 1*, you create a new FSRM report to discover large files (over 10 MB in size) on the C:\ drive. The output from this step looks like this:

```
PS C:\Foo> # 1. Creating a new FSRM storage report for large files on C:\ on FS1
PS C:\Foo> $NewReportHT = @{
           Name            = 'Large Files on FS1'
           NameSpace       = 'C:\'
           ReportType      = 'LargeFiles'
           LargeFileMinimum = 10MB
           Interactive     = $true
           }
PS C:\Foo> New-FsrmStorageReport @NewReportHT

FileGroupIncluded         :
FileOwnerFilePattern      :
FileOwnerUser             :
FileScreenAuditDaysSince  : 0
FileScreenAuditUser       :
FolderPropertyName        :
Interactive               : True
LargeFileMinimum          : 10485760
LargeFilePattern          :
LastError                 :
LastReportPath            :
LastRun                   :
LeastAccessedFilePattern  :
LeastAccessedMinimum      : 0
MailTo                    :
MostAccessedFilePattern   :
MostAccessedMaximum       : 0
Name                      : Large Files on FS1
Namespace                 : {C:\}
PropertyFilePattern       :
PropertyName              :
QuotaMinimumUsage         : 0
ReportFormat              : {DHtml, XML}
ReportType                : LargeFiles
Schedule                  :
Status                    : Queued
PSComputerName            :
```

Figure 8.43: Creating a new FSRM storage report

In *step 2*, you view the available FSRM reports, with output like this:

```
PS C:\Foo> # 2. Getting existing FSRM reports
PS C:\Foo> Get-FsrmStorageReport -Name * |
             Format-Table -Property Name, NameSpace,
                                     ReportType, ReportFormat


Name                   NameSpace ReportType ReportFormat
----                   --------- ---------- ------------
Large Files on FS1 {C:\}         LargeFiles {DHtml, XML}
```

Figure 8.44: Viewing available FSRM storage reports

In *step 3*, you examine the completed reports and output in the C:\StorageReports folder. The
output looks like this:

```
PS C:\Foo> # 3. Viewing Interactive reports available on FS1
PS C:\Foo> $Path = 'C:\StorageReports\Interactive'
PS C:\Foo> Get-ChildItem -Path $Path

    Directory: C:\StorageReports\Interactive

Mode            LastWriteTime        Length Name
----            -------------        ------ ----
d----       28/08/2022     13:04            LargeFiles2_2022-08-28_13-03-47_files
-a---       28/08/2022     13:04     235866 LargeFiles2_2022-08-28_13-03-47.html
-a---       28/08/2022     13:04     430926 LargeFiles2_2022-08-28_13-03-47.xml
```

Figure 8.45: Viewing completed FSRM storage reports

In *step 4*, you examine the large file report in your default browser, which looks like this:

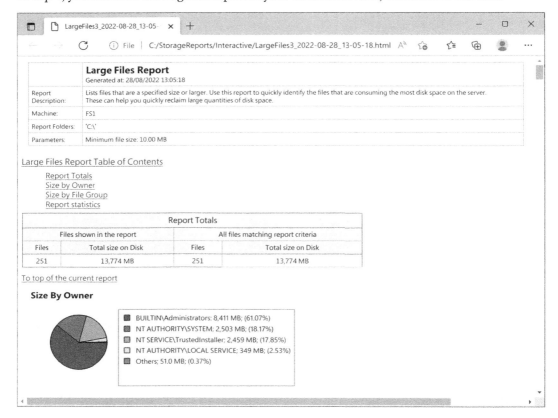

Figure 8.46: Viewing a large file report from FS1

In *step 5*, you extract the critical information from the report XML file and output it to the console. The output looks like this:

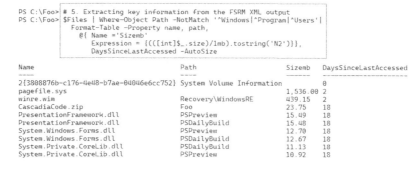

Figure 8.47: Viewing large file information

In *step 6*, you create a new scheduled task to run monthly. The task runs the `FilesbyFileGroup` report. This step produces no output.

In *step 7*, you examine the details of the scheduled task, with output like this:

```
PS C:\Foo> # 7. Getting details of the task
PS C:\Foo> Get-ScheduledTask |
             Where-Object TaskName -Match 'Monthly' |
               Format-Table -AutoSize


TaskPath                                              TaskName                              State
--------                                              --------                              -----
\Microsoft\Windows\File Server Resource Manager\ StorageReport-Monthly Files by files group report Ready
```

Figure 8.48: Getting details of the scheduled task

In *step 8*, you execute the scheduled task immediately, with output like this:

```
PS C:\Foo> # 8. Running the task now
PS C:\Foo> Get-ScheduledTask -TaskName '*Monthly*' |
             Start-ScheduledTask
PS C:\Foo> Get-ScheduledTask -TaskName '*Monthly*'


TaskPath                                              TaskName                              State
--------                                              --------                              -----
\Microsoft\Windows\File Server Resource Manag… StorageReport-Monthly Files by f… Running
```

Figure 8.49: Executing the scheduled FSRM task

In *step 9*, after FSRM completes running the report, you view the report output like this:

```
PS C:\Foo> # 9. Viewing the report in the StorageReports folder
PS C:\Foo> $Path   = 'C:\StorageReports\Scheduled'
PS C:\Foo> $Report = Get-ChildItem -Path $Path\*.html
PS C:\Foo> $Report


    Directory: C:\StorageReports\Scheduled

Mode              LastWriteTime         Length Name
----              -------------         ------ ----
-a---        28/08/2022     16:13        94620 FilesByType4_2022-08-28_16-12-40.html
```

Figure 8.50: Viewing the report data

In the final step in this recipe, *step 10*, you view the report in the browser, with output like this:

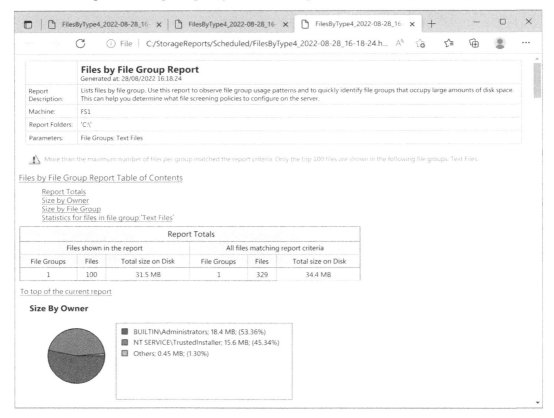

Figure 8.51: Viewing the report in the browser

There's more...

In *step 1*, you create a new FSRM interactive report. FSRM starts running this command immediately. If you are not quick enough, you might see no output when you attempt to view the FSRM reports in *step 3*. If the step shows you no output, this indicates that the report is complete. You can then view the report output, as you do in *step 4*.

When you view the report content folder, for example, in *step 3*, you may initially see no report output. It can take FSRM some time to produce the report, so you must be patient.

In *step 4*, you view the HTML report created by FSRM using your default browser. Depending on the configuration of your host, you may see a prompt asking which application you wish to use to view the report.

As you can see from this recipe, FSRM creates report output as HTML and XML. You cannot change the HTML format – but it is probably good enough for most uses. If you want a specific design or just some data, you get the same information from the XML and format it to suit your needs.

Implementing FSRM Filestore Screening

FSRM has a file screening option. This feature allows you to control the types of files you allow to be stored on your file server. You could, for example, define a file screen to prohibit a user from saving music files (files with the MP3 or FLAC extension) to your file server. With FSRM's file screening, if a user attempts to save a file such as GD71-02-18.T09.FLAC, and FSRM prevents the saving of the file.

To configure FSRM file screening, you need to specify the folder FSRM should protect and a file screen template that describes the characteristics of files that FSRM should block. FSRM comes with five built-in file screen templates. You can create additional templates to suit your requirements.

FSRM has eleven built-in file groups that cover common content types and can be updated and extended. Each file screen template contains a set of file groups. Each file group defines a set of file extensions that FSRM can block.

One built-in FSRM file group is audio and video files. This group, for example, includes a wide variety of audio and video file extensions, including AAC, MP3, FLAC, and more. Interestingly, this built-in file group does not block **SHN (Shorten)** files. You could easily add this extension to the relevant file group, should you wish.

Note that file screening works solely based on file extensions. FSRM, for example, might block you from saving a file such as GD71-02-18.T09.FLAC. However, if you tried to store this file as GD71-02-18.T09.CALF, FSRM allows a user to save the file. The FSRM file screening does not examine the file to ascertain the actual file type. In most cases, file screening stops the more obvious policy infractions.

Getting ready

This recipe uses FS1, a domain-joined host in the Reskit.Org domain, on which you have installed PowerShell 7 and VS Code. In a previous recipe, *Implementing FSRM quotas*, you installed FSRM on FS1.

How to do it...

1. Examining the existing FSRM file groups

    ```
    Get-FsrmFileGroup |
      Format-Table -Property Name, IncludePattern
    ```

2. Examining the existing file screening templates

    ```
    Get-FsrmFileScreenTemplate |
      Format-Table -Property Name, IncludeGroup, Active
    ```

3. Creating a new folder

    ```
    $Path = 'C:\FileScreen'
    If (-Not (Test-Path $Path)) {
      New-Item -Path $Path -ItemType Directory  |
        Out-Null
    }
    ```

4. Creating a new file screen

    ```
    $FileScreenHT =  @{
      Path         = $Path
      Description  = 'Block Executable Files'
      IncludeGroup = 'Executable Files'
    }
    New-FsrmFileScreen @FileScreenHT
    ```

5. Testing file screen by copying notepad.exe

    ```
    $FSTestHT = @{
      Path         = "$Env:windir\notepad.exe"
      Destination = 'C:\FileScreen\notepad.exe'
    }
    Copy-Item  @FSTestHT
    ```

6. Setting up an active email notification

    ```
    $MailBody =
    "[Source Io Owner] attempted to save an executable program to
    [File Screen Path].
    ```

```
This is not allowed!
"

$FSAction = @{
  Type            = 'Email'
  MailTo          = 'DoctorDNS@Gmail.Com'
  Subject         = 'Warning: attempted to save an executable file'
  Body            = $MailBody
  RunLimitInterval = 60
}
$Notification = New-FsrmAction @FSAction
$NewFileScreenHT = @{
  Path        = $Path
  Notification = $Notification
  IncludeGroup = 'Executable Files'
  Description  = 'Block any executable file'
  Active       = $true
}
Set-FsrmFileScreen @NewFileScreenHT
```

7. Getting FSRM notification limits

```
Get-FsrmSetting |
    Format-List -Property "*NotificationLimit"
```

8. Changing FSRM notification limits

```
$FSNotificationHT = @{
  CommandNotificationLimit = 1
  EmailNotificationLimit   = 1
  EventNotificationLimit   = 1
  ReportNotificationLimit  = 1
}
Set-FsrmSetting @FSNotificationHT
```

9. Retesting the file screen and viewing the FSRM email

```
Copy-Item @FSTestHT
```

How it works...

In *step 1*, you examine the initial set of FSRM file groups. The output looks like this:

```
PS C:\Foo> # 1. Examining the existing FSRM file groups
PS C:\Foo> Get-FsrmFileGroup |
              Format-Table -Property Name, IncludePattern

Name                   IncludePattern
----                   --------------
Audio and Video Files  {*.aac, *.aif, *.aiff, *.asf, *.asx, *.au, *.avi, *.flac, *.m3u, *.mid, *.midi, *.mov,
                        *.mp1, *.mp2, *.mp3, *.mp4, *.mpa, *.mpe, *.mpeg, *.mpeg2, *.mpeg3, *.mpg, *.ogg, *.qt,
                        *.qtw, *.ram, *.rm, *.rmi, *.rmvb, *.snd, *.swf, *.vob, *.wav, *.wax, *.wma, *.wmv,
                        *.wvx}
Image Files            {*.bmp, *.dib, *.eps, *.gif, *.img, *.jfif, *.jpe, *.jpeg, *.jpg, *.pcx, *.png, *.ps,
                        *.psd, *.raw, *.rif, *.spiff, *.tif, *.tiff}
Office Files           {*.accdb, *.accde, *.accdr, *.accdt, *.adn, *.adp, *.doc, *.docm, *.docx, *.dot, *.dotm,
                        *.dotx, *.grv, *.gsa, *.gta, *.mad, *.maf, *.mda, *.mda, *.mdb, *.mde, *.mdf,
                        *.mdf, *.mdm, *.mdt, *.mdw, *.mdw, *.mdw, *.mdz, *.mpd, *.mpp, *.mpt, *.obt, *.odb,
                        *.one, *.onepkg, *.pot, *.potm, *.potx, *.ppa, *.ppam, *.pps, *.ppsm, *.ppsx, *.ppt,
                        *.pptm, *.pptx, *.pub, *.pwz, *.rqy, *.rtf, *.rwz, *.sldm, *.sldx, *.slk, *.thmx, *.vdx,
                        *.vsd, *.vsl, *.vss, *.vst, *.vsu, *.vsw, *.vsx, *.vtx, *.wbk, *.wri, *.xla, *.xlam,
                        *.xlb, *.xlc, *.xld, *.xlk, *.xll, *.xlm, *.xls, *.xlsb, *.xlsm, *.xlsx, *.xlt, *.xltm,
                        *.xltx, *.xlv, *.xlw, *.xsf, *.xsn}
E-mail Files           {*.eml, *.idx, *.mbox, *.mbx, *.msg, *.oft, *.ost, *.pab, *.pst}
Executable Files       {*.bat, *.cmd, *.com, *.cpl, *.exe, *.inf, *.js, *.jse, *.msh, *.msi, *.msp, *.ocx,
                        *.pif, *.pl, *.ps1, *.scr, *.vb, *.vbs, *.wsf, *.wsh}
System Files           {*.acm, *.dll, *.ocx, *.sys, *.vxd}
Compressed Files       {*.ace, *.arc, *.arj, *.bhx, *.bz2, *.cab, *.gz, *.gzip, *.hpk, *.hqx, *.jar, *.lha,
                        *.lzh, *.lzx, *.pak, *.pit, *.rar, *.sea, *.sit, *.sqz, *.tgz, *.uu, *.uue, *.z, *.zip,
                        *.zoo}
Web Page Files         {*.asp, *.aspx, *.cgi, *.css, *.dhtml, *.hta, *.htm, *.html, *.mht, *.php, *.php3,
                        *.shtml, *.url}
Text Files             {*.asc, *.text, *.txt}
Backup Files           {*.bak, *.bck, *.bkf, *.old}
Temporary Files        {*.temp, *.tmp, ~*}
```

Figure 8.52: Examining existing FSRM file groups

In *step 2*, you examine the built-in FSRM file screening templates. The output from this step is:

```
PS C:\Foo> # 2. Examining the existing file screening templates
PS C:\Foo> Get-FsrmFileScreenTemplate |
              Format-Table -Property Name, IncludeGroup, Active

Name                                   IncludeGroup                          Active
----                                   ------------                          ------
Block Audio and Video Files            {Audio and Video Files}               True
Block Executable Files                 {Executable Files}                    True
Block Image Files                      {Image Files}                         True
Block E-mail Files                     {E-mail Files}                        True
Monitor Executable and System Files    {Executable Files, System Files}      False
```

Figure 8.53: Viewing file screen templates

In *step 3*, you create a new folder for testing FSRM file screening, which produces no output. In *step 4*, you create a new FSRM file screen. The output from this step looks like this:

```
PS C:\Foo> # 4. Creating a new file screen
PS C:\Foo> $FileScreenHT = @{
               Path        = $Path
               Description = 'Block Executable Files'
               IncludeGroup = 'Executable Files'
           }
PS C:\Foo> New-FsrmFileScreen @FileScreenHT

Active          : True
Description     : Block Executable Files
IncludeGroup    : {Executable Files}
MatchesTemplate : False
Notification    :
Path            : C:\FileScreen
Template        :
PSComputerName  :
```

Figure 8.54: Creating a new file screen

To test the file screen, in *step 5*, you copy notepad.exe from the Windows folder to the file screen folder, with output like this:

```
PS C:\Foo> # 5. Testing file screen by copying notepad.exe
PS C:\Foo> $FSTestHT = @{
               Path        = "$Env:windir\notepad.exe"
               Destination = 'C:\FileScreen\notepad.exe'
           }
PS C:\Foo> Copy-Item  @FSTestHT
Copy-Item: Access to the path 'C:\FileScreen\notepad.exe' is denied.  ⬅━━━━━━━
```

Figure 8.55: Testing a file screen

In *step 6*, you set up an active email notification to notify you any time a user attempts to save an executable file to the screened folder. This step creates no output.

In *step 7*, you examine the FSRM notification limits with output like this:

```
PS C:\Foo> # 7. Getting FSRM Notification Limits
PS C:\Foo> Get-FsrmSetting |
               Format-List -Property "*NotificationLimit"

CommandNotificationLimit : 60
EmailNotificationLimit   : 60
EventNotificationLimit   : 60
ReportNotificationLimit  : 60
```

Figure 8.56: Examining FSRM notification limits

In *step 8*, you reduce the email notification limits to one second to speed up the creation of email notifications for testing. This step creates no console output.

In *step 9*, you test the updated file screen by re-attempting to save an executable to the screened folder. You then get the following output:

```
PS C:\Foo> # 9. Re-testing the file screen to check the action
PS C:\Foo> Copy-Item @FSTestHT
Copy-Item: Access to the path 'C:\FileScreen\notepad.exe' is denied.
```

Figure 8.57: Retesting the file screen

Having set up an email notification for the file screen, you can look at your email client and view the FSRM-generated email, which looks like this:

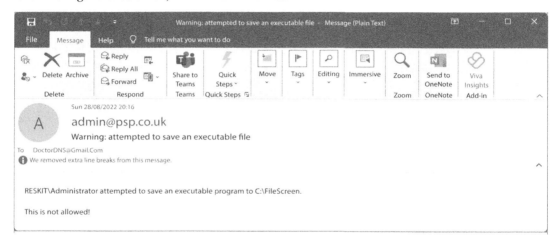

Figure 8.58: Viewing the File Screen email

There's more...

In *step 1*, you look at the file extensions that FSRM recognizes by default. These file extensions cover most of the common scenarios. One small omission is that the audio and video files should include the extension SHN. Files with the SHN extension are lossless audio files using the Shorten compression algorithm. You can find a wealth of legal SHN-based concert recordings of many bands, such as The Grateful Dead. For this reason, in production, you might want to update the FSRM file group to enable FSRM to screen SHN files when you use that FSRM file group in a screening rule.

FSRM's file screening feature does a good job of stopping a user from accidentally saving files that would violate the organization's file storage policies. For example, the organization might stipulate that users may not save audio or video files to the organization's file server.

If a user "accidentally" saves an MP3 file, FSRM would politely refuse. However, as noted earlier, FSRM file screening is based solely on the file's extension. Thus, if the user saves a file and changes the extension to 3MP, FSRM does not object. Of course, in doing so, the user is deliberately breaking an organizational policy, which could be a career-limiting move.

Join our community on Discord

Join our community's Discord space for discussions with the author and other readers:

```
https://packt.link/SecNet
```

9

Managing Printing

This chapter covers the following recipes:

- Installing and Sharing Printers
- Publishing a Printer to Active Directory
- Changing the Spooler Directory
- Changing Printer Drivers
- Printing a Test Page
- Managing Printer Security
- Creating a Printer Pool

Introduction

Printing is a feature that Microsoft has incorporated into various versions of the Windows operating system and has evolved over the years. Printer configuration and management in Windows Server 2022 hasn't changed much from earlier versions. Windows Server 2022 provides you with a printing platform for your organization and the ability to create print servers that you can share with users in your organization.

When printing in Windows, the physical device that renders output onto paper is known as a print device. A printer is a queue of documents to be printed on a print device. A print server can support multiple printers. Each printing device has an associated printer driver that converts your documents to a printed form on a given print device. Most printer drivers are vendor and printer model-dependent.

Some drivers come with Windows; others you need to obtain from a printer vendor. In some cases, these drivers are downloadable from the internet; in other cases, you may need to download and run a driver installation program to add the correct drivers to your print server.

Printers print to the print device by using a printer port (such as USB, parallel, or a network address). You define the printer port before creating a Windows printer for network printers. Microsoft hasn't changed the basic print architecture with Windows Server 2022. Windows Server 2012 introduced a new driver architecture that Windows Server 2022 supports. This driver model enables you to make use of two different driver types: printer class drivers and model-specific drivers. The former provides a single driver for various specific printing device models, whereas you use the model-specific drivers for just a single model. Increasingly, print device manufacturers are implementing more generic drivers that can simplify the organizational rollout of shared printing.

Another change in Windows Server 2012, carried into Windows Server 2022, is that you no longer have to use the print server to distribute printer drivers (which is especially relevant for network printers). You can use tools, such as the Microsoft Endpoint Manager or Group Policies, to distribute print drivers to clients in such cases.

This chapter covers installing, managing, and updating printers, print drivers, and printer ports on a Windows Server 2022 server. You may find that some of the administration tools used in this chapter aren't available on Windows Server Core systems. You must have the full Windows Server GUI (including the Desktop Experience) for any GUI utilities to enable full management.

In the *Installing and Sharing Printers* recipe, you install a printer and share it. In the *Publishing a Printer to Active Directory* recipe, you'll publish the printer to **Active Directory (AD)**, enabling users in the domain to search AD to find the printer. When you create a print server (by adding printer ports, printers, and so on), you may find that the default spool folder (underneath C:\Windows) may not be in an ideal location. When you print a document, Windows uses this spool folder to hold the temporary files required for the print device to render the document. Occasionally, this folder can get quite large, such as when a physical print device runs out of paper, and no one fixes the problem. In production, you might move the spool folder to a separate physical storage device, which can also improve the performance of a busy print server. In the *Changing the Spooler Directory* recipe, you change the default location for the printer spool.

In the *Changing Printer Drivers* recipe, you change the driver for the printer you created earlier. If you need to replace a specific print device with a different model, you may need to use other printer drivers. The printer vendor could also release updated drivers that you can deploy.

When you install a printer, a good step is to print a test page, as you can see in the *Printing a Test Page* recipe.

A Windows Printer can have an **Access Control List (ACL)** like a file or folder. You can also modify the ACL, as shown in the *Managing Printer Security* recipe. In most organizations, print devices deployed via a print server are shared resources. You see how to deploy a shared printer in the *Installing and Sharing Printers* recipe.

In Windows, a printer pool is a printer that has two or more associated printing devices. This means having two or more physical printers (print devices on separate ports) that users see as just a single printer. A printer pool could be useful when users create large numbers of printed documents. You can deploy multiple physical printers but expose these as a single Windows printer. In the *Creating a Printer Pool* recipe, you see how you can automate the creation of a printer pool using rundll32.exe.

The systems used in the chapter

This chapter uses a domain-joined server, PSRV, a member server in the Reskit.org domain on which you have installed PowerShell 7 (and VS Code). You also need the domain controller for the domain online as well, DC1, as follows:

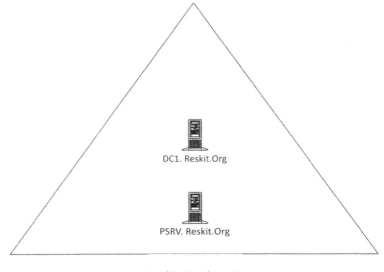

Figure 9.1: Hosts in use for this chapter

Installing and Sharing Printers

The first step in creating a print server for your organization involves installing the print server feature, printer drivers, and printer ports to the print server. Once you do that, you can create and share printers for others to access. In this recipe, you download and install two Xerox printer drivers. This recipe uses one of the drivers, while you use the second in the *Changing Printer Drivers* recipe. This internet download comes as a .zip archive that you must extract before using the drivers.

Note: if you're using this recipe to support other printer makes and models, you may need to make some changes. In some cases, such as with some Hewlett-Packard printers, the manufacturer designed the printer drivers to install them by running a downloadable executable. You must run the downloaded executable on each print server to add the necessary drivers. Thus, this recipe may not apply to all printing devices.

Getting ready

You run this recipe on PSRV after you have installed PowerShell 7.

How to do it...

1. Installing the Print-Server features on PSRV

    ```
    Install-WindowsFeature -Name Print-Server,
                                 Print-Services,
                                 RSAT-Print-Services
    ```

2. Creating a folder for the Xerox printer drivers

    ```
    $NewItemHT = @{
      Path        = 'C:\Foo\Xerox'
      ItemType    = 'Directory'
      Force       = $true
      ErrorAction = "Silentlycontinue"
    }
    New-Item @NewItemHT | Out-Null
    ```

3. Downloading printer drivers for the Xerox printers

    ```
    $URL='http://download.support.xerox.com/pub/drivers/6510/'+
         'drivers/win10x64/ar/6510_5.617.7.0_PCL6_x64.zip'
    $Target='C:\Foo\Xerox\Xdrivers.zip'
    ```

```
Start-BitsTransfer -Source $URL -Destination $Target
```

4. Expanding the .zip file

```
$Drivers = 'C:\Foo\Xerox\Drivers'
Expand-Archive -Path $Target -DestinationPath $Drivers
```

5. Installing the drivers

```
$Model1 = 'Xerox Phaser 6510 PCL6'
$P =  'C:\Foo\Xerox\Drivers\6510_5.617.7.0_PCL6_x64_Driver.inf\'+
      'x3NSURX.inf'
rundll32.exe printui.dll,PrintUIEntry /ia /m "$Model1"  /f "$P"
$Model2 = 'Xerox WorkCentre 6515 PCL6'
rundll32.exe printui.dll,PrintUIEntry /ia /m "$Model2"  /f "$P"
```

6. Adding a `PrinterPort` for a new printer

```
$PrintPortHT = @{
  Name              = 'SalesPP'
  PrinterHostAddress = '10.10.10.61'
}
Add-PrinterPort @PrintPortHT
```

7. Adding the printer to PSRV

```
$PrinterHT = @{
  Name = 'SalesPrinter1'
  DriverName = $Model1
  PortName   = 'SalesPP'
}
Add-Printer @PrinterHT
```

8. Sharing the printer

```
Set-Printer -Name SalesPrinter1 -Shared $True
```

9. Reviewing what you have done

```
Get-PrinterPort -Name SalesPP |
  Format-Table -Autosize -Property Name, Description,
                            PrinterHostAddress, PortNumber
Get-PrinterDriver -Name xerox* |
```

```
    Format-Table -Property Name, Manufacturer,
                                DriverVersion, PrinterEnvironment
Get-Printer -ComputerName PSRV -Name SalesPrinter1 |
    Format-Table -Property Name, ComputerName,
                                Type, PortName, Location, Shared
```

10. Checking the status of the shared printer

```
net view \\PSRV
```

How it works...

In *step 1*, you install both the Print Server Windows feature and the printing RSAT, with output
like this:

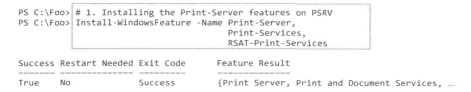

Figure 9.2: Installing printer features to PSRV

In *step 2*, you create a new folder to hold the printer driver download. In *step 3*, you download the
drivers (as a compressed .zip file) into the folder you just created. In *step 4*, you expand the .ZIP
files, and in *step 5*, you install these printer drivers. In *step 6*, you add a new printer port to PSRV,
and in *step 7*, you add a new printer using the printer port you just created and the Xerox printer
drivers you downloaded. Finally, in *step 8*, you share the printer so other users can print to this
printer. These seven steps produce no output.

In *step 9*, you examine the printer ports, printer drivers, and printers available on PSRV, with
output like this:

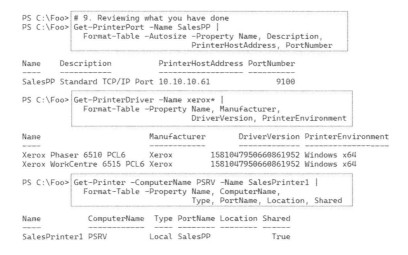

```
PS C:\Foo> # 9. Reviewing what you have done
PS C:\Foo> Get-PrinterPort -Name SalesPP |
             Format-Table -Autosize -Property Name, Description,
                                     PrinterHostAddress, PortNumber

Name     Description          PrinterHostAddress PortNumber
----     -----------          ------------------ ----------
SalesPP  Standard TCP/IP Port 10.10.10.61              9100

PS C:\Foo> Get-PrinterDriver -Name xerox* |
             Format-Table -Property Name, Manufacturer,
                                     DriverVersion, PrinterEnvironment

Name                      Manufacturer    DriverVersion      PrinterEnvironment
----                      ------------    -------------      ------------------
Xerox Phaser 6510 PCL6    Xerox           1581047950660861952 Windows x64
Xerox WorkCentre 6515 PCL6 Xerox          1581047950660861952 Windows x64

PS C:\Foo> Get-Printer -ComputerName PSRV -Name SalesPrinter1 |
             Format-Table -Property Name, ComputerName,
                                     Type, PortName, Location, Shared

Name          ComputerName  Type PortName Location Shared
----          ------------  ---- -------- -------- ------
SalesPrinter1 PSRV          Local SalesPP          True
```

Figure 9.3: Viewing printer components on PSRV

In *step 10*, you use the net.exe command to view the shared printers that SRV1 provides, with output like this:

```
PS C:\Foo> # 10. Checking the status of the shared printer
PS C:\Foo> net view \\PSRV
Shared resources at \\PSRV

Share name      Type    Used as  Comment

-------------------------------------------------------------------------------
SalesPrinter1   Print            SalesPrinter1
The command completed successfully.
```

Figure 9.4: Viewing the shared printer on PSRV

There's more...

In this recipe, you create a printer on PSRV based on Xerox printers. The fact that you may not have this printer model in your environment means you can't physically print to such a print device, but you can set up the printer as shown in the recipe.

In *step 5*, you use PrintUI.DLL and RunDLL32.EXE. The former, PrintUI.DLL, is a library of printer management functionalities. If you use the Printer Management GUI tool to manage printers, the GUI calls this DLL to perform your chosen action. Since Microsoft designed and built this DLL to support the Windows printer GUI, the DLL can create additional dialog boxes, which are not useful for automation. You can rely on the help information generated to resolve any problems.

In *step 10*, you use the net.exe command to view the shared printer on PSRV. There is currently no cmdlet that provides this information.

Publishing a Printer to Active Directory

After you create and share a printer (as shown in the previous recipe), you can publish it to Active Directory. You publish the printer you created in the last recipe and examine the results in this recipe. When you publish a printer, you can also specify a physical location for it. Your users can search for published printers based on location and capabilities (such as color printers).

Getting ready

Before running this recipe, you must set up the PSRV printer server (you did this in the *Installing and Sharing Printers* recipe). Additionally, you need SalesPrinter1 created.

How to do it...

1. Getting the printer to publish and store the returned object in $Printer

   ```
   $Printer = Get-Printer -Name SalesPrinter1
   ```

2. Viewing the printer details

   ```
   $Printer | Format-Table -Property Name, Published
   ```

3. Publishing and sharing the printer to AD

   ```
   $Printer | Set-Printer -Location '10th floor 10E4'
   $Printer | Set-Printer -Shared $true -Published $true
   ```

4. Viewing the updated publication status

   ```
   Get-Printer -Name SalesPrinter1 |
     Format-Table -Property Name, Location, Drivername, Published
   ```

How it works...

In *step 1*, you obtain details of the printer you wish to share and store this into the variable `$Printer`, producing no output. In *step 2*, you examine the printer details contained in `$Printer` with output like this:

```
PS C:\Foo> # 2. Viewing the printer details
PS C:\Foo> $Printer | Format-Table -Property Name, Published

Name          Published
----          ---------
SalesPrinter1     False
```

Figure 9.5: Viewing the SalesPrinter1 printer on PSRV

In *step 3*, you publish the printer to the `Reskit.Org` AD, and you share the printer explicitly. This step produces no output. In *step 4*, you use `Get-Printer` to review the publication status of the printer, with output like this:

```
PS C:\Foo> # 4. Viewing the updated publication status
PS C:\Foo> Get-Printer -Name SalesPrinter1 |
             Format-Table -Property Name, Location, Drivername, Published

Name          Location       Drivername             Published
----          --------       ----------             ---------
SalesPrinter1 10th floor 10E4 Xerox Phaser 6510 PCL6     True
```

Figure 9.6: Viewing the SalesPrinter1 printer details

There's more...

Publishing a printer to AD allows users to locate printers near them using the **Add Printer** dialog to search for published printers. For example, if you log on to any computer in the domain, you can get to this dialog box by clicking **Start** | **Settings** | **Devices** | **Printers & scanners** to bring up the **Add printers & scanners** dialog. From this dialog box, click **Add a printer or scanner**.

Wait until the search is complete, then click on **The printer that I want isn't listed**, which brings up the **Add Printer** dialog, like this:

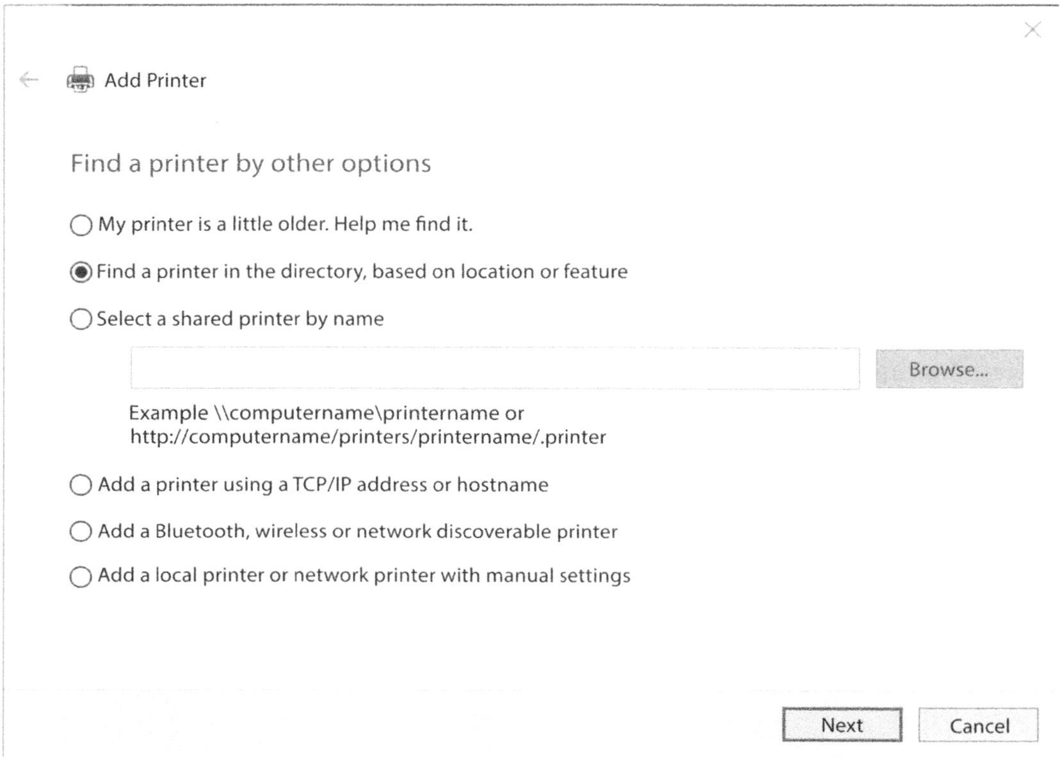

Figure 9.7: Using the Add Printer dialog

From this dialog box, click on **Next** to bring up the **Find Printers** dialog, which looks like this:

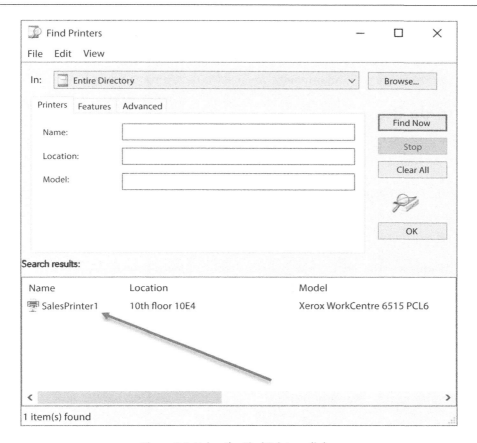

Figure 9.8: Using the Find Printers dialog

In larger organizations, publishing printers to the AD can be very useful in helping users find the corporate printers available.

Changing the Spooler Directory

During the printing process, the Windows printer spooler in Windows uses an on-disk folder to hold the temporary files the printing process creates. If multiple users each print large documents to a single printer, the print queue, and the temporary folder can get quite large. By default, this folder is C:\Windows\System32\spool\PRINTERS. You may wish to change the default spool folder on a separate physical storage device for a busy print server with multiple printers. Also, consider ensuring the volume is fail-safe (e.g. using hardware or software RAID).

Getting ready

Before running this recipe, you must set up the PSRV printer server (you did this in the *Installing and Sharing Printers* recipe). Additionally, you need `SalesPrinter1` created.

How to do it...

1. Loading the `System.Printing` namespace and classes

    ```
    Add-Type -AssemblyName System.Printing
    ```

2. Defining the required permissions

    ```
    $Permissions =
        [System.Printing.PrintSystemDesiredAccess]::AdministrateServer
    ```

3. Creating a `PrintServer` object with the required permissions

    ```
    $NewObjHT = @{
      TypeName     = 'System.Printing.PrintServer'
      ArgumentList = $Permissions
    }
    $PrintServer = New-Object @NewObjHT
    ```

4. Displaying print server properties

    ```
    $PrintServer
    ```

5. Observing the default spool folder

    ```
    "The default spool folder is: [{0}]" -f $PringServer.
    DefaultSpoolDirectory
    ```

6. Creating a new spool folder

    ```
    $NewItemHT = @{
      Path        = 'C:\SpoolPath'
      ItemType    = 'Directory'
      Force       = $true
      ErrorAction = 'SilentlyContinue'
    }
    New-Item @NewItemHT | Out-Null
    ```

7. Updating the default spool folder path

```
$NewPath = 'C:\SpoolPath'
$PrintServer.DefaultSpoolDirectory = $NewPath
```

8. Committing the change

```
$PrintServer.Commit()
```

9. Restarting the spooler to accept the new folder

```
Restart-Service -Name Spooler
```

10. Verifying the new spooler folder

```
New-Object -TypeName System.Printing.PrintServer |
  Format-Table -Property Name,
                  DefaultSpoolDirectory
```

Another way to set the spooler directory is by directly editing the registry as follows:

11. Stopping the spooler service

```
Stop-Service -Name Spooler
```

12. Creating a new spool directory

```
$SpoolFolder2 = 'C:\SpoolViaRegistry'
$NewItemHT2 = @{
  Path        = $SpoolFolder2
  Itemtype    = 'Directory'
  ErrorAction = 'SilentlyContinue'
}
New-Item @NewItemHT2 | Out-Null
```

13. Creating the spooler folder and configuring it in the registry

```
$RegistryPath = 'HKLM:\SYSTEM\CurrentControlSet\Control\' +
                  'Print\Printers'
$ItemPropHT = @{
  Path    = $RegistryPath
  Name    = 'DefaultSpoolDirectory'
  Value   = $SPL
}
Set-ItemProperty @ItemPropHT
```

14. Restarting the spooler service

```
Start-Service -Name Spooler
```

15. Viewing the results

```
New-Object -TypeName System.Printing.PrintServer |
  Format-Table -Property Name, DefaultSpoolDirectory
```

How it works...

In *step 1*, you load the System.Printing namespace, which produces no output. In *step 2*, you create a variable holding the desired access to the printer. In *step 3*, you create a PrintServer object with the appropriate permissions. Then, in *step 4*, you examine the default spooler folder for a newly installed Windows Server 2022 host, which produces output like this:

```
PS C:\Foo> # 4. Displaying print server properties
PS C:\Foo> $PrintServer

Name                         : \\COOKHAM216
SubSystemVersion             : 0
RestartJobOnPoolEnabled      : True
RestartJobOnPoolTimeout      : 600
MinorVersion                 : 0
MajorVersion                 : 3
EventLog                     : LogPrintingErrorEvents
NetPopup                     : False
BeepEnabled                  : False
DefaultSchedulerPriority     : Normal
SchedulerPriority            : Normal
DefaultPortThreadPriority    : Normal
PortThreadPriority           : Normal
DefaultSpoolDirectory        : C:\Windows\system32\spool\PRINTERS
Parent                       :
PropertiesCollection         : {EventLog, RestartJobOnPoolTimeout, SchedulerPriority,
                                 MinorVersion, Name, MajorVersion, DefaultSpoolDirectory,
                                 DefaultPortThreadPriority, DefaultSchedulerPriority,
                                 PortThreadPriority, BeepEnabled, RestartJobOnPoolEnabled, NetPopup}
```

Figure 9.9: Examining the default spool folder

In *step 5*, you create a new folder on PSRV to serve as your print server's spool folder. In *step 6*, you update the printer spool folder path. In *step 7*, you commit this change. These three steps produce no console output. In *step 8*, you restart the spooler service. Depending on the speed of your system, you may see output as follows:

```
PS C:\Foo> # 9. Restarting the Spooler to accept the new folder
PS C:\Foo> Restart-Service -Name Spooler
WARNING: Waiting for service 'Print Spooler (Spooler)' to start...
```

Figure 9.10: Restarting the print spooler service

In *step 10*, you view the printer details with output like this:

```
PS C:\Foo> # 10. Verifying the new spooler folder
PS C:\Foo> New-Object -TypeName System.Printing.PrintServer |
             Format-Table -Property Name,
                            DefaultSpoolDirectory

Name    DefaultSpoolDirectory
----    ---------------------
\\PSRV  C:\SpoolPath
```

Figure 9.11: Examining the default spool folder

From *step 1* through to *step 9*, you set and validate the spool folder using .NET. There is another separate way to change the spool folder that involves using WMI, which we will use next.

In *step 11*, you stop the spooler service. In *step 12*, you create a new folder, and in *step 13*, you configure the necessary registry settings to contain the path to the new spool folder. Then in *step 14*, you restart the spooler. These four steps produce no console output. With the changes made to the spool folder within the registry, in *step 15*, you can view the updated spool folder with output like this:

```
PS C:\Foo> # 15. Viewing the results
PS C:\Foo> New-Object -TypeName System.Printing.PrintServer |
             Format-Table -Property Name, DefaultSpoolDirectory

Name    DefaultSpoolDirectory
----    ---------------------
\\PSRV  C:\WINDOWS\system32\spool\PRINTERS
```

Figure 9.12: Examining the updated spool folder

There's more...

For most organizations with a larger number of shared printers, configuring the print server to use another folder for spooling is a good idea. If possible, use a large separate storage volume to avoid the risk of the spool folder filling up. And ensure that the disk volume is fault tolerant (i.e., using software or hardware RAID).

You used two mechanisms in this recipe to change the spooler folder. One uses a .NET object, while the other involves directly editing the registry.

Many of the steps in this recipe produce no output. This lack of output is normal when dealing directly with .NET classes and methods and editing the registry.

In *step 1*, you add the .NET System.Printing namespace DLL into the current PowerShell session. This namespace DLL contains the classes involved with managing printing. When PowerShell loads, it does not load this DLL, so you have to load it, as shown in this step, before you can use the classes, types, etc. inside the namespace. For details on what is inside this namespace, see https://learn.microsoft.com/dotnet/api/system.printing.

Changing Printer Drivers

It may be necessary to change the printer driver for a Windows printer. For example, you might replace an existing print device with a new or different model, or the printer vendor may have released a new driver for your printer. In these cases, you want the printer's name to remain the same, but you need to update the printer's print driver. In the *Installing and Sharing Printers* recipe, you downloaded and installed two Xerox printer drivers. You used the first driver, Xerox Phaser 6510 PCL6, when you defined the SalesPrinter1 printer.

In this recipe, you change the driver for the printer and use the other previously installed driver, Xerox Phaser 6515 PCL6.

Keeping the printer name (and port) unchanged makes swapping a printer relatively straightforward. In this recipe, you change the printer driver while leaving the printer's name and the printer's port (including the printer's IP address and port number) unchanged. This scenario might occur if you replace the physical printing device with a newer model, or even change the printer type/manufacturer.

Getting ready

You run this recipe on PSRV after you have installed PowerShell 7.

How to do it...

1. Adding the print driver for the new printing device

   ```
   $Model2 = 'Xerox WorkCentre 6515 PCL6'
   Add-PrinterDriver -Name $Model2
   ```

2. Viewing loaded printer drivers

   ```
   Get-PrinterDriver
   ```

3. Getting the Sales Group printer object and store it in $Printer

   ```
   $PrinterName = 'SalesPrinter1'
   $Printer     = Get-Printer -Name $PrinterName
   ```

4. Updating the driver using the Set-Printer cmdlet

```
$Printer | Set-Printer -DriverName $Model2
```

5. Observing the updated printer driver

```
Get-Printer -Name $PrinterName |
    Format-Table -Property Name, DriverName, PortName,
                    Published, Shared
```

How it works...

In *step 1*, you use the Add-PrinterDriver cmdlet to add the printer driver for the printer. In *step 2*, you view the loaded print drivers without output like this:

```
PS C:\Foo> # 2. Viewing loaded printer drivers:
PS C:\Foo> Get-PrinterDriver

Name                                    PrinterEnvironment MajorVersion    Manufacturer
----                                    ------------------ ------------    ------------
Microsoft XPS Document Writer v4        Windows x64        4               Microsoft
Microsoft Software Printer Driver       Windows x64        4               Microsoft
Microsoft Print To PDF                  Windows x64        4               Microsoft
Xerox WorkCentre 6515 PCL6              Windows x64        3               Xerox
Xerox Phaser 6510 PCL6                  Windows x64        3               Xerox
Remote Desktop Easy Print               Windows x64        3               Microsoft
Microsoft Shared Fax Driver             Windows x64        3               Microsoft
Microsoft enhanced Point and Print...   Windows x64        3               Microsoft
Microsoft enhanced Point and Print...   Windows NT x86     3               Microsoft
```

Figure 9.13: Viewing loaded printer drivers

In *step 3*, you obtain the printer details, and in *step 4*, you update the printer to use the updated driver. These steps produce no console output.

In *step 5*, you use the Get-Printer cmdlet to observe that you have installed the updated driver for the SalesPrinter1 printer, which looks like this:

```
PS C:\Foo> Get-Printer -Name $PrinterName |
            Format-Table -Property Name, DriverName, PortName,
                            Published, Shared

Name          DriverName                  PortName Published Shared
----          ----------                  -------- --------- ------
SalesPrinter1 Xerox WorkCentre 6515 PCL6  SalesPP       True   True
```

Figure 9.14: Viewing the updated printer driver for SalesPrinter1

As you see in this recipe, changing a printer driver is straightforward – after you install a new printer driver, you use Set-Printer to inform Windows which driver it should use when printing to the printer.

Printing a Test Page

There are occasions when you may wish to print a test page on a printer – for example, after you change the toner or printer ink on a physical printer or after changing the print driver (as shown in the *Changing Printer Drivers* recipe). In those cases, the test page helps you to ensure that the printer is working properly.

Getting ready

This recipe uses the PSRV print server that you set up in the *Installing and Sharing Printers* recipe.

How to do it...

1. Getting the printer objects from WMI

    ```
    $Printers = Get-CimInstance -ClassName Win32_Printer
    ```

2. Displaying the number of printers defined on PSRV

    ```
    '{0} Printers defined on this system' -f $Printers.Count
    ```

3. Getting the Sales Group printer WMI object

    ```
    $Printer = $Printers |
      Where-Object Name -eq 'SalesPrinter1'
    ```

4. Displaying the printer's details

    ```
    $Printer | Format-Table -AutoSize
    ```

5. Printing a test page

    ```
    Invoke-CimMethod -InputObject $Printer -MethodName PrintTestPage
    ```

6. Checking on test page print job

    ```
    Get-PrintJob -PrinterName SalesPrinter1
    ```

How it works...

In *step 1*, you get details of the printers installed on PSRV using WMI and store them in the variable `$Printers`, producing no output. In *step 2*, you display how many printers you have are defined on your printer server, with output like this:

```
PS C:\Foo> # 2. Displaying the number of printers defined on PSRV
PS C:\Foo> '{0} Printers defined on this system' -f $Printers.Count
7 Printers defined on this system
```

Figure 9.15: Viewing printers on PSRV

In *step 3*, you get the specific WMI instance for the `SalesPrinter1` printer, creating no console output. In *step 4*, you view the details of this printer, with output like this:

```
PS C:\Foo> # 4. Displaying the printer's details
PS C:\Foo> $Printer | Format-Table -AutoSize

Name          ShareName     SystemName PrinterState PrinterStatus Location
----          ---------     ---------- ------------ ------------- --------
SalesPrinterl SalesPrinterl PSRV       0            3             10th floor 10E4
```

Figure 9.16: Viewing details of SalesPrinter1

In *step 5*, you use `Invoke-CimMethod` to run the `PrintTestPage()` method on the printer, generating output like this:

```
PS C:\Foo> # 5. Printing a test page
PS C:\Foo> Invoke-CimMethod -InputObject $Printer -MethodName PrintTestPage

ReturnValue PSComputerName
----------- --------------
          0
```

Figure 9.17: Invoking the PrintTestPage method

In the final step in this recipe, *step 6*, you view the print jobs on the `SalesPrinter1` printer, where you can see your test page output generated in the previous step. The output from this step looks like this:

```
PS C:\Foo> # 6. Checking on test page print job
PS C:\Foo> Get-PrintJob -PrinterName SalesPrinterl
Id ComputerName   PrinterName   DocumentName   SubmittedTime        JobStatus
-- ------------   -----------   ------------   -------------        ---------
2                 SalesPrinterl Test Page      03/09/2022 13:16:18  Printing, Reta...
```

Figure 9.18: Viewing printer jobs to observe the test page

There's more...

In this recipe, you used WMI to create a test page on the SalesPrinter1 printer. As you saw in *step 6*, the printer's queue has the print job. In theory, the document should appear on the print device immediately. If you do not get any physical output, you must troubleshoot your printer infrastructure: is the printer turned on, is the network cable plugged in and working, does the printer have the correct IP address, etc.?

Managing Printer Security

Every Windows printer has a discretionary **ACL**. The ACL contains one or more **Access Control Entries (ACEs)**. Each ACE defines a specific permission for some particular group or user. You could define a group (such as SalesAdmins) and permit that group to manage documents while you give another group (such as Sales) access to print to the printer.

By default, when you create a printer, Windows adds some ACEs to the printer's ACL. The default ACL includes permitting the Everyone group to print to the printer. For some printers, this may not be appropriate. For this reason, you may need to adjust the ACL, as shown in this recipe.

The PrintManagement module contains several cmdlets that help you manage the printers. However, there are no cmdlets for managing ACLs on printers. You can always use .NET directly to manage the ACL or use third-party scripts that do the job for you. But this code can be complex (and easy to mess up). Make sure you test any recipes that modify printer ACLs very carefully. Always have a way to reset any ACL back to defaults should you make a mistake and need to start again to define the printer ACL. And as ever, you can always manage the ACL using the GUI if you need to!

Getting ready

Run this recipe on the PSRV printer server after you have installed and configured the SalesPrinter1 printer. This recipe uses the SalesPrinter1 printer and creates two new groups, Sales and SalesAdmin, in the AD.

How to do it...

1. Setting up AD for this recipe

```
$ScriptBlock = {
  # 1.1 Creating Sales OU
  $OUHT = @{
    Name = 'Sales'
```

```
            Path = 'DC=Reskit,DC=Org'
        }
        New-ADOrganizationalUnit @OUHT
        # 1.2 Creating Sales Group
        $G1HT = @{
          Name      = 'SalesGroup'
          GroupScope = 'Universal'
          Path      = 'OU=Sales,DC=Reskit,DC=Org'
        }
        New-ADGroup @G1HT
        # 1.3 Creating SalesAdmin Group
         $G2HT = @{
           Name      = 'SalesAdmins'
           GroupScope = 'Universal'
           Path      = 'OU=Sales,DC=Reskit,DC=Org'
         }
         New-ADGroup @G2HT
       }
       # 1.4 Running Script block on DC1
       Invoke-Command -ComputerName DC1 -ScriptBlock $ScripBlock
```

2. Getting the group to allow access

```
$GroupHT1 = @{
    Typename     = 'Security.Principal.NTAccount'
    Argumentlist = 'SalesGroup'
}
$SalesGroup = New-Object @GroupHT1
$GroupHT2 = @{
    Typename     = 'Security.Principal.NTAccount'
    Argumentlist = 'SalesAdmins'
}
$SalesAdminGroup = New-Object @GroupHT2
```

3. Getting the group SIDs

```
$SalesGroupSid =
    $SalesGroup.Translate([Security.Principal.Securityidentifier]).
Value
```

```
$SalesAdminGroupSid =
    $SalesAdminGroup.Translate(
    [Security.Principal.Securityidentifier]).Value
```

4. Defining the SDDL for this printer

    ```
    $SDDL = 'O:BAG:DUD:PAI(A;OICI;FA;;;DA)' +
            "(A;OICI;0x3D8F8;;;$SalesGroupSid)"+
            "(A;;LCSWSDRCWDWO;;;$SalesAdminGroupSid)"
    ```

5. Getting the Sales Group printer object

    ```
    $SGPrinter = Get-Printer -Name SalesPrinter1 -Full
    ```

6. Setting the permissions

    ```
    $SGPrinter | Set-Printer -Permission $SDDL
    ```

7. Viewing the permissions from the GUI.

Check the printer's security settings from the **Settings** applet in Windows.

How it works...

In *step 1*, you create a new OU in the Reskit.Org domain (Sales), then create two new Universal security groups (SalesGroup and SalesAdmins).

In *step 2*, you create two Security.Principal.NTAccount objects with the properties for the two security groups. In *step 3*, you use these two new objects to retrieve the **Security IDs (SIDs)** for each of the groups. In *step 4*, you create a **Security Descriptor Description Language (SDDL)** permission set.

In *step 5*, you use the Get-Printer to return a WMI object that describes the printer. Then in *step 6*, you use Set-Printer to set the ACL for your printer. These first six steps produce no console output.

In *step 7*, you observe the ACL by using the Windows Printer GUI. The output looks like this:

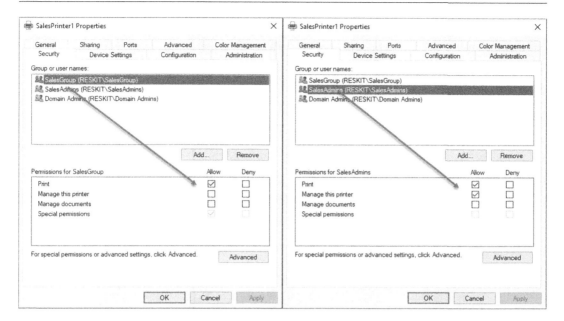

Figure 9.19: Viewing printer security settings

There's more...

In this recipe, you update the ACL for the Sales Group printer `SalesPrinter1`. The recipe uses a .NET object to obtain the SIDs for two security groups. Then you hand-construct the SDDL and apply it to the printer.

Unlike NTFS, there are no third-party printer ACL management tools readily available to simplify the setting of ACLs. SDDL is the default mechanism, but it is not always straightforward. For some details on SDDL, see `https://protect-eu.mimecast.com/s/oCRPC1YnptYWwjHLzb-o?domain=learn.microsoft.com`.

Creating a Printer Pool

Windows allows you to create a *printer pool*, a printer with two or more print devices (each with a separate printer port). With a printer pool, Windows sends a given print job to any of the pool's printers. This feature is helpful in environments where users print large numbers of documents and need the speed additional printers can provide, without asking the user to choose the specific print device.

There are no PowerShell cmdlets to enable you to create a printer pool. Also, WMI does not provide a mechanism to create a printer pool. As with other recipes in this chapter, you use PrintUI. DLL and RunDLL32 to deploy your printer pool. This recipe is another example of utilizing older console applications to achieve your objective.

Getting ready

You run this recipe on PSRV, on which you have set up a new printer, SalesPrinter1.

How to do it...

1. Adding a port for the printer

   ```
   $P = 'SalesPP2' # new printer port name
   Add-PrinterPort -Name $P -PrinterHostAddress 10.10.10.62
   ```

2. Creating the printer pool for SalesPrinter1

   ```
   $Printer = 'SalesPrinter1'
   $P1      = 'SalesPP'   # First printer port
   $P2      = 'SalesPP2'  # Second printer port
   rundll32.exe printui.dll,PrintUIEntry /Xs /n $Printer Portname
   "$P1,$P2"
   ```

3. Viewing the printer pool

   ```
   Get-Printer $Printer |
       Format-Table -Property Name, Type, DriverName, PortName -AutoSize
   ```

How it works...

In *step 1*, you add a new printer port, SalesPP2. In *step 2*, you create a new printer pool by using printui.dll and setting two printer ports. In the final step, *step 3*, you view the output to confirm you have set up a printer pool of two print devices/ports. The output of this final step looks like this:

```
PS C:\Foo> Get-Printer $Printer |
              Format-Table -Property Name, Type, DriverName, PortName -AutoSize

Name           Type  DriverName                PortName
----           ----  ----------                --------
SalesPrinter1  Local Xerox WorkCentre 6515 PCL6 SalesPP,SalesPP2
```

Figure 9.20: Viewing the printer pool

There's more...

In *step 3*, you use the Get-Printer command to retrieve details about the printer to verify you have set up a printer pool. You can also view this pool using the printer GUI, which looks like this:

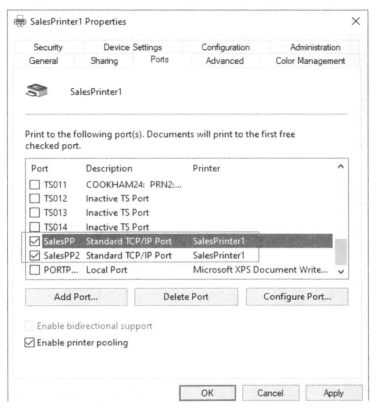

Figure 9.21: Viewing the printer pool from the GUI

Join our community on Discord

Join our community's Discord space for discussions with the author and other readers:

https://packt.link/SecNet

10

Exploring Windows Containers

This chapter covers the following recipes:

- Configuring a container host
- Deploying sample containers
- Deploying IIS in a container
- Using a Dockerfile to create a custom container

Introduction

Containers and container technology have been around on the Linux platform for some time and can also be run on Windows (both Windows 10/11 and Windows Server 2022). Containers can assist in deploying applications. The opensource Docker initiative popularized containers. Windows Server 2022 supports both Docker and Docker containerization integrated with Hyper-V.

With containers in Windows Server 2022, you perform most administration tasks not by using PowerShell cmdlets but by using a command-line tool called docker.exe. For those used to PowerShell's object-oriented and task-focused approach, you may find this application hard to use. I daresay you are not alone. The docker.exe application works in PowerShell, and you can use PowerShell to wrap the command. As ever with command-line tools, you can wrap the command-line application with a PowerShell function to get the benefits of object orientation.

To use containers with Windows Server 2019, you must download and install several components, including container base images. These downloads require an internet connection and are not particularly small. So be sure to have lots of disk space.

Containers provide scalability by enabling you to run multiple containers directly on top of Windows Server 2022. Containers can take up considerably fewer resources than if you run each container in separate **virtual machines (VMs)**. In theory, running multiple containers on a single host could be a security risk because malware could enable bad actors to access the contents of one container from another unfriendly container. To reduce those risks, you can run containers virtualized inside Hyper-V. With Hyper-V containers, Windows runs the container inside a virtualized environment that provides additional hardware-level security, albeit at the price of performance. Hyper-V containers are also useful in a shared tenant environment, where one container host can run containers belonging to different organizations.

By default, you cannot run a container that uses one version of Windows Server within another version of Windows Server. So if you base a container on Windows Server 2019 Server Core, you cannot, by default, run it on top of Windows Server 2022. This does incur a small performance overhead when you start and stop the container. To get around this issue, you can run the container virtualized.

The first step in deploying containers in Windows Server 2022 is configuring your container host, including adding several downloaded components. In the *Configuring a container host* recipe, you configure a host, CH1, to run containers.

Once you have configured a container host, it's a great idea to test that you can run containers successfully. You can download many sample containers to test out the basic container functionality (and the use of docker.exe). You explore and download key base container images and sample containers in the *Deploying sample containers* recipe.

A common application that you can deploy using containers is **Internet Information Server (IIS)**. In the *Deploying IIS in a container* recipe, you download a container base image containing IIS and then run this image inside a container.

You can also build customized container images containing your applications, as seen in the *Using a Dockerfile to create a custom container* recipe.

The recipes in this chapter use the command-line tool docker.exe. For those familiar and comfortable with all of PowerShell's awesomeness, this may come as a bit of a shock. As you can observe, docker.exe has no tab completion, all output is minimal text blobs (no objects), parameter names seem random and curious, the online help is not very helpful, and the error reporting is downright atrocious. All in all, docker.exe takes time to get to grips with, is less easy to automate than other Windows features, and feels very, very slow even on a well-equipped workstation. But if you plan to use the awesome container features in Windows Server, consider spending some time building a good framework and framework tools for your environment. One example is the Get-ContainerImage function you create in the *Deploying IIS in a container* recipe.

It's also worth noting that if you use most major search engines to discover aspects of containers, searches tend to yield many useful pages. However, many pages focus on Linux as a container host and using tools and features not available under Windows. It can be a struggle to find good Windows-based documentation.

There is much more to explore with containers. This chapter only introduces containers, container images, docker.exe, and Dockerfile files. Topics including Docker networking, Docker Swarm, and more are outside the scope of this book. To discover more about containers than we can fit here, look at Packt's book: *Learning Windows Server Containers* by Srikanth Machiraju. And, for more on the endearingly awful docker.exe application, take a look at *Docker on Windows* by Elton Stoneman.

For more information on Windows containers, see this link: https://learn.microsoft.com/ virtualization/windowscontainers/about/

The systems used in the chapter

In this chapter, you configure and manage containers on the Windows Server 2022 host CH1. You have installed PowerShell 7 (and VS Code) on this host. You also need the domain controller and DNS server for the Reskit.Org domain, DC1, online.

The hosts are as follows:

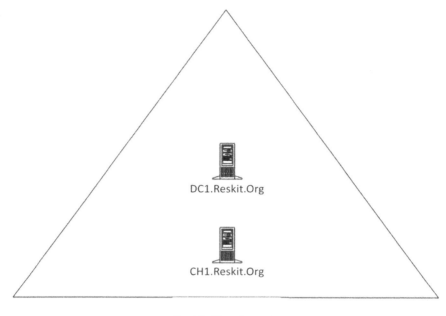

Reskit.Org domain

Figure 10.1: Host in use for this chapter

Configuring a container host

The first step in containerization is to configure a container host. The container host is a Windows system (virtual or physical). You have installed the Windows Server 2022 host with just PowerShell loaded.

Configuring the host requires you to add Windows features and download/install the Docker components you need to manage containers.

You can also run containers on Windows 11, and this recipe would mostly work on that platform but would need some modifications. These changes and containers on Windows 11 are outside the scope of this chapter.

Getting ready

You run this recipe on CH1 after you have installed PowerShell 7 (and VS Code).

How to do it...

1. Installing the Docker provider module

```
$InstallHT1 = @{
  Name       = 'DockerMSFTProvider'
  Repository = 'PSGallery'
  Force      = $True
}
Install-Module @InstallHT1
```

2. Installing the latest version of the Docker package

```
$InstallHT2 = @{
  Name         = 'Docker'
  ProviderName = 'DockerMSFTProvider'
  Force        = $True
}
Install-Package @InstallHT2
```

3. Ensuring that the Hyper-V and related tools are added

```
Add-WindowsFeature -Name Hyper-V -IncludeManagementTools |
  Out-Null
```

4. Removing Defender, as it interferes with Docker

```
Remove-WindowsFeature -Name Windows-Defender |
  Out-Null
```

5. Restarting the computer to enable Docker and containers

```
Restart-Computer
```

6. Checking Windows containers and Hyper-V features are installed on CH1

```
Get-WindowsFeature -Name Containers, Hyper-v
```

7. Checking Docker service

```
Get-Service -Name Docker
```

8. Checking Docker version information

```
docker version
```

9.   Displaying Docker configuration information

```
docker info
```

How it works...

In *step 1*, you download and install the Docker provider module for Windows. This step produces no console output. In *step 2*, you install the latest version of the Docker provider, which produces the following output:

```
PS C:\Foo> # 2. Installing the latest version of the docker package
PS C:\Foo> $InstallHT2 = @{
             Name          = 'Docker'
             ProviderName = 'DockerMSFTProvider'
             Force         = $True
           }
PS C:\Foo> Install-Package @InstallHT2

WARNING: A restart is required to enable the containers feature. Please restart your machine.

Name     Version    Source          Summary
----     -------    ------          -------
Docker   20.10.9    DockerDefault   Contains Docker EE for use with Windows Server.
```

Figure 10.2: Installing the Docker package

In *step 3*, you add the Hyper-V feature to CH1 and add the Hyper-V management tools, producing output like this:

```
PS C:\Foo> # 2. Installing the latest version of the docker package
PS C:\Foo> $InstallHT2 = @{
             Name          = 'Docker'
             ProviderName = 'DockerMSFTProvider'
             Force         = $True
           }
PS C:\Foo> Install-Package @InstallHT2

WARNING: A restart is required to enable the containers feature. Please restart your machine.

Name     Version    Source          Summary
----     -------    ------          -------
Docker   20.10.9    DockerDefault   Contains Docker EE for use with Windows Server.
```

Figure 10.3: Adding Hyper-V Windows Server feature to CH1

The Windows Defender package can interfere with the operation of containers. For that reason, in *step 4,* you remove this feature. To complete the setup of the components added and removed so far, you need to reboot the machine, which you do in *step 5*. These two steps produce no console output.

After rebooting CH1, in *step 6*, you confirm that you have added the containers and Hyper-V features successfully, producing output like this:

```
PS C:\Foo> # 6. Checking Windows Containers and Hyper-V features are installed on CH1
PS C:\Foo> Get-WindowsFeature -Name Containers, Hyper-V

Display Name Name          Install State
------------ ----          -------------
             Hyper-V       Installed
             Containers    Installed
```

Figure 10.4: Checking the Hyper-V and Containers features on CH1

Within Windows Server, the Docker service does much of the work of running containers. In *step 7*, you verify that the Docker service is running. This step produces output like this:

```
PS C:\Foo> # 7. Checking Docker service
PS C:\Foo> Get-Service -Name Docker

Status    Name       DisplayName
------    ----       -----------
Running   Docker     Docker Engine
```

Figure 10.5: Checking the Hyper-V and Containers features on CH1

In *step 8*, you use the docker.exe command to display Docker's version information, with output like this:

```
PS C:\Foo> # 8. Checking Docker Version information
PS C:\Foo> docker version
Client: Mirantis Container Runtime
 Version:           20.10.9
 API version:       1.41
 Go version:        go1.16.12m2
 Git commit:        591094d
 Built:             12/21/2021 21:34:30
 OS/Arch:           windows/amd64
 Context:           default
 Experimental:      true

Server: Mirantis Container Runtime
 Engine:
  Version:          20.10.9
  API version:      1.41 (minimum version 1.24)
  Go version:       go1.16.12m2
  Git commit:       9b96ce992b
  Built:            12/21/2021 21:33:06
  OS/Arch:          windows/amd64
  Experimental:     false
```

Figure 10.6: Checking the Docker version information

In *step 9*, you display the Docker configuration details with output like this:

```
PS C:\Foo> # 9. Displaying Docker configuration information
PS C:\Foo> docker info
Client:
 Context:    default
 Debug Mode: false
 Plugins:
  app: Docker App (Docker Inc., v0.9.1-beta3)
  cluster: Manage Mirantis Container Cloud clusters (Mirantis Inc., v1.9.0)
  registry: Manage Docker registries (Docker Inc., 0.1.0)

Server:
 Containers: 0
  Running: 0
  Paused: 0
  Stopped: 0
 Images: 7
 Server Version: 20.10.9
 Storage Driver: windowsfilter
  Windows:
 Logging Driver: json-file
 Plugins:
  Volume: local
  Network: ics internal l2bridge l2tunnel nat null overlay private transparent
  Log: awslogs etwlogs fluentd gcplogs gelf json-file local logentries splunk syslog
 Swarm: inactive
 Default Isolation: process
 Kernel Version: 10.0 20348 (20348.1.amd64fre.fe_release.210507-1500)
 Operating System: Windows Server 2022 Datacenter Version 2009 (OS Build 20348.169)
 OSType: windows
 Architecture: x86_64
 CPUs: 6
 Total Memory: 4.124GiB
 Name: CH1
 ID: VUDQ:UPUI:ZMI4:G53V:WTFT:VTZK:6YBB:SQI2:K34F:F7OZ:DXW7:NEJ2
 Docker Root Dir: C:\ProgramData\docker
 Debug Mode: false
 Registry: https://index.docker.io/v1/
 Labels:
 Experimental: false
 Insecure Registries:
  127.0.0.0/8
 Live Restore Enabled: false
```

Figure 10.7: Displaying the Docker configuration

There's more...

In *step 2*, you install the DockerMSFTProvider package. This package also has the necessary Windows components to run containers. On Windows Server, this includes the containers Windows feature (as you check in *step 6*).

In *step 5*, you remove Defender. This is a simple fix to avoid issues that can arise when you test this recipe. For production, you should consult the Docker documentation at https://docs.docker.com/engine/security/antivirus/.

Deploying sample containers

Once you have a container host configured, you should check that you have set up your environment successfully and your container host can utilize containers. A really simple way to check that your container host is fully able to run containers is by downloading and running a simple container image. Docker publishes a useful hello-world container image you can use. Or you can download and run one of the standard OS images.

Before you can run a container, you must acquire a container image. There are several ways to obtain images, as you see in this chapter. Using the docker command, you can search and download images either to use directly or to use as the basis of a custom-built container. Docker maintains an online registry that contains a variety of container images for you to leverage.

This recipe demonstrates using the Docker registry to obtain images and then using those images locally. This recipe looks at some basic container management tasks and shows some methods to automate the docker.exe command.

Getting ready

You run this recipe in the container host, CH1. You set up this host in the *Configuring a container host* recipe.

How to do it...

1. Finding hello-world container images at the Docker hub

   ```
   docker search hello-world
   ```

2. Pulling the Docker official hello-world image

   ```
   docker pull hello-world
   ```

3. Checking the image just downloaded

   ```
   docker image ls
   ```

4. Running the hello-world container image

   ```
   docker run hello-world
   ```

5. Getting Server Core base image

   ```
   $ServerCore = 'mcr.microsoft.com/windows/servercore:ltsc2022'
   docker pull $ServerCore
   ```

6. Checking the images available now on CH1

```
docker image ls
```

7. Running the ServerCore container image

```
docker run $ServerCore
```

8. Creating a function to get the Docker image details as objects

```
Function Get-DockerImage {
  # Getting the images
  $Images = docker image ls | Select-Object -Skip 1
  # Regex for getting the fields
  $Regex = '^(\S+)\s+(\S+)\s+(\S+)\s+([ \w]+)\s+(\S+)$'
  # Creating an object for each image and emit
  foreach ($Image in $Images) {
  $image -match $Regex  | Out-Null
  $ContainerHT = [ordered] @{
      Name    = $Matches.1
      Tag     = $Matches.2
      ImageId = $Matches.3
      Created = $Matches.4
      Size    = $Matches.5
    } # end hash table
    New-Object -TypeName pscustomobject -Property $ContainerHT
  } # end foreach
} # end function
```

9. Inspecting ServerCore image

```
$ServerCoreImage = Get-DockerImage | Where-Object name -match
servercore
docker inspect $ServerCoreImage.ImageId | ConvertFrom-Json
```

10. Pulling a Server 2019 container image

```
$Server2019Image = 'mcr.microsoft.com/windows:1809'
docker pull $Server2019Image
```

11. Running older server image

```
docker run $Server2019Image
```

12. Running the image with `isolation`

```
docker run --isolation=hyperv $Server2019Image
```

13. Checking difference in run times with Hyper-V

```
# Running with no isolation
$Start1 = Get-Date
docker run hello-world |
    Out-Null
$End1 = Get-Date
$Time1 = ($End1-$Start1).TotalMilliseconds
# Running with isolation
$Start2 = Get-Date
docker run --isolation=hyperv hello-world | Out-Null
$End2 = get-date
$Time2 = ($End2-$Start2).TotalMilliseconds
# Displaying the time differences
"Without isolation, took : $Time1 milliseconds"
"With isolation, took    : $Time2 milliseconds"
```

14. Viewing system disk usage

```
docker system df
```

15. Viewing active containers

```
docker container ls -a
```

16. Removing active containers

```
$Actives = docker container ls -q -a
foreach ($Active in $actives) {
  docker container rm $Active -f
}
```

17. Removing all Docker images

```
docker rmi $(docker images -q) -f  | Out-Null
```

18. Removing other Docker detritus

```
docker prune -f
```

19. Checking images and containers

```
docker image ls
docker container ls
```

How it works...

In *step 1*, you use the docker.exe search command to find hello-world containers at Docker hub. The output looks like this:

```
PS C:\Foo> # 1. Finding hello-world container images at the Docker Hub
PS C:\Foo> docker search hello-world
NAME                                       DESCRIPTION                                   STARS    OFFICIAL    AUTOMATED
hello-world                                Hello World! (an example of minimal Dockeriz…  1835     [OK]
kitematic/hello-world-nginx                A light-weight nginx container that demonstr…  152
tutum/hello-world                          Image to test docker deployments. Has Apache…  89                   [OK]
dockercloud/hello-world                    Hello World!                                   19                   [OK]
crccheck/hello-world                       Hello World web server in under 2.5 MB         15                   [OK]
vad1mo/hello-world-rest                    A simple REST Service that echoes back all t…  5                    [OK]
ppc64le/hello-world                        Hello World! (an example of minimal Dockeriz…  2
rancher/hello-world                                                                       2
ansibleplaybookbundle/hello-world-db-apb   An APB which deploys a sample Hello World! a…  2                    [OK]
thomaspoignant/hello-world-rest-json       This project is a REST hello-world API to bu…  1
ansibleplaybookbundle/hello-world-apb      An APB which deploys a sample Hello World! a…  1                    [OK]
strimzi/hello-world-consumer                                                              0
armswdev/c-hello-world                     Simple hello-world C program on Alpine Linux…  0
strimzi/hello-world-producer                                                              0
koudaiii/hello-world                                                                      0
businessgeeks00/hello-world-nodejs                                                        0
strimzi/hello-world-streams                                                               0
tacc/hello-world                                                                          0
garystafford/hello-world                   Simple hello-world Spring Boot service for t…  0                    [OK]
freddiedevops/hello-world-spring-boot                                                     0
tsepotesting123/hello-world                                                               0
okteto/hello-world                                                                        0
rsperling/hello-world3                                                                    0
dandando/hello-world-dotnet                                                               0
kevindockercompany/hello-world
```

Figure 10.8: Discovering hello-world container images

In *step 2*, you use the docker.exe command to pull the Docker official hello-world image with output like this:

```
PS C:\Foo> # 2. Pulling the Docker official hello-world image
PS C:\Foo> docker pull hello-world
Using default tag: latest
latest: Pulling from library/hello-world
2ebf439f800c: Pull complete
59d9f62c09b7: Pull complete
d6884bc3f6c7: Pull complete
Digest: sha256:7d246653d0511db2a6b2e0436cfd0e52ac8c066000264b3ce63331ac66dca625
Status: Downloaded newer image for hello-world:latest
docker.io/library/hello-world:latest
```

Figure 10.9: Downloading the hello-world official Docker container from the Docker hub

In *step 3*, you use the docker image command to view the images that reside on CH1, with output like this:

```
PS C:\Foo> # 3. Checking the Image just downloaded
PS C:\Foo> docker image is
REPOSITORY    TAG       IMAGE ID       CREATED       SIZE
hello-world   latest    d4d88879abb0   3 weeks ago   297MB
```

Figure 10.10: Viewing Docker image on CH1

With the container image downloaded, in *step 4*, you run this image in the container to validate your container installation and configuration. The output looks like this:

```
PS C:\Foo> # 4. Running the hello-world container image
PS C:\Foo> docker run hello-world

Hello from Docker!
This message shows that your installation appears to be working correctly.

To generate this message, Docker took the following steps:
 1. The Docker client contacted the Docker daemon.
 2. The Docker daemon pulled the "hello-world" image from the Docker Hub.
    (windows-amd64, nanoserver-ltsc2022)
 3. The Docker daemon created a new container from that image which runs the
    executable that produces the output you are currently reading.
 4. The Docker daemon streamed that output to the Docker client, which sent it
    to your terminal.

To try something more ambitious, you can run a Windows Server container with:
 PS C:\> docker run -it mcr.microsoft.com/windows/servercore:ltsc2022 powershell

Share images, automate workflows, and more with a free Docker ID:
 https://hub.docker.com/

For more examples and ideas, visit:
 https://docs.docker.com/get-started/
```

Figure 10.11: Running the hello-world container image

In *step 5*, you download another container image, a Windows ServerCore image. The output from this step is as follows:

```
PS C:\Foo> # 5. Getting Server Core image base image
PS C:\Foo> docker pull mcr.microsoft.com/windows/servercore:ltsc2022
ltsc2022: Pulling from windows/servercore
97f65a0ec59e: Pull complete
97b25a378238: Pull complete
Digest: sha256:35c3cb29ef2c9f05e36070de4c79d7fc861c035fa5df2df64ae607a276db42c6
Status: Downloaded newer image for mcr.microsoft.com/windows/servercore:ltsc2022
mcr.microsoft.com/windows/servercore:ltsc2022
```

Figure 10.12: Pulling a Windows Server Core container image

In *step 6*, you check the container images on CH1, where you can see the newly downloaded server core container image. The output looks like this:

```
PS C:\Foo> # 6. Checking the images available now on CH1
PS C:\Foo> docker image is
REPOSITORY                                TAG        IMAGE ID        CREATED        SIZE
hello-world                               latest     d4d88879abb0    3 weeks ago    297MB
mcr.microsoft.com/windows/servercore      ltsc2022   5798b78d003a    4 weeks ago    5.08GB
```

Figure 10.13: Listing container images on CH1

In *step 7*, you run the container, returning output like this:

```
PS C:\Foo> # 7. Running the servercore container image
PS C:\Foo> docker run $ServerCore
Microsoft Windows [Version 10.0.20348.887]
(c) Microsoft Corporation. All rights reserved.
```

Figure 10.14: Executing the servercore container image

The docker.exe command produces simple string output, unlike PowerShell cmdlets, which produce rich objects. One way to overcome that limitation is to create objects on the fly using a wrapper function.

In *step 8*, you create a new PowerShell function (Get-DockerImage), which gets the images but returns the information as custom objects. There is no output directly from this step. Within this step, you create a hash table, which you then convert to a custom object. You could have created the object directly – as always you have choices.

In *step 9*, you use the Get-DockerImage function to get a specific container image, then you do a detailed examination of this container image, with output like this:

```
PS C:\Foo> # 9. Inspecting Server Core Image
PS C:\Foo> $ServerCoreImage = Get-DockerImage | Where-Object name -match servercore
PS C:\Foo> docker inspect $ServerCoreImage.ImageId | ConvertFrom-Json
```

```
Id              : sha256:5798b78d003a0eb4c52ddc590a333254e974bdc400f262bd7b4442bb2c6e49a2
RepoTags        : {mcr.microsoft.com/windows/servercore:ltsc2022}
RepoDigests     : {mcr.microsoft.com/windows/servercore@sha256:
                    35c3cb29ef2c9f05e36070d04c79d7fc861c035fa5df2df64ae607a276db42c6}
Parent          :
Comment         :
Created         : 06/08/2022 02:59:35
Container       :
ContainerConfig : @{Hostname=; Domainname=; User=; AttachStdin=False; AttachStdout=False;
                    AttachStderr=False; Tty=False; OpenStdin=False; StdinOnce=False; Env=;
                    Cmd=; Image=; Volumes=; WorkingDir=; Entrypoint=; OnBuild=; Labels=}
DockerVersion   :
Author          :
Config          : @{Hostname=; Domainname=; User=; AttachStdin=False; AttachStdout=False;
                   AttachStderr=False; Tty=False; OpenStdin=False; StdinOnce=False; Env=;
                   Cmd=System.Object[]; Image=; Volumes=;
                   WorkingDir=; Entrypoint=; OnBuild=; Labels=}
Architecture    : amd64
Os              : windows
OsVersion       : 10.0.20348.887
Size            : 5083872027
VirtualSize     : 5083872027
GraphDriver     : @{Data=; Name=windowsfilter}
RootFS          : @{Type=layers; Layers=System.Object[]}
Metadata        : @{LastTagTime=01/01/0001 00:00:00}
```

Figure 10.15: Inspecting the server core image

In *step 10*, you pull a Windows Server image for an older version (Windows Server 2019):

```
PS C:\Foo> # 10. Pulling a Server 2019 container image
PS C:\Foo> $Server2019Image = imcr.microsoft.com/windows:1809'
PS C:\Foo> docker pull $Server2019Image
1809: Pulling from windows
b079fa252589: Pull complete
3100d4854554: Pull complete
Digest: sha256:14241ad3587eb63e81c07e227adfc5b1ee4702d5b047599886fd82144210c479
Status: Downloaded newer image for mcr.microsoft.com/windows:1809
mcr.microsoft.com/windows:1809
```

Figure 10.16: Inspecting the server core image

In *step 11*, you attempt to run this downloaded image with the following output:

```
PS C:\Foo> # 11. Running older server image
PS C:\Foo> docker run $Server2019Image
docker: Error response from daemon: hcsshim::CreateComputeSystem
        3c8495f8debb5bf0cb39d141dbf2ba85c20e4c94b1c465e7228331dacf5de2b3:
        The container operating system does not match the host operating system.
```

Figure 10.17: Running a Windows Server 2019 image natively

Since the Windows kernel in the container host is different from the kernel in the container image, Windows cannot natively run the Windows Server 2019 images. You can work around this by using Hyper-V isolation, like this:

```
PS C:\Foo> # 12. run it with isolation
PS C:\Foo> PS C:\Foo> docker run --isolation=hypery $Server2019Image
Microsoft Windows [Version 10.0.17763.3287]
(c) 2018 Microsoft Corporation. All rights reserved.
```

Figure 10.18: Running a Windows Server 2019 image inside Hyper-V

While Hyper-V isolation can help with incompatible kernel version issues, there is a performance hit with using virtualization. In *step 13*, you run the hello-world container image natively and in Hyper-V. Then the step displays how to Windows run the container with and without virtualization. The output looks like this:

```
PS C:\Foo> # 13. Checking difference in run times with Hyper-V
PS C:\Foo> # Running with no isolation
PS C:\Foo> $Start1 = Get-Date
PS C:\Foo> docker run hello-world | Out-Null
PS C:\Foo> $End1 = Get-Date
PS C:\Foo> $Time1 = ($End1-$Start1).TotalMilliseconds
PS C:\Foo> # Running with isolation
PS C:\Foo> $Start2 = Get-Date
PS C:\Foo> docker run --isolation=hyperv hello-world | Out-Null
PS C:\Foo> $End2 = get-date
PS C:\Foo> $Time2 = ($End2-$Start2).TotalMilliseconds
PS C:\Foo> # Displaying the time differences
PS C:\Foo> "Without isolation, took : $Time1 milliseconds"
PS C:\Foo> "With isolation, took    : $Time2 milliseconds"
Without isolation, took : 2989.7237 milliseconds
With isolation, took    : 5881.3702 milliseconds
```

Figure 10.19: Measuring the performance impact of running a container inside Hyper-V

In *step 14*, you use the docker system command to view the disk usage for containers on CH1 with output like this:

```
PS C:\Foo> # 14. Viewing system disk usage
PS C:\Foo> docker system dF
TYPE            TOTAL      ACTIVE      SIZE        RECLAIMABLE
Images          3          3           21.14GB     0B (0%)
Containers      5          0           0B          0B
Local Volumes   0          0           0B          0B
Build Cache     0          0           0B          0B
```

Figure 10.20: Viewing container image disk space usage

In *step 15*, you view the containers currently active on CH1, with output like this:

```
PS C:\Foo> # 15. Viewing active containers
PS C:\Foo> docker container ls -a
CONTAINER ID   IMAGE                                         COMMAND                 CREATED         STATUS                    PORTS   NAMES
13e6b90c2a2a   hello-world                                   "cmd /C 'type C:\\hel…"  4 minutes ago   Exited (0) 4 minutes ago          dreamy_cannon
8287cd70030b   hello-world                                   "cmd /C 'type C:\\hel…"  4 minutes ago   Exited (0) 4 minutes ago          objective_ardinghelli
6c0cb5e6505f   mcr.microsoft.com/windows:1809                "c:\\windows\\system32…" 8 minutes ago   Exited (0) 7 minutes ago          condescending_hugle
3c8495f8debb   mcr.microsoft.com/windows:1809                "c:\\windows\\system32…" 9 minutes ago   Created                           kind_bassi
c42a3e2b23aa   mcr.microsoft.com/windows/servercore:ltsc2022 "c:\\windows\\system32…" 47 minutes ago  Exited (0) 46 minutes ago         vigilant_swirles
```

Figure 10.21: Viewing active containers on CH1

In *step 16*, you remove all active containers on CH1. In *step 17*, you remove all Docker images from CH1. These two steps produce no console output. In *step 18*, you use the prune command to remove all other Docker-related resources with output like this:

```
PS C:\Foo> # 18. Removing other docker detritus
PS C:\Foo> docker system prune -f
Total reclaimed space: 0B
```

Figure 10.22: Using the Docker prune command

In *step 19*, you verify that you have removed all containers and container images from CH1, with output like this:

```
PS C:\Foo> # 19. Checking images and containers
PS C:\Foo> docker image is

REPOSITORY    TAG        IMAGE ID    CREATED    SIZE

PS C:\Foo> docker container is

CONTAINER ID    IMAGE      COMMAND      CREATED      STATUS      PORTS      NAMES
```

Figure 10.23: Checking on remaining containers and container images

There's more...

In *step 4*, you run the hello-world container you downloaded in *step 2*. When Windows runs this container, the container prints out some text, then exits. These sample container images are a great demonstration that your container host is up, running, and able to host containers.

Docker.exe returns the images on the system as an array of strings (that is, not objects!). The first ($Images[0]) entry is a string of the line of column headers. The next two entries in the $Images array relate to the ServerCore and hello-world images, respectively.

In *step 8*, you create a simple PowerShell function that uses docker.exe to get and return the container images. This function returns the container image details as rich objects, not simple strings. If you are doing a lot of work with docker.exe, consider writing wrapper functions like this to simplify scripting.

In step 10, you download a container whose built-in base OS is a different version from the OS running on the container host (CH1). In step 11, you run it and see an error. You should expect this error. You have two options. The first is to use a more up-to-date container image that matches yours. The other alternative is to use Hyper-V isolation, which works fine, as you see in *step 12*.

In *step 13*, you could have used the measure command to measure how long it took Windows to load and execute the container.

Using Hyper-V isolation has a performance implication that involves the overhead of Hyper-V. But when you use Hyper-V for containers, you can experience a startup performance hit. But once the container is up and running, the hit is not usually significant. Also, using virtualization can provide added security, which may be appropriate, particularly in a shared-hosting environment.

Deploying IIS in a container

A popular containerized application is IIS. Microsoft publishes a container image that contains everything you need to run IIS containerized.

In this recipe, you download and run a container with IIS running and serving web pages.

Getting ready

This recipe uses the CH1 host, which you configured in the *Configuring a container host* recipe.

How to do it...

1. Creating the reskitapp folder

```
$EA = @{ErrorAction='SilentlyContinue'}
New-Item -Path C:\ReskitApp -ItemType Directory @EA
```

2. Creating a web page

```
$FileName = 'C:\Reskitapp\Index.htm'
$Index = @"
<!DOCTYPE html>
<html><head><title>
ReskitApp Container Application</title></head>
<body><p><center><b>
HOME PAGE FOR RESKITAPP APPLICATION</b></p>
Running in a container in Windows Server 2022<p>
</center><br><hr></body></html>
"@
$Index | Out-File -FilePath $FileName
```

3. Getting a server core with an IIS image from the Docker registry

```
$Image = 'mcr.microsoft.com/windows/servercore/iis'
docker pull $Image
```

4. Running the image as a container named rkwebc

```
docker run -d -p80:80 --name rkwebc "$Image"
```

5. Copying the page into the container

```
Set-Location -Path C:\Reskitapp
docker cp .\index.htm rkwebc:c:\inetpub\wwwroot\index.htm
```

6. Viewing the page

```
Start-Process "Http://CH1.Reskit.Org/Index.htm"
```

7. Cleaning up

```
docker rm rkwebc -f | Out-Null
docker image rm  mcr.microsoft.com/windows/servercore/iis |
  Out-Null
```

How it works...

In *step 1*, you create a new folder to hold the new application you are going to create, with output like this:

```
PS C:\Foo> # 1.  Creating the reskitapp folder
PS C:\Foo> $EA = @{ErrorAction='SilentlyContinue'}
PS C:\Foo> New-Item -Path C:\ReskitApp -ItemType Directory @EA


    Directory: C:\

Mode                 LastWriteTime         Length Name
----                 -------------         ------ ----
d----        05/09/2022     16:13                 ReskitApp
```

Figure 10.24: Creating the c:\ReskitApp folder

In *step 2*, you create a simple web page and store it in the `C:\ReskitApp` folder, producing no console output.

In *step 3*, you download a server core image that contains IIS, with output like this:

```
PS C:\Foo> # 3. Getting a server core with IIS image from the Docker registry:
PS C:\Foo> $Image = 'mcr.microsoft.com/windows/servercore/iis'
PS C:\Foo> docker pull $Image
Using default tag: latest
latest: Pulling from windows/servercore/iis
97f65a0ec59e: Pull complete
97b25a378238: Pull complete
7ebd66ebabd1: Pull complete
fa560e2e7835: Pull complete
39278cebafe6: Pull complete
Digest: sha256:d1821f5d785e5e17f4cb4194525dbcb57b7ec2e819d4db4738c14b6f2f2c2ad0
Status: Downloaded newer image for mcr.microsoft.com/windows/servercore/iis:latest
mcr.microsoft.com/windows/servercore/iis:latest
```

Figure 10.25: Pulling a container image with IIS

In *step 4*, you run the container image as a detached (i.e., permanently running) container. This step creates a small bit of console output as follows:

```
PS C:\Foo> # 4. Running the image as a container named rkwebc
PS C:\Foo> docker run -d -p80:80 --name rkwebc "$Image"
244189ade083393e734bf9aff4fb3339e4a6f340922ba812504327255fcaab20
```

Figure 10.26: Running a detached container

Now you have the container running (and running IIS), you can use your browser to connect to the website published by IIS. In *step 5*, you start the browser to view the default home page for the default website, with output like this:

Figure 10.27: Running a detached container

In *step 7*, you clean up by first stopping the container and then removing the IIS container image. This step creates no output.

There's more...

This recipe creates a new web page (in *step 1* and *step 2*) on the CH1 host, then copies that file into the running container (*step 5*). When you run the container, you use port forwarding to instruct Docker to forward port 80 on the container host to port 80 in the container.

With containers, although you do not have IIS loaded on CH1, you can run a container in which IIS is active and provides a website (although, in this case, a default website with no site content).

In this recipe, you use the existing network address/name (that is, of the CH1 host) to access the container's website. You can see another method to push data into a container in the *Using a Dockerfile to create a custom container* recipe.

In *step 5*, you use the docker cp command to copy files from the container host into the container. In this recipe, you only add (and in *step 6*, view) a single page to the existing default website loaded by installing IIS. You can always use the docker exec command to create a new website inside the container and run that, much like you did in the recipes in the IIS chapter. You could also copy all the files and other resources necessary for a rich website, set up SSL, and use host headers to support multiple containers. There are other ways to transfer information between your container and other hosts in your environment. See https://markheath.net/post/transfer-files-docker-windows-containers and take a look at some methods you can use to transfer data into and out of your containers.

In this recipe, you forwarded traffic inbound to port 80 on the container host to port 80 in the container. This is a very simple way to use containers and container networking. You could also create a Docker network and give your container unique IP settings. For more on Docker networking, see the following: http://rafalgolarz.com/blog/2017/04/10/networking_golang_app_with_docker_containers/ and https://docs.docker.com/v17.09/engine/userguide/networking/. You can, as ever, use your search engine to discover more about containers and networking. One thing to keep in mind as you search is that much of the search results relate to running containers on Linux, where the networking stack is quite different and differently managed.

Using a Dockerfile to create a custom container

You can use containers in various ways, depending on your needs. In most cases, you may find it useful to build custom container images, complete with an OS, OS features, and applications. A great way to make your image is to use a Dockerfile containing the instructions for building a new image and then use the docker build command to create a customized container you can then run.

In this recipe, you create a custom container image that provides an IIS website.

Getting ready

In this recipe, you use the container host, CH1, that you set up in the *Configuring a container host* recipe.

How to do it...

1. Creating folder and setting location to the folder on CH1

    ```
    $SitePath = 'C:\RKWebContainer'
    $NewItemHT = @{
      Path        = $SitePath
      ItemType    = 'Directory'
      ErrorAction = 'SilentlyContinue'
    }
    New-Item @NewItemHT | Out-Null
    Set-Location -Path $SitePath
    ```

2. Creating a script to run in the container to create a new site in the container

    ```
    $ScriptBlock = {
    # 2.1 Creating folder in the container
    $SitePath = 'C:\RKWebContainer'
    ```

```powershell
$NewItemHT2 = @{
  Path        = $SitePath
  ItemType    = 'Directory'
  ErrorAction = 'SilentlyContinue'
}
New-Item @NewItemHT2 | Out-Null
Set-Location -Path $NewItemHT2.Path
# 2.1 Creating a page for the site
$PAGE = @'
<!DOCTYPE html>
<html>
<head><title>Main Page for RKWeb.Reskit.Org</title></head>
<body><p><center><b>
Home Page For RKWEB.RESKIT.ORG
</b></p>
Windows Server 2002, Containers, and PowerShell Rock!
</center/</body></html>
'@
$PAGE | OUT-FILE $SitePath\Index.html | Out-Null
#2.2 Creating a new web site in the container that uses Host headers
$WebSiteHT = @{
  PhysicalPath = $SitePath
  Name         = 'RKWeb'
  HostHeader   = 'RKWeb.Reskit.Org'
}
New-Website @WebSiteHT
} # End of script block
# 2.5 Save script block to file
$ScriptBlock | Out-File $SitePath\Config.ps1
```

3. Creating a new a record for our soon to be containerized site

```powershell
Invoke-Command -Computer DC1.Reskit.Org -ScriptBlock {
  $DNSHT = @{
    ZoneName  = 'Reskit.Org'
    Name      = 'RKWeb'
    IpAddress = '10.10.10.221'
  }
```

```
    Add-DnsServerResourceRecordA @DNSHT
}
```

4. Creating Dockerfile

```
$DockerFile = @"
FROM mcr.microsoft.com/windows/servercore/iis
LABEL Description="RKWEB Container" Vendor="PS Partnership"
Version="1.0.0.42"
RUN powershell -Command Add-WindowsFeature Web-Server
RUN powershell -Command GIP
WORKDIR C:\\RKWebContainer
COPY Config.ps1 \Config.ps1
RUN powershell -command ".\Config.ps1"
"@
$DockerFile  | Out-File -FilePath .\Dockerfile -Encoding ascii
```

5. Building the image

```
docker build -t rkwebc .
```

6. Running the image

```
docker run -d --name rkwebc -p 80:80 rkwebc
```

7. Navigating to the container

```
Invoke-WebRequest -UseBasicParsing HTTP://RKweb.Reskit.Org
```

8. Viewing the web page in the browser

```
Start-Process "http://RKWeb.Reskit.Org"
```

9. Testing network connection

```
Test-NetConnection -ComputerName localhost -Port 80
```

10. Cleaning up forcibly

```
docker container rm rkwebc -f
```

How it works...

In *step 1,* you create a new folder to hold a new IIS website and navigate to the folder. In *step 2,* you create a script you later run inside a container to create a new website (within the container). In *step 3,* you run a script block on DC1 that creates a new A record for the containerized website. In *step 4,* you create a Dockerfile that contains the Docker build instructions that enable docker build to create your container image. These four setup steps generate no output.

In *step 5*, you use the Docker command to build your new customized container. The (voluminous) output from this step looks like this:

```
PS C:\RKWebContainer> # 5. Build the Images
PS C:\RKWebContainer> docker build -t rkwebc .
Sending build context to Docker daemon  3.584kB
Step 1/7 : FROM mcr.microsoft.com/windows/servercore/iis
latest: Pulling from windows/servercore/iis
97f65a0ec59e: Pull complete
97b25a378238: Pull complete
7ebd66ebabd1: Pull complete
fa560e2e7835: Pull complete
39278cebafe6: Pull complete
Digest: sha256:d1821f5d785e5e17f4cb4194525dbcb57b7ec2e819d4db4738c14b6f2f2c2ad0
Status: Downloaded newer image for mcr.microsoft.com/windows/servercore/iis:lates
 ---> 8397e926fa67
Step 2/7 : LABEL Description="RKWEB Container" Vendor="PS Partnership" Version="1
 ---> Running in 451b28258dc5
Removing intermediate container 451b28258dc5
 ---> b18bdcdfe1df
Step 3/7 : RUN powershell -Command Add-WindowsFeature Web-Server
 ---> Running in bc01c1831a2e

Success Restart Needed Exit Code     Feature Result
------- -------------- ---------     --------------
True    No             NoChangeNeeded {}

Removing intermediate container bc01c1831a2e
 ---> fbe8fcd9327a
Step 4/7 : RUN powershell -Command GIP
 ---> Running in ae9fa7a4d55c

InterfaceAlias       : vEthernet (Ethernet)
InterfaceIndex       : 21
InterfaceDescription : Hyper-V Virtual Ethernet Container Adapter
IPv4Address          : 172.26.216.230
IPv6DefaultGateway   :
IPv4DefaultGateway   : 172.26.208.1
DNSServer            : 172.26.208.1
                       10.10.10.10

Removing intermediate container ae9fa7a4d55c
 ---> f87f6d9a3836
Step 5/7 : WORKDIR C:\\RKWebContainer
 ---> Running in baee270860dd
Removing intermediate container baee270860dd
 ---> 15c07d026d4a
Step 6/7 : COPY Config.ps1 \Config.ps1
 ---> a2c8e08456d6
Step 7/7 : RUN powershell -command ".\Config.ps1"
 ---> Running in 7382f69c7cda

Name      ID   State   Physical Path          Bindings
----      --   -----   -------------          --------
RKWeb     1299 Started C:\RKWebContainer      http *:80:RKWeb
          8361                                .Reskit.Org
          53

Removing intermediate container 7382f69c7cda
 ---> 8e710ffdf906
Successfully built 8e710ffdf906
Successfully tagged rkwebc:latest
```

Figure 10.28: Running a detached container

In *step 6*, you run a detached container with your new customized container image, producing output like this:

```
PS C:\RKWebContainer> # 6. Running the image
PS C:\RKWebContainer> docker run -d --name rkwebc -p 80:80 rkwebc
e48e53b8bd46e7ca86991ca7c161b57037df3e2dc2989f44946a8d03942865ba
```

Figure 10.29: Running a detached container

In *step 7*, you use the Invoke-WebRequest command to get the web page from the container. This step produces output like this:

```
PS C:\RKWebContainer> # 7. Navigating to the container
PS C:\RKWebContainer> Invoke-WebRequest -UseBasicParsing HTTP://RKweb.Reskit.Org

StatusCode        : 200
StatusDescription : OK
Content           : yp<!DOCTYPE html>
                    <html>
                    <head><title>Main Page for RKWeb.Reskit.Org</title></head>
                    <body><p><cen...
RawContent        : HTTP/1.1 200 OK
                    Accept-Ranges: bytes
                    ETag: "bae994ef43c1d81:0"
                    Server: Microsoft-IIS/10.0
                    Date: Mon, 05 Sep 2022 16:44:23 GMT
InputFields       : {}
Links             : {}
RawContentLength  : 416
RelationLink      : {}
```

Figure 10.30: Getting the web page from the container

In *step 8*, you view the web page from the containerized website within the browser, with output like this:

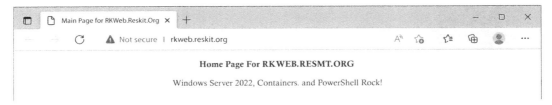

Figure 10.31: Getting the web page from the container

In *step 9*, you view the network connection to port 80 on the local host. Docker binds this local port to port 80 in the container. The output from this step looks like this:

```
PS C:\RKWebContainer> # 9. Testing network connection
PS C:\RKWebContainer> Test-NetConnection -ComputerName localhost -Port 80

ComputerName     : localhost
RemoteAddress    : 127.0.0.1
RemotePort       : 80
InterfaceAlias   : Loopback Pseudo-Interface 1
SourceAddress    : 127.0.0.1
TcpTestSucceeded : True
```

Figure 10.32: Viewing port 80 on the local host

In the final step in this recipe, *step 10*, you stop and close the container producing no output.

There's more...

In this recipe, you use a base container image that you have to download from the Docker registry (mcr.microsoft.com/windows/servercore/iis). Then, you build a container that has the web server feature added and in which you can run the Config.ps1 file to configure the container to run your website. For more information on Dockerfiles, see this link: https://docs.docker.com/engine/reference/builder/

Join our community on Discord

Join our community's Discord space for discussions with the author and other readers:

https://packt.link/SecNet

11

Managing Hyper-V

This chapter covers the following recipes:

- Installing Hyper-V inside Windows Server
- Creating a Hyper-V VM
- Using PowerShell Direct
- Using Hyper-V VM groups
- Configuring the VM hardware
- Configuring VM networking
- Implementing nested virtualization
- Managing a VM's state
- Managing storage movement
- Configuring VM replication
- Managing VM checkpoints
- Clustering Hyper-V servers

Introduction

Hyper-V is Microsoft's **virtual machine (VM)** hypervisor. Microsoft has made Hyper-V available in all versions of Windows Server 2022 and the Enterprise, Professional, and Education editions of Windows 11. Windows Server 2022 and Windows 11 include Hyper-V as an option you can install.

Microsoft first released Hyper-V with Server 2008 and has improved it significantly with each successive version of Windows Server. Improvements include features, support for the latest hardware, and significantly increased scalability.

A useful feature of Hyper-V is nested virtualization, the ability to run Hyper-V inside a Hyper-V VM. Nested virtualization has some good use cases, such as in training. You could give each student a VM on a large blade containing the VMs needed for the course labs. Nested virtualization also provides an additional layer of security that might be useful in multi-tenant scenarios.

Microsoft previously shipped a free version of Hyper-V, Microsoft Hyper-V Server. Hyper-V Server runs VMs with no GUI. You configure and manage it remotely using recipes like the ones in this chapter. The product was free, although you did need to license any guest VMs. For Server 2022, Microsoft has dropped this. You can now only use Hyper-V inside Windows 11 or Windows Server.

This chapter starts with installing and configuring the Hyper-V feature. After installing Hyper-V, you will go on to create a VM, `PSDirect`, which requires you to download an ISO image of Windows Server from the internet.

After you create the `PSDirect` VM, you will use the VM. You will use PowerShell Direct to set up a remoting session into a VM without a network connection. You will also configure the VM's hardware and networking capability. You will then use the PowerShell cmdlets to manage the state of the VM.

Hyper-V allows you to move a VM and/or a VM's storage between Hyper-V hosts. For disaster recovery, you can replicate a running VM (and use that replica should the primary VM fail).

You can take snapshots, or checkpoints, of a VM to save a VM's state and restore your VM to that point, as you will see in the *Managing VM Checkpoints* recipe.

The systems used in the chapter

This chapter uses two Hyper-V host systems, `HV1` and `HV2` – both domain-joined servers in the `Reskit.Org` domain. You will also use a domain-joined host, `SRV1`. Finally, you will make use of a domain controller in the domain (`DC1`), so that host must be online as well. The hosts used in this chapter are as shown here:

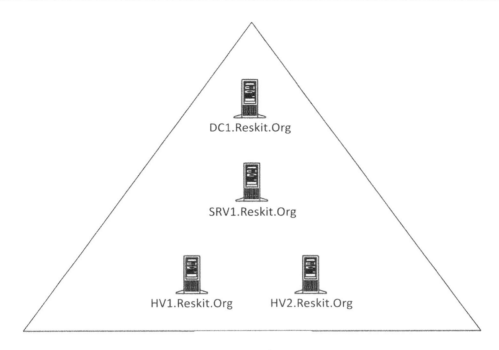

Figure 11.1: Hosts in use for this chapter

Installing Hyper-V inside Windows Server

In Windows Server, Hyper-V is a Windows feature you can add using the Install-WindowsFeature cmdlet. You also have the choice of whether to add the Hyper-V management tools. These tools include the Hyper-V Manager GUI tool and the PowerShell cmdlets that you will use in this chapter.

Once you have installed Hyper-V, you must reboot to complete the installation. Once fully installed, you can configure Hyper-V and the Hyper-V VMs using PowerShell, as you will see in later recipes in this chapter. One configuration setting you may wish to set initially is the location Hyper-V should use to store, by default, both the VM details and where to store the **Virtual Hard Disks** (**VHDs**). Another configuration setting you can make is to specify **Non-Uniform Memory Address** (**NUMA**) topology for the VM host. For more details on NUMA in Hyper-V, see: https://petri.com/customize-non-uniform-memory-access-numa-configuration-of-vm/#:~:text=You%20can%20find%20the%20NUMA%20topology%20settings%20if,machine%20starts%20up.%20You%20can%20customize%20three%20settings.

Getting ready

You should run this recipe on HV1 after you have installed PowerShell 7. You must also have HV2 online and configured.

How to do it...

1. Installing the Hyper-V feature on HV1, HV2

```
$InstallSB = {
  Install-WindowsFeature -Name Hyper-V -IncludeManagementTools
}
Invoke-Command -ComputerName HV1, HV2 -ScriptBlock $InstallSB
```

2. Rebooting the servers to complete the installation

```
Restart-Computer -ComputerName HV2 -Force
Restart-Computer -ComputerName HV1 -Force
```

3. Creating a PSSession with both HV Servers (after reboot)

```
$Sessions = New-PSSession HV1, HV2
```

4. Creating and setting the location for the VMs and VHDs on HV1 and HV2

```
$ConfigSB1 = {
    New-Item -Path C:\VM -ItemType Directory -Force |
        Out-Null
    New-Item -Path C:\VM\VHDS -ItemType Directory -Force |
        Out-Null
    New-Item -Path C:\VM\VMS -ItemType Directory -force |
        Out-Null
}
Invoke-Command -ScriptBlock $ConfigSB1 -Session $Sessions |
  Out-Null
```

5. Setting default paths for the Hyper-V VM disk/config information

```
$ConfigSB2 = {
  $VHDS = 'C:\VM\VHDS'
  $VMS  = 'C:\VM\VMS'
  Set-VMHost -ComputerName Localhost -VirtualHardDiskPath $VHDS
  Set-VMHost -ComputerName Localhost -VirtualMachinePath $VMS
}
Invoke-Command -ScriptBlock $ConfigSB2 -Session $Sessions
```

6. Setting NUMA spanning

```
$ConfigSB3 = {
  Set-VMHost -NumaSpanningEnabled $true
}
Invoke-Command -ScriptBlock $ConfigSB3 -Session $Sessions
```

7. Setting EnhancedSessionMode

```
$ConfigSB4 = {
 Set-VMHost -EnableEnhancedSessionMode $true
}
Invoke-Command -ScriptBlock $ConfigSB4 -Session $Sessions
```

8. Setting host resource metering on HV1, HV2

```
$ConfigSB5 = {
 $RMInterval = New-TimeSpan -Hours 0 -Minutes 15
 Set-VMHost -ResourceMeteringSaveInterval $RMInterval
}
Invoke-Command -ScriptBlock $ConfigSB5 -Session $Sessions
```

9. Reviewing key VM host settings

```
$CheckVMHostSB = {
  Get-VMHost
}
$Properties = 'Name', 'V*Path','Numasp*', 'Ena*','RES*'
Invoke-Command -Scriptblock $CheckVMHostSB -Session $Sessions |
  Format-Table -Property $Properties
```

How it works...

In *step 1*, you install the Hyper-V feature to both HV1 and HV2. The output from this step looks like this:

```
PS C:\Foo> # 1. Installing the Hyper-V feature on HV1, HV2
PS C:\Foo> $InstallSB = {
              Install-WindowsFeature -Name Hyper-V -IncludeManagementTools
           }
PS C:\Foo> Invoke-Command -ComputerName HV1, HV2 -ScriptBlock $InstallSB

PSComputerName : HV2
RunspaceId     : 628a05c7-b80b-40e4-8feb-d5bdb93c694d
Success        : True
RestartNeeded  : Yes
FeatureResult  : {Hyper-V, Hyper-V Module for Windows PowerShell,
                 Hyper-V GUI Management Tools, Remote Server Administration Tools,
                 Hyper-V Management Tools, Role Administration Tools}
ExitCode       : SuccessRestartRequired

WARNING: You must restart this server to finish the installation process

PSComputerName : HV1
RunspaceId     : 3f0df3e9-33bd-4cbb-9b5e-63454533d361
Success        : True
RestartNeeded  : Yes
FeatureResult  : {Hyper-V, Hyper-V Module for Windows PowerShell,
                 Hyper-V GUI Management Tools, Remote Server Administration Tools,
                 Hyper-V Management Tools, Role Administration Tools}
ExitCode       : SuccessRestartRequired
```

Figure 11.2: Installing Hyper-V on HV1 and HV2

To complete the installation of Hyper-V, in *step 2*, you reboot both HV1 and HV2. This step creates no output but does reboot both hosts.

After rebooting HV1 and HV2, you log back into the host using Reskit/Administrator. In *step 3*, you create two new PowerShell remoting sessions for HV1 and HV2. In *step 4*, you use the remoting sessions to create new folders for HV1 and HV2 to hold the Hyper-V VMs and Hyper-V virtual disks. In *step 5*, you configure Hyper-V on both hosts to use these new locations to store the VMs and virtual drives, and in *step 6,* you specify that the host should support NUMA spanning. Then, in *step 7*, you set EnhancedSessionMode to improve VM connections using the VMConnect.exe application. Finally, in *step 8*, you set the two Hyper-V hosts to use resource metering. These six steps produce no console output.

In *step 9*, you review the key Hyper-V host settings on your two Hyper-V hosts, with output like this:

```
PS C:\Foo> # 9. Reviewing key VM host settings
PS C:\Foo> $CheckVMHostSB = {
               Get-VMHost
           }
PS C:\Foo> $Properties = 'Name', 'V*Path','Numasp*', 'Ena*','RES*'
PS C:\Foo> Invoke-Command -Scriptblock $CheckVMHostSB -Session $Sessions |
               Format-Table -Property $Properties

Name VirtualHardDiskPath VirtualMachinePath NumaSpanningEnabled EnableEnhancedSessionMode ResourceMeteringSaveInterval
---- ------------------- ------------------ ------------------- ------------------------- ----------------------------
HV2  C:\VM\VHDS          C:\VM\VMS                 True                    True 01:00:00
HV1  C:\VM\VHDS          C:\VM\VMS                 True                    True 01:00:00
```

Figure 11.3: Viewing Hyper-V settings on HV1 and HV2

There's more...

In *step 1*, you install the Hyper-V feature on two servers. You can only do this successfully if your host supports the necessary virtualization capabilities and you have enabled them in your system's BIOS. To ensure that your system supports Hyper-V, see this link: http://mikefrobbins.com/2012/09/06/use-powershell-to-check-for-processor-cpu-second-level-address-translation-slat-support/. Additionally, double-check that you have enabled virtualization in the VM host's BIOS before running this step.

In *step 2*, you restart both servers. Install-WindowsFeature (used in *step 1*) can restart the servers automatically by using the -Restart switch. In automation terms, this would mean that the system starts rebooting before the remote script completes, which could cause Invoke-Command to error out. The recipe avoids this by not rebooting after installing the Hyper-V features. You then reboot the host in a controlled way in a later step. Once you complete the restart, your script can carry on managing the servers.

In *steps 4* through *step 8,* you set up one aspect of the VM hosts in each step. You could have combined these steps and just called Set-VMHost once with all Hyper-V server properties specified.

See also

You can find more information on some of the Hyper-V features used in this recipe (details of which are outside the scope of this book) as follows:

Features	Links for more information
Connecting to a VM, including enhanced session mode	https://learn.microsoft.com/windows-server/virtualization/hyper-v/learn-more/hyper-v-virtual-machine-connect

Understanding the hard disk options	`https://www.altaro.com/hyper-v/understanding-working-vhdx-files/`
Hyper-V and NUMA	`https://blogs.technet.microsoft.com/pracheta/2014/01/22/numa-understand-it-its-usefulness-with-windows-server-2012/`
Configuring Hyper-V resource metering	`https://redmondmag.com/articles/2013/08/15/hyper-v-resource-metering.aspx`

Creating a Hyper-V VM

Creating a Hyper-V VM is relatively straightforward and consists of simple steps. First, you need to create the VM itself inside your Hyper-V host. Then, you create the VM's virtual hard disk and add it to the VM. You may also wish to adjust the number of processors and memory for the VM and set the VM's DVD drive contents. Once you have created your VM, you need to install the VM's **Operating System (OS)**. You have numerous options for deploying Windows (or Linux) in a Hyper-V VM.

Windows Assessment and Deployment Kit, a free product from Microsoft, contains various tools to assist in the automation of deploying Windows. These include **Deployment Image Servicing and Management (DISM)**, **Windows Imaging and Configuration Designer (Windows ICD)**, **Windows System Image Manager (Windows SIM)**, **User State Migration Tool (USMT)**, and a lot more. For more information on the tools and deploying Windows, see `https://learn.microsoft.com/en-us/windows/deployment/windows-deployment-scenarios-and-tools`.

Another way to install the OS into a VM is to create the VM (either with PowerShell or Hyper-V Manager) and attach the OS's ISO image to the VM's DVD drive. After starting the VM, you do a manual installation, and once you complete the OS installation, you can use the recipes in this book to configure the server to your needs.

In this recipe, you will create a VM, `PSDirect`. Initially, this has a VM name of `PSDirect` but a Windows-assigned hostname. In a later recipe, you will change this hostname to `Wolf`. In building the VM, you assign the Windows Server 2022 DVD to the VM's DVD drive. This step ensures that Windows commences the GUI setup process when you start the VM. The result should be a fully installed OS inside the VM. The details of performing the actual installation are outside the scope of this recipe.

There are two minor issues with using the GUI to install Windows Server 2022. Firstly, the Windows setup process randomly generates a machine name. Secondly, the VM is set up as a workgroup computer and not joined to the domain. You can easily script both renaming the server and joining the domain to the VM. The scripts used to generate the VM farm used in this book are examples of deploying Windows Server 2022 in a more automated fashion using a SETUP.XML file that specifies the installation's details. The scripts that create the VMs used are available online at GitHub. See https://github.com/doctordns/ReskitBuildScripts for the scripts and documentation on them.

Getting ready

You need to run this recipe on the VM host HV1 you created in the *Installing Hyper-V inside Windows Server* recipe. You also need the Windows Server ISO image. For testing purposes, this could be an evaluation version or a complete retail edition – and for this chapter, you could use an image of Windows Server 2022. To get an evaluation version of Windows Server, visit the Microsoft Evaluation Center at https://www.microsoft.com/evalcenter/evaluate-windows-server-2022.

You can also download an ISO of the latest preview copy of Windows Server and use ISO when installing the VM. See https://www.microsoft.com/en-us/software-download/windowsinsiderpreviewserver for preview build downloads, and https://techcommunity.microsoft.com/t5/windows-server-insiders/bd-p/WindowsServerInsiders for more information about Windows Insider builds. For this, you need to be a member of the Windows Insider program – membership is free. For more details on getting started with the Windows Insider program, see https://learn.microsoft.com/windows-insider/get-started.

How to do it...

1. Setting up the VM name and paths for this recipe

```
$VMName      = 'PSDirect'
$VMLocation  = 'C:\VM\VMS'
$VHDlocation = 'C:\VM\VHDS'
$VhdPath     = "$VHDlocation\PSDirect.Vhdx"
$ISOPath     = 'C:\Builds\en_windows_server_x64.iso'
If ( -not (Test-Path -Path $ISOPath -PathType Leaf)) {
  Throw "Windows Server ISO DOES NOT EXIST"
}
```

2. Creating a new VM

```
New-VM -Name $VMName -Path $VMLocation -MemoryStartupBytes 1GB
```

3. Creating a virtual disk file for the VM

```
New-VHD -Path $VhdPath -SizeBytes 128GB -Dynamic | Out-Null
```

4. Adding the virtual hard disk to the VM

```
Add-VMHardDiskDrive -VMName $VMName -Path $VhdPath
```

5. Setting ISO image in the VM's DVD drive

```
$IsoHT = @{
  VMName           = $VMName
  ControllerNumber = 1
  Path             = $ISOPath
}
Set-VMDvdDrive @IsoHT
```

6. Starting the VM

```
Start-VM -VMname $VMName
```

7. Viewing the VM

```
Get-VM -Name $VMName
```

How it works...

In *step 1*, you specify the VMs and the locations of the VMs' hard disk and assign them to variables. You also check to ensure that the Windows Server ISO is in the correct place with the correct name. Assuming the ISO exists and you have named it correctly, this step produces no output. If the step fails to find the file, it aborts with a suitable error message. Depending on which Windows Server 2022 ISO image you get and from where, the filename may vary. You can either change the filename on the disk to match this step or change the script.

In *step 2*, you create a new VM using the New-VM cmdlet, with output that looks like this:

```
PS C:\Foo> # 2.  Creating a new VM
PS C:\Foo> New-VM -Name $VMName -Path $VMLocation -MemoryStartupBytes 1GB

Name      State CPUUsage(%) MemoryAssigned(M) Uptime   Status             
----      ----- ----------- ----------------- ------   ------             
PSDirect  Off   0           0                 00:00:00 Operating normally 10.0
```

Figure 11.4: Creating a new VM

In *step 3*, you create a virtual disk file for the VM and add this VHDX to the PSDirect VM in *step 4*. In *step 5*, you add the ISO image to the PSDirect VM, and then, in *step 6*, you start the VM. These four steps generate no output.

In the final step in this recipe, you use Get-VM to view the VM details, producing output like this:

```
PS C:\Foo> # 7. Viewing the VM
PS C:\Foo> Get-VM –Name $VMName

Name      State    CPUUsage(%) MemoryAssigned(M) Uptime          Status            Version
----      -----    ----------- ----------------- ------          ------            -------
PSDirect  Running  4           1024              00:00:21.8460000 Operating normally 10.0
```

Figure 11.5: Viewing the new Hyper-V VM

There's more…

In *step 1*, you specify the name of the ISO image for Windows Server 2022. Depending on which image you are using, the filename of the ISO you download may be different. Either adjust the filename to match this step or change it to match the ISO's filename. You can find ISO images for evaluation versions at the Microsoft Evaluation Center for released versions of Windows Server. If you like living in the fast lane, consider using a Windows Insider preview build.

In *step 2*, you create a new VM. Although this step should succeed, you cannot run this VM yet, as you need to define at least one virtual hard disk to use with the VM. You will carry out these configuration steps in subsequent steps.

Once you start the VM, in *step 6*, the VM runs and completes Windows Server's installation. To complete the installation of Windows Server, you need to use the GUI. For this chapter's purposes, accept all the installation defaults and ensure that you set the Administrator password to Pa$$w0rd. As with all the passwords used in this book, feel free to use whatever passwords you wish – but ensure that you don't forget them later.

Using PowerShell Direct

PowerShell Direct is a Hyper-V feature that allows you to open PowerShell remoting sessions to a VM without a network connection. This feature enables you to create a PowerShell remoting session to a VM to fix issues, such as networking misconfiguration. You can't fix the issue without a working network connection to the VM, but until you fix the issue, you cannot make a connection to the VM. A "Catch-22" situation. With PowerShell Direct, you can create a remoting session in the VM, as seen in this recipe.

Getting ready

This recipe uses HV1, a Windows Server Datacenter host on which you have installed the Hyper-V feature. You should have also created a VM of Windows Server called PSDirect. This recipe demonstrates how to use PowerShell Direct, so it doesn't matter which version of Windows Server you install so long as it is Windows Server 2016 or later (and you complete the installation of the OS inside the PSDirect VM).

You will run the final steps of this recipe on DC1, showing how to connect to a VM remotely from the Hyper-V host.

How to do it...

1. Creating a credential object for Reskit\Administrator

```
$Admin = 'Administrator'
$PS    = 'Pa$$w0rd'
$RKP   = ConvertTo-SecureString -String $PS -AsPlainText -Force
$Cred  = [System.Management.Automation.PSCredential]::New(
            $Admin, $RKP)
```

2. Viewing the PSDirect VM

```
Get-VM -Name PSDirect
```

3. Invoking a command on the VM specifying the VM name

```
$CommandHT = @{
  VMName      = 'PSDirect'
  Credential  = $Cred
  ScriptBlock = {HOSTNAME.EXE}
}
Invoke-Command @CommandHT
```

4. Invoking a command based on the VMID

```
$VMID = (Get-VM -VMName PSDirect).VMId.Guid
Invoke-Command -VMid $VMID -Credential $Cred  -ScriptBlock
{ipconfig}
```

5. Entering a PS remoting session with the PSDirect VM

```
Enter-PSSession -VMName PSDirect -Credential $Cred
```

```
Get-CimInstance -Class Win32_ComputerSystem
Exit
```

Run the rest of this recipe from DC1.

6. Creating credential for PSDirect on DC1

```
$Admin = 'Administrator'
$PS    = 'Pa$$w0rd'
$RKP   = ConvertTo-SecureString -String $PS -AsPlainText -Force
$Cred  = [System.Management.Automation.PSCredential]::New(
             $Admin, $RKP)
```

7. Creating a remoting session to HV1 (Hyper-V host)

```
$RemoteSession = New-PSSession -ComputerName HV1 -Credential $Cred
```

8. Entering an interactive session with HV1

```
Enter-PSSession $RemoteSession
```

9. Creating credentials for PSDirect inside HV1

```
$Admin = 'Administrator'
$PS    = 'Pa$$w0rd'
$RKP   = ConvertTo-SecureString -String $PS -AsPlainText -Force
$Cred  = [System.Management.Automation.PSCredential]::New(
             $Admin, $RKP)
```

10. Entering and using the remoting session inside PSDirect

```
$PSDRS = New-PSSession -VMName PSDirect -Credential $Cred
Enter-PSSession -Session $PSDRS
HOSTNAME.EXE
```

11. Closing sessions

```
Exit-PSSession  # exits from session to PSDirect
Exit-PSSession  # exits from session to HV1
```

How it works...

In *step 1*, you create a PowerShell credential object. You use this object later in this recipe to enable a connection to the PSDirect VM. This step creates no output.

In *step 2*, you use the Get-VM cmdlet to view the PSDirect VM with output like this:

```
PS C:\Foo> # 2. Viewing the PSDirect VM
PS C:\Foo> Get-VM -Name PSDirect

Name      State   CPUUsage(%) MemoryAssigned(M) Uptime              Status             Version
----      -----   ----------- ----------------- ------              ------             -------
PSDirect Running 0            1024              02:18:03.4980000 Operating normally 10.0
```

Figure 11.6: Viewing the PSDirect Hyper-V VM

In *step 3*, you use Invoke-Command to run the hostname command in the PSDirect VM, with output like this:

```
PS C:\Foo> # 3. Invoking a command on the VM specifying VM name
PS C:\Foo> $CommandHT = @{
             VMName      = 'PSDirect'
             Credential  = $Cred
             ScriptBlock = {HOSTNAME.EXE}
           }
PS C:\Foo> Invoke-Command @CommandHT
WIN-LRBCORRT59T
```

Figure 11.7: Checking the hostname of the PSDirect VM

In *step 4*, you invoke a command inside the PSDirect VM, but using the VM's GUID, with output like this:

```
PS C:\Foo> # 4. Invoking a command based on VMID
PS C:\Foo> $VMID = (Get-VM -VMName PSDirect).VMId.Guid
PS C:\Foo> Invoke-Command -VMid $VMID -Credential $Cred  -ScriptBlock {ipconfig}

Windows IP Configuration


Ethernet adapter Ethernet:

   Media State . . . . . . . . . . . : Media disconnected
   Connection-specific DNS Suffix  . :
```

Figure 11.8: Checking the hostname of the PSDirect VM by VM GUID

In *step 5*, you use the Enter-PSSession command to enter an interactive session with the PSDirect VM. Inside the remoting session, you run Get-CimInstance to return details of the computer system of the VM. The output should look like this:

```
PS C:\Foo> # 5. Entering a PS remoting session with the psdirect VM
PS C:\Foo> Enter-PSSession -VMName PSDirect -Credential $Cred
[PSDirect]: PS C:\Users\Administrator\Documents> Get-CimInstance -Class Win32_ComputerSystem

Name            PrimaryOwnerName Domain    TotalPhysicalMemory Model           Manufacturer
----            ---------------- ------    ------------------- -----           ------------
WIN-LKBCORRT59T Windows User     WORKGROUP 1073270784          Virtual Machine Microsoft Corporation

[PSDirect]: PS C:\Users\Administrator\Documents> Exit
```

Figure 11.9: Entering a PS remoting session with the PSDirect VM

Now that you have created a working VM in HV1, you run the remainder of the VM setup steps remotely on DC1. In *step 6*, you create a credential object. In *step 7*, you use this credential object to create a PowerShell remoting session from DC1 to the Hyper-V host (HV1). These two steps produce no console output.

In *step 8*, you enter a remoting session with HV1. Inside the remoting session (effectively on HV1), you create a PSDirect-based remoting session with the PSDirect VM, with output like this:

```
PS C:\Foo> # 8. Entering an interactive session with HV1
PS C:\Foo> Enter-PSSession $RS
[HV1]: PS C:\Users\Administrator\Documents>
```

Figure 11.10: Using the remoting session on HV1

In *step 9*, you create a credential object for the PSDirect VM, generating no output. Then, in *step 10*, you enter the remote session to the PSDirect VM using the credential object and run the HOSTNAME.EXE command. The result of this step looks like this:

```
[HV1]: PS C:\Users\Administrator\Documents> # 10. Entering and using the remoting session inside PSDirect
[HV1]: PS C:\Users\Administrator\Documents> $PSDRS = New-PSSession -VMName PSDirect -Credential $Cred
[HV1]: PS C:\Users\Administrator\Documents> Enter-PSSession -Session $PSDRS
[HV1]: [PSDirect]: PS C:\Users\Administrator\Documents> HOSTNAME.EXE
WIN-LRBCORRT59T
[HV1]: [PSDirect]: PS C:\Users\Administrator\Documents>
```

Figure 11.11: Running HOSTNAME.EXE in session to PSDirect from HV1

In the final step in this recipe, *step 11*, you exit the interactive sessions on the PSDirect and HV1 VMs. The output from this step looks like this:

```
[HV1]: [PSDirect]: PS C:\Users\Administrator\Documents> # 11. Closing sessions
[HV1]: [PSDirect]: PS C:\Users\Administrator\Documents> Exit-PSSession  # exits from session to PSDirect
[HV1]: PS C:\Users\Administrator\Documents> Exit-PSSession  # exits from session to HV1
PS C:\Foo>
```

Figure 11.12: Exiting the remoting sessions

There's more...

In *step 3*, you use PowerShell Direct to enter a VM session and run a command. Assuming you installed Windows in the PSDirect VM using a supported version of Windows, the setup process generates a random machine name. This machine name is different for each installation; therefore, the machine name of the host in your VM is certain to be different.

In *step 4*, you use the PowerShell Direct feature to run a command inside the PSDirect VM. As you can see from the output in *Figure 12.8*, the NIC for this VM is disconnected. Once inside this remote session, you can use the normal Windows Server troubleshooting tools to view and restore networking.

In *step 6*, you create and later use a credential object. Since HV1 is already domain-joined, this is not, strictly speaking, necessary.

Using Hyper-V VM groups

Hyper-Vs VM groups allow you to group VMs for automation. There are two types of VM groups you can create, VMCollectionType and ManagementCollectionType:

- A VMCollectionType VM group contains VMs.
- A ManagementCollectionType VM group contains VMCollectionType VM groups.

You might have two VMCollectionType VM groups, SQLAccVMG (which contains the SQLAcct1, SQLAcct2, and SQLAcct3 VMs), and a group, SQLMfgVMG, that contains the SQLMfg1 and SQLMfg2 VMs. You could create a ManagementCollectionType VM group, VM-All, containing the two VMCollectionType VM groups.

The VMGroup feature feels incomplete. For example, no -VMGroup parameters exist on any of the Hyper-V cmdlets. Thus, you can't easily execute any Hyper-V commands on all the members of a VM group, and having two types of groups seems confusing and possibly unhelpful. That said, this feature could be useful for large VM hosts running hundreds of VMs, if only from an organizational perspective.

Getting ready

You will run this recipe on the HV2, a Windows Server 2022 server with the added Hyper-V feature. You configured this host in the *Installing Hyper-V inside Windows Server* recipe.

How to do it...

1. Creating five VMs on HV2

```
$VMLocation = 'C:\Vm\VMs'    # Created in earlier recipe
# Create SQLAcct1
$VMN1        = 'SQLAcct1'
New-VM -Name $VMN1 -Path "$VMLocation\$VMN1"
# Create SQLAcct2
$VMN2        = 'SQLAcct2'
New-VM -Name $VMN2 -Path "$VMLocation\$VMN2"
# Create SQLAcct3
$VMN3        = 'SQLAcct3'
New-VM -Name $VMN3 -Path "$VMLocation\$VMN3"
```

```
# Create SQLMfg1
$VMN4        = 'SQLMfg1'
New-VM -Name $VMN4 -Path "$VMLocation\$VMN4"
# Create SQLMfg2
$VMN5        = 'SQLMfg2'
New-VM -Name $VMN5 -Path "$VMLocation\$VMN5"
```

2. Viewing SQL VMs

```
Get-VM -Name SQL*
```

3. Creating Hyper-V VM groups

```
$VHGHT1 = @{
  Name      = 'SQLAccVMG'
  GroupType = 'VMCollectionType'
}
$VMGroupACC = New-VMGroup @VHGHT1
$VHGHT2 = @{
  Name      = 'SQLMfgVMG'
  GroupType = 'VMCollectionType'
}
$VMGroupMFG = New-VMGroup @VHGHT2
```

4. Displaying the VM groups on HV2

```
Get-VMGroup |
    Format-Table -Property Name, *Members, ComputerName
```

5. Creating arrays of group member VM names

```
$AccountingVMs   = 'SQLAcct1', 'SQLAcct2','SQLAcct3'
$ManfacturingVMs = 'SQLMfg1', 'SQLMfg2'
```

6. Adding members to the Accounting SQL VM group

```
Foreach ($Server in $AccountingVMs) {
    $VM = Get-VM -Name $Server
    Add-VMGroupMember -Name SQLAccVMG -VM $VM
}
```

7. Adding members to the Manufacturing SQL VM group

```
Foreach ($Server in $ManfacturingVMs) {
    $VM = Get-VM -Name $Server
    Add-VMGroupMember -Name SQLMfgVMG -VM $VM
}
```

8. Viewing VM groups on HV2

```
Get-VMGroup |
  Format-Table -Property Name, *Members, ComputerName
```

9. Creating a management collection VM group

```
$VMGroupHT = @{
  Name      = 'VMMGSQL'
  GroupType = 'ManagementCollectionType'
}
$VMManufacturingSQL = New-VMGroup  @VMGroupHT
```

10. Adding the two VMCollectionType groups to the VMManagement group

```
Add-VMGroupMember -Name VMMGSQL -VMGroupMember $VMGroupACC,
                                              $VMGroupMFG
```

11. Setting FormatEnumerationLimit to 99

```
$FormatEnumerationLimit = 99
```

12. Viewing VM groups by type

```
Get-VMGroup | Sort-Object -Property GroupType |
   Format-Table -Property Name, GroupType, VMGroupMembers,
                          VMMembers
```

13. Stopping all the SQL VMs

```
Foreach ($VM in ((Get-VMGroup VMMGSQL).VMGroupMembers.vmmembers)) {
  Stop-VM -Name $VM.Name -WarningAction SilentlyContinue
}
```

14. Setting CPU count in all SQL VMs to 4

```
Foreach ($VM in ((Get-VMGroup VMMGSQL).VMGroupMembers.VMMembers)) {
  Set-VMProcessor -VMName $VM.name -Count 4
}
```

15. Setting `Accounting` SQL VMs to have 6 processors

```
Foreach ($VM in ((Get-VMGroup SQLAccVMG).VMMembers)) {
  Set-VMProcessor -VMName $VM.name -Count 6
}
```

16. Checking processor counts for all VMs sorted by CPU count

```
$VMS = (Get-VMGroup -Name VMMGSQL).VMGroupMembers.VMMembers
Get-VMProcessor -VMName $VMS.Name |
  Sort-Object -Property Count -Descending |
    Format-Table -Property VMName, Count
```

17. Remove VMs from the VM groups

```
$VMs = (Get-VMGroup -Name SQLAccVMG).VMMEMBERS
Foreach ($VM in $VMS)  {
  $X = Get-VM -vmname $VM.name
  Remove-VMGroupMember -Name SQLAccVMG -VM $x
  }
$VMs = (Get-VMGroup -Name SQLMFGVMG).VMMEMBERS
Foreach ($VM in $VMS)  {
  $X = Get-VM -vmname $VM.name
  Remove-VMGroupMember -Name SQLmfgvMG -VM $x
}
```

18. Removing VM groups from `VMManagementGroups`

```
$VMGS = (Get-VMGroup -Name VMMGSQL).VMMembers
Foreach ($VMG in $VMGS)  {
  $X = Get-VMGroup -vmname $VMG.name
  Remove-VMGroupMember -Name VMMGSQL -VMGroupName $x
}
```

19. Removing all the VM groups

```
Remove-VMGroup -Name SQLACCVMG  -Force
Remove-VMGroup -Name SQLMFGVMG  -Force
Remove-VMGroup -Name VMMGSQL    -Force
```

How it works...

In *step 1*, you create several VMs using the New-VM cmdlet, with the output of this step looking like this:

```
PS C:\Foo> # 1. Creating five VMs on HV2
PS C:\Foo> $VMLocation = 'C:\Vm\VMs'   # Created in earlier recipe
PS C:\Foo> # Create SQLAcct1
PS C:\Foo> $VMN1        = 'SQLAcct1'
PS C:\Foo> New-VM -Name $VMN1 -Path "$VMLocation\$VMN1"

Name      State CPUUsage(%) MemoryAssigned(M) Uptime    Status             Version
----      ----- ----------- ----------------- ------    ------             -------
SQLAcct1  Off   0           0                  00:00:00 Operating normally 10.0

PS C:\Foo> # Create SQLAcct2
PS C:\Foo> $VMN2        = 'SQLAcct2'
PS C:\Foo> New-VM -Name $VMN2 -Path "$VMLocation\$VMN2"

Name      State CPUUsage(%) MemoryAssigned(M) Uptime    Status             Version
----      ----- ----------- ----------------- ------    ------             -------
SQLAcct2  Off   0           0                  00:00:00 Operating normally 10.0

PS C:\Foo> # Create SQLAcct3
PS C:\Foo> $VMN3        = 'SQLAcct3'
PS C:\Foo> New-VM -Name $VMN3 -Path "$VMLocation\$VMN3"

Name      State CPUUsage(%) MemoryAssigned(M) Uptime    Status             Version
----      ----- ----------- ----------------- ------    ------             -------
SQLAcct3  Off   0           0                  00:00:00 Operating normally 10.0

PS C:\Foo> # Create SQLMfg1
PS C:\Foo> $VMN4        = 'SQLMfg1'
PS C:\Foo> New-VM -Name $VMN4 -Path "$VMLocation\$VMN4"

Name      State CPUUsage(%) MemoryAssigned(M) Uptime    Status             Version
----      ----- ----------- ----------------- ------    ------             -------
SQLMfg1   Off   0           0                  00:00:00 Operating normally 10.0

PS C:\Foo> # Create SQLMfg2
PS C:\Foo> $VMN5        = 'SQLMfg2'
PS C:\Foo> New-VM -Name $VMN5 -Path "$VMLocation\$VMN5"

Name      State CPUUsage(%) MemoryAssigned(M) Uptime    Status             Version
----      ----- ----------- ----------------- ------    ------             -------
SQLMfg2   Off   0           0                  00:00:00 Operating normally 10.0
```

Figure 11.13: Creating new SQL VMs on HV2

In *step 2*, you use the Get-VM cmdlet to look at the five VMs you just created, with output like this:

```
PS C:\Foo> # 2. Viewing SQL VMs
PS C:\Foo> Get-VM -Name SQL*

Name      State CPUUsage(%) MemoryAssigned(M) Uptime    Status             Version
----      ----- ----------- ----------------- ------    ------             -------
SQLAcct3  Off   0           0                  00:00:00 Operating normally 10.0
SQLMfg2   Off   0           0                  00:00:00 Operating normally 10.0
SQLMfg1   Off   0           0                  00:00:00 Operating normally 10.0
SQLAcct1  Off   0           0                  00:00:00 Operating normally 10.0
SQLAcct2  Off   0           0                  00:00:00 Operating normally 10.0
```

Figure 11.14: Viewing the VMs on HV2

In *step 3*, you create several Hyper-V VM CollectionType VM groups, generating no output. In *step 4*, you examine the existing VM groups on HV2 with console output like this:

```
PS C:\Foo> # 4. Displaying the VM groups on HV2
PS C:\Foo> Get-VMGroup |
             Format-Table -Property Name, *Members, ComputerName

Name       VMMembers VMGroupMembers ComputerName
----       --------- -------------- ------------
SQLMfgVMG  {}                       HV2
SQLAccVMG  {}                       HV2
```

Figure 11.15: Viewing VM groups on HV2

To simplify the creation of the VM collection groups, in *step 5*, you create arrays of the VM names. In *step 6*, you add VMs to the SQLAccVMG VM group, while in *step 7*, you add VMs to the SQLMfgVMG VM group. These three steps produce no console output.

Then, in *step 8*, you view the VM groups again, with output like this:

```
PS C:\Foo> # 8. Viewing VM groups on HV2
PS C:\Foo> Get-VMGroup |
             Format-Table -Property Name, *Members, ComputerName

Name       VMMembers                      VMGroupMembers ComputerName
----       ---------                      -------------- ------------
SQLMfgVMG  {SQLMfg2, SQLMfg1}                            HV2
SQLAccVMG  {SQLAcct3, SQLAcct1, SQLAcct2}                HV2
```

Figure 11.16: Viewing the VM groups on HV2

In *step 9*, you create a VM management collection group, and in *step 10*, you populate the VM management collection group. To simplify the output, in *step 11*, you set the $FormatEnumerationLimit to 99. These three steps create no console output.

In *step 12*, you view all the fully populated VM groups, sorted by VM group type, with output like this:

```
PS C:\Foo> # 12. Viewing VM groups by type
PS C:\Foo> Get-VMGroup | Sort-Object -Property GroupType |
             Format-Table -Property Name, GroupType, VMGroupMembers,
                             VMMembers

Name       GroupType                VMGroupMembers        VMMembers
----       ---------                --------------        ---------
SQLMfgVMG  VMCollectionType                               {SQLMfg2, SQLMfg1}
SQLAccVMG  VMCollectionType                               {SQLAcct3, SQLAcct1, SQLAcct2}
VMMGSQL    ManagementCollectionType {SQLMfgVMG, SQLAccVMG}
```

Figure 11.17: Viewing the fully populated VM groups on HV2

In *step 13*, you use the VM groups you have created to stop all the SQL VMs. In *step 14*, you set the VMs in the VMMGSQL VM management collection group to have four virtual processors, and in *step 15*, you set the VMs in the SQLAccVMG VM collection group to each have six virtual processors. These three steps produce no output to the console.

In *step 16*, you review the virtual processors assigned to each SQL VM like this:

```
PS C:\Foo> # 16. Checking processor counts for all VMs sorted by CPU count
PS C:\Foo> $VMS = (Get-VMGroup -Name VMMGSQL).VMGroupMembers.VMMembers
PS C:\Foo> Get-VMProcessor -VMName $VMS.Name |
             Sort-Object -Property Count -Descending |
               Format-Table -Property VMName, Count

VMName     Count
------     -----
SQLAcct3     6
SQLAcct1     6
SQLAcct2     6
SQLMfg2      4
SQLMfg1      4
```

Figure 11.18: Viewing the processor counts for the VMs on HV2

In *step 17*, you remove all the VMs from the VM collection groups, and in *step 18*, you remove all the members from the VM management groups. Finally, in *step 19*, you remove all the VM groups. These three steps produce no output.

There's more...

In *step 11*, you set a value for the $FormatEnumerationLimit automatic variable. This variable controls how many repeating groups the Format-* cmdlets display. By default, PowerShell initializes this variable with a value of 4. Using this default, in *step 11*, you will see at most four members of each of the VM groups, with PowerShell displaying "…" to indicate that you have more than four members. If you set $FormatEnumerationLImit to 0 (zero), PowerShell displays all the members, irrespective of the number. With this step, PowerShell can display up to 99 VM members for each VM group. You may wish to set this preference variable in your profile or inside specific scripts in production.

In this recipe, you used five supposed SQL Server VMs to illustrate the use of VM groups. There are no actual usable VMs (each of the five VMs you create does not have an OS or SQL Server loaded). You can, should you wish to, add steps to install Windows Server and SQL Server on these VMs.

VM groups provide few benefits for most Hyper-V customers, and as mentioned, VM groups feel half-implemented. In production, you could easily create string variables holding VM names and use these instead of VM groups.

Configuring the VM hardware

Configuring hardware in your VM is like configuring a physical computer without needing a screwdriver. With a physical computer, you can adjust the CPUs and BIOS settings and change physical RAM, network interfaces, disk interfaces, disk devices, DVD drives (with/without a loaded DVD), and more. You can find each of these virtual components within a Hyper-V VM. As you will see in the recipe, the PowerShell cmdlets make it simple to configure the virtual hardware available to any Hyper-V VM.

In this recipe, you will adjust the VM's BIOS, CPU count, and memory and then add a SCSI controller. With the controller in place, you will create a new virtual disk and assign it to the SCSI controller. Then, you will view the results.

Like most physical servers, you cannot change all of these virtual hardware components while your virtual server is up and running. You will run this recipe from HV1 and turn the PSDirect VM off before configuring the virtual hardware.

This recipe does not cover the VM's virtual NIC. By default, VMs (such as those created in the *Creating a Hyper-V VM* recipe) contain a single virtual NIC. You can add additional NICs to any VM should you wish to. You will configure VM networking in the *Configuring VM Networking* recipe later in this chapter.

Getting ready

This recipe uses HV1, a Windows Server 2022 host on which you have installed the Hyper-V feature. You should also have created a Windows Server VM called PSDirect.

How to do it...

1. Turning off the PSDirect VM

    ```
    Stop-VM -VMName PSDirect
    Get-VM -VMName PSDirect
    ```

2. Setting the startup order in the VM's BIOS

    ```
    $Order = 'IDE','CD','LegacyNetworkAdapter','Floppy'
    Set-VMBios -VmName PSDirect -StartupOrder $Order
    Get-VMBios PSDirect
    ```

3. Setting and viewing CPU count for PSDirect

    ```
    Set-VMProcessor -VMName PSDirect -Count 2
    ```

```
Get-VMProcessor -VMName PSDirect |
  Format-Table VMName, Count
```

4. Setting and viewing PSDirect memory

```
$VMConfigurationHT = [ordered] @{
  VMName              = 'PSDirect'
  DynamicMemoryEnabled = $true
  MinimumBytes        = 512MB
  StartupBytes        = 1GB
  MaximumBytes        = 2GB
}
Set-VMMemory @VMConfigurationHT
Get-VMMemory -VMName PSDirect
```

5. Adding and viewing a ScsiController in the PSDirect VM

```
Add-VMScsiController -VMName PSDirect
Get-VMScsiController -VMName PSDirect
```

6. Starting the PSDirect VM

```
Start-VM -VMName PSDirect
Wait-VM  -VMName PSDirect -For IPAddress
```

7. Creating a new VHDX file for the PSDirect VM

```
$VHDPath = 'C:\VM\VHDs\PSDirect-D.VHDX'
New-VHD -Path $VHDPath -SizeBytes 8GB -Dynamic
```

8. Getting controller number of the newly added ScsiController

```
$VM             = Get-VM -VMName PSDirect
$SCSIController = Get-VMScsiController -VM $VM |
                  Select-Object -Last 1
```

9. Adding the VHD to the SCSIController

```
$VMNewDiskHT = @{
    VMName            = 'PSDirect'
    ControllerType    = $SCSIController.ControllerNumber
    ControllerNumber  = 0
    ControllerLocation = 0
```

```
        Path                    = $VHDPath
    }
    Add-VMHardDiskDrive @VMNewDiskHT
```

10. Viewing drives in the PSDirect VM

```
    Get-VMScsiController -VMName PSDirect |
        Select-Object -ExpandProperty Drives
```

How it works...

In *step 1*, you turn off the PSDirect VM and check the status of the VM, with output like this:

```
PS C:\Foo> # 1. Turning off the PSDirect VM
PS C:\Foo> Stop-VM -VMName PSDirect
PS C:\Foo> Get-VM -VMName PSDirect

Name     State CPUUsage(%) MemoryAssigned(M) Uptime   Status            Version
----     ----- ----------- ----------------- ------   ------            -------
PSDirect Off   0           0                 00:00:00 Operating normally 10.0
```

Figure 11.19: Stopping the PSDirect VM

In *step 2*, you set the startup order for the VM's BIOS. Then, you view the BIOS details. The output of this step is:

```
PS C:\Foo> # 2. Setting the startup order in the VM's BIOS
PS C:\Foo> $Order = 'IDE','CD','LegacyNetworkAdapter','Floppy'
PS C:\Foo> Set-VMBios –VmName PSDirect –StartupOrder $Order
PS C:\Foo> Get-VMBios PSDirect

VMName    StartupOrder                              NumLockEnabled
------    ------------                              --------------
PSDirect {IDE, CD, LegacyNetworkAdapter, Floppy} False
```

Figure 11.20: Updating and viewing the VM's BIOS

In *step 3*, you adjust and then view the number of virtual processors for the PSDirect VM, with an output like this:

```
PS C:\Foo> # 3. Setting and viewing CPU count for PSDirect
PS C:\Foo> Set-VMProcessor -VMName PSDirect -Count 2
PS C:\Foo> Get-VMProcessor -VMName PSDirect |
               Format-Table VMName, Count

VMName    Count
------    -----
PSDirect  2
```

Figure 11.21: Updating and viewing the VM's BIOS

In *step 4*, you set the virtual memory for the PSDirect VM and then view the memory settings with the following output:

```
PS C:\Foo> # 4. Setting and viewing PSDirect memory
PS C:\Foo> $VMConfigurationHT = [ordered] @{
             VMName              = 'PSDirect'
             DynamicMemoryEnabled = $true
             MinimumBytes        = 512MB
             StartupBytes        = 1GB
             MaximumBytes        = 2GB
           }
PS C:\Foo> Set-VMMemory @VMConfigurationHT
PS C:\Foo> Get-VMMemory -VMName PSDirect

VMName     DynamicMemoryEnabled Minimum(M) Startup(M) Maximum(M)
------     -------------------- ---------- ---------- ----------
PSDirect   True                 512        1024       2048
```

Figure 11.22: Changing and viewing the VM memory

In *step 5*, you add a second SCSI controller to the PSDirect VM. You then view the SCSI controllers inside the PSDirect VM. You should see output like this:

```
PS C:\Foo> # 5. Adding and viewing a ScsiController in the PSDirect VM
PS C:\Foo> Add-VMScsiController -VMName PSDirect
PS C:\Foo> Get-VMScsiController -VMName PSDirect

VMName     ControllerNumber Drives
------     ---------------- ------
PSDirect   0                {}
PSDirect   1                {}
```

Figure 11.23: Adding and viewing virtual disk controllers

Now that you have adjusted the virtual hardware for the PSDirect VM, in *step 6*, you restart the VM and wait for the VM to come up. This step generates no output.

In *step 7*, you create a new virtual disk file for the PSDirect VM, with output like this:

```
PS C:\Foo> # 7. Creating a new VHDX file for the PSDirect VM
PS C:\Foo> $VHDPath = 'C:\VM\VHDs\PSDirect-D.VHDX'
PS C:\Foo> New-VHD -Path $VHDPath -SizeBytes 8GB -Dynamic

ComputerName            : HV1
Path                    : C:\VM\VHDs\PSDirect-D.VHDX
VhdFormat               : VHDX
VhdType                 : Dynamic
FileSize                : 4194304
Size                    : 8589934592
MinimumSize             :
LogicalSectorSize       : 512
PhysicalSectorSize      : 4096
BlockSize               : 33554432
ParentPath              :
DiskIdentifier          : 49F1E70B-A66D-4F60-A536-53FB87042BAC
FragmentationPercentage : 0
Alignment               : 1
Attached                : False
DiskNumber              :
IsPMEMCompatible        : False
AddressAbstractionType  : None
Number                  :
```

Figure 11.24: Creating a new virtual disk drive

In *step 8*, you get the SCSI controllers in the PSDirect VM and the controller you added in *step 5*. Then, in *step 9*, you add the newly created virtual disk drive to the recently added SCSI controller. These two steps produce no console output.

In *step 10*, you attach the disk drives to the SCSI controllers in the PSDirect VM, with an output like this:

```
PS C:\Foo> # 10. Viewing drives in the PSDirect VM
PS C:\Foo> Get-VMScsiController -VMName PSDirect
              Select-Object -ExpandProperty Drives

VMName   ControllerType ControllerNumber ControllerLocation DiskNumber Path
------   -------------- ---------------- ------------------ ---------- ----
PSDirect SCSI           0                0                             C:\VM\VHDs\PSDirect-D.VHDX
```

Figure 11.25: Viewing the SCSI disk drives in the PSDirect VM

There's more...

With Hyper-V, you can only update some VM hardware configuration settings when you have turned off the VM. In *step 1*, you switch the VM off to enable you to make virtual BIOS settings. Once you have completed these BIOS (and possibly other) changes, you can restart the VM.

In *step 2*, you set the startup order for the VM and view the settings. In production, you may have scripts like this that set VM settings to a preferred corporate standard, irrespective of the default values.

In *step 3*, you set the number of processors in the nested VM to 2. You should ensure that the Hyper-V host has at least two virtual CPUs if not more.

Some settings, such as the SCSI disk controllers and disk drives, can be added and removed from a running VM. In *step 9*, you add a newly created virtual disk drive to the running PSDirect VM.

In *step 10*, you view the SCSI disks in the PSDirect VM. This VM has an IDE-based boot disk. Hence, you see a single disk in the output of this step.

Configuring VM networking

In the *Creating a Hyper-V VM* recipe, you created a VM, PSDirect. This VM has, by default, a single network card that Hyper-V sets to acquire IP address details from DHCP. In this recipe, you create a new switch, assign the VM's NIC to a switch, and configure the IP address details for the virtual network adapter.

Getting ready

You will run this recipe on HV1, which uses the PSDirect VM you created in the *Creating a Hyper-V VM* recipe. This recipe also makes use of a DHCP server running on DC1. In *Chapter 5, Managing Networking*, you set the DHCP service up in the *Installing DHCP* recipe. Then, you configured the DHCP server in the *Configuring DHCP scopes and options* recipe.

This chapter uses the PSDirect VM you created earlier. When you build this machine using the normal setup routine, Windows assigns a random machine name, which you saw in a previous recipe (*Using PowerShell Direct*). In this recipe, you will also change the name of the host inside to Wolf.

In this recipe, you will set the PSDirect VM's networking card to enable MAC address spoofing. This step lets the VM see the network and get an IP address from the DHCP server on DC1. If you are running HV1 as a VM, you must also enable MAC spoofing on the NIC(s) in this VM on the VM host of HV1.

How to do it...

1. Setting the PSDirect VM's NIC

```
Get-VM PSDirect |
    Set-VMNetworkAdapter -MacAddressSpoofing On
```

2. Getting NIC details and any IP addresses from the PSDirect VM

```
Get-VMNetworkAdapter -VMName PSDirect
```

3. Creating a credentials then getting VM networking details

```
$Administrator = 'localhost\Administrator'
$Password      = 'Pa$$w0rd'
$RKPassword =
    ConvertTo-SecureString -String $Password -AsPlainText -Force
$RKCred       = [System.Management.Automation.PSCredential]::new(
                                        $Administrator,
                                        $RKPassword)

$VMHT = @{
    VMName      = 'PSDirect'
    ScriptBlock = {ipconfig}
    Credential  = $RKCred
}
Invoke-Command @VMHT
```

4. Creating a new virtual switch on HV1

```
$VirtSwitchHT = @{
    Name           = 'Internal'
    NetAdapterName = 'Ethernet'
    Notes          = 'Created on HV1'
}
New-VMSwitch @VirtSwitchHT
```

5. Connecting the PSDirect VM's NIC to the internal switch

```
Connect-VMNetworkAdapter -VMName PSDirect -SwitchName Internal
```

6. Viewing VM networking information

```
Get-VMNetworkAdapter -VMName PSDirect
```

7. Observing the IP address in the PSDirect VM

    ```
    $CommandHT = @{
        VMName      = 'PSDirect'
        ScriptBlock = {ipconfig}
        Credential  = $RKCred
    }
    Invoke-Command @CommandHT
    ```

8. Viewing the hostname on PSDirect

    ```
    $CommandHT.ScriptBlock = {hostname}
    Invoke-Command @CommandHT
    ```

9. Changing the name of the host in the PSDirect VM

    ```
    $CommandHT.ScriptBlock = {Rename-Computer -NewName Wolf -Force}
    Invoke-Command @CommandHT
    ```

10. Rebooting and wait for the restarted PSDirect VM

    ```
    Restart-VM -VMName PSDirect -Wait -For IPAddress -Force
    ```

11. Getting hostname of the PSDirect VM

    ```
    $CommandHT.ScriptBlock = {HOSTNAME}
    Invoke-Command @CommandHT
    ```

How it works...

In *step 1*, you set the PSDirect VM's NIC to enable MAC address spoofing. There is no output from this step.

In *step 2*, you get the NIC details for the NIC assigned to the PSDirect VM, with output like this:

```
PS C:\Foo> # 2. Getting NIC details and any IP addresses from the PSDirect VM
PS C:\Foo> Get-VMNetworkAdapter -VMName PSDirect

Name                   IsManagementOs VMName   SwitchName MacAddress   Status IPAddresses
----                   -------------- ------   ---------- ----------   ------ -----------
Network Adapter False                 PSDirect            00155D0AC900 {0k}   {169.254.17.230, fe80::351e:a5ce:b8d7:11e6}
```

Figure 11.26: Viewing the NIC details for the PSDirect VM

In *step 3*, you create a credential object for the PSDirect VM. Then, you use the credentials to run the ipconfig.exe command from inside the VM, with output like this:

```
PS C:\Foo> # 3. Creating a credential then getting VM networking details
PS C:\Foo> $RKAdministrator = 'localhost\Administrator'
PS C:\Foo> $Password        = 'Pa$$w0rd'
PS C:\Foo> $RKPassword = ConvertTo-SecureString -String $Password -AsPlainText -Force
PS C:\Foo> $RKCred = [System.Management.Automation.PSCredential]::new(
                                              $RKAdministrator,
                                              $RKPassword)
PS C:\Foo> $VMHT = @{
              VMName      = 'PSDirect'
              ScriptBlock = {ipconfig}
              Credential  = $RKCred
           }
PS C:\Foo> Invoke-Command @VMHT
```

```
Windows IP Configuration


Ethernet adapter Ethernet:

   Media State . . . . . . . . . . . : Media disconnected
   Connection-specific DNS Suffix  . :
```

Figure 11.27: Viewing the IP configuration inside the PSDirect VM

In *step 4*, you create a new Hyper-V VM switch inside the HV1 VM host, which produces the following output:

```
PS C:\Foo> # 4. Creating a virtual switch on HV1
PS C:\Foo> $VirtSwitchHT = @{
              Name          = 'iNTGERNAL'
              NetAdapterName = 'Ethernet'
              Notes         = 'Created on HV1'
           }
PS C:\Foo> New-VMSwitch @VirtSwitchHT
```

```
Name     SwitchType NetAdapterInterfaceDescription
----     ---------- ------------------------------
Internal External   Microsoft Hyper-V Network Adapter
```

Figure 11.28: Creating a new virtual switch inside HV1

In *step 5*, you connect the NIC in the PSDirect VM to the VM switch, creating no output. In *step 6*, you can review the networking information for the PSDirect VM with output like this:

```
PS C:\Foo> # 6. Viewing VM networking inFormation
PS C:\Foo> Get-VMNetworkAdapter -VMName PSDirect
```

```
Name            IsManagementOs VMName   SwitchName MacAddress   Status IPAddresses
----            -------------- ------   ---------- ----------   ------ -----------
Network Adapter False          PSDirect External   00155D0AC900 {OK}   {10.10.10.179, fe80::351e:a5ce:b8d7:11e6}
```

Figure 11.29: Viewing the PSDirect NIC settings

In *step 7*, you execute a script block inside the PSDirect VM to return the VM's network details, which produces output that looks like this:

```
PS C:\Foo> # 7. Observing the IP address in the PSDirect VM
PS C:\Foo> $CommandHT = @{
             VMName      = 'PSDirect'
             ScriptBlock = {ipconfig}
             Credential  = $RKCred
           }
PS C:\Foo> Invoke-Command @CommandHT

Windows IP Configuration

Ethernet adapter Ethernet 2:

   Connection-specific DNS Suffix  . : Reskit.Org
   Link-local IPv6 Address . . . . . : fe80::94d5:e366:7bf7:320a%7
   IPv4 Address. . . . . . . . . . . : 10.10.10.179
   Subnet Mask . . . . . . . . . . . : 255.255.255.0
   Default Gateway . . . . . . . . . :
```

Figure 11.30: Observing the PSDirect network settings

In *step 8*, you view the existing hostname of the PSDirect VM with output that looks like this:

```
PS C:\Foo> # 8. Viewing the hostname on PSDirect
PS C:\Foo> $CommandHT.ScriptBlock = {hostname}
PS C:\Foo> Invoke-Command @CommandHT
WIN-LKBC0RRT59T
```

Figure 11.31: Viewing the hostname of the PSDirect VM

In *step 9*, you use the Rename-Computer cmdlet, running inside the PSDirect VM. This step changes the hostname of the VM to Wolf and produces the following output:

```
PS C:\Foo> # 9. Changing the name of the host in the PSDirect VM
PS C:\Foo> $CommandHT.ScriptBlock = {Rename-Computer -NewName Wolf -Force}
PS C:\Foo> Invoke-Command @CommandHT
WARNING: The changes will take effect after you restart the computer WIN-LKBCORRT59T.
```

Figure 11.32: Changing the VM's hostname

In *step 10*, you reboot the PSDirect VM, generating no console output. After the VM has restarted, in *step 11*, you run the HOSTNAME command inside the VM, with console output like this:

```
PS C:\Foo> # 11. Getting hostname of the PSDirect VM
PS C:\Foo> $CommandHT.ScriptBlock = {HOSTNAME}
PS C:\Foo> Invoke-Command @CommandHT
Wolf
```

Figure 11.33: Viewing the updated hostname in the PSDirect VM

There's more...

In *step 1*, you set the PSDirect VM's NIC to enable MAC address spoofing. You can read more about MAC address spoofing with Hyper-V at https://charbelnemnom.com/how-to-set-dynamic-mac-address-on-a-hyper-v-vm-with-powershell/.

In *step 5*, you connect the PSDirect VM's NIC to the virtual switch you created on HV1. Since the PSDirect VM's NIC is (by default) set to get IP addresses via DHCP, as soon as you connect the virtual NIC to the switch, the VM should acquire the IP address configuration from the DC1 host, which is running DHCP. You can see the DHCP-acquired IP configuration details in the output from *step 6*.

Implementing nested virtualization

Nested virtualization is a feature that enables a Hyper-V VM to host VMs that also have virtualization enabled. You could, for example, take a Hyper-V host (say, HV1) and, on that host, run a VM (say, PSDirect). With nested virtualization, you could enable your PSDirect VM to host VMs. You could then create a nested VM inside the PSDirect VM called NestedVM.

Nested VMs have many uses. First, nested VMs hosted in one VM are provided hardware isolation from nested VMs run in other VMs. In this case, nested virtualization offers additional security for VMs.

Nested virtualization is also helpful for testing and education or training. You can give students a single VM (on a large blade server, for example). Nested virtualization enables them to create additional VMs for the course lab work. And most IT pros find it cool! You can, for example, run all the recipes in this chapter using nested virtualization.

Enabling nested Hyper-V is very simple. First, you must update the virtual CPU in the VM that you want to support nesting. Therefore, you will adjust the virtual CPU in the PSDirect VM to expose the virtualization extensions in this recipe. Changing the BIOS to do this must be done after you turn off the VM. After you restart the VM, you will install the Hyper-V feature and create the NestedVM nested VM. This recipe does not show the details of configuring the NestedVM VM. To expose the virtualization extensions for any Hyper-V VM, you use the Set-VMProcessor -ExposeVirtualizationExtensions $True, and specify a VM name.

Getting ready

This recipe uses the HV1 Hyper-V host, with an existing Hyper-V VM, PSDirect, available. The recipe assumes that you have set up PSDirect as discussed in the *Creating a Hyper-V VM* recipe earlier in this chapter.

How to do it...

1. Stopping the PSDirect VM

    ```
    Stop-VM -VMName PSDirect
    ```

2. Setting the VM's processor to support virtualization

    ```
    $VMHT = @{
      VMName                          = 'PSDirect'
      ExposeVirtualizationExtensions = $true
    }
    Set-VMProcessor @VMHT
    Get-VMProcessor -VMName PSDirect |
      Format-Table -Property Name, Count,
                             ExposeVirtualizationExtensions
    ```

3. Starting the PSDirect VM

    ```
    Start-VM -VMName PSDirect
    Wait-VM  -VMName PSDirect -For Heartbeat
    Get-VM   -VMName PSDirect
    ```

4. Creating credentials for PSDirect

    ```
    $User = 'Wolf\Administrator'
    $PasswordHT = @{
      String      = 'Pa$$w0rd'
      AsPlainText = $true
      Force       = $true
    }
    $SecurePW  = ConvertTo-SecureString @PasswordHT
    $Cred = [System.Management.Automation.PSCredential]::new(
                                              $User, $SecurePW)
    ```

5. Creating a script block for remote execution

```
$ScriptBlock = {
  Install-WindowsFeature -Name Hyper-V -IncludeManagementTools
}
```

6. Creating a remoting session to PSDirect

```
$Session = New-PSSession -VMName PSDirect -Credential $Cred
```

7. Installing Hyper-V inside PSDirect

```
$InstallHT = @{
  Session     = $Session
  ScriptBlock = $ScriptBlock
}
Invoke-Command @InstallHT
```

8. Restarting the VM to finish adding Hyper-V to PSDirect

```
Stop-VM   -VMName PSDirect
Start-VM -VMName PSDirect
Wait-VM   -VMName PSDirect -For IPAddress
Get-VM    -VMName PSDirect
```

9. Creating a nested VM inside the PSDirect VM

```
$ScriptBlock2 = {
        $VMName = 'NestedVM'
        New-VM -Name $VMName -MemoryStartupBytes 1GB | Out-Null
        Get-VM
}
$InstallHT2 = @{
  VMName = 'PSDirect'
  ScriptBlock = $ScriptBlock2
}
Invoke-Command @InstallHT2 -Credential $Cred
```

How it works...

In *step 1*, you ensure that the PSDirect VM has stopped. This step creates no console output. In *step 2*, you configure the VM's virtual processor to support virtualization. Then, you review the VM's processor settings, which look like this:

```
PS C:\Foo> # 2. Setting the VM's processor to support virtualization
PS C:\Foo> $VMHT = @{
             VMName                              = 'PSDirect'
             ExposeVirtualizationExtensions = $true
           }
PS C:\Foo> Set-VMProcessor @VMHT
PS C:\Foo> Get-VMProcessor -VMName PSDirect |
             Format-Table -Property Name, Count,
                                     ExposeVirtualizationExtensions

Name       Count ExposeVirtualizationExtensions
----       ----- ------------------------------
Processor    2                                True
```

Figure 11.34: Viewing the virtual processor inside PSDirect

In *step 3*, you start the PSDirect VM and then use Get-VM to view details about the VM, which look like this:

```
PS C:\Foo> # 3. Starting the PSDirect VM
PS C:\Foo> Start-VM -VMName PSDirect
PS C:\Foo> Wait-VM  -VMName PSDirect -For Heartbeat
PS C:\Foo> Get-VM   -VMName PSDirect

Name     State   CPUUsage(%) MemoryAssigned(M) Uptime           Status             Version
----     -----   ----------- ----------------- ------           ------             -------
PSDirect Running 23          1024              00:00:35.7060000 Operating normally 10.0
```

Figure 11.35: Starting and viewing PSDirect

In *step 4*, you create a PowerShell credential object for the PSDirect VM. In *step 5*, you create a script block that installs the Hyper-V feature. Then, in *step 6*, you create a PowerShell remoting session with the PSDirect VM. These three steps produce no output to the console.

In *step 7*, you use the remoting session to install the Hyper-V feature inside the PSDirect VM, producing output like this:

```
PS C:\Foo> # 7. Installing Hyper-V inside PSDirect
PS C:\Foo> $InstallHT = @{
              Session    = $Session
              ScriptBlock = $ScriptBlock
           }
PS C:\Foo> Invoke-Command @InstallHT

PSComputerName : PSDirect
RunspaceId     : 2449adca-f238-4333-a0c2-425f4e7e2f2a
Success        : True
RestartNeeded  : Yes
FeatureResult  : {Hyper-V, Hyper-V Module for Windows PowerShell,
                  Hyper-V GUI Management Tools, Remote Server Administration Tools,
                  Hyper-V Management Tools, Role Administration Tools}
ExitCode       : SuccessRestartRequired

WARNING: You must restart this server to finish the installation process.
```

Figure 11.36: Installing Hyper-V inside the PSDirect VM

As you can see from the output, after installing the Hyper-V feature inside PSDirect, you need to reboot the VM to complete the installation process. In *step 8*, you restart PSDirect, wait for it to start, and finally view the VM details with output like this:

```
PS C:\Foo> # 8. Restarting the VM to finish adding Hyper-V to PSDirect
PS C:\Foo> Stop-VM  -VMName PSDirect
PS C:\Foo> Start-VM -VMName PSDirect
PS C:\Foo> Wait-VM  -VMName PSDirect -For IPAddress
PS C:\Foo> Get-VM   -VMName PSDirect
```

Name	State	CPUUsage(%)	MemoryAssigned(M)	Uptime	Status	Version
PSDirect	Running	29	1024	00:00:41.8930000	Operating normally	10.0

Figure 11.37: Restarting the PSDirect VM

In the final step in this recipe, *step 9*, you create a new nested VM, NestedVM, inside the PSDirect VM, which produces console output like this:

```
PS C:\Foo> # 9. Creating a nested VM inside the PSDirect VM
PS C:\Foo> $ScriptBlock2 = {
              $VMName = 'NestedVM'
              New-VM -Name $VMName -MemoryStartupBytes 1GB | Out-Null
              Get-VM
           }
PS C:\Foo> $InstallHT2 = @{
              VMName = 'PSDirect'
              ScriptBlock = $ScriptBlock2
           }
PS C:\Foo> Invoke-Command @InstallHT2 -Credential $Cred
```

Name	State	CPUUsage(%)	MemoryAssigned(M)	Uptime	Status	Version	PSComputerName
NestedVM	Off	0	0	00:00:00	Operating normally	10.0	PSDirect

Figure 11.38: Creating a nested VM inside PSDirect

There's more...

In *step 7*, you install the Hyper-V feature in the nested VM (NestedVM) inside the PSDirect VM. The installation of Hyper-V inside the PSDirect VM is successful, as you can see in this step's output. Had the PSDirect VM not supported virtualization, the Install-WindowsFeature cmdlet would have thrown an error. Likewise, had you not installed Hyper-V in PSDirect, *step 9* would have failed without creating the VM. If you wish to, you can adjust the *Creating a Hyper-V VM* recipe steps to install and configure an OS in the NestedVM.

Managing the VM state

Hyper-V allows you to start, stop, and pause a Hyper-V VM. You can also save the VM and its state and then restore the VM. You use the Hyper-V cmdlets to manage your VMs locally (on the Hyper-V host in a **remote desktop (RDP)** or PowerShell remoting session) or use RSAT tools to manage the state of VMs on remote Hyper-V hosts.

You can start and stop VMs either directly or via the task scheduler. You might want to start up a few VMs every working morning and stop them every evening. If you have provisioned your Hyper-V host with spinning disks, starting multiple VMs at once stresses the storage subsystem, especially if you are using any form of RAID on the disk drives you use to hold your virtual disks. Depending on your hardware, you can sometimes hear the IO Blender effect starting up a small VM farm. Even with solid-state disks, starting several VMs simultaneously puts a considerable load on the Windows storage system. In such cases, you might pause a VM and let others start faster.

Saving a VM can help avoid a long startup process. If you have created multiple VMs to test the recipes in this book, you can save VMs and restart them as you move through the chapters.

Getting ready

You will run this recipe on the HV1 host once you have created the PSDirect VM. You created that VM in the *Creating a Hyper-V VM* recipe.

How to do it...

1. Getting the VM's state to check if it is off

```
Stop-VM -Name PSDirect -WarningAction SilentlyContinue
Get-VM -Name PSDirect
```

2. Starting the VM

    ```
    Start-VM -VMName PSDirect
    Wait-VM -VMName PSDirect -For IPAddress
    Get-VM -VMName PSDirect
    ```

3. Suspending and viewing the PSDirect VM

    ```
    Suspend-VM -VMName PSDirect
    Get-VM -VMName PSDirect
    ```

4. Resuming the PSDirect VM

    ```
    Resume-VM -VMName PSDirect
    Get-VM -VMName PSDirect
    ```

5. Saving the VM

    ```
    Save-VM -VMName PSDirect
    Get-VM -VMName PSDirect
    ```

6. Resuming the saved VM and viewing the status

    ```
    Start-VM -VMName PSDirect
    Get-VM -VMName PSDirect
    ```

7. Restarting the PSDirect VM

    ```
    Restart-VM -VMName PSDirect -Force
    Get-VM      -VMName PSDirect
    ```

8. Waiting for the PSDirect VM to get an IP address

    ```
    Wait-VM     -VMName PSDirect -For IPaddress
    Get-VM      -VMName PSDirect
    ```

9. Performing a hard power-off on the PSDirect VM

    ```
    Stop-VM -VMName PSDirect -TurnOff
    Get-VM  -VMname PSDirect
    ```

How it works...

In *step 1*, you stop the PSDirect VM and check its status. The output looks like this:

```
PS C:\Foo> # 1. Getting the VM's state to check if it is off
PS C:\Foo> Stop-VM -Name PSDirect -WarningAction SilentlyContinue
PS C:\Foo> Get-VM -Name PSDirect

Name       State CPUUsage(%) MemoryAssigned(M) Uptime     Status             Version
----       ----- ----------- ----------------- ------     ------             -------
PSDirect   Off   0           0                 00:00:00   Operating normally 10.0
```

Figure 11.39: Stopping the PSDirect VM

In *step 2*, you use the Start-VM cmdlet to start the PSDirect VM and then use Wait-VM to wait for the VM to start up and get an IP address. The output from this step looks like this:

```
PS C:\Foo> # 2. Starting the VM
PS C:\Foo> Start-VM -VMName PSDirect
PS C:\Foo> Wait-VM -VMName PSDirect -For IPAddress
PS C:\Foo> Get-VM -VMName PSDirect

Name       State   CPUUsage(%) MemoryAssigned(M) Uptime             Status             Version
----       -----   ----------- ----------------- ------             ------             -------
PSDirect   Running 27          1024              00:00:42.4010000   Operating normally 10.0
```

Figure 11.40: Starting the PSDirect VM

In *step 3*, you use Suspend-VM to pause the PSDirect VM and observe its status with the following output:

```
PS C:\Foo> # 3. Suspending and viewing the PSDirect VM
PS C:\Foo> Suspend-VM -VMName PSDirect
PS C:\Foo> Get-VM -VMName PSDirect

Name       State  CPUUsage(%) MemoryAssigned(M) Uptime             Status             Version
----       -----  ----------- ----------------- ------             ------             -------
PSDirect   Paused 0           1024              00:01:16.8060000   Operating normally 10.0
```

Figure 11.41: Suspending the PSDirect VM

Having paused the PSDirect VM, in *step 4*, you use the Resume-VM cmdlet to unpause the VM with the following output:

```
PS C:\Foo> # 4. Resuming the PSDirect VM
PS C:\Foo> Resume-VM -VMName PSDirect
PS C:\Foo> Get-VM -VMName PSDirect

Name       State   CPUUsage(%) MemoryAssigned(M) Uptime             Status             Version
----       -----   ----------- ----------------- ------             ------             -------
PSDirect   Running 0           1024              00:01:17.1490000   Operating normally 10.0
```

Figure 11.42: Resuming the PSDirect VM

In *step 5*, you save the PSDirect VM, with output like this:

```
PS C:\Foo> # 5. Saving the VM
PS C:\Foo> Save-VM -VMName PSDirect
PS C:\Foo> Get-VM -VMName PSDirect

Name       State CPUUsage(%) MemoryAssigned(M) Uptime   Status           Version
----       ----- ----------- ----------------- ------   ------           -------
PSDirect Saved 0               0                00:00:00 Operating normally 10.0
```

Figure 11.43: Saving the PSDirect VM

You can resume a saved VM by using the Start-VM command, as you can see in *step 6*, which creates output like this:

```
PS C:\Foo> # 6. Resuming the saved VM and viewing the status
PS C:\Foo> Start-VM -VMName PSDirect
PS C:\Foo> Get-VM -VMName PSDirect

Name       State   CPUUsage(%) MemoryAssigned(M) Uptime         Status           Version
----       -----   ----------- ----------------- ------         ------           -------
PSDirect Running 0               1024              00:00:00.1320000 Operating normally 10.0
```

Figure 11.44: Resuming the PSDirect VM (after you have saved it)

Step 7 demonstrates how to use the Restart-VM cmdlet to restart the PSDirect VM. The output from this step looks like this:

```
PS C:\Foo> # 7. Restarting the PSDirect VM
PS C:\Foo> Restart-VM -VMName PSDirect -Force
PS C:\Foo> Get-VM      -VMName PSDirect

Name       State   CPUUsage(%) MemoryAssigned(M) Uptime         Status           Version
----       -----   ----------- ----------------- ------         ------           -------
PSDirect Running 0               1024              00:00:00.2240000 Operating normally 10.0
```

Figure 11.45: Restarting the PSDirect VM (after you have saved it)

In the previous step, you restart the VM, which can take some time, depending on your VM host and VM size. In *step 8*, you use the Wait-VM cmdlet to wait for the VM to restart and then use the Get-VM cmdlet to observe the status of the PSDirect VM like this:

```
PS C:\Foo> # 8. Waiting for the PSDirect VM to get an IP address
PS C:\Foo> Wait-VM      -VMName PSDirect -For IPaddress
PS C:\Foo> Get-VM       -VMName PSDirect

Name       State   CPUUsage(%) MemoryAssigned(M) Uptime         Status           Version
----       -----   ----------- ----------------- ------         ------           -------
PSDirect Running 5               1024              00:00:52.6320000 Operating normally 10.0
```

Figure 11.46: Waiting for the PSDirect VM to restart

In the final step in this recipe, *step 9*, you perform a hard power-off of the PSDirect VM, with an output like this:

```
PS C:\Foo> # 9. Performing a hard power off on the PSDirect VM
PS C:\Foo> Stop-VM -VMName PSDirect -TurnOff
PS C:\Foo> Get-VM  -VMname PSDirect

Name         State CPUUsage(%) MemoryAssigned(M) Uptime   Status             Version
----         ----- ----------- ----------------- ------   ------             -------
PSDirect Off       0           0                 00:00:00 Operating normally 10.0
```

Figure 11.47: Turning off the PSDirect VM

There's more...

Managing the state of VMs is straightforward with the cmdlets in the Hyper-V module. You can start and stop a VM just like with physical machines. The Hyper-V cmdlets allow you to start a VM on a Hyper-V host and wait until it is far enough through the startup process to enable you to interact with the VM. This is an important feature of automation.

In some scenarios, saving a VM is very useful. If you have VMs that you use infrequently, you can save them rather than shutting them down, thereby improving the VM startup time. You can also save all the VMs when you need to reboot the VM host.

One thing to be aware of – if your VM host updates itself via Windows Update or WSUS, you may find from time to time that Windows cannot restart a saved VM. You can remove the saved state and restart.

Managing a VM and VM storage movement

Hyper-V enables you to move a VM to a new VM host and move a VM's storage to a new location. Moving a VM and moving a VM's storage are two important features you can use to manage your Hyper-V hosts.

Hyper-V's Live Migration feature allows you to move a Hyper-V VM to a different VM host without any downtime. You can also move a VM's storage (any VHD/VHDX associated with the VM) to a different location. You can combine these and move a VM supported by local storage to another Hyper-V host, moving both the VM and the underlying storage. Storage migration works best when the VM is held on shared storage (via a fiber channel SAN, iSCSI, or SMB).

In this recipe, first, you move the storage for the PSDirect VM. You created this VM in the *Creating a Hyper-V VM* recipe and stored the VM configuration and the VM's VHD on the hard disk. To move the storage, you will create a new SMB share and then move the VM's storage to the new SMB share.

In the second part of this recipe, you will perform the live migration of the PSDirect VM from HV1 to HV2. This VM movement is known as live migration because you are migrating a live VM that stays up and running during migration.

Getting ready

In this recipe, you will use the HV1 and HV2 systems (Windows 2022 Server with Hyper-V loaded) as set up in the *Installing Hyper-V inside Windows Server* recipe, and the PSDirect VM created in the *Creating a Hyper-V VM* recipe.

In the first part of this recipe, you will move the storage for the PSDirect VM. You created this VM in the *Creating a Hyper-V VM* recipe. You should ensure that this VM is up and running.

You will run the first part of this recipe on HV1 to move the PSDirect VM from HV1 to HV2. Once you have moved the VM to HV2, you will run the final part of this recipe on HV2 to move the VM back to HV1. If you attempt to run the last part of this recipe remotely, for example, for a client machine or from HV1 (suitably wrapped up in a script block you run with Invoke-Command), you will see a Kerberos error due to the Kerberos Double Hop problem. You can deploy Windows **Credential Security System Provider (CredSSP)** to overcome that issue.

How to do it...

1. Viewing the PSDirect VM on HV1 and verifying that it is turned on and running

```
Start-VM -VMName PSDirect
Get-VM -Name PSDirect -Computer HV1
```

2. Getting the VM configuration location

```
(Get-VM -Name PSDirect).ConfigurationLocation
```

3. Getting the virtual hard disk locations

```
Get-VMHardDiskDrive -VMName PSDirect |
    Format-Table -Property VMName, ControllerType, Path
```

4. Moving the VMs to the C:\PSDirectNew folder

```
$MoveStorageHT = @{
  Name                 = 'PSDirect'
  DestinationStoragePath = 'C:\PSDirectNew'
}
Move-VMStorage @MoveStorageHT
```

5. Viewing the configuration details after moving the VM's storage

```
(Get-VM -Name PSDirect).ConfigurationLocation
Get-VMHardDiskDrive -VMName PSDirect |
  Format-Table -Property VMName, ControllerType, Path
```

6. Getting the VM details for the VMs from HV2

```
Get-VM -ComputerName HV2
```

7. Creating Internal virtual switch on HV2

```
$ScriptBlock = {
  $NSHT = @{
    Name            = 'Internal'
    NetAdapterName = 'Ethernet'
    ALLOWmAnagementOS = $true
  }
  New-VMSwitch @NSHT
}
Invoke-Command -ScriptBlock $ScriptBlock -ComputerName HV2
```

8. Enabling VM migration for both HV1 and HV2

```
Enable-VMMigration -ComputerName HV1, HV2
```

9. Configuring VM migration on both hosts

```
$MigrationHT = @{
  UseAnyNetworkForMigration                   = $true
  ComputerName                                = 'HV1', 'HV2'
  VirtualMachineMigrationAuthenticationType = 'Kerberos'
  VirtualMachineMigrationPerformanceOption  = 'Compression'
}
Set-VMHost @MigrationHT
```

10. Moving the PSDirect VM to HV2

```
$Start = Get-Date
$VMMoveHT = @{
  Name            = 'PSDirect'
  ComputerName    = 'HV1'
  DestinationHost = 'HV2'
```

```
    IncludeStorage          =  $true
    DestinationStoragePath = 'C:\PSDirect' # on HV2
}
Move-VM @VMMoveHT
$Finish = Get-Date
```

11. Displaying the time taken to migrate

```
$OS = "Migration took: [{0:n2}] minutes"
($OS -f ($($Finish-$Start).TotalMinutes))
```

12. Checking the VMs on HV1

```
Get-VM -ComputerName HV1
```

13. Checking the VMs on HV2

```
Get-VM -ComputerName HV2
```

14. Looking at the details of the PSDirect VM on HV2

```
((Get-VM -Name PSDirect -Computer HV2).ConfigurationLocation)
Get-VMHardDiskDrive -VMName PSDirect -Computer HV2  |
   Format-Table -Property VMName, Path
```

Run the remainder of this recipe on HV2.

15. Moving the PSDirect VM back to HV1

```
$Start2 = Get-Date
$VMHT2  = @{
    Name                    = 'PSDirect'
    ComputerName            = 'HV2'
    DestinationHost         = 'HV1'
    IncludeStorage          =  $true
    DestinationStoragePath = 'C:\vm\vhds\PSDirect' # on HV1
}
Move-VM @VMHT2
$Finish2  = Get-Date
```

16. Displaying the time taken to migrate back to HV1

```
$OS = "Migration back to HV1 took: [{0:n2}] minutes"
($OS -f ($($fINISH2 - $Start2).TotalMinutes))
```

17. Check VMs on HV1

```
Get-VM -Computer HV1
```

How it works...

In *step 1*, you check the status of the PSDirect VM to confirm that it is up and running. The output should look like this:

```
PS C:\Foo> # 1. Viewing the PSDirect VM on HV1 and verifying that it is turned on and running
PS C:\Foo> Start-VM –VMName PSDirect
PS C:\Foo> Get–VM –Name PSDirect –Computer HV1

Name      State     CPUUsage(%) MemoryAssigned(M) Uptime          Status              Version
----      -----     ----------- ----------------- ------          ------              -------
PSDirect  Running 0               1024             00:00:00.3600000 Operating normally 10.0
```

Figure 11.48: Checking the status of the PSDirect VM

In *step 2*, you determine the location that Hyper-V is using to store the VM configuration for the PSDirect VM, with console output like this:

```
PS C:\Foo> # 2. Getting the VM configuration location
PS C:\Foo> (Get–VM –Name PSDirect).ConfigurationLocation
C:\VM\VMS\PSDirect
```

Figure 11.49: Checking the PSDirect VM configuration location

In *step 3*, you view the locations that Hyper-V is using to store the virtual hard disks for the PSDirect VM, with output like this:

```
PS C:\Foo> # 3. Getting the virtual hard drive locations
PS C:\Foo> Get-VMHardDiskDrive –VMName PSDirect |
              Format–Table –Property VMName, ControllerType, Path

VMName    ControllerType Path
------    -------------- ----
PSDirect             IDE C:\VM\VHDS\PSDirect.Vhdx
PSDirect            SCSI C:\VM\VHDs\PSDirect-D.VHDX
```

Figure 11.50: Viewing PSDirect's virtual hard disks

In *step 4*, you move the storage of the running PSDirect VM. This step generates no output. After moving the VM's storage, in *step 5*, you review the VM configuration location and the details of the hard disks for the PSDirect VM. The output of this step looks like this:

```
PS C:\Foo> # 5. Viewing the configuration details after moving the VM's storage
PS C:\Foo> (Get-VM -Name PSDirect).ConfigurationLocation C:\PSDirectNew
PS C:\Foo> Get-VMHardDiskDrive -VMName PSDirect |
              Format-Table -Property VMName, ControllerType, Path

VMName     ControllerType Path
------     -------------- ----
PSDirect             IDE C:\PSDirectNew\Virtual Hard Disks\PSDirect.Vhdx
PSDirect            SCSI C:\PSDirectNew\Virtual Hard Disks\PSDirect-D.VHDX
```

Figure 11.51: Viewing PSDirect's virtual hard disks after moving the storage

In *step 6*, you check to see which VMs remain available on HV2, with output like this:

```
PS C:\Foo> # 6. Getting the VM details for VMs from HV2
PS C:\Foo> Get-VM -ComputerName HV2

Name     State CPUUsage(%) MemoryAssigned(M) Uptime   Status             Version
----     ----- ----------- ----------------- ------   ------             -------
SQLAcct1 Off   0           0                 00:00:00 Operating normally 10.0
SQLAcct2 Off   0           0                 00:00:00 Operating normally 10.0
SQLAcct3 Off   0           0                 00:00:00 Operating normally 10.0
SQLMfg1  Off   0           0                 00:00:00 Operating normally 10.0
SQLMfg2  Off   0           0                 00:00:00 Operating normally 10.0
```

Figure 11.52: Viewing the VMs on HV2

In *step 7*, you create a new VM networking switch on HV2 to enable VM networking. The output you see is as follows:

```
PS C:\Foo> # 7. Creating Internal virtual switch on HV2
PS C:\Foo> $ScriptBlock = {
             $NSHT = @{
               Name            = 'Internal'
               NetAdapterName = 'Ethernet'
               ALLOWmAnagementOS = $true
             }
             New-VMSwitch @NSHT
           }
PS C:\Foo> Invoke-Command -ScriptBlock $ScriptBlock -ComputerName HV2

Name     SwitchType NetAdapterInterfaceDescription        PSComputerName
----     ---------- ------------------------------        --------------
Internal External   Microsoft Hyper-V Network Adapter HV2
```

Figure 11.53: Creating a new VM switch on HV2

In *step 8*, you enable VM migration on both HV1 and HV2. In *step 9*, you configure Hyper-V VM migration on both servers. Next, in *step 10*, you perform a live migration of the PSDirect VM to HV2. These three steps produce no output.

In *step 11*, you display how long it took Hyper-V to migrate the PSDirect VM, with output like this:

```
PS C:\Foo> # 11. Displaying the time taken to migrate
PS C:\Foo> $OS = "Migration took: [{0:n2}] minutes"
PS C:\Foo> ($OS -f ($($Finish-$Start).TotalMinutes))
Migration took: [1.16] minutes
```

Figure 11.54: Displaying the VM migration time

In *step 12*, you use the Get-VM cmdlet to view the VMs on HV1. Since you migrated the PSDirect VM to HV2, there are no VMs on HV2. Thus, there is no console output from this step. Then, in *step 13*, you view the VMs on HV2, which produces output like this:

```
PS C:\Foo> # 13. Checking the VMs on HV2
PS C:\Foo> Get-VM -ComputerName HV2

Name      State    CPUUsage(%) MemoryAssigned(M) Uptime             Status             Version
----      -----    ----------- ----------------- ------             ------             -------
PSDirect  Running  0           830               00:06:34.0690000   Operating normally 10.0
SQLAcct1  Off      0           0                 00:00:00           Operating normally 10.0
SQLAcct2  Off      0           0                 00:00:00           Operating normally 10.0
SQLAcct3  Off      0           0                 00:00:00           Operating normally 10.0
SQLMfg1   Off      0           0                 00:00:00           Operating normally 10.0
SQLMfg2   Off      0           0                 00:00:00           Operating normally 10.0
```

Figure 11.55: Displaying VMs on HV2

In *step 14*, you examine the details of where Hyper-V has stored the VM configuration and virtual hard disks for the PSDirect VM. The output of this step looks like this:

```
PS C:\Foo> # 14. Looking at the details of the PSDirect VM on HV2
PS C:\Foo> ((Get-VM -Name PSDirect -Computer HV2).ConfigurationLocation)
C:\PSDirect
PS C:\Foo> Get-VMHardDiskDrive -VMName PSDirect -Computer HV2  |
             Format-Table -Property VMName, Path

VMName    Path
------    ----
PSDirect  C:\PSDirect\Virtual Hard Disks\PSDirect.Vhdx
PSDirect  C:\PSDirect\Virtual Hard Disks\PSDirect-D.VHDX
```

Figure 11.56: Displaying the hard disks for the PSDirect VM

In *step 15* (which you run from HV2), you migrate the PSDirect VM back to HV1, producing no console output. In the final step in this recipe, *step 16*, you view how long it took Hyper-V to migrate the VM back to HV1, with output like this:

```
PS C:\Foo> # 16. Displaying the time taken to migrate back to HV1
PS C:\Foo> $OS = "Migration back to HV1 took: [{0:n2}] minutes"
PS C:\Foo> ($OS -F ($($fINISH2 - $Start2).TotalMinutes))
Migration back to HV1 took: [0.96] minutes
```

Figure 11.57: Viewing the PSDirect migration time

There's more...

In *step 1*, you check the status of the PSDirect VM to ensure it is running. If the output you see shows that the VM is not running, you should use the Start-VM cmdlet to start it before proceeding with this recipe.

In *step 6*, you used Get-VM to view the VMs defined on HV2. The output shows the VMs created in the earlier recipe, *Using Hyper-V VM groups*.

In *step 13*, you view the VMs on HV2, which now shows the PSDirect VM. Note that the VM has continued running since you performed a live migration. Consider opening a remote desktop connection using mstsc.exe, or use the VMConnect feature of the Hyper-V management console and open a session to the PSDirect VM. With either method, you can use and view the VM as you carry out the migration. When the migration is complete, you may need to log in to your VM session again.

Managing VM replication

VM replication is a disaster recovery feature within Hyper-V. Hyper-V creates a VM replica on a remote Hyper-V server and keeps that replica up to date as the original VM changes. You can make the replica active should the VM's host fail for some reason. The VM on the remote host is not active during the normal operation of the original VM.

With Hyper-V replication, the source VM host bundles up the changes in a running VM's VHD file(s) and regularly sends them to the replica server. The replica server then applies those changes to the dormant replica.

Once you have established a VM replica, you can test the replica to ensure that it can start should you need it. Also, you can fail over to the replica, bringing the replicated VM up based on the most recently replicated data. If the source VM host becomes inoperable before it can replicate changes on the source VM, there is a risk of the replication process losing those changes.

In this recipe, you will create and use a replica of the PSDirect VM, which you have used in previous recipes in this chapter.

Getting ready

This recipe creates a Hyper-V VM replica of the PSDirect VM running in HV1 to HV2. You created this VM in the *Creating a Hyper-V VM* recipe. You also use this VM in the *Managing VM and storage movement* recipe.

You should have loaded the Hyper-V management tools on DC1. If you have not already done so, do the following on DC1:

```
Install-WindowsFeature -Name RSAT-Hyper-V-Tools, Hyper-V-PowerShell |
  Out-Null
```

Additionally, remember that these recipes assume you have turned off any firewalls on your VMs (and host). This simplifies the environment and enables the recipe to focus on, in this case, VM replication.

How to do it...

1. Configuring HV1 and HV2 to be trusted for delegation in AD on DC1

```
$ScriptBlock = {
  Set-ADComputer -Identity HV1 -TrustedForDelegation $True
  Set-ADComputer -Identity HV2 -TrustedForDelegation $True
}
Invoke-Command -ComputerName DC1 -ScriptBlock $ScriptBlock
```

2. Rebooting the HV1 and HV2 hosts

```
Restart-Computer -ComputerName HV2 -Force
Restart-Computer -ComputerName HV1 -Force
```

3. Configuring Hyper-V replication on HV1 and HV2

```
$VMReplHT = @{
  ReplicationEnabled                = $true
  AllowedAuthenticationType         = 'Kerberos'
  KerberosAuthenticationPort        = 42000
  DefaultStorageLocation            = 'C:\Replicas'
  ReplicationAllowedFromAnyServer   = $true
  ComputerName                      = 'HV1.Reskit.Org',
                                      'HV2.Reskit.Org'
}
Set-VMReplicationServer @VMReplHT
```

4. Enabling PSDirect on HV1 to be a replica source

```
$VMReplicaSourceHT = @{
  VMName           = 'PSDirect'
```

```
    Computer            = 'HV1'
    ReplicaServerName   = 'HV2'
    ReplicaServerPort   = 42000
    AuthenticationType  = 'Kerberos'
    CompressionEnabled  = $true
    RecoveryHistory     = 5
  }
  Enable-VMReplication  @VMReplicaSourceHT -Verbose
```

5. Viewing the replication status of HV1

```
  Get-VMReplicationServer -ComputerName HV1
```

6. Checking PSDirect on Hyper-V hosts

```
  Get-VM -ComputerName HV1 -VMName PSDirect
  Get-VM -ComputerName HV2 -VMName PSDirect
```

7. Starting the initial replication

```
  Start-VMInitialReplication -VMName PSDirect -ComputerName HV1
```

8. Examining the replication state on HV1 just after you start the initial replication

```
  Measure-VMReplication -ComputerName HV1
```

9. Examine the replication status on HV1 after replication completes

```
  Measure-VMReplication -ComputerName HV1
```

10. Testing PSDirect failover to HV2

```
  $FOScriptBlock = {
    $VM = Start-VMFailover -AsTest -VMName PSDirect -Confirm:$false
    Start-VM $VM
  }
  Invoke-Command -ComputerName HV2 -ScriptBlock $FOScriptBlock
```

11. Viewing the status of the PSDirect VMs on HV2

```
  $VMsOnHV1 = Get-VM -ComputerName HV2 -VMName PSDirect*
  $VMsOnHV1
```

12. Examining networking on PSDirect Test VM

```
$TestVM = $VMsOnHV1 | Where-Object Name -Match 'Test'
Get-VMNetworkAdapter -CimSession HV2 -VMName $TestVM.Name
```

13. Stopping the failover test

```
$StopScriptBlock = {
  Stop-VMFailover -VMName PSDirect
}
Invoke-Command -ComputerName HV2 -ScriptBlock $StopScriptBlock
```

14. Viewing the status of VMs on HV1 and HV2 after failover has stopped

```
Get-VM -ComputerName HV1 -VMName PSDirect*
Get-VM -ComputerName HV2 -VMName PSDirect*
```

15. Stopping VM on HV1 before performing a planned failover

```
Stop-VM PSDirect -ComputerName HV1
```

16. Starting VM failover from HV1 to HV2

```
Start-VMFailover -VMName PSDirect -ComputerName HV2 -Confirm:$false
```

17. Completing the failover

```
$CHT = @{
  VMName       = 'PSDIrect'
  ComputerName = 'HV2'
  Confirm      = $false
}
Complete-VMFailover @CHT
```

18. Viewing VM status on both Hyper-V hosts

```
Get-VM -ComputerName HV1 -VMName PSDirect*
Get-VM -ComputerName HV2 -VMName PSDirect*
```

19. Starting the replicated VM on HV2

```
Start-VM -VMname PSDirect -ComputerName HV2
```

20. Checking PSDirect VM networking for HV2

```
Get-VMNetworkAdapter -ComputerName HV2 -VMName PSDirect
```

21. Connecting PSDirect to the VM switch

```
$ConnectHT = @{
  VMName       = 'PSDirect'
  ComputerName = 'HV2'
  SwitchName   = 'Internal'
}
Connect-VMNetworkAdapter @ConnectHT
```

22. Checking PSDirect VM networking for HV2

```
Get-VMNetworkAdapter -ComputerName HV2 -VMName PSDirect
```

How it works...

In *step 1*, you configure HV1 and HV2 to be trusted for delegation as required to support VM replication, and then in *step 2*, you reboot both hosts to complete the process of trusting these hosts for delegation. These two steps produce no console output.

After rebooting both hosts, in *step 3*, you configure both Hyper-V hosts to support VM replication. In *step 4*, you set up a Hyper-V replication partnership between HV1 and HV2. These two steps create no output.

In *step 5*, you review the replication status of the HV1 Hyper-V host, which creates output like this:

```
PS C:\Foo> # 5. Viewing the replication status of HV1
PS C:\Foo> Get-VMReplicationServer -ComputerName HV1

RepEnabled AuthType KerbAuthPort CertAuthPort AllowAnyServer
---------- -------- ------------ ------------ --------------
True       Kerb     42000        443          True
```

Figure 11.58: Viewing the replication status of HV1

Next, in *step 6*, you check the replication status of the PSDirect VM, which you do on both Hyper-V servers. The output of this step looks like this:

```
PS C:\Foo> # 6. Checking PSDirect on Hyper-V hosts
PS C:\Foo> Get-VM -ComputerName HV1 -VMName PSDirect

Name      State   CPUUsage(%) MemoryAssigned(M) Uptime              Status              Version
----      -----   ----------- ----------------- ------              ------              -------
PSDirect  Running 3           1024              00:11:43.8010000    Operating normally  10.0

PS C:\Foo> Get-VM -ComputerName HV2 -VMName PSDirect

Name      State CPUUsage(%) MemoryAssigned(M) Uptime          Status              Version
----      ----- ----------- ----------------- ------          ------              -------
PSDirect  Off   0           0                 00:00:00        Operating normally  10.0
```

Figure 11.59: Checking the PSDirect VM status on HV1 and HV2

In *step 7*, you start the VM replication process. This step involves Hyper-V creating a duplicate VM on HV2, essentially a full copy of the PSDirect VM. This step produces no output.

If you run *step 8* immediately after completing *step 7*, you can observe the initial replication process. You should see output like this:

```
PS C:\Foo> # 8. Examining the initial replication state on HV1 just after
PS C:\Foo> #    you start the initial replication
PS C:\Foo> Measure-VMReplication -ComputerName HV1

VMName    State                       Health LReplTime PReplSize(M) AvgLatency AvgReplSize(M) Relationship
------    -----                       ------ --------- ------------ ---------- -------------- ------------
PSDirect  InitialReplicationInProgress Normal          7,650.41                0.00           Simple
```

Figure 11.60: Viewing the replication process

The initial replication process should take a few minutes. However, the replication speed also depends on the Hyper-V host hardware components, VM memory and virtual processors, and the underlying network and disk subsystem speeds. The disk sizes of a VM's virtual disks are also a significant factor that affects the initial replication speed. After Hyper-V completes the initial replication of PSDirect, you can view the replication status, as shown in *step 9*. The output of this step looks like this:

```
PS C:\Foo> # 9. Examining the replication status on HV1 after replication completes
PS C:\Foo> Measure-VNReplication -ComputerName HV1

VMName    State       Health LReplTime           PReplSize(M) AvgLatency AvgReplSize(M) Relationship
------    -----       ------ ---------           ------------ ---------- -------------- ------------
PSDirect  Replicating Normal 28/09/2022 12:14:53 16.01        00:01:24   2,248.00       Simple
```

Figure 11.61: Viewing the replication once the initial replication is complete

Once the PSDirect replication is invoked, and Hyper-V has completed an initial replication, you can test the failover capability. In *step 10*, you run a test failover of the PSDirect VM from HV1 to HV2. This step generates no console output.

In *step 11*, you can view the status of the PSDirect VMs on HV2, with an output like this:

```
PS C:\Foo> # 11. Viewing the status of PSDirect VMs on HV2
PS C:\Foo> $VMsOnHV1 = Get-VM —ComputerName HV2 —VMName PSDirect*
PS C:\Foo> $VMsOnHV1

Name                State   CPUUsage(%) MemoryAssigned(M) Uptime           Status             Version
----                -----   ----------- ----------------- ------           ------             -------
PSDirect — Test Running 3          1024              00:05:34.2340000 Operating normally 10.0
PSDirect            Off     0          0                 00:00:00         Operating normally 10.0
```

Figure 11.62: Viewing PSDirect VMs on HV2

In *step 12*, you examine the networking in the PSDirect test VM with output like this:

```
PS C:\Foo> # 12. Examining networking on PS DIrtect Test VM
PS C:\Foo> $TestVM = $VMsOnHV1 1 Where—Object Name —Match 'Test'
PS C:\Foo> Get-VMNetworkAdapter —CimSession HV2 —VMName $TestVM.Name

Name            IsManagementOs VMName       SwitchName MacAddress   Status IPAddresses
----            -------------- ------       ---------- ----------   ------ -----------
Network Adapter False          PSDirect — Test          00155D0ACA03 {0k}   {169.254.12.154, fe80::904d:130b:5e89:c9a}
```

Figure 11.63: Viewing the status of PSDirect networking

In *step 13*, you stop the PSDirect VM before carrying out a *planned* failover. Next, in *step 15*, you perform the planned failover of PSDirect from HV1 to HV2. Once you have initiated the planned failover (that is, once the cmdlet completes), in *step 16*, you complete the VM failover process. In *step 17*, you start the PSDirect VM on HV2. These four steps produce no console output.

In *step 18*, you check the status of the PSDirect VM on both Hyper-V hosts. This step generates the following output:

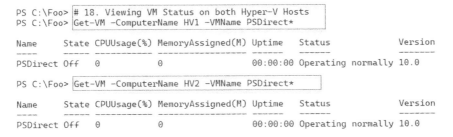

```
PS C:\Foo> # 18. Viewing VM Status on both Hyper-V Hosts
PS C:\Foo> Get-VM —ComputerName HV1 —VMName PSDirect*

Name      State CPUUsage(%) MemoryAssigned(M) Uptime   Status             Version
----      ----- ----------- ----------------- ------   ------             -------
PSDirect Off   0          0                 00:00:00 Operating normally 10.0

PS C:\Foo> Get-VM —ComputerName HV2 —VMName PSDirect*

Name      State CPUUsage(%) MemoryAssigned(M) Uptime   Status             Version
----      ----- ----------- ----------------- ------   ------             -------
PSDirect Off   0          0                 00:00:00 Operating normally 10.0
```

Figure 11.64: Checking the VM status of PSDirect on both Hyper-V hosts

In *step 19*, you start the PSDirect VM on the HV2 Hyper-V host. This step creates no output. In *step 20*, you check the networking for the PSDirect VM with an output like this:

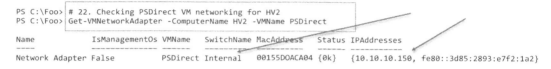

```
PS C:\Foo> # 20. Checking PSDirect VM networking for HV2
PS C:\Foo> Get-VMNetworkAdapter -ComputerName HV2 -VMName PSDirect

Name               IsManagementOs VMName    SwitchName MacAddress   Status IPAddresses
----               -------------- ------    ---------- ----------   ------ -----------
Network Adapter    False          PSDirect             00155D0ACA04 {OK}   {169.254.1.162, fe80::3d85:2893:e7f2:1a2}
```

Figure 11.65: Checking the VM networking on PSDirect

In *step 20*, you add the NIC in the PSDirect VM into the Internal VM switch on HV2, creating no console output. In *step 22*, you re-check the networking on PSDirect with an output like this:

```
PS C:\Foo> # 22. Checking PSDirect VM networking for HV2
PS C:\Foo> Get-VMNetworkAdapter -ComputerName HV2 -VMName PSDirect

Name               IsManagementOs VMName    SwitchName MacAddress   Status IPAddresses
----               -------------- ------    ---------- ----------   ------ -----------
Network Adapter    False          PSDirect  Internal   00155D0ACA04 {0k}   {10.10.10.150, fe80::3d85:2893:e7f2:1a2}
```

Figure 11.66: Checking the VM networking on PSDirect

There's more...

In *step 11*, you view the two PSDirect VMs on HV2. The first is the VM that you are replicating from HV1. During this step, PSDirect is up and running on HV1 and replicates any changes to HV2. You see a separate test VM showing that the replica VM is up and running on HV2. It is always good to run a test failover after setting up replication to ensure that the replication and failover work as you wish.

In *step 18*, you view the PSDirect VM status on both of your Hyper-V hosts. As you can see in the output from this step, *Figure 11.64*, the PSDirect VM is up and running on HV2. On HV1, you still have an (older) copy of the VM with the VM failed over (and running) on HV2.

Managing VM checkpoints

With Hyper-V in Server 2022, a checkpoint captures the state of a VM as a restore point. Hyper-V then enables you to roll back a VM to a checkpoint. Windows Server 2008's version of Hyper-V provided this feature, although these restore points were called snapshots at that time.

In Server 2012, Microsoft changed the name to "checkpoint." This terminology change was consistent with System Center and avoided any confusion with the **Volume Shadow Copy Service (VSS)** snapshots used by many backup systems. While the Hyper-V team changed the terminology, some of the cmdlet names remain unchanged. For instance, to restore a VM to a checkpoint, you use the Restore-VMSnapshot cmdlet.

You can create a variety of checkpoints for a VM. When you create a checkpoint, Hyper-V temporarily pauses the VM. Hyper-V creates a new differencing disk (AVHD). Hyper-V then resumes the VM, which writes all data to the differencing disk.

Checkpoints are excellent for a variety of scenarios. They can be helpful in troubleshooting. You can trigger a bug in the VM and take a checkpoint. Then, you can try a fix—if it doesn't work, you can just roll the VM back to the checkpoint and try another fix. Checkpoints are also helpful for training. You can create a VM in which you perform all the lab exercise steps and create a checkpoint after each successful lab. That way, the student can make a mistake in a lab exercise and skip forward to a later checkpoint to carry on.

Using checkpoints in production is a different matter. In general, you should avoid using checkpoints on your production systems for several reasons. If your servers use any replication or transaction-based applications, the impact of rolling back a VM to an earlier time can lead to issues. Since checkpoints rely on differencing disks that feature constantly growing physical disk files, using checkpoints can also result in poor performance.

In this recipe, you will create a checkpoint of the PSDirect VM, and then you create a file inside the VM. You will take a further checkpoint and create a second file. Then, you will revert to the first checkpoint, observing that there are no files (thus far) created. You roll forward to the second checkpoint to see that the first file is there but not the second (because you created the second file after taking the checkpoint). Then, you remove all the checkpoints. After each checkpoint operation, you observe the VHDX and AVHD files that Hyper-V uses in the PSDirect VM.

Getting ready

You will run this recipe on HV1. This recipe uses the PSDirect VM you created and used earlier in this chapter. Depending on which other recipes you have run from this chapter, the virtual disks may be in different folders, but the recipe copes with the disk files in any folder known to Hyper-V.

How to do it...

1. Ensuring PSDirect VM is running

```
$VMState = Get-VM -VMName PSDirect | Select-Object -ExpandProperty
State
If ($VMState -eq 'Off') {
  Start-VM -VMName PSDirect
}
```

2. Creating credentials for PSDirect

```
$RKAdmin     = 'Wolf\Administrator'
$Pass        = 'Pa$$w0rd'
$RKPassword  =
    ConvertTo-SecureString -String $Pass -AsPlainText -Force
$RKCred = [System.Management.Automation.PSCredential]::new(
    $RKAdmin,$RKPassword)
```

3. Examining the C:\ in the PSDirect VM before we start

```
$ScriptBlock = { Get-ChildItem -Path C:\ | Format-Table}
$InvocationHT = @{
  VMName      = 'PSDirect'
  ScriptBlock = $ScriptBlock
  Credential  = $RKCred
}
Invoke-Command @InvocationHT
```

4. Creating a checkpoint of PSDirect on HV1

```
$CPHT = @{
  VMName        = 'PSDirect'
  ComputerName  = 'HV1'
  SnapshotName  = 'Snapshot1'
}
Checkpoint-VM @CPHT
```

5. Examining the files created to support the checkpoints

```
$Parent = Split-Path -Parent (Get-VM -Name PSdirect |
            Select-Object -ExpandProperty HardDrives).Path |
              Select-Object -First 1
Get-ChildItem -Path $Parent
```

6. Creating some content in a file on PSDirect and displaying it   .

```
$ScriptBlock = {
  $FileName1 = 'C:\File_After_Checkpoint_1'
  Get-Date | Out-File -FilePath $FileName1
  Get-Content -Path $FileName1
}
```

```
$InvocationHT = @{
  VMName      = 'PSDirect'
  ScriptBlock = $ScriptBlock
  Credential  = $RKCred
}
Invoke-Command @InvocationHT
```

7. Taking a second checkpoint

```
$SecondChkpointHT = @{
  VMName        = 'PSDirect'
  ComputerName  = 'HV1'
  SnapshotName  = 'Snapshot2'
}
Checkpoint-VM @SecondChkpointHT
```

8. Viewing the VM checkpoint details for PSDirect

```
Get-VMSnapshot -VMName PSDirect
```

9. Looking at the files supporting the two checkpoints

```
Get-ChildItem -Path $Parent
```

10. Creating and displaying another file in PSDirect

```
$ScriptBlock2 = {
  $FileName2 = 'C:\File_After_Checkpoint_2'
  Get-Date | Out-File -FilePath $FileName2
  Get-ChildItem -Path C:\ -File | Format-Table
}
$InvocationHT2 = @{
  VMName      = 'PSDirect'
  ScriptBlock = $ScriptBlock2
  Credential  = $RKCred
}
Invoke-Command @InvocationHT2
```

11. Restoring the PSDirect VM back to the checkpoint named Snapshot1

```
$Snap1 = Get-VMSnapshot -VMName PSDirect -Name Snapshot1
Restore-VMSnapshot -VMSnapshot $Snap1 -Confirm:$false
```

```
Start-VM -Name PSDirect
Wait-VM -For IPAddress -Name PSDirect
```

12. Seeing what files we have now on PSDirect

```
$ScriptBlock3 = {
  Get-ChildItem -Path C:\ | Format-Table
}
$InvocationHT3 = @{
  VMName      = 'PSDirect'
  ScriptBlock = $ScriptBlock3
  Credential  = $RKCred
}
Invoke-Command @InvocationHT3
```

13. Rolling forward to Snapshot2

```
$Snap2 = Get-VMSnapshot -VMName PSdirect -Name Snapshot2
Restore-VMSnapshot -VMSnapshot $Snap2 -Confirm:$false
Start-VM -Name PSDirect
Wait-VM -For IPAddress -Name PSDirect
```

14. Observe the files you now have supporting PSDirect

```
$ScriptBlock4 = {
    Get-ChildItem -Path C:\ | Format-Table
}
$InvocationHT4 = @{
  VMName      = 'PSDirect'
  ScriptBlock = $ScriptBlock4
  Credential  = $RKCred
}
Invoke-Command @InvocationHT4
```

15. Restoring to Snapshot1 again

```
$Snap1 = Get-VMSnapshot -VMName PSDirect -Name Snapshot1
Restore-VMSnapshot -VMSnapshot $Snap1 -Confirm:$false
Start-VM -Name PSDirect
Wait-VM -For IPAddress -Name PSDirect
```

16. Checking checkpoints and VM data files again

```
Get-VMSnapshot -VMName PSDirect
Get-ChildItem -Path $Parent | Format-Table
```

17. Removing all the checkpoints from HV1

```
Get-VMSnapshot -VMName PSDirect |
    Remove-VMSnapshot
```

18. Checking VM data files again

```
Get-ChildItem -Path $Parent
```

How it works...

In *step 1*, you ensure that the PSDirect VM is running (on HV1). Next, in *step 2*, you create a Windows credential object to use when invoking script blocks inside the PSDirect VM. These steps generate no console output.

In *step 3*, using the credential object you created earlier, you invoke a script block that examines the C:\ drive inside the PSDirect VM. This step creates output like this:

```
PS C:\Foo> # 3. Examining the C:\ in the PSDirect VM before we start
PS C:\Foo> $ScriptBlock = { Get-ChildItem -Path C:\ | Format-Table}
PS C:\Foo> $InvocationHT = @{
             VMName      = 'PSDirect'
             ScriptBlock = $ScriptBlock
             Credential  = $RKCred
           }
PS C:\Foo> Invoke-Command @InvocationHT


    Directory: C:\


Mode                 LastWriteTime         Length Name
----                 -------------         ------ ----
d-----          5/8/2021    1:20 AM                PerfLogs
d-r---          9/26/2022   9:47 AM                Program Files
d-----          5/8/2021    2:39 AM                Program Files (x86)
d-r---          9/16/2022   5:50 AM                Users
d-----          9/17/2022   5:55 AM                Windows
```

Figure 11.67: Viewing the C:\ drive inside the PSDirect VM

In *step 4*, you use the Checkpoint-VM cmdlet to create a new VM checkpoint, which you name Snapshot1. This step creates no output.

With *step 5*, you determine where Hyper-V has stored the virtual disks for the PSDirect VM, and then you display the associated files with an output like this:

```
PS C:\Foo> # 5. Examining the files created to support the checkpoints
PS C:\Foo> $Parent = Split-Path -Parent (Get-VM -Name PSdirect |
                     Select-Object -ExpandProperty HardDrives).Path |
                     Select-Object -First 1
PS C:\Foo> Get-ChildItem -Path $Parent


    Directory: C:\VM\VHDS\PSDirect\Virtual Hard Disks

Mode                 LastWriteTime         Length Name
----                 -------------         ------ ----
-a---       18/10/2022     17:23        37748736 PSDirect_FB257654-AAF1-4BF0-815D-BA73754FA7FA.avhdx
-a---       18/10/2022     17:22         4194304 PSDirect-D_13E2C8CF-E339-4D79-B2B9-9414EB86AB3F.avhdx
-a---       18/10/2022     17:13         4194304 PSDirect-D.VHDX
-a---       18/10/2022     17:22     11815354368 PSDirect.Vhdx
```

Figure 11.68: Examining files supporting a checkpoint

In *step 6*, you create a new file on the C:\ drive in the PSDirect VM. Then, you view the contents of this file. The output looks like this:

```
PS C:\Foo> # 6. Creating some content in a file on PSDirect and displaying it
PS C:\Foo> $ScriptBlock = {
              $FileName1 = 'C:\File_After_Checkpoint_1'
              Get-Date | Out-File -FilePath $FileName1
              Get-Content -Path $FileName1
           }
PS C:\Foo> $InvocationHT = @{
              VMName      = 'PSDirect'
              ScriptBlock = $ScriptBlock
              Credential  = $RKCred
           }
PS C:\Foo> Invoke-Command @InvocationHT

Tuesday, October 18, 2022 4:20:55 AM
```

Figure 11.69: Creating a file in the PSDirect VM

After creating a file inside the VM, in *step 7*, you create a second checkpoint that generates no output. In *step 8*, you use the Get-VMSnapshot cmdlet to view the checkpoint for the PSDirect VM currently on HV1, which looks like this:

```
PS C:\Foo> # 8. Viewing the VM checkpoint details for PSDirect
PS C:\Foo> Get-VMSnapshot -VMName PSDirect

VMName    Name      SnapshotType CreationTime         ParentSnapshotName
------    ----      ------------ ------------         ------------------
PSDirect  Snapshot1 Standard     18/10/2022 17:23:03
PSDirect  Snapshot2 Standard     18/10/2022 17:27:54  Snapshot1
```

Figure 11.70: Viewing snapshots of the PSDirect VM

In *step 9*, again, you examine the files that Hyper-V uses to store your virtual disk images and both sets of checkpoint files for the PSDirect VM like this:

```
PS C:\Foo> # 9. Looking at the files supporting the two checkpoints
PS C:\Foo> Get-ChildItem -Path $Parent

    Directory: C:\VM\VHDS\PSDirect\Virtual Hard Disks

Mode                 LastWriteTime         Length Name
----                 -------------         ------ ----
-a---        18/10/2022     17:28        71303168 PSDirect_30F65FC1-08E3-478E-8D33-291E1001F8B4.avhdx
-a---        18/10/2022     17:27       442499072 PSDirect_FB257654-AAF1-4BF0-815D-BA73754FA7FA.avhdx
-a---        18/10/2022     17:27         4194304 PSDirect-D_13E2C8CF-E339-4D79-B2B9-9414EB86AB3F.avhdx
-a---        18/10/2022     17:27         4194304 PSDirect-D_78C6477B-5603-4639-B0A7-9C37D6063830.avhdx
-a---        18/10/2022     17:13         4194304 PSDirect-D.VHDX
-a---        18/10/2022     17:22     11815354368 PSDirect.Vhdx
```

Figure 11.71: Viewing snapshots of the PSDirect VM

In *step 10*, you create a new file in the PSDirect VM, add contents to the file, and then view those files created so far like this:

```
PS C:\Foo> # 10. Creating and displaying another file in PSDirect
PS C:\Foo> #      (i.e. after you have taken Snapshot2)
PS C:\Foo> $ScriptBlock2 = {
               $FileName2 = 'C:\File_After_Checkpoint_2'
               Get-Date | Out-File -FilePath $FileName2
               Get-ChildItem -Path C:\ -File | Format-Table
           }
PS C:\Foo> $InvocationHT2 = @{
               VMName      = 'PSDirect'
               ScriptBlock = $ScriptBlock2
               Credential  = $RKCred
           }
PS C:\Foo> Invoke-Command @InvocationHT2

    Directory: C:\

Mode                 LastWriteTime         Length Name
----                 -------------         ------ ----
-a----        10/18/2022     9:25 AM           90 File_After_Checkpoint_1
-a----        10/18/2022     9:30 AM           90 File_After_Checkpoint_2
```

Figure 11.72: Creating a second file in PSDirect

In *step 11*, you revert the PSDirect VM back to the first checkpoint (i.e. Snapshot1), which generates no output to the console. In *step 12*, you see what files you now have on the C:\ drive (after you have reverted to the earlier checkpoint), with output like this:

```
PS C:\Foo> # 12. Seeing what files we have now on PSDirect
PS C:\Foo> $ScriptBlock3 = {
                Get-ChildItem -Path C:\ | Format-Table
            }
PS C:\Foo> $InvocationHT3 = @{
              VMName      = 'PSDirect'
              ScriptBlock = $ScriptBlock3
              Credential  = $RKCred
            }
PS C:\Foo> Invoke-Command @InvocationHT3
```

```
    Directory: C:\


Mode                 LastWriteTime         Length Name
----                 -------------         ------ ----
d-----        5/8/2021     1:20 AM                PerfLogs
d-r---        9/26/2022    9:47 AM                Program Files
d-----        5/8/2021     2:39 AM                Program Files (x86)
d-r---        9/16/2022    5:50 AM                Users
d-----        9/17/2022    5:55 AM                Windows
```

Figure 11.73: Checking the files in PSDirect

In *step 13*, you roll forward the PSDirect VM to the second checkpoint, which generates no output. In *step 14*, you examine the files created in PSDirect (in the second checkpoint), which looks like this:

```
PS C:\Foo> # 14. Observe the files you now have supporting PSDirect
PS C:\Foo> $ScriptBlock4 = {
                Get-ChildItem -Path C:\ | Format-Table
            }
PS C:\Foo> $InvocationHT4 = @{
              VMName      = 'PSDirect'
              ScriptBlock = $ScriptBlock4
              Credential  = $RKCred
            }
PS C:\Foo> Invoke-Command @InvocationHT4
```

```
    Directory: C:\


Mode                 LastWriteTime         Length Name
----                 -------------         ------ ----
d-----        5/8/2021     1:20 AM                PerfLogs
d-r---        9/26/2022    9:47 AM                Program Files
d-----        5/8/2021     2:39 AM                Program Files (x86)
d-r---        9/16/2022    5:50 AM                Users
d-----        9/17/2022    5:55 AM                Windows
-a----        10/18/2022   9:25 AM             90 File_After_Checkpoint_1
```

Figure 11.74: Checking files in PSDirect after restoring Snapshot2

In *step 15*, you restore PSDirect to the first checkpoint, a step that generates no console output. In *step 16*, you check the checkpoints and the virtual disk files again, with output like this:

```
PS C:\Foo> # 16. Checking checkpoints and VM data files again
PS C:\Foo> Get-VMSnapshot -VMName PSDirect

VMName   Name      SnapshotType CreationTime        ParentSnapshotName
------   ----      ------------ ------------        ------------------
PSDirect Snapshot1 Standard     18/10/2022 17:23:03
PSDirect Snapshot2 Standard     18/10/2022 17:27:54 Snapshot1

PS C:\Foo> Get-ChildItem -Path $Parent | Format-Table

    Directory: C:\VM\VHDS\PSDirect\Virtual Hard Disks

Mode          LastWriteTime      Length Name
----          -------------      ------ ----
-a--- 18/10/2022     20:41    473956352 PSDirect_414F9F70-521F-42F0-9325-EEA16590E12F.avhdx
-a--- 18/10/2022     17:27    442499072 PSDirect_FB257654-AAF1-4BF0-815D-BA73754FA7FA.avhdx
-a--- 18/10/2022     17:27      4194304 PSDirect-D_13E2C8CF-E339-4D79-B2B9-9414EB86AB3F.avhdx
-a--- 18/10/2022     20:40      4194304 PSDirect-D_37ADA8DF-DDB0-4F1E-9E16-CD5103C7A7A4.avhdx
-a--- 18/10/2022     17:13      4194304 PSDirect-D.VHDX
-a--- 18/10/2022     17:22  11815354368 PSDirect.Vhdx
```

Figure 11.75: Checking the checkpoints on HV1

In *step 17*, you remove all the checkpoints for PSDirect on HV1, which generates no output to the console. In the final step in this recipe, *step 18*, you check the VM data files on HV1, which produces the following output:

```
PS C:\Foo> # 18. Checking VM data files again
PS C:\Foo> Get-ChildItem -Path $Parent

    Directory: C:\VM\VHDS\PSDirect\Virtual Hard Disks

Mode              LastWriteTime         Length Name
----              -------------         ------ ----
-a---        18/10/2022     20:42      4194304 PSDirect-D.VHDX
-a---        18/10/2022     20:42  11815354368 PSDirect.Vhdx
```

Figure 11.76: Viewing the disk files after removing the checkpoints for the PSDirect VM

There's more...

In *step 9*, you examine the files that Hyper-V uses to support the PSDirect VM checkpoints. The first VHDX file holds the starting state at which you took the first checkpoint. Then, you see another AVHDX file (one per virtual disk in the VM) representing the state after the second snapshot. You have taken snapshots of the AVHDX files for both virtual disks, representing any work you have done after taking a checkpoint and before taking another.

In *step 10*, you view the two files you have created in the PSDirect VM. After reverting to the first checkpoint, in *step 12*, you see that neither of the two files you created exists on the C:\ drive. This is because you created those files after creating the first checkpoint. This situation is the expected result of restoring a checkpoint. It also illustrates that you need to take care when reverting to a snapshot, as you can lose work.

A final point about checkpoints/snapshots – this is a great bit of technology but is not a long-term backup or recovery strategy. Backup products, such as VEAAM, can take a snapshot of a VM and back up the now-static VHDX. Once the backup is complete, you remove the snapshot and allow Hyper-V to merge any updates back into the base disk.

Creating a Hyper-V report

Your Hyper-V hosts are almost certainly mission-critical. Indeed, any Hyper-V host you deploy is critical to your IT infrastructure. If a Hyper-V host goes down or starts suffering from performance or capacity issues, it can affect all the VMs running on that host.

If you deploy Hyper-V, you must report on and monitor the health of your HyperV host, as well as the health of the VMs. By monitoring the reports, you can detect issues before they become critical. If your VM host, for example, has a slowly increasing CPU load, you can consider moving a VM to another VM host.

Reports that you use to monitor the health of a Hyper-V host fall into two broad categories – firstly, details about the VM host itself. Secondly, you need to monitor the VMs running on that host. This recipe creates a report containing both sets of information.

Getting ready

This recipe runs on the Hyper-V host HV1. The host should be set up as per the *Installing Hyper-V inside Windows Server* recipe. This host should be up and running and have one VM defined and running. The VM is PSDirect, which you created in the *Creating a Hyper-V VM* recipe.

How to do it...

1. Creating a basic report object hash table

   ```
   $ReportHT = [Ordered] @{}
   ```

2. Adding host details to the report hash table

   ```
   $HostDetails = Get-CimInstance -ClassName Win32_ComputerSystem
   $ReportHT.HostName = $HostDetails.Name
   ```

```
$ReportHT.Maker = $HostDetails.Manufacturer
$ReportHT.Model = $HostDetails.Model
```

3. Adding PowerShell and OS version information

```
$ReportHT.PSVersion = $PSVersionTable.PSVersion.tostring()
$OS = Get-CimInstance -Class Win32_OperatingSystem
$ReportHT.OSEdition   = $OS.Caption
$ReportHT.OSArch      = $OS.OSArchitecture
$ReportHT.OSLang      = $OS.OSLanguage
$ReportHT.LastBootTime = $OS.LastBootUpTime
$Now = Get-Date
$UpdateTime = [float] ("{0:n3}" -f (($Now -$OS.LastBootUpTime).
Totaldays))
$ReportHT.UpTimeDays = $UpdateTime
```

4. Adding a count of processors in the host

```
$ProcessorHT = @{
    ClassName = 'MSvm_Processor'
    Namespace = 'root/virtualization/v2'
}
$Proc = Get-CimInstance @ProcessorHT
$ReportHT.CPUCount = ($Proc |
  Where-Object elementname -match 'Logical Processor').Count
```

5. Adding the current host CPU usage

```
$ClassName = 'Win32_PerfFormattedData_PerfOS_Processor'
$CPU = Get-CimInstance  -ClassName $ClassName |
         Where-Object Name -eq '_Total'    |
           Select-Object -ExpandProperty PercentProcessorTime
$ReportHT.HostCPUUsage = $CPU
```

6. Adding the total host physical memory

```
$Memory = Get-Ciminstance -Class Win32_ComputerSystem
$HostMemory = [float] ( "{0:n2}" -f ($Memory.
TotalPhysicalMemory/1GB))
$ReportHT.HostMemoryGB = $HostMemory
```

7. Adding the memory allocated to VMs

```
$Sum = 0
Get-VM | Foreach-Object {$sum += $_.MemoryAssigned + $Total}
$Sum = [float] ( "{0:N2}" -f ($Sum/1gb) )
$ReportHT.AllocatedMemoryGB = $Sum
```

8. Creating a report header object

```
$HostDetails = $ReportHT | Format-Table | Out-String
```

9. Creating two new VMs to populate the VM report:

```
New-VM -Name VM2 | Out-Null
New-VM -Name VM3 | Out-Null
```

10. Getting VM details on the local VM host

```
$VMs        = Get-VM -Name *
$VMDetails = @()
```

11. Getting VM details for each VM

```
Foreach ($VM in $VMs) {
  # Create VM Report hash table
    $VMReport = [ordered] @{}
  # Add VM's Name
    $VMReport.VMName    = $VM.VMName
  # Add Status
    $VMReport.Status    = $VM.Status
  # Add Uptime
    $VMReport.Uptime    = $VM.Uptime
  # Add VM CPU
    $VMReport.VMCPUUsage = $VM.CPUUsage
  # Replication Mode/Status
    $VMReport.ReplMode  = $VM.ReplicationMode
    $VMReport.ReplState = $Vm.ReplicationState
  # Creating object from Hash table, adding to array
    $VMR = New-Object -TypeName PSObject -Property $VMReport
    $VMDetails += $VMR
}
```

12. Getting the array of VM objects as a table

```
$VMReportDetails =
  $VMDetails |
    Sort-Object -Property VMName |
      Format-Table |
        Out-String
```

13. Creating final report

```
$Report   = "VM Host Details: 'n" +
              $HostDetails   +
              "'nVM Details: 'n" +
              $VMReportDetails
```

14. Displaying the final report

```
$Report
```

How it works...

Except for the final step, none of the steps in this recipe produce a console output.

In *step 1*, you create a report hash table to collect details about the Hyper-V host. In *step 2*, you add the host details to this hash table. In *step 3*, you add the PowerShell and OS details. In *step 4*, you add a count of processors in the Hyper-V host.

In *step 5*, you add the current host's CPU utilization to the hash table. In *step 6*, you add the total physical memory of the host. In *step 7*, you add the memory allocated to VMs. Then, in *step 8*, you create the first part of the Hyper-V report, containing the host system details.

In *step 9*, you create two new VMs to HV1 to add some additional content to the final report. In *step 10*, you collect the details of each VM and create a new hash table.

In *step 11*, you collect details for each VM and add these to the $VMDetails array. In *step 12*, you convert this array into a report fragment. With *step 13*, you create the final report, adding the details about the host and the details of each VM.

In the final step, *step 14*, you display the report, which looks like this:

```
PS C:\Foo> # 14. Displaying final report
PS C:\Foo> $Report

VM Host Details:

Name               Value
----               -----
HostName           HV1
Maker              Microsoft Corporation
Model              Virtual Machine
PSVersion          7.2.6
OSEdition          Microsoft Windows Server 2022 Datacenter
OSArch             64-bit
OSLang             1033
LastBootTime       28/09/2022 11:41:47
UpTimeDays         23.171
CPUCount           6
HostCPUUsage       63
HostMemoryGB       8
AllocatedMemoryGB  1


VM Details:

VMName   Status             Uptime               VMCPUsage ReplMode ReplState
------   ------             ------               --------- -------- ---------
PSDirect Operating normally 2.19:06:58.0580000           6     None Disabled
VM2      Operating normally 00:00:00                     0     None Disabled
VM3      Operating normally 00:00:00                     0     None Disabled
```

Figure 11.77: Viewing disk files after removing the checkpoints for the PSDirect VM

There's more...

This recipe uses various methods to obtain key performance and usage metrics. Once this information has been retrieved, the recipe converts this information into an object, which you can then display.

The recipe first creates a report object, containing the VM host's details. Then, the recipe gets key information about each VM and creates an object for each VM on the host, which the recipe adds to the overall Hyper-V report. At the end of the recipe, you display the combined report. This approach lets you sort and filter the objects to create whatever kind of reporting you need. The technique used here is to create hash tables that hold the host and VM details and then turn these hash tables into full-fledged objects.

This recipe reports some, but not all, of the details of the host or the VMs. You can adjust either part of the recipe to add (or remove) details from the report.

In *step 14*, you view a report of the HV1 Hyper-V host, which is running a limited set of VMs. On a busier and larger system, this report might look like this:

```
VM Host Details:

Name                 Value
----                 -----
HostName             COOKHAM216
Maker                Dell Inc.
Model                Precision 7920 Tower
PSVersion            7.2.6
OSEdition            Microsoft Windows 11 Enterprise Insider Preview
OSArch               64-bit
OSLang               1033
LastBootTime         24/09/2022 18:02:05
UpTimeDays           27.101
CPUCount             64
HostCPUUsage         3
HostMemoryGB         127.51
AllocatedMemoryGB    27.29


VM Details:

VMName         Status              Uptime                VMCPUUsage  ReplMode  ReplState
------         ------              ------                ----------  --------  ---------
***Cookham1 Operating normally 27.02:25:13.2360000              0      None   Disabled
CH1         Operating normally 00:00:00                         0      None   Disabled
DC1         Operating normally 27.02:09:26.9510000              0      None   Disabled
DC2         Operating normally 27.02:09:26.4410000              0      None   Disabled
FS1         Operating normally 00:00:00                         0      None   Disabled
FS2         Operating normally 00:00:00                         0      None   Disabled
HV1         Operating normally 23.08:46:13.1760000              0      None   Disabled
HV2         Operating normally 23.08:46:17.8320000              0      None   Disabled
PSRV        Operating normally 00:00:00                         0      None   Disabled
SMTP-2019   Operating normally 00:00:00                         0      None   Disabled
SRV1        Operating normally 00:00:00                         0      None   Disabled
SRV2        Operating normally 00:00:00                         0      None   Disabled
SS1         Operating normally 00:00:00                         0      None   Disabled
UKDC1       Operating normally 00:00:00                         0      None   Disabled
```

Figure 11.78: Viewing the report on a real Hyper-V host

Join our community on Discord

Join our community's Discord space for discussions with the author and other readers:

`https://packt.link/SecNet`

12

Debugging and Troubleshooting Windows Server

This chapter covers the following recipes:

- Using PSScriptAnalyzer
- Using Best Practices Analyzer
- Exploring PowerShell Script Debugging
- Performing BASIC Network Troubleshooting
- Using Get-NetView to Diagnose Network Issues

Introduction

You can think of debugging as the art and science of removing bugs from your PowerShell scripts. A script may not do what you or your users want, both during the development of a script and after you deploy the script into production. Troubleshooting is a process you go through to determine why your script is not doing what you want, and then it helps you resolve your issues.

There are three broad classes of problems that you encounter:

- Syntax errors
- Logic errors
- Runtime errors

Syntax errors are very common – especially if your typing is less than perfect. It is so easy to type `Get-ChildTiem` as opposed to `Get-ChildItem`. The good news is that your script won't run successfully until you resolve your syntax errors. There are several ways to avoid syntax errors and to simplify the task of finding and removing them. One simple way is to use a good code editor, such as VS Code. Just like Microsoft Word, VS Code highlights potential syntax errors to help you identify, fix, and eliminate them as you make them.

Another way to reduce typos or syntax issues is to use tab completion in the PowerShell console or the VS Code editor. You type some of the necessary text, hit the *tab* key, and PowerShell does the rest of the typing.

Logic errors, on the other hand, are bits of code that do not do what you want or expect. There are many reasons why code could have a logic error. One issue many IT pros encounter is defining a variable but not using it later or typing the variable name incorrectly. Tools such as the PowerShell Script Analyzer can analyze your code and help you track down potential issues in your code.

You can also encounter runtime errors. For example, your script to add and configure a user in your AD could encounter a runtime problem. The AD service on a DC may have crashed, the NIC in your DC might have failed, or the network path from a user to the DC might have a failed router or one with an incorrect routing table. Checking network connectivity ensures that the network path from your user to the relevant servers is working as required. But you also need to confirm that your networking configuration itself is correct.

Troubleshooting network issues in large and complex networks can be a challenge. The `Get-NetView` module (and cmdlet) enables you to gather important information about networking on a given host, which can help resolve issues. Windows and PowerShell do not install this module by default, but it is readily available from the PowerShell Gallery.

The `Get-NetView` command produces a vast amount of detail that can be hard to use. In many cases, there are a few very common networking issues you may face. You will examine some of these problems and their solution in the *Checking Network Connectivity* recipe.

You may have a working system or service that, in some cases, could become problematic if you are unlucky. The Best Practices Analyzer enables you to examine core Windows services to ensure that you run these services in the best possible way.

Windows comes with the **best practices analyzer (BPA)** tool, which can help you analyze your hosts to check whether you have deployed using best practices. You can use the built-in analyzer to assess your systems and possibly implement best practice recommendations, such as always having at least two domain controllers. Some BPA recommendations may not be appropriate for your environment. Running BPA regularly to avoid configuration creep is a great approach.

The systems used in the chapter

This chapter primarily uses the server SRV1, a domain-joined server in the Reskit.Org domain. You have used this server, and the domain, in previous chapters of this book. You also need access to the domain's two DCs (DC1 and DC2). Additionally, you should ensure that SRV1 has access to the internet.

The hosts used in this chapter are as shown here:

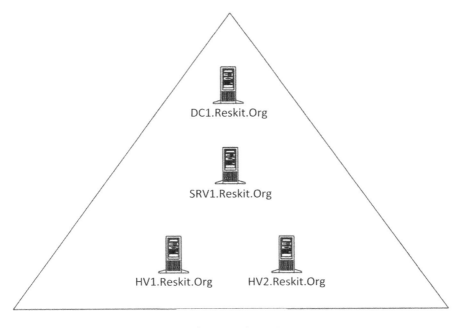

Reskit.Org domain

Figure 12.1: Host in use for this chapter

Using PSScriptAnalyzer

The PowerShell Script Analyzer is a PowerShell module produced by the PowerShell team that analyzes your code and provides opportunities to improve. You can download the latest version of the module from the PowerShell Gallery. Like many PowerShell modules, the Script Analyzer is subject to constant updating. You can always download the newest version of this module directly from GitHub.

Using the VS Code editor to develop your code, you should know that the Script Analyzer is built into VS Code. So as you are creating your PowerShell script, VS Code highlights any errors the Script Analyzer finds. VS Code, therefore, helps you to write better code straightaway.

Another feature of the PowerShell Script Analyzer is the ability to reformat PowerShell code to be more readable. You can configure numerous settings to define how the Script Analyzer should reformat your code.

Getting ready

You run this recipe on SRV1, a domain-joined host. You have installed PowerShell 7 on thius host.

How to do it...

1. Discovering the Powershell Script Analyzer module

```
Find-Module -Name PSScriptAnalyzer |
  Format-List Name, Version, Type, Desc*, Author, Company*, *Date,
*URI*
```

2. Installing the script analyzer module

```
Install-Module -Name PSScriptAnalyzer -Force
```

3. Discovering the commands in the Script Analyzer module

```
Get-Command -Module PSScriptAnalyzer
```

4. Discovering analyzer rules

```
Get-ScriptAnalyzerRule |
  Group-Object -Property Severity |
    Sort-Object -Property Count -Descending
```

5. Examining a rule

    ```
    Get-ScriptAnalyzerRule |
      Select-Object -First 1 |
        Format-List
    ```

6. Creating a script file with issues

    ```
    @'
    # Bad.ps1
    # A file to demonstrate Script Analyzer
    #
    ### Uses an alias
    $Procs = gps
    ### Uses positional parameters
    $Services = Get-Service 'foo' 21
    ### Uses poor function header
    Function foo {"Foo"}
    ### Function redefines a built in command
    Function Get-ChildItem {"Sorry Dave I cannot do that"}
    ### Command uses a hard-coded computer name
    Test-Connection -ComputerName DC1
    ### A line that has trailing white space
    $foobar = "foobar"
    ### A line using a global variable
    $Global:foo
    '@ | Out-File -FilePath "C:\Foo\Bad.ps1"
    ```

7. Checking the newly created script file

    ```
    Get-ChildItem C:\Foo\Bad.ps1
    ```

8. Analyzing the script file

    ```
    Invoke-ScriptAnalyzer -Path C:\Foo\Bad.ps1 |
      Sort-Object -Property Line
    ```

9. Defining a function to format more nicely

    ```
    $Script1 = @'
    function foo {"hello!"
    ```

```
Get-ChildItem -Path C:\FOO
}
'@
```

10. Defining formatting settings

```
$Settings = @{
  IncludeRules = @("PSPlaceOpenBrace", "PSUseConsistentIndentation")
  Rules = @{
    PSPlaceOpenBrace = @{
      Enable = $true
      OnSameLine = $true
    }
    PSUseConsistentIndentation = @{
      Enable = $true
    }
  }
}
```

11. Invoking formatter

```
Invoke-Formatter -ScriptDefinition $Script1 -Settings $Settings
```

12. Changing settings and reformatting

```
$Settings.Rules.PSPlaceOpenBrace.OnSameLine = $False
Invoke-Formatter -ScriptDefinition $Script1 -Settings $Settings
```

How it works...

In *step 1*, you use the Find-Module command to find the PSScriptAnalyzer module in the PowerShell Gallery. The output of this step looks like this:

```
PS C:\Foo> # 1. Discovering the Powershell Script Analyzer module
PS C:\Foo> Find-Module -Name PSScriptAnalyzer |
               Format-List Name, Version, Type, Desc*, Author, Company*, *Date, *URI*
```

```
Name            : PSScriptAnalyzer
Version         : 1.21.0
Type            : Module
Description     : PSScriptAnalyzer provides script analysis and checks for
                  potential code defects in the scripts by applying a group
                  of built-in or customized rules on the scripts being analyzed.
Author          : Microsoft Corporation
CompanyName     : {PowerShellTeam, JamesTruher-MSFT, rjmholt}
PublishedDate   : 29/09/2022 20:14:59
InstalledDate   :
UpdatedDate     :
LicenseUri      : https://github.com/PowerShell/PSScriptAnalyzer/blob/master/LICENSE
ProjectUri      : https://github.com/PowerShell/PSScriptAnalyzer
IconUri         : https://raw.githubusercontent.com/powershell/psscriptanalyzer/master/logo.png
```

Figure 12.2: Finding the PowerShell Script Analyzer module

In *step 2*, you install the PSScriptAnalyzer module, which generates no console output. In *step 3*, you use the Get-Command cmdlet to discover the commands inside the PSScriptAnalyzer module, with output like this:

```
PS C:\Foo> # 3. Discovering the commands in the Script Analyzer module
PS C:\Foo> Get-Command -Module PSScriptAnalyzer
```

```
CommandType Name                  Version Source
----------- ----                  ------- ------
Cmdlet      Get-ScriptAnalyzerRule 1.21.0  PSScriptAnalyzer
Cmdlet      Invoke-Formatter       1.21.0  PSScriptAnalyzer
Cmdlet      Invoke-ScriptAnalyzer  1.21.0  PSScriptAnalyzer
```

Figure 12.3: Getting the commands in the Script Analyzer module

The PowerShell Script Analyzer uses a set of rules that define potential problems with your scripts. In *step 4*, you use Get-ScriptAnalyzerRule to examine the types of rules available, with output like this:

```
PS C:\Foo> # 4. Discovering analyzer rules
PS C:\Foo> Get-ScriptAnalyzerRule |
               Group-Object -Property Severity |
               Sort-Object -Property Count -Sescebding
```

```
Count Name        Group
----- ----        -----
   50 Warning     {PSAlignAssignmentStatement, PSAvoidUsingCmdletAliases, PSAvoidAssignmentT…
   11 Information {PSAvoidUsingPositionalParameters, PSAvoidTrailingWhitespace, PSAvoidUsing…
    7 Error       {PSAvoidUsingUsernameAndPasswordParams, PSAvoidUsingComputerNameHardcoded,…
```

Figure 12.4: Examining Script Analyzer rule types

You can view one of the Script Analyzer rules using the `Get-ScriptAnalyzerRule`, as shown in *step 5*, with output like this:

```
PS C:\Foo> # 5. Examining a rule
PS C:\Foo> Get-ScriptAnalyzerRule |
             Select-Object -First 1 |
               Format-List

Name        :
Severity    : Warning
Description : Line up assignment statements such that the assignment operator are aligned.
SourceName  : PS
```

Figure 12.5: Examining a Script Analyzer rule

In *step 6*, which generates no console output, you create a new script file (bad.ps1). This script has issues that possibly need attention. In *step 7*, you check on the newly created script file with output like this:

```
PS C:\Foo> # 7. Checking the newly created script file
PS C:\Foo> Get-ChildItem C:\Foo\Bad.ps1

       Directory: C:\Foo

Mode              LastWriteTime   Length Name
----              -------------   ------ ----
-a---       26/10/2022     19:38     567 Bad.ps1
```

Figure 12.6: Checking the newly created script file

In *step 8*, you use the `Invoke-ScriptAnalyzer` command to check the C:\Foo\Bad.ps1 file for potential issues. The output from this step looks like this:

```
PS C:\Foo> PS C:\Foo> # 8. Analyzing the script file
PS C:\Foo> Invoke-ScriptAnalyzer -Path C:\Foo\Bad.ps1 |
           Sort-Object -Property Line

RuleName                                Severity     ScriptName Line  Message
--------                                --------     ---------- ----  -------
PSAvoidUsingCmdletAliases               Warning      Bad.ps1    5     'gps' is an alias of 'Get-Process'.
                                                                      Alias can introduce possible problems
                                                                      and make scripts hard to maintain.
                                                                      Please consider changing alias to its
                                                                      full content.
PSUseDeclaredVarsMoreThanAssignments    Warning      Bad.ps1    5     The variable 'Procs' is assigned but
                                                                      never used.
PSUseDeclaredVarsMoreThanAssignments    Warning      Bad.ps1    7     The variable 'Services' is assigned but
                                                                      never used.
PSAvoidOverwritingBuiltInCmdlets        Warning      Bad.ps1    11    'Get-ChildItem' is a cmdlet that is
                                                                      included with PowerShell (version
                                                                      core-6.1.0-windows) whose definition
                                                                      should not be overridden
PSAvoidUsingComputerNameHardcoded       Error        Bad.ps1    13    The ComputerName parameter of cmdlet
                                                                      'Test-Connection' is hardcoded. This
                                                                      will expose sensitive information about
                                                                      the system if the script is shared.
PSAvoidTrailingWhitespace               Information  Bad.ps1    15    Line has trailing whitespace
PSUseDeclaredVarsMoreThanAssignments    Warning      Bad.ps1    15    The variable 'foobar' is assigned but
                                                                      never used.
PSAvoidGlobalVars                       Warning      Bad.ps1    17    Found global variable 'Global:foo'.
```

Figure 12.7: Analyzing the script

A second and useful feature of Script Analyzer is to reformat a script file to improve the script's layout. Reformatting can be useful, for example, if you are cutting and pasting code from various internet sources (each with its own unique formatting styles). Here, you define a simple PowerShell with no formatting applied. This step generates no console output.

IT pros may never agree on what constitutes a good code layout. Script Analyzer lets you specify exactly how you want it to format your code. In *step 10*, you specify a set of formatting rules, which generates no output.

In *step 11*, you invoke the script formatter using the settings specified in the previous step. The output of this step is as follows:

```
PS C:\Foo> # 11. Invoking formatter
PS C:\Foo> Invoke-Formatter -ScriptDefinition $Script1 -Settings $Settings
function foo {
    "hello!"
    Get-ChildItem -Path C:\FOO
}
```

Figure 12.8: Using the script formatter and formatting rules

In *step 12*, you update the formatting rules. These changes ask the formatter to place the start of a function definition's script block. You have the option to have the formatter put the open brace character ({) that follows the function keyword and function name on the same line or, as in this case, on a separate line. The output of this step looks like this:

```
PS C:\Foo> # 12. Changing settings and reformatting
PS C:\Foo> $Settings.Rules.PSPlaceOpenBrace.OnSameLine = $False
PS C:\Foo> Invoke-Formatter -ScriptDefinition $Script1 -Settings $Settings
function foo
{
    "hello!"
    Get-ChildItem -Path C:\FOO
}
```

Figure 12.9: Changing formatter rules reformatting the function definition

There's more...

In *step 1*, you view details about the PSScriptAnalyzer module. The version shown in the output may differ from what you see if you test the recipe. The module developers update this module regularly. Microsoft regularly posts details about what is new in an updated module version. For example, you can read details about the latest (at the time of writing!) update to the module here: https://devblogs.microsoft.com/powershell/psscriptanalyzer-pssa-1-21-0-has-been-released/.

Note that the author of this module was a long-time PowerShell team member, Jim Truher. Interestingly, Jim did some demonstrations the first time Microsoft displayed Monad (as PowerShell was then named) at the PDC in the autumn of 2003. This book's author was in the room!

In the final part of this recipe, you use the formatting feature to format a small function. The goal of the formatter is to help you create easier-to-read code. That can be very useful for long production scripts or when you have hundreds of scripts that you want to format consistently. A consistent layout makes it easier to find issues, as well as simplifying subsequent script maintenance.

Step 12 sets a rule that makes the Script Analyzer's formatter put a script block's opening brace on a separate line. Opinion varies as to whether this is a good approach. Therefore, the formatting rules provide you with options such as lining up the "=" sign in a set of assignment statements, and many more. The documentation on these rules is not particularly helpful, but you can start here: https://www.powershellgallery.com/packages/PSScriptAnalyzer/1.21.0/Content/Settings%5CCodeFormatting.psd1. If Microsoft issues an update to this module, adjust this URL to point to the latest version.

And for the curious, you can look at the module and its contents on the project's GitHub repository at `https://github.com/PowerShell/PSScriptAnalyzer`.

Performing BASIC Network Troubleshooting

For many common network problems, some simple steps may help you resolve your more common issues or point you toward a solution.

In this recipe, you carry out some basic troubleshooting on a local SRV1, a domain-joined host running Windows Server 2022. A common adage amongst many IT pros is that the problem is DNS, irrespective of the problem (until you prove otherwise). You start this recipe by getting the host's **fully qualified domain name (FQDN)** and the IPv4 address of the DNS server, and then you check whether the DNS server(s) is online.

You then use the configured DNS server to determine the names of the DCs in your domain and ensure you can reach each DC over TCP port 389 (LDAP) and TCP port 445 (for GPOs). Next, you test the default gateway's availability. Finally, you test the ability to reach a remote host over port 80 (HTTP) and port 443 (HTTP over SSL/TLS).

In most cases, the simple tests in this recipe, run on the afflicted host, should help you find some of the more common problems.

Getting ready

You run this recipe on SRV1, a domain-joined host. You must have both DC1 and DC2 running, providing a DNS service for the domain. You should also ensure you have configured SRV1 to point to these two DCs for DNS.

How to do it...

1. Getting and displaying the DNS name of this host

   ```
   $DNSDomain = $Env:USERDNSDOMAIN
   $FQDN      = "$Env:COMPUTERNAME.$DNSDomain"
   "Host FQDN: $FQDN"
   ```

2. Getting DNS server address

   ```
   $DNSHT = @{
     InterfaceAlias = "Ethernet"
     AddressFamily  = 'IPv4'
   }
   ```

```
$DNSServers = (Get-DnsClientServerAddress @DNSHT).ServerAddresses
$DNSServers
```

3. Checking if the DNS servers are online

```
Foreach ($DNSServer in $DNSServers) {
  $TestDNS = Test-NetConnection -Port 53 -ComputerName $DNSServer
  $Result  = $TestDNS ? "Available" : ' Not reachable'
  "DNS Server [$DNSServer] is $Result"
}
```

4. Defining a search for DCs in our domain

```
$DNSRRName = "_ldap._tcp." + $DNSDomain
$DNSRRName
```

5. Getting the DC SRV records

```
$DCRRS = Resolve-DnsName -Name $DNSRRName -Type all |
    Where-Object IP4address -ne $null
$DCRRS
```

6. Testing each DC for availability over LDAP

```
ForEach ($DNSRR in $DCRRS){
  $TestDC = Test-NetConnection -Port 389 -ComputerName $DNSRR.
IPAddress
  $Result  = $TestDC ? 'DC Available' : 'DC Not reachable'
  "DC [$($DNSRR.Name)]  at [$($DNSRR.IPAddress)]   $Result for LDAP"
}
```

7. Testing DC availability for SMB

```
ForEach ($DNSRR in $DCRRS){
  $TestDC =
    Test-NetConnection -Port 445 -ComputerName $DNSRR.IPAddress
  $Result  = $TestDC ? 'DC Available' : 'DC Not reachable'
  "DC [$($DNSRR.Name)]  at [$($DNSRR.IPAddress)]   $Result for SMB"
}
```

8. Testing default gateway

```
$NIC     = Get-NetIPConfiguration -InterfaceAlias Ethernet
$DGW     = $NIC.IPv4DefaultGateway.NextHop
$TestDG  = Test-NetConnection $DGW
$Result  = $TestDG.PingSucceeded ? "Reachable" : ' NOT Reachable'
"Default Gateway for [$($NIC.Interfacealias) is [$DGW] - $Result"
```

9. Testing a remote web site using ICMP

```
$Site     = "WWW.Packt.Com"

$TestIP   = Test-NetConnection -ComputerName $Site
$ResultIP = $TestIP ? "Ping OK" : "Ping FAILED"
"ICMP to $Site - $ResultIP"
```

10. Testing a remote web site using port 80

```
$TestPort80 = Test-Connection -ComputerName $Site -TcpPort 80
$Result80   = $TestPort80 ? 'Site Reachable' : 'Site NOT reachable'
"$Site over port 80   : $Result80"
```

11. Testing a remote web site using port 443

```
$TestPort443 = Test-Connection -ComputerName $Site -TcpPort 443
$Result443   = $TestPort443 ? 'Site Reachable' : 'Site NOT
reachable'
"$Site over port 443  : $Result443"
```

How it works...

In *step 1*, you create a variable to hold the FQDN of the host. Then, you display the value with output like this:

```
PS C:\Foo> # 1. Getting and displaying the DNS name of this host
PS C:\Foo> $DNSDomain = $Env:USERDNSDOMAIN
PS C:\Foo> $FQDN      = "$Env:COMPUTERNAME.$DNSDomain"
PS C:\Foo> "Host FQDN: $FQDN"
Host FQDN: SRV1.RESKIT.ORG
```

Figure 12.10: Displaying the FQDN of this host

In *step 2*, you use Get-DNSClientServerAddress to get the IP addresses of the DNS servers that you (or DHCP) have configured on the host. The output looks like this:

```
PS C:\Foo> # 2. Getting DNS server address
PS C:\Foo> $DNSHT = @{
             InterfaceAlias = "Ethernet"
             AddressFamily  = 'IPv4'
           }
PS C:\Foo> $DNSServers = (Get-DnsClientServerAddress @DNSHT).ServerAddresses
PS C:\Foo> $DNSServers
10.10.10.10
10.10.10.11
```

Figure 12.11: Discovering configured DNS servers

In *step 3*, you check whether each configured DNS server is available, with output like this:

```
PS C:\Foo> # 3. Checking if the DNS servers are online
PS C:\Foo> Foreach ($DNSServer in $DNSServers) {
             $TestDNS = Test-NetConnection -Port 53 -ComputerName $DNSServer
             $Result  = $TestDNS ? "Available" : ' Not reachable'
             "DNS Server [$DNSServer] is $Result"
           }
DNS Server [10.10.10.10] is Available
DNS Server [10.10.10.11] is Available
```

Figure 12.12: Checking the reachability of each configured DNS server

In *step 4*, you determine the DNS **resource record (RR)** name for the SRV records registered by active DCs for a given domain. The output looks like this:

```
PS C:\Foo> # 4. Defining a search for DCs in our domain
PS C:\Foo> $DNSRRName = "_ldap._tcp." + $DNSDomain
PS C:\Foo> $DNSRRName
_ldap._tcp.RESKIT.ORG
```

Figure 12.13: Defining an RR name for DC SRV records

In *step 5*, you retrieve the SRV RRs for the DCs in the Reskit.Org domain. Each RR represents a server that can act as a DC in the Reskit.Org domain. The output of this step looks like this:

```
PS C:\Foo> # 5. Getting the DC SRV records
PS C:\Foo> $DCRRS = Resolve-DnsName -Name $DNSRRName -Type all |
            Where-Object IP4address -ne $null
PS C:\Foo> $DCRRS
```

```
Name                 Type   TTL   Section     IPAddress
----                 ----   ---   -------     ---------
dc2.reskit.org       A      3600  Additional  10.10.10.11
dc1.reskit.org       A      3600  Additional  10.10.10.10
```

Figure 12.14: Querying for DNS RRs for DCs

In *step 6*, you test each discovered DC for LDAP connectivity, with output like this:

```
PS C:\Foo> # 6. Testing each DC for availability over LDAP
PS C:\Foo> ForEach ($DNSRR in $DCRRS){
             $TestDC = Test-NetConnection -Port 389 -ComputerName $DNSRR.IPAddress
             $Result = $TestDC ? 'DC Available' : 'DC Not reachable'
             "DC [$($DNSRR.Name)] at [$($DNSRR.IPAddress)]   $Result for LDAP"
           }
DC [dc2.reskit.org]  at [10.10.10.11]   DC Available for LDAP
DC [dc1.reskit.org]  at [10.10.10.10]   DC Available for LDAP
```

Figure 12.15: Testing LDAP connectivity to domain controllers

For each host's Group Policy agent to download GPOs from a DC, the host uses an SMB connection to the SYSVOL share on a DC. In *step 7*, you check connectivity to each DC's SMB port (port 445). The output of this step looks like this:

```
PS C:\Foo> # 7. Testing DC availability for SMB
PS C:\Foo> ForEach ($DNSRR in $DCRRS){
             $TestDC =
              Test-NetConnection -Port 445 -ComputerName $DNSRR.IPAddress
             $Result = $TestDC ? 'DC Available' : 'DC Not reachable'
             "DC [$($DNSRR.Name)] at [$($DNSRR.IPAddress)]   $Result for SMB"
           }
DC [dc2.reskit.org]  at [10.10.10.11]   DC Available for SMB
DC [dc1.reskit.org]  at [10.10.10.10]   DC Available for SMB
```

Figure 12.16: Testing SMB connectivity to domain controllers

In *step 8*, you check whether your host can reach its configured default gateway. The output of this step looks like this:

```
PS C:\Foo> # 8. Testing default gateway
PS C:\Foo> $NIC    = Get-NetIPConfiguration -InterfaceAlias Ethernet
PS C:\Foo> $DGW    = $NIC.IPv4DefaultGateway.NextHop
PS C:\Foo> $TestDG = Test-NetConnection $DGW
WARNING: Ping to 10.10.10.254 failed with status: DestinationHostUnreachable
PS C:\Foo> $Result = $TestDG.PingSucceeded ? "Reachable" : ' NOT Reachable'
PS C:\Foo> "Default Gateway for [$($NIC.Interfacealias) is [$DGW] - $Result"
Default Gateway for [Ethernet is [10.10.10.254] -  NOT Reachable
```

Figure 12.17: Testing the default gateway

In *step 9*, you check to see if you can reach an external internet-based host using ICMP (aka ping). The output of this step looks like this:

```
PS C:\Foo> # 9. Testing a remote web site using ICMP
PS C:\Foo> $Site = "WWW.Packt.Com"
PS C:\Foo> $TestIP    = Test-NetConnection -ComputerName $Site
PS C:\Foo> $ResultIP  = $TestIP ? "Ping OK" : "Ping FAILED"
PS C:\Foo> "ICMP to $Site - $ResultIP"
ICMP to WWW.Packt.Com - Ping OK
```

Figure 12.18: Testing connectivity to an internet site

In *step 10*, you check to see whether you can reach the same server, via the HTTP port, port 80, with output like this:

```
PS C:\Foo> # 10. Testing a remote web site using port 80
PS C:\Foo> $TestPort80 = Test-Connection -ComputerName $Site -TcpPort 80
PS C:\Foo> $Result80   = $TestPort80 ? 'Site Reachable' : 'Site NOT reachable'
PS C:\Foo> "$Site over port 80    : $Result80"
WWW.Packt.Com over port 80    : Site Reachable
```

Figure 12.19: Testing connectivity over port 80

Finally, in *step 11*, you check to see whether you can reach the same server via HTTP over SSL/TLS, port 443, with output like this:

```
PS C:\Foo> # 11. Testing a remote web site using port 443
PS C:\Foo> $TestPort443 = Test-Connection -ComputerName $Site -TcpPort 443
PS C:\Foo> $Result443   = $TestPort443 ? 'Site Reachable' : 'Site NOT reachable'
PS C:\Foo> "$Site over port 443   : $Result443"
WWW.Packt.Com over port 443   : Site Reachable
```

Figure 12.20: Testing connectivity over port 443

There's more...

In *step 1*, you create a variable to hold the FQDN of the host and then display this value at the console. You should ensure you have configured the hostname correctly and want to use this to ensure that your host has properly registered your host's FQDN in any configured DNS server. If DNS misregistration is causing problems, you may wish to adapt this script to check for correct DNS resource record registration.

In *step 3*, you use the ternary operator. This operator is a new feature in PowerShell 7.0. For more details on the ternary operator, see https://learn.microsoft.com/powershell/module/microsoft.powershell.core/about/about_if?view=powershell-7.3.

In *step 4*, you create a DNS RR name, which you then use in *step 5* to query for any SRV records of that name. AD uses DNS as a locator service – each DC registers SRV records to advertise its ability to serve as a DC. The SRV record contains the FQDN name of the advertised DC. The approach taken by these two steps is similar to how any domain client finds a domain controller. The Windows Netlogon service on a DC registers all the appropriate SRV records each time the service starts or every 24 hours. One troubleshooting technique is to use Restart-Service to restart the Netlogon service on each DC.

If you have a large routed network, you may wish to move the default gateway check, performed here in *step 8*, earlier in your production version of this recipe, and possibly before *step 3*. If you can't reach your default gateway and your DNS server and your DCs are on different subnetworks, the earlier steps are going to fail due to a default gateway issue. For the remaining steps to work, you need to resolve the problem with the default gateway not being reachable (e.g., by turning on the default gateway VM).

In *steps 9, 10*, and *11*, you test connectivity to a remote host via ICMP and ports 80 and 443. A host or an intermediate router may drop ICMP traffic yet allow port 80/443 traffic in many cases. So just because a ping has not succeeded does not necessarily suggest a point of failure at all – it may be a deliberate feature and by design.

In some of the steps in this recipe, you used the PowerShell 7 ternary operator to construct the message output. These steps provide a good example of this operator. For more details on the ternary operator, see https://learn.microsoft.com/powershell/module/microsoft.powershell.core/about/about_operators.

Using Get-NetView to Diagnose Network Issues

In most cases, network issues are relatively easy to resolve. But in some cases, especially in larger networks, problems can be much more complex. Getting a resolution can require a lot of information. As shown in the *Performing Basic Network Troubleshooting* recipe, a few steps can point you to the issue's cause.

Get-NetView is a tool that collects details about your network environment, which can help you troubleshoot network issues. This tool gathers everything you might want to know about a host to enable you to resolve complex issues.

The Get-NetView module contains a single function, Get-NetView. The command pulls together a range of network details. The command creates a set of text files for you to peruse and a ZIP file containing those same details. You can view the text files directly on the host or email the ZIP file to a central network team for deeper analysis.

Get-NetView output includes the following details:

- Get-NetView metadata
- The host environment (including OS, hardware, domain, and hostname)
- Physical, virtual, and container NICs
- Network configuration (including IP addresses, MAC addresses, neighbors, and IP routes)
- Physical switch configuration, including QoS policies
- Hyper-V VM configuration
- Hyper-V virtual switches, bridges, and NATs
- Windows device drivers
- Performance counters
- System and application events

The output provided by Get-NetView, as the above list suggests, is voluminous. To help troubleshoot a given issue, only a very small amount of the information is likely to be useful to you. However, if there is an issue in your network, this information can help you troubleshoot.

Getting ready

This recipe uses SRV1, a domain-joined Windows Server 2022 host. You have installed PowerShell 7 and VS Code on this host.

How to do it...

1. Finding the Get-NetView module on the PS Gallery

   ```
   Find-Module -Name Get-NetView
   ```

2. Installing the latest version of Get-NetView

   ```
   Install-Module -Name Get-NetView -Force -AllowClobber
   ```

3. Checking the installed version of Get-NetView

   ```
   Get-Module -Name Get-NetView -ListAvailable | ft -au
   ```

4. Importing Get-NetView

   ```
   Import-Module -Name Get-NetView -Force
   ```

5. Creating a new folder for NetView output

   ```
   $FolderName = 'C:\NetViewOutput'
   New-Item -Path $FolderHName -ItemType Directory | Out-Null
   ```

6. Running Get-NetView

   ```
   Get-NetView -OutputDirectory $FolderHName
   ```

7. Viewing the output folder using Get-ChildItem:

   ```
   $OutputDetails = Get-ChildItem -Path $FolderName
   $OutputDetails
   ```

8. Viewing the output folder contents using Get-ChildItem

   ```
   $Results = $OutputDetails | Select-Object -First 1
   Get-ChildItem -Path $Results
   ```

9. Viewing the IP configuration

   ```
   Get-Content -Path $Results\_ipconfig.txt
   ```

How it works...

In *step 1*, you find the Get-NetView module on the PowerShell Gallery. The output from this step looks like this:

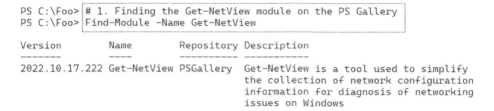

```
PS C:\Foo> # 1. Finding the Get-NetView module on the PS Gallery
PS C:\Foo> Find-Module -Name Get-NetView

Version        Name         Repository Description
-------        ----         ---------- -----------
2022.10.17.222 Get-NetView  PSGallery  Get-NetView is a tool used to simplify
                                        the collection of network configuration
                                        information for diagnosis of networking
                                        issues on Windows
```

Figure 12.21: Finding the Get-NetView module

In *step 2*, you download and install the latest version of this module, which generates no output. In *step 3*, you check which version (or versions) of the Get-NetView module are on SRV1, with output like this:

```
PS C:\Foo> # 3. Checking installed version of Get-NetView
PS C:\Foo> Get-Module -Name Get-NetView -ListAvailable

    Directory: C:\Users\administrator.RESKIT\Documents\PowerShell\Modules

ModuleType Version        PreRelease Name        PSEdition  ExportedCommands
---------- -------        ---------- ----        ---------  ----------------
Script     2022.10.17.222            Get-NetView Core,Desk  Get-NetView
```

Figure 12.22: Checking the installed version of the Get-NetView module

In *step 4*, you import the Get-NetView module. In *step 5*, you create a new folder on the C:\ drive to hold the output that Get-NetView generates. These two steps produce no output.

In *step 6*, you run Get-NetView. As you can see, as it runs, the command logs a series of network configuration details and outputs a running commentary. This command generates a lot of console output, a subset of which looks like this:

```
PS C:\Foo> # 6. Running Get-View
PS C:\Foo> Get-NetView -OutputDirectory $FolderName
Transcript started, output file is C:\NetViewOutput\msdbg.SRV1\Get-NetView.log
(   988 ms) Get-Service "*" | Sort-Object Name | Format-Table -AutoSize
( 1,181 ms) Get-Service "*" | Sort-Object Name | Format-Table -Property * -AutoSize
( 2,658 ms) Get-ChildItem HKLM:\SYSTEM\CurrentControlSet\Services\vmsmp -Recurse
Get-VMSwitch: The Hyper-V Management Tools could not access an expected WMI class on computer 'SRV1'.
This may indicate that the Hyper-V Platform is not installed on the computer or that the version
of the Hyper-V Platform is incompatible with these management tools.

(    45 ms) Get-NetAdapterQos
(    49 ms) Get-NetAdapterQos -IncludeHidden
(    26 ms) Get-NetAdapterQos -IncludeHidden | Format-List -Property *
HNSDetail: hns service not found, skipping.
(     0 ms) [Unavailable] Get-NetIntent -ClusterName Get-Cluster
(     0 ms) [Unavailable] Get-NetIntentStatus -ClusterName Get-Cluster
(     0 ms) [Unavailable] Get-NetIntentAllGoalStates -ClusterName Get-Cluster | ConvertTo-Json -Depth 10
(    54 ms) pktmon status
(   107 ms) pktmon stop
(    16 ms) pktmon filter list
(    82 ms) pktmon list
(    59 ms) pktmon list --all
(    50 ms) pktmon list --all --include-hidden
(    46 ms) pktmon start --capture --counters-only --comp all
... remainder of output snipped for brevity
```

Figure 12.23: Running Get-NetView

In *step 7*, you view the output folder to view the files created by Get-NetView, with output like this:

```
PS C:\NetViewOutput> # 7. Viewing the output folder using Get-ChildItem
PS C:\NetViewOutput> $OutputDetails = Get-ChildItem $FolderName
PS C:\NetViewOutput> $OutputDetails


    Directory: C:\NetViewOutput


Mode                 LastWriteTime         Length Name
----                 -------------         ------ ----
d----          03/11/2022     13:44               msdbg.SRV1
-a---          03/11/2022     13:44       76218062 msdbg.SRV1-2022.11.03_01.43.12.zip
```

Figure 12.24: Viewing the Get-NetView output folder

In *step 8*, you view the output folder that Get-NetView populates with detailed network configuration information, with output like this:

```
PS C:\Foo> # 8. Viewing the output folder contents using Get-ChildItem
PS C:\Foo> $Results = $OutputDetails | Select-Object -First 1
PS C:\Foo> Get-ChildItem -Path $Results

    Directory: C:\NetViewOutput\msdbg.SRV1

Mode                 LastWriteTime         Length Name
----                 -------------         ------ ----
d----        03/11/2022     13:44                _Localhost
d----        03/11/2022     13:44                _Logs
d----        03/11/2022     13:44                802.1X
d----        03/11/2022     13:43                ATC
d----        03/11/2022     13:43                Counters
d----        03/11/2022     13:44                NetIp
d----        03/11/2022     13:44                NetNat
d----        03/11/2022     13:44                NetQoS
d----        03/11/2022     13:43                NetSetup
d----        03/11/2022     13:44                Netsh
d----        03/11/2022     13:43                NIC.5.Ethernet 2.Microsoft Hyper-V Network Adapter #2
d----        03/11/2022     13:43                NIC.7.Ethernet.Microsoft Hyper-V Network Adapter
d----        03/11/2022     13:43                NIC.Hidden
d----        03/11/2022     13:43                Pktmon
d----        03/11/2022     13:44                SMB
d----        03/11/2022     13:43                VMSwitch.Detail
-a---        03/11/2022     13:43           2233 _advfirewall.txt
-a---        03/11/2022     13:43            776 _arp.txt
-a---        03/11/2022     13:43           1783 _ipconfig.txt
-a---        03/11/2022     13:43         498394 _netcfg.txt
-a---        03/11/2022     13:43          10717 _netstat.txt
-a---        03/11/2022     13:43             69 _nmbind.txt
-a---        03/11/2022     13:43           6897 Environment.txt
-a---        03/11/2022     13:43          12811 Get-ComputerInfo.txt
-a---        03/11/2022     13:43          19460 Get-NetAdapter.txt
-a---        03/11/2022     13:43           3747 Get-NetAdapterStatistics.txt
-a---        03/11/2022     13:43           6574 Get-NetIpAddress.txt
-a---        03/11/2022     13:43            254 Get-NetLbfoTeam.txt
-a---        03/11/2022     13:43           1164 Get-NetOffloadGlobalSetting.txt
-a---        03/11/2022     13:43            894 Get-VMNetworkAdapter.txt
-a---        03/11/2022     13:43            782 Get-VMSwitch.txt
-a---        03/11/2022     13:43            354 Powercfg.txt
-a---        03/11/2022     13:43           1312 Verifier.txt
```

Figure 12.25: Viewing the Get-NetView output folder

In *step 9*, you examine one of the files created by Get-NetView. This file contains details of the IP
configuration of the server, with output that looks like this:

```
PS C:\NetViewOutput> # 9. Viewing IP configuration
PS C:\NetViewOutput> Get-Content -Path $Results\_ipconfig.txt
administrator @ SRV1:
PS C:\NetViewOutput> ipconfig

Windows IP Configuration


Ethernet adapter Ethernet:

    Connection-specific DNS Suffix  . :
    Link-local IPv6 Address . . . . . : fe80::a125:4dcc:684b:bfa2%7
    IPv4 Address. . . . . . . . . . . : 10.10.10.50
    Subnet Mask . . . . . . . . . . . : 255.255.255.0
    Default Gateway . . . . . . . . . :
administrator @ SRV1:
PS C:\NetViewOutput> ipconfig /allcompartments /all

Windows IP Configuration


=================================================================================
Network Information for Compartment 1 (ACTIVE)
=================================================================================
    Host Name . . . . . . . . . . . . : SRV1
    Primary Dns Suffix  . . . . . . . : Reskit.Org
    Node Type . . . . . . . . . . . . : Hybrid
    IP Routing Enabled. . . . . . . . : No
    WINS Proxy Enabled. . . . . . . . : No
    DNS Suffix Search List. . . . . . : Reskit.Org

Ethernet adapter Ethernet:

    Connection-specific DNS Suffix  . :
    Description . . . . . . . . . . . : Microsoft Hyper-V Network Adapter
    Physical Address. . . . . . . . . : 00-15-5D-01-2A-2E
    DHCP Enabled. . . . . . . . . . . : No
    Autoconfiguration Enabled . . . . : Yes
    Link-local IPv6 Address . . . . . : fe80::a125:4dcc:684b:bfa2%7(Preferred)
    IPv4 Address. . . . . . . . . . . : 10.10.10.50(Preferred)
    Subnet Mask . . . . . . . . . . . : 255.255.255.0
    Default Gateway . . . . . . . . . :
    DHCPv6 IAID . . . . . . . . . . . : 100668765
    DHCPv6 Client DUID. . . . . . . . : 00-01-00-01-2A-BE-82-5D-00-15-5D-01-2A-2E
    DNS Servers . . . . . . . . . . . : 10.10.10.10
                                        10.10.10.11
    NetBIOS over Tcpip. . . . . . . . : Enabled
```

Figure 12.26: Viewing IP configuration

There's more...

In *step 3*, you check the version or versions of the Get-NetView module on your system. You may see a later version of this module.

In *step 7*, you view the files output by Get-NetView. As you can see, there is a folder and a ZIP archive file in the output folder. Get-NetView adds all the network information to separate files in the output folder and then compresses all that information into a single archive file that you can send to a network technician for resolution. This approach allows the remote technician to view the ZIP file's contents, even if they do not have access to the host (and can read the files in the output folder).

In *step 9*, you view one of the many bits of information created by Get-NetView. In this case, you look at the IP configuration information, including the IP address, subnet mask, and the default gateway, as well as the configured DNS servers.

Using Best Practices Analyzer

One way to avoid needing to perform troubleshooting is to deploy your services in a more trouble-free, or at least trouble-tolerant, manner. There are many ways to deploy and operate your environment, and some methods are demonstrably better than others. For example, having two DCs, two DNS servers with AD-integrated zones, and two DHCP servers in a failover relationship means that you can experience numerous issues in these core services and still deploy a reliable end-user service. While you may still need to troubleshoot to resolve any issue, your services are running acceptably, with your users unaware that there is an issue.

Along with industry experts, MVPs, and others, Microsoft product teams have identified recommendations for deploying a Windows infrastructure. Some product teams, such as Exchange, publish extensive guidance and have developed a self-contained tool.

The Windows Server BPA is a built-in Windows Server tool that analyzes your on-premises servers for adherence to best practices. A best practice is a guideline that industry experts agree is the best way to configure your servers. For example, most AD experts recommend you have at least TWO domain controllers for each domain. But for a test environment, that may be overkill. So while best practices are ones to strive for, sometimes they may be inappropriate for your needs. It is, therefore, important to use some judgment when reviewing the results of BPA.

 Important note: BPA does not work natively in PowerShell 7 on any supported Windows Server version, including (at the time of writing) Windows Server 2022. There is, however, a way around this that involves using PowerShell remoting and running the BPA in Windows PowerShell, as you can see from this recipe.

BPA with Windows Server 2022 comes with 14 BPA models. Each model is a set of rules that you can use to test your AD environment. The AD team, for example, has built a BPA model for Active Directory, `Microsoft/Windows/DirectoryServices`, which you can run to determine issues with AD on a domain controller.

In this recipe, you create a PowerShell remoting session with DC1. You use the `Invoke-Command` cmdlet to run the BPA cmdlets, allowing you to analyze, in this recipe, the Active Directory model. In effect, you run the actual cmdlets in Windows PowerShell via remoting.

Getting ready

This recipe uses SRV1, a domain-joined Windows 2022 server in the `Reskit.Org` domain. You also need the domain controllers in the `Reskit.Org` (DC1 and DC2) online for this recipe.

How to do it...

1. Creating a remoting session to Windows PowerShell on DC1

```
$BPASession = New-PSSession -ComputerName DC1
```

2. Discovering the BPA module on DC1

```
$ScriptBlock1 = {
  Get-Module -Name BestPractices -List |
    Format-Table -AutoSize
}
Invoke-Command -Session $BPASession -ScriptBlock $ScriptBlock1
```

3. Discovering the commands in the BPA module

```
$ScriptBlock2 = {
    Get-Command -Module BestPractices  |
      Format-Table -AutoSize
}
Invoke-Command -Session $BPASession -ScriptBlock $ScriptBlock2
```

4. Discovering all available BPA models on DC1

```
$ScriptBlock3 = {
  Get-BPAModel  |
    Format-Table -Property Name, Id, LastScanTime -AutoSize
}
Invoke-Command -Session $BPASession -ScriptBlock $ScriptBlock3
```

5. Running the BPA DirectoryServices model on DC1

```
$ScriptBlock4 = {
  Invoke-BpaModel -ModelID Microsoft/Windows/DirectoryServices -Mode
ALL |
    Format-Table -AutoSize
}
Invoke-Command -Session $BPASession -ScriptBlock $ScriptBlock4
```

6. Getting BPA results from DC1

```
$ScriptBlock5 = {
  Get-BpaResult -ModelID Microsoft/Windows/DirectoryServices  |
    Where-Object Resolution -ne $null|
      Format-List -Property Problem, Resolution
}
Invoke-Command -Session $BPASession -ScriptBlock $ScriptBlock5
```

How it works...

In *step 1*, you create a PowerShell remoting session with your domain controller, DC1. This step creates no output. In *step 2*, you run the Get-Module command on DC1 using the remoting session. The output of this step looks like this:

```
PS C:\Foo> # 2. Discovering the BPA module on DC1
PS C:\Foo> $ScriptBlock1 = {
             Get-Module -Name BestPractices -List |
               Format-Table -AutoSize
           }
PS C:\Foo> Invoke-Command -Session $BPASession -ScriptBlock $ScriptBlock1

    Directory: C:\WINDOWS\system32\WindowsPowerShell\v1.0\Modules

ModuleType Version Name           ExportedCommands
---------- ------- ----           ----------------
Manifest   1.0     BestPractices  {Get-BpaModel, Get-BpaResult, Invoke-BpaModel, Set-BpaResult}
```

Figure 12.27: Viewing the BPA module on DC1

In *step 3*, you discover the commands contained in the BPA module (on DC1), with output like this:

```
PS C:\Foo> # 3. Discovering the commands in the BPA module
PS C:\Foo> $ScriptBlock2 = {
               Get-Command -Module BestPractices  |
                 Format-Table -AutoSize
           }
PS C:\Foo> Invoke-Command -Session $BPASession -ScriptBlock $ScriptBlock2

CommandType Name             Version Source
----------- ----             ------- ------
Cmdlet      Get-BpaModel     1.0     BestPractices
Cmdlet      Get-BpaResult    1.0     BestPractices
Cmdlet      Invoke-BpaModel  1.0     BestPractices
Cmdlet      Set-BpaResult    1.0     BestPractices
```

Figure 12.28: Discovering the commands inside the BPA module

In *step 4*, you discover the BPA models, which are available on DC1. The output looks like this:

```
PS C:\Foo> # 4. Discovering all available BPA models on DC1
PS C:\Foo> $ScriptBlock3 = {
               Get-BPAModel  |
                 Format-Table -Property Name,Id, LastScanTime -AutoSize
           }
PS C:\Foo> Invoke-Command -Session $BPASession -ScriptBlock $ScriptBlock3

Name                                                    Id                                                       LastScanTime
----                                                    --                                                       ------------
RightsManagementServices                                Microsoft/Windows/ADRMS                                  Never
CertificateServices                                     Microsoft/Windows/CertificateServices                    Never
Microsoft DHCP Server Configuration Analysis Model      Microsoft/Windows/DHCPServer                             Never
DirectoryServices                                       Microsoft/Windows/DirectoryServices                      Never
Microsoft DNS Server Configuration Analysis Model       Microsoft/Windows/DNSServer                              Never
File Services                                           Microsoft/Windows/FileServices                           Never
Hyper-V                                                 Microsoft/Windows/Hyper-V                                 Never
LightweightDirectoryServices                            Microsoft/Windows/LightweightDirectoryServices           Never
Network Policy and Access Services (NPAS)               Microsoft/Windows/NPAS                                    Never
Microsoft Remote Access Server Configuration Analysis Model Microsoft/Windows/RemoteAccessServer                 Never
TerminalServices                                        Microsoft/Windows/TerminalServices                       Never
Windows Server Update Services                          Microsoft/Windows/UpdateServices                         Never
Microsoft Volume Activation Configuration Analysis Model Microsoft/Windows/VolumeActivation                      Never
WebServer                                               Microsoft/Windows/WebServer                              Never
```

Figure 12.29: Discovering the BPA models available on DC1

In *step 5*, you use the `Invoke-BpaModel` command to run the Directory Services BPA model on DC1. Invoking the model produces minimal output, as follows:

```
PS C:\Foo> # 5. Running the BPA DirectoryServices model on DC1
PS C:\Foo> $ScriptBlock4 = {
               Invoke-BpaModel -ModelID Microsoft/Windows/DirectoryServices -Mode ALL |
                 Format-Table -AutoSize
           }
PS C:\Foo> Invoke-Command -Session $BPASession -ScriptBlock $ScriptBlock4

ModelId                                 SubModelId Success ScanTime                ScanTimeUtcOffset Detail
-------                                 ---------- ------- --------                ----------------- ------
Microsoft/Windows/DirectoryServices                True    04/11/2022 11:41:35     01:00:00          {DC1, DC1}
```

Figure 12.30: Running the Directory Services BPA

To obtain the detailed results of the BPA scan, you use the Get-BpaResult command, as you can see in *step 6*, which produces the following output:

```
PS C:\Foo> # 6. Getting BPA results from DC1
PS C:\Foo> $ScriptBlock5 = {
             Get-BpaResult -ModelID Microsoft/Windows/DirectoryServices   |
               Where-Object Resolution -ne $null|
                 Format-List -Property Problem, Resolution
           }
PS C:\Foo> Invoke-Command -Session $BPASession -ScriptBlock $ScriptBlock5
```

```
Problem     : The primary domain controller (PDC) emulator operations master in this
              forest is not configured to correctly synchronize time from a valid time
              source.
Resolution  : Set the PDC emulator master in this forest to synchronize time with a
              reliable external time source. If you have not configured a reliable time
              server (GTIMESERV) in the forest root domain, set the PDC emulator master
              days.
Resolution  : To ensure that recent system state backups are available to recover Active
              Directory data that was recently added, deleted, or modified, perform
              daily backups of all directory partitions in your forest or keep the time
              between Active Directory backups to a maximum of 8 days.

Problem     : The directory partition DC=DomainDnsZones,DC=Reskit,DC=Org on the domain
              controller DC1.Reskit.Org has not been backed up within the last 8 days.
Resolution  : To ensure that recent system state backups are available to recover Active
              Directory data that was recently added, deleted, or modified, perform
              daily backups of all directory partitions in your forest or keep the time
              between Active Directory backups to a maximum of 8 days.

Problem     : The directory partition DC=ForestDnsZones,DC=Reskit,DC=Org on the domain
              controller DC1.Reskit.Org has not been backed up within the last 8 days.
Resolution  : To ensure that recent system state backups are available to recover Active
              Directory data that was recently added, deleted, or modified, perform
              daily backups of all directory partitions in your forest or keep the time
              between Active Directory backups to a maximum of 8 days.

Problem     : The Active Directory Domain Services (AD DS) server role on the domain
              controller DC1.Reskit.Org is installed on a virtual machine (VM).
Resolution  : Make sure that the domain controller DC1.Reskit.Org complies with the best
              practice guidelines that are described in the Help to avoid performance
              issues and replication and security failures in the Active Directory
              environment.
```

Figure 12.31: Viewing BPA results

There's more...

BPA results include details of unsuccessful tests. The unsuccessful results, where BPA finds that your deployment does not implement a best practice, are the ones you may need to review and take action.

In *step 6*, you retrieve the results of the BPA scan you ran in the previous step. The results show three fundamental issues:

- You have not synchronized time on the DC holding the PDC emulator FSMO role with some reliable external source. This issue means that time on your hosts could "wander" from real-world time, possibly leading to problems later on. See `https://blogs.msmvps.com/acefekay/tag/pdc-emulator-time-configuration` for more information on configuring your DCs with a reliable time source.

- You have not backed up your AD environment. Even with multiple DCs, performing regular backups is best practice. See `https://learn.microsoft.com/en-us/windows/win32/ad/backing-up-and-restoring-an-active-directory-server` for more information on backing up and restoring a DC.

- DC1 is a DC you are running in a VM. While Microsoft supports such a deployment, there are some best practices you should adhere to to ensure the reliable running of your AD service. See `https://learn.microsoft.com/windows-server/identity/ad-ds/get-started/virtual-dc/virtualized-domain-controllers-hyper-v` for more details on virtualizing DCs using Hyper-V.

For a test environment, these issues are inconsequential, and you can probably ignore them. If you are using Hyper-V for test VMs, you can configure Hyper-V to update the VMs' local time, at least for the DCs you run in a VM. A backup of your AD is unnecessary in a test environment. And running a domain controller in a Hyper-V, at least for a testing environment, is not an issue with the latest, supported Windows Server versions.

Exploring PowerShell Script Debugging

PowerShell 7, as well as Windows PowerShell, contains some great debugging features. You use these debugging tools to find and remove errors in your scripts. You can set breakpoints in a script. When you run the script, PowerShell stops execution at the breakpoint. You can set a breakpoint to stop at a particular line in the script, any time the script reads or writes a PowerShell variable, or any time PowerShell calls a named cmdlet.

When PowerShell encounters a breakpoint, it suspends processing and presents you with a debugging prompt, as you see in this recipe. You can then examine the results that your script has produced. When you hit a breakpoint, PowerShell enters a debug terminal from which you can run additional commands. This helps to ensure your script produces the output and results you expect. Suppose your script adds a user to the AD and then performs an action on that user (adding the user to a group, for example). You could stop the script just after the Add-ADUser command completes. You could then use Get-AdUser or other commands to check whether your script has added the user as you expected. You can then use the continue statement to resume your script. PowerShell then resumes running your script until it either completes or hits another breakpoint.

Getting ready

This recipe uses SRV1, a domain-joined host controller in the Reskit.Org domain. You have installed PowerShell 7 on this host. You run this script from the PowerShell console.

How to do it...

1. Creating a script to debug

```
$Script = @'
# Script to illustrate breakpoints
Function Get-Foo1 {
  param ($J)
  $K = $J*2            # NB: line 4
  $M = $K              # NB: $M written to
  $M
  $BIOS = Get-CimInstance -Class Win32_Bios
}
Function Get-Foo {
  param ($I)
  (Get-Foo1 $I)        # Uses Get-Foo1
}
Function Get-Bar {
  Get-Foo (21)}
# Start of ACTUAL script
  "In Breakpoint.ps1"
  "Calculating Bar as [{0}]" -f (Get-Bar)
'@
```

2. Saving the script

```
$FileName = 'C:\Foo\Breakpoint.ps1'
$Script| Out-File -FilePath $FileName
```

3. Executing the script

```
& $FileName
```

4. Adding a breakpoint at a line in the script

```
Set-PSBreakpoint -Script $FileName -Line 4 |  # breaks at line 4
    Out-Null
```

5. Adding a breakpoint on the script using a specific command

```
Set-PSBreakpoint -Script $FileName -Command "Get-CimInstance" |
    Out-Null
```

6. Adding a breakpoint when the script writes to $M

```
Set-PSBreakpoint -Script $FileName -Variable M -Mode Write |
    Out-Null
```

7. Viewing the breakpoints set in this session

```
Get-PSBreakpoint | Format-Table -AutoSize
```

8. Running the script - until the first breakpoint is hit

```
& $FileName
```

9. Viewing the value of $J from the debug console

```
$J
```

10. Viewing the value of $K from the debug console

```
$K
```

11. Continuing script execution from the DBG prompt until the next breakpoint

```
continue
```

12. Continuing script execution until the execution of Get-CimInstance

    ```
    continue
    ```

13. Continuing script execution until the end of the script

    ```
    continue
    ```

How it works...

In *step 1*, you create a script to allow you to examine PowerShell script debugging. In *step 2*, you save this file to the C: drive. These steps generate no output.

In *step 3*, you execute the script, which produces some output to the console like this:

```
PS C:\Foo> # 3. Executing the script
PS C:\Foo> & $FileName
In Breakpoint.ps1
Calculating Bar as [42]
```

Figure 12.32: Executing the script

In *step 4*, you set a breakpoint in the script at a specific line. In *step 5*, you set another breakpoint whenever your script calls a particular command (Get-CimInstance). In *step 6*, you set a breakpoint to stop whenever you write to a specific variable ($M). Setting these three breakpoints produces no output (since you piped the command output to Out-Null).

In *step 7*, you view the breakpoints you have set thus far in the current PowerShell session. The output looks like this:

```
PS C:\Foo> # 7. Viewing the breakpoints set in this session
PS C:\Foo>
PS C:\Foo> Get-PSBreakpoint | Format-Table -AutoSize

ID Script          Line Command          Variable Action
-- ------          ---- -------          -------- ------
 1 Breakpoint.ps1     4
 2 Breakpoint.ps1          Get-CimInstance
 3 Breakpoint.ps1                              M
```

Figure 12.33: Viewing the breakpoints

Having set three break points in the script, in *step 8*, you run the script. PowerShell stops execution when it reaches the first breakpoint (in line 4 of the script file), with output like this:

```
PS C:\Foo> # 8. Running the script - until the first breakpoint is hit
PS C:\Foo> & $FileName
In Breakpoint.ps1
Entering debug mode. Use h or ? for help.

Hit Line breakpoint on 'C:\Foo\Breakpoint.ps1:4'

At C:\Foo\Breakpoint.ps1:4 char:3
+     $k = $J*2              # NB: line 4
+     ~~~~~~~~~~
[DBG]: PS C:\Foo>>
```

Figure 12.34: Running the script until PowerShell hits the first breakpoint

From the DBG prompt, you can enter any PowerShell command, for example, to view the value of $J, which you do in *step 9*. This step produces the following console output:

```
[DBG]: PS C:\Foo>> # 9. Viewing the value of $J from the debug console
[DBG]: PS C:\Foo>> $J
21
```

Figure 12.35: Viewing the value of the $J variable

In *step 10*, you attempt to view the value of the $K variable. Since PowerShell stopped execution *before* the line executes and before your script can create and write a value to this variable, this step displays no output, as you can see here:

```
[DBG]: PS C:\Foo>> # 10. Viewing the value of $k from the debug console
[DBG]: PS C:\Foo>> $k
[DBG]: PS C:\Foo>>
```

Figure 12.36: Attempting to view the value of the $K variable

To continue the script execution, in *step 11*, you type continue to have PowerShell continue running the script until it hits the next breakpoint. The console output looks like this:

```
[DBG]: PS C:\Foo>> # 11. Continuing script execution from the DBG prompt until the next breakpoint
[DBG]: PS C:\Foo>> continue
Hit Variable breakpoint on 'C:\Foo\Breakpoint.ps1:$M' (Write access)

At C:\Foo\Breakpoint.ps1:5 char:3
+     $M = $k              # NB: $M written to
+     ~~~~~~~
[DBG]: PS C:\Foo>>
```

Figure 12.37: Running the script until PowerShell hits the second breakpoint

As in the previous step, at the debug console, you can examine the script's actions thus far. Then, you can continue script execution, in *step 12*, by typing continue, which produces output like this:

```
[DBG]: PS C:\Foo>> # 12. Continuine script executiont until the execution of Get-CimInstance
[DBG]: PS C:\Foo>> continue
Hit Command breakpoint on 'C:\Foo\Breakpoint.ps1:Get-CimInstance'

At C:\Foo\Breakpoint.ps1:7 char:3
+     $BIOS = Get-CimInstance -Class Win32_Bios
+     ~~~~~~~~~~~~~~~~~~~~~~~~~~~~~~~~~~~~~~~~~~
```

Figure 12.38: Running the script until PowerShell hits the third and final breakpoint

In *step 13*, you continue running the script, which now completes, with output like this:

```
[DBG]: PS C:\Foo>> # 13. Continuing script execution from until the end of the script
[DBG]: PS C:\Foo>> continue
Calculating Bar as [42]
```

Figure 12.39: Running the script to completion

There's more...

In *step 4*, you set a line breakpoint, instructing PowerShell to stop execution once it reaches a specific line (and column) in our script. In *step 5*, you set a command breakpoint, telling PowerShell to break whenever the script invokes a particular command, in this case, Get-CimInstance. In *step 6*, you set a variable breakpoint – you tell PowerShell to stop whenever your script reads from or writes to a specific variable.

When debugging, whenever you reach a breakpoint, you should check to see if the value of variables is what you expect to see. In *step 8*, you run this instrumented script – which breaks at the first breakpoint. From the debug console, as you see in *step 9*, you can view the value of any variable, such as $J. In *step 10*, you also view the value of $K. Since PowerShell has not yet processed the assignment, this variable has no value.

In *step 11*, you continue execution until PowerShell hits the second breakpoint. As before, you could examine the values of key variables.

After continuing again, your script hits the final breakpoint just before PowerShell invokes Get-CimInstance and assigns the output to $BIOS. From the debug console, you could invoke the cmdlet to check what the result would be.

Finally, in *step 13*, you continue to complete the execution of the script. Note that you now see the normal PowerShell prompt.

If you have an especially complex script, you could set the breakpoints using another script similar to this recipe. You would use Set-PSBreakpoint whenever your script executes important commands, writes to specific variables, or reaches a key line in the script. You could later use that script file when you perform subsequent debugging.

Join our community on Discord

Join our community's Discord space for discussions with the author and other readers:

https://packt.link/SecNet

13

Managing Windows Server with Window Management Instrumentation (WMI)

This chapter covers the following recipes:

- Exploring WMI Architecture in Windows
- Exploring WMI Namespaces
- Exploring WMI Classes
- Obtaining WMI Class Instances
- Using WMI Methods
- Using WMI Events
- Implementing Permanent WMI Eventing

Introduction

Windows Management Instrumentation (WMI) is a Windows component you use to help manage Windows systems. WMI is Microsoft's proprietary implementation of the standards-based **Web-Based Enterprise Management (WBEM)**. WBEM is an open standard promulgated by the **Distributed Management Task Force (DMTF)** that aims to unify the management of distributed computing environments by using open standards-based internet technologies.

In addition to WMI, there are other implementations of WBEM, including OpenWBEM. You can read more about the DMTF and WBEM at `https://www.dmtf.org/about/faq/wbem_faq`, and check out OpenWBEM over at `http://openwbem.sourceforge.net/`. That said, WMI is most useful today on Windows.

Microsoft first introduced WMI as an add-on component for Windows NT 4. They later integrated WMI as an essential component of the Windows client from Windows XP onward, and Windows Server versions since Windows Server 2000. Subsequently, several feature teams inside the Windows group heavily used WMI. For example, the storage and networking stacks within Windows use WMI. Many of the cmdlets, such as `Get-NetAdapter`, are based directly on WMI.

The WBEM standards originally specified that the components of WMI communicate using HTTP. To improve performance, Microsoft instead used **Component Object Model (COM)** technology, which was a popular environment in the early days of Windows NTG.

Internally, WMI itself remains largely based on COM.

PowerShell 1.0 came with a set of cmdlets that you could use to access WMI. These were basic cmdlets that worked in all subsequent versions of Windows PowerShell. However, there is no support for these cmdlets directly in PowerShell 7. You can invoke older WMI cmdlet-based scripts on a machine using PowerShell remoting if you really need to.

With PowerShell V3, Microsoft did some significant work on WMI, resulting in a new module, `CimCmdlets`. There were several reasons behind the new module and the associated updates to some of the WMI internals to assist developers. In this chapter, you use the `CimCmdlets` module to access the features of WMI. You can read more about why the team built new cmdlets in a blog post at `https://devblogs.microsoft.com/powershell/introduction-to-cim-cmdlets/`. If you have scripts that use the older WMI cmdlets, consider upgrading them to use the later `CimCmdlets` module instead. These newer cmdlets are faster, which is always a nice benefit.

WMI architecture

WMI is a complex subject with a lot of parts. As an IT professional, it is useful to understand the WMI architecture within Windows before getting to know the **Common Information Model (CIM)** cmdlets. The runtime architecture of WMI is the same in Windows 10/11 and Windows Server 2022. The following diagram shows the conceptual view of the WMI architecture:

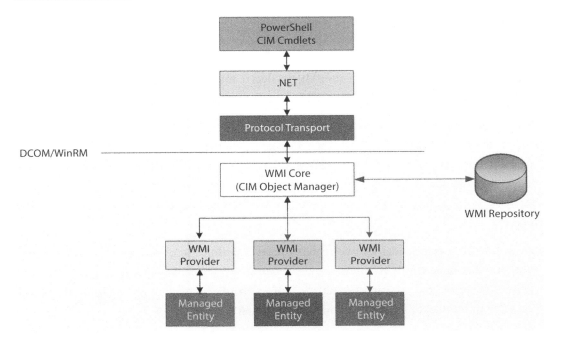

Figure 13.1: WMI architecture

As an IT pro, you use the cmdlets in the CimCmdlets module to access WMI. These cmdlets use .NET to communicate, via an underlying transport protocol (such as WinRM and Named Pipes), with the WMI core and the CIM Object Manager. The connection can be to either a local or remote host. The core components of WMI, particularly the **CIM Object Manager (CIMOM)**, are all COM components you find on every Windows host.

The CIMOM stores information in the WMI repository, sometimes called the (CIM) or the CIM database. This database is, in effect, a subset of an ANSI-SQL database. The CIM cmdlets enable you to access the information within the database. The CIM database organizes the data into namespaces of classes. .NET also uses namespaces to collect .NET classes. However, .NET classes include the namespace name as part of the class name. For example, you can create a new email message using the .NET class System.Net.Mail.Mailmessage, where the namespace is System.Net.Mail. Thus, the full class name contains the namespace and class names. With WMI, namespace names and class names are separate – you supply them to the CIM cmdlets using different cmdlet parameters.

In the WMI database, WMI classes contain data instances that hold information about managed entities. For example, the WMI namespace Root\CimV2 has the class Win32_Share. Each instance within this WMI class represents one of the **Server Message Block (SMB)** shares within your host. With PowerShell, you normally use the SMB cmdlets to manage SMB shares. There is often useful information in other WMI classes for which there is no cmdlet support.

Strictly speaking, inside PowerShell, a WMI object instance is an instance of a specialized .NET class with data returned from WMI. For this reason, you can treat WMI objects using the same mechanisms you employ with other .NET objects and the output from PowerShell cmdlets. When you retrieve instances of, for example, the Win32_Share class, .NET gets the instance information and returns it in a .NET wrapper object. You can then manipulate that share detail like any other object.

Many WMI classes have methods you can invoke that perform some operation on either a given WMI instance or statically based on the class. The Win32_Share class, for example, has a static Create() method that you can use to create a new share. Each instance of the Win32_Share class has a dynamic Delete() method, which deletes the SMB share.

An important architectural feature of WMI is the WMI provider. A WMI provider is an add on to WMI that implements WMI classes inside a given host. The Win32 WMI provider, for example, implements hundreds of WMI classes, including Win32_Share and Win32_Bios. A provider also implements class methods and class events. For example, the Win32 provider performs the Delete() method to delete an SMB share and the Create() method to create a new SMB share.

In production, you are more likely to manage SMB shares using the SMB cmdlets and less likely to use WMI directly. Since SMB shares should be very familiar, they make a great example to help you understand more about WMI, and this chapter's recipes use the class Win32_Share. That being said, using WMI directly to create SMB shares is a little faster than using New-SMBShare.

WMI and WMI providers both provide a rich eventing system. WMI and WMI provider classes can implement events to which you can subscribe. When the event occurs, the eventing system notifies you, and you can take some action to handle the event occurrence. For example, you can register for a WMI event when someone changes an AD group's membership. When this happens, WMI eventing allows you to take some actions, such as emailing a security administrator to inform them of the group's membership change. WMI also implements permanent WMI events. This feature allows you to configure WMI to trap and handle events with no active PowerShell session. Permanent events even survive a reboot of the host, which is extremely powerful in a lights-off environment.

There is much more detail about WMI than can fit in this chapter. For more information about WMI and how you can interact with it in more detail, consult Richard Siddaway's PowerShell and WMI book ($^{©}$ Manning, Aug 2012 - `https://www.manning.com/books/powershell-and-wmi`). Richard's book details WMI, but all the code samples use the older WMI cmdlets. You should be able to translate the samples to use the CIM cmdlets. A key value of the book is the discussion of WMI features and how they work. The basic functioning of WMI has not changed significantly since that book was published.

The systems used in the chapter

This chapter primarily uses the server SRV1, a domain-joined server in the Reskit.Org domain. You have used this server, and the domain, in previous chapters of this book. You also need access to the domain's two DCs (DC1 and DC2) and another member server, SRV2.

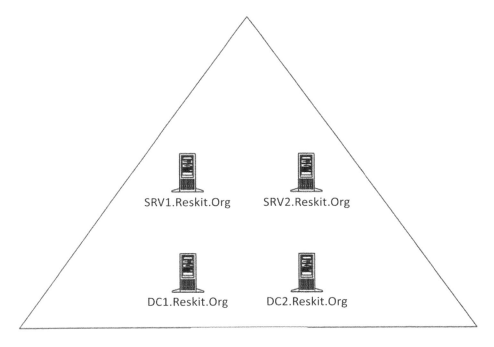

Reskit.Org domain

Figure 13.2: Host in use for this chapter

Exploring WMI Architecture in Windows

Windows installs WMI during the installation of the OS. The installation process puts most of the WMI components, including the repository, tools, and the WMI providers, into a folder `C:\Windows\System32\WBEM`.

Inside a running Windows host, WMI runs as a service, the winmgmt service (`WinMgmt.exe`). Windows runs this service inside a shared service process (`svchost.exe`). In the early versions of WMI in Windows, WMI loaded all the WMI providers into the winmgmt service. The failure of a single provider could cause the entire WMI service to fail. Later, with Windows XP and beyond, Microsoft improved WMI to load providers in a separate process, `Wmiprvse.exe`. WMI loads individual providers as needed.

In this recipe, you examine the contents of the WBEM folder, the WMI service, and the runtime components of WMI.

Getting ready

This recipe uses SRV1, a domain-joined host. You have installed PowerShell 7 and VS code on this host.

How to do it...

1. Viewing the WBEM folder

   ```
   $WBEMFOLDER = "$Env:windir\system32\wbem"
   Get-ChildItem -Path $WBEMFOLDER |
     Select-Object -First 20
   ```

2. Viewing the WMI repository folder

   ```
   Get-ChildItem -Path $WBEMFOLDER\Repository
   ```

3. Viewing the WMI service details

   ```
   Get-Service -Name Winmgmt |
     Format-List -Property *
   ```

4. Getting process details

   ```
   $Service = tasklist.exe /svc /fi "SERVICES eq winmgmt" |
                  Select-Object -Last 1
   $Process = [int] ($Service.Substring(30,4))
   ```

```
Get-Process -Id $|Process
```

5. Examining DLLs loaded by the WMI service process

```
Get-Process -Id $Process |
  Select-Object -ExpandProperty Modules |
    Where-Object ModuleName -match 'wmi' |
      Format-Table -Property FileName, Description, FileVersion
```

6. Discovering WMI providers

```
Get-ChildItem -Path $WBEMFOLDER\*.dll |
  Select-Object -ExpandProperty Versioninfo |
    Where-Object FileDescription -match 'prov' |
      Format-Table -Property Internalname,
                             FileDescription,
                             ProductVersion
```

7. Examining the WmiPrvSE process

```
Get-CimInstance -ClassName Win32_Bios | Out-Null
Get-Process -Name WmiPrvSE
```

8. Finding the WMI event log

```
$Log = Get-WinEvent -ListLog *wmi*
$Log
```

9. Looking at the event types in the WMI log

```
$Events = Get-WinEvent -LogName $Log.LogName
$Events | Group-Object -Property LevelDisplayName
```

10. Examining WMI event log entries

```
$Events |
  Select-Object -First 5 |
    Format-Table -Wrap
```

11. Viewing executable programs in the WBEM folder

```
$Files = Get-ChildItem -Path $WBEMFOLDER\*.exe
"{0,15}  {1,-40}" -f 'File Name','Description'
Foreach ($File in $Files){
```

```
    $Name = $File.Name
    $Desc = ($File |
             Select-Object -ExpandProperty VersionInfo).FileDescription
    "{0,15}  {1,-40}" -f $Name,$Desc
    }
```

12. Examining the CimCmdlets module

```
Get-Module -Name CimCmdlets |
  Select-Object -ExcludeProperty Exported*
    Format-List -Property *
```

13. Finding cmdlets in the CimCmdlets module

```
Get-Command -Module CimCmdlets
```

14. Examining the .NET type returned from Get-CimInstance

```
Get-CimInstance -ClassName Win32_Share | Get-Member
```

How it works...

The WMI service and related files are in the Windows installation folder's System32\WBEM folder. In *step 1*, you view part of the contents of that folder, with output like this:

```
PS C:\Foo> # 1. Viewing the WBEM folder
PS C:\Foo> $WBEMFOLDER = "$Env:windir\system32\wbem"
PS C:\Foo> Get-ChildItem -Path $WBEMFOLDER |
              Select-Object -First 20
```

```
   Directory: C:\Windows\System32\wbem

Mode              LastWriteTime       Length Name
----              -------------       ------ ----
d----       23/09/2022     16:35             AutoRecover
d----       08/05/2021     10:41             en
d----       22/09/2022     16:24             en-US
d----       08/05/2021     09:20             Logs
d----       22/09/2022     13:49             MOF
d----       26/10/2022     17:23             Performance
d----       24/09/2022     16:09             Repository
d----       08/05/2021     09:20             tmf
d----       08/05/2021     09:20             xml
-a---       08/05/2021     09:14         2852 aeinv.mof
-a---       08/05/2021     10:41        17510 AgentWmi.mof
-a---       08/05/2021     09:15          693 AgentWmiUninstall.mof
-a---       08/05/2021     09:14          852 appbackgroundtask_uninstall.mof
-a---       08/05/2021     09:14        65536 appbackgroundtask.dll
-a---       08/05/2021     09:14         2902 appbackgroundtask.mof
-a---       08/05/2021     09:15         1112 AttestationWmiProvider_Uninstall.mof
-a---       08/05/2021     09:15         3376 AttestationWmiProvider.mof
-a---       08/05/2021     09:14         1724 AuditRsop.mof
-a---       08/05/2021     09:14         1092 authfwcfg.mof
-a---       08/05/2021     09:14        12120 bcd.mof
```

Figure 13.3: Examining the WBEM folder

WMI stores the CIM repository in a separate folder. In *step 2*, you examine the files that make up the database, with output like this:

```
PS C:\Foo> # 2. Viewing the WMI repository folder
PS C:\Foo> Get-ChildItem -Path $WBEMFOLDER\Repository
```

```
   Directory: C:\Windows\System32\wbem\Repository

Mode              LastWriteTime       Length Name
----              -------------       ------ ----
-a---       05/11/2022     22:20      5750784 INDEX.BTR
-a---       05/11/2022     19:32       105640 MAPPING1.MAP
-a---       05/11/2022     22:20       105640 MAPPING2.MAP
-a---       05/11/2022     06:52       105640 MAPPING3.MAP
-a---       05/11/2022     22:20     31899648 OBJECTS.DATA
```

Figure 13.4: Examining the files making up the CIM repository

In *step 3*, you use the Get-Service cmdlet to examine the WMI service, with a console output that looks like this:

```
PS C:\Foo> # 3. Viewing the WMI service details
PS C:\Foo> Get-Service -Name Winmgmt   |
              Format-List -Property *

UserName             : localSystem
Description          : Provides a common interface and object model to access management
                       information about operating system, devices, applications and
                       services. If this service is stopped, most Windows-based software will
                       not function properly. If this service is disabled, any services that
                       explicitly depend on it will fail to start.
DelayedAutoStart     : False
BinaryPathName       : C:\WINDOWS\system32\svchost.exe -k netsvcs -p
StartupType          : Automatic
Name                 : Winmgmt
RequiredServices     : {RPCSS}
CanPauseAndContinue  : True
CanShutdown          : True
CanStop              : True
DisplayName          : Windows Management Instrumentation
DependentServices    : {UALSVC, HgClientService}
MachineName          : .
ServiceName          : Winmgmt
ServicesDependedOn   : {RPCSS}
StartType            : Automatic
ServiceHandle        : Microsoft.Win32.SafeHandles.SafeServiceHandle
Status               : Running
ServiceType          : Win32OwnProcess, Win32ShareProcess
Site                 :
Container            :
```

Figure 13.5: Viewing the WMI service

In *step 4*, you examine the Windows process that runs the WMI service, with output like this:

```
PS C:\Foo> # 4. Getting process details
PS C:\Foo> $Service = tasklist.exe /svc /fi "SERVICES eq winmgmt" |
                        Select-Object -Last 1
PS C:\Foo> $Process = [int] ($Service.Substring(30,4))
PS C:\Foo> Get-Process -Id $Process

NPM(K)    PM(M)    WS(M)    CPU(s)     Id SI ProcessName
------    -----    -----    ------     -- -- -----------
    17    16.25    36.81     90.09   3392  0 svchost
```

Figure 13.6: Viewing the WMI service

In *step 5*, you look at the DLLs loaded by the WMI service process with the following output:

```
PS C:\Foo> # 5. Examining DLLs loaded by the WMI service process
PS C:\Foo> Get-Process -Id $Process |
              Select-Object -ExpandProperty Modules |
                Where-Object ModuleName -match 'wmi' |
                  Format-Table -Property FileName, Description, FileVersion

FileName                                 Description      FileVersion
--------                                 -----------      -----------
c:\windows\system32\wbem\wmisvc.dll      WMI              10.0.20348.1 (WinBuild.160101.0800)
C:\WINDOWS\SYSTEM32\WMICLNT.dll          WMI Client API   10.0.20348.1 (WinBuild.160101.0800)
C:\WINDOWS\system32\wbem\wmiutils.dll    WMI              10.0.20348.1 (WinBuild.160101.0800)
C:\WINDOWS\system32\wbem\wmiprvsd.dll    WMI              10.0.20348.1 (WinBuild.160101.0800)
```

Figure 13.7: Viewing the DLLs loaded by the WMI service process

Each WMI provider is a DLL that the WMI service can use. In *step 6*, you look at the WMI providers on SRV1, with output like this:

```
DhcpServerPsProvider.dll      DHCP WMIv2 Provider                             10.0.20348.1
DMWmiBridgeProv.dll           DM WMI Bridge Provider                          10.0.20348.1
DMWmiBridgeProv1.dll          DM WMI Bridge Provider                          10.0.20348.1
DnsClientPsProvider.dll       DNS Client WMIv2 Provider                       10.0.20348.1
DnsServerPsProvider.dll       DNS WMIv2 Provider                              10.0.20348.1
dsprov.dll                    WMI DS Provider                                 10.0.20348.1
"EventTracingManagement.dll"  WMI Provider for ETW                            10.0.20348.1
ipmiprr.dll                   IPMI Provider Resource                          10.0.20348.1
IPMIPRV.dll                   WMI IPMI PROVIDER                               10.0.20348.1
MDMAppProv.dll                MDM Application Provider                        10.0.20348.1
MDMSettingsProv.dll           MDM Settings Provider                           10.0.20348.1
mgmtprovider.dll              Server Manager Managment Provider               10.0.20348.1
mistreamprov.dll              SIL Composable Streams Provider                 10.0.20348.1
DtcCIMProvider.dll            DTC WMIv2 Provider                              10.0.20348.1
msiprov.dll                   WMI MSI Provider                                10.0.20348.1
MspsProv.exe                  Msps Prov                                       10.0.20348.1
mttmprov.dll                  Mangement Tools Task Manager CIM Provider       10.0.20348.1
NCObjAPI                      Non-COM WMI Event Provision APIs                10.0.20348.1
ndisimplatwmi.DLL             NDIS IM Platform WMI Provider                   10.0.20348.1
NetAdapter.dll                Network Adapter WMI Provider                    10.0.20348.1
netdacim.dll                  Microsoft Direct Access WMI Provider            10.0.20348.1
NetEventPacketCapture.dll     NetEvent Packet Capture Provider                10.0.20348.1
NetNat.dll                    Windows NAT WMI Provider                        10.0.20348.1
netnccim.dll                  DA Network Connectivity WMI Provider            10.0.20348.1
NetPeerDistCim.dll            BranchCache WMI Provider                        10.0.20348.1
netswitchteamcim.DLL          VM Switch Teaming WMI Provider                  10.0.20348.1
NetTCPIP.dll                  TCPIP WMI Provider                              10.0.20348.1
nlmcim.dll                    Network Connection Profiles WMI Provider        10.0.20348.1
ntevt.dll                     WMI Event Log Provider                          10.0.20348.1
PLATID.DLL                    WMIv2 Provider to Retrieve Platform Identifiers 10.0.20348.1
PrintManagementProvider.DLL   Print WMI Provider                              10.0.20348.1
RacWmiProv.dll                Reliability Metrics WMI Provider                10.0.20348.1
RAMgmtPSProvider.dll          RAMgmtPSProvider                                10.0.20348.1
regprov.dll                   Registry Provider                               10.0.20348.1
schedprov.dll                 Task Scheduler WMIv2 Provider                   10.0.20348.1
SDNDiagnosticsProvider.dll    SDNDiagnosticsProvider                          10.0.20348.1
servercompprov.dll            Windows Server Feature WMI Provider             10.0.20348.1
sllprovider.dll               Server License Logging CIM Provider             10.0.20348.1
vdswmi.dll                    WMI Provider for VDS                            10.0.20348.1
viewprov.dll                  WMI View Provider                               10.0.20348.1
VpnClientPsProvider.dll       VPN Client WMIv2 Provider                       10.0.20348.1
VSSPROV.DLL                   WMI Provider for VSS                            10.0.20348.1
WdacWmiProv.dll               WDAC WMI Providers                              10.0.20348.1
Win32_EncryptableVolume.DLL   Win32_Encryptable Volume Provider               10.0.20348.143
Win32_Tpm.DLL                 TPM WMI Provider                                10.0.20348.1
WMIPCIMA.dll                  WMI Win32Ex Provider                            10.0.20348.1
wmipdfs.dll                   WMI DFS Provider                                10.0.20348.1
WMIPDskQ.dll                  WMI Provider for Disk Quota Information          10.0.20348.1
WbemPerfClass.dll             WbemPerf V2 Class Provider                      10.0.20348.1
WbemPerfInst.dll              WbemPerf V2 Instance Provider                   10.0.20348.1
wmipicmp.dll                  WMI ICMP Echo Provider                          10.0.20348.1
WMIPIpRt.dll                  WBEM Provider for IP4 Routes                    10.0.20348.1
wmipjobj.dll                  WMI Windows Job Object Provider                 10.0.20348.1
WMIPSess.dll                  WMI Provider for Sessions and Connections       10.0.20348.1
```

Figure 13.8: Viewing WMI provider DLLs

In *step 7*, you examine the WmiPrvSE process, with output like this:

```
PS C:\Foo> # 7. Examining the WmiPrvSE process
PS C:\Foo> Get-CimInstance -ClassName Win32_Bios | Out-Null
PS C:\Foo> Get-Process -Name WmiPrvSE

 NPM(k)    PM(M)    WS(M)   CPU(s)     Id  SI ProcessName
 ------    -----    -----   ------     --  -- -----------
     11     2.75     9.10     0.03  10012   0 WmiPrvSE
```

Figure 13.9: Viewing the WmiPrvSE process

Like other Windows services, WMI writes details of events to an event log, which can help troubleshoot WMI issues. In *step 8*, you look for the WMI event log, with output like this:

```
PS C:\Foo> # 8. Finding the WMI event log
PS C:\Foo> $Log = Get-WinEvent -ListLog *wmi*
PS C:\Foo> $Log

LogMode   MaximumSizeInBytes RecordCount LogName
-------   ------------------ ----------- -------
Circular             1052672        1457 Microsoft-Windows-WMI-Activity/Operational
```

Figure 13.10: Viewing the WMI event log

In *step 9*, you get the events from the log to view the different log levels, with output like this:

```
PS C:\Foo> # 9. Looking at the Event Types in the WMI log
PS C:\Foo> $Events = Get-WinEvent -LogName $Log.LogName
PS C:\Foo> $Events | Group-Object -Property LevelDisplayName

Count Name        Group
----- ----        -----
  728 Error       {System.Diagnostics.Eventing.Reader.EventLogRecord, System.Diagnostics.Eventing.Reader.EventLogRecor…
  729 Information {System.Diagnostics.Eventing.Reader.EventLogRecord, System.Diagnostics.Eventing.Reader.EventLogRecor…
```

Figure 13.11: Discovering WMI event types

In *step 10*, you view the first five WMI event log entries on SRV1. The output looks like this:

```
PS C:\Foo> # 10. Examining WMI event log entries
PS C:\Foo> $Events |
             Select-Object -First 5 |
               Format-Table -Wrap

   ProviderName: Microsoft-Windows-WMI-Activity

TimeCreated             Id LevelDisplayName Message
-----------             -- ---------------- -------
06/11/2022 20:51:39   5857 Information      CIMWin32 provider started with result code 0x0. HostProcess = wmiprvse.exe; ProcessID
                                            = 10012; ProviderPath = %systemroot%\system32\wbem\cimwin32.dll
06/11/2022 20:50:53   5857 Information      WMIProv provider started with result code 0x0. HostProcess = wmiprvse.exe; ProcessID =
                                            8304; ProviderPath = %systemroot%\system32\wbem\wmiprov.dll
06/11/2022 20:50:52   5860 Information      Namespace = ROOT\CIMV2; NotificationQuery = SELECT * FROM Win32_ProcessStartTrace
                                            WHERE ProcessName = 'wsmprovhost.exe'; UserName = NT AUTHORITY\SYSTEM; ClientProcessID
                                            = 6780, ClientMachine = SRV1; PossibleCause = Temporary
06/11/2022 20:50:52   5857 Information      WMI Kernel Trace Event Provider provider started with result code 0x0. HostProcess =
                                            wmiprvse.exe; ProcessID = 3392; ProviderPath = C:\Windows\System32\wbem\krnlprov.dll
06/11/2022 20:50:51   5857 Information      WmiPerfClass provider started with result code 0x0. HostProcess = wmiprvse.exe;
                                            ProcessID = 8304; ProviderPath = C:\Windows\System32\wbem\WmiPerfClass.dll
```

Figure 13.12: Viewing WMI event log entries

In *step 11*, you view the executable programs in the WBEM folder, with output like this:

```
PS C:\Foo> # 11. Viewing executable programs in WBEM folder
PS C:\Foo> $Files = Get-ChildItem -Path $WBEMFOLDER\*.exe
PS C:\Foo> "{0,15}  {1,-40}" -f 'File Name','Description'
PS C:\Foo> Foreach ($File in $Files){
              $Name = $File.Name
              $Desc = ($File |
                    Select-Object -ExpandProperty VersionInfo).FileDescription
              "{0,15}  {1,-40}" -f $Name,$Desc
              }

      File Name  Description
    mofcomp.exe  The Managed Object Format (MOF) Compiler
    scrcons.exe  WMI Standard Event Consumer - scripting
   unsecapp.exe  Sink to receive asynchronous callbacks for WMI client application
   wbemtest.exe  WMI Test Tool
    WinMgmt.exe  WMI Service Control Utility
   WMIADAP.exe  WMI Reverse Performance Adapter Maintenance Utility
  WmiApSrv.exe  WMI Performance Reverse Adapter
       WMIC.exe  WMI Commandline Utility
  WmiPrvSE.exe  WMI Provider Host
```

Figure 13.13 Viewing the executable programs in the WBEM folder

With PowerShell 7 (and, optionally, with Windows PowerShell), you access WMI's functionality using the cmdlets in the CimCmdlets module. The Windows installation program installed a version of this module when you installed the host OS, and the PowerShell 7 installation process adds an updated version of this module.

In *step 12*, you examine the properties of this module, with output like this:

```
PS C:\Foo> # 12. Examining the CimCmdlets module
PS C:\Foo> Get-Module -Name CimCmdlets |
              Select-Object -ExcludeProperty Exported*

LogPipelineExecutionDetails : False
Name                        : CimCmdlets
Path                        : C:\Program Files\PowerShell\7\Microsoft.Management.Infrastructure.CimCmdlets.dll
ImplementingAssembly        : Microsoft.Management.Infrastructure.CimCmdlets, Version=7.2.6.500, Culture=neutral,
                              PublicKeyToken=31bf3856ad364e35
Definition                  :
Description                 :
Guid                        : fb6cc51d-c096-4b38-b78d-0fed6277096a
HelpInfoUri                 : https://aka.ms/powershell72-help
ModuleBase                  : C:\program files\powershell\7\Modules\CimCmdlets
PrivateData                 :
ExperimentalFeatures        : {}
Tags                        : {}
ProjectUri                  :
IconUri                     :
LicenseUri                  :
ReleaseNotes                :
RepositorySourceLocation    :
Version                     : 7.0.0.0
ModuleType                  : Binary
Author                      : PowerShell
AccessMode                  : ReadWrite
ClrVersion                  :
CompanyName                 : Microsoft Corporation
Copyright                   : Copyright (c) Microsoft Corporation.
DotNetFrameworkVersion      :
Prefix                      :
FileList                    : {}
CompatiblePSEditions        : {Core}
ModuleList                  : {}
NestedModules               : {}
PowerShellHostName          :
PowerShellHostVersion       :
PowerShellVersion           : 3.0
ProcessorArchitecture       : None
Scripts                     : {}
RequiredAssemblies          : {Microsoft.Management.Infrastructure.CimCmdlets.dll, Microsoft.Management.Infrastructure.Dll}
RequiredModules             : {}
RootModule                  : Microsoft.Management.Infrastructure.CimCmdlets
SessionState                : System.Management.Automation.SessionState
OnRemove                    :
```

Figure 13.14: Viewing the CimCmdlets module details

In *step 13*, you use the Get-Command cmdlet to discover the cmdlets within the CimCmdlets module, which looks like this:

```
PS C:\Foo> # 13. Finding cmdlets in the CimCmdlets module
PS C:\Foo> Get-Command -Module CimCmdlets

CommandType Name                         Version Source
----------- ----                         ------- ------
Cmdlet      Get-CimAssociatedInstance    7.0.0.0 CimCmdlets
Cmdlet      Get-CimClass                 7.0.0.0 CimCmdlets
Cmdlet      Get-CimInstance              7.0.0.0 CimCmdlets
Cmdlet      Get-CimSession               7.0.0.0 CimCmdlets
Cmdlet      Invoke-CimMethod             7.0.0.0 CimCmdlets
Cmdlet      New-CimInstance              7.0.0.0 CimCmdlets
Cmdlet      New-CimSession               7.0.0.0 CimCmdlets
Cmdlet      New-CimSessionOption         7.0.0.0 CimCmdlets
Cmdlet      Register-CimIndicationEvent  7.0.0.0 CimCmdlets
Cmdlet      Remove-CimInstance           7.0.0.0 CimCmdlets
Cmdlet      Remove-CimSession            7.0.0.0 CimCmdlets
Cmdlet      Set-CimInstance              7.0.0.0 CimCmdlets
```

Figure 13.15: Viewing the cmdlets in the CimCmdlets *module*

In *step 14*, you examine the properties of an object returned from WMI after using the Get-CimInstance command. The output from this step looks like this:

```
PS C:\Foo> # 14. Examining the .NET type returned from Get-CimInstance
PS C:\Foo> Get-CimInstance -ClassName Win32_Share | Get-Member

   TypeName: Microsoft.Management.Infrastructure.CimInstance#root/cimv2/Win32_Share

Name                        MemberType  Definition
----                        ----------  ----------
Dispose                     Method      void Dispose(), void IDisposable.Dispose()
Equals                      Method      bool Equals(System.Object obj)
GetCimSessionComputerName   Method      string GetCimSessionComputerName()
GetCimSessionInstanceId     Method      guid GetCimSessionInstanceId()
GetHashCode                 Method      int GetHashCode()
GetType                     Method      type GetType()
ToString                    Method      string ToString()
AccessMask                  Property    uint AccessMask {get;}
AllowMaximum                Property    bool AllowMaximum {get;}
Caption                     Property    string Caption {get;}
Description                 Property    string Description {get;}
InstallDate                 Property    CimInstance#DateTime InstallDate {get;}
MaximumAllowed              Property    uint MaximumAllowed {get;}
Name                        Property    string Name {get;}
Path                        Property    string Path {get;}
PSComputerName              Property    string PSComputerName {get;}
Status                      Property    string Status {get;}
Type                        Property    uint Type {get;}
PSStatus                    PropertySet PSStatus {Status, Type, Name}
```

Figure 13.16: Examining the output from Get-CimInstance

There's more...

In *step 1*, you viewed the first 20 files/folders in the WBEM folder. There are a lot more files than you see in the figure. These include the DLL files for the WMI providers available on your system.

In *step 7*, you view the WmiPrvSE process. This process hosts WMI providers. Depending on the actions WMI is currently doing, you may see zero, one, or more occurrences of this process on your hosts.

In *step 9* and *step 10*, you discover and examine the WMI system event log. On SRV1, you can see both Error and Information event log entries. As you can see in *step 10*, the information entries mostly indicate that WMI has loaded and invoked a particular provider. In most cases, the error event messages you see are transient or benign.

In *step 14*, you looked at the data returned by Get-CimInstance. As you can see from the output, the cmdlet returns the data obtained from the WMI class. This data is wrapped in a .NET object and has a class of Microsoft.Management.Infrastructure.CimInstance, with a suffix indicating the path to the WMI class, in this case, the Win32_Share class in the ROOT/CIMV2 WMI namespace.

As you can see from the output, the returned object and its contents differ from that produced by the Get-WMIObject cmdlet. This could be an issue if you upgrade Windows PowerShell scripts that previously used the older WMI cmdlets.

Exploring WMI Namespaces

The PowerShell CIM cmdlets enable you to retrieve, update, and remove information from the CIM database and subscribe to and handle WMI events. The CIM database organizes its data into sets of classes within a hierarchical set of namespaces. A namespace is, in effect, a container holding WMI classes.

The name of the root WMI namespace is ROOT, although WMI is not overly consistent about capitalization, as you may notice. A namespace can contain classes as well as additional child namespaces. For example, the root namespace has a child namespace, CIMV2, which you refer to as ROOT\CIMV2. This namespace also has child namespaces.

Every namespace in the CIM database, including ROOT, has a special system class called __NAMESPACE. This class contains the names of child namespaces within the current namespaces. Thus, in the namespace ROOT, the __NAMESPACE class includes an instance for the CIMV2 child namespace. Since this class exists inside every namespace, it is straightforward to discover all the namespaces on your system.

There are many namespaces and classes within WMI on any given system. The specific namespaces and classes depend on what applications and Windows features you run on a host. Additionally, not all the namespaces or classes are useful to the IT pro. Other classes or namespaces may contain classes useful for IT professionals, while most are typically only useful for developers implementing WMI components or WMI providers. The Win32 WMI provider implements the ROOT\CimV2 namespace. This namespace contains classes of interest to IT pros.

Another less commonly used namespace is ROOT\directory\LDAP, which contains classes related to the Active Directory. While you perform most of the AD management using the AD cmdlets, there are features of this namespace, specifically eventing, that are not available with the AD cmdlets and that you may find useful. And these classes can be utilized even if you do not have the AD **Remote Server Administration Tools (RSAT)** tools loaded.

Getting ready

This recipe uses SRV1, a domain-joined host. You have installed PowerShell 7 and VS Code on this host.

How to do it...

1. Viewing WMI classes in the root namespace

    ```
    Get-CimClass -Namespace 'ROOT' |
      Select-Object -First 10
    ```

2. Viewing the __NAMESPACE class in ROOT

    ```
    Get-CimInstance -Namespace 'ROOT' -ClassName __NAMESPACE |
      Sort-Object -Property Name
    ```

3. Getting and counting classes in ROOT\CIMV2

    ```
    $Classes = Get-CimClass -Namespace 'ROOT\CIMV2'
    "There are $($Classes.Count) classes in ROOT\CIMV2"
    ```

4. Discovering all the namespaces on SRV1

```
$EAHT = @{ErrorAction = 'SilentlyContinue'}
Function Get-WMINamespaceEnum {
  [CmdletBinding()]
  Param($NS)
  Write-Output $NS
  Get-CimInstance "__Namespace" -Namespace $NS @EAHT |
    ForEach-Object { Get-WMINamespaceEnum "$ns\$($_.name)"    }
}  # End of function
$Namespaces = Get-WMINamespaceEnum 'ROOT' |
  Sort-Object
"There are $($Namespaces.Count) WMI namespaces on SRV1"
```

5. Viewing first 25 namespaces on SRV1

```
$Namespaces |
  Select-Object -First 25
```

6. Creating a script block to count namespaces and classes

```
$ScriptBlock = {
 Function Get-WMINamespaceEnum {
   [CmdletBinding()]
   Param(
     $NameSpace
    )
   Write-Output $NameSpace
   $EAHT = @{ErrorAction = 'SilentlyContinue'}
   Get-CimInstance "__Namespace" -Namespace $NameSpace @EAHT |
     ForEach-Object {
       Get-WMINamespaceEnum "$NameSpace\$($_.Name)"
     }
 }  # End of function
 $Namespaces = Get-WMINamespaceEnum 'ROOT' | Sort-Object
 $WMIClasses = @()
```

```
    Foreach ($WMINameSpace in $Namespaces) {
    $WMIClasses += Get-CimClass -Namespace $WMINameSpace
  }
  "There are $($Namespaces.Count) WMI namespaces on $(hostname)"
  "There are $($WMIClasses.Count) classes on $(hostname)"
}
```

7. Running the script block locally on SRV1

```
Invoke-Command -ComputerName SRV1 -ScriptBlock $ScriptBlock
```

8. Running the script block on SRV2

```
Invoke-Command -ComputerName SRV2 -ScriptBlock $ScriptBlock
```

9. Running the script block on DC1

```
Invoke-Command -ComputerName DC1 -ScriptBlock $ScriptBlock
```

How it works...

In *step 1*, you view the WMI classes in the WMI root namespace on SRV1, with output like this:

```
PS C:\Foo> # 1. Viewing WMI classes in the root namespace
PS C:\Foo> Get-CimClass -Namespace 'ROOT' |
              Select-Object -First 10

   NameSpace: ROOT

CimClassName                           CimClassMethods CimClassProperties
------------                           --------------- ------------------
__SystemClass                          {}              {}
__thisNAMESPACE                        {}              {SECURITY_DESCRIPTOR}
__CacheControl                         {}              {}
__EventConsumerProviderCacheControl    {}              {ClearAfter}
__EventProviderCacheControl            {}              {ClearAfter}
__EventSinkCacheControl                {}              {ClearAfter}
__ObjectProviderCacheControl           {}              {ClearAfter}
__PropertyProviderCacheControl         {}              {ClearAfter}
__NAMESPACE                            {}              {Name}
__ArbitratorConfiguration              {}              {OutstandingTasksPerUser, OutstandingTasksTotal…
```

Figure 13.17: WMI classes in the ROOT namespace

In *step 2*, you examine the instances of the __NAMESPACE class in the ROOT WMI namespace. The output looks like this:

```
PS C:\Foo> # 2. Viewing the __NAMESPACE class in ROOT
PS C:\Foo> Get-CimInstance -Namespace 'ROOT' -ClassName __NAMESPACE |
             Sort-Object -Property Name

Name                PSComputerName
----                --------------
AccessLogging
Appv
CIMV2
Cli
DEFAULT
directory
Hardware
Interop
InventoryLogging
Microsoft
msdtc
MSPS
PEH
Policy
RSOP
SECURITY
ServiceModel
StandardCimv2
subscription
WMI
```

Figure 13.18: Examining the __NAMESPACE class in the ROOT namespace

With *step 3*, you get and then count the classes in the ROOT\CIMV2 namespace, with output like this:

```
PS C:\Foo> # 3. Getting and counting classes in ROOT\CIMV2
PS C:\Foo> $Classes = Get-CimClass -Namespace 'ROOT\CIMV2'
PS C:\Foo> "There are $($Classes.Count) classes in ROOT\CIMV2"
There are 1196 classes in ROOT\CIMV2
```

Figure 13.19: Getting and counting the classes in Root\CIMV2

In *step 4*, you define and then use a function to discover all the namespaces in WMI on this host, sorted alphabetically, and then display a count of the namespaces found. The output of this step looks like this:

```
PS C:\Foo> # 4. Discovering all the namespaces on SRV1
PS C:\Foo> $EAHT = @{ErrorAction = 'SilentlyContinue'}
PS C:\Foo> Function Get-WMINamespaceEnum {
               [CmdletBinding()]
               Param($NS)
               Write-Output $NS
               Get-CimInstance "__Namespace" -Namespace $NS @EAHT |
               ForEach-Object { Get-WMINamespaceEnum "$ns\$($_.name)"    }
           }  # End of function
PS C:\Foo> $Namespaces = Get-WMINamespaceEnum 'ROOT' |
               Sort-Object
PS C:\Foo> "There are $($Namespaces.Count) WMI namespaces on SRV1"

There are 126 WMI namespaces on SRV1
```

Figure 13.20: Discovering all the WMI namespaces on SRV1

In *step 5*, you view the first 25 namespace names, with output like this:

```
PS C:\Foo> # 5. Viewing first 25 namespaces on SRV1
PS C:\Foo> $Namespaces |
               Select-Object -First 25
ROOT
ROOT\AccessLogging
ROOT\Appv
ROOT\CIMV2
ROOT\CIMV2\mdm
ROOT\CIMV2\mdm\dmmap
ROOT\CIMV2\mdm\MS_409
ROOT\CIMV2\ms_409
ROOT\CIMV2\power
ROOT\CIMV2\power\ms_409
ROOT\CIMV2\Security
ROOT\CIMV2\Security\MicrosoftTpm
ROOT\CIMV2\Security\MicrosoftVolumeEncryption
ROOT\CIMV2\TerminalServices
ROOT\CIMV2\TerminalServices\ms_409
ROOT\Cli
ROOT\Cli\MS_409
ROOT\DEFAULT
ROOT\DEFAULT\ms_409
ROOT\directory
ROOT\directory\LDAP
ROOT\directory\LDAP\ms_409
ROOT\Hardware
ROOT\Hardware\ms_409
ROOT\Interop
```

Figure 13.21: Listing the first 25 namespaces in WMI on SRV1

In *step 6*, you create a script that counts WMI namespaces and classes for a given host. This step generates no console output. In *step 7*, you run this function against SRV1, with output like this:

```
PS C:\Foo> # 7. Running the script block locally on SRV1
PS C:\Foo> Invoke-Command -ComputerName SRV1 -ScriptBlock $ScriptBlock
There are 126 WMI namespaces on SRV1
There are 17213 classes on SRV1
```

Figure 13.22: Counting the namespaces and classes in WMI on SRV1

In *step 8*, you run the script block on SRV2, with output like this:

```
PS C:\Foo> # 8. Running the script block on SRV2
PS C:\Foo> Invoke-Command -ComputerName SRV2 -ScriptBlock $ScriptBlock
There are 102 WMI namespaces on SRV2
There are 14150 classes on SRV2
```

Figure 13.23: Counting the namespaces and classes in WMI on SRV2

In the final step, *step 9*, you run the script block on a domain controller, DC1. The output of this step is as follows:

```
PS C:\Foo> # 9. Running the script block on DC1
PS C:\Foo> Invoke-Command -ComputerName DC1 -ScriptBlock $$ScriptBlock
There are 114 WMI namespaces on DC1
There are 16492 classes on DC1
```

Figure 13.24: Counting the namespaces and classes in WMI on DC1

There's more...

In *step 2*, you determine the child namespaces of the root namespaces. Each instance contains a string with the child's namespace name. The first entry is AccessLogging. Therefore the full namespace name of this child namespace is ROOT\AccessLogging.

In *step 3*, you count the classes in the ROOT\CIMV2. As mentioned, not all of these classes are useful to an IT pro, although many are. You can use your search engine to find classes that might be useful.

In *step 4*, you define a recursive function. When you call this function, specifying the ROOT namespace, the function retrieves the child namespace names from the __NAMESPACE class in the ROOT namespace. Then, for each child's namespace of the root, the function calls itself with a child namespace name. Eventually, this function returns the names of every namespace in WMI. You then sort this alphabetically by namespace name. Note that you can sort the output of GET-WMINamespaceEnum without specifying a property – you are sorting on the contents of the strings returned from the function.

In *step 5*, you view some of the namespaces in WMI on SRV1. Two important namespaces are the ROOT\CIMV2 and the ROOT\directory\LDAP. The former contains classes provided by the Win32 WMI provider. These classes include details about the software and hardware on your system, including the bios, the OS, files, and much more.

Step 7, *step 8*, and *step 9* run the function (defined in *step 6*) remotely. These steps count and display a count of the namespaces and classes on all three systems. For this reason, you should expect that the number of classes and namespaces differs.

Exploring WMI Classes

A WMI class defines a WMI-managed object such as a file share, a disk file, etc. All WMI classes live within a namespace. WMI classes, like .NET classes, contain members that include properties, methods, and events. An example class is Win32_Share, which you find in the root\CIMV2 namespace. This class defines an SMB share on a Windows host. Within WMI, the Win32 WMI provider implements this class (along with multiple other OS and host-related classes).

As mentioned, you typically use the SMB cmdlets to manage SMB shares (as discussed in *Chapter 8, Managing Shared Data*, including the *Creating and securing SMB shares* recipe). Likewise, you carry out most AD management activities using AD cmdlets rather than accessing the information via WMI. Nevertheless, you can do things with WMI, such as event handling, that can be very useful to the IT professional.

A WMI class contains one or more properties that are attributes of an occurrence of a WMI class. Classes can also include methods that act on a WMI occurrence. For example, the Win32_Share class contains a Name property that holds that share's name. The Win32_Share class also has a Create() method to create a new SMB share and a Delete() method to remove a specific SMB share. A WMI method can be either dynamic (or instance-based) or static (class-related). The Win32_Share's Delete() method is a dynamic method you use to delete a particular SMB share. The Create() method is a static method that the class can perform to create a new SMB share. You can learn more about WMI methods in the *Using WMI Methods* recipe later in this chapter.

In this recipe, you use the CIM cmdlets to discover information about classes and what a class can contain. You first examine a class within the default root\CIMV2 namespace. You also look at a class in a non-default namespace and discover the objects contained in the class.

Getting ready

This recipe uses SRV1, a domain-joined host. You have installed PowerShell 7 and VS Code on this host.

How to do it...

1. Viewing Win32_Share class

    ```
    Get-CimClass -ClassName Win32_Share
    ```

2. Viewing Win32_Share class properties

    ```
    Get-CimClass -ClassName Win32_Share |
      Select-Object -ExpandProperty CimClassProperties |
        Sort-Object -Property Name |
          Format-Table -Property Name, CimType
    ```

3. Getting methods of Win32_Share class

    ```
    Get-CimClass -ClassName Win32_Share |
      Select-Object -ExpandProperty CimClassMethods
    ```

4. Getting classes in a non-default namespace

    ```
    Get-CimClass -Namespace root\directory\LDAP |
      Where-Object CimClassName -match '^ds_group'
    ```

5. Viewing the instances of the ds_group class

    ```
    Get-CimInstance -Namespace root\directory\LDAP -Classname 'DS_Group'
    |
      Select-Object -First 10 |
        Format-Table -Property DS_name, DS_Member
    ```

How it works...

In *step 1*, you view a specific class, the Win32_Share class, with output like this:

```
PS C:\Foo> # 1. Viewing Win32_Share class
PS C:\Foo> Get-CimClass -ClassName Win32_Share

   NameSpace: ROOT/cimv2

CimClassName CimClassMethods          CimClassProperties
------------ ---------------          ------------------
Win32_Share  {Create, SetShareInfo,   {Caption, Description, InstallDate, Name,
             GetAccessMask, Delete}    Status, AccessMask, AllowMaximum, MaximumAllowed,
                                       Path, Type}
```

Figure 13.25: Viewing the Win32_Share WMI class

In *step 2*, you view the properties of the Win32_Share class. The output of this step looks like this:

```
PS C:\Foo> # 2. Viewing Win32_Share class properties
PS C:\Foo> Get-CimClass -ClassName Win32_Share |
              Select-Object -ExpandProperty CimClassProperties |
                Sort-Object -Property Name |
                  Format-Table -Property Name, CimType

Name             CimType
----             -------
AccessMask       UInt32
AllowMaximum     Boolean
Caption          String
Description      String
InstallDate      DateTime
MaximumAllowed   UInt32
Name             String
Path             String
Status           String
Type             UInt32
```

Figure 13.26: Viewing the Win32_Share class properties

In *step 3*, you use the Get-CimClass cmdlet to view the methods available with the Win32_Share class, with output like this:

```
PS C:\Foo> # 3. Getting methods of Win32_Share class
PS C:\Foo> Get-CimClass -ClassName Win32_Share |
              Select-Object -ExpandProperty CimClassMethods

Name           ReturnType Parameters                                                              Qualifiers
----           ---------- ----------                                                              ----------
Create         UInt32 {Access, Description, MaximumAllowed, Name, Password, Path, Type} {Constructor, Implemented, MappingStrings, Static}
SetShareInfo   UInt32 {Access, Description, MaximumAllowed}                             {Implemented, MappingStrings}
GetAccessMask  UInt32 {}                                                               {Implemented, MappingStrings}
Delete         UInt32 {}                                                               {Destructor, Implemented, MappingStrings}
```

Figure 13.27: Viewing the methods in the Win32_Share class

In *step 4*, you get group-related classes in the ROOT\directory\LDAP namespace. The step returns just those classes that have the name ds_group. As you can see, this matches a few of the classes in this namespace, as follows:

```
PS C:\Foo> # 4. Getting classes in a non-default namespace
PS C:\Foo> Get-CimClass -Namespace root\directory\LDAP |
              Where-Object CimClassName -match '^ds_group'

   NameSpace: ROOT/directory/LDAP

CimClassName              CimClassMethods   CimClassProperties
------------              ---------------   ------------------
ds_groupofuniquenames     {}                {ADSIPath, DS_adminDescription, DS_adminDisplayName...
ds_groupofnames           {}                {ADSIPath, DS_adminDescription, DS_adminDisplayName...
ds_group                  {}                {ADSIPath, DS_adminDescription, DS_adminDisplayName...

ds_grouppolicycontainer   {}                {ADSIPath, DS_adminDescription, DS_adminDisplayName...
```

Figure 13.28: Finding AD group-related classes in the LDAP namespace

In *step 5*, you get the first ten instances of the ds_group WMI class (ten of the groups in AD). The output, shown here, includes both the AD group's name and the current members of each AD group. The output of this step looks like this:

```
PS C:\Foo> # 5. Viewing the instances of the ds_group class
PS C:\Foo> Get-CimInstance -Namespace root\directory\LDAP -Classname 'DS_Group' |
           Select-Object -First 10 |
             Format-Table -Property DS_name, DS_Member

DS_name                                DS_Member
-------                                ---------
Administrators                         {CN=Domain Admins,CN=Users,DC=Reskit,DC=Org, CN=Enterprise Admins,CN=Users,DC=Reskit,DC=Org,
                                       CN=Administrator,CN=Users,DC=Reskit,DC=Org}
Users                                  {CN=Domain Users,CN=Users,DC=Reskit,DC=Org,
                                       CN=S-1-5-11,CN=ForeignSecurityPrincipals,DC=Reskit,DC=Org,
                                       CN=S-1-5-4,CN=ForeignSecurityPrincipals,DC=Reskit,DC=Org]
Guests                                 {CN=Domain Guests,CN=Users,DC=Reskit,DC=Org, CN=Guest,CN=Users,DC=Reskit,DC=Org}
Print Operators
Backup Operators
Replicator
Remote Desktop Users
Network Configuration Operators
Performance Monitor Users
Performance Log Users
```

Figure 13.29: Finding AD groups and group members

There's more...

In *step 3*, you view the methods in the Win32_Share class using Get-CimClass. Since you did not specify a namespace, the WMI cmdlet assumes you are interested in the ROOT\CIV2 namespace. Note that, in this step, the Create() method has two important qualifiers – constructor and status. These two constructor qualifiers tell you that you use the static Create() method to construct a new instance of this class (and a new SMB share). Likewise, you use the Delete() method to remove an instance of the class.

You can see in the output that a provider, in this case, the Win32 provider, is specified. This provider implements all of the methods shown. You may find that some classes have no implementation, although this is not common.

In *step 5*, you view the first instances in the ds_group class. This class contains an instance for every group in the Reskit.Org domain. This class contains more information for each group returned by your use of the Get-ADGroup cmdlet.

Obtaining WMI Class Instances

In the *Exploring WMI Classes* recipe, you discovered that WMI provides many (over 100) namespaces on each host and thousands of WMI classes. You use the Get-CimInstance cmdlet to return the instances of a WMI class. These classes can reside on either the local or a remote host, as you can see in the recipe. This cmdlet returns the WMI instances for a specified WMI class wrapped in a .NET object.

With WMI, you have three ways in which you can use Get-CimInstance:

- The first way is to use the cmdlet to return all class occurrences and properties.
- The second way is to use the -Filter parameter to specify a WMI filter. When used with Get-CimInstance, the WMI filter instructs the command to filter and return some instances of the desired class.
- The third method uses a WMI query using the **WMI Query Language** (**WQL**). A WQL query is, in effect, a SQL statement that instructs WMI to return some or all properties of some or all occurrences of the specified WMI class.

When you use WMI across the network, specifying a filter or a full WMI query can reduce the amount of data transiting the wire and improve performance. This happens as there is there less data transmiteed.

As in previous recipes, you use the Get-CimInstance to retrieve WMI class instances using each of these three approaches.

Getting ready

This recipe uses SRV1, a domain-joined host. You have installed PowerShell 7 and VS Code on this host.

How to do it...

1. Using Get-CimInstance in the default namespace

```
Get-CimInstance -ClassName Win32_Share
```

2. Getting WMI objects from a non-default namespace

```
$Instance1 = @{
  Namespace = 'ROOT\directory\LDAP'
  ClassName = 'ds_group'
}
Get-CimInstance @Instance1 |
  Sort-Object -Property Name |
    Select-Object -First 10 |
      Format-Table -Property DS_name, DS_distinguishedName
```

3. Using a WMI filter

```
$Filter = "ds_Name LIKE '%operator%' "
Get-CimInstance @Instance1  -Filter $Filter |
  Format-Table -Property DS_Name
```

4. Using a WMI query

```
$Query = @"
  SELECT * from ds_group
    WHERE ds_Name like '%operator%'
"@
Get-CimInstance -Query $Query -Namespace 'root\directory\LDAP' |
  Format-Table DS_Name
```

5. Getting a WMI object from a remote system (DC1)

```
Get-CimInstance -CimSession DC1 -ClassName Win32_ComputerSystem |
  Format-Table -AutoSize
```

How it works...

In *step 1*, you use Get-CimInstance to return all the instances of the Win32_Share class on SRV1, with output like this:

```
PS C:\Foo> # 1. Using Get-CimInstance in the default namespace
PS C:\Foo> Get-CimInstance -ClassName Win32_Share

Name    Path       Description
----    ----       -----------
ADMIN$  C:\WINDOWS Remote Admin
C$      C:\        Default share
IPC$               Remote IPC
```

Figure 13.30: Retrieving Win32_Share class instances on SRV1

In *step 2*, you use Get-CimInstance to retrieve instances of a class in a non-default namespace that you name explicitly, with output like this:

```
PS C:\Foo> # 2. Getting WMI objects from a non-default namespace
PS C:\Foo> $Instance1 = @{
            Namespace = 'ROOT\directory\LDAP'
            ClassName = 'ds_group'
           }
PS C:\Foo> Get-CimInstance @Instance1 |
            Sort-Object -Property Name |
              Select-Object -First 10 |
                Format-Table -Property DS_name, DS_distinguishedName


DS_name                                   DS_distinguishedName
-------                                   --------------------
Administrators                            CN=Administrators,CN=Builtin,DC=Reskit,DC=Org
Group Policy Creator Owners               CN=Group Policy Creator Owners,CN=Users,DC=Reskit,DC=Org
Pre-Windows 2000 Compatible Access        CN=Pre-Windows 2000 Compatible Access,CN=Builtin,DC=Reskit,DC=Org
Windows Authorization Access Group        CN=Windows Authorization Access Group,CN=Builtin,DC=Reskit,DC=Org
Allowed RODC Password Replication Group   CN=Allowed RODC Password Replication Group,CN=Users,DC=Reskit,DC=Org
Denied RODC Password Replication Group    CN=Denied RODC Password Replication Group,CN=Users,DC=Reskit,DC=Org
Enterprise Read-only Domain Controllers   CN=Enterprise Read-only Domain Controllers,CN=Users,DC=Reskit,DC=Org
Cloneable Domain Controllers              CN=Cloneable Domain Controllers,CN=Users,DC=Reskit,DC=Org
Protected Users                           CN=Protected Users,CN=Users,DC=Reskit,DC=Org
Key Admins                                CN=Key Admins,CN=Users,DC=Reskit,DC=Org
```

Figure 13.31: Retrieving WMI objects in an explicitly named namespace

In *step 3*, you use a WMI filter, specified with the -Filter parameter to the Get-CimInstance cmdlet. The output looks like this:

```
PS C:\Foo> # 3. Using a WMI filter
PS C:\Foo> $Filter = "ds_Name LIKE '%operator%' "
PS C:\Foo> Get-CimInstance @Instance1  -Filter $Filter |
            Format-Table -Property DS_Name


DS_Name
-------
Network Configuration Operators
Cryptographic Operators
Access Control Assistance Operators
Print Operators
Account Operators
Server Operators
Backup Operators
```

Figure 13.32: Retrieving WMI objects using a WMI filter

In *step 4*, you use a full WMI query that contains the namespace/class you wish to retrieve and details of which properties and instances WMI should return, like in the following output:

```
PS C:\Foo> # 4. Using a WMI query
PS C:\Foo> $Query = @"
              SELECT * from ds_group
                WHERE ds_Name like '%operator%'
           "@
PS C:\Foo> Get-CimInstance -Query $Query -Namespace 'root\directory\LDAP' |
              Format-Table DS_Name


DS_Name
-------
Network Configuration Operators
Cryptographic Operators
Access Control Assistance Operators
Print Operators
Account Operators
Server Operators
Backup Operator
```

Figure 13.33: Retrieving WMI objects using a WMI query

In *step 5*, you retrieve a WMI object from a remote host, DC1. The class retrieved by this step, Win32_ComputerSystem, holds details of the host, such as hostname, domain name, and total physical memory, as you can see in the following output:

```
PS C:\Foo> # 5. Getting a WMI object from a remote system (DC1)
PS C:\Foo> Get-CimInstance -CimSession DC1 -ClassName Win32_ComputerSystem
              Format-Table -AutoSize

Name PrimaryOwnerName Domain    TotalPhysicalMemory Model  Manufacturer           PSComputerName
---- ---------------- ------    ------------------- -----  ------------           --------------
DC1  Book Readers     Reskit.Org 4331601920               Virtual Machine Microsoft Corporation DC1
```

Figure 13.34: Retrieving WMI information from DC1

There's more...

In *step 4*, you create a WMI query and use it in a call to Get-CimInstance. The cmdlet uses this query to return all properties on any class instance whose name contains the character "operator", using WMI's wildcard syntax. This query returns all properties in the groups that include printer operators and server operators, as you can see in the output from this step.

In *step 5*, you return details of the DC1 host. You used Get-CimInstance to return the single occurrence of the Win32_ComputerSystem class. The output shows that the DC1 host has 4 GB of memory. If you are using virtualization to implement this host, you may see a different value depending on how you configured the VM.

Using WMI Methods

In many object-oriented programming languages, including PowerShell, a method is an action that an object can carry out. With WMI, any WMI class can have methods that do something useful in relation to an instance or the class itself. For example, the Win32_Share class has a Delete() method to delete a given SMB share. The class also has the Create() static method, which creates a new SMB share.

In many cases, WMI methods duplicate what you can do with other PowerShell cmdlets. You could, for example, use the New-SmbShare cmdlet to create a new SMB share rather than using the Create() static method of the Win32_Share class.

WMI methods are of two types: instance methods and static methods. An instance method operates on a specific instance – for example, deleting a particular SMB share. Classes also provide static methods, which do not need a reference to any existing class instances. For example, you can use the Create() static method to create a new SMB share (and a new occurrence in the Win32_Share class).

Getting ready

This recipe uses SRV1, a domain-joined host. You have installed PowerShell 7 and VS Code on this host.

How to do it...

1. Reviewing methods of Win32_Share class on SRV1

    ```
    Get-CimClass -ClassName Win32_Share |
      Select-Object -ExpandProperty CimClassMethods
    ```

2. Reviewing properties of Win32_Share class

    ```
    Get-CimClass -ClassName Win32_Share |
      Select-Object -ExpandProperty CimClassProperties |
        Format-Table -Property Name, CimType
    ```

3. Creating a new SMB share using the `Create()` static method

```
$NewShareDetails = @{
  Name        = 'TestShare1'
  Path        = 'C:\Foo'
  Description = 'Test Share'
  Type        = [uint32] 0 # disk
}
$CimShareHT = @{
  ClassName  = 'Win32_Share'
  MethodName = 'Create'
  Arguments  = $NewShareDetails
}
Invoke-CimMethod @CimShareHT
```

4. Viewing the new SMB share

```
Get-SMBShare -Name 'TestShare1'
```

5. Viewing the new SMB share using `Get-CimInstance`

```
Get-CimInstance -Class Win32_Share -Filter "Name = 'TestShare1'"
```

6. Removing the share

```
Get-CimInstance -Class Win32_Share -Filter "Name = 'TestShare1'" |
  Invoke-CimMethod -MethodName Delete
```

How it works...

In *step 1*, you use `Get-CimClass` to retrieve and display the methods provided by the `Win32_Share` WMI class. The output is as follows:

```
PS C:\Foo> # 1. Reviewing methods of Win32_Share class on SRV1
PS C:\Foo> Get-CimClass -ClassName Win32_Share |
             Select-Object -ExpandProperty CimClassMethods

Name          ReturnType Parameters                                                 Qualifiers
----          ---------- ----------                                                 ----------
Create        UInt32     {Access, Description, MaximumAllowed, Name, Password, Path, Type} {Constructor, Implemented, MappingStrings, Static}
SetShareInfo  UInt32     {Access, Description, MaximumAllowed}                       {Implemented, MappingStrings}
GetAccessMask UInt32     {}                                                         {Implemented, MappingStrings}
Delete        UInt32     {}                                                         {Destructor, Implemented, MappingStrings}
```

Figure 13.35: Reviewing the methods contained in the Win32_Share WMI class

In *step 2*, you use the Get-CimClass cmdlet to get the properties of each instance of the Win32_Share class, producing the following:

```
PS C:\Foo> # 2. Reviewing properties of Win32_Share class
PS C:\Foo> Get-CimClass -ClassName Win32_Share |
             Select-Object -ExpandProperty CimClassProperties |
             Format-Table -Property Name, CimType

Name                CimType
----                -------
Caption              String
Description          String
InstallDate        DateTime
Name                 String
Status               String
AccessMask           UInt32
AllowMaximum        Boolean
MaximumAllowed       UInt32
Path                 String
Type                 UInt32
```

Figure 13.36: Reviewing the properties of an instance of the Win32_Share class

With *step 3*, you use the Invoke-CimMethod cmdlet to invoke the Create() method of the Win32_ Share class and create a new SMB share on SRV1, with output like this:

```
PS C:\Foo> # 3. Creating a new SMB share using the Create() static method
PS C:\Foo> $NewShareDetails = @{
             Name        = 'TestShare1'
             Path        = 'C:\Foo'
             Description = 'Test Share'
             Type        = [uint32] 0 # disk
           }
PS C:\Foo> $CimShareHT = @{
             ClassName  = 'Win32_Share'
             MethodName = 'Create'
             Arguments  = $NewShareDetails
           }
PS C:\Foo> Invoke-CimMethod @CimShareHT

ReturnValue PSComputerName
----------- --------------
          0
```

Figure 13.37: Creating a new SMB share using WMI

In *step 4*, you use the Get-SMBShare cmdlet to get the SMB share information for the share you created in the previous step, producing output like this:

```
PS C:\Foo> # 4. Viewing the new SMB share
PS C:\Foo> Get-SMBShare -Name 'TestShare1'

Name        ScopeName Path    Description
----        --------- ----    -----------
TestShare1  *         C:\Foo  Test Share
```

Figure 13.38: Viewing the newly created SMB share using Get-SMBShare

In *step 5*, you use Get-CimInstance to view the details of the share via WMI. This step produces the following output:

```
PS C:\Foo> # 5. Viewing the new SMB share using Get-CimInstance
PS C:\Foo> Get-CimInstance -Class Win32_Share -Filter "Name = 'TestShare1'"

Name        Path    Description
----        ----    -----------
TestShare1  C:\Foo  Test Share
```

Figure 13.39: Viewing the newly created SMB share using Get-CimInstance

In the final step in this recipe, *step 6*, you use Invoke-CimMethod to delete a specific share (the one you created in *step 3*). The output is as follows:

```
PS C:\Foo> # 6. Removing the share
PS C:\Foo> Get-CimInstance -Class Win32_Share -Filter "Name = 'TestShare1'" |
             Invoke-CimMethod -MethodName Delete

ReturnValue PSComputerName
----------- --------------
          0
```

Figure 13.40: Removing the SMB share

There's more...

In *step 3*, you create a new SMB share using the Invoke-CimMethod cmdlet. This cmdlet takes a hash table containing the properties and property values for the new SMB share. The cmdlet returns an object containing a ReturnCode property. A return code of 0 indicates success – in this case, it means that WMI has created a new share.

You need to consult the documentation for other values of the return code. For the Win32_Share class, you can find more online documentation at https://learn.microsoft.com/windows/win32/cimwin32prov/create-method-in-class-win32-share. This page shows the return codes that the Create() method could generate and what those return codes indicate.

For example, a return code of 8 would suggest that you attempted to create a share whose name already exists. If you plan to use WMI in production scripting, consider testing for non-zero return codes and handling common errors gracefully.

In *step 6*, you use a WMI method, `Delete()`, to delete the previously created SMB share. You delete this share by first using the `Get-CimInstance` with a WMI filter to retrieve the share(s) to be deleted. You then pipe these share objects to the `Invoke-CimMethod` cmdlet and invoke the `Delete()` method on the instance passed in the pipeline. The approach taken in *step 6* is a common way to remove WMI class instances of this class and, for that matter, any WMI class.

Using WMI Events

A key feature of WMI is its event handling. Thousands of events can occur within a Windows system that might possibly be of interest. For example, you might want to know if someone adds a new member to a high-privilege AD group such as Enterprise Admins. You can tell WMI to notify you when such an event occurs, then take whatever action is appropriate. For example, you might print out an updated list of group members when group membership changes occur. You could also check a list of users who should be members of the group and take some action if the user added is not authorized.

Events are handled both by WMI itself and by WMI providers. WMI can signal an event should a change be detected in a CIM class – that is, any new, updated, or deleted class instance. You can detect changes too in entire classes or namespaces. WMI calls these events **intrinsic** events. One common intrinsic event would occur when you (or Windows) start a new process and, by doing so, WMI adds a new instance to the `Win32_Process` class (contained in the `ROOT/CIMV2` namespace).

WMI providers can also implement events. These are known as **extrinsic** WMI events. The AD WMI provider, for example, implements an event that fires any time the membership of an AD group changes. The Windows registry provider also provides an extrinsic event that detects changes to the registry, such as a new registry key or an updated registry value.

To use WMI event management, you first create an event subscription. The event subscription tells WMI which event you want it to track. Additionally, you can define an event handler that tells WMI what you want to do if the event occurs. For example, if a new process starts, you may wish to display the event's details. If an AD group membership changes, you might want to check to see if any group members are not authorized and report the fact, or possibly even delete the invalid group member.

For more details on how you can receive WMI events, see https://learn.microsoft. com//windows/win32/wmisdk/receiving-a-wmi-event.

For information about the types of events to receive, see https://learn.microsoft. com/windows/win32/wmisdk/determining-the-type-of-event-to-receive.

There are two types of WMI eventing you can utilize. In this recipe, you create and handle temporary WMI events that work within a PowerShell session. If you close a session, WMI stops tracking all the events you registered for in that session. In the *Implementing Permanent WMI Eventing* recipe, you will look at creating event subscriptions independent of the current PowerShell session.

When you register for a temporary event, you can provide WMI with a script block that you want WMI to execute when the event occurs. WMI runs this script block in the background, inside a PowerShell job.

When you register for a WMI event, PowerShell creates this job in which it runs the action script. As with all PowerShell jobs, you use Receive-Job to view any output generated by the script. If your script block contains Write-Host statements, PowerShell sends any output directly to the console (not the background job). You can also register for a WMI event without specifying an action block. In that case, WMI queues the events, and you can use Get-WinEvent to retrieve the event details.

When WMI detects an event, it generates an event record containing the event's details. These event records can be useful in helping you with more information on the event, but the records are not a complete snapshot of the event. You can register for a WMI event should the membership of an AD group change, and receive details such as the new member. However, the event record does not contain details of the user who modified the group's membership or of the host's IP address used to effect the unauthorized change.

Getting ready

This recipe uses DC1, a domain controller in the Reskit domain. You have used this host in many of the previous chapters. You have installed PowerShell 7 and VS Code on this host. Also, you should have previously created the user Malcolm in the AD.

How to do it...

1. Registering an intrinsic event

```
$Query1 = "SELECT * FROM __InstanceCreationEvent WITHIN 2
           WHERE TargetInstance ISA 'Win32_Process'"
$EventHT = @{
  Query           = $Query1
  SourceIdentifier = 'NewProcessEvent'
}
Register-CimIndicationEvent @EventHT
```

2. Running Notepad to trigger the event

```
notepad.exe
```

3. Getting the new process event

```
$NotepadEvent = Get-Event -SourceIdentifier 'NewProcessEvent' |
                  Select-Object -Last 1
```

4. Displaying event details

```
$NotepadEvent.SourceEventArgs.NewEvent.TargetInstance
```

5. Unregistering the event

```
Unregister-Event -SourceIdentifier 'NewProcessEvent'
```

6. Registering an event query based on the registry provider

```
New-Item -Path 'HKLM:\SOFTWARE\Packt' | Out-Null
$Query2 = "SELECT * FROM RegistryValueChangeEvent
           WHERE Hive='HKEY_LOCAL_MACHINE'
              AND KeyPath='SOFTWARE\\Packt' AND ValueName='MOLTUAE'"
$Action2 = {
  Write-Host -Object "Registry Value Change Event Occurred"
  $Global:RegEvent = $Event
}
$RegisterHT = @{
  Query  = $Query2
  Action = $Action2
  Source = 'RegChange'
```

```
    }
    Register-CimIndicationEvent @RegisterHT
```

7. Creating a new registry key and setting a value entry

```
    $Query3HT = [ordered] @{
      Type  = 'DWord'
      Name  = 'MOLTUAE'
      Path  = 'HKLM:\Software\Packt'
      Value = 42
    }
    Set-ItemProperty @Query3HT
    Get-ItemProperty -Path HKLM:\SOFTWARE\Packt
```

8. Unregistering the event

```
    Unregister-Event -SourceIdentifier 'RegChange'
```

9. Examining event details

```
    $RegEvent.SourceEventArgs.NewEvent
```

10. Creating a WQL event query

```
    $Group = 'Enterprise Admins'
    $Query1 = @"
      SELECT * From __InstanceModificationEvent Within 5
        WHERE TargetInstance ISA 'ds_group' AND
              TargetInstance.ds_name = '$Group'
    "@
```

11. Creating a temporary WMI event registration

```
    $EventHT= @{
      Namespace = 'ROOT\directory\LDAP'
      SourceID  = 'DSGroupChange'
      Query     = $Query1
      Action    = {
        $Global:ADEvent = $Event
        Write-Host 'We have a group change'
      }
    }
    Register-CimIndicationEvent @EventHT
```

12. Adding a user to the Enterprise Admins group

```
Add-ADGroupMember -Identity 'Enterprise Admins' -Members Malcolm
```

13. Viewing the newly added user within the group

```
$ADEvent.SourceEventArgs.NewEvent.TargetInstance |
  Format-Table -Property DS_sAMAccountName,DS_Member
```

14. Unregistering the event

```
Unregister-Event -SourceIdentifier 'DSGroupChange'
```

How it works...

In *step 1*, you register for an intrinsic event that occurs whenever Windows starts a process. The registration does not include an action block. In *step 2*, you run Notepad.exe to trigger the event. In *step 3*, you use Get-WinEvent to retrieve details of the event. These three steps produce no console output.

In *step 4*, you view details of the process startup event, with output like this:

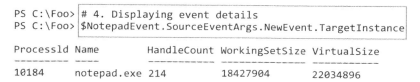

Figure 13.41: Displaying event details

In *step 5*, you remove the registration for the process start event. This step generates no output. In *step 6*, you register a new event subscription using a WMI query that targets the WMI provider, with output like this:

```
PS C:\Foo> # 6. Registering an event query based on the registry provider
PS C:\Foo> New-Item -Path 'HKLM:\SOFTWARE\Packt' | Out-Null
PS C:\Foo> $Query2 = "SELECT * FROM RegistryValueChangeEvent
                      WHERE Hive='HKEY_LOCAL_MACHINE'
                        AND KeyPath='SOFTWARE\\Packt' AND ValueName='MOLTUAE'"
PS C:\Foo> $Action2 = {
               Write-Host -Object "Registry Value Change Event Occurred"
               $Global:RegEvent = $Event
           }
PS C:\Foo> $RegisterHT = @{
               Query  = $Query2
               Action = $Action2
               Source = 'RegChange'
           }
PS C:\Foo> Register-CimIndicationEvent @RegisterHT
```

Id	Name	PSJobTypeName	State	HasMoreData	Location	Command
--	----	-------------	-----	-----------	--------	-------
1	RegChange		NotStarted	False		...

Figure 13.42: Registering for a registry provider-based event

With the event registration complete, in *step 7*, you create a new registry key and set a registry key value to test the event subscription. The output of this step looks like this:

```
PS C:\Foo> # 7. Creating a new registry key and setting a value entry
PS C:\Foo> $Query2HT = [ordered] @{
               Type  = 'DWord'
               Name  = 'MOLTUAE'
               Path  = 'HKLM:\Software\Packt'
               Value = 42
           }
PS C:\Foo> Set-ItemProperty @Query2HT

Registry Value Change Event Occurred   ←━━━━━━━━━━━━━━━━━━━━━━━

PS C:\Foo> Get-ItemProperty -Path HKLM:\SOFTWARE\Packt

MOLTUAE      : 42
PSPath       : Microsoft.PowerShell.Core\Registry::HKEY_LOCAL_MACHINE\SOFTWARE\Packt
PSParentPath : Microsoft.PowerShell.Core\Registry::HKEY_LOCAL_MACHINE\SOFTWARE
PSChildName  : Packt
PSDrive      : HKLM
PSProvider   : Microsoft.PowerShell.Core\Registry
```

Figure 13.43: Invoking the WMI registry event

In *step 8*, you remove the registry event to avoid more event handling and event output. This step generates no console output.

In *step 9*, you examine the output WMI generated based on the registry changes you made in *step 7*. The event details look like this:

```
PS C:\Foo> # 9. Examining event details
PS C:\Foo> $RegEvent.SourceEventArgs.NewEvent

SECURITY_DESCRIPTOR :
TIME_CREATED        : 133136814589107181
Hive                : HKEY_LOCAL_MACHINE
keyPath             : SOFTWARE\Packt
ValueName           : MOLTUAE
PSComputerName      :
```

Figure 13.44: Examining a registry change WMI event

In *step 10*, you create a WQL query that captures changes to the Enterprise Admins AD group, generating no output. In *step 11*, you use the query to create a temporary WMI event that fires when the group membership changes. The output looks like this:

```
PS C:\Foo> # 11. Creating a temporary WMI event registration
PS C:\Foo> $EventHT= @{
              Namespace = 'ROOT\directory\LDAP'
              SourceID  = 'DSGroupChange'
              Query     = $Query1
              Action    = {
                $Global:ADEvent = $Event
                Write-Host 'We have a group change'
              }
           }
PS C:\Foo> Register-CimIndicationEvent @EventHT

Id   Name             PSJobTypeName    State       HasMoreData  Location  Command
--   ----             -------------    -----       -----------  --------  -------
2    DSGroupChange                     NotStarted  False                  ...
```

Figure 13.45: Examining a registry change WMI event

To test this new directory change event, in *step 12*, you add a user to the Enterprise Admins AD group, generating output like this:

```
PS C:\Foo> # 12. Adding a user to the Enterprise Admins group
PS C:\Foo> Add-ADGroupMember -Identity 'Enterprise Admins' -Members Malcolm
PS C:\Foo> We have a group change  ◄─────────
```

Figure 13.46: Triggering an AD group membership change event

In *step 13*, you examine the details of the event you generated in the previous step, with output like this:

```
PS C:\Foo> # 13. Viewing the newly added user within the group
PS C:\Foo> $ADEvent.SourceEventArgs.NewEvent.SourceInstance |
              Format-Table -Property DS_sAMAccountName,DS_Member

DS_sAMAccountName DS_Member
----------------- ---------
Enterprise Admins {CN=Malcolm,OU=IT,DC=Reskit,DC=Org,
                   CN=Jerry Garcia,OU=IT,DC=Reskit,DC=Org,
                   CN=Administrator,CN=Users,DC=Reskit,DC=Org}
```

Figure 13.47: Examining the details of the AD group membership change event

In the final step in this recipe, *step 14*, you unregister for the AD group membership change. This step generates no output.

There's more...

In *step 7*, you test the registry event handling, which includes an event action script block that you want PowerShell to execute when the event occurs. Since the script block you specified in *step 6* contains a Write-Host statement, you see the output on the PowerShell console.

In *step 9*, you examine the details WMI generated when the WMI registry change event occurred. As with other events, the event details omit potentially critical information. For example, the event does not tell you which user made this change or provide the new value of the registry value. You can examine the Windows Security event log to discover the user logged on to that system (and, therefore, the user who made the change). And you can use Get-ItemProperty to determine the new value for this registry key property.

The registry value name, MOLTUAE, is an acronym for "meaning of life, the universe, and everything" – a famous line from a well-known book. The value, of course, is 42.

In *step 12*, you add the user Malcolm to the group, You created the Malcolm user in *Chapter 5*, in the recipe *Adding users to active directory using a CSV file*.

In *step 14*, you explicitly remove the registration for the AD change event. Alternatively, you could have closed the current PowerShell session, removing the event subscriptions.

If you use WMI eventing, you may find other inconsistencies between different event types. In *step 7*, you examine the output from a registry change event, while in *step 13*, you review the result from an AD change event. In the latter, you can see in the event details the membership of the Enterprise Admins group, but in the registry change event, you do not see the new registry value.

Implementing Permanent WMI Eventing

In the *Managing WMI events* recipe, you used PowerShell's WMI event handling capability and used temporary event handling – the event handlers are active only as long as the PowerShell session is active and a user logs in to the host. You created an event subscription in that recipe and handled the events as your system generated them. This temporary event handling is a great troubleshooting tool that works well if you are logged in and running PowerShell.

WMI also provides permanent event handling. WMI permanent event registrations enable WMI to detect and act on some events, even if no one is logged on. You configure WMI to subscribe and handle events as they occur without using an active and open session. With permanent event handling, you configure WMI to subscribe to specific events, for instance, adding a new member to a high-privilege AD group such as Enterprise Admins, along with an action that WMI should perform when that event occurs. For example, you could create a log entry, a complete report, or possibly send an email message to report on the event if/when it occurs.

WMI in Windows defines several different types of permanent event consumers you can use to set a permanent event:

- **Active Script Consumer**: You use this to run a specific VBS script.
- **Log File Consumer**: This handler writes details of events to event log files.
- **NT Event Log Consumer**: This consumer writes event details into the Windows event log.
- **SMTP Event Consumer**: You can use this consumer to send a simple SMTP email message when an event occurs.
- **Command Line Consumer**: With this consumer, you can run a program, such as PowerShell 7, and pass a script filename. When the event occurs, the script has access to the event details and can do pretty much anything you can do in PowerShell.

Microsoft developed the Active Script consumer in the days of Visual Basic and VBS scripts. Unfortunately, this consumer does not support PowerShell scripts. On the other hand, the command-line WMI permanent event handler enables you to run any programs you wish when the event handler detects an event occurrence. In this recipe, you ask WMI to run pwsh.exe and execute a specific script file when the event fires.

Managing permanent event handling is similar to the temporary WMI events you explored in the *Managing WMI events* recipe. But there are some significant differences. You tell WMI which event to trap and what to do when that event occurs.

You add a WMI class occurrence to three WMI classes, as you see in the recipe, to implement a permanent event handler as follows:

1. Define an event filter: The event filter specifies the specific event that WMI should handle. You do this by adding a new instance to the particular event class you want WMI to detect. This event filter is the same as in the previous recipe, *Managing WMI events*.

2. Define an event consumer: In this step, you define the action you want WMI to take when the event occurs.

3. Bind the event filter and event consumer: This step adds a new occurrence to an event-binding class. This occurrence directs WMI to act (invoke the event consumer) whenever WMI detects that a specific WMI event (specified in the event filter) has occurred.

The AD WMI provider implements a wide range of AD-related events to which you can subscribe. WMI namespaces typically contain specific event classes that can detect when anything changes within the namespace. The namespace ROOT/Directory/LDAP has a system class named __InstanceModificationEvent.

A small word of caution is appropriate. You need to be very careful when working with WMI permanent event handling. A best practice is understanding how you remove the objects related to the permanent event handler. Until you explicitly remove these records, WMI continues to monitor your host for the events, which can unnecessarily consume host resources.

This recipe also demonstrates a useful approach – creating PowerShell functions to display the event subscription and then remove the subscription fully. This can be useful to ensure you do not end up with unnecessary event details in WMI.

Finally, be careful when changing an event filter's refresh time (specified in the WMI event filter). Decreasing the event refresh time can consume additional CPU and memory. A refresh rate of once per second or every 5 seconds is possibly overly excessive. For testing, shorter refresh times can be helpful, but checking every 10 seconds or longer is more than adequate for production.

Getting ready

This recipe uses DC1, a domain-joined host. You have installed PowerShell 7 and VS Code on this host.

Also, ensure that the user Malcolm is not an Enterprise Admins AD group member.

How to do it...

1. Creating a list of valid users for the Enterprise Admins group

    ```
    $OKUsersFile = 'C:\Foo\OKUsers.Txt'
    $OKUsers  =  @'
    Administrator
    JerryG
    '@
    $OKUsers |
      Out-File -FilePath $OKUsersFile
    ```

2. Defining helper functions to get/remove permanent events

    ```
    Function Get-WMIPE {
      '*** Event Filters Defined ***'
      Get-CimInstance -Namespace root\subscription -ClassName __
    EventFilter |
        Where-Object Name -eq "EventFilter1" |
          Format-Table Name, Query
      '***Consumer Defined ***'
      $NS = 'ROOT\subscription'
      $CN = 'CommandLineEventConsumer'
      Get-CimInstance -Namespace $ns -Classname  $CN |
        Where-Object {$_.name -eq "EventConsumer1"}  |
          Format-Table Name, Commandlinetemplate
      '***Bindings Defined ***'
      Get-CimInstance -Namespace root\subscription -ClassName __
    FilterToConsumerBinding |
        Where-Object -FilterScript {$_.Filter.Name -eq "EventFilter1"} |
          Format-Table Filter, Consumer
    }
    Function Remove-WMIPE {
      Get-CimInstance -Namespace root\subscription __EventFilter |
        Where-Object Name -eq "EventFilter1" |
          Remove-CimInstance
      Get-CimInstance -Namespace root\subscription
    CommandLineEventConsumer |
        Where-Object Name -eq 'EventConsumer1' |
    ```

```
        Remove-CimInstance
    Get-CimInstance -Namespace root\subscription __
FilterToConsumerBinding  |
      Where-Object -FilterScript {$_.Filter.Name -eq 'EventFilter1'}
  |
        Remove-CimInstance
 }
```

3. Creating an event filter query

```
$Group = 'Enterprise Admins'
$Query = @"
  SELECT * From __InstanceModificationEvent Within 10
    WHERE TargetInstance ISA 'ds_group' AND
          TargetInstance.ds_name = '$Group'
"@
```

4. Creating the event filter

```
$Param = @{
  QueryLanguage =  'WQL'
  Query          = $Query
  Name           = "EventFilter1"
  EventNameSpace = "root/directory/LDAP"
}
$IHT = @{
  ClassName = '__EventFilter'
  Namespace = 'root/subscription'
  Property  = $Param
}
$InstanceFilter = New-CimInstance @IHT
```

5. Creating the Monitor.ps1 script run when the WMI event occurs

```
$Monitor = @'
$LogFile   = 'C:\Foo\Grouplog.Txt'
$Group     = 'Enterprise Admins'
"On: [$(Get-Date)] Group [$Group] was changed" |
  Out-File -Force $LogFile -Append -Encoding Ascii
$ADGM = Get-ADGroupMember -Identity $Group
```

```
# Display who's in the group
"Group Membership"
$ADGM | Format-Table Name, DistinguishedName |
  Out-File -Force $LogFile -Append  -Encoding Ascii
$OKUsers = Get-Content -Path C:\Foo\OKUsers.txt
# Look at who is not authorized
foreach ($User in $ADGM) {
  if ($User.SamAccountName -notin $OKUsers) {
    "Unauthorized user [$($User.SamAccountName)] added to $Group"  |
      Out-File -Force $LogFile -Append  -Encoding Ascii
  }
}
"**********************************'n'n"  |
Out-File -Force $LogFile -Append -Encoding Ascii
'@
$Monitor | Out-File -Path C:\Foo\Monitor.ps1
```

6.   Creating a WMI event consumer which consumer runs PowerShell 7 to execute C:\Foo\
     Monitor.ps1

```
$CLT = 'Pwsh.exe -File C:\Foo\Monitor.ps1'
$Param =[ordered] @{
  Name                 = 'EventConsumer1'
  CommandLineTemplate = $CLT
}
$ECHT = @{
  Namespace = 'root/subscription'
  ClassName = "CommandLineEventConsumer"
  Property  = $param
}
$InstanceConsumer = New-CimInstance @ECHT
```

7.   Binding the filter and consumer

```
$Param = @{
  Filter   = [ref]$InstanceFilter
  Consumer = [ref]$InstanceConsumer
}
```

```
$IBHT = @{
  Namespace = 'root/subscription'
  ClassName = '__FilterToConsumerBinding'
  Property  = $Param
}
$InstanceBinding = New-CimInstance    @IBHT
```

8. Viewing the event registration details

```
Get-WMIPE
```

9. Adding a user to the `Enterprise Admins` group

```
Add-ADGroupMember -Identity 'Enterprise admins' -Members Malcolm
```

10. Viewing `Grouplog.txt` file

```
Get-Content -Path C:\Foo\Grouplog.txt
```

11. Tidying up

```
Remove-WMIPE    # invoke this function you defined above
$RGMHT = @{
 Identity = 'Enterprise admins'
 Member   = 'Malcolm'
 Confirm  = $false
}
Remove-ADGroupMember @RGMHT
Get-WMIPE           # ensure you have removed the event handling
```

How it works...

In *step 1*, you create a text file containing the SAMAccountName of users that you have specified should be a member of the Enterprise Admins group. In *step 2*, you create two helper functions to view and delete the WMI class instances that handle the event. In *step 3*, you create an event filter query, which, in *step 4*, you add to WMI. These steps produce no output.

When you change the group membership, the permanent WMI event occurs. At that point, you want WMI to run a specific PowerShell script. In *step 5*, you create a file, C:\Foo\Monitor.ps1. This step creates no console output.

In *step 6*, you create a new event consumer, telling WMI to run the monitor script to detect the event. Then in *step 7*, you bind the event consumer and the event filter to complete setting up a permanent event handler. These two steps also produce no output.

In *step 8*, you use the Get-WMIPE function you defined in *step 2* earlier. The function outputs the details of the event filter, with the output of this step as follows:

```
PS C:\Foo> # 8. Viewing the event registration details
PS C:\Foo> Get-WMIPE

*** Event Filters Defined ***

Name        Query
----        -----
EventFilter1   SELECT * From __InstanceModificationEvent Within 10
               WHERE TargetInstance ISA 'ds_group' AND
                     TargetInstance.ds_name = 'Enterprise Admins'

***Consumer Defined ***

Name           Commandlinetemplate
----           -------------------
EventConsumer1 Pwsh.exe -File C:\Foo\Monitor.ps1

***Bindings Defined ***

Filter                              Consumer
------                              --------
__EventFilter (Name = "EventFilter1") CommandLineEventConsumer (Name = "EventConsumer1")
```

Figure 13.48: Viewing event registration details

In *step 9*, you test the permanent event handling by adding a new user (Malcolm) to the Enterprise Admins group. This step does not generate console output because you did not add Write-Host statements to Monitor.ps1.

In *step 10*, you view the Grouplog.txt file, with output like this:

```
PS C:\Foo> # 10. Viewing Grouplog.txt file
PS C:\Foo> Get-Content -Path C:\Foo\Grouplog.txt

On:  [11/25/2022 15:44:54]  Group [Enterprise Admins] was changed

Name          DistinguishedName
----          -----------------
Malcolm       CN=Malcolm,OU=IT,DC=Reskit,DC=Org
Jerry Garcia  CN=Jerry Garcia,OU=IT,DC=Reskit,DC=Org
Administrator CN=Administrator,CN=Users,DC=Reskit,DC=Org

Unauthorized user [Malcolm] added to Enterprise Admins
********************************
```

Figure 13.49: Viewing event registration details

In the final step in this recipe, *step 11*, you tidy up by invoking the `Remove-WMIPE` function you defined in *step 2*. This removes the event details from WMI. At the end of this step, you run the `Get-WMIPE` function to ensure you have deleted all the event subscription class instances. The output of this step looks like this:

```
PS C:\Foo> # 11. Tidying up
PS C:\Foo> Remove-WMIPE    # invoke this function you defined above
PS C:\Foo> $RGMHT = @{
             Identity = 'Enterprise admins'
             Member   = 'Malcolm'
             Confirm  = $false
           }
PS C:\Foo> Remove-ADGroupMember @RGMHT
PS C:\Foo> Get-WMIPE         # ensure you have removed the event handling

*** Event Filters Defined ***
***Consumer Defined ***
***Bindings Defined ***
```

Figure 13.50: Tidying up

There's more...

In *step 5*, you create a script that you want WMI to run any time the membership of the `Enterprise Admins` group changes. This script writes details to a text file (`Grouplog.txt`) containing the time the event occurred, the new membership, and whether this group now includes any unauthorized users. You could modify `Monitor.ps1` to send an email to an administrative mailbox or remove the unauthorized user. You could also look in the Windows Security event log to find the most recent user to log on to the server.

In *step 10*, you view the output generated by the `Monitor.ps1` script. Note that it can take a few seconds for the permanent event handler to run the script to completion and generate output to the log file.

Join our community on Discord

Join our community's Discord space for discussions with the author and other readers:

`https://packt.link/SecNet`

14

Managing Windows Update Services

This chapter covers the following recipes:

- Installing Windows Server Update Services
- Configuring WSUS Update Synchronization
- Configuring the Windows Update Client
- Creating Computer Target Groups
- Configuring WSUS Automatic Approvals
- Managing WSUS Updates

Introduction

Keeping your client and server systems updated with patches and updates is an important task undertaken by Windows administrators. **Windows Server Update Services (WSUS)** is a feature of Windows Server 2019 that enables you to manage the download and distribution of updates to your organization's computers.

In addition to updating Windows, WSUS enables you to manage patches and updates for various Microsoft software products. Thus, an update you download from Microsoft and distribute via WSUS may apply to Windows, Microsoft Office, and many other Microsoft software products.

This chapter shows how to install and configure the WSUS server and WSUS client computers. The recipes examine the management, approval, and installation of updates and how you can report on the status of update installation.

Note: Windows Update is one of the few Windows services you can not administer using PowerShell 7 directly. The design of the WSUS module means you can not use the cmdlets directly using PowerShell 7 or the Windows PowerShell compatibility mechanism. WSUS cmdlets use .NET Framework classes that the .NET team has not migrated to work with the open-source .NET implementation used by PowerShell 7. Additionally, the WSUS team designed the cmdlets, so you use object instance methods rather than cmdlets. Thus, if you load the module using the compatibility mechanism, the methods are lost, and you cannot use them directly within PowerShell 7. You can, however, create a remoting session using a Windows PowerShell endpoint and run these otherwise incompatible cmdlets within that remoting session.

This chapter demonstrates that you can manage WSUS using PowerShell 7 and Windows PowerShell remoting. This method is a lot more work, and it is more work to debug scripts – but it does work.

The systems used in the chapter

This chapter uses two primary hosts: SRV1 and WSUS1. You run recipes remotely from SRV1 against the WSUS host. You also need the domain's domain controller, DC1, as well. The hosts used in this chapter are as shown here:

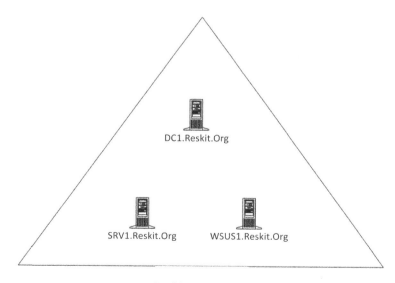

Reskit.Org domain

Figure 14.1: Hosts in use for this chapter

Installing Windows Server Update Services

WSUS is an installable feature within Windows Server 2022 that Windows setup does not install by default. To use Windows Update Services, you first install the WSUS Windows feature and do basic configuration and setup. Once installed, you can use the Windows PowerShell cmdlets to deploy WSUS in your environment.

In this recipe, you install WSUS and review the results of that installation. In subsequent recipes, you manage and use the WSUS service.

Note that this recipe uses remoting from SRV1 to WSUS1. The steps demonstrate the complexity of installing WSUS and configuring it for initial use in general and within PowerShell 7.

Getting ready

You run this recipe on SRV1, a domain-joined Windows Server 2022 host. The recipe also uses the WSUS1 server, another member server in the Reskit.Org domain. At the start of this recipe, WSUS1 has no additional features or software loaded.

How to do it...

1. Creating a remoting session for WSUS1

```
$SessionHT = @{
  ConfigurationName = 'microsoft.powershell'
  ComputerName      = 'WSUS1'
  Name              = 'WSUS'
}
$Session = New-PSSession @SessionHT
```

2. Installing WSUS on WSUS1

```
$ScriptBlock1 = {
  $InstallHT = @{
    Name                 = 'UpdateServices'
    IncludeManagementTools = $true
  }
  Install-WindowsFeature @InstallHT |
    Format-Table -AutoSize -Wrap
}
Invoke-Command -Session $Session -ScriptBlock $ScriptBlock1
```

3. Determining features installed on WSUS1

```
Invoke-Command -Session $Session -ScriptBlock {
  Get-WindowsFeature |
    Where-Object Installed |
      Format-Table
}
```

4. Creating a folder for WSUS update content on WSUS1

```
$ScriptBlock2 = {
  $WSUSDir = 'C:\WSUS'
  If (-Not (Test-Path -Path $WSUSDir -ErrorAction SilentlyContinue))
      {New-Item -Path $WSUSDir -ItemType Directory | Out-Null}
}
Invoke-Command -Session $Session -ScriptBlock $ScriptBlock2
```

5. Performing the post-installation configuration using wsusutil.exe

```
$ScriptBlock3 = {
  $WSUSDir = 'C:\WSUS'
  $Child = 'Update Services\Tools\wsusutil.exe'
  $CMD = Join-Path -Path "$env:ProgramFiles\" -ChildPath $Child
  & $CMD Postinstall CONTENT_DIR="$WSUSDir"
}
Invoke-Command -ComputerName WSUS1 -ScriptBlock $ScriptBlock3
```

6. Viewing the WSUS website on WSUS1

```
Invoke-Command -ComputerName WSUS1 -ScriptBlock {
  Get-Website -Name ws* | Format-Table -AutoSize
}
```

7. View the cmdlets in the UpdateServices module

```
Invoke-Command -ComputerName WSUS1 -ScriptBlock {
  Get-Command -Module UpdateServices |
    Format-Table -AutoSize
}
```

8. Inspecting properties of the object created with Get-WsusServer

```
Invoke-Command -Session $Session -ScriptBlock {
```

```
    $WSUSServer = Get-WsusServer
    $WSUSServer.GetType().Fullname
    $WSUSServer | Select-Object -Property *
}
```

9. Viewing details of the WSUS server object

```
Invoke-Command -Session $Session -ScriptBlock {
  ($WSUSServer | Get-Member -MemberType Method).count
  $WSUSServer | Get-Member -MemberType Method
}
```

10. Viewing WSUS server configuration

```
Invoke-Command -Session $Session -ScriptBlock {
  $WSUSServer.GetConfiguration() |
    Select-Object -Property SyncFromMicrosoftUpdate, LogFilePath
}
```

11. Viewing product categories after initial install

```
Invoke-Command -Session $Session -ScriptBlock {
  $WSUSProducts = Get-WsusProduct -UpdateServer $WSUSServer
  "{0} WSUS Products discovered" -f $WSUSProducts.Count
  $WSUSProducts |
    Select-Object -ExpandProperty Product |
      Format-Table -Property Title,
                            Description
}
```

12. Displaying subscription information

```
Invoke-Command -Session $Session -ScriptBlock {
  $WSUSSubscription = $WSUSServer.GetSubscription()
  $WSUSSubscription |
    Select-Object -Property * |
      Format-List
}
```

13. Getting latest categories of products available from Microsoft Update

```
Invoke-Command -Session $Session -ScriptBlock {
```

```
$WSUSSubscription.StartSynchronization()
Do {
  Write-Output $WSUSSubscription.GetSynchronizationProgress()
  Start-Sleep -Seconds 30
}
While ($WSUSSubscription.GetSynchronizationStatus() -ne
                                    'NotProcessing')
}
```

14. Checking the results of the synchronization

```
Invoke-Command -Session $Session -ScriptBlock {
  $WSUSSubscription.GetLastSynchronizationInfo()
}
```

15. Reviewing the categories of the products available after synchronization

```
Invoke-Command -Session $Session -ScriptBlock {
  $WSUSProducts = Get-WsusProduct -UpdateServer $WSUSServer
  "{0} Product found on WSUS1" -f $WSUSProducts.Count
  $WSUSProducts |
    Select-Object -ExpandProperty Product -First 25 |
      Format-Table -Property Title,
                                Description
}
```

How it works...

In *step 1*, you create a remoting session from SRV1 to WUS1. This step produces no console output. Next, in *step 2*, you install the Windows Update Services feature and the associated tools via the remoting session. The output looks like this:

```
PS C:\Foo> # 2. Installing WSUS on WSUS1
PS C:\Foo> $ScriptBlock1 = {
            $InstallHT = @{
              Name                   = 'UpdateServices'
              IncludeManagementTools = $true
            }
            Install-WindowsFeature @InstallHT |
              Format-Table
          }
PS C:\Foo> Invoke-Command -Session $Session -ScriptBlock $ScriptBlock1

Success Restart Needed Exit Code Feature Result
------- -------------- --------- --------------
True    No             Success   {ASP.NET 4.8, HTTP Activation,
                                 Remote Server Administration Tools,
                                 Role Administration Tools...}

WARNING: Additional configuration may be required. Review the article Managing WSUS Using
PowerShell at TechNet Library (http://go.microsoft.com/fwlink/?LinkId=235499) for more
information on the recommended steps to perform WSUS installation using PowerShell.
```

Figure 14.2: Installing WSUS on WSUS1 via remoting

When you install the Windows Update Services, the installation process adds several additional related services, as you can see in *step 3*, which looks like this:

```
PS C:\Foo> # 3. Determining features installed on WSUS1
PS C:\Foo> Invoke-Command -Session $Session -ScriptBlock {
              Get-WindowsFeature |
                Where-Object Installed |
                  Format-Table
           }
```

```
Display Name                                              Name                        Install Sta
------------                                              ----                        -----------
[X] File and Storage Services                             FileAndStorage-Services     Installed
    [X] Storage Services                                  Storage-Services            Installed
[X] Web Server (IIS)                                      Web-Server                  Installed
    [X] Web Server                                        Web-WebServer               Installed
        [X] Common HTTP Features                          Web-Common-Http             Installed
            [X] Default Document                          Web-Default-Doc             Installed
            [X] Static Content                            Web-Static-Content          Installed
        [X] Performance                                   Web-Performance             Installed
            [X] Dynamic Content Compression               Web-Dyn-Compression         Installed
        [X] Security                                      Web-Security                Installed
            [X] Request Filtering                         Web-Filtering               Installed
            [X] Windows Authentication                    Web-Windows-Auth            Installed
        [X] Application Development                       Web-App-Dev                 Installed
            [X] .NET Extensibility 4.8                    Web-Net-Ext45               Installed
            [X] ASP.NET 4.8                               Web-Asp-Net45               Installed
            [X] ISAPI Extensions                          Web-ISAPI-Ext               Installed
            [X] ISAPI Filters                             Web-ISAPI-Filter            Installed
    [X] Management Tools                                  Web-Mgmt-Tools              Installed
        [X] IIS Management Console                        Web-Mgmt-Console            Installed
        [X] IIS 6 Management Compatibility                Web-Mgmt-Compat             Installed
            [X] IIS 6 Metabase Compatibility              Web-Metabase                Installed
[X] Windows Server Update Services                        UpdateServices              Installed
    [X] WID Connectivity                                  UpdateServices-WidDB        Installed
    [X] WSUS Services                                     UpdateServices-Services     Installed
[X] .NET Framework 4.8 Features                           NET-Framework-45-Featu...   Installed
    [X] .NET Framework 4.8                                NET-Framework-45-Core       Installed
    [X] ASP.NET 4.8                                       NET-Framework-45-ASPNET     Installed
    [X] WCF Services                                      NET-WCF-Services45          Installed
        [X] HTTP Activation                               NET-WCF-HTTP-Activatio...   Installed
        [X] TCP Port Sharing                              NET-WCF-TCP-PortSharin...   Installed
[X] Microsoft Defender Antivirus                          Windows-Defender            Installed
[X] Remote Server Administration Tools                    RSAT                        Installed
    [X] Role Administration Tools                         RSAT-Role-Tools             Installed
        [X] Windows Server Update Services Tools          UpdateServices-RSAT         Installed
            [X] API and PowerShell cmdlets                UpdateServices-API          Installed
            [X] User Interface Management Console         UpdateServices-UI           Installed
[X] System Data Archiver                                  System-DataArchiver         Installed
[X] Windows Internal Database                             Windows-Internal-Datab...   Installed
[X] Windows PowerShell                                    PowerShellRoot              Installed
    [X] Windows PowerShell 5.1                            PowerShell                  Installed
[X] Windows Process Activation Service                    WAS                         Installed
    [X] Process Model                                     WAS-Process-Model           Installed
    [X] Configuration APIs                                WAS-Config-APIs             Installed
[X] WoW64 Support                                         WoW64-Support               Installed
[X] XPS Viewer                                            XPS-Viewer                  Installed
```

Figure 14.3: Viewing the installed features on WSUS1

In *step 4*, you create a folder that you use to hold WSUS content on WSUS1. This step produces no console output.

In *step 5*, you perform the post-installation task using the wsusutil.exe console command, which produces some limited output like this:

```
PS C:\Foo> # 5. Performing post-installation configuration using WsusUtil.exe
PS C:\Foo> $ScriptBlock3 = {
             $WSUSDir = 'C:\WSUS'
             $Child = 'Update Services\Tools\wsusutil.exe'
             $CMD = Join-Path -Path "$env:ProgramFiles\" -ChildPath $Child
             & $CMD —% Postinstall CONTENT_DIR=$WSUSDir
           }
PS C:\Foo> Invoke-Command -ComputerName WSUS1 -ScriptBlock $ScriptBlock3
Log file is located at C:\Users\Administrator\ApoData\Local\Temp\\WSUS Postinstall_20221202T165613.10g
Post install is starting
Post install has successfully completed
```

Figure 14.4: Viewing Installed features on WSUS1

When you execute *step 5*, the wsusutil.exe utility creates an IIS website on WSUS1 to communicate with WSUS clients. In *step 6*, you view the site, as you can see here:

```
PS C:\Foo> # 6. Viewing the WSUS website on WSUS1
PS C:\Foo> Invoke-Command -ComputerName WSUS1 -ScriptBlock {
             Get-Website -Name ws* | Format-Table -AutoSize
           }

Name               ID        State   Physical Path                                    Bindings
----               --        -----   -------------                                    --------
WSUS Administration 624931287 Started C:\Program Files\Update Services\WebServices\Root\ http :8530:
                                                                                        https :8531: sslFlags=0
```

Figure 14.5: Viewing the WSUS website

In *step 7*, you examine the commands contained in the UpdateServices module you installed earlier (in *step 1*). The output of this step looks like this:

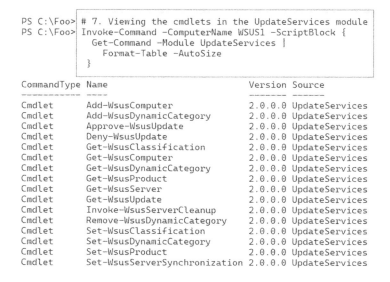

Figure 14.6: Viewing the WSUS cmdlets

You examine the key properties of your WSUS server, in *step 8*, by using the Get-WsusServer cmdlet. The cmdlet returns a UpdateServer object, which looks like this:

```
PS C:\Foo> # 8. Inspecting properties of the object created with Get-WsusServer
PS C:\Foo> Invoke-Command -Session $Session -ScriptBlock {
              $WSUSServer = Get-WsusServer
              $WSUSServer.GetType().Fullname
              $WSUSServer | Select-Object -Property *
          }

  TypeName: Microsoft.UpdateServices.Internal.BaseApi.UpdateServer

WebServiceUrl                     : http://WSUS1:8530/ApiRemoting30/WebService.asmx
BypassApiRemoting                 : False
IsServerLocal                     : True
Name                              : WSUS1
Version                           : 10.0.20348.143
IsConnectionSecureForApiRemoting  : True
PortNumber                        : 8530
PreferredCulture                  : en
ServerName                        : WSUS1
UseSecureConnection               : False
ServerProtocolVersion             : 1.20
PSComputerName                    : WSUS1
RunspaceId                        : 80977ba5-ba38-4d97-95d5-a5057610dbb1
```

Figure 14.7: Viewing the WSUS server properties

The $WSUSServer object you instantiated in *step 8* also contains many methods you can call to manage aspects of the WSUS server. There are a large number of methods, as you can see from the output of *step 9*:

```
PS C:\Foo> # 9. Viewing details of the WSUS Server object
PS C:\Foo> Invoke-Command -Session $Session -ScriptBlock {
             ($WSUSServer | Get-Member -MemberType Method).count
             $WSUSServer | Get-Member -MemberType Method
           }

   TypeName: Microsoft.UpdateServices.Internal.BaseApi.UpdateServer

Name                                   MemberType Definition
----                                   ---------- ----------

AddDynamicCategories                   Method     void AddDynamicCategories(Sys...
AddDynamicCategory                     Method     void AddDynamicCategory(Micro...
CancelAllDownloads                     Method     void CancelAllDownloads(), vo...
CreateComputerTargetGroup              Method     Microsoft.UpdateServices.Admi...
CreateDynamicCategory                  Method     Microsoft.UpdateServices.Admi...
CreateInstallApprovalRule              Method     Microsoft.UpdateServices.Admi...
CreateObjRef                           Method     System.Runtime.Remoting.ObjRe...
DeleteDynamicCategory                  Method     void DeleteDynamicCategory(st...
DeleteUpdate                           Method     void DeleteUpdate(guid update...
Equals                                 Method     bool Equals(System.Object obj...
ExpirePackage                          Method     void ExpirePackage(Microsoft....
ExportPackageMetadata                  Method     void ExportPackageMetadata(Mi...
ExportUpdates                          Method     void ExportUpdates(string pac...
GetChildServers                        Method     Microsoft.UpdateServices.Admi...
GetCleanupManager                      Method     Microsoft.UpdateServices.Admi...
GetComponentsWithErrors                Method     System.Collections.Specialize...
GetComputersNotContactedSinceCount     Method     int GetComputersNotContactedS...
GetComputersWithRecentNameChange       Method     System.Collections.Specialize...
GetComputerTarget                      Method     Microsoft.UpdateServices.Admi...
GetComputerTargetByName                Method     Microsoft.UpdateServices.Admi...
GetComputerTargetCount                 Method     int GetComputerTargetCount(),...
GetComputerTargetGroup                 Method     Microsoft.UpdateServices.Admi...
GetComputerTargets                     Method     Microsoft.UpdateServices.Admi...
GetContentDownloadProgress             Method     Microsoft.UpdateServices.Admi...
GetCurrentUserRole                     Method     Microsoft.UpdateServices.Admi...
GetDatabaseConfiguration               Method     Microsoft.UpdateServices.Admi...
GetDownstreamServer                    Method     Microsoft.UpdateServices.Admi...
GetDownstreamServers                   Method     Microsoft.UpdateServices.Admi...
GetDynamicCategories                   Method     System.Collections.Generic.IE...
GetDynamicCategory                     Method     Microsoft.UpdateServices.Admi...
GetEmailNotificationConfiguration      Method     Microsoft.UpdateServices.Admi...
GetFailedToDownloadUpdatesCount        Method     int GetFailedToDownloadUpdate...
GetFrontEndServers                     Method     System.Collections.ObjectMode...
GetHashCode                            Method     int GetHashCode()
```

Figure 14.8: Viewing the WSUS server object's methods

A key troubleshooting feature of WSUS is the `SoftwareDistribution.log`. In *step 10*, you view the WSUS configuration to discover the filename, which looks like this:

```
PS C:\Foo> # 10. Viewing WSUS server configuration
PS C:\Foo> Invoke-Command -Session $Session -ScriptBlock {
             $WSUSServer.GetConfiguration() |
               Select-Object -Property SyncFromMicrosoftUpdate,LogFilePath
           }

SyncFromMicrosoftUpdate : True
LogFilePath             : C:\Program Files\Update Services\LogFiles\SoftwareDistribution.log
PSComputerName          : WSUS1
RunspaceId              : 262cd894-b585-4b58-b7c4-6bdedebfb635
```

Figure 14.9: Viewing the WSUS configuration

Following the initial installation and configuration in *step 11*, you can see that the WSUS1 server gets updates for a very small set of products (17 in all), as shown here:

```
PS C:\Foo> # 11. Viewing product categories after initial install
PS C:\Foo> Invoke-Command -Session $Session -ScriptBlock {
             $WSUSProducts = Get-WsusProduct -UpdateServer $WSUSServer
             "{0} WSUS Products discovered" -f $WSUSProducts.Count
             $WSUSProducts |
               Select-Object -ExpandProperty Product |
                 Format-Table -Property Title,
                                        Description
           }

17 WSUS Products discovered

Title                                         Description
-----                                         -----------
Exchange 2000 Server                          For Exchange 2000 Products
Exchange Server 2003                          For Exchange 2003 Products
Exchange                                      Exchange
Local Publisher                               The local publisher (not Microsoft Update) of patches and applications.
Locally published packages                    Patches and applications that are published locally, not synchronized from Microsoft Update.
Microsoft Corporation                         Microsoft Corporation
Office 2003                                   Office 2003
Office XP                                      Office XP
Office                                        Office
SQL Server                                    SQL Server Catergory Description
SQL                                           SQL
Windows 2000 family                           Windows 2000 family
Windows Server 2003 family                    Windows Server 2003 family
Windows Server 2003, Datacenter Edition       Windows Server 2003, Datacenter Edition
Windows XP 64-Bit Edition Version 2003        Windows XP 64-Bit Edition Version 2003
Windows XP family                             Windows XP family
Windows                                       Windows
```

Figure 14.10: Viewing the WSUS configuration

You can configure the WSUS server to subscribe to and automatically retrieve new updates. In *step 12*, you retrieve and view the WSUS server's subscription details, which look like this:

```
PS C:\Foo> # 12. Displaying subscription information
PS C:\Foo> Invoke-Command -Session $Session -ScriptBlock {
             $WSUSSubscription = $WSUSServer.GetSubscription()
             $WSUSSubscription |
               Select-Object -Property * |
                 Format-List
           }
```

```
UpdateServer                        : Microsoft.UpdateServices.Internal.BaseApi.UpdateServer
SynchronizeAutomatically            : False
SynchronizeAutomaticallyTimeOfDay   : 09:15:52
LastModifiedTime                    : 03/12/2022 11:31:41
LastModifiedBy                      : RESKIT\Administrator
LastSynchronizationTime             : 01/01/0001 00:00:00
Anchor                              : 0,2000-01-01 00:00:01.000
DeploymentAnchor                    :
NumberOfSynchronizationsPerDay      : 1
IsCategoryOnlySync                  : False
```

Figure 14.11: Viewing the WSUS subscription information

In *step 13*, you perform a full synchronization by invoking the StartSynchronization() method of the WSUS server object. This method invokes an asynchronous operation – after calling this method, WSUS carries out the server update process in the background. You can call the GetSynchronizizationStatus() method to view the status, as you can see in *step 13*.

The synchronization process is not overly fast and can take several hours to complete. Truncated for brevity, the output of this step looks something like this:

```
PS C:\Foo> # 13. Getting latest categories of products available from Microsoft Update
PS C:\Foo> Invoke-Command -Session $Session -ScriptBlock {
             $WSUSSubscription.StartSynchronization()
             Do {
               Write-Output $WSUSSubscription.GetSynchronizationProgress()
               Start-Sleep -Seconds 30
             }
             While ($WSUSSubscription.GetSynchronizationStatus() -ne
                                                  'NotProcessing')
           }
```

```
PSComputerName : WSUS1
RunspaceId     : 262cd894-b585-4b58-b7c4-6bdedebfb635
TotalItems     : 0
ProcessedItems : 0
Phase          : NotProcessing

PSComputerName : WSUS1
RunspaceId     : 262cd894-b585-4b58-b7c4-6bdedebfb635
TotalItems     : 3954
ProcessedItems : 0
Phase          : Categories

... snipped for brevity

PSComputerName : WSUS1
RunspaceId     : 262cd894-b585-4b58-b7c4-6bdedebfb635
TotalItems     : 103642
ProcessedItems : 5451
Phase          : Updates

PSComputerName : WSUS1
RunspaceId     : 262cd894-b585-4b58-b7c4-6bdedebfb635
TotalItems     : 103642
ProcessedItems : 104202
Phase          : Updates
```

Figure 14.12: Synchronizing WSUS

After WSUS has completed the synchronization, in *step 14*, you review a summary of the results, showing the successful result. The output looks like this:

```
PS C:\Foo> # 14. Checking the results of the synchronization
PS C:\Foo> Invoke-Command -Session $Session -ScriptBlock {
               $WSUSSubscription.GetLastSynchronizationInfo()
           }

PSComputerName  : WSUS1
RunspaceId      : 77ec8cff-d1c6-4c90-a11d-4cef89201968
Id              : f2db6a4e-da3a-41b5-9330-2630cfb7d724
StartTime       : 04/12/2022 11:36:04
EndTime         : 04/12/2022 11:37:33
StartedManually : True
Result          : Succeeded
Error           : NotApplicable
ErrorText       :
UpdateErrors    : {}
```

Figure 14.13: Reviewing results of the most recent synchronization

Now that this first full synchronization has taken place, WSUS can support a larger number of Microsoft products, as you can see in the output from *step 15*, which looks like this:

```
PS C:\Foo> # 15.Reviewing the categories of the products available after synchronzation
PS C:\Foo> Invoke-Command -Session $Session -ScriptBlock {
               $WSUSProducts = Get-WsusProduct -UpdateServer $WSUSServer
               "{0} Product found on WSUS1" -f $WSUSProducts.Count
               $WSUSProducts |
                 Select-Object -ExpandProperty Product -First 25 |
                   Format-Table -Property Title,
                                          Description
           }

391 Product found on WSUS1

Title                                                   Description
-----                                                   -----------
.NET 5.0                                                .NET 5.0
.NET 6.0                                                .NET 6.0
.NET Core 2.1                                           .NET Core 2.1
.NET Core 3.1                                           .NET Core 3.1
Active Directory Rights Management Services Client 2.0  Active Directory Rights Management Services Client 2.0 (AD...
Active Directory                                        Active Directory Product Family Category
Antigen for Exchange/SMTP                               Defines the category for Antigen Updates. This will make s...
Antigen                                                 Antigen Product Family Category
ASP.NET Web and Data Frameworks                         ASP.NET Web and Data Frameworks product family
ASP.NET Web Frameworks                                  ASP.NET Web Framework
Azure Connected Machine Agent 3                         Updates for the Azure Connected Machine Agent
Azure Connected Machine Agent                           Product Family for Azure Connected Machine Agent
Azure File Sync agent updates for Windows Server 2012 R2 Azure File Sync agent updates for Windows Server 2012 R2
Azure File Sync agent updates for Windows Server 2016   Azure File Sync agent updates for Windows Server 2016
Azure File Sync agent updates for Windows Server 2019   Azure File Sync agent updates for Windows Server 2019
Azure File Sync agent updates for Windows Server 2022   Azure File Sync agent updates for Windows Server 2022
Azure File Sync                                         Azure File Sync
Azure IoT Edge for Linux on Windows Category            Updates for Azure IoT Edge for Linux on Windows Category. ...
Azure IoT Edge for Linux on Windows                     Product Family for Azure IoT Edge for Linux on Windows
Azure Stack HCI                                         Azure Stack HCI and above
Bing Bar                                                Get quick access to Bing and MSN, as well as handy tools f...
Bing Growth                                             Product Family for Bing Growth
Bing Service v2.0                                       Bing Service 2.0 update
Bing                                                    Live Search Product Family Category
BizTalk Server 2002                                     Category for BizTalk 2002. It requires SP1 as the minimum ...
```

Figure 14.14: Reviewing product categories now available to WSUS

There's more...

In *step 2*, you use the Install-WindowsFeature command to install WSUS. As you can see in the output, you must perform additional configuration before using WSUS, which you do in later recipe steps, particularly in *step 5*. Also, note that the URL shown in the output is invalid at the time of writing. Microsoft has removed the mentioned TechNet Library article; sadly, the associated content also appears lost.

In *step 3*, you create a folder to hold downloaded updates you intend to review and then deploy to your organization. This folder can get large, especially when you implement multilingual updates. You should hold your updates on a volume that is likely to have adequate space in the future. Making the volume fault-tolerant is also important as you plan and deploy WSUS.

In *step 5*, you run the wsusutil.exe command remotely on WSUS1 to complete the service installation. This executable comes with the WSUS installation. This command is useful and valuable because the WSUS team did not support certain operations via Windows PowerShell cmdlets. In this step, you run the command to perform the initial configuration of your WSUS server, including creating the WSUS database. If the command does not complete successfully, recovery is not particularly straightforward. If you use a VM to run WSUS1 (both in your testing and production scenario), taking VM snapshots after each step makes it much easier to recover.

In *step 13*, you perform a full sync with the Windows Update servers. The initial synchronization can take several hours. You may wish to change the value used in the Start-Sleep command to a larger value (otherwise, you could end up with thousands of lines of output!).

In this recipe, you installed WSUS on a single server. You can use WSUS on multiple servers, which is appropriate for supporting larger networks. You can set up a WSUS server to synchronize from other WSUS servers on the network, use web proxies, and work with SQL Server instead of the Windows Internal Database.

The objects created by WSUS are complex. In most cases, you can use standard PowerShell discovery techniques to discover more about these objects. There is more detailed information about the WSUS objects at https://learn.microsoft.com/previous-versions/windows/desktop/mt748187(v=vs.85). Microsoft last updated this documentation in 2016 and does not update it regularly. That said, the information is accurate for WSUS in Windows Server 2022.

Configuring WSUS Update Synchronization

As you can see, WSUS can update hundreds of products, although many may not be useful in your organization. After you install WSUS and do the initial synchronization, you can configure WSUS to identify the specific products for which your organization requires product updates. You can also define the classifications of updates WSUS should download.

Once you define the updates to be obtained (and later provided to WSUS clients), you can configure WSUS to synchronize subsequent updates manually. You can also build an update schedule and have WSUS update automatically. In this way, you can have WSUS download only the updates for the product categories and the classifications you have selected at your chosen time. The first initial synchronization can take hours, depending on your selections. Subsequent synchronizations pull only the newest updates since the last synchronization.

Getting ready

You run this recipe on SRV1, a domain-joined Windows Server 2022 host. The recipe also uses the WSUS1 server, another member server in the Reskit.Org domain. At the start of this recipe, WSUS1 has no additional features or software loaded.

How to do it...

1. Creating a remote session on WSUS1

   ```
   $Session = New-PSSession -ComputerName WSUS1
   ```

2. Locating versions of Windows Server supported by Windows Update

   ```
   Invoke-Command -Session $Session -ScriptBlock {
     Get-WsusProduct |
       Where-Object -FilterScript {$_.product.title -match
                                   '^Windows Server'} |
         Select-Object -ExpandProperty Product |
           Format-Table Title, UpdateSource
   }
   ```

3. Discovering updates for Windows 11

   ```
   Invoke-Command -Session $Session -ScriptBlock {
     Get-WsusProduct -TitleIncludes 'Windows 11' |
       Select-Object -ExpandProperty Product |
         Format-Table -Property Title
   }
   ```

4. Create and view a list of software product titles to include

```
Invoke-Command -Session $Session -ScriptBlock {
$Products =
  (Get-WsusProduct |
    Where-Object -FilterScript {$_.product.title -match
                                '^Windows Server'}).Product.Title
  $Products += @('Microsoft SQL Server 2016','Windows 11')
  $Products
}
}
```

5. Assigning the desired products to include in Windows Update

```
Invoke-Command -Session $Session -ScriptBlock {
  Get-WsusProduct |
    Where-Object {$PSItem.Product.Title -in $Products} |
        Set-WsusProduct
}
```

6. Getting WSUS classification

```
Invoke-Command -Session $Session -ScriptBlock {
  Get-WsusClassification |
    Select-Object -ExpandProperty Classification |
      Format-Table -Property Title, Description  -Wrap
}
```

7. Building a list of desired update classifications

```
Invoke-Command -Session $Session -ScriptBlock {
  $UpdateList = @('Critical Updates',
                  'Definition Updates',
                  'Security Updates',
                  'Service Packs',
                  'Update Rollups',
                  'Updates')
}
```

8. Setting the list of desired update classifications in WSUS

```
Invoke-Command -Session $Session -ScriptBlock {
```

```
    Get-WsusClassification |
      Where-Object {$_.Classification.Title -in $UpdateList} |
        Set-WsusClassification
  }
```

9. Getting synchronization details

```
Invoke-Command -Session $Session -ScriptBlock {
  $WSUSServer = Get-WsusServer
  $WSUSSubscription = $WSUSServer.GetSubscription()
}
```

10. Starting synchronizing available updates

```
Invoke-Command -Session $Session -ScriptBlock {
  $WSUSSubscription.StartSynchronization()
}
```

11. Looping and waiting for synchronization to complete

```
Invoke-Command -Session $Session -ScriptBlock {
  $IntervalSeconds = 15
  $NP = 'NotProcessing'
  Do {
    $WSUSSubscription.GetSynchronizationProgress()
    Start-Sleep -Seconds $IntervalSeconds
    } While ($WSUSSubscription.GetSynchronizationStatus() -eq $NP)
}
```

12. Synchronizing the updates which can take a long while to complete

```
Invoke-Command -Session $Session -ScriptBlock {
  $IntervalSeconds = 15
  $NP = 'NotProessing'
  #   Wait for synchronizing to start
  Do {
  Write-Output $WSUSSubscription.GetSynchronizationProgress()
  Start-Sleep -Seconds $IntervalSeconds
  }
  While ($WSUSSubscription.GetSynchronizationStatus() -eq $NP)
  #    Wait for all phases of process to end
```

```
    Do {
    Write-Output $WSUSSubscription.GetSynchronizationProgress()
    Start-Sleep -Seconds $IntervalSeconds
    } Until ($WSUSSubscription.GetSynchronizationStatus() -eq $NP)
}
```

13. Checking the results of the synchronization

```
Invoke-Command -Session $Session -ScriptBlock {
  $WSUSSubscription.GetLastSynchronizationInfo()
}
```

14. Configure automatic synchronization to run once per day

```
Invoke-Command -Session $Session -ScriptBlock {
  $WSUSSubscription = $WSUSServer.GetSubscription()
  $WSUSSubscription.SynchronizeAutomatically = $true
  $WSUSSubscription.NumberOfSynchronizationsPerDay = 1
  $WSUSSubscription.Save()
}
```

How it works...

In *step 1*, you create a remoting session from SRV1 to WUS1. This step produces no console output. Next, in *step 2*, you determine the different versions of Windows Server supported by WSUS, with output that looks like this:

```
PS C:\Foo> # 2. Locating versions of Windows Server supported by Windows Update
PS C:\Foo> Invoke-Command -Session $Session -ScriptBlock {
              Get-WsusProduct |
                Where-Object -FilterScript {$_.product.title -match
                                             '^Windows Server'} |
                  Select-Object -ExpandProperty Product |
                    Format-Table Title, UpdateSource
           }
```

```
Title                                                                   UpdateSource
-----                                                                   ------------
Windows Server 2003, Datacenter Edition                                 MicrosoftUpdate
Windows Server 2003                                                     MicrosoftUpdate
Windows Server 2008 R2                                                  MicrosoftUpdate
Windows Server 2008 Server Manager Dynamic Installer                    MicrosoftUpdate
Windows Server 2008                                                     MicrosoftUpdate
Windows Server 2012 Language Packs                                      MicrosoftUpdate
Windows Server 2012 R2  and later drivers                               MicrosoftUpdate
Windows Server 2012 R2 Drivers                                          MicrosoftUpdate
Windows Server 2012 R2 Language Packs                                   MicrosoftUpdate
Windows Server 2012 R2                                                  MicrosoftUpdate
Windows Server 2012                                                     MicrosoftUpdate
Windows Server 2016 and Later Servicing Drivers                         MicrosoftUpdate
Windows Server 2016 for RS4                                             MicrosoftUpdate
Windows Server 2016                                                     MicrosoftUpdate
Windows Server 2016                                                     MicrosoftUpdate
Windows Server 2019 and later, Servicing Drivers                        MicrosoftUpdate
Windows Server 2019 and later, Upgrade & Servicing Drivers              MicrosoftUpdate
Windows Server 2019 Datacenter: Azure Edition Hotpatch                  MicrosoftUpdate
Windows Server 2019                                                     MicrosoftUpdate
Windows Server 2019                                                     MicrosoftUpdate
Windows Server Drivers                                                  MicrosoftUpdate
Windows Server Manager - Windows Server Update Services (WSUS) Dynamic Installer MicrosoftUpdate
Windows Server Solutions Best Practices Analyzer 1.0                    MicrosoftUpdate
Windows Server Technical Preview Language Packs                         MicrosoftUpdate
Windows Server, version 1903 and later                                  MicrosoftUpdate
Windows Server, version 1903 and later                                  MicrosoftUpdate
```

Figure 14.15: Reviewing product categories now available to WSUS

In *step 3*, you view the version(s) of Windows 11 that you can update using WSUS and Windows Update, like this:

```
PS C:\Foo> # 3. Discovering updates for for Windows 11
PS C:\Foo> Invoke-Command -Session $Session -ScriptBlock {
              Get-WsusProduct -TitleIncludes 'Windows 11' |
                Select-Object -ExpandProperty Product |
                  Format-Table -Property Title
           }
```

```
Title
-----
Windows 11 Client S, version 22H2 and later, Servicing Drivers
Windows 11 Client S, version 22H2 and later, Upgrade & Servicing Drivers
Windows 11 Client, version 22H2 and later, Servicing Drivers
Windows 11 Client, version 22H2 and later, Upgrade & Servicing Drivers
Windows 11 Dynamic Update
Windows 11 GDR-DU
Windows 11
```

Figure 14.16: Versions of Windows 11 supported by WSUS

In most cases, you probably do not want or need to support all Microsoft products. Rather, you most likely want to get updates for a subset of products that exist in your environment. To achieve that, you begin, in *step 4*, by creating a list of the products you DO want to support. In this step, you include all versions of Windows Server, SQL Server 2016, and all versions of Windows 11, which looks like this:

```
PS C:\Foo> # 4. Create and view a list of software product titles to include
PS C:\Foo> Invoke-Command -Session $Session -ScriptBlock {
             $Products =
              (Get-WsusProduct |
                Where-Object -FilterScript {$_.product.title -match
                                            '^Windows Server'}).Product.Title
             $Products += @('Microsoft SQL Server 2016','Windows 11')
             $Products
           }

Windows Server 2003, Datacenter Edition
Windows Server 2003
Windows Server 2008 R2
Windows Server 2008 Server Manager Dynamic Installer
Windows Server 2008
Windows Server 2012 Language Packs
Windows Server 2012 R2  and later drivers
Windows Server 2012 R2 Drivers
Windows Server 2012 R2 Language Packs
Windows Server 2012 R2
Windows Server 2012
Windows Server 2016 and Later Servicing Drivers
Windows Server 2016 for RS4
Windows Server 2016
Windows Server 2016
Windows Server 2019 and later, Servicing Drivers
Windows Server 2019 and later, Upgrade & Servicing Drivers
Windows Server 2019 Datacenter: Azure Edition Hotpatch
Windows Server 2019
Windows Server 2019
Windows Server Drivers
Windows Server Manager - Windows Server Update Services (WSUS) Dynamic Installer
Windows Server Solutions Best Practices Analyzer 1.0
Windows Server Technical Preview Language Packs
Windows Server, version 1903 and later
Windows Server, version 1903 and later
Microsoft SQL Server 2016
Windows 11
```

Figure 14.17: Creating a list of products for WSUS to support

In *step 5*, you specify that your WSUS server should get updates for the products in the $Products array you created in the previous step. There is no output from this step.

For any given product supported, Windows Update can provide many different kinds, or classifications, of updates. In *step 6*, you get the classifications of update types available, which look like this:

```
PS C:\Foo> # 6. Getting WSUS classification
PS C:\Foo> Invoke-Command -Session $Session -ScriptBlock {
             Get-WsusClassification |
               Select-Object -ExpandProperty Classification |
                 Format-Table -Property Title, Description  -Wrap
           }
```

```
Title                Description
-----                -----------
Applications         Products or line of business applications.
Critical Updates     A broadly released fix for a specific problem addressing a critical,
                     non-security related bug.
Definition Updates   A broadly-released and frequent software update containing additions to a
                     product's definition database. Definition databases are often used to
                     detect objects with specific attributes, such as malicious code, phishing
                     Web sites, or junk e-mail.
Driver Sets          A package of software modules that is designed to support the hardware of
                     a specific model of computing device.
Drivers              A software component necessary to control or regulate another device.
Feature Packs        New product functionality that is first distributed outside the context
                     of a product release, and usually included in the next full product
                     release.
Security Updates     A broadly released fix for a product-specific security-related
                     vulnerability. Security vulnerabilities are rated based on their severity
                     which is indicated in the Microsoft® security bulletin as critical,
                     important, moderate, or low.
Service Packs        A tested, cumulative set of all hotfixes, security updates, critical
                     updates and updates, as well as additional fixes for problems found
                     internally since the release of the product. Service packs may also
                     contain a limited number of customer-requested design changes or features.
Tools                A utility or feature that aids in accomplishing a task or set of tasks.
Update Rollups       A tested, cumulative set of hotfixes, security updates, critical updates,
                     and updates packaged together for easy deployment. A rollup generally
                     targets a specific area, such as security, or a component of a product,
                     such as Internet Information Services "IIS".
Updates              A broadly released fix for a specific problem addressing a noncritical,
                     non-security-related bug.
Upgrades             A new product release bringing a device to the next version, containing
                     bug fixes, design changes and new features.
```

Figure 14.18: Reviewing WSUS update classifications

You may not want all these kinds of updates. For example, you may wish not to download driver updates, perhaps preferring manual updates for drivers if/when needed. To achieve this, in *step 7*, you build a list of the update classifications you wish WSUS to support. In *step 8*, you configure your WSUS server with this list. In *step 9*, you obtain the synchronization status of WSUS1, and in *step 10*, you initiate synchronization of update categories of WSUS1 from Windows Update. Then in *step 11*, you wait for the synchronization to complete. These four steps produce no console output.

In *step 12*, you initiate a loop that gets the category synchronization status. If category updating is still processing, wait a bit longer. This synchronization should not take too long, but be patient. The console output looks like this:

```
PS C:\Foo> # 12. Synchronizing the updates which can take a long while to complete
PS C:\Foo> Invoke-Command -Session $Session -ScriptBlock {
              $IntervalSeconds = 15
              $NP = 'NotProcessing'
              Do {
                $WSUSSubscription.GetSynchronizationProgress()
                Start-Sleep -Seconds $IntervalSeconds
                } While ($WSUSSubscription.GetSynchronizationStatus() -eq $NP)
           }
```

```
PSComputerName : WSUS1
Runspaceld     : 77ec8cff-d1f6-4c90-alld-4cef89201968
TotalItems     : 31327
Processedltems : 420
Phase          : Updates

PSComputerName : WSUS1
Runspaceld     : 77ec8cff-d1f6-4c90-alld-4cef89201968
TotalItems     : 31327
Processedltems : 730
Phase          : Updates
PS C:\Foo>
```

Figure 14.19: Synchronizing update categories

With the update categories synchronized, you can now synchronize the updates available to your WSUS server – updates for specified properties with a specific update category. You do this in *step 13*. This step can take a long time. The (trimmed) output from this step looks like this:

```
PS C:\Foo> # 13. Synchronize the updates which can take a long while to compelete.
PS C:\Foo> Invoke-Command -Session $Session -ScriptBlock {
               $IntervalSeconds = 15
               $NP = 'NotProessing'
               #   Wait for synchronizing to start
               Do {
               Write-Output $WSUSSubscription.GetSynchronizationProgress()
               Start-Sleep -Seconds $IntervalSeconds
               }
               While ($WSUSSubscription.GetSynchronizationStatus() -eq $NP)
               #    Wait for all phases of process to end
               Do {
               Write-Output $WSUSSubscription.GetSynchronizationProgress()
               Start-Sleep -Seconds $IntervalSeconds
               } Until ($WSUSSubscription.GetSynchronizationStatus() -eq $NP)
           }

PSComputerName : WSUS1
RunspaceId     : 77ec8cff-d1f6-4c90-a11d-4cef89201968
TotalItems     : 31327
ProcessedItems : 3576
Phase          : Updates

PSComputerName : WSUS1
RunspaceId     : 77ec8cff-d1f6-4c90-a11d-4cef89201968
TotalItems     : 31327
ProcessedItems : 24204
Phase          : Updates
PS C:\Foo>
```

Figure 14.20: Synchronizing updates

Once this synchronization is complete, in *step 14*, you view the WSUS synchronization status, which now looks like this:

```
PS C:\Foo> # 14. Checking the results of the synchronization
PS C:\Foo> Invoke-Command -Session $Session -ScriptBlock {
               $WSUSSubscription.GetLastSynchronizationInfo()
           }

PSComputerName  : WSUS1
RunspaceId      : 77ec8cff-d1f6-4c90-a11d-4cef89201968
Id              : 10aee80a-2746-49af-b78e-27fd12c6ec09
StartTime       : 04/12/2022 12:12:28
EndTime         : 04/12/2022 14:38:41
StartedManually : True
Result          : Succeeded
Error           : NotApplicable
ErrorText       :
UpdateErrors    : {}
```

Figure 14.21: Viewing synchronization status

In *step 14*, you configure WSUS1 to download new updates every day for those products and classifications you previously specified. This step produces no output.

There's more...

In *step 2*, you examined the updates available for all versions of Windows Server. As you can see, this even includes very old versions of Windows Server, such as Windows Server 2003, which is now out of support and, hopefully, you no longer use within your organization.

Inevitably, some organizations are still running Windows Server 2003, hopefully for good business reasons. It's comforting to know that you can still get updates even if you should have updated or replaced them years ago. That said, it would be highly unusual for Microsoft to issue further updates for such old and out-of-support versions of Windows.

WSUS supports a range of products and different classifications of updates. Consider carefully what products you wish to get updates for and what update types to support. You could err on the side of caution, but that can involve many updates you may never need.

In *step 13*, you see the synchronization status every 15 seconds. At each check, you can see how many updates have been downloaded. The initial update downloads can take a long time.

Configuring the Windows Update Client

By default, Windows computers, both the server and client version, download updates from Microsoft's Windows Update servers on the internet. To configure Windows hosts to take updates from an internal WSUS server, you need to update the configuration of the built-in Windows Update Client in Windows.

Using Group Policy is the easiest method of configuring the Windows Update Client. You create a **Group Policy Object (GPO)**, configure the policy with server names, and so on, and then assign the policy.

You can apply a single GPO to the domain as a whole (configuring Windows Update Client on every domain-joined host) or apply policies at the site or OU level, depending on the complexity of your WSUS implementation. A small company located on a single site might use just one policy at the domain or site level. Large multinational organizations may have multiple WSUS servers around the globe and need multiple Windows Update policies applied throughout a large multi-forest network.

In this recipe, you configure SRV1 to get updates from the WSUS server WSUS1.

Getting ready

You run this recipe on SRV1 after you have installed and configured WSUS on the WSUS1 server.

How to do it...

1. Ensuring the GP management tools are available on SRV1

    ```
    Install-WindowsFeature -Name GPMC -IncludeManagementTools | Out-Null
    ```

2. Creating a new policy and linking it to the domain

    ```
    $PolicyName = 'Reskit WSUS Policy'
    New-GPO -Name $PolicyName
    ```

3. Configuring SRV1 to use WSUS for updates

    ```
    $WSUSKEY = 'HKLM\Software\Policies\Microsoft\Windows\WindowsUpdate\
    AU'
    $RVHT1 = @{
      Name       = $PolicyName
      Key        = $WSUSKEY
      ValueName  = 'UseWUServer'
      Type       = 'DWORD'
      Value      = 1
    }
    Set-GPRegistryValue @RVHT1 | Out-Null
    ```

4. Setting AU options

    ```
    $KEY2 = 'HKLM\Software\Policies\Microsoft\Windows\WindowsUpdate\AU'
    $RVHT2 = @{
      Name       = $PolicyName
      Key        = $KEY2
      ValueName  = 'AUOptions'
      Type       = 'DWORD'
      Value      = 2
    }
    Set-GPRegistryValue  @RVHT2 | Out-Null
    ```

5. Setting the WSUS server URL

```
$Session = New-PSSession -ComputerName WSUS1

$WSUSServer = Invoke-Command -Session $Session -ScriptBlock {
  Get-WSUSServer
}
$FS  = "http{2}://{0}:{1}"
$N   = $WSUSServer.Name
$P   = 8530 # default WSUS port
$WSUSURL = $FS -f $n, $p, ('','s')[$WSUSServer.UseSecureConnection]
$KEY3 = 'HKLM\Software\Policies\Microsoft\Windows\WindowsUpdate'
$RVHT3 = @{
Name      = $PolicyName
Key       = $KEY3
ValueName = 'WUServer'
Type      = 'String'
Value     = $WSUSURL
}
Set-GPRegistryValue @RVHT3  | Out-Null
```

6. Setting the WU status server URL

```
$KEY4 = 'HKLM\Software\Policies\Microsoft\Windows\WindowsUpdate'
$RVHT4 = @{
Name      = $PolicyName
Key       = $KEY4
ValueName = 'WUStatusServer'
Type      = 'String'
Value     = $WSUSURL
}
Set-GPRegistryValue @RVHT4 | Out-Null
```

7. Viewing a report on the GPO

```
$RHT = @{
Name        = $PolicyName
ReportType  = 'Html'
Path        = 'C:\foo\out.html'
}
Get-GPOReport @RHT
Invoke-Item -Path $RHT.Path
```

How it works...

In *step 1*, you install the Group Policy Management Console and related tools (in case you have not previously installed the feature on this host in previous recipes). This step creates no console output.

In *step 2*, you create a new GPO in the Reskit.Org domain, generating output like this:

```
PS C:\Foo> # 2. Creating a new policy and linking it to the domain
PS C:\Foo> $PolicyName = 'Reskit WSUS Policy'
PS C:\Foo> New-GPO -Name $PolicyName

DisplayName      : Reskit WSUS Policy
DomainName       : Reskit.Org
Owner            : RESKIT\Domain Admins
Id               : 9c6e0c02-75ef-43c7-8148-366e23da186e
GpoStatus        : AllSettingsEnabled
Description      :
CreationTime     : 08/12/2022 17:08:43
ModificationTime : 08/12/2022 17:08:43
UserVersion      :
ComputerVersion  :
WmiFilter        :
```

Figure 14.22: Creating a new GPO

In *step 3*, you configure SRV1 to accept updates from WSUS (versus Microsoft Update). In *step 4*, you set the options for Windows Update to download and install any approved updates. In *step 5*, you create and configure Windows Update with the URL to use to get WSUS-approved updates. In *step 6*, you specify the status server (the server to which Windows Update sends status reports on updates). These four steps create no output.

In the final step, *step 7*, you generate and view a management report showing the policy details. There is no console output, but this step opens a browser window with the report like this:

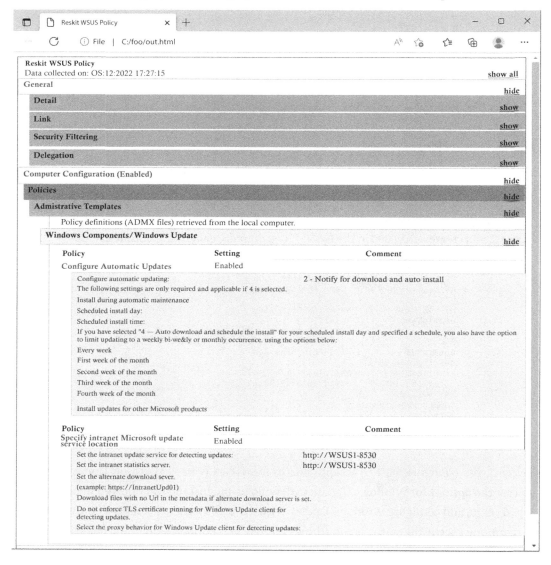

Figure 14.23: Viewing the GPO

There's more...

In *step 2*, you created the WSUS policy and linked it to the domain. For large organizations, separate policies may be appropriate, each connected to separate OUs or sites in your AD. This can facilitate distributed administration where different AD OUs or AD sites might need different settings, and for very large organizations, multiple independent WSUS implementations worldwide.

In this recipe, you configured the GPO object with four registry-based settings. The recipe used Out-Null to limit the amount of output. If you experiment with this recipe, consider removing the pipe to Null to see the output generated.

In *step 7*, you view the GPO report. This report shows what settings are included in the GPO.

Creating Computer Target Groups

With the recipes so far in this chapter, you have set up a WSUS server and created a GPO to configure the Windows Update Client on your computers. The next step is to create target groups—the computers you plan to use when targeting WSUS updates.

In any organization, different groups of hosts can have other update requirements. Your Windows client hosts run software such as Microsoft Office that you do not normally see on a server.

Your mission-critical servers might require a separate testing and sign-off process for updates that you then approve for use. For efficient management of updates, you define target groups (for example, **domain controllers (DCs)**, SQL servers, and so on) and then determine the computers in the target group.

In this recipe, you create a target group for domain servers, including SRV1 and SRV2.

Getting ready

You run this recipe on SRV1, with SRV1 and WSU1 online. You should have installed and configured WSUS on WSUS1. Additionally, you need at least one of the domain controllers in the Reskit.org domain up and running.

How to do it...

1. Creating a remoting session to WSUS1

    ```
    $SessionHT = @{
        ConfigurationName = 'microsoft.powershell'
        ComputerName      = 'WSUS1'
    ```

```
    Name                = 'WSUS'
  }
$Session = New-PSSession @SessionHT
```

2. Creating a WSUS computer target group for servers

```
Invoke-Command -Session $Session -ScriptBlock {
  $WSUSServer = Get-WsusServer  -Name WSUS1 -port 8530
  $WSUSServer.CreateComputerTargetGroup('Domain Servers')
}
```

3. Viewing all computer target groups on WSUS1

```
Invoke-Command -Session $Session -ScriptBlock {
  $WSUSServer.GetComputerTargetGroups() |
    Format-Table -Property Name
}
```

4. Finding the servers whose name includes SRV

```
Invoke-Command -Session $Session -ScriptBlock {
  Get-WsusComputer -NameIncludes SRV |
    Format-Table -Property FullDomainName, OSDescription
}
```

5. Adding SRV1, SRV2 to the Domain Servers target group

```
Invoke-Command -Session $Session -ScriptBlock {
  Get-WsusComputer -NameIncludes SRV |
    Where-Object FullDomainName -match '^SRV' |
      Add-WsusComputer -TargetGroupName 'Domain Servers'
}
```

6. Getting the Domain Servers computer target group

```
Invoke-Command -Session $Session -ScriptBlock {
  $SRVGroup = $WSUSServer.GetComputerTargetGroups() |
                Where-Object Name -eq 'Domain Servers'
}
```

7. Finding the computers in the group

```
Invoke-Command -Session $Session -ScriptBlock {
```

```
Get-WsusComputer |
  Where-Object ComputerTargetGroupIDs -Contains $SRvGroup.id |
    Sort-Object -Property FullDomainName |
        Format-Table -Property FullDomainName, ClientVersion,
                                LastSyncTime
}
```

How it works...

In *step 1*, you create a remoting session to WSUS1, using a Windows PowerShell 5.1 endpoint. This step creates no console output.

In *step 2*, you create a new computer target group called Domain Servers, which looks like this:

```
PS C:\Foo> # 2.  Creating a WSUS computer target group for servers
PS C:\Foo> Invoke-Command -Session $Session -ScriptBlock {
              $WSUSServer = Get-WsusServer  -Name WSUS1 -port 8530
              $WSUSServer.CreateComputerTargetGroup('Domain Servers')
           }

PSComputerName   WSUS1
RunspaceId       c174bdae-e697-4fb4-8be2-3c9da9701920
UpdateServer     Microsoft.UpdateServices.Internal.BaseApi.UpdateServer
Id               3a409534-50c7-4159-af22-caea674d5ff1
Name             Domain Servers  ◄━━━━━━━━━━━
```

Figure 14.24: Creating a computer target group

In *step 3*, you use the $WSUSServer object to get and then display the current target groups, including the one you just created, which looks like this:

```
PS C:\Foo> # 3. Viewing all computer target groups on WSUS1
PS C:\Foo> Invoke-Command -Session $Session -ScriptBlock {
              $WSUSServer.GetComputerTargetGroups() |
                Format-Table -Property Name
           }

Name
----
All Computers
Domain Servers  ◄━━━━━━━━━
Unassigned Computers
```

Figure 14.25: Viewing computer target groups on WSUS1

Managing Windows Update Services

In *step 4*, you retrieve the computers whose name contains SRV and that have registered with the WSUS server, which looks like this:

```
PS C:\Foo> # 4. Finding the Servers whose name includes SRV
PS C:\Foo> Invoke-Command -Session $Session -ScriptBlock {
             Get-WsusComputer -NameIncludes SRV |
               Format-Table -Property FultDomainName, OSDescription
           }

FultDomainName   OSDescription
--------------   -------------
srvl.reskit.org  Windows Server 2022 Datacenter
srv2.reskit.org  Windows Server 2022 Datacenter
psrv.reskit.org  Windows Server 2022 Datacenter
```

Figure 14.26: Viewing computer target groups on WSUS1

In *step 5*, which creates no output, you add just the two servers (SRV1 and SRV2) into the Domain Servers computer target group. In *step 6*, which also creates no console output, you instantiate the Domain Servers target group and store it in the SRVGroup variable.

In the final step, you view the servers in the Domain Servers target group with output like this:

```
PS C:\Foo> # 7. Finding the computers in the group:
PS C:\Foo> Invoke-Command -Session $Session -ScriptBlock {
             Get-WsusComputer |
               Where-Object ComputerTargetGroupIDs -Contains $SRvGroup.id |
                 Sort-Object -Property FullDomainName |
                   Format-Table -Property FullDomainName, ClientVersion,
                                             LastSyncTime
           }

FullDomainName   ClientVersion   LastSyncTime
--------------   -------------   ------------
srvl.reskit.org  10.0.20348.1070 09/12/2022 10:03:01
srvl.reskit.org  10.0.20348.1070 09/12/2022 08:49:28
```

Figure 14.27: Viewing members of the Domain Servers computer target group

There's more...

In *step 2*, you create a target group. In WSUS, a target group is a collection of computer systems that an administrator defines and uses to specify the computers that should receive updates from the WSUS server. You can use the target groups that organize computers based on various criteria, such as their location, role, or hardware configuration. This allows you to configure which specific updates are needed by each target group.

In *step 7*, you display the computers in the Domain Servers computer target group. Once you create the GPO object (as in *step 2*), it can take 24 hours or longer to have all the computers in your domain begin working with WSUS for the computers in the Domain Servers target group. Since it can take a lot of time to set up a WSUS server and create and populate computer target groups, it may be a task you leave for a long weekend.

Configuring WSUS Automatic Approvals

Microsoft's Windows Update can produce many updates for you to manage (inspect, accept/ decline, and deploy). Some update types, for example, critical updates, may be ones you want to automatically approve, so as soon as you receive one of these, you can start deploying it.

Configuring automatic approvals can be a good thing in that you ask WSUS to push more urgent updates automatically. At the same time, automatically pushing an update can be problematic if, for some reason, the update has issues.

Getting ready

You run this recipe on SRV1 after installing and configuring WSUS on WSUS1.

How to do it...

1. Creating a remoting session to WSUS1

    ```
    $SessionHT = @{
            ConfigurationName = 'microsoft.powershell'
            ComputerName      = 'WSUS1'
            Name              = 'WSUS'
        }
    $Session = New-PSSession @SessionHT
    ```

2. Creating the auto-approval rule

    ```
    Invoke-Command -Session $Session -ScriptBlock {
      $WSUSServer = Get-WsusServer
      $ApprovalRule =
        $WSUSServer.CreateInstallApprovalRule('Critical Updates')
    }
    ```

3. Defining a deadline for the rule

    ```
    Invoke-Command -Session $Session -ScriptBlock {
      $Type = 'Microsoft.UpdateServices.Administration.' +
              'AutomaticUpdateApprovalDeadline'
      $RuleDeadLine = New-Object -Typename $Type
      $RuleDeadLine.DayOffset = 3
      $RuleDeadLine.MinutesAfterMidnight = 180
      $ApprovalRule.Deadline = $RuleDeadLine
    }
    ```

4. Adding update classifications to the rule

```
Invoke-Command -Session $Session -ScriptBlock {
  $UpdateClassifications = $ApprovalRule.GetUpdateClassifications()
  $CriticalUpdates = $WSUSServer.GetUpdateClassifications() |
    Where-Object -Property Title -eq 'Critical Updates'
  $UpdateClassifications.Add($CriticalUpdates) | Out-Null
  $Defs = $WSUSServer.GetUpdateClassifications() |
            Where-Object -Property Title -eq 'Definition Updates'
  $UpdateClassifications.Add($Defs) | Out-Null
  $ApprovalRule.SetUpdateClassifications($UpdateClassifications)
}
```

5. Assigning the rule to a computer target group

```
Invoke-Command -Session $Session -ScriptBlock {
  $Type = 'Microsoft.UpdateServices.Administration.'+
            'ComputerTargetGroupCollection'
  $TargetGroups = New-Object $Type
  $TargetGroups.Add(($WSUSServer.GetComputerTargetGroups() |
    Where-Object -Property Name -eq 'Domain Servers'))
  $ApprovalRule.SetComputerTargetGroups($TargetGroups) |
    Out-Null
}
```

6. Enabling the rule

```
Invoke-Command -Session $Session -ScriptBlock {
  $ApprovalRule.Enabled = $true
  $ApprovalRule.Save()
}
```

7. Getting a list of approval rules

```
Invoke-Command -Session $Session -ScriptBlock{
  $WSUSServer.GetInstallApprovalRules()   |
    Format-Table -Property Name, Enabled, Action
}
```

How it works...

In this recipe, you configure automatic approval for certain updates. This rule automatically approves updates that are either critical updates or definition updates. Updates of these two types you approve for use by clients.

In *step 1*, you create a PowerShell remoting session on the WSUS1 server using a Windows PowerShell remoting endpoint. In *step 2*, you create an in-memory object for an approval rule. Next, in *step 3*, you define a deadline for the rule. In *step 4*, you add some update classifications to the rule. Then, in *step 5*, you assign the rule to a computer target group. In *step 5*, you enable this new approval rule and save it. These six steps produce no output.

In *step 7*, you get a list of the current approval rules on WSUS1, with output like this:

```
PS C:\Foo> # 7. Geting a list of approval rules
PS C:\Foo> Invoke-Command -Session $Session -ScriptBlock{
             $WSUSServer.GetInstallApprovalRules()    |
               Format-Table -Property Name, Enabled, Action
           }


Name                                   Enabled  Action
----                                   -------  ------
Default Automatic Approval Rule        False    Install
Critical Updates                       True     Install
```

Figure 14.28: Viewing a list of approval rules

There's more...

For many operations, the WSUS team did not provide cmdlets and also did not provide GUI support. Instead, you need to rely on the properties and particularly the methods of many WSUS objects. A key object is the WSUS server object. This object, which you instantiate using the Get-WSUSServer cmdlet, contains methods such as GetInstallApprovalRules(), which gets the installed approval rules. The WSUS team chose not to create a Get-InstallApprovalRule cmdlet.

How you write scripts to manage WSUS is similar to how you might have developed older-style Windows applications using the **Component Object Model (COM)**. PowerShell's built-in help system does not provide much assistance in discovering details about the methods or how to use them. There is little current, up-to-date documentation on the methods and objects either. This approach makes it harder to access all of the richness of WSUS simply through cmdlets.

Managing WSUS Updates

Microsoft produces a large number of updates and has ever since Microsoft first introduced WSUS. You can manage these updates via the GUI or PowerShell. As with other aspects of managing WSUS, managing updates via PowerShell means using the WSUS server object and its associated methods.

Getting ready

You run this recipe on SRV1 after installing and configuring WSUS on WSUS1.

How to do it...

1. Creating a remoting session to WSUS1

    ```
    $SessionHT = @{
      ConfigurationName = 'microsoft.powershell'
      ComputerName      = 'WSUS1'
      Name              = 'WSUS'
    }
    $Session = New-PSSession @SessionHT
    ```

2. Viewing the status of WSUS1

    ```
    Invoke-Command -Session $Session -ScriptBlock {
      $WSUSServer = Get-WsusServer
      $WSUSServer.GetStatus()
    }
    ```

3. Viewing computer targets

    ```
    Invoke-Command -Session $Session -ScriptBlock {
      $WSUSServer.GetComputerTargets() |
        Sort-Object -Property FullDomainName |
          Format-Table -Property FullDomainName, IPAddress, Last*
    }
    ```

4. Searching for updates with titles containing Windows Server 2022

    ```
    Invoke-Command -Session $Session -ScriptBlock {
      $Title   = 'Windows Server 2022'
      $Updates = 'Security Updates'
      $SecurityUpdates = $WSUSServer.SearchUpdates($Title)
    }
    ```

5. Viewing the matching updates (first 10)

```
Invoke-Command -Session $Session -ScriptBlock {
  $SecurityUpdates |
    Sort-Object -Property Title |
      Select-Object -First 10 |
        Format-Table -Property Title, Description
}
```

6. Selecting one of the updates to approve based on the **Knowledge Based** (**KB**) article ID

```
Invoke-Command -Session $Session -ScriptBlock {
  $SelectedUpdate = $SecurityUpdates |
    Where-Object KnowledgebaseArticles -eq 5019080
}
```

7. Defining the computer target group

```
Invoke-Command -Session $Session -ScriptBlock {
  $SRVTargetGroup = $WSUSServer.GetComputerTargetGroups() |
    Where-Object -Property Name -eq 'Domain Servers'
}
```

8. Approving the update for installation in the target group

```
Invoke-Command -Session $Session -ScriptBlock {
  $SelectedUpdate.Approve('Install',$SRVTargetGroup)
}
```

9. Selecting one of the updates to decline based on a KB article ID

```
Invoke-Command -Session $Session -ScriptBlock {
$DeclinedUpdate = $SecurityUpdates |
  Where-Object -Property KnowledgebaseArticles -eq 5019080
}
```

10. Declining the update

```
Invoke-Command -Session $Session -ScriptBlock {
  $DeclinedUpdate.Decline($DCTargetGroup)
}
```

How it works...

In *step 1*, you create a PowerShell remoting session on the WSUS1 server using a Windows PowerShell remoting endpoint. In *step 2*, you use the Get-WsusServer cmdlet to instantiate a UpdateServer object inside the persistent remoting session to WSUS1. This object and its methods are at the core of automating WSUS. You then use the GetStatus() method to return the status of your WSUS server, which looks like this:

```
PS C:\Foo> # 2. Viewing the status of WSUS1
PS C:\Foo> Invoke-Command -Session $Session -ScriptBlock {
             $WSUSServer = Get-WsusServer
             $WSUSServer.GetStatus()
           }
```

```
PSComputerName                                        : WSUS1
RunspaceId                                            : aaeea23c-8aff-4460-abc8-5580828dfb01
UpdateCount                                           : 26471
DeclinedUpdateCount                                   : 539
ApprovedUpdateCount                                   : 18
NotApprovedUpdateCount                                : 25914
UpdatesWithStaleUpdateApprovalsCount                  : 0
ExpiredUpdateCount                                    : 0
CriticalOrSecurityUpdatesNotApprovedForInstallCount   : 15474
WsusInfrastructureUpdatesNotApprovedForInstallCount   : 0
UpdatesWithClientErrorsCount                          : 0
UpdatesWithServerErrorsCount                          : 0
UpdatesNeedingFilesCount                              : 0
UpdatesNeededByComputersCount                         : 46
UpdatesUpToDateCount                                  : 25886
CustomComputerTargetGroupCount                        : 1
ComputerTargetCount                                   : 13
ComputerTargetsNeedingUpdatesCount                    : 12
ComputerTargetsWithUpdateErrorsCount                  : 0
ComputersUpToDateCount                                : 0
UnrecognizedClientRequestedTargetGroupNames           : {}
ShouldDeleteUnneededRevisions                         : False
```

Figure 14.29: Viewing status of WSUS1

In *step 3*, you use the GetComputerTargets() method to retrieve the names of the host computers served by your WSUS server, which looks like this:

```
PS C:\Foo> # 3. Viewing computer targets
PS C:\Foo> Invoke-Command -Session $Session -ScriptBlock {
               $WSUSServer.GetComputerTargets() |
                 Sort-Object -Property FullDomainName |
                   Format-Table -Property FullDomainName, IPAddress, Last*
           }

FullDomainName    IPAddress               LastSyncTime         LastSyncResult LastReportedStatusTime LastReportedInventoryTime
--------------    ---------               ------------         -------------- ---------------------- -------------------------
ch1.reskit.org    10.10.10.221            11/12/2022 13:58:36  Succeeded 11/12/2022 14:06:54  01/01/0001 00:00:00
dc1.reskit.org    10.10.10.10             11/12/2022 15:56:15  Succeeded 11/12/2022 16:04:22  01/01/0001 00:00:00
dc2.reskit.org    10.10.10.11             11/12/2022 14:28:41  Succeeded 11/12/2022 14:36:46  01/01/0001 00:00:00
fs1.reskit.org    10.10.10.101            11/12/2022 13:58:50  Succeeded 11/12/2022 14:06:59  01/01/0001 00:00:00
fs2.reskit.org    10.10.10.102            11/12/2022 13:58:26  Succeeded 11/12/2022 14:06:36  01/01/0001 00:00:00
hv1.reskit.org    10.10.10.201            11/12/2022 13:58:49  Succeeded 11/12/2022 14:06:59  01/01/0001 00:00:00
hv2.reskit.org    10.10.10.202            11/12/2022 13:58:51  Succeeded 11/12/2022 14:07:00  01/01/0001 00:00:00
psrv.reskit.org   10.10.10.60             11/12/2022 14:59:07  Succeeded 11/12/2022 15:07:19  01/01/0001 00:00:00
smtp.reskit.org   10.10.10.49             11/12/2022 10:54:59  Succeeded 11/12/2022 10:57:01  01/01/0001 00:00:00
srv1.reskit.org   10.10.10.50             11/12/2022 16:23:24  Succeeded 11/12/2022 13:06:36  01/01/0001 00:00:00
srv2.reskit.org   10.10.10.52             11/12/2022 11:52:24  Succeeded 11/12/2022 12:00:32  01/01/0001 00:00:00
ss1.reskit.org    10.10.10.111            11/12/2022 13:58:51  Succeeded 11/12/2022 14:06:59  01/01/0001 00:00:00
wsus1.reskit.org  fe80::8672:8cc3:1e91:da0f%3 11/12/2022 06:00:52  Succeeded 11/12/2022 06:09:01  01/01/0001 00:00:00
```

Figure 14.30: Viewing WSUS computers

In *step 4*, you use the SearchUpdates() method to get the security updates for hosts running Windows Server 2022. This step produces no output. In *step 5*, you review the first 10 security updates for Windows Server 2022, which looks like this:

```
Title                                                                                                                                                               Description
-----                                                                                                                                                               -----------
2021-11 Cumulative security Hotpatch for Azure Stack HCI, version 21H2 and Windows Server 2022 Datacenter: Azure Edition for x64-based Systems (KB5007386) Install this update to resol…
2021-12 Cumulative security Hotpatch for Azure Stack HCI, version 21H2 and Windows Server 2022 Datacenter: Azure Edition for x64-based Systems (KB5008286) Install this update to resol…
2022-02 Cumulative security Hotpatch for Azure Stack HCI, version 21H2 and Windows Server 2022 Datacenter: Azure Edition for x64-based Systems (KB5010456) Install this update to resol…
2022-03 Cumulative security Hotpatch for Azure Stack HCI, version 21H2 and Windows Server 2022 Datacenter: Azure Edition for x64-based Systems (KB5011580) Install this update to resol…
2022-06 Cumulative security Hotpatch for Azure Stack HCI, version 21H2 and Windows Server 2022 Datacenter: Azure Edition for x64-based Systems (KB5014677) Install this update to resol…
2022-09 Cumulative security Hotpatch for Azure Stack HCI, version 21H2 and Windows Server 2022 Datacenter: Azure Edition for x64-based Systems (KB5017392) Install this update to resol…
2022-11 Cumulative security Hotpatch for Azure Stack HCI, version 21H2 and Windows Server 2022 Datacenter: Azure Edition for x64-based Systems (KB5019080) Install this update to resol…
```

Figure 14.31: Viewing available updates

In *step 6*, you select a specific update based on a KB article number. In *step 7*, you define a target group to which to apply the selected update. These two steps produce no output.

In *step 8*, you approve this selected patch for installation for all members of the Domain Servers computer target groups. The output of this step looks like this:

```
PS C:\Foo> # 8. Approving the update for installation in the target group
PS C:\Foo> Invoke-Command -Session $Session -ScriptBlock {
               $SelectedUpdate.Approve('Install',$SRVTargetGroup)
           }

PSComputerName        : WSUS1
RunspaceId            : aaeea23c-8aff-4460-abc8-5580828dfb01
UpdateServer          : Microsoft.UpdateServices.Internal.BaseApi.UpdateServer
Id                    : 678c6d2f-f575-4ade-95b1-9521942a8df6
CreationDate          : 11/12/2022 19:26:26
Action                : Install
GoLiveTime            : 11/12/2022 19:26:26
Deadline              : 31/12/9999 23:59:59
IsOptional            : False
State                 : Pending
AdministratorName     : RESKIT\Administrator
UpdateId              : Microsoft.UpdateServices.Administration.UpdateRevisionId
ComputerTargetGroupId : 3a409534-50c7-4159-af22-caea674d5ff1
IsAssigned            : True
```

Figure 14.32: Approving an update explicitly

In *step 9*, select an update you don't wish to install. This step produces no output. In *step 10*, you decline that update for the `Domain Servers` computer target group, which also creates no console output.

There's more...

In *step 4*, you examined the security updates for Windows Server 2022. You could also have looked for any updates or critical updates. You can also update this step to search for different targets, such as Windows 10 or Office.

In *step 6*, you selected a specific update based on a KB article ID that you want to approve explicitly. Suppose you are an IT pro responsible for Windows Update Services inside your organization. In that case, you must keep up to date on critical updates and deploy urgent patches as quickly as possible.

In *step 9*, you declined a specific update for one computer target group, also based on the KB article number. As you administer WSUS, you may discover certain updates that you can decline, since they do not impact certain target groups, or experience says they are not good to deploy in your organization. Keeping on top of which patches to approve or decline can be a lot of work, but it is vital to ensure that your systems are updated promptly.

Join our community on Discord

Join our community's Discord space for discussions with the author and other readers:

`https://packt.link/SecNet`

packt.com

Subscribe to our online digital library for full access to over 7,000 books and videos, as well as industry leading tools to help you plan your personal development and advance your career. For more information, please visit our website.

Why subscribe?

- Spend less time learning and more time coding with practical eBooks and Videos from over 4,000 industry professionals
- Improve your learning with Skill Plans built especially for you
- Get a free eBook or video every month
- Fully searchable for easy access to vital information
- Copy and paste, print, and bookmark content

At www.packt.com, you can also read a collection of free technical articles, sign up for a range of free newsletters, and receive exclusive discounts and offers on Packt books and eBooks.

Other Books You May Enjoy

If you enjoyed this book, you may be interested in these other books by Packt:

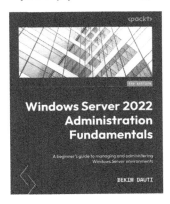

Windows Server 2022 Administration Fundamentals

Bekim Dauti

ISBN: 9781803232157

- Grasp the fundamentals of Windows Server 2022
- Understand how to deploy Windows Server 2022
- Discover Windows Server post-installation tasks
- Add roles to your Windows Server environment
- Apply Windows Server 2022 GPOs to your network
- Delve into virtualization and Hyper-V concepts
- Tune, maintain, update, and troubleshoot Windows Server 2022
- Get familiar with Microsoft's role-based certifications

Mastering PowerShell Scripting

Chris Dent

ISBN: 9781800206540

- Optimize code with functions, switches, and looping structures

- Test and debug your scripts as well as raising and catching errors

- Work with objects and operators to test and manipulate data

- Parse and manipulate different data types

- Use jobs, runspaces, and runspace pools to run code asynchronously

- Write .NET classes with ease within PowerShell

- Create and implement regular expressions in PowerShell scripts

- Make use of advanced techniques to define and restrict the behavior of parameters

Packt is searching for authors like you

If you're interested in becoming an author for Packt, please visit authors.packtpub.com and apply today. We have worked with thousands of developers and tech professionals, just like you, to help them share their insight with the global tech community. You can make a general application, apply for a specific hot topic that we are recruiting an author for, or submit your own idea.

Share your thoughts

Now you've finished *Windows Server Automation with PowerShell Cookbook, Fifth Edition*, we'd love to hear your thoughts! Scan the QR code below to go straight to the Amazon review page for this book and share your feedback or leave a review on the site that you purchased it from.

https://packt.link/r/1-804-61423-8

Your review is important to us and the tech community and will help us make sure we're delivering excellent quality content.

Index

Download a free PDF copy of this book

Thanks for purchasing this book!

Do you like to read on the go but are unable to carry your print books everywhere? Is your eBook purchase not compatible with the device of your choice?

Don't worry, now with every Packt book you get a DRM-free PDF version of that book at no cost.

Read anywhere, any place, on any device. Search, copy, and paste code from your favorite technical books directly into your application.

The perks don't stop there, you can get exclusive access to discounts, newsletters, and great free content in your inbox daily

Follow these simple steps to get the benefits:

1. Scan the QR code or visit the link below

https://packt.link/free-ebook/9781804614235

2. Submit your proof of purchase
3. That's it! We'll send your free PDF and other benefits to your email directly

Made in United States
North Haven, CT
20 June 2023

38014944R00389